II. the GIRLFRIEND

One night Günther, who would turn the occasional trick, brought a girl home.

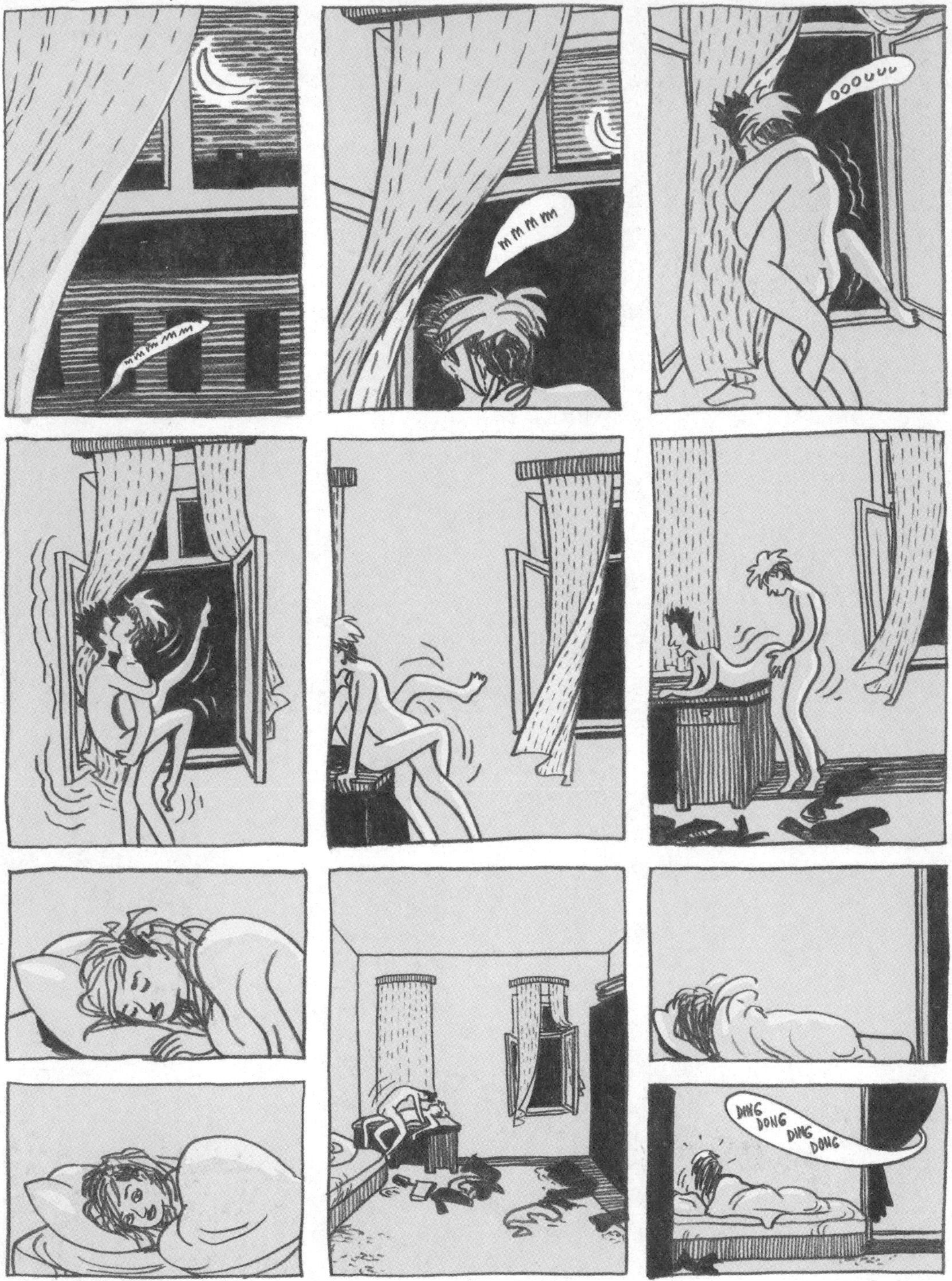
mmmm
OOOUUU
DING DONG DING DONG

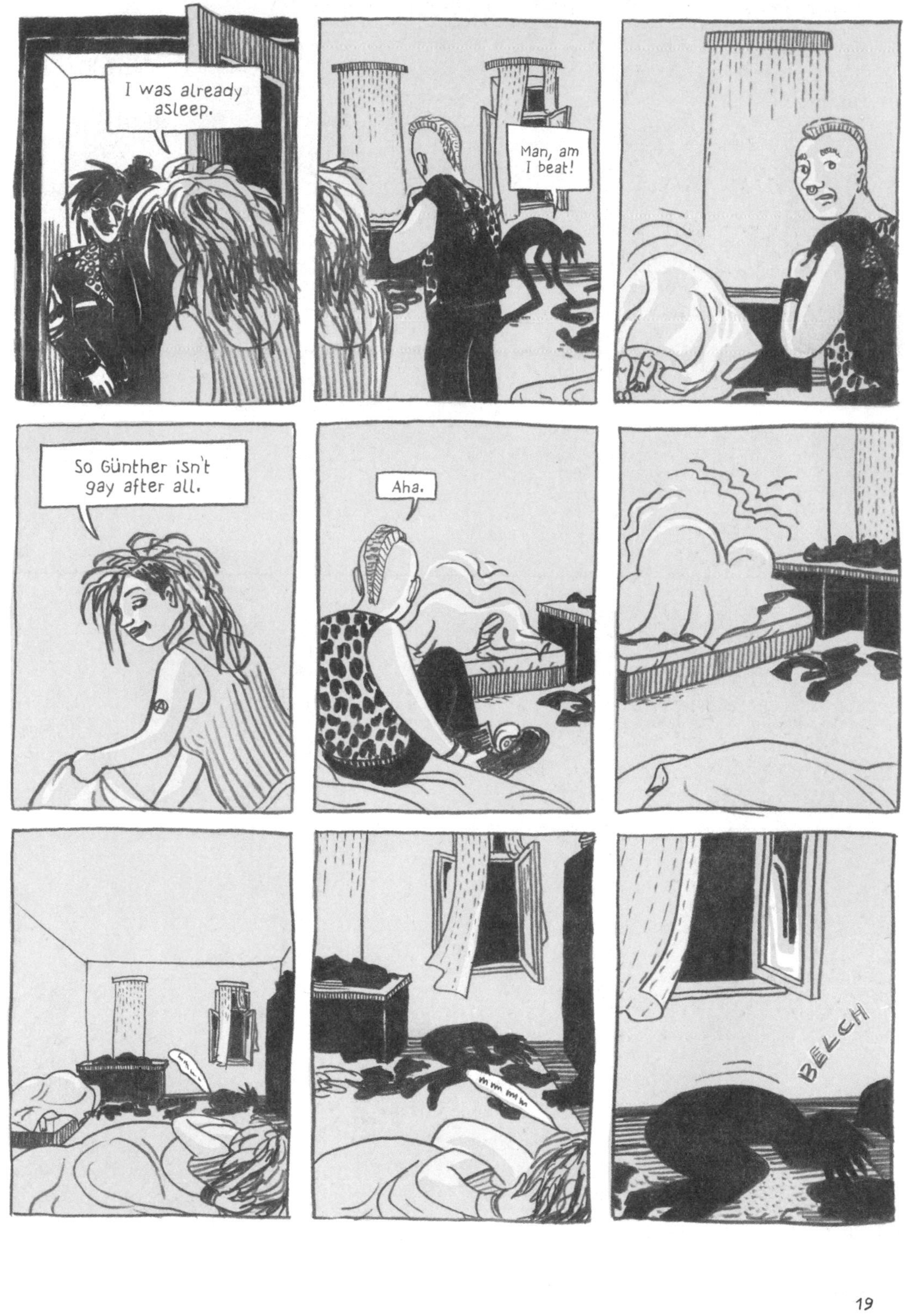
I was already asleep.
Man, am I beat!
So Günther isn't gay after all.
Aha.
BELCH

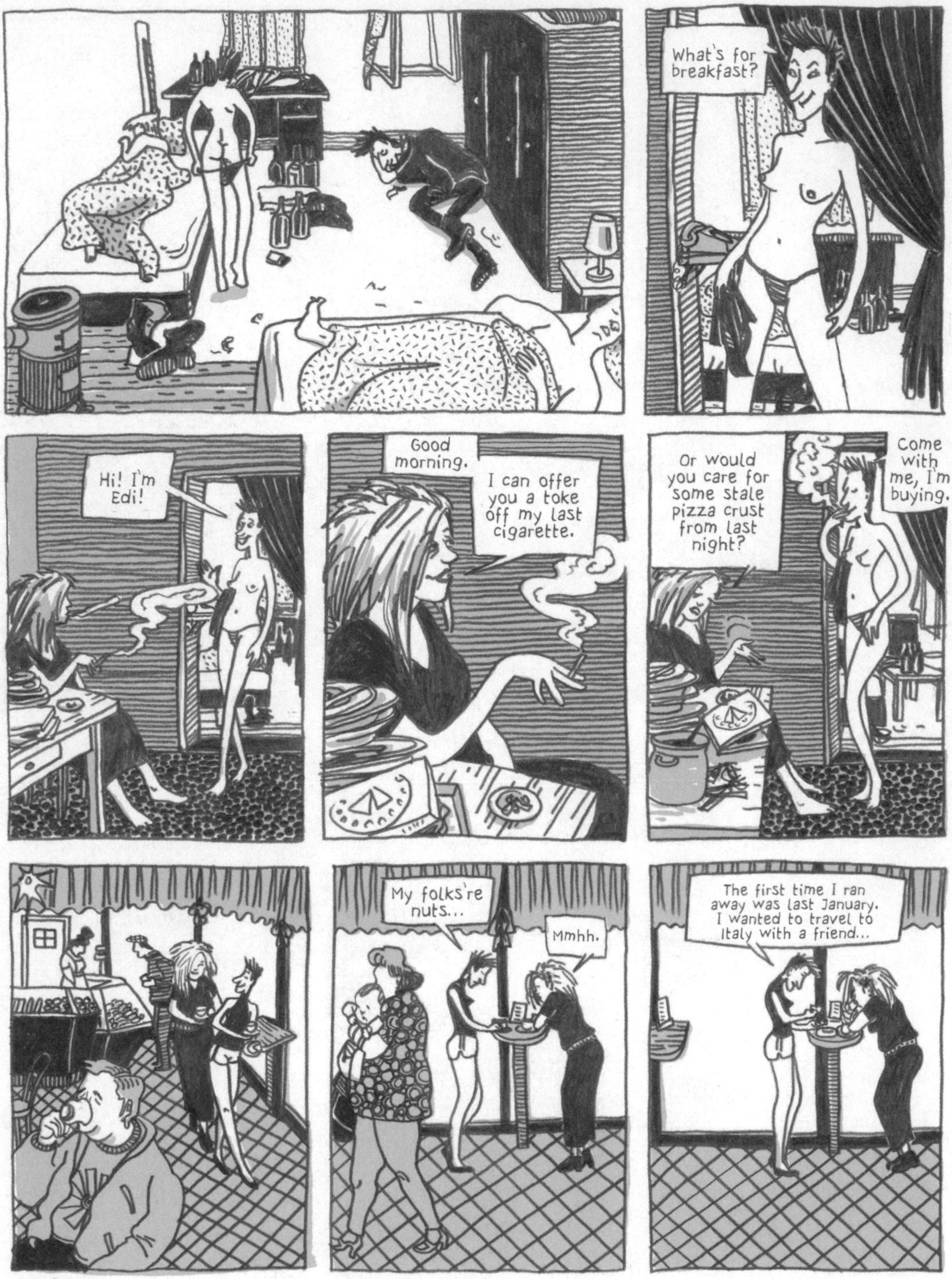
What's for breakfast?
Hi! I'm Edi!
Good morning.
I can offer you a toke off my last cigarette.
Or would you care for some stale pizza crust from last night?
Come with me, I'm buying.
My folks're nuts...
Mmhh.
The first time I ran away was last January. I wanted to travel to Italy with a friend...

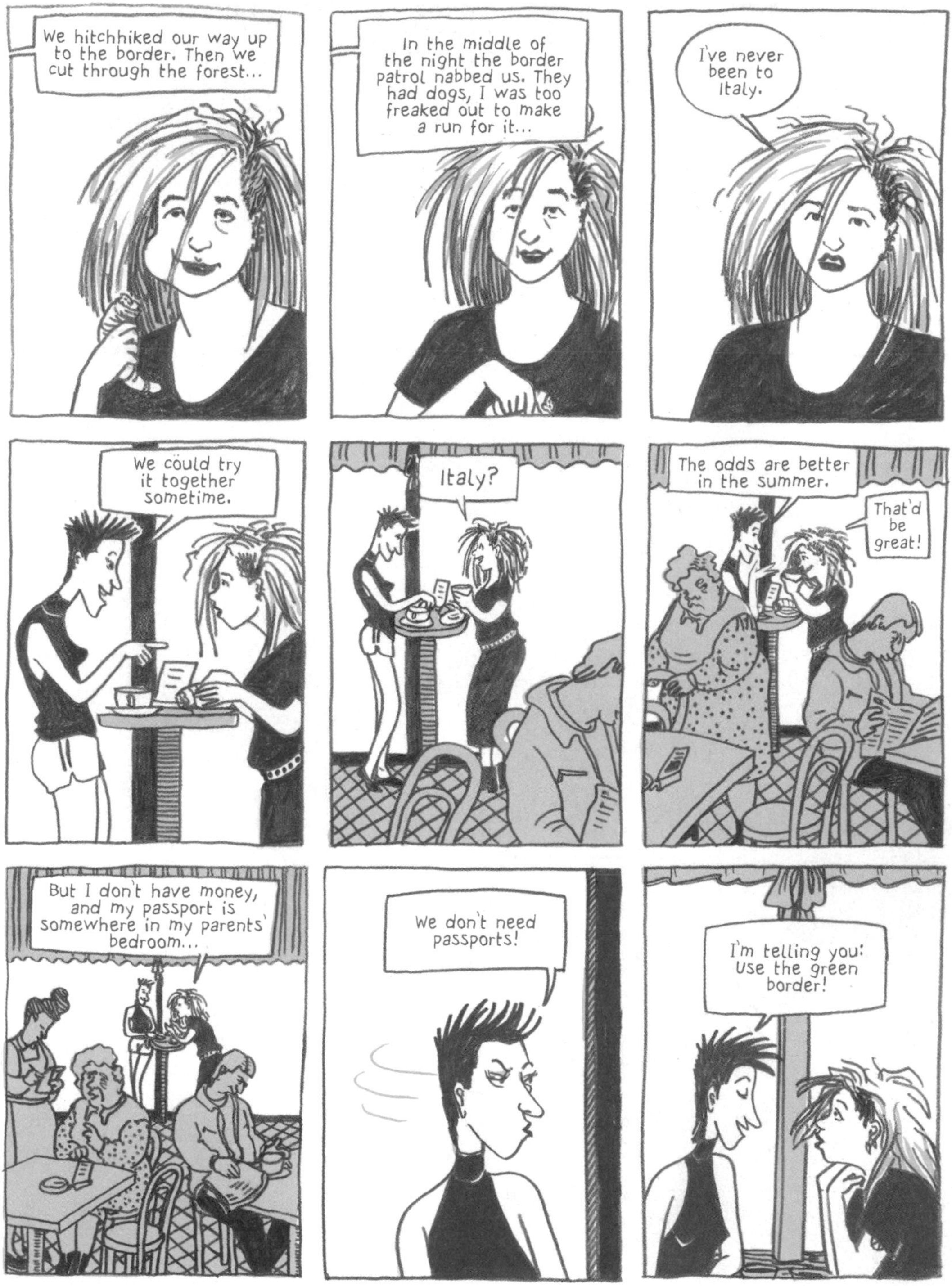
We hitchhiked our way up to the border. Then we cut through the forest...
In the middle of the night the border patrol nabbed us. They had dogs, I was too freaked out to make a run for it...
I've never been to Italy.
We could try it together sometime.
Italy?
The odds are better in the summer.
That'd be great!
But I don't have money, and my passport is somewhere in my parents' bedroom...
We don't need passports!
I'm telling you: Use the green border!

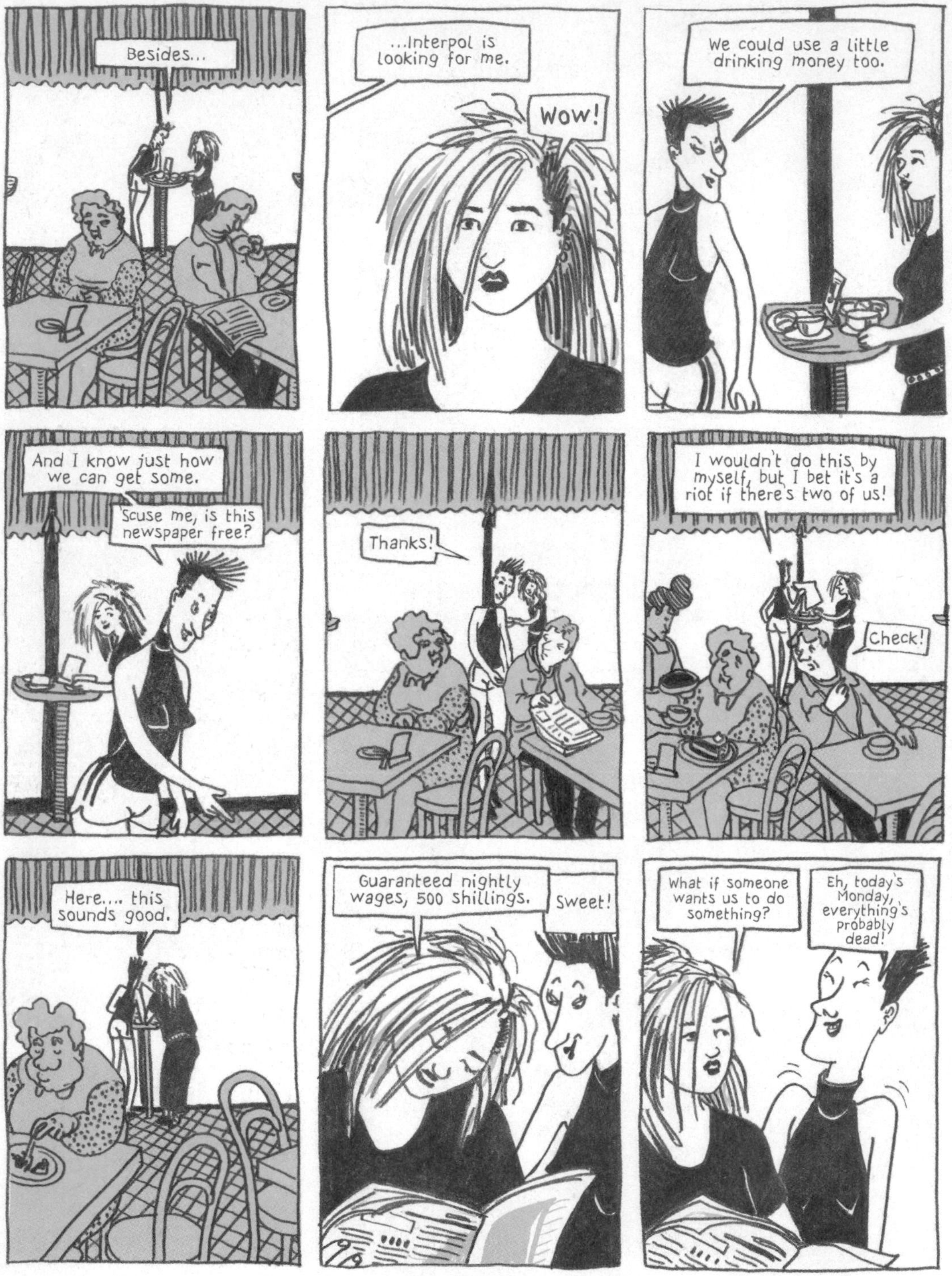
Besides...
...Interpol is looking for me.
Wow!
We could use a little drinking money too.
And I know just how we can get some.
'Scuse me, is this newspaper free?
Thanks!
I wouldn't do this by myself, but I bet it's a riot if there's two of us!
Check!
Here.... this sounds good.
Guaranteed nightly wages, 500 shillings.
Sweet!
What if someone wants us to do something?
Eh, today's Monday, everything's probably dead!

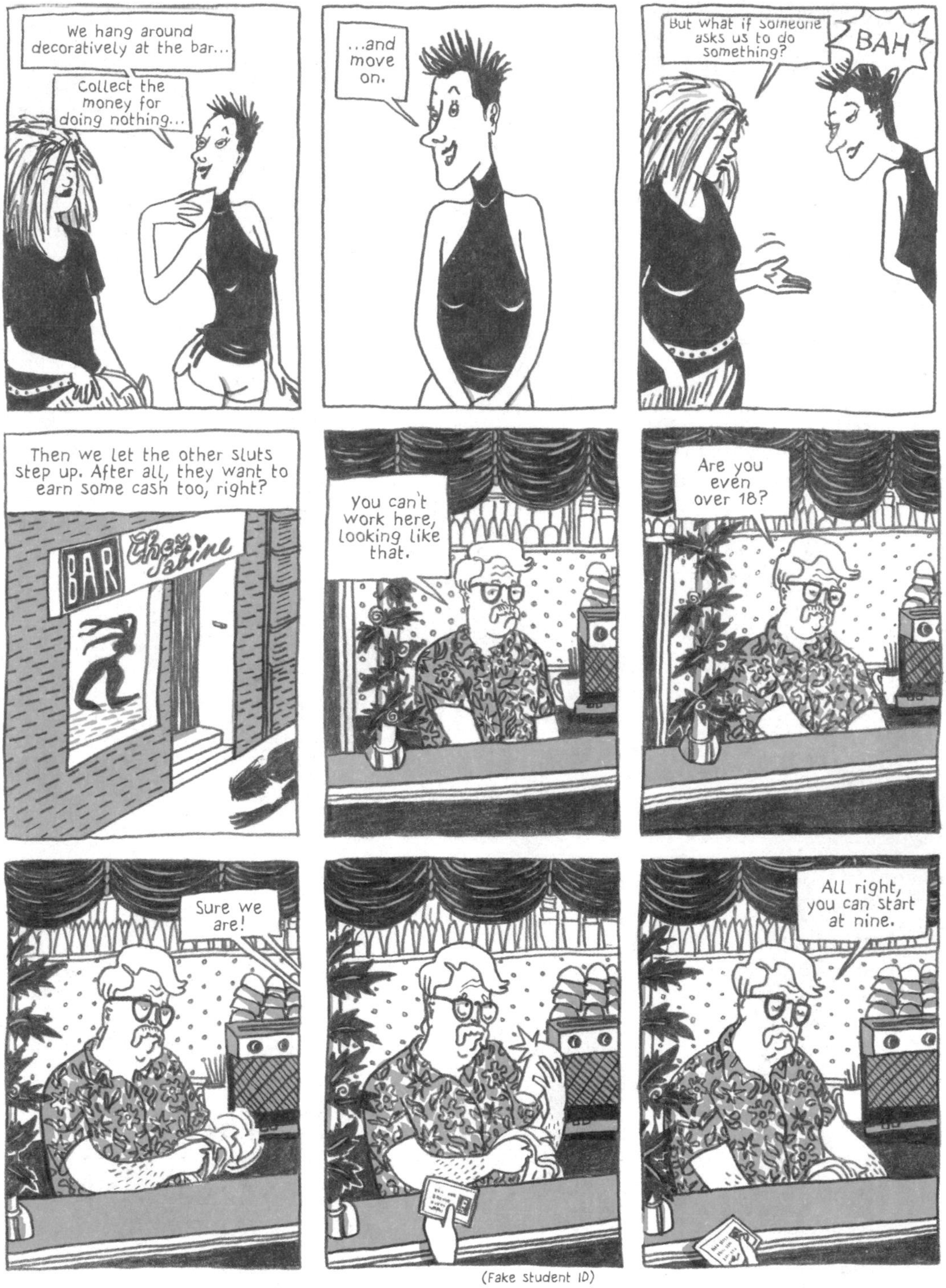
We hang around decoratively at the bar...
Collect the money for doing nothing...
...and move on.
But what if someone asks us to do something?
BAH
Then we let the other sluts step up. After all, they want to earn some cash too, right?
BAR
Chez Sabine
You can't work here, looking like that.
Are you even over 18?
Sure we are!
All right, you can start at nine.

(Fake student ID)

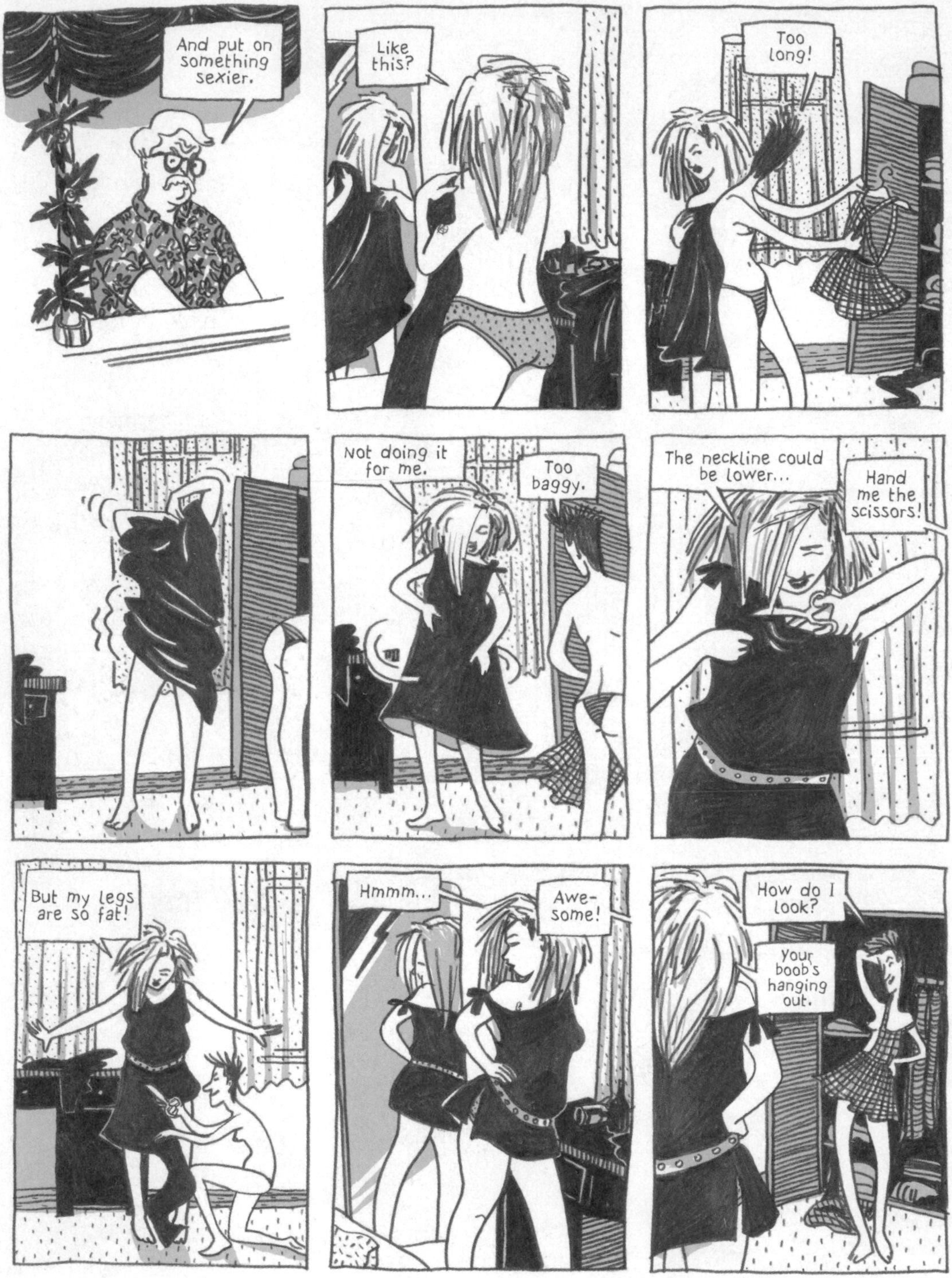
And put on something sexier.
Like this?
Too long!
Not doing it for me.
Too baggy.
The neckline could be lower...
Hand me the scissors!
But my legs are so fat!
Hmmm...
Awe-some!
How do I look?
Your boob's hanging out.

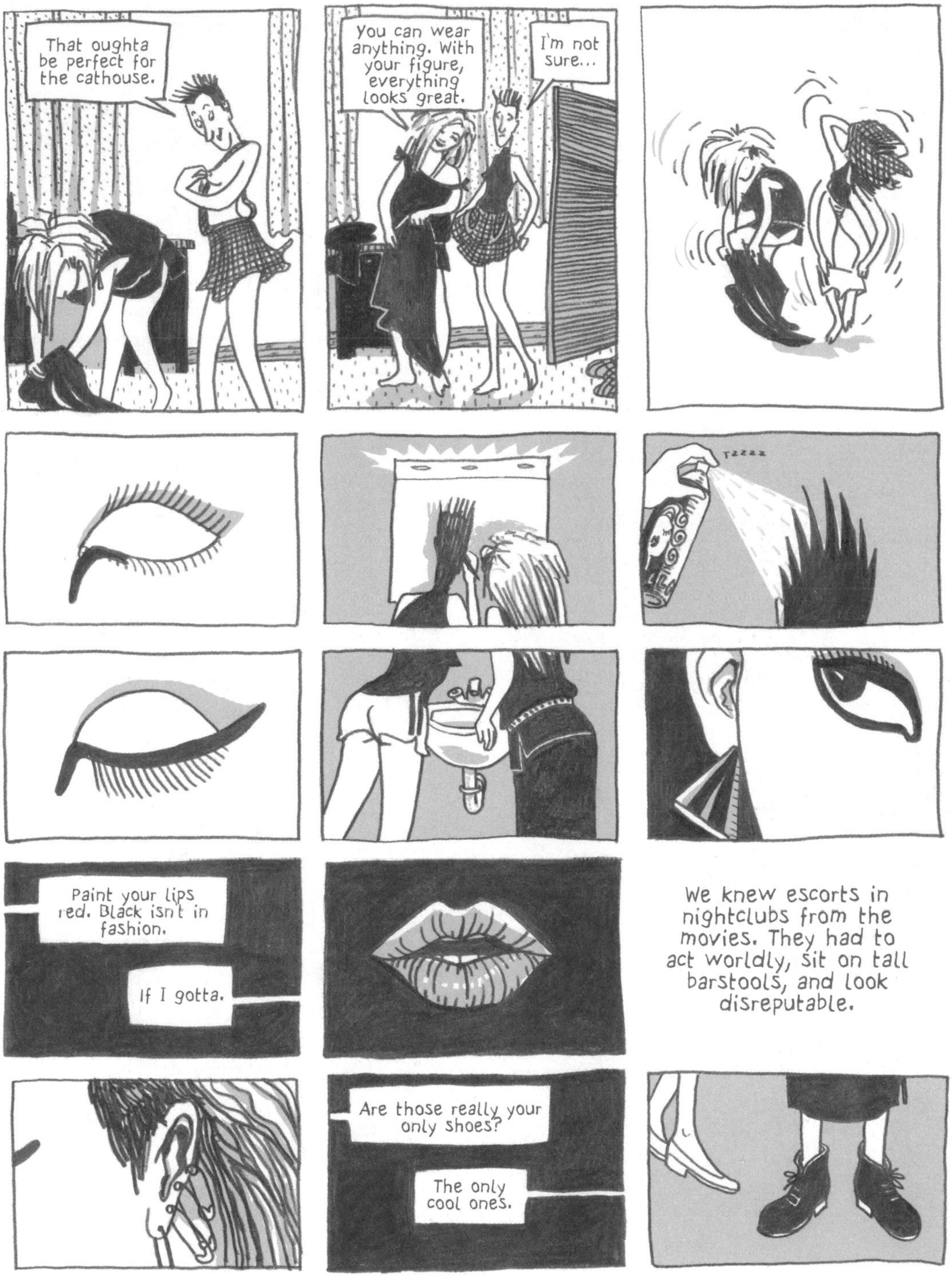
That oughta be perfect for the cathouse.
You can wear anything. With your figure, everything looks great.
I'm not sure...
TZZZZ
Paint your lips red. Black isn't in fashion.
If I gotta.
We knew escorts in nightclubs from the movies. They had to act worldly, sit on tall barstools, and look disreputable.
Are those really your only shoes?
The only cool ones.

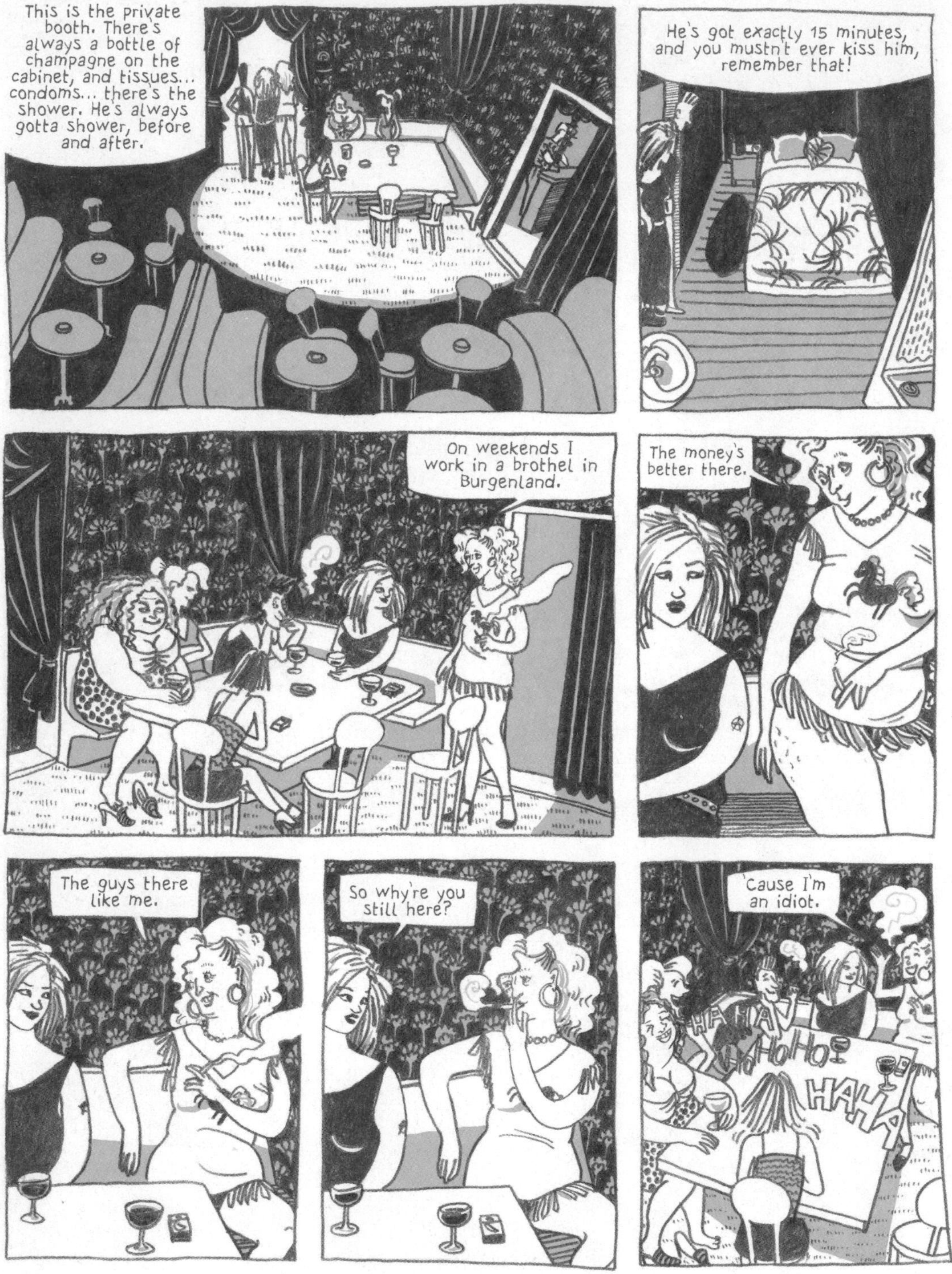
This is the private booth. There's always a bottle of champagne on the cabinet, and tissues... condoms... there's the shower. He's always gotta shower, before and after.
He's got exactly 15 minutes, and you mustn't ever kiss him, remember that!
On weekends I work in a brothel in Burgenland.
The money's better there.
The guys there like me.
So why're you still here?
'Cause I'm an idiot.
HAHA
HoHoHo
HAHA

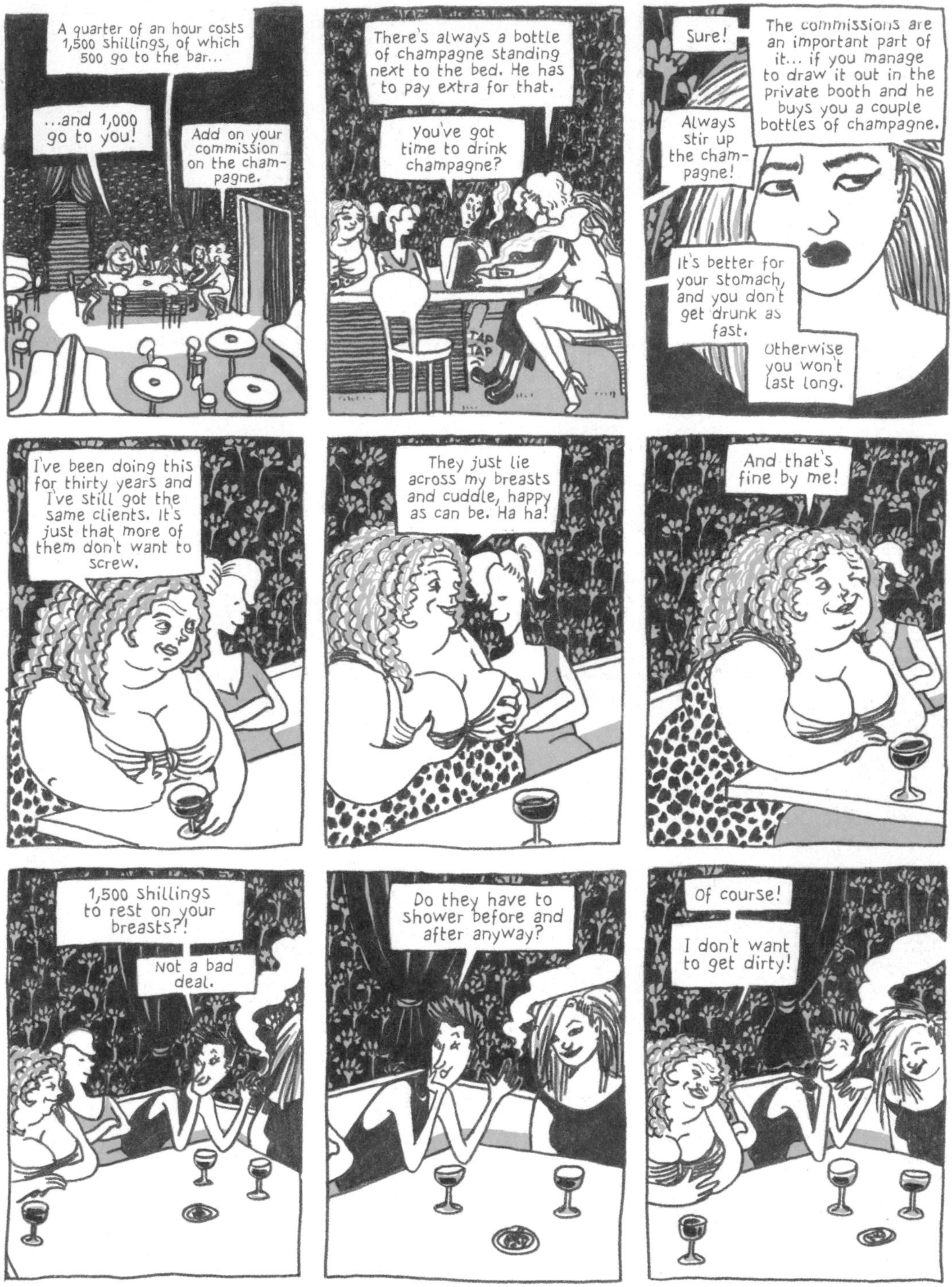
A quarter of an hour costs 1,500 shillings, of which 500 go to the bar...
...and 1,000 go to you!
Add on your commission on the champagne.
There's always a bottle of champagne standing next to the bed. He has to pay extra for that.
You've got time to drink champagne?
TAP TAP
Sure!
The commissions are an important part of it... if you manage to draw it out in the private booth and he buys you a couple bottles of champagne.
Always stir up the champagne!
It's better for your stomach, and you don't get drunk as fast.
Otherwise you won't last long.
I've been doing this for thirty years and I've still got the same clients. It's just that more of them don't want to screw.
They just lie across my breasts and cuddle, happy as can be. Ha ha!
And that's fine by me!
1,500 shillings to rest on your breasts?!
Not a bad deal.
Do they have to shower before and after anyway?
Of course!
I don't want to get dirty!

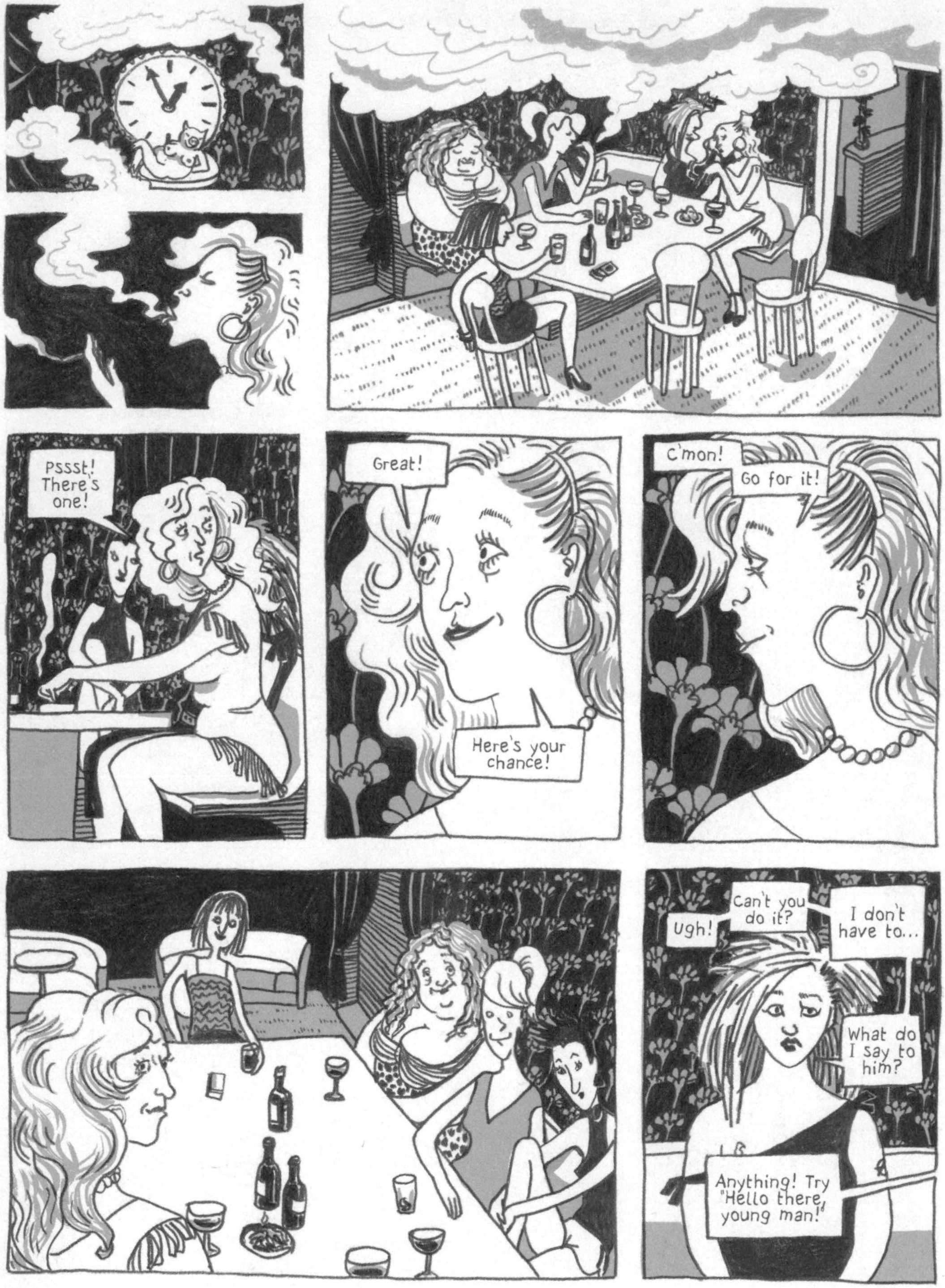
Pssst! There's one!
Great!
Here's your chance!
C'mon!
Go for it!
Ugh!
Can't you do it?
I don't have to...
What do I say to him?
Anything! Try "Hello there, young man!"

These whores had hearts of gold.

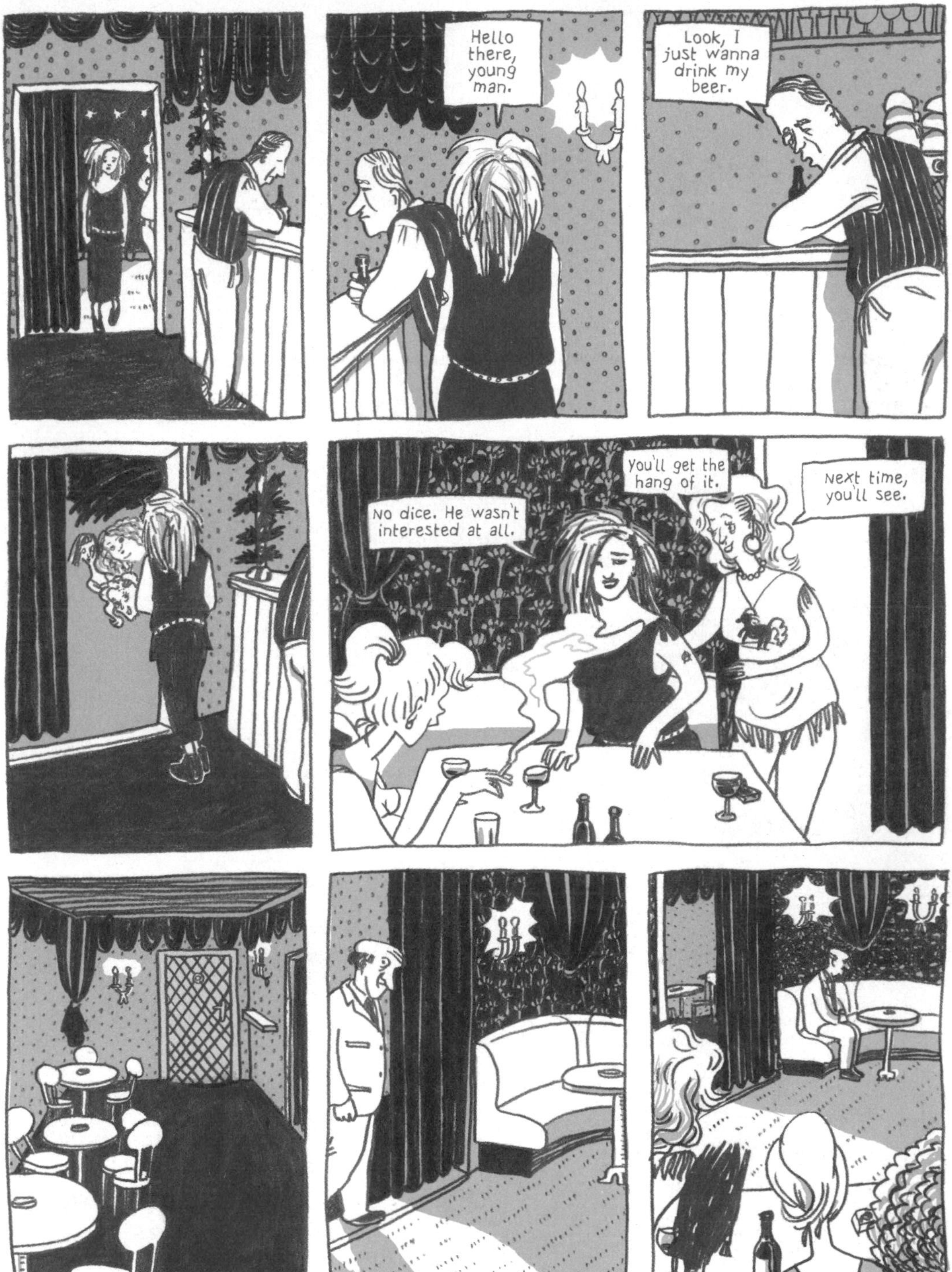
Hello there, young man.
Look, I just wanna drink my beer.
No dice. He wasn't interested at all.
You'll get the hang of it.
Next time, you'll see.

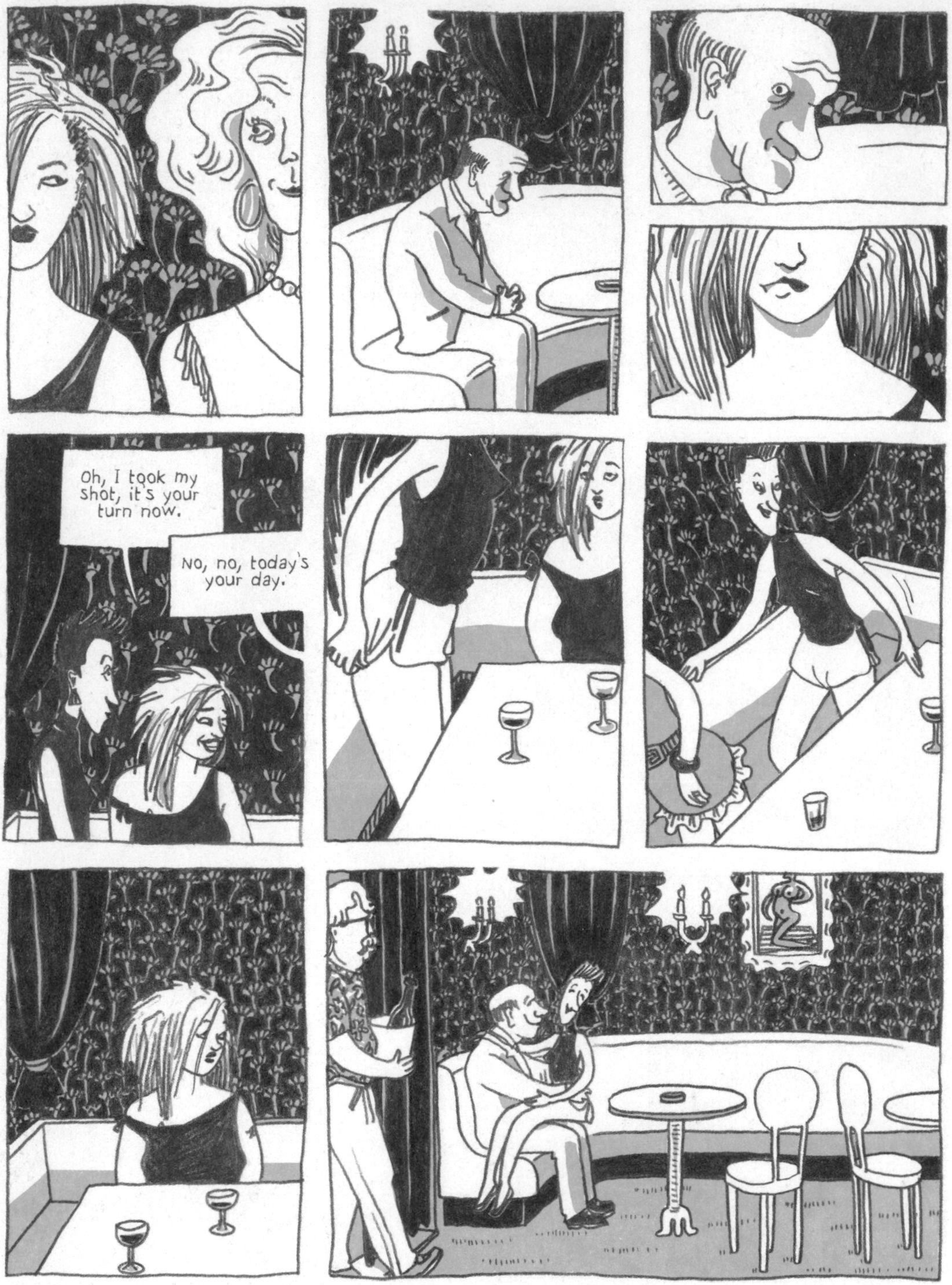

Oh, I took my shot, it's your turn now.
No, no, today's your day.

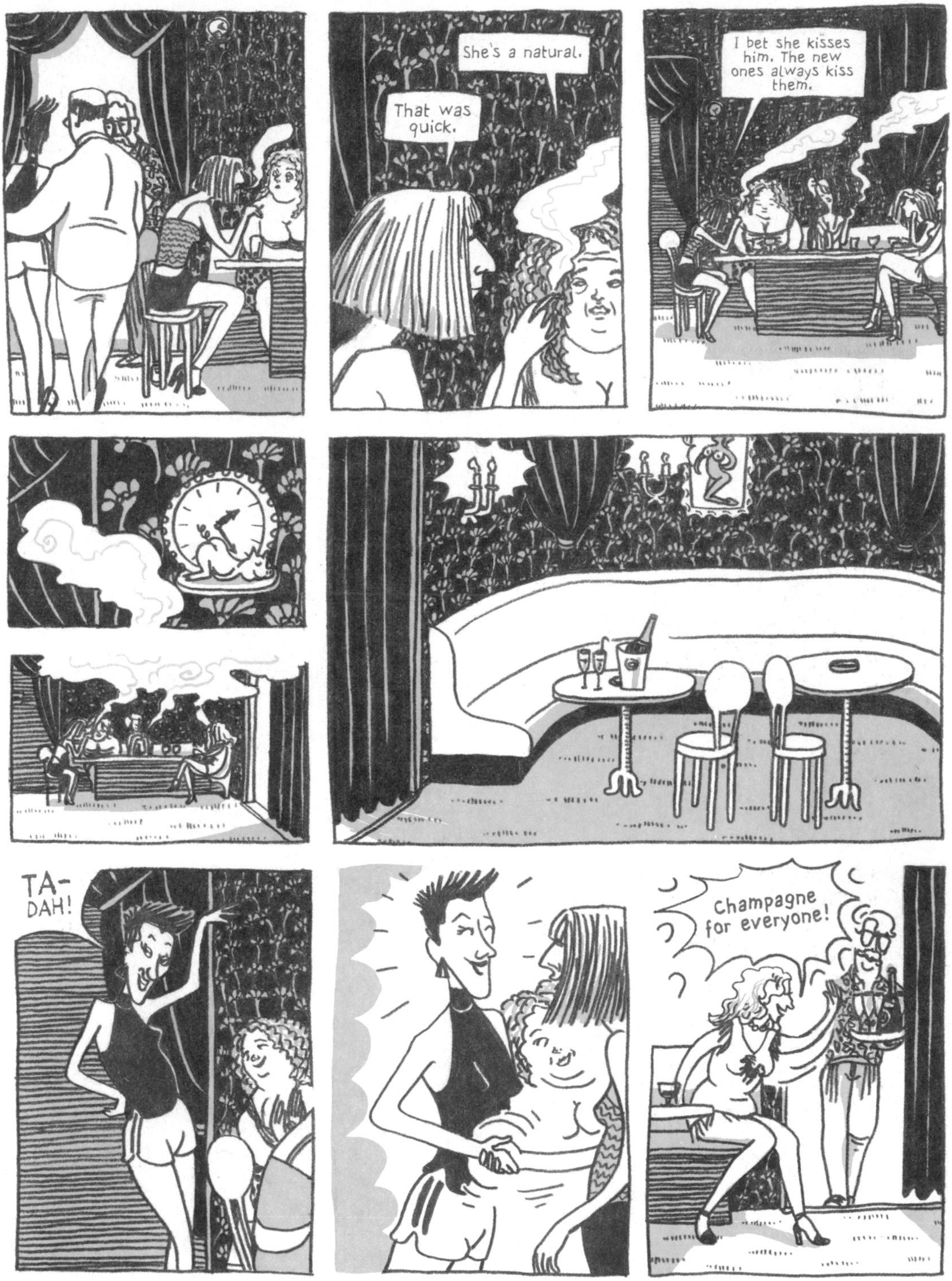

That was quick.
She's a natural.
I bet she kisses him. The new ones always kiss them.
TA-DAH!
Champagne for everyone!

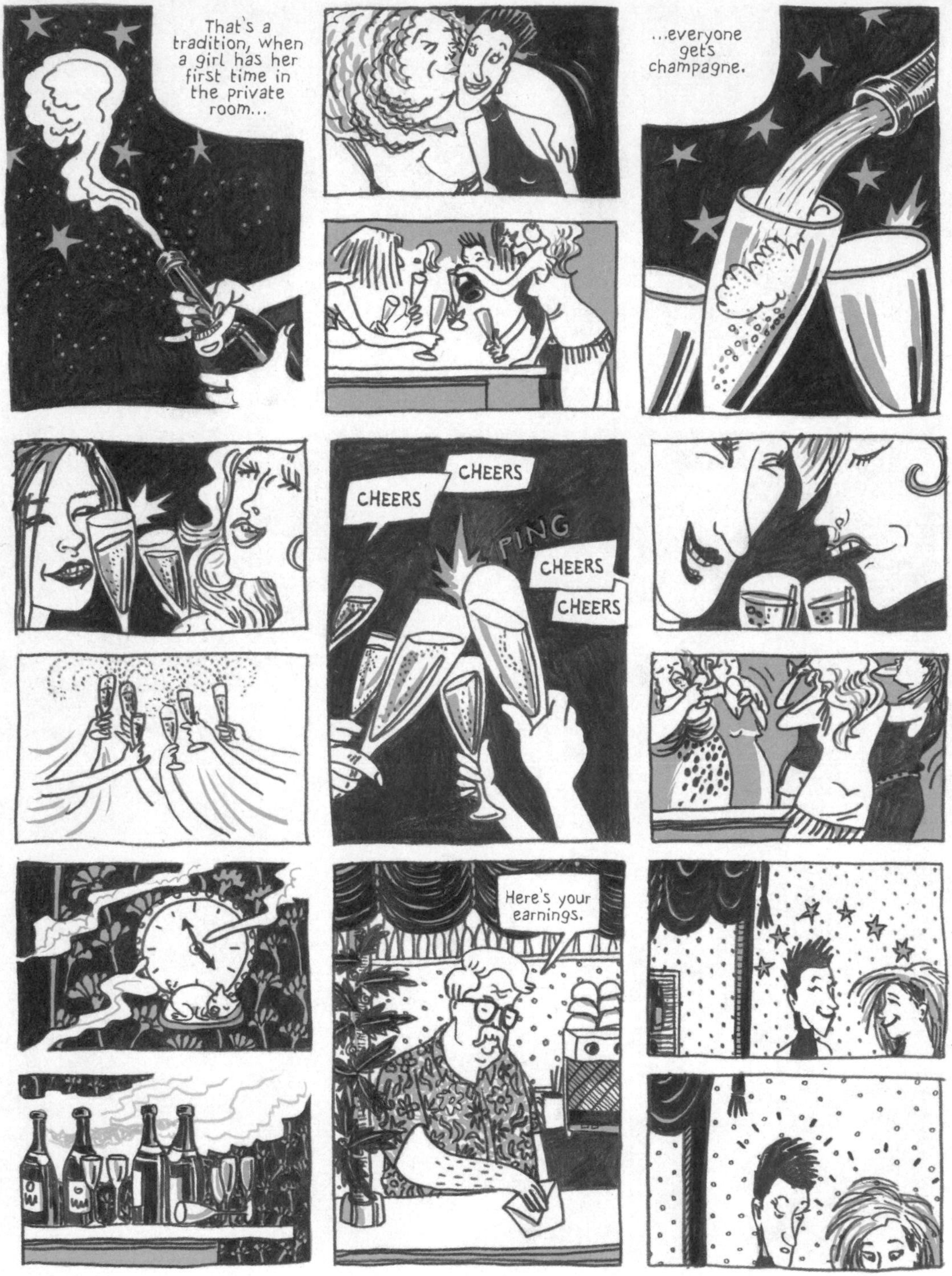
That's a tradition, when a girl has her first time in the private room...
...everyone gets champagne.
CHEERS
CHEERS
PING
CHEERS
CHEERS
Here's your earnings.

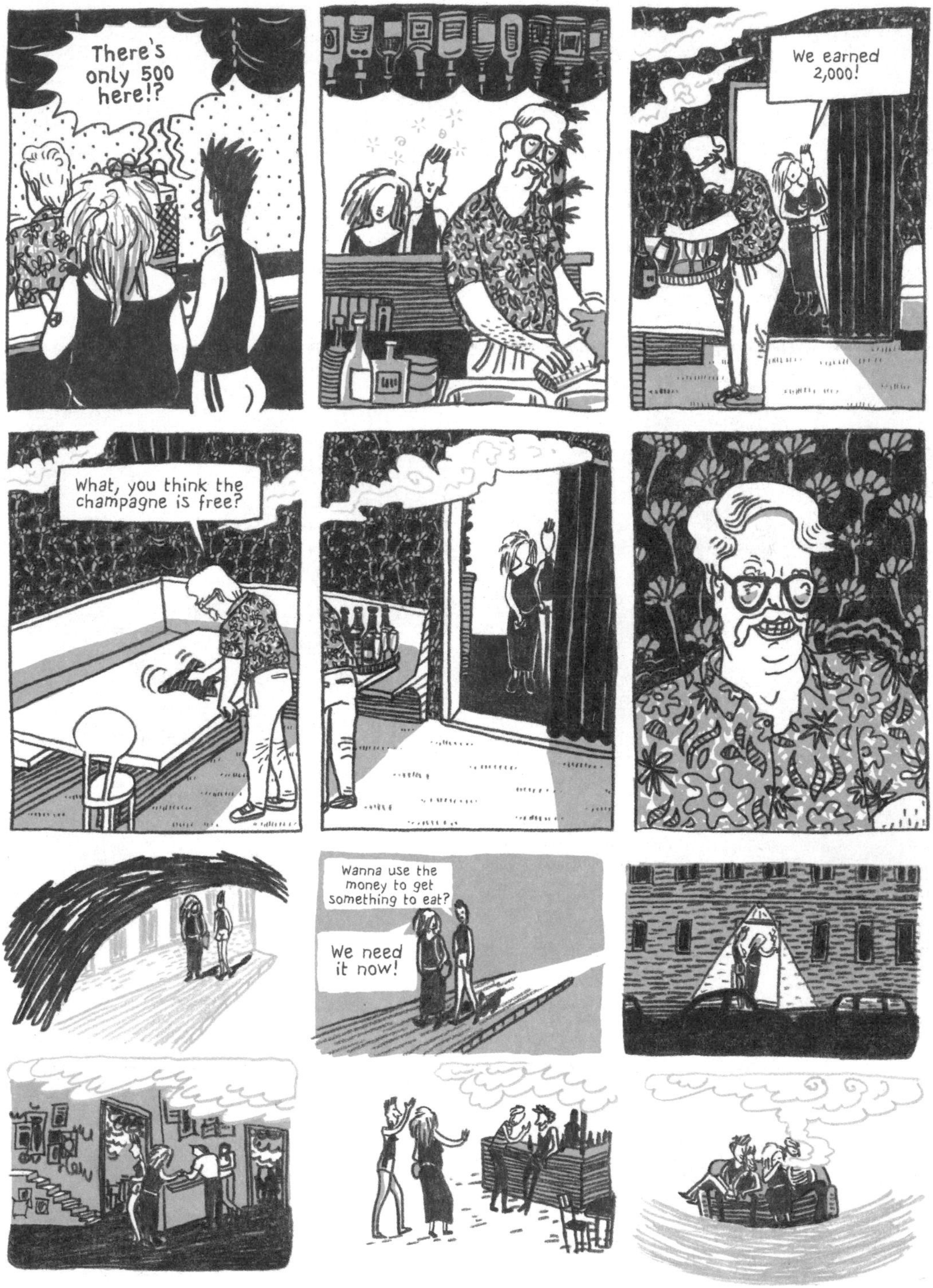
There's only 500 here!?
We earned 2,000!
What, you think the champagne is free?
Wanna use the money to get something to eat?
We need it now!

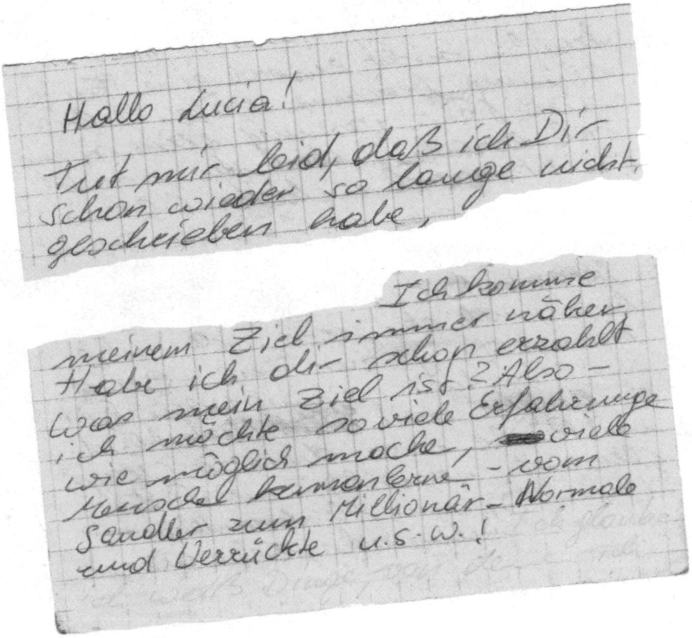

Hallo Lucia!
Tut mir leid, daß ich Dir
schon wieder so lange nicht
geschrieben habe,
Ich komme
meinem Ziel immer näher.
Habe ich dir schon erzählt
was mein Ziel ist? Also —
ich möchte soviele Erfahrunge
wie möglich mache, viele
Menschen kennenlerne — vom
Sandler zum Millionär — Normale
und Verrückte u.s.w.!

Hey, Lucia!

I'm sorry that I haven't written for such a long time again… I'm getting closer and closer to my goal. What is my goal? Well — I'd like to accumulate as much experience as possible, to meet as many people as possible — from the bum to the millionaire, normal people and crazy ones…

(Letter to a childhood friend, never mailed)

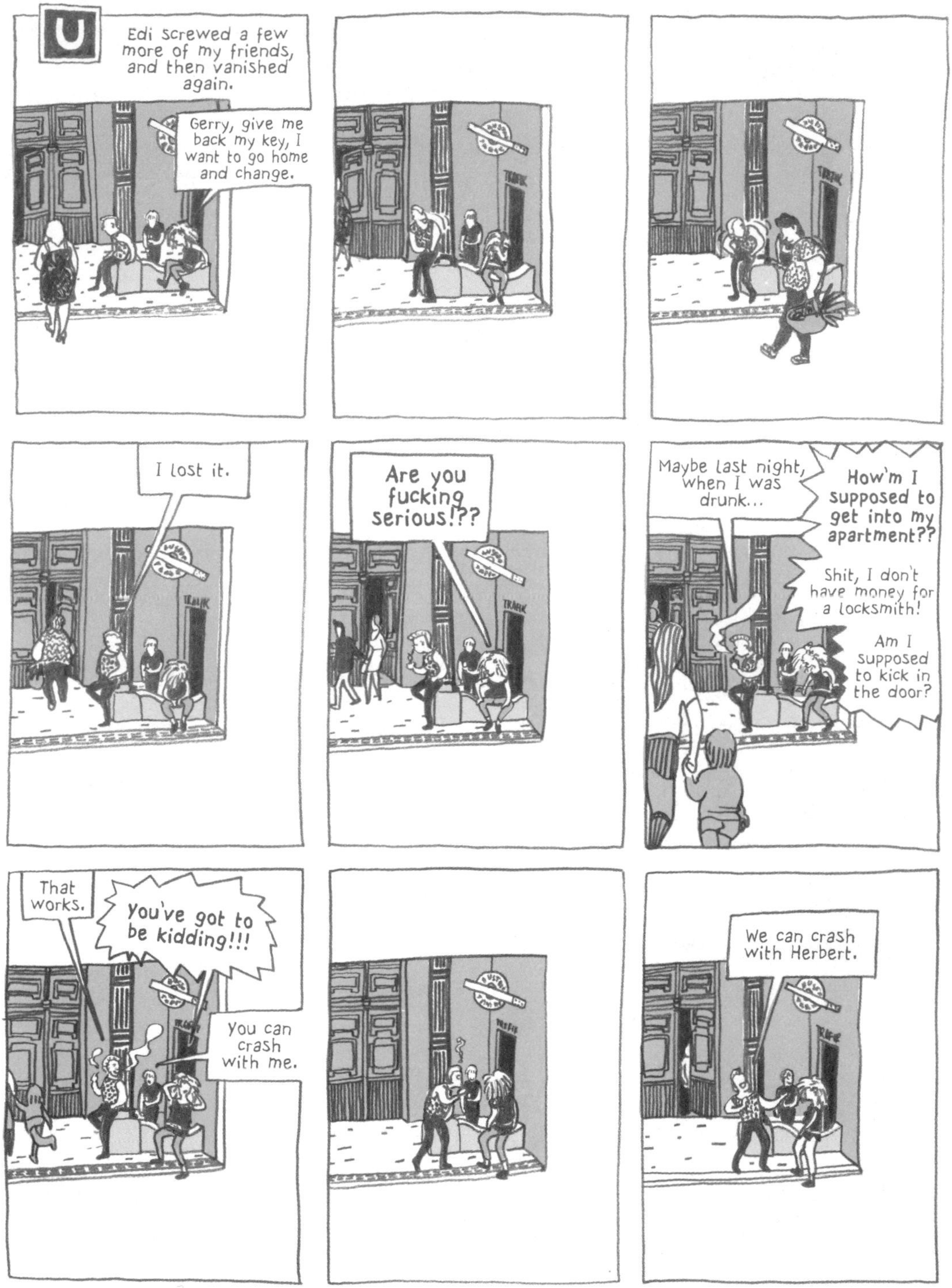
U
Edi screwed a few more of my friends, and then vanished again.
Gerry, give me back my key, I want to go home and change.
I lost it.
Are you fucking serious!??
Maybe last night, when I was drunk...
How'm I supposed to get into my apartment??
Shit, I don't have money for a locksmith!
Am I supposed to kick in the door?
That works.
You've got to be kidding!!!
You can crash with me.
We can crash with Herbert.

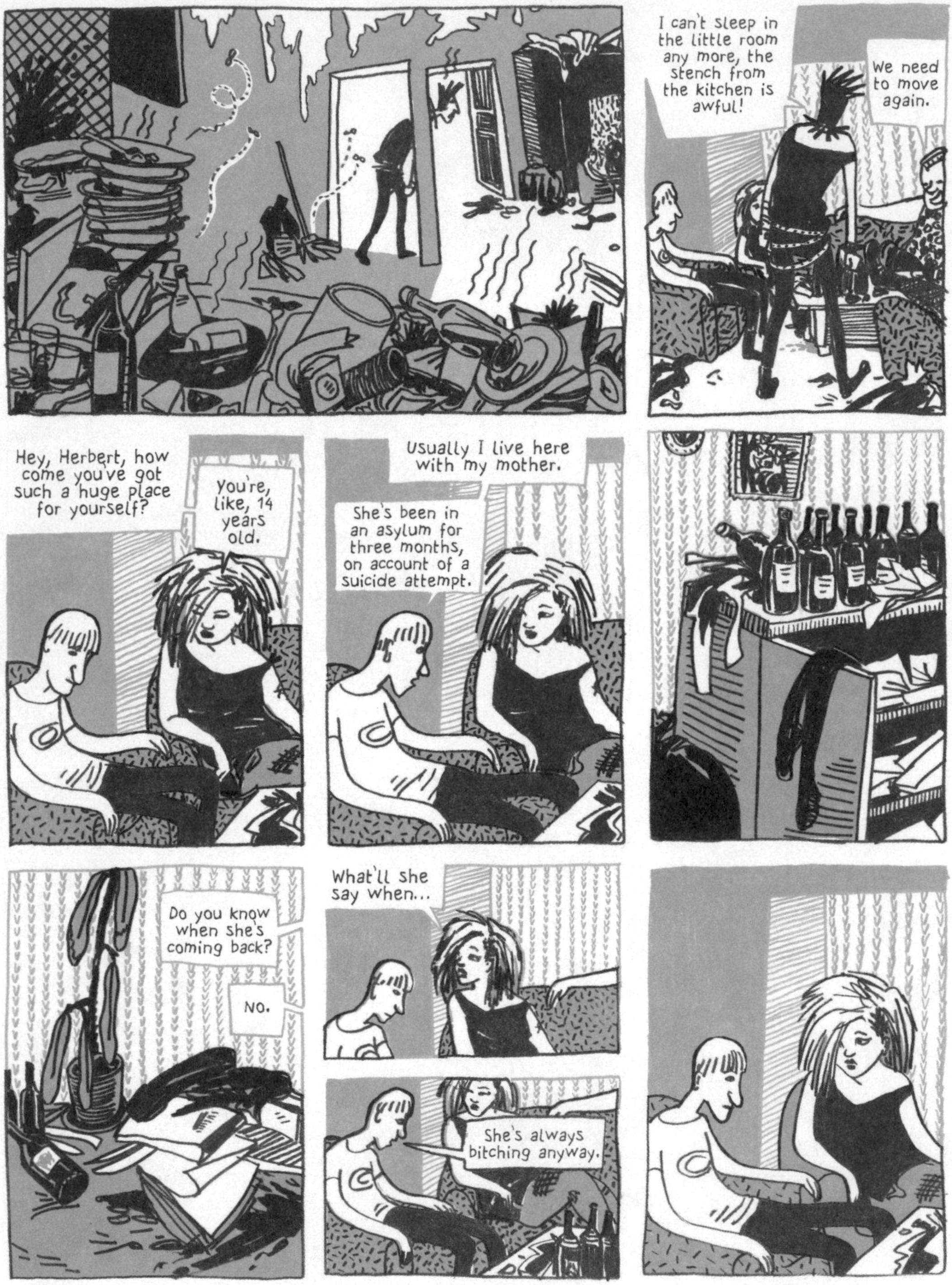
I can't sleep in the little room any more, the stench from the kitchen is awful!
We need to move again.
Hey, Herbert, how come you've got such a huge place for yourself?
You're, like, 14 years old.
Usually I live here with my mother.
She's been in an asylum for three months, on account of a suicide attempt.
Do you know when she's coming back?
No.
What'll she say when...
She's always bitching anyway.

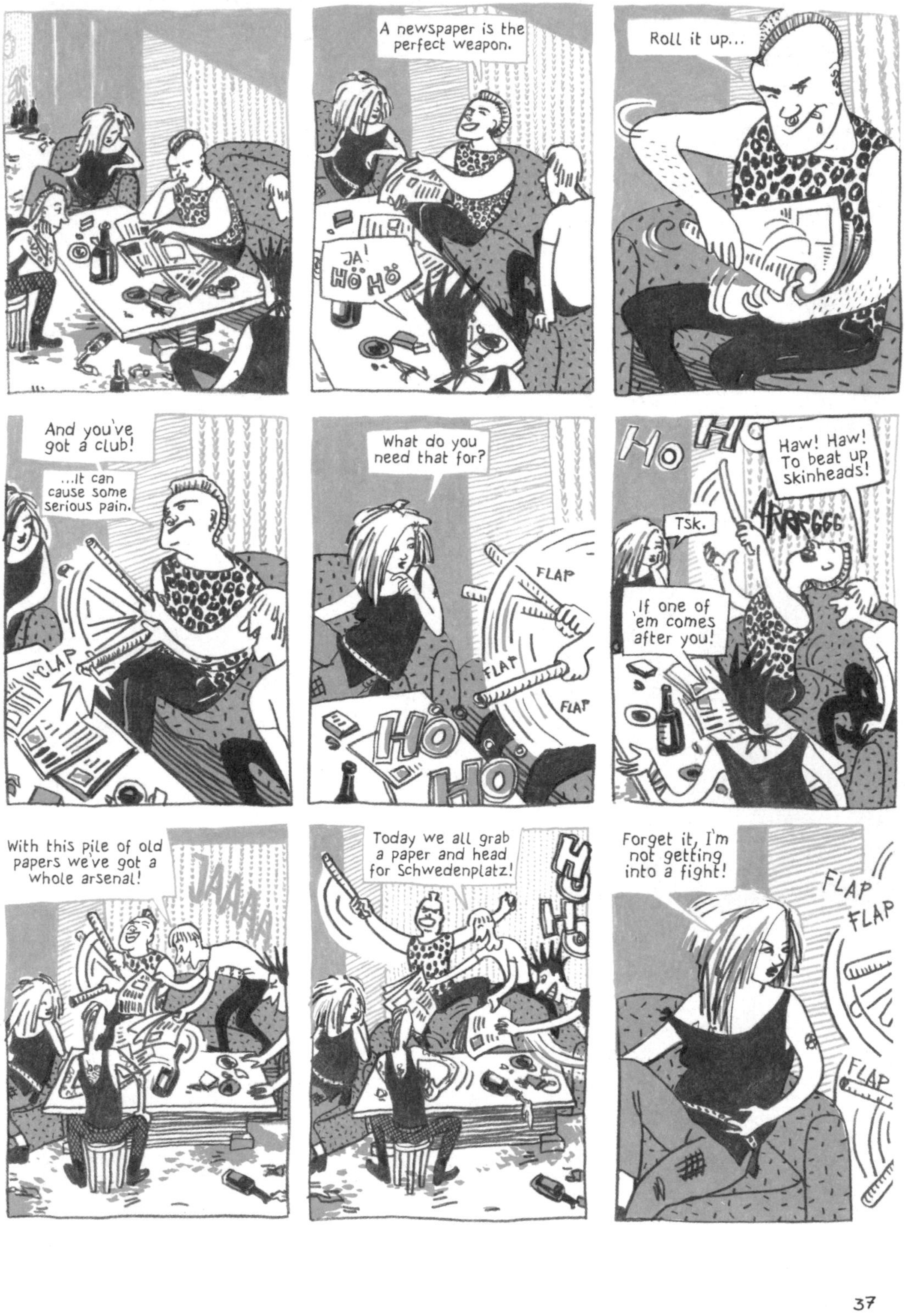
A newspaper is the perfect weapon.
JA! HÖ HÖ
Roll it up...
And you've got a club!
...It can cause some serious pain.
CLAP
What do you need that for?
FLAP
FLAP
FLAP
HÖ
HO
Ho
Haw! Haw! To beat up skinheads!
ARRRGGG
Tsk.
If one of 'em comes after you!
With this pile of old papers we've got a whole arsenal!
JAAAA
Today we all grab a paper and head for Schwedenplatz!
Forget it, I'm not getting into a fight!
FLAP
FLAP
FLAP

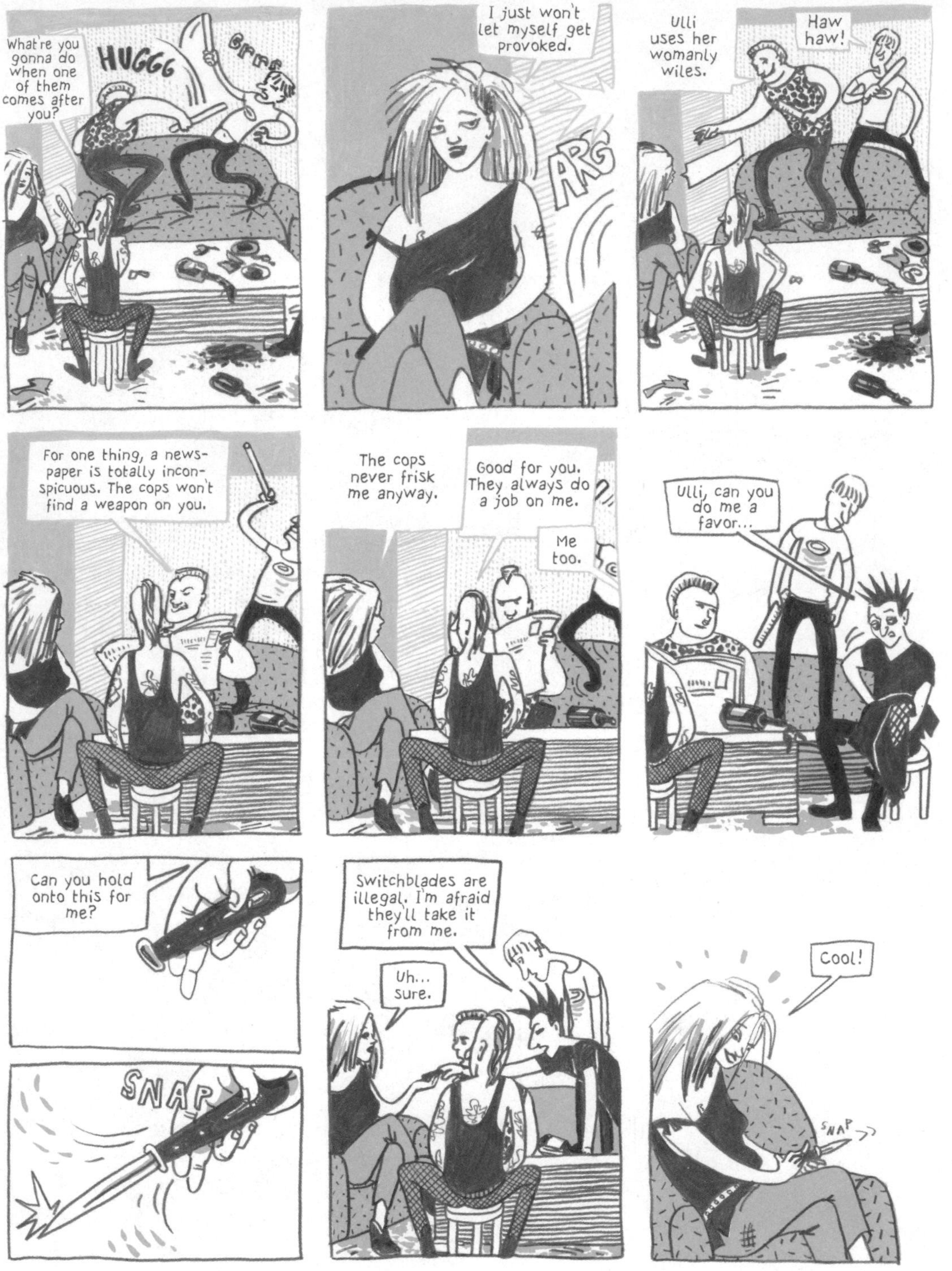
What're you gonna do when one of them comes after you?
HUGGG
GRRR
I just won't let myself get provoked.
ARG
Ulli uses her womanly wiles.
Haw haw!
For one thing, a news-paper is totally incon-spicuous. The cops won't find a weapon on you.
The cops never frisk me anyway.
Good for you. They always do a job on me.
Me too.
Ulli, can you do me a favor...
Can you hold onto this for me?
SNAP
Switchblades are illegal. I'm afraid they'll take it from me.
Uh... sure.
Cool!
SNAP

SKINHEAD VOR BEGEGNUNG MI
PUNK

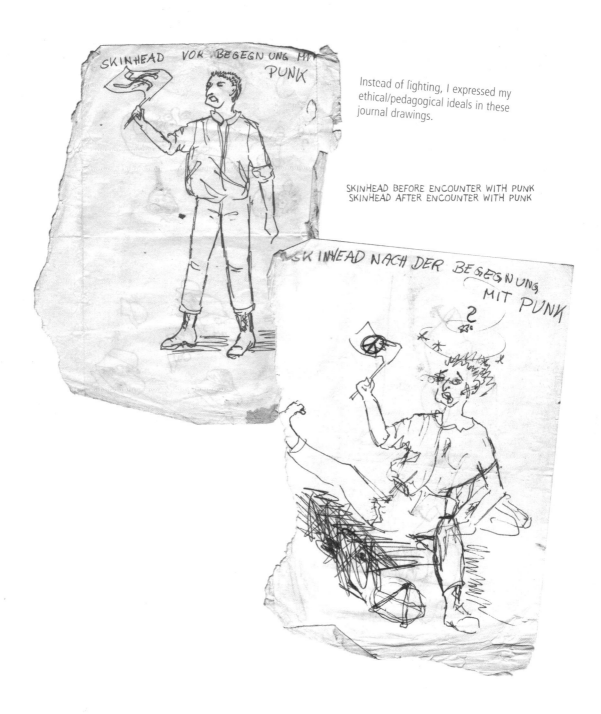

Instead of fighting, I expressed my ethical/pedagogical ideals in these journal drawings.

SKINHEAD BEFORE ENCOUNTER WITH PUNK
SKINHEAD AFTER ENCOUNTER WITH PUNK

SKINHEAD NACH DER BEGEGNUNG
MIT PUNK

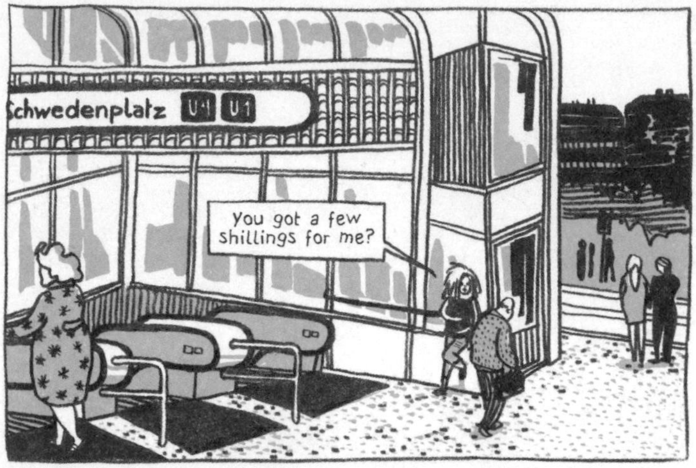
Schwedenplatz U4 U1
You got a few shillings for me?

I'll skip a week that we spent with the drunken wife of a former veteran of the Foreign Legion. She was afraid of being alone, because her husband might show up at her door at any moment, to bash in her skull.

Schwedenplatz was our real home base. You'd always score a few shillings, a sip of wine, or a meatball sandwich.

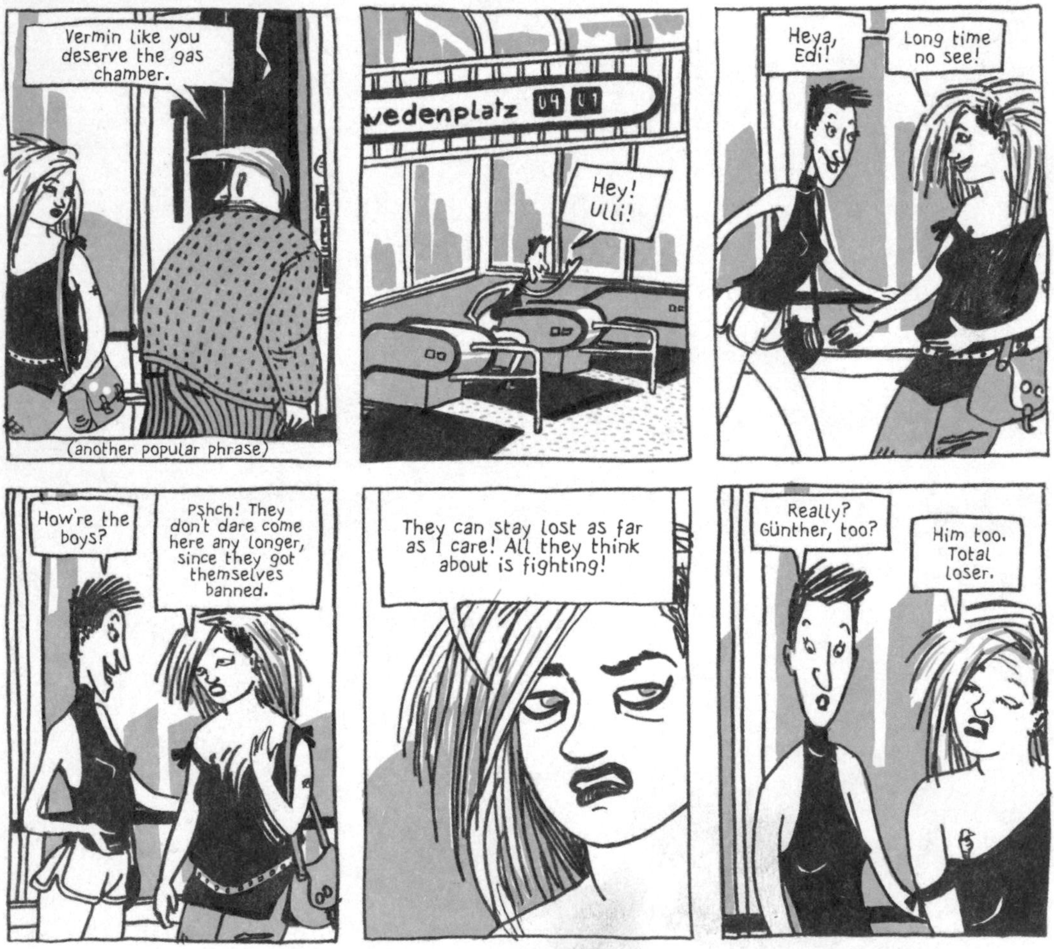
Vermin like you deserve the gas chamber.
(another popular phrase)
wedenplatz U4 U1
Hey! Ulli!
Heya, Edi!
Long time no see!
How're the boys?
Pshch! They don't dare come here any longer, since they got themselves banned.
They can stay lost as far as I care! All they think about is fighting!
Really? Günther, too?
Him too. Total loser.

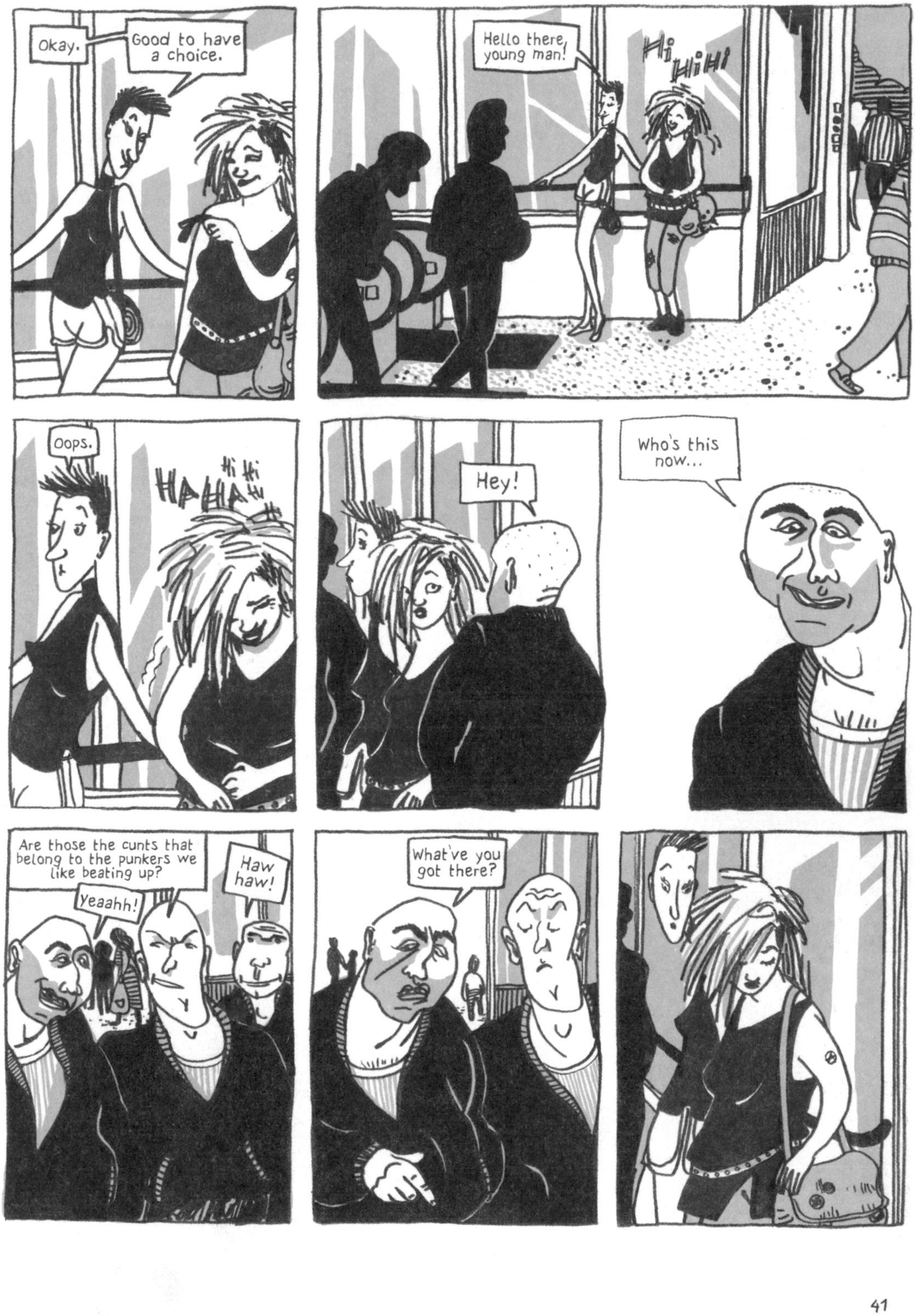
Okay.
Good to have a choice.
Hello there, young man!
Hi HiHi
Oops.
Hi Hi
HAHA
Hey!
Who's this now...
Are those the cunts that belong to the punkers we like beating up?
Yeaahh!
Haw haw!
What've you got there?

What's that?

That!

A crossed-out swastika.

Why d'you have that there?

'Cause I think nazis suck.

Grrr... Let's go for a walk around the corner!

CRAC

C'mon, don't be shy...

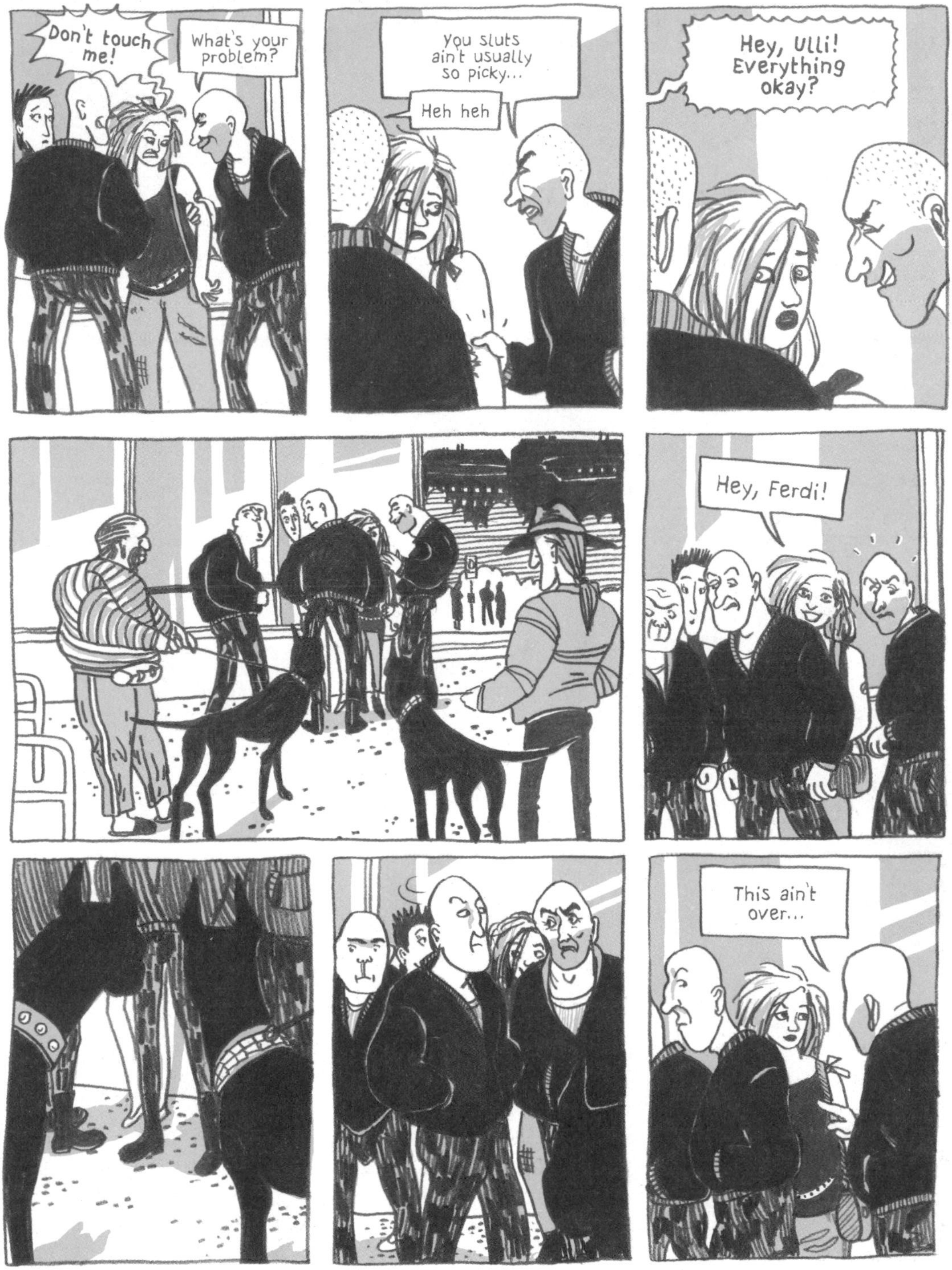
Don't touch me!
What's your problem?
You sluts ain't usually so picky...
Heh heh
Hey, Ulli! Everything okay?
Hey, Ferdi!
This ain't over...

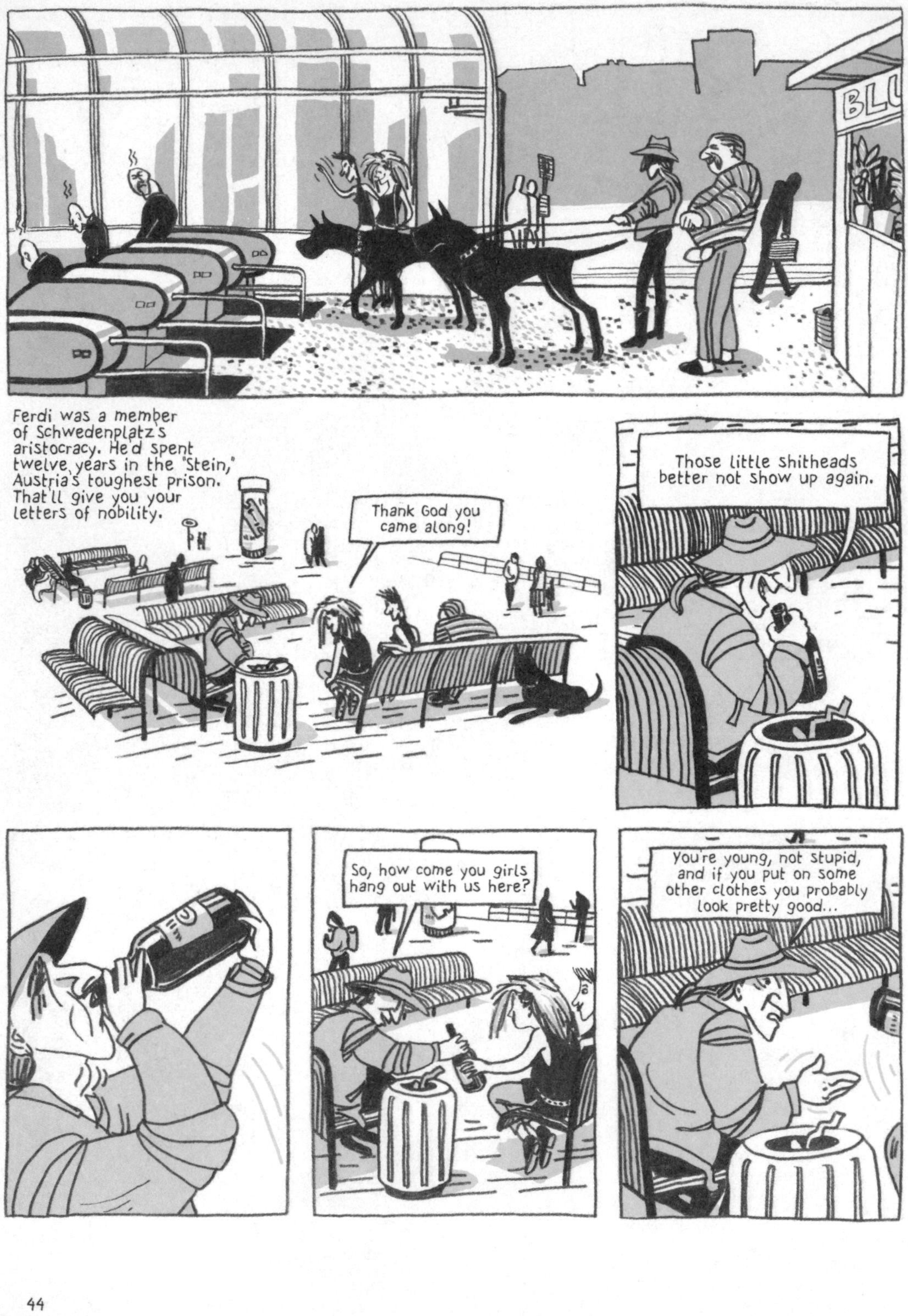
BLU
Ferdi was a member of Schwedenplatz's aristocracy. He'd spent twelve years in the "Stein," Austria's toughest prison. That'll give you your letters of nobility.
Thank God you came along!
Those little shitheads better not show up again.
So, how come you girls hang out with us here?
You're young, not stupid, and if you put on some other clothes you probably look pretty good...

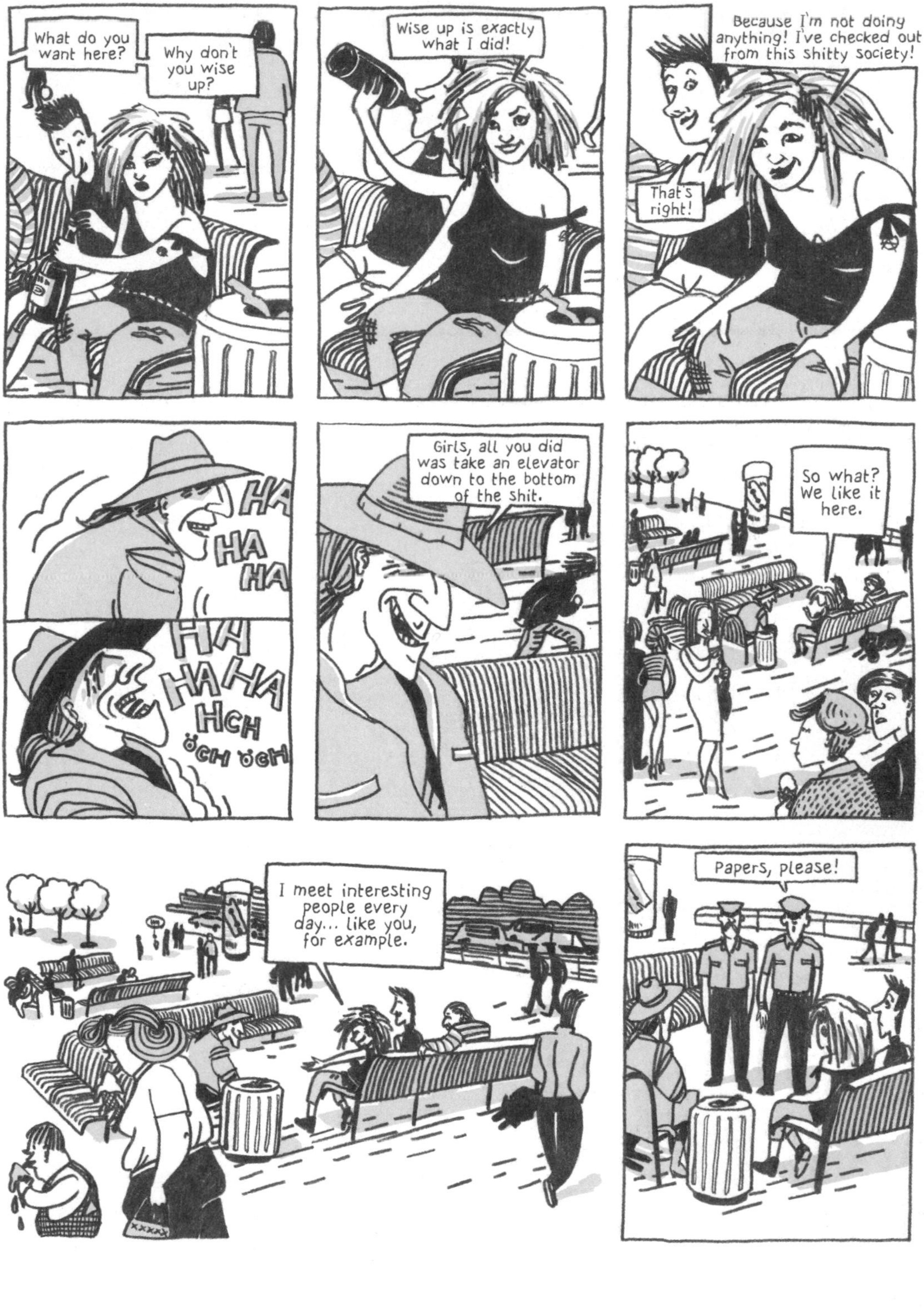
What do you want here?
Why don't you wise up?
Wise up is exactly what I did!
Because I'm not doing anything! I've checked out from this shitty society!
That's right!
HA HA HA
HA HAHA HCH ÖCH ÖCH
Girls, all you did was take an elevator down to the bottom of the shit.
So what? We like it here.
I meet interesting people every day... like you, for example.
Papers, please!

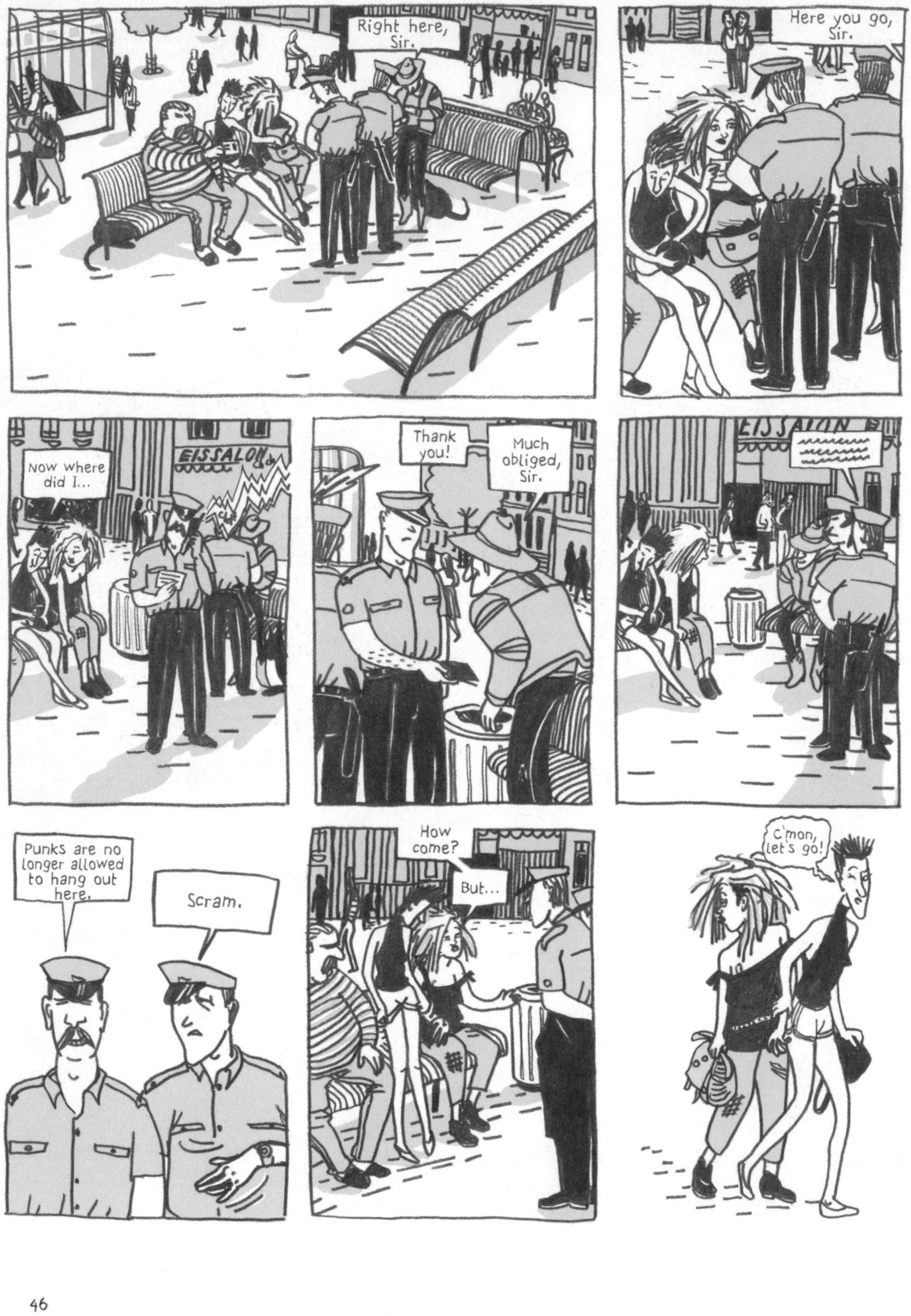
Right here, Sir.
Here you go, Sir.
Now where did I...
Thank you!
Much obliged, Sir.
Punks are no longer allowed to hang out here.
Scram.
How come?
But...
C'mon, let's go!

SSENBAHN
LTESTELL
THEKE
ANKE
ANK

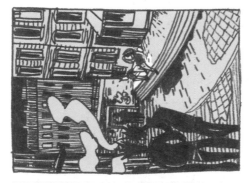

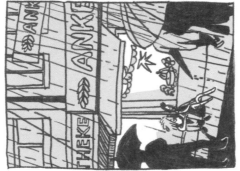

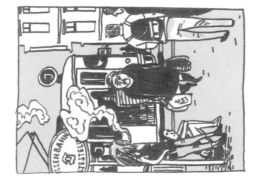

III. the PLAN

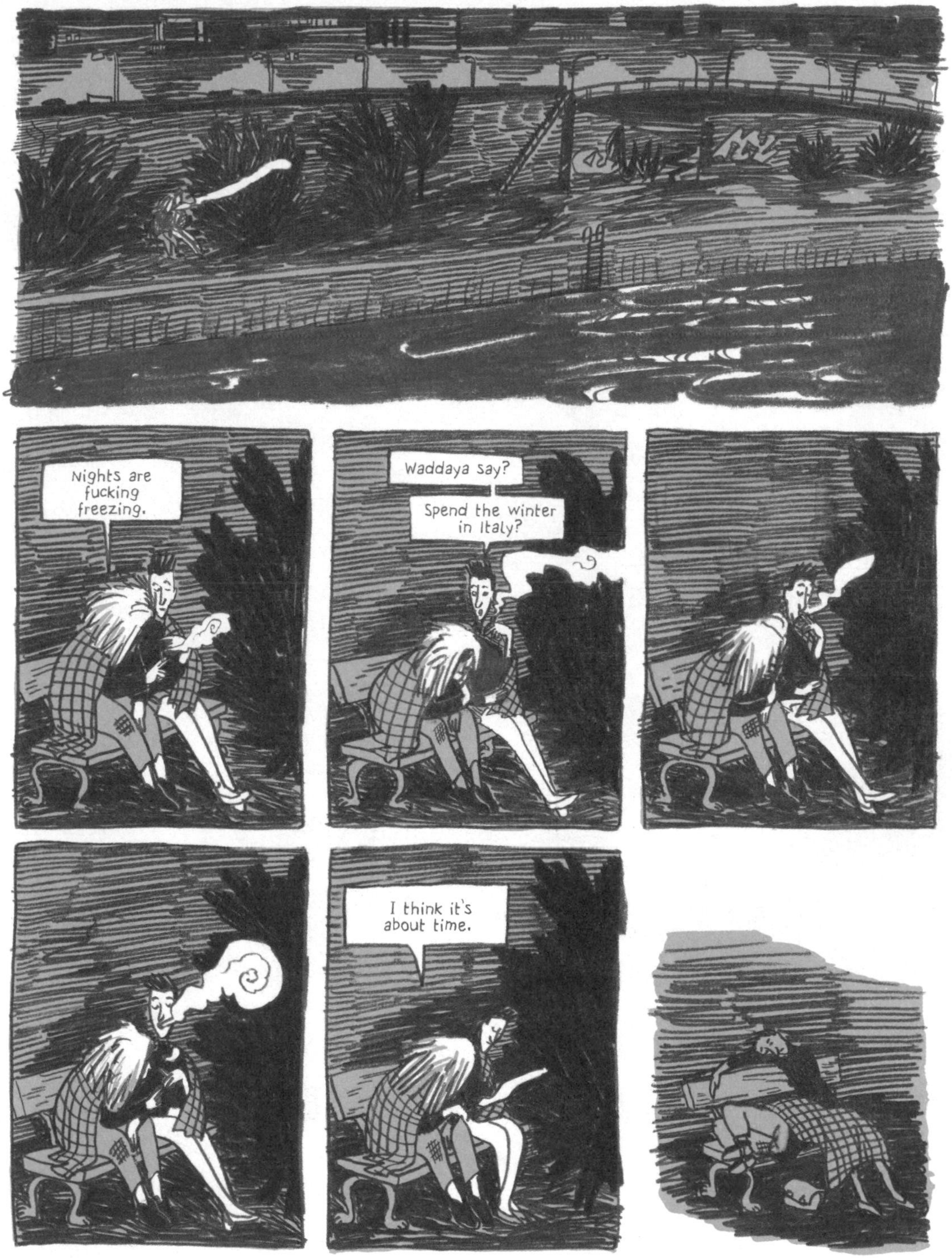

Nights are fucking freezing.
Waddaya say?
Spend the winter in Italy?
I think it's about time.

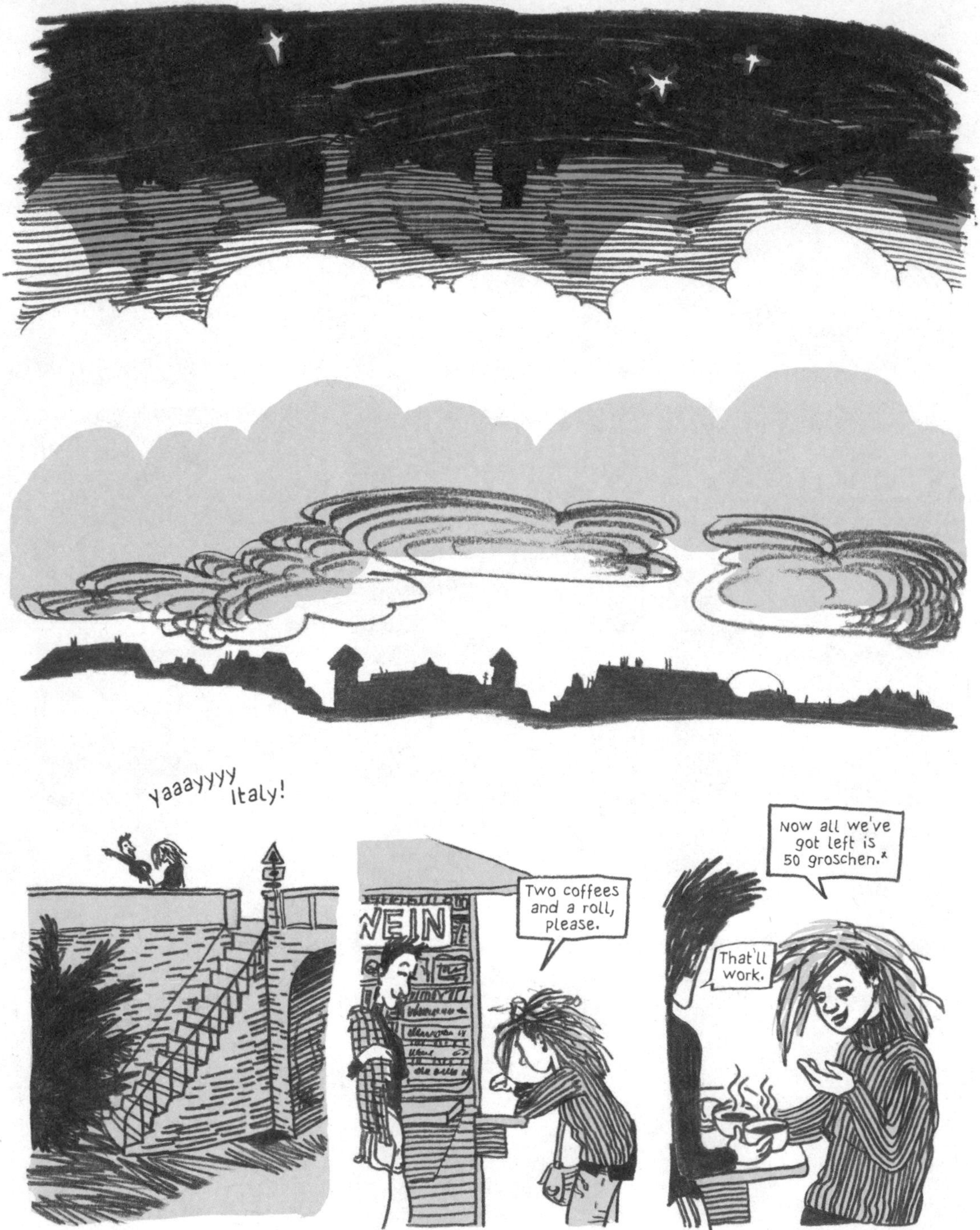
Yaaayyyy
Italy!
WEIN
Two coffees and a roll, please.
Now all we've got left is 50 groschen.*
That'll work.

* about 0.03 Euros

IV the DEED

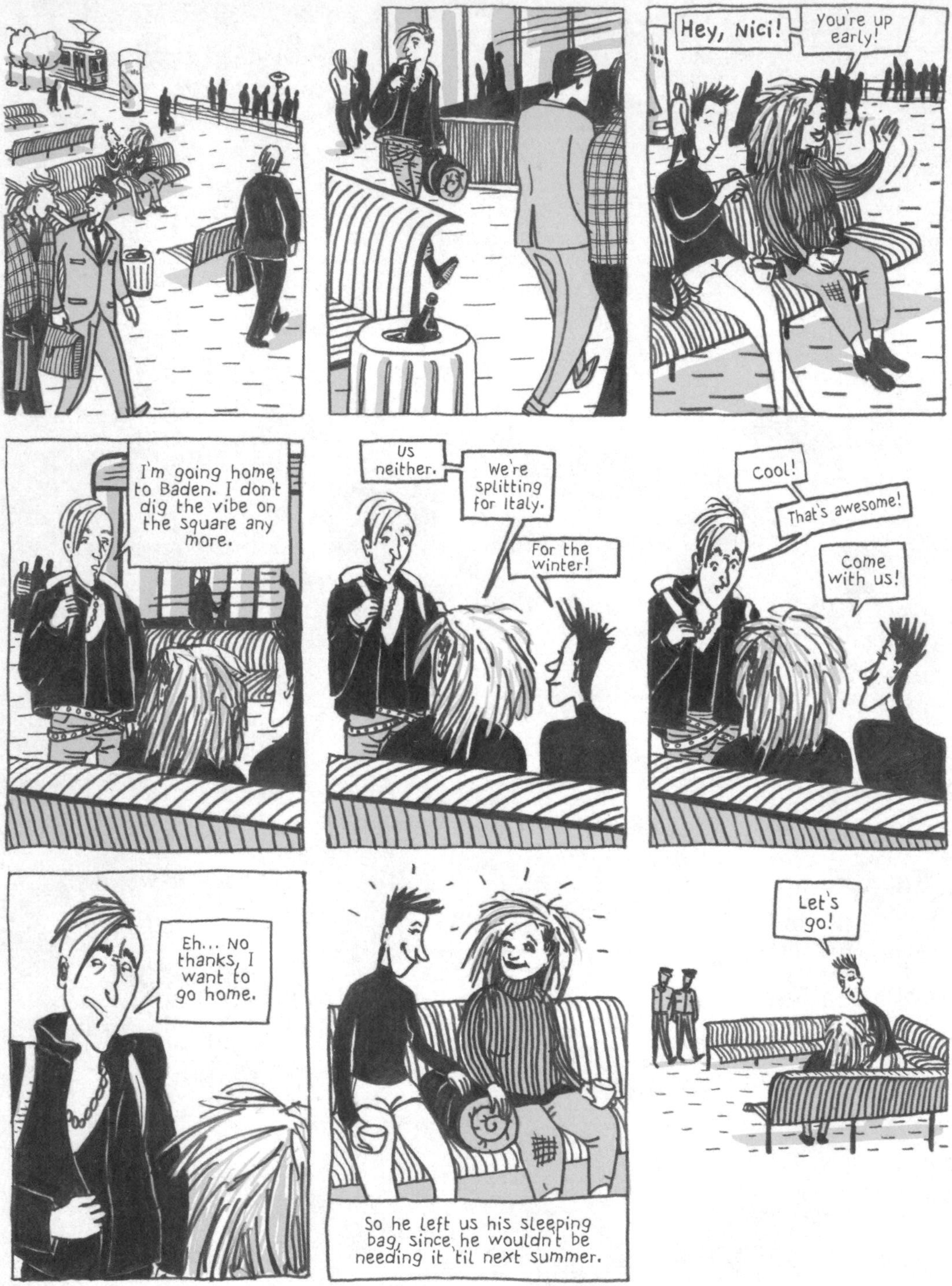
Hey, Nici!
You're up early!
I'm going home to Baden. I don't dig the vibe on the square any more.
Us neither.
We're splitting for Italy.
For the winter!
Cool!
That's awesome!
Come with us!
Eh... No thanks, I want to go home.
So he left us his sleeping bag, since he wouldn't be needing it 'til next summer.
Let's go!

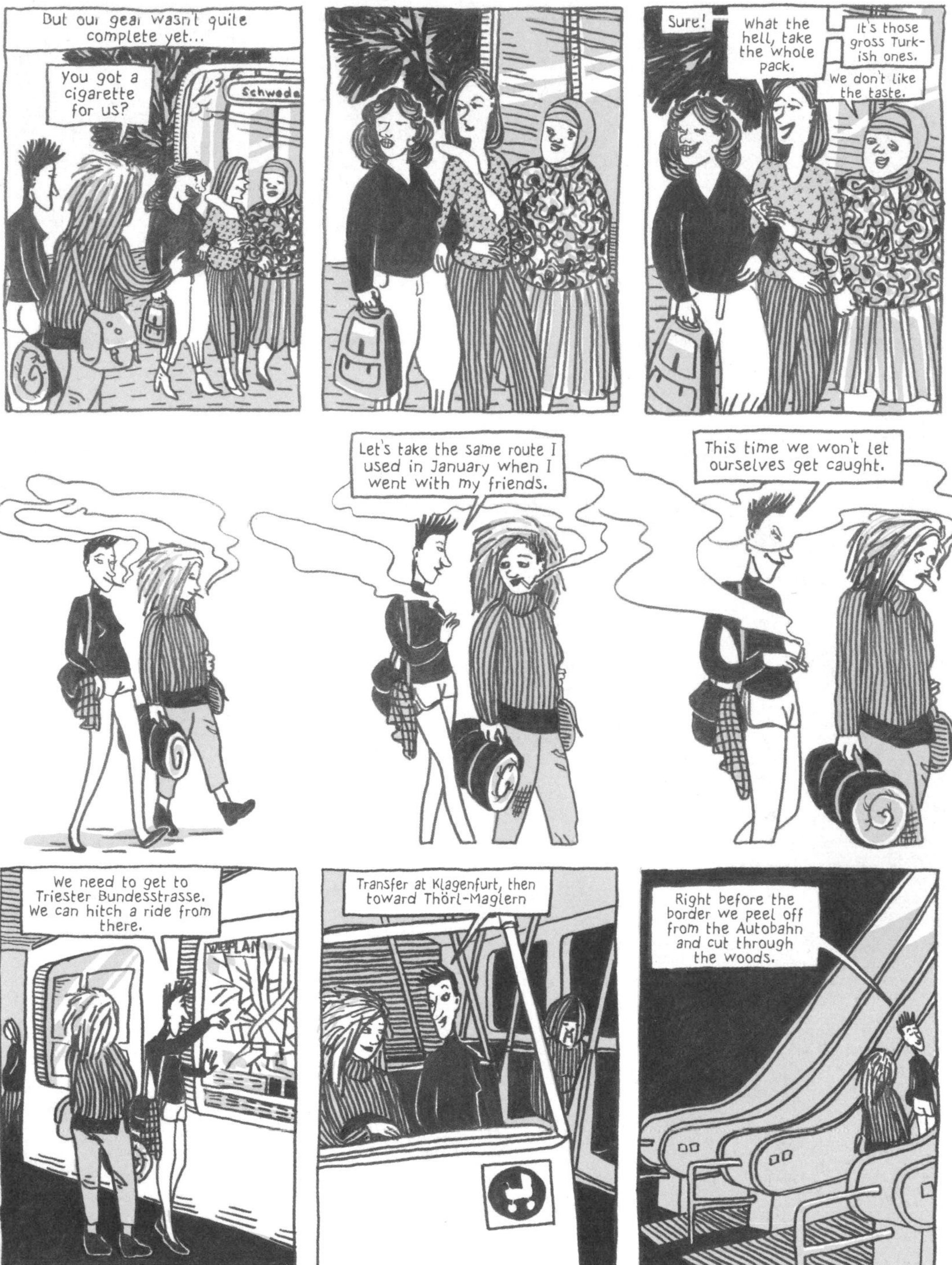
But our gear wasn't quite complete yet...
You got a cigarette for us?
Schwede
Sure!
What the hell, take the whole pack.
It's those gross Turk-ish ones.
We don't like the taste.
Let's take the same route I used in January when I went with my friends.
This time we won't let ourselves get caught.
We need to get to Triester Bundesstrasse. We can hitch a ride from there.
Transfer at Klagenfurt, then toward Thörl-Maglern
Right before the border we peel off from the Autobahn and cut through the woods.

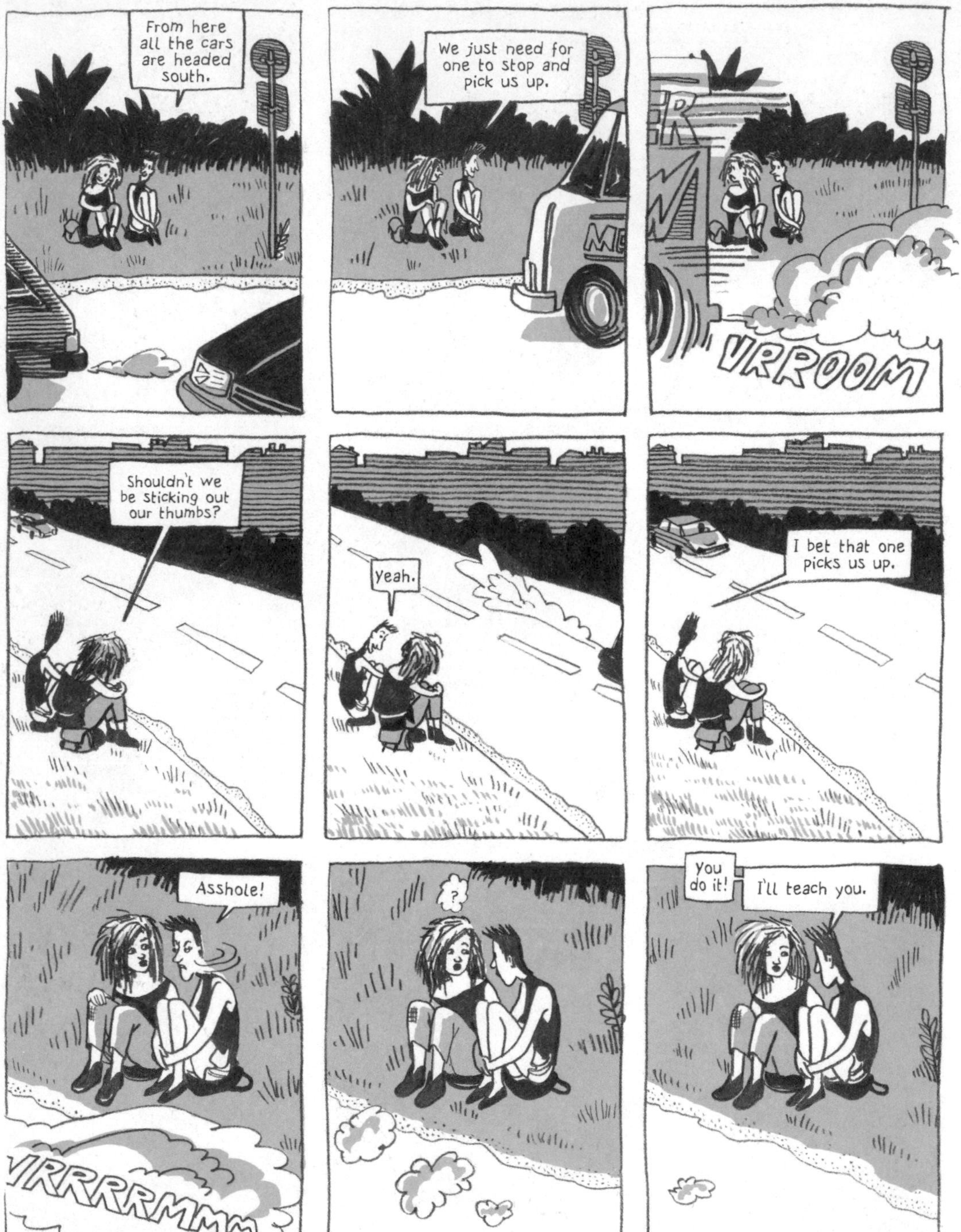
From here all the cars are headed south.
We just need for one to stop and pick us up.
VRROOM
Shouldn't we be sticking out our thumbs?
Yeah.
I bet that one picks us up.
Asshole!
VRRRRRMMMM
?
You do it!
I'll teach you.

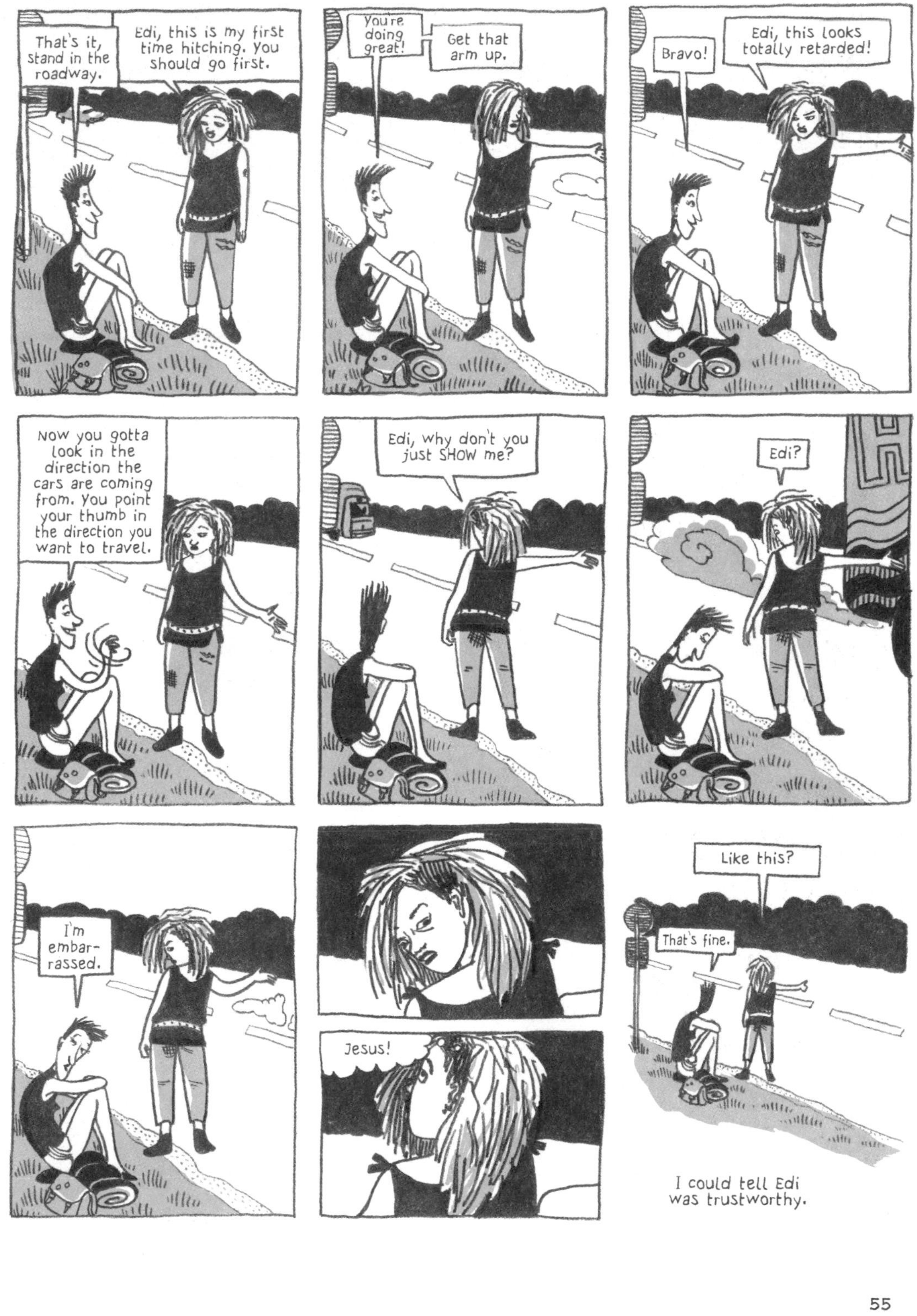
That's it, stand in the roadway.
Edi, this is my first time hitching. You should go first.
You're doing great!
Get that arm up.
Bravo!
Edi, this looks totally retarded!
Now you gotta look in the direction the cars are coming from. You point your thumb in the direction you want to travel.
Edi, why don't you just SHOW me?
Edi?
I'm embar-rassed.
Jesus!
Like this?
That's fine.
I could tell Edi was trustworthy.

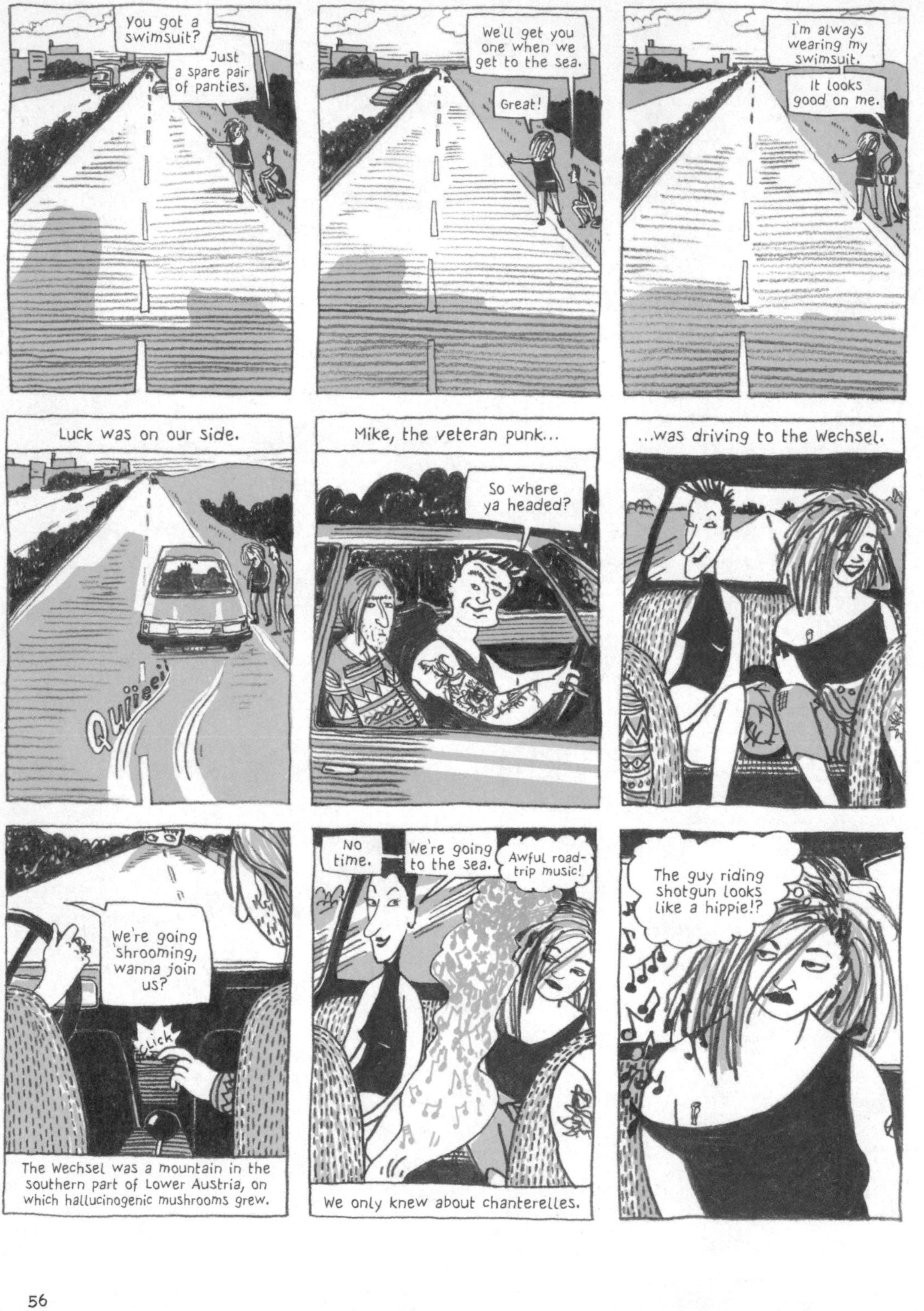
You got a swimsuit?
Just a spare pair of panties.
We'll get you one when we get to the sea.
Great!
I'm always wearing my swimsuit.
It looks good on me.
Luck was on our side.
Quiieei
Mike, the veteran punk...
So where ya headed?
...was driving to the Wechsel.
We're going shrooming, wanna join us?
Click
The Wechsel was a mountain in the southern part of Lower Austria, on which hallucinogenic mushrooms grew.
No time.
We're going to the sea.
Awful road-trip music!
We only knew about chanterelles.
The guy riding shotgun looks like a hippie!?

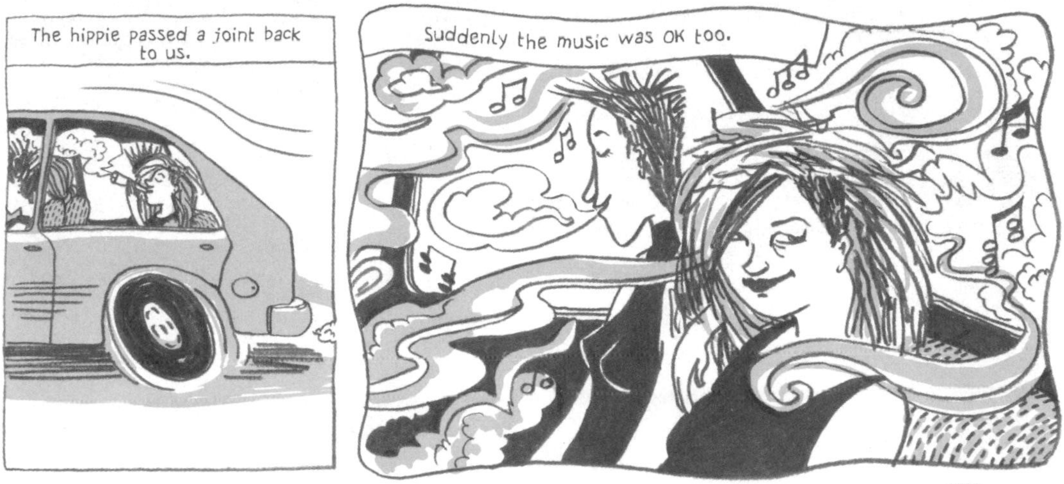
The hippie passed a joint back to us.
Suddenly the music was OK too.

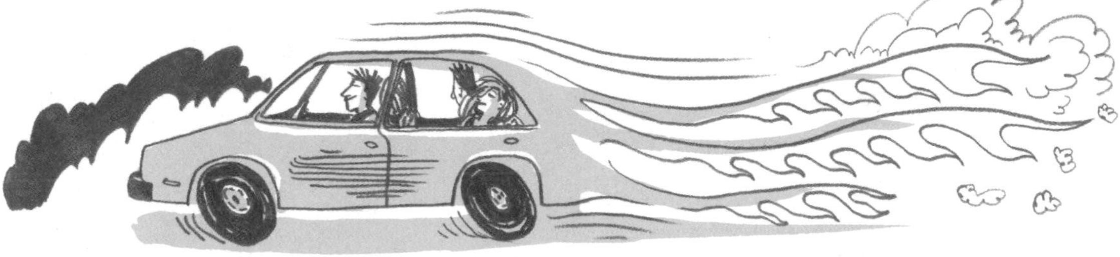

From my travel diary:

"I realized the craziness of our situation: Two 17-year-old girls hitchhiking to Italy —

" — a country which I only knew from books and movies — with just a sleeping bag —

"— a blanket, no spare clothes, no money, no papers. We felt like global explorers!!!"

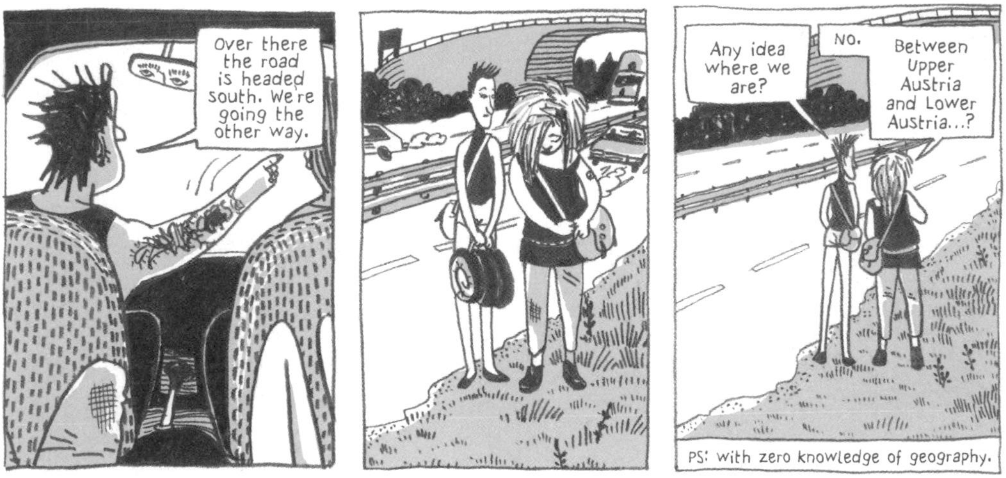
Over there the road is headed south. We're going the other way.
Any idea where we are?
No.
Between Upper Austria and Lower Austria...?
PS: with zero knowledge of geography.

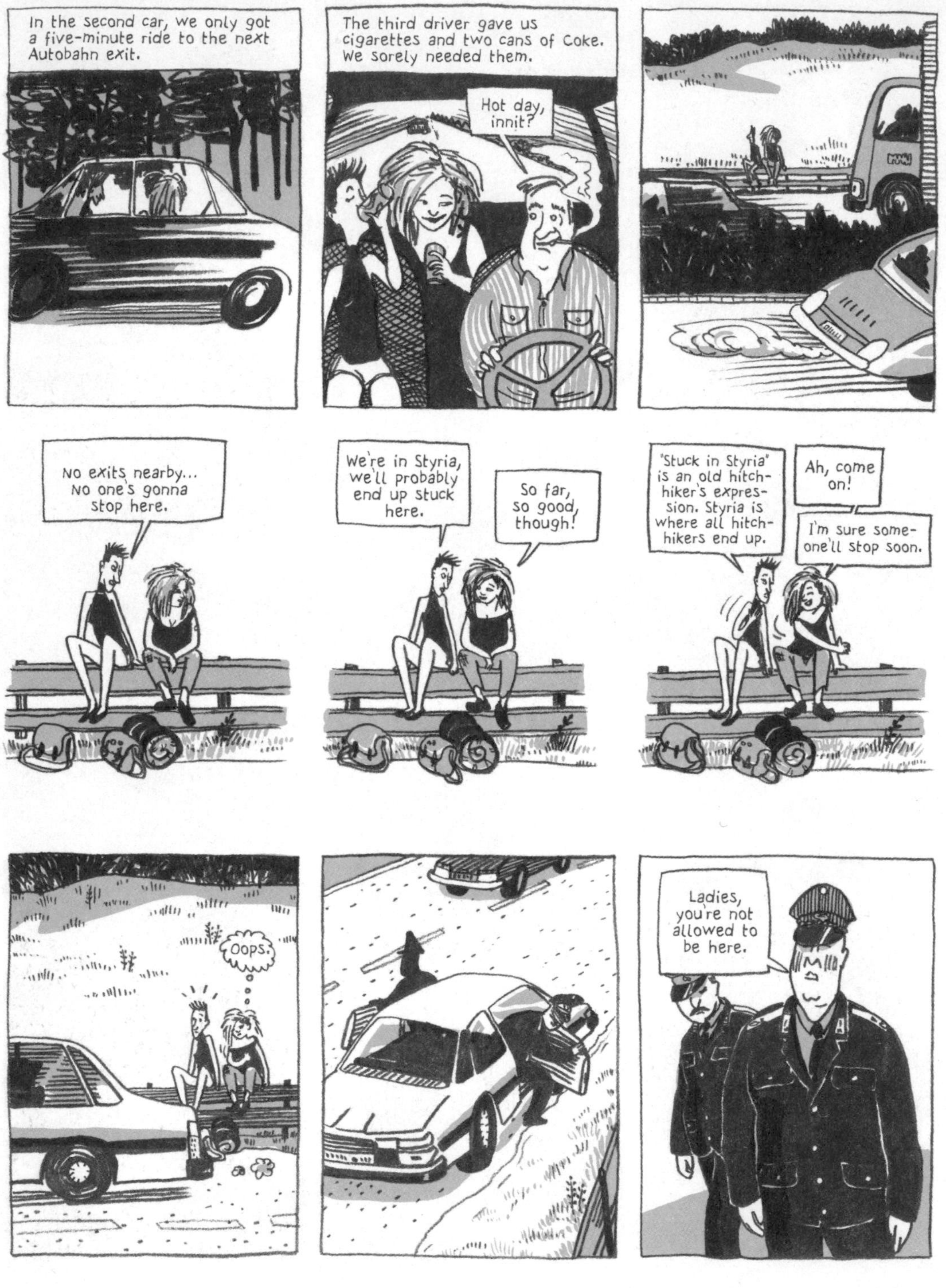

In the second car, we only got a five-minute ride to the next Autobahn exit.
The third driver gave us cigarettes and two cans of Coke. We sorely needed them.
Hot day, innit?
No exits nearby... No one's gonna stop here.
We're in Styria, we'll probably end up stuck here.
So far, so good, though!
"Stuck in Styria" is an old hitch-hiker's expres-sion. Styria is where all hitch-hikers end up.
Ah, come on!
I'm sure some-one'll stop soon.
Oops.
Ladies, you're not allowed to be here.

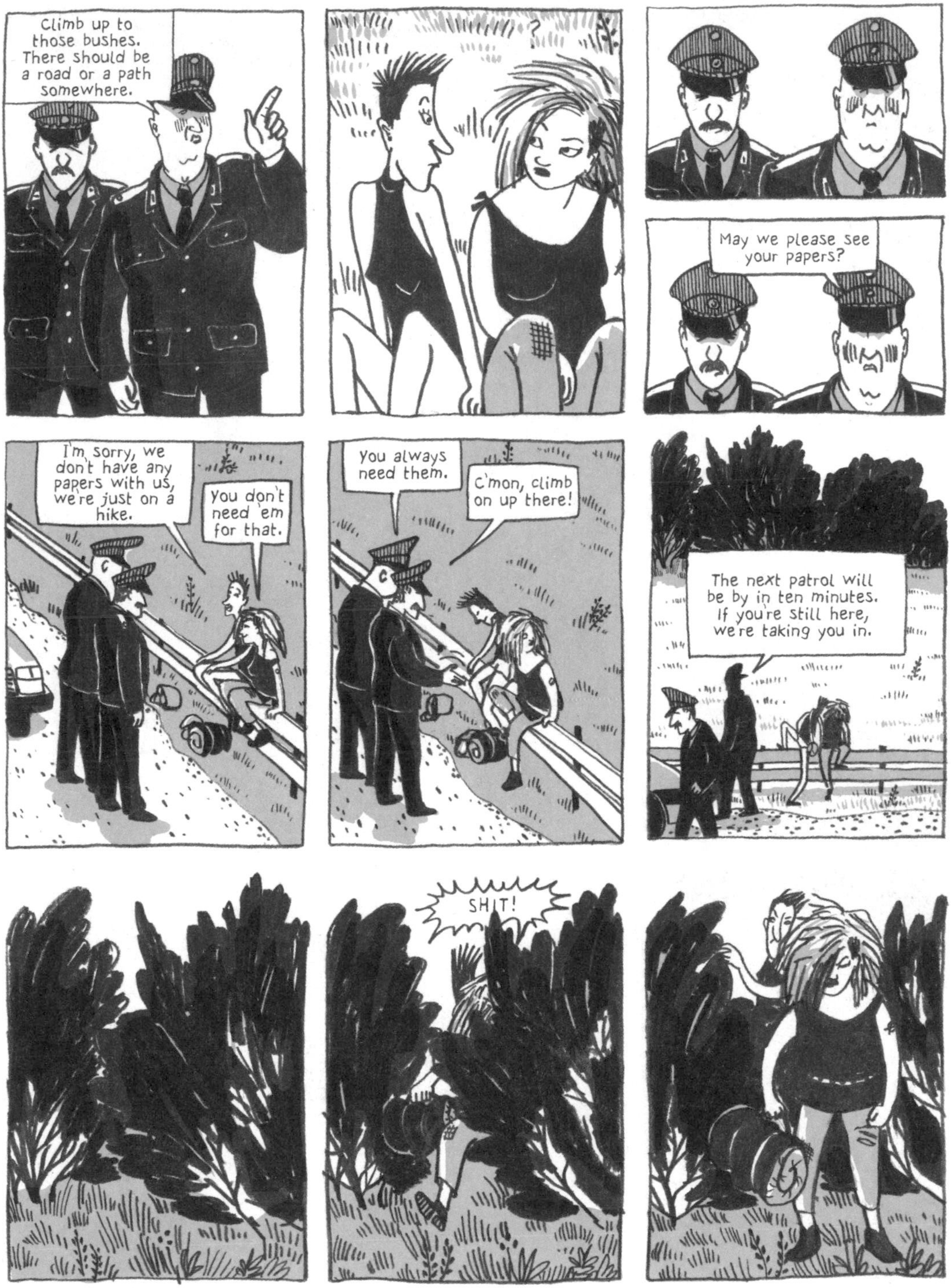

Climb up to those bushes. There should be a road or a path somewhere.
?
May we please see your papers?
I'm sorry, we don't have any papers with us, we're just on a hike.
You don't need 'em for that.
You always need them.
C'mon, climb on up there!
The next patrol will be by in ten minutes. If you're still here, we're taking you in.
SHIT!

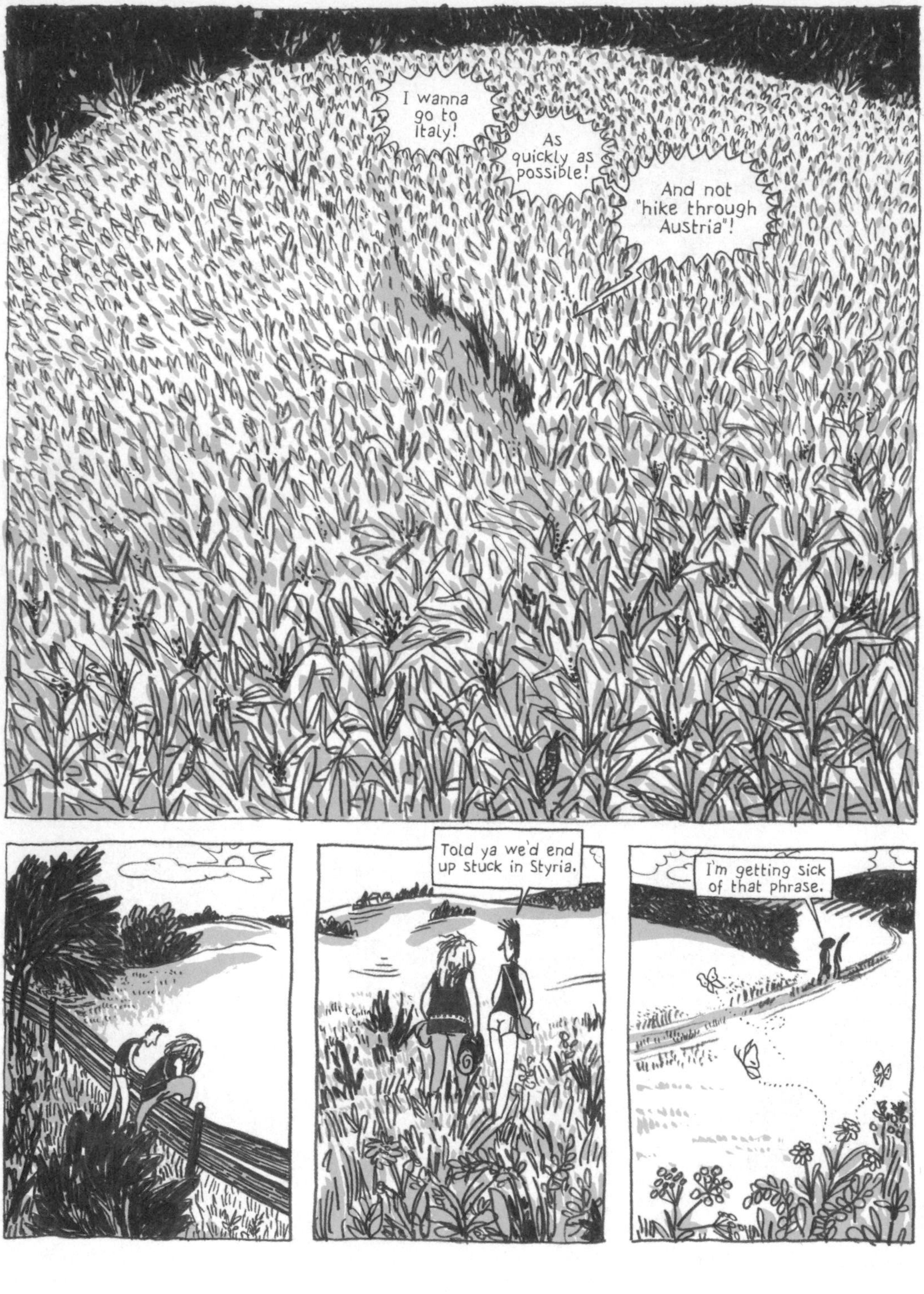
I wanna go to Italy!
As quickly as possible!
And not "hike through Austria"!
Told ya we'd end up stuck in Styria.
I'm getting sick of that phrase.

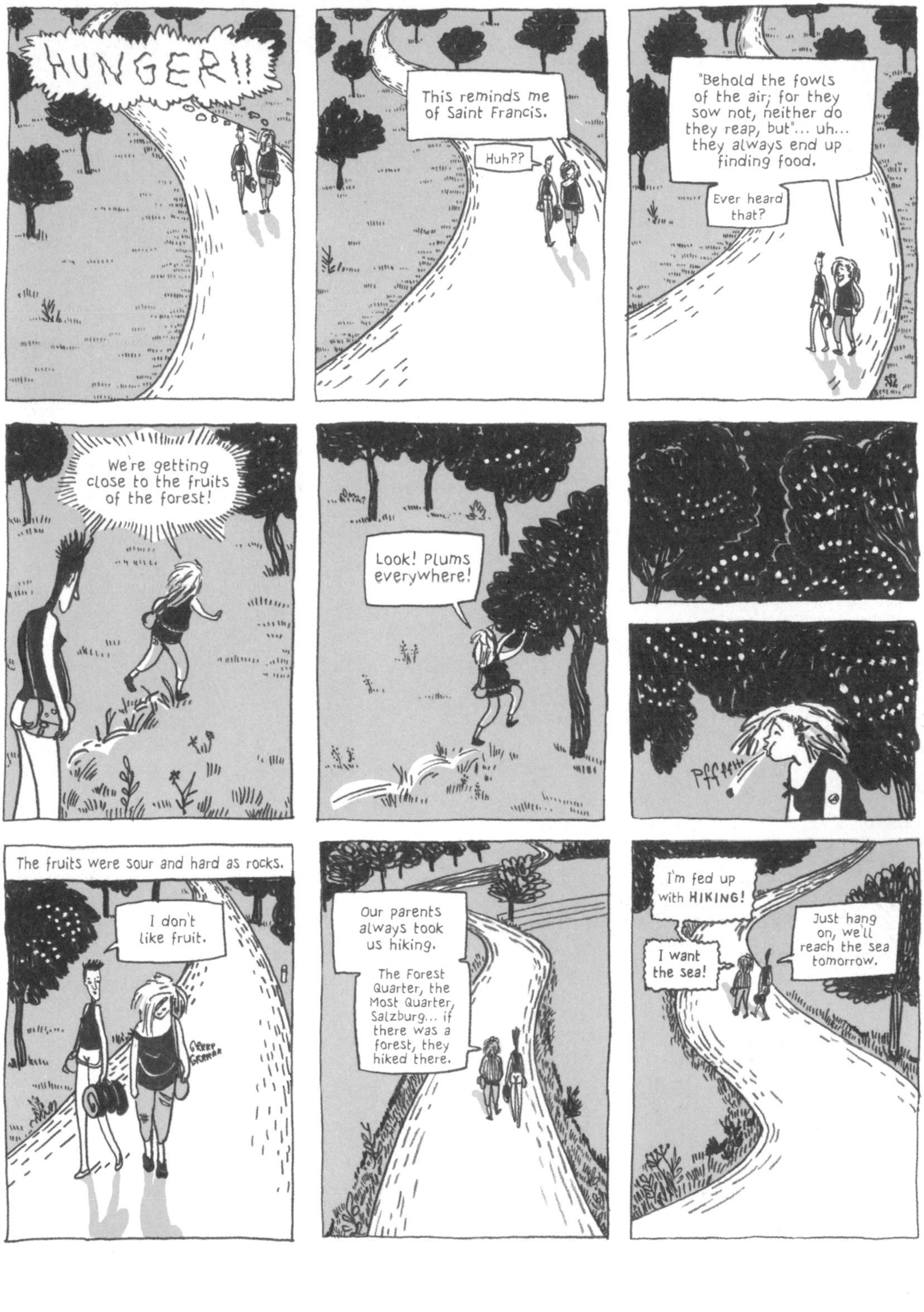
HUNGER!!
This reminds me of Saint Francis.
Huh??
"Behold the fowls of the air; for they sow not, neither do they reap, but"... uh... they always end up finding food.
Ever heard that?
We're getting close to the fruits of the forest!
Look! Plums everywhere!
The fruits were sour and hard as rocks.
I don't like fruit.
Our parents always took us hiking.
The Forest Quarter, the Most Quarter, Salzburg... if there was a forest, they hiked there.
I'm fed up with HIKING!
I want the sea!
Just hang on, we'll reach the sea tomorrow.

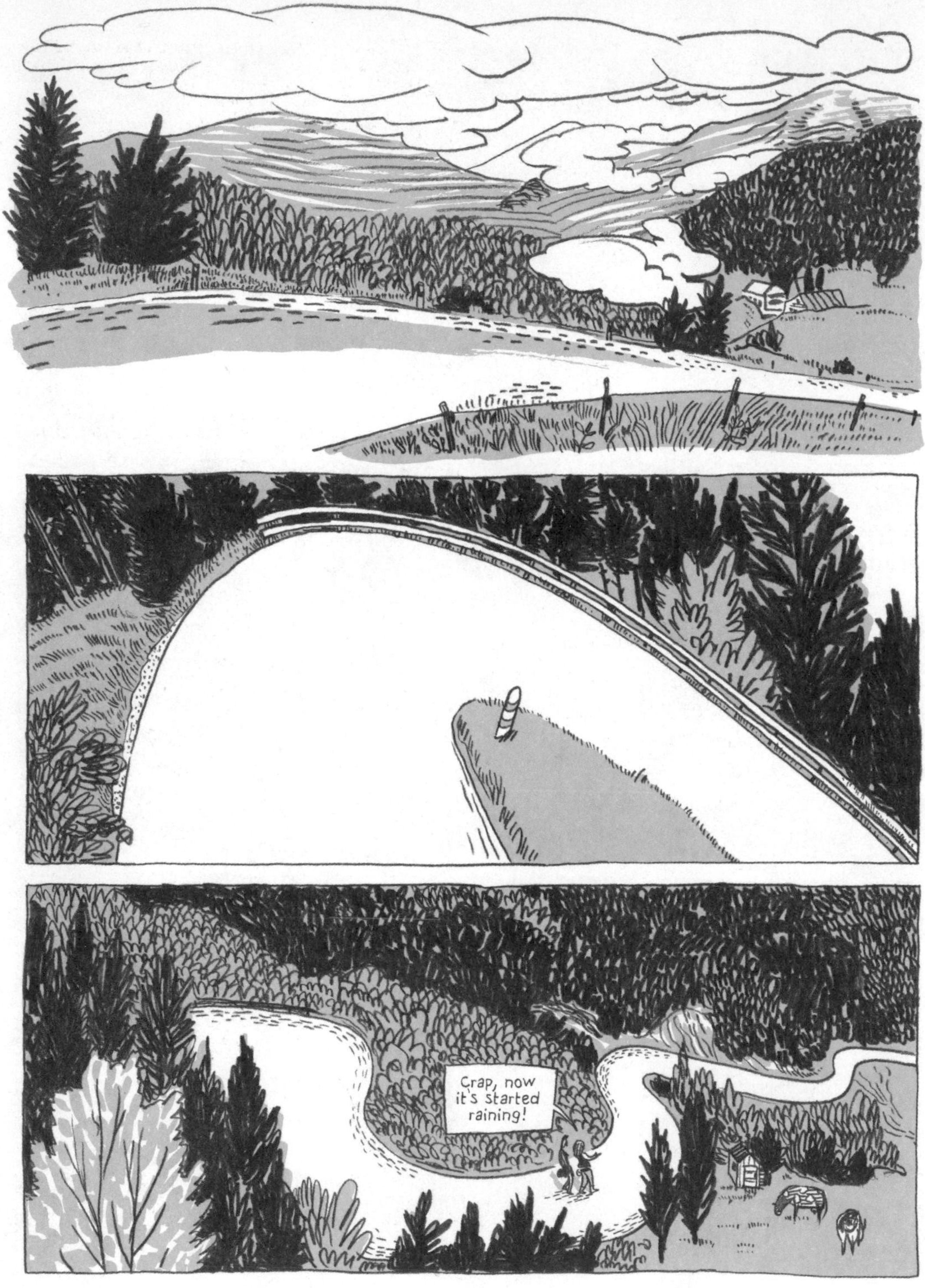
Crap, now it's started raining!

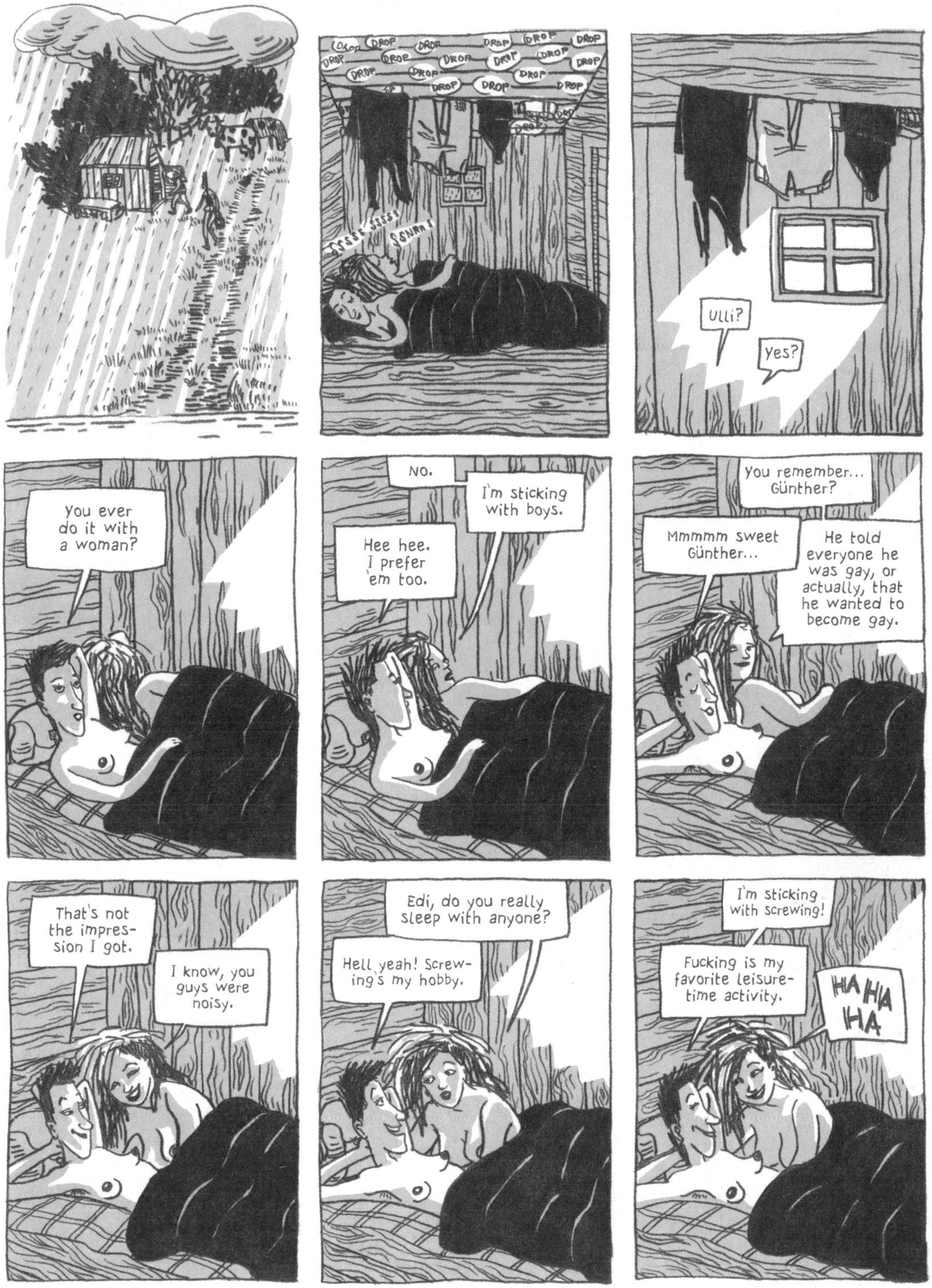
DROP DROP DROP DROP DROP DROP
SSSSS SSSSS SCHNARR
Ulli?
Yes?
You ever do it with a woman?
No.
I'm sticking with boys.
Hee hee. I prefer 'em too.
You remember... Günther?
Mmmmm sweet Günther...
He told everyone he was gay, or actually, that he wanted to become gay.
That's not the impression I got.
I know, you guys were noisy.
Edi, do you really sleep with anyone?
Hell yeah! Screwing's my hobby.
I'm sticking with screwing!
Fucking is my favorite leisure-time activity.
HA HA HA

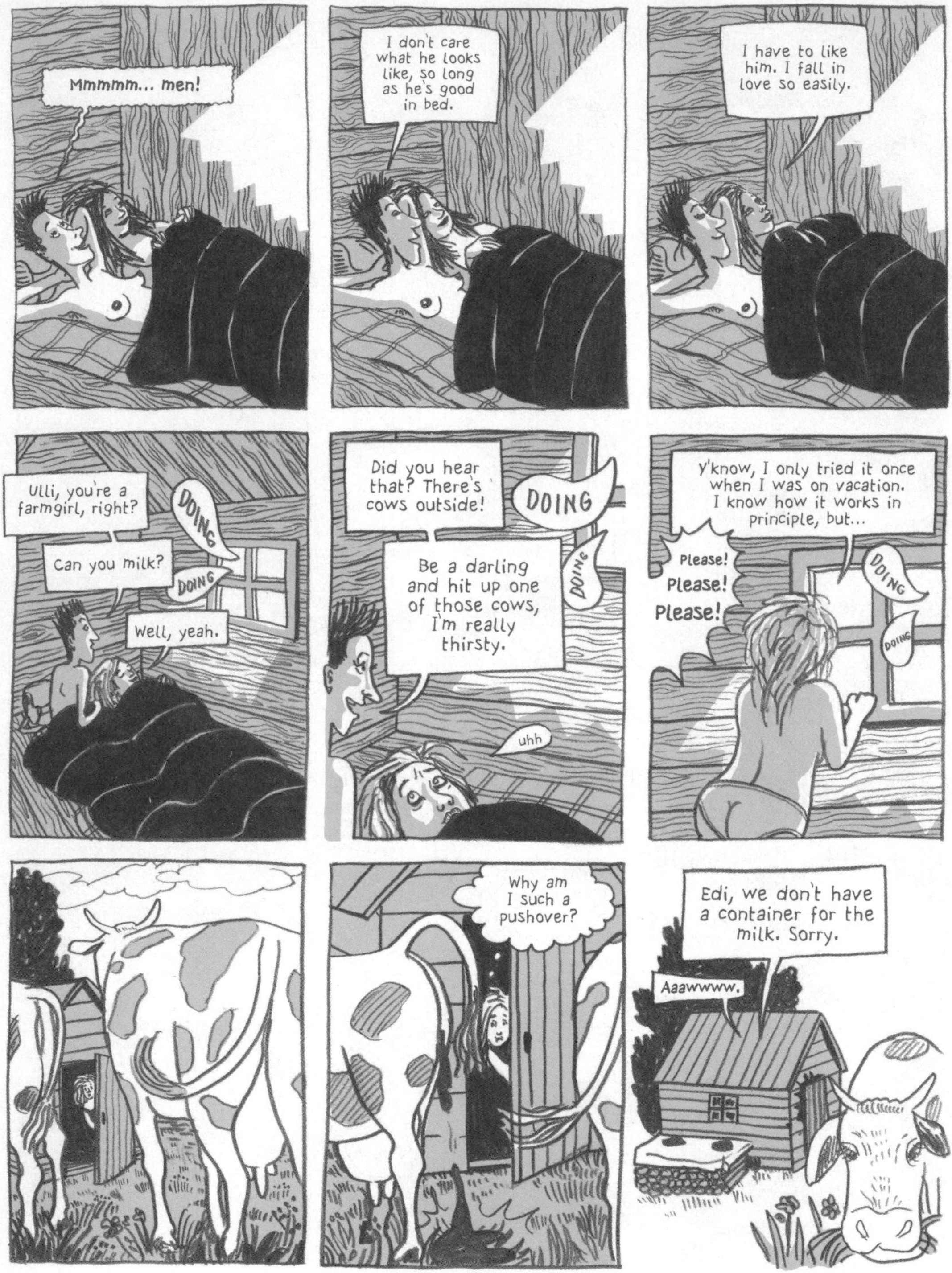
Mmmmm... men!
I don't care what he looks like, so long as he's good in bed.
I have to like him. I fall in love so easily.
Ulli, you're a farmgirl, right?
DOING
Can you milk?
DOING
Well, yeah.
Did you hear that? There's cows outside!
DOING
Be a darling and hit up one of those cows, I'm really thirsty.
DOING
uhh
Y'know, I only tried it once when I was on vacation. I know how it works in principle, but...
Please! Please! Please!
DOING
DOING
Why am I such a pushover?
Edi, we don't have a container for the milk. Sorry.
Aaawwww.

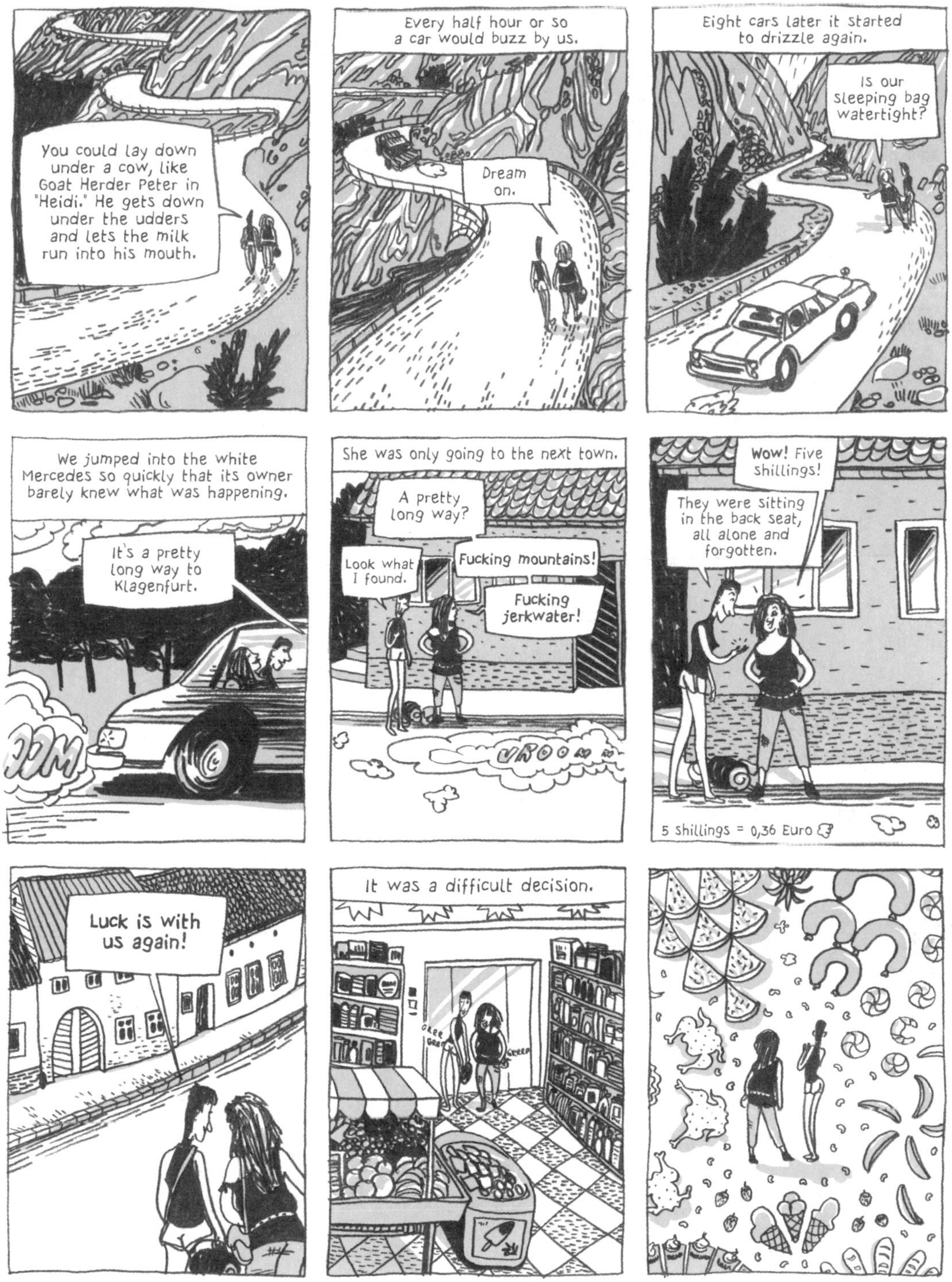
You could lay down under a cow, like Goat Herder Peter in "Heidi." He gets down under the udders and lets the milk run into his mouth.
Every half hour or so a car would buzz by us.
Dream on.
Eight cars later it started to drizzle again.
Is our sleeping bag watertight?
We jumped into the white Mercedes so quickly that its owner barely knew what was happening.
It's a pretty long way to Klagenfurt.
She was only going to the next town.
A pretty long way?
Look what I found.
Fucking mountains!
Fucking jerkwater!
VROOM
Wow! Five shillings!
They were sitting in the back seat, all alone and forgotten.
5 Shillings = 0,36 Euro
Luck is with us again!
It was a difficult decision.

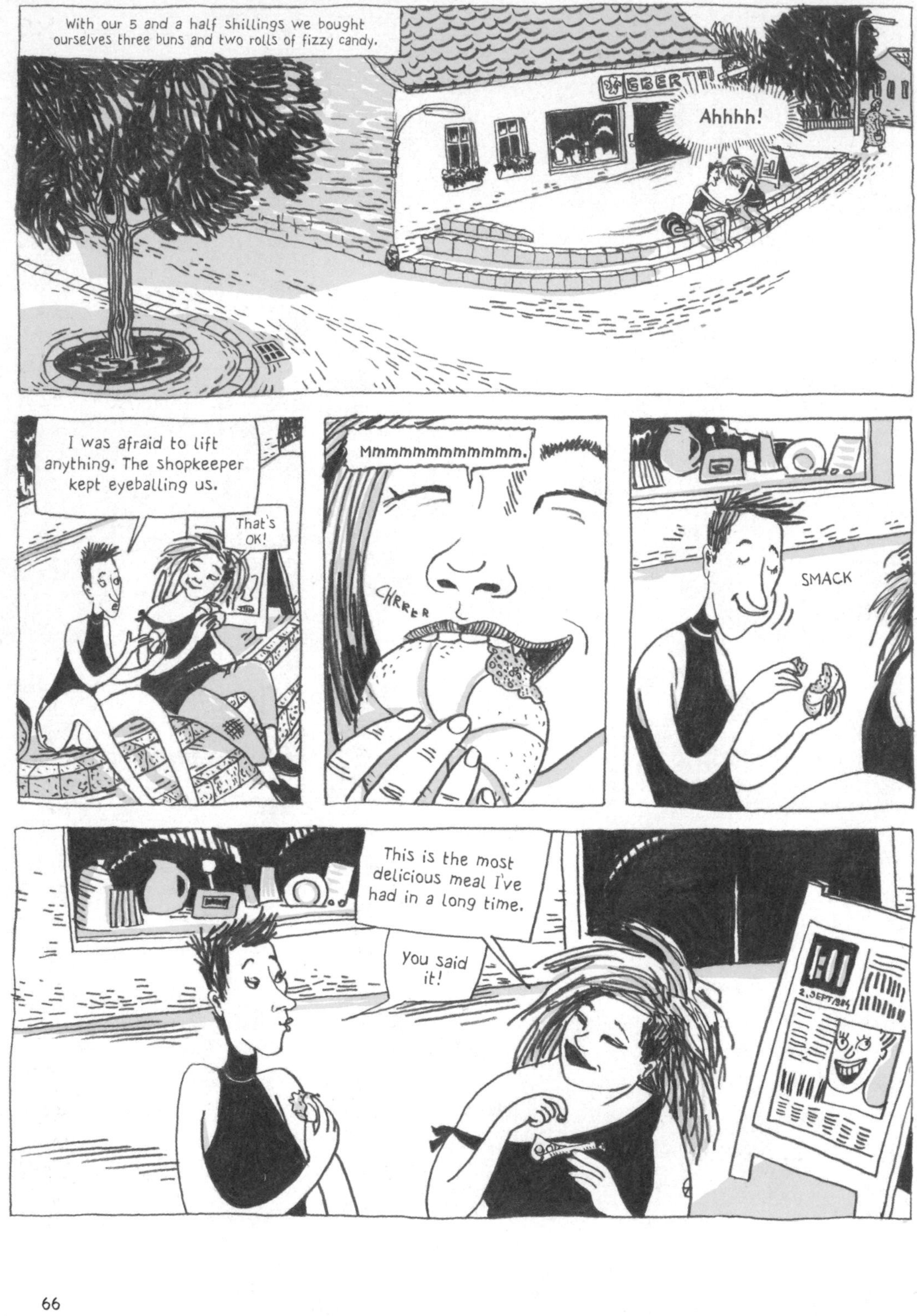
With our 5 and a half shillings we bought ourselves three buns and two rolls of fizzy candy.
EBERT
Ahhhh!
I was afraid to lift anything. The shopkeeper kept eyeballing us.
That's OK!
Mmmmmmmmmmmm.
CHRRRR
SMACK
This is the most delicious meal I've had in a long time.
You said it!

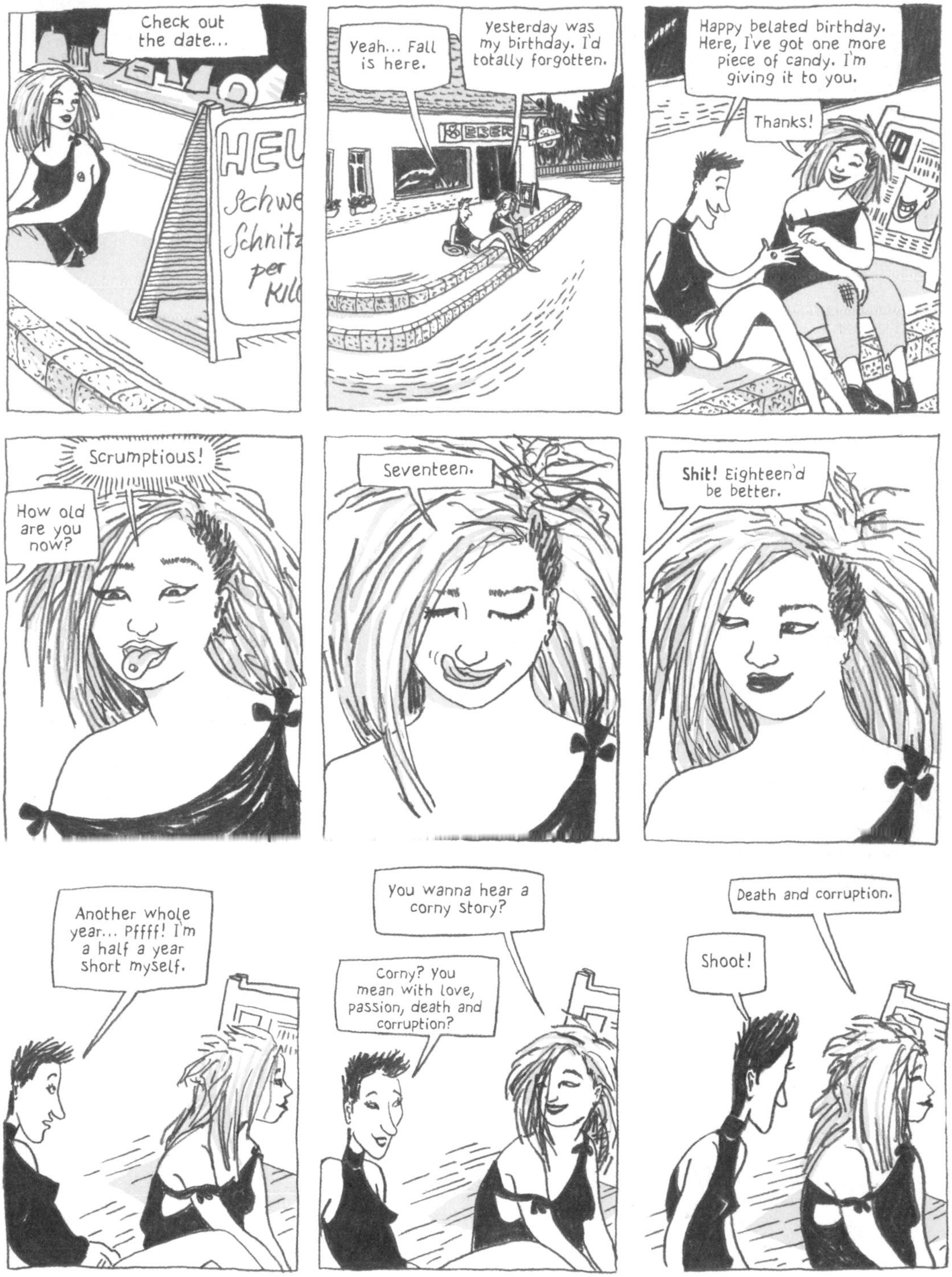

Check out the date...
HEU
Schwe
Schnitz
per
Kil
Yeah... Fall is here.
Yesterday was my birthday. I'd totally forgotten.
EBERL
Happy belated birthday. Here, I've got one more piece of candy. I'm giving it to you.
Thanks!
Scrumptious!
How old are you now?
Seventeen.
Shit! Eighteen'd be better.
Another whole year... Pffff! I'm a half a year short myself.
You wanna hear a corny story?
Corny? You mean with love, passion, death and corruption?
Death and corruption.
Shoot!

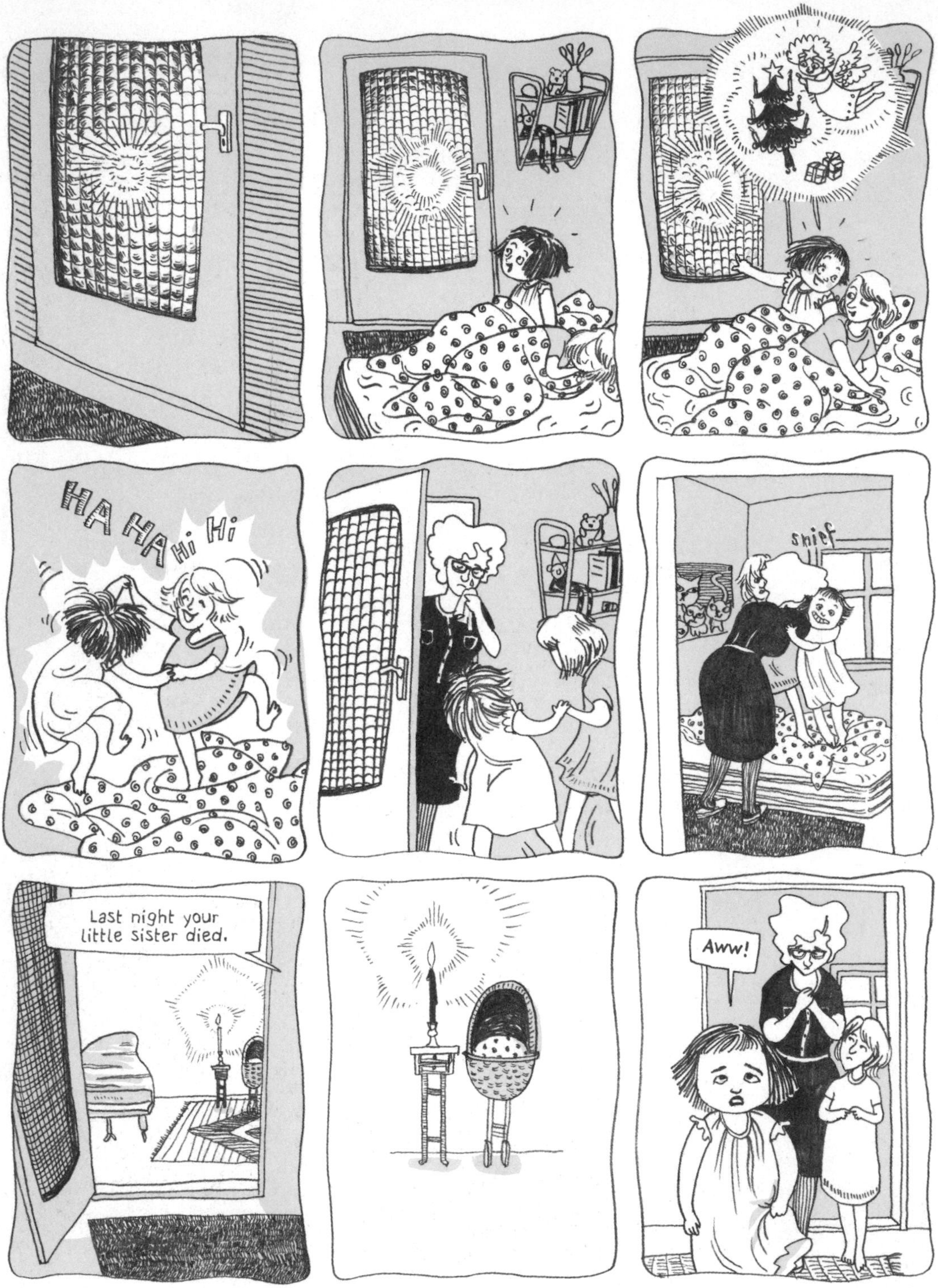
HA HA Hi Hi
snief
Last night your little sister died.
Aww!

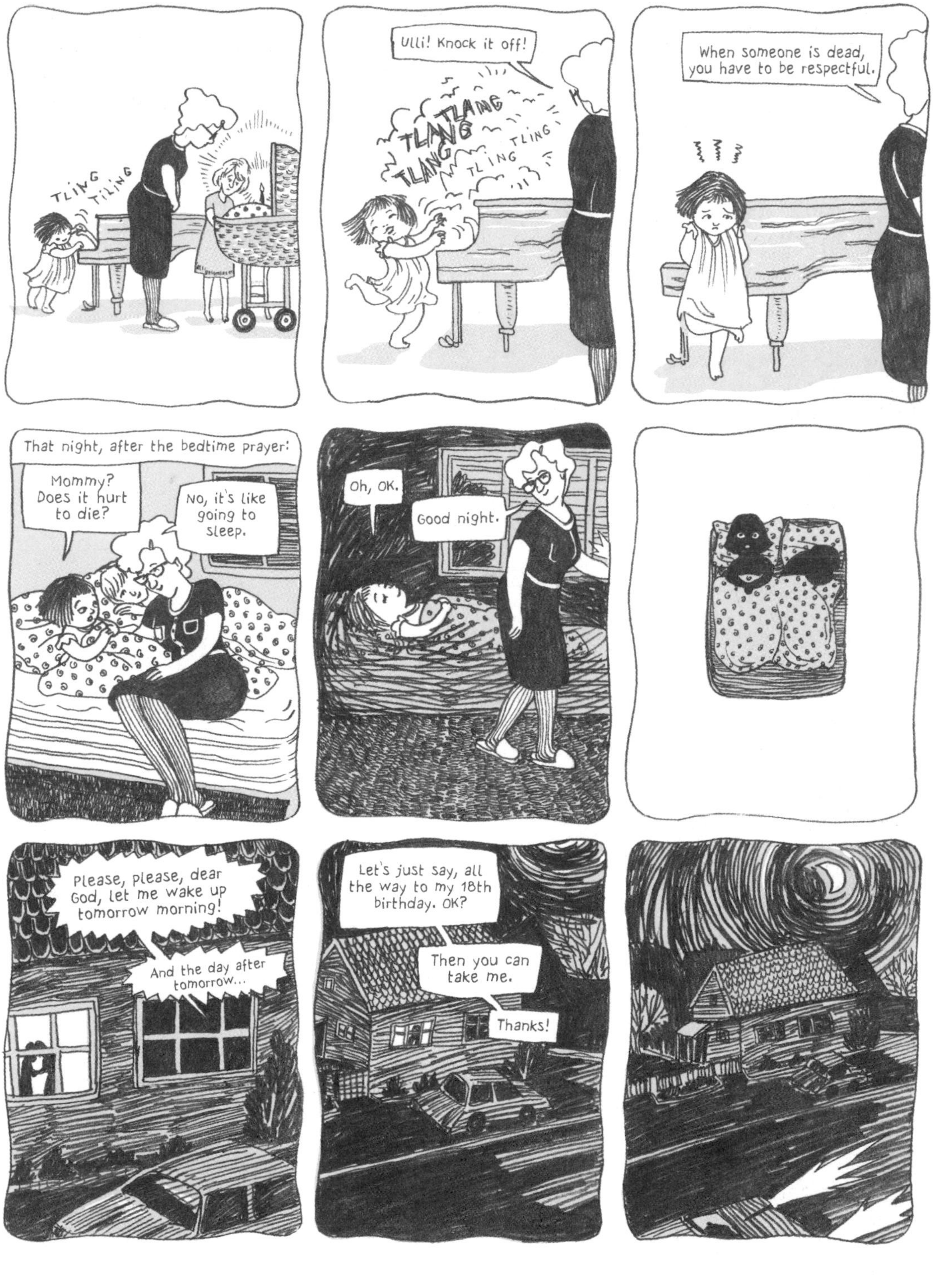

TLING TILING
Ulli! Knock it off!
TLANG TLANG TLANG TLING TLING
When someone is dead, you have to be respectful.
That night, after the bedtime prayer:
Mommy? Does it hurt to die?
No, it's like going to sleep.
Oh, OK.
Good night.
Please, please, dear God, let me wake up tomorrow morning!
And the day after tomorrow...
Let's just say, all the way to my 18th birthday. OK?
Then you can take me.
Thanks!

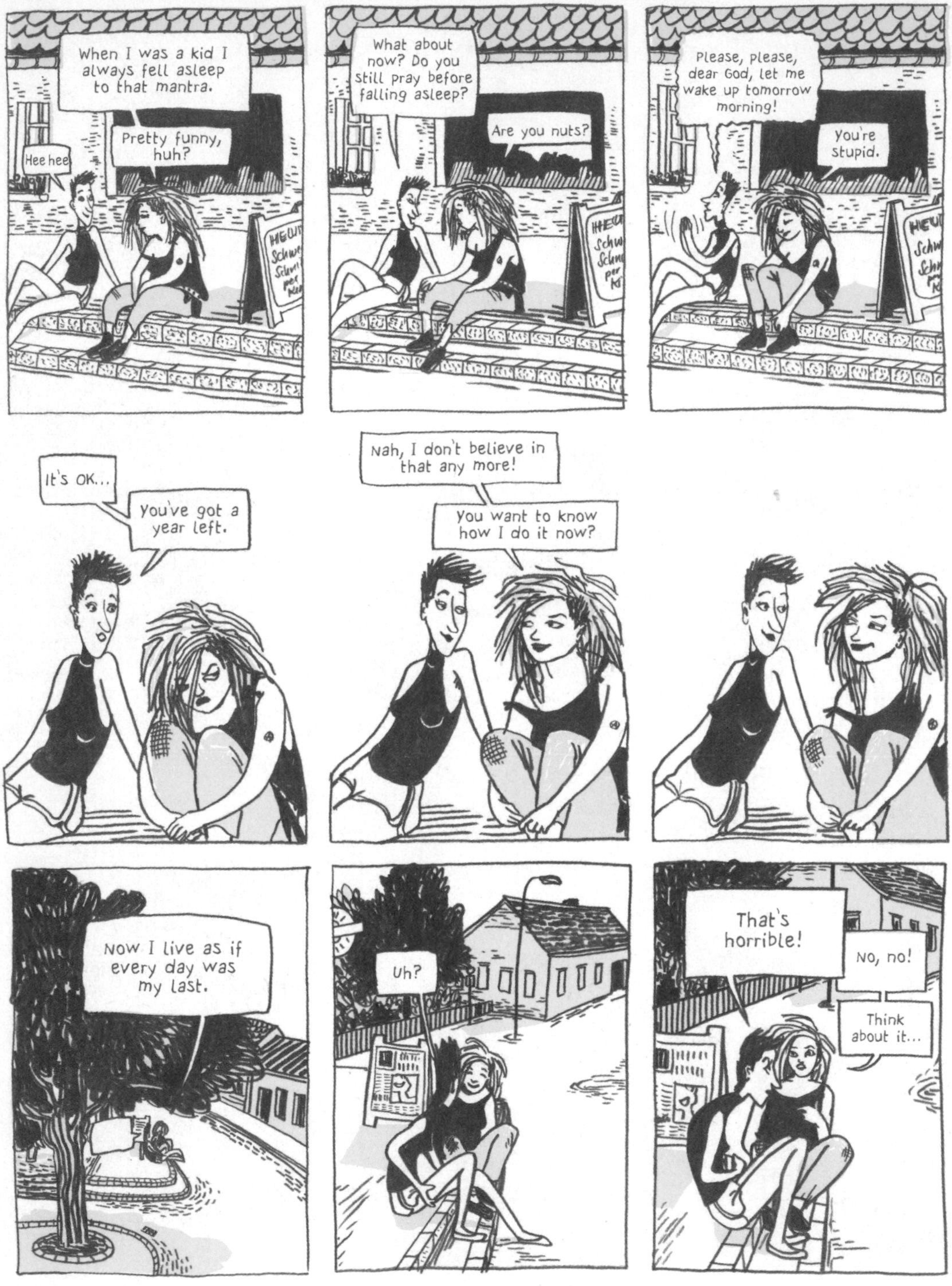
When I was a kid I always fell asleep to that mantra.
Pretty funny, huh?
Hee hee
What about now? Do you still pray before falling asleep?
Are you nuts?
Please, please, dear God, let me wake up tomorrow morning!
You're stupid.
It's OK...
You've got a year left.
Nah, I don't believe in that any more!
You want to know how I do it now?
Now I live as if every day was my last.
Uh?
That's horrible!
No, no!
Think about it...

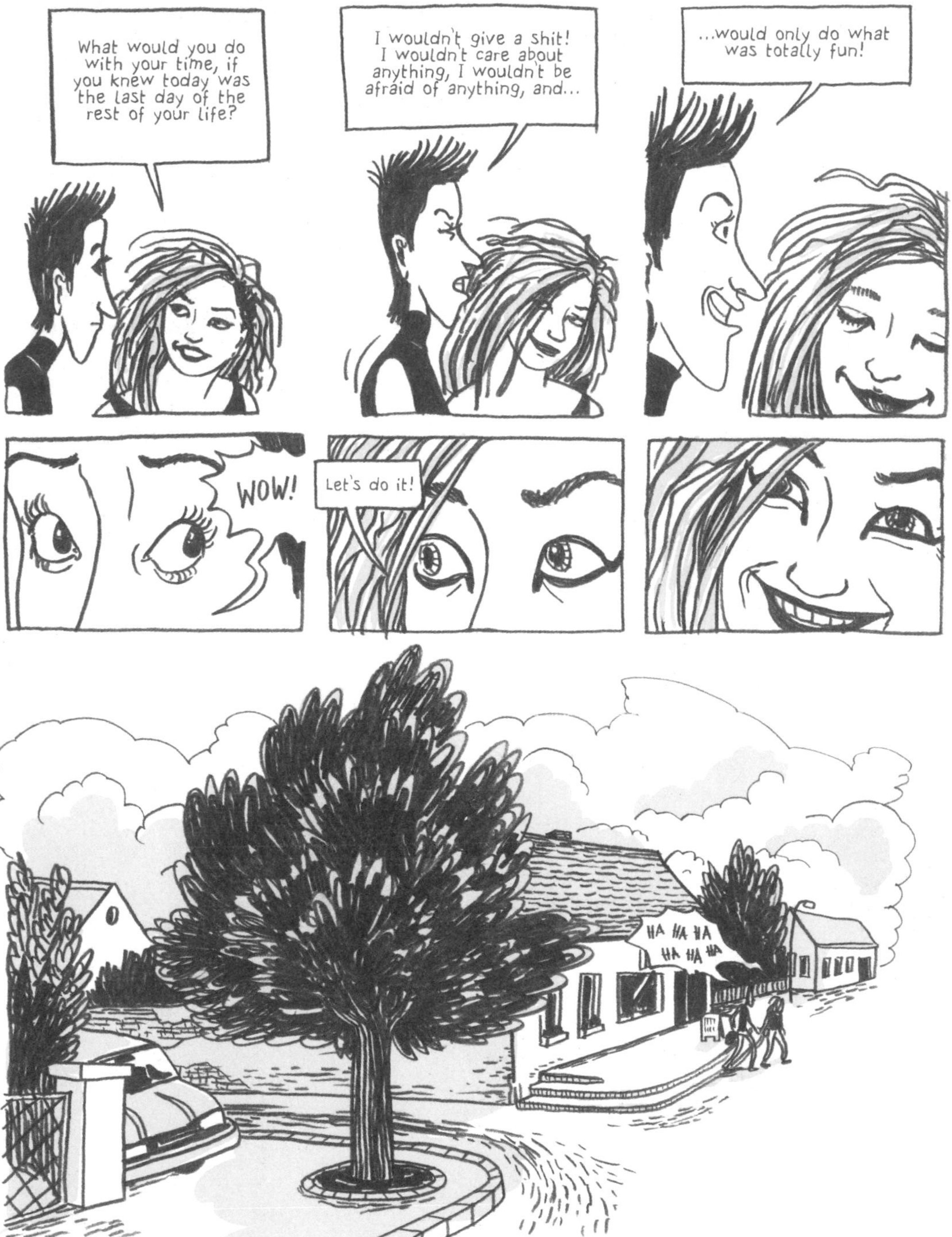

What would you do with your time, if you knew today was the last day of the rest of your life?
I wouldn't give a shit! I wouldn't care about anything, I wouldn't be afraid of anything, and...
...would only do what was totally fun!
WOW!
Let's do it!
HA HA HA
HA HA HA

V. the WILD LIFE

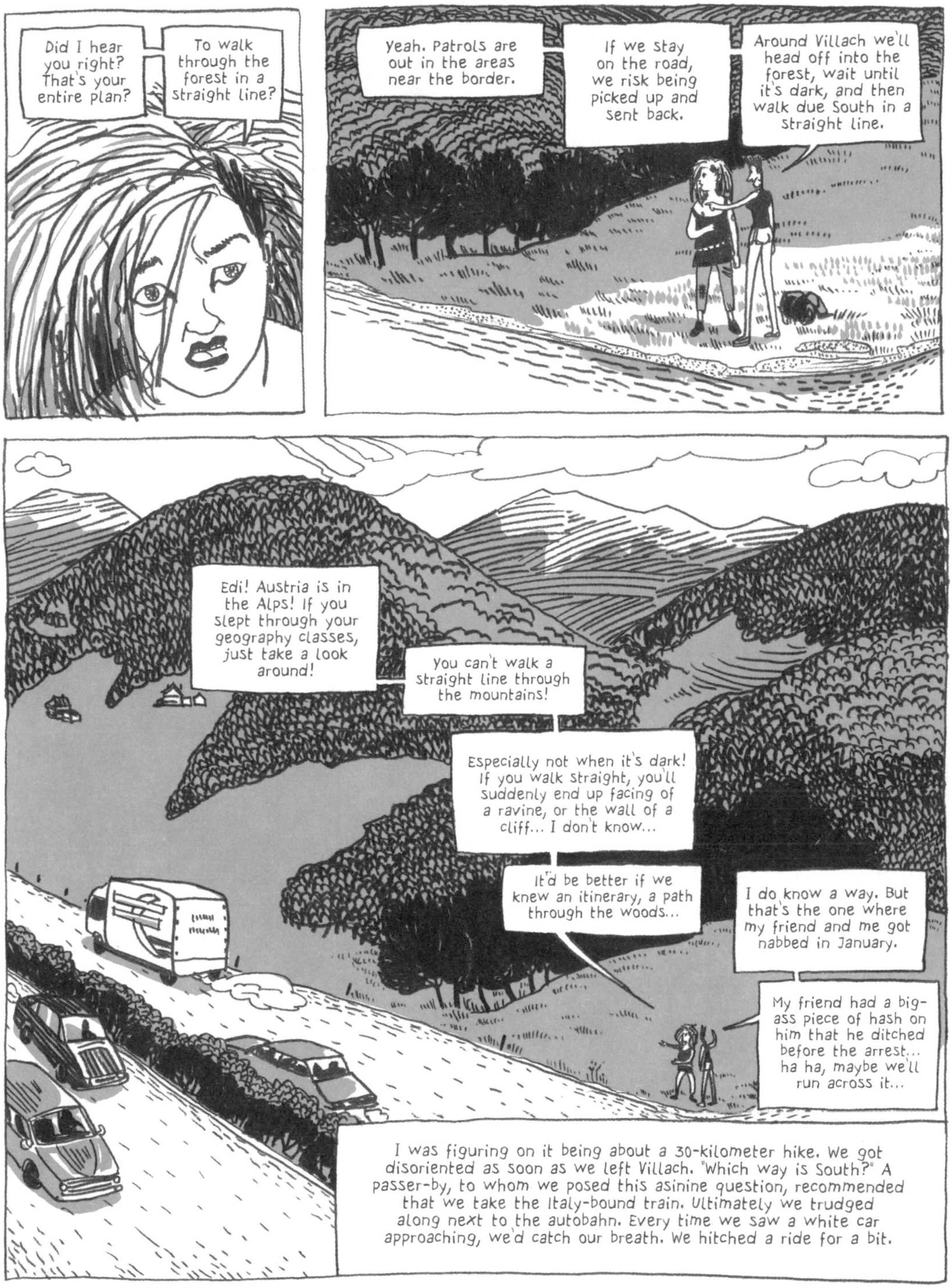
Did I hear you right? That's your entire plan?
To walk through the forest in a straight line?
Yeah. Patrols are out in the areas near the border.
If we stay on the road, we risk being picked up and sent back.
Around Villach we'll head off into the forest, wait until it's dark, and then walk due South in a straight line.
Edi! Austria is in the Alps! If you slept through your geography classes, just take a look around!
You can't walk a straight line through the mountains!
Especially not when it's dark! If you walk straight, you'll suddenly end up facing of a ravine, or the wall of a cliff... I don't know...
It'd be better if we knew an itinerary, a path through the woods...
I do know a way. But that's the one where my friend and me got nabbed in January.
My friend had a big-ass piece of hash on him that he ditched before the arrest... ha ha, maybe we'll run across it...
I was figuring on it being about a 30-kilometer hike. We got disoriented as soon as we left Villach. "Which way is South?" A passer-by, to whom we posed this asinine question, recommended that we take the Italy-bound train. Ultimately we trudged along next to the autobahn. Every time we saw a white car approaching, we'd catch our breath. We hitched a ride for a bit.

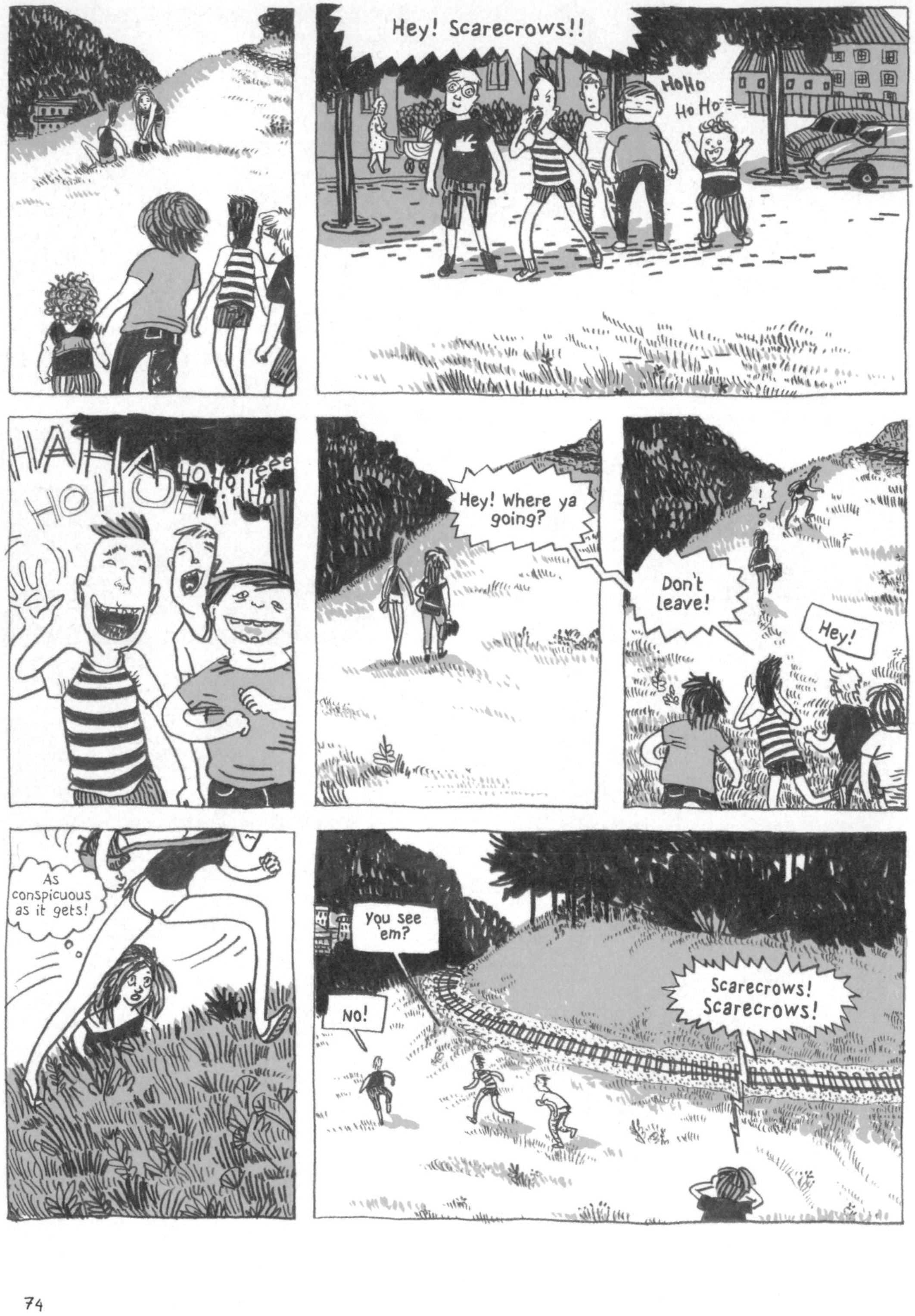
Hey! Scarecrows!!
HoHo
Ho Ho
HAHA
HOHOH
HoHo
Hey! Where ya going?
!
Don't leave!
Hey!
As conspicuous as it gets!
You see 'em?
No!
Scarecrows! Scarecrows!

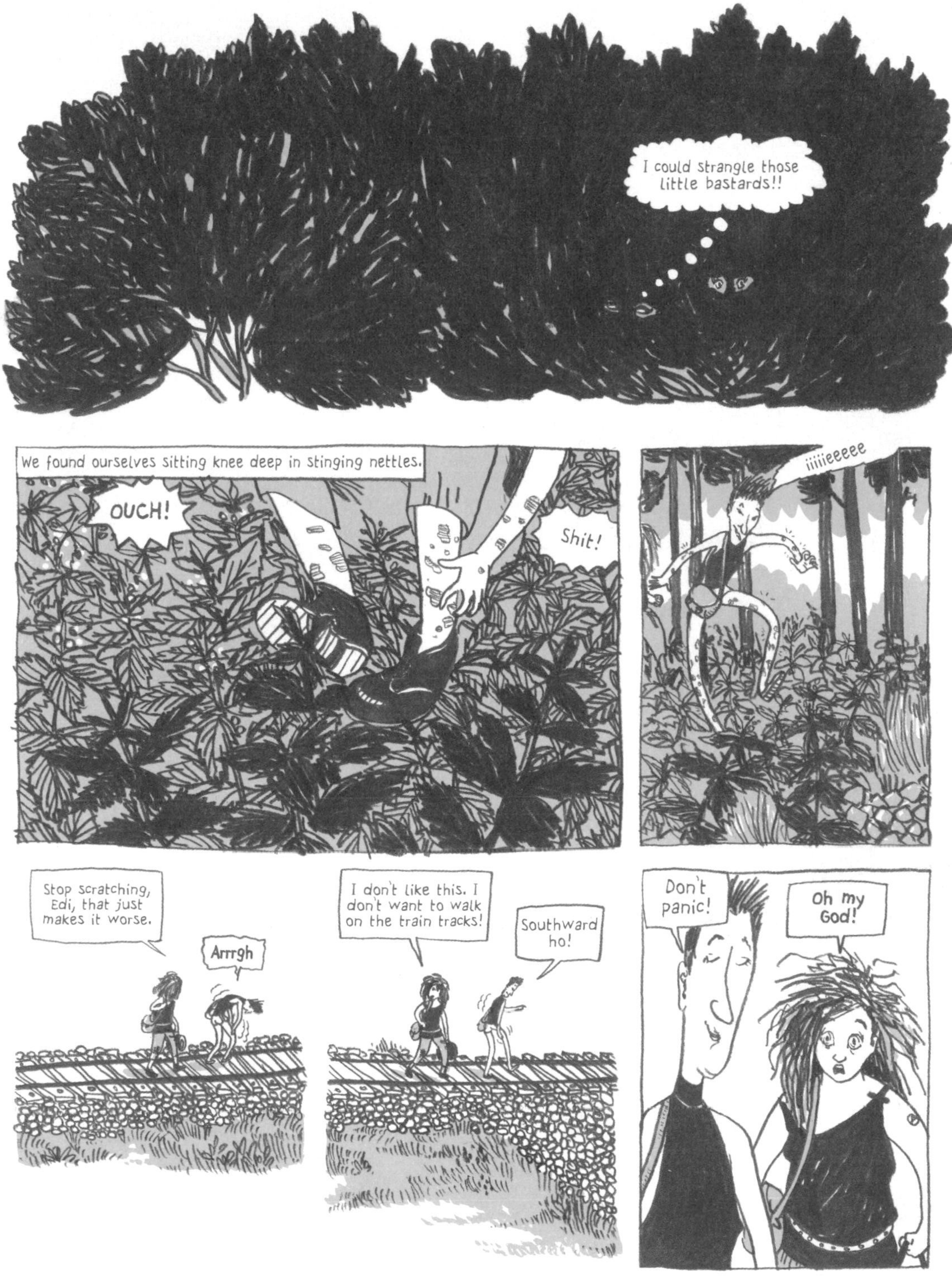
I could strangle those little bastards!!
We found ourselves sitting knee deep in stinging nettles.
OUCH!
Shit!
iiiiieeeee
Stop scratching, Edi, that just makes it worse.
Arrrgh
I don't like this. I don't want to walk on the train tracks!
Southward ho!
Don't panic!
Oh my God!

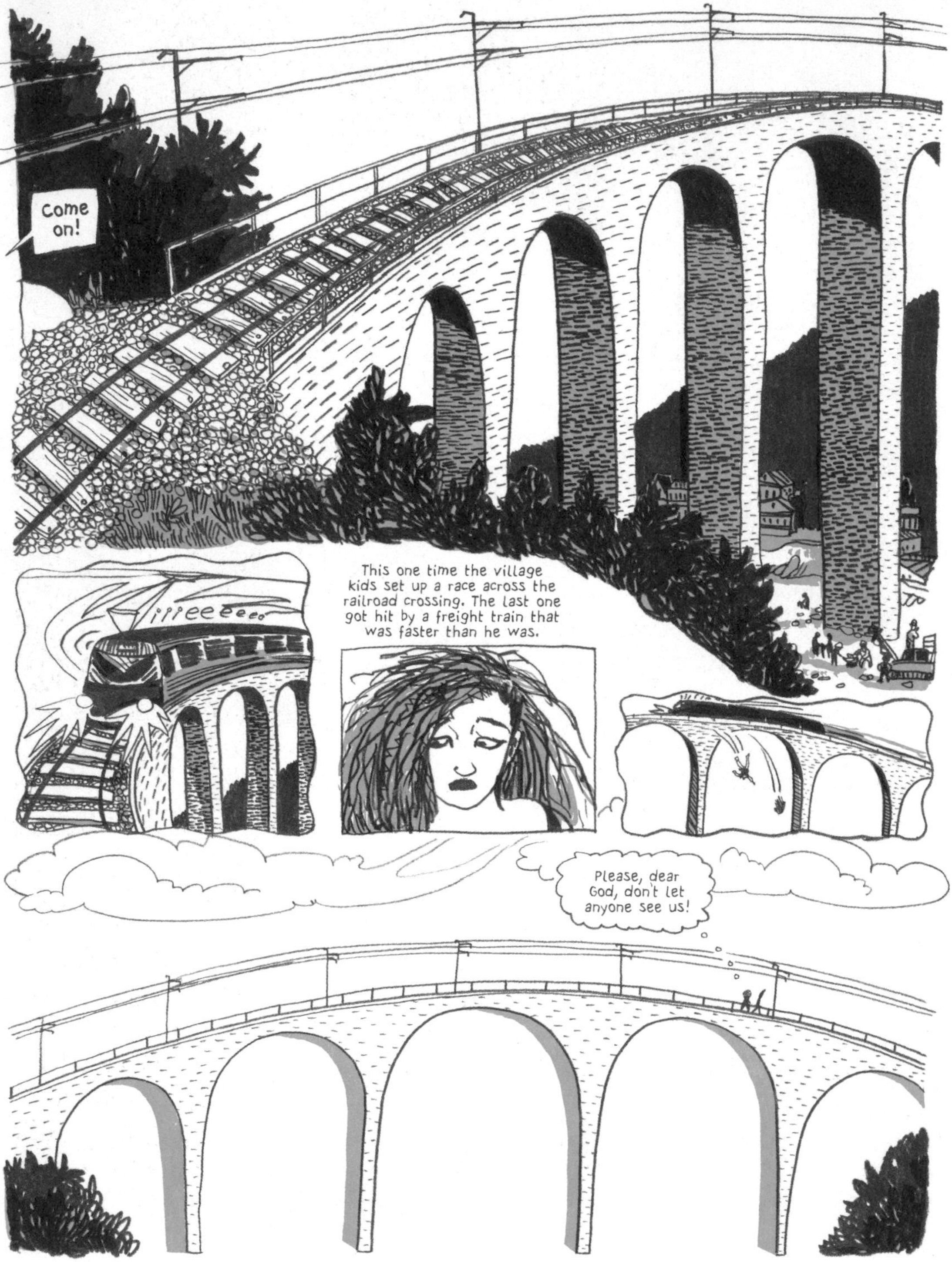
Come on!
IPPEEEEEEE
This one time the village kids set up a race across the railroad crossing. The last one got hit by a freight train that was faster than he was.
Please, dear God, don't let anyone see us!

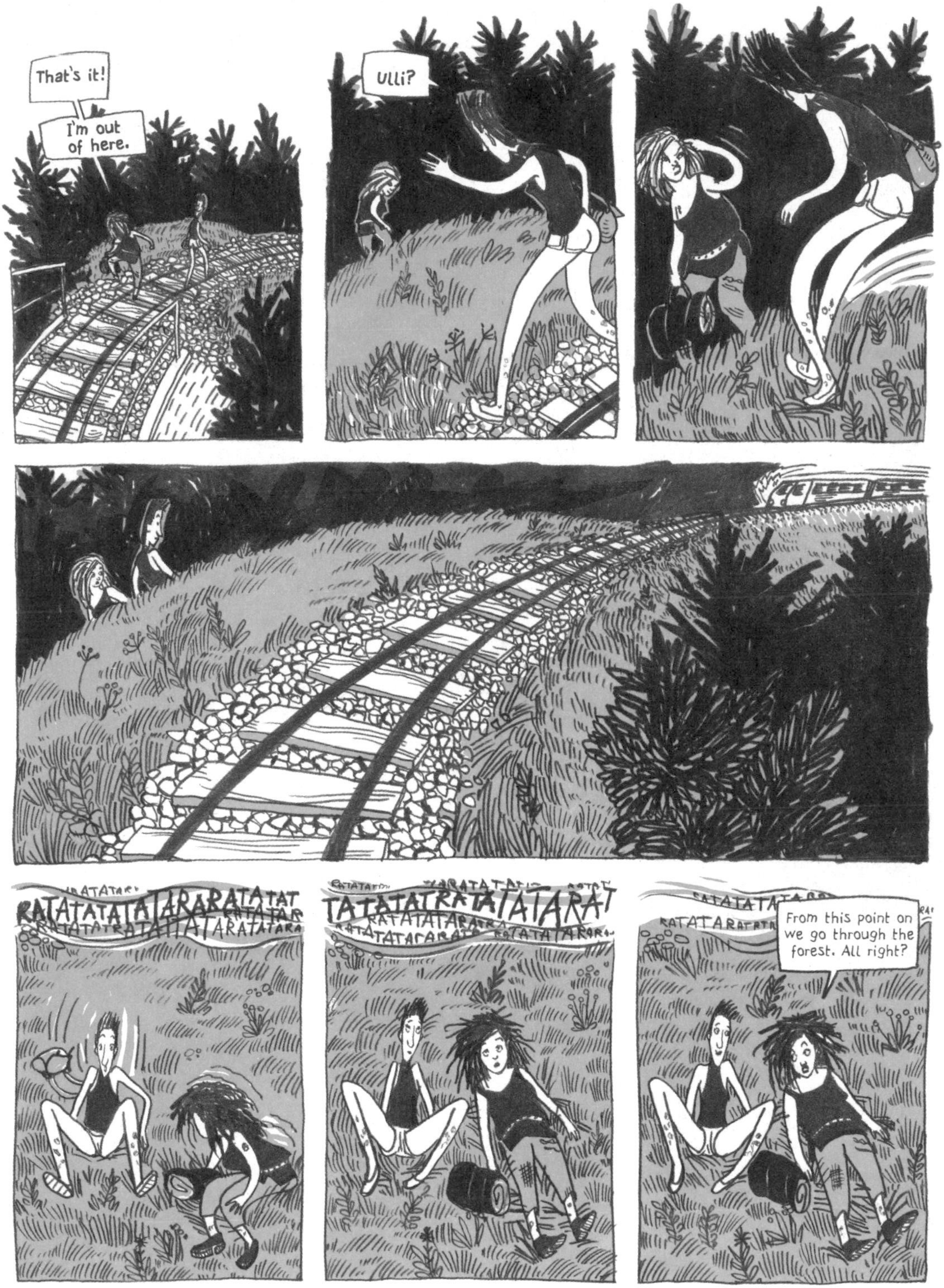

That's it!
I'm out of here.
Ulli?
RATATATATATARARATATAT
TATATATRATATATARAT
From this point on we go through the forest. All right?

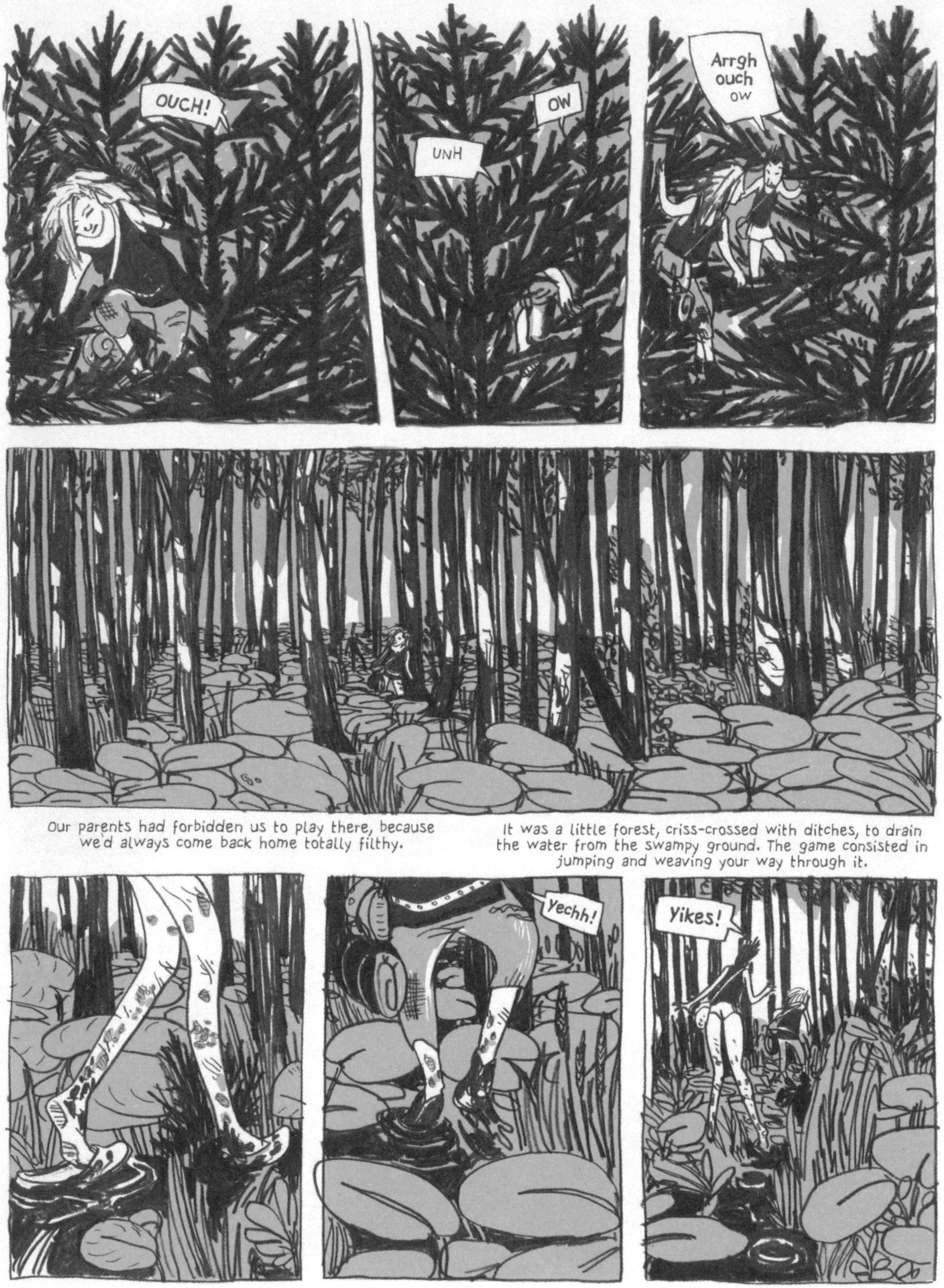
OUCH!
UNH
OW
Arrgh ouch ow
Our parents had forbidden us to play there, because we'd always come back home totally filthy.
It was a little forest, criss-crossed with ditches, to drain the water from the swampy ground. The game consisted in jumping and weaving your way through it.
Yechh!
Yikes!

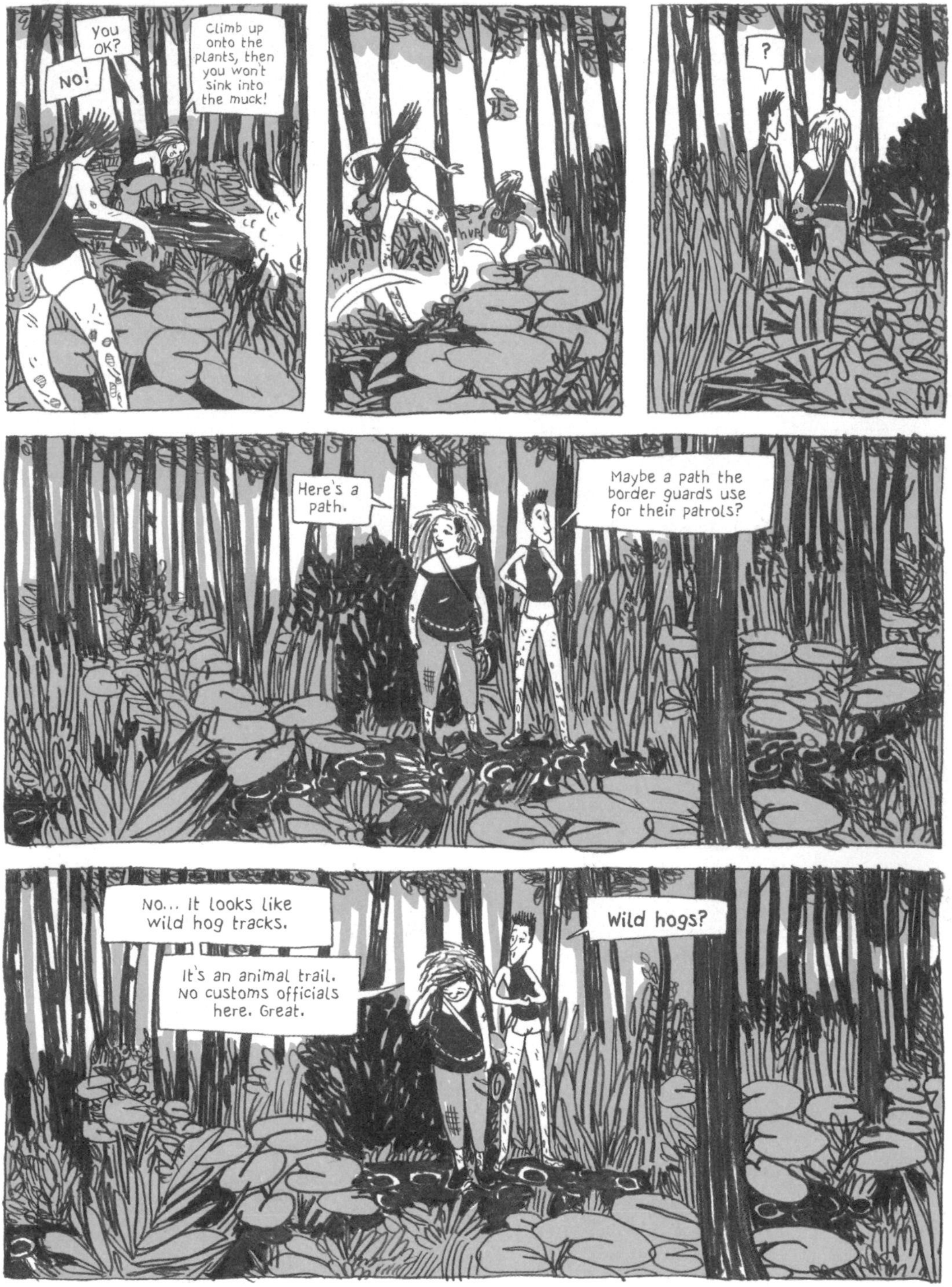

You OK?
No!
Climb up onto the plants, then you won't sink into the muck!
?
Here's a path.
Maybe a path the border guards use for their patrols?
No... It looks like wild hog tracks.
It's an animal trail. No customs officials here. Great.
Wild hogs?

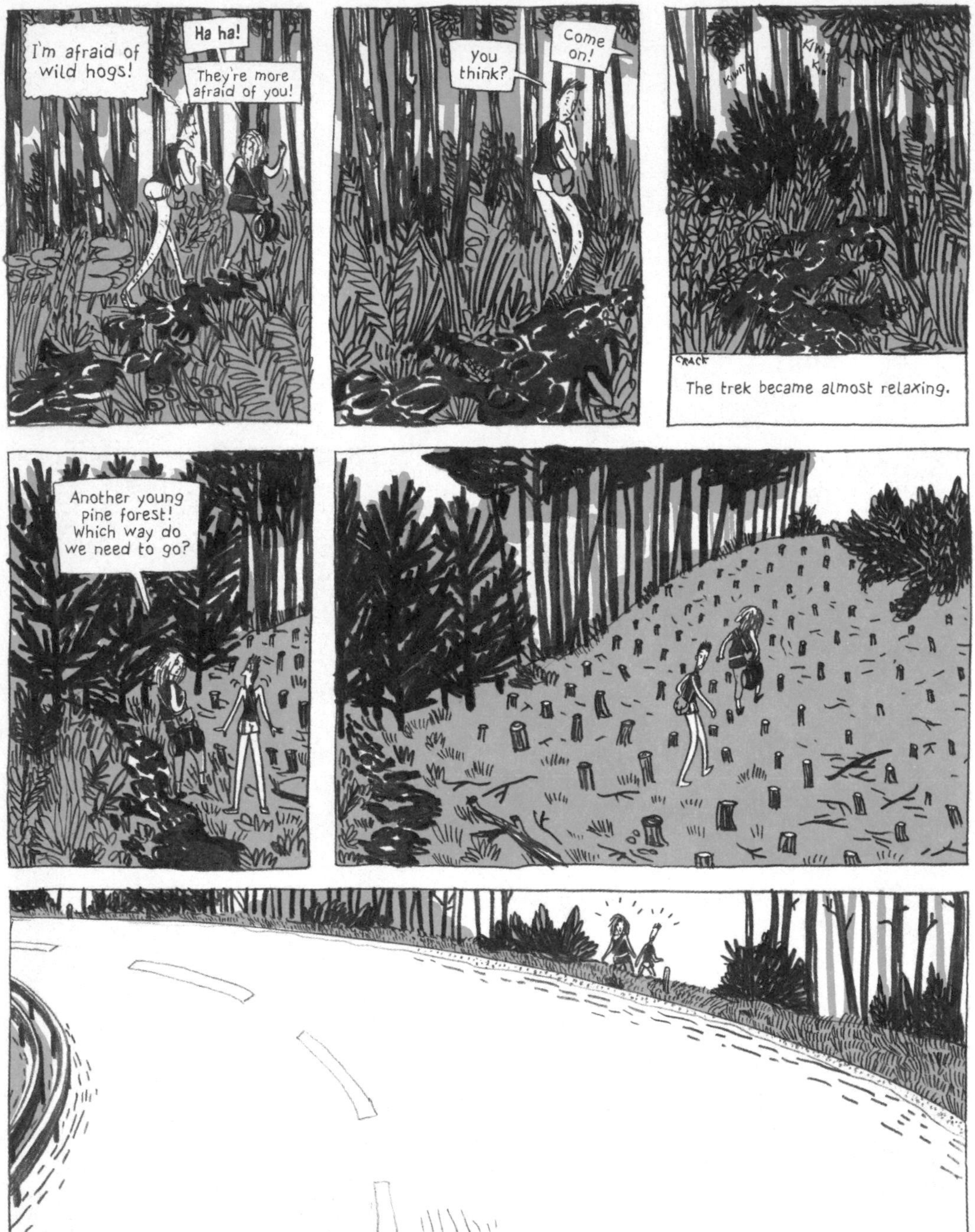

I'm afraid of wild hogs!
Ha ha!
They're more afraid of you!
You think?
Come on!
KIWIT
KIWIT
CRACK
The trek became almost relaxing.
Another young pine forest! Which way do we need to go?

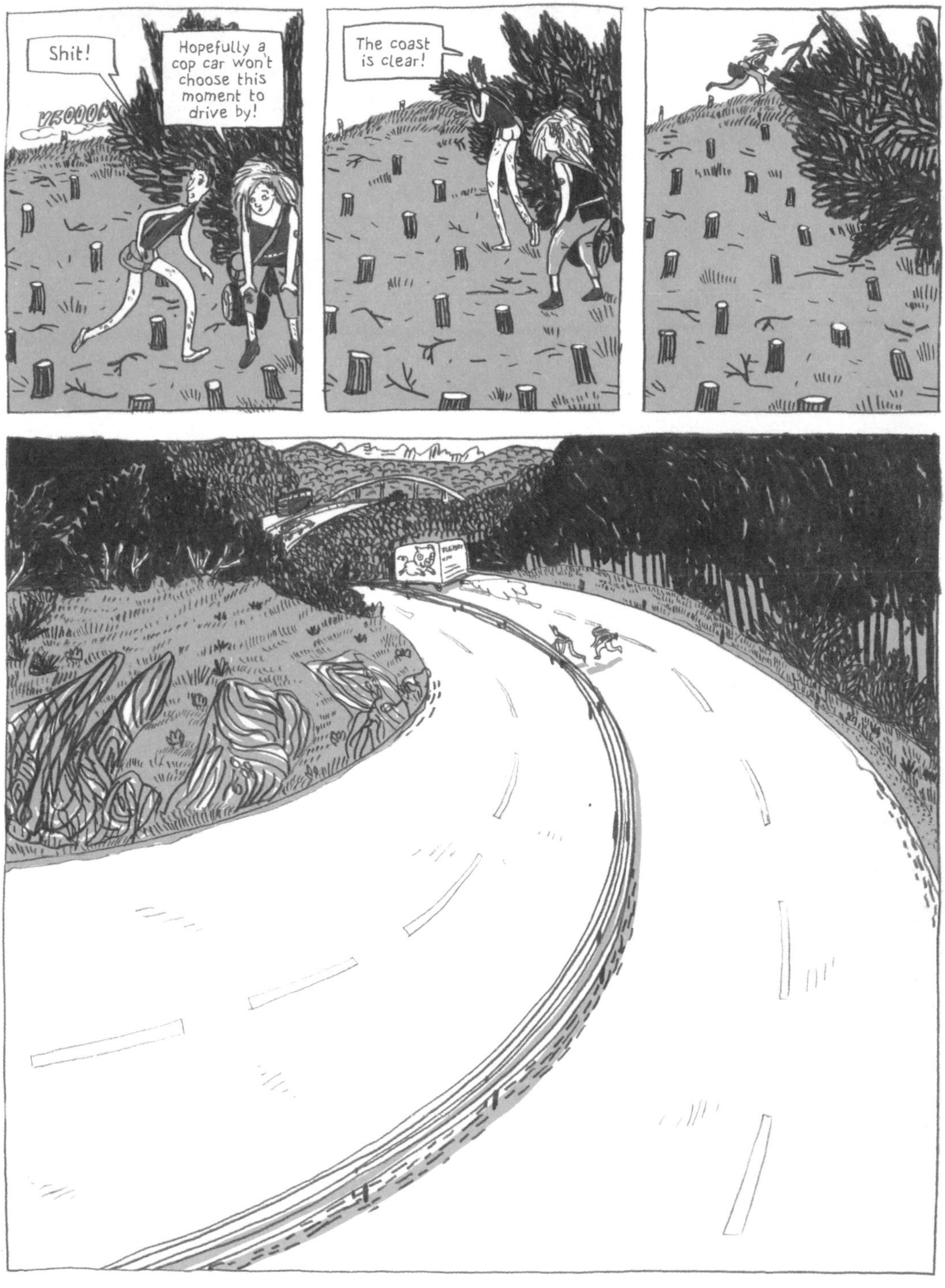

VROOOM
Shit!
Hopefully a cop car won't choose this moment to drive by!
The coast is clear!

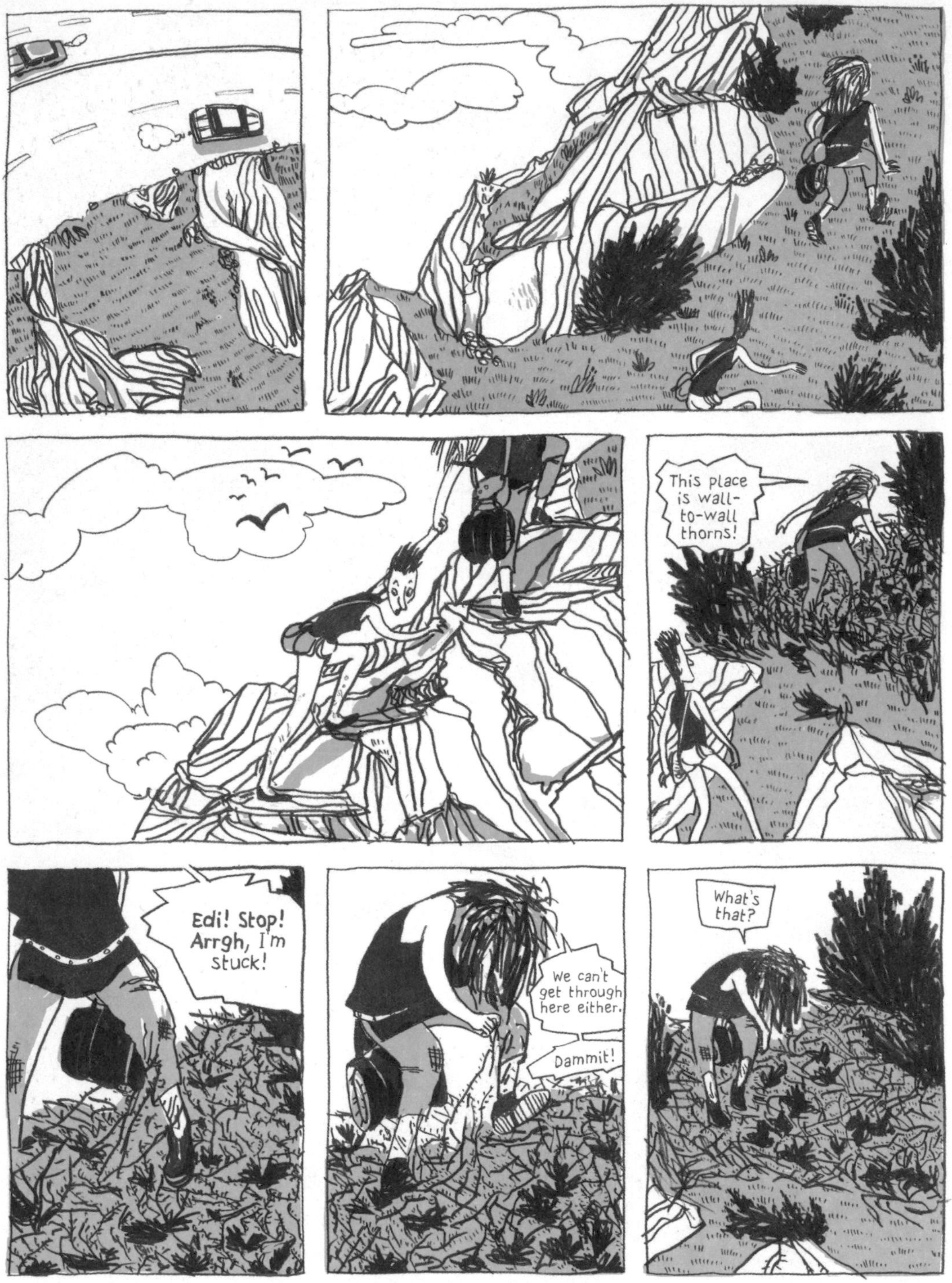
This place is wall-to-wall thorns!
Edi! Stop! Arrgh, I'm stuck!
We can't get through here either.
Dammit!
What's that?

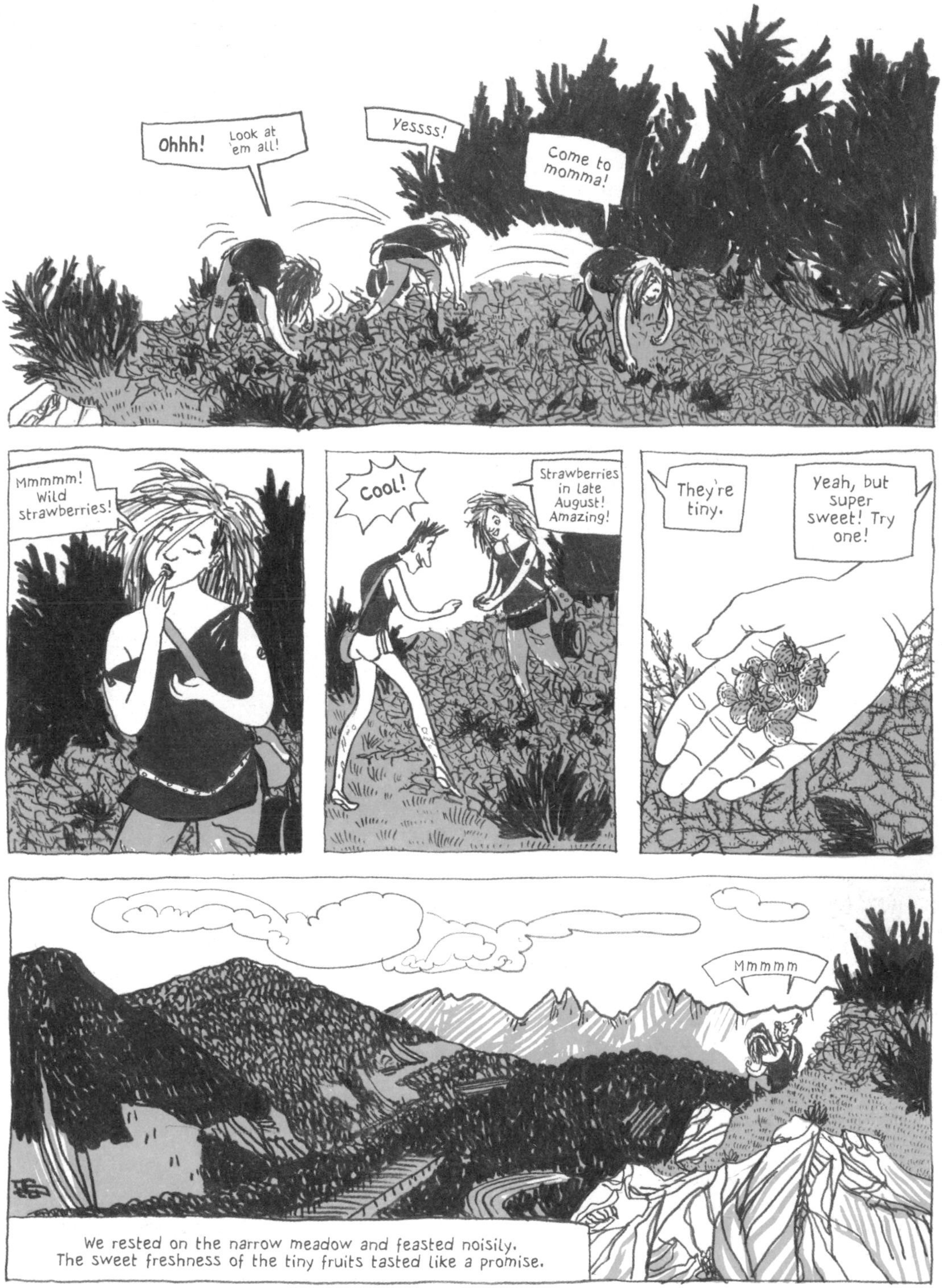
Ohhh!
Look at 'em all!
Yessss!
Come to momma!
Mmmmm! Wild strawberries!
Cool!
Strawberries in late August! Amazing!
They're tiny.
Yeah, but super sweet! Try one!
Mmmmm
We rested on the narrow meadow and feasted noisily.
The sweet freshness of the tiny fruits tasted like a promise.

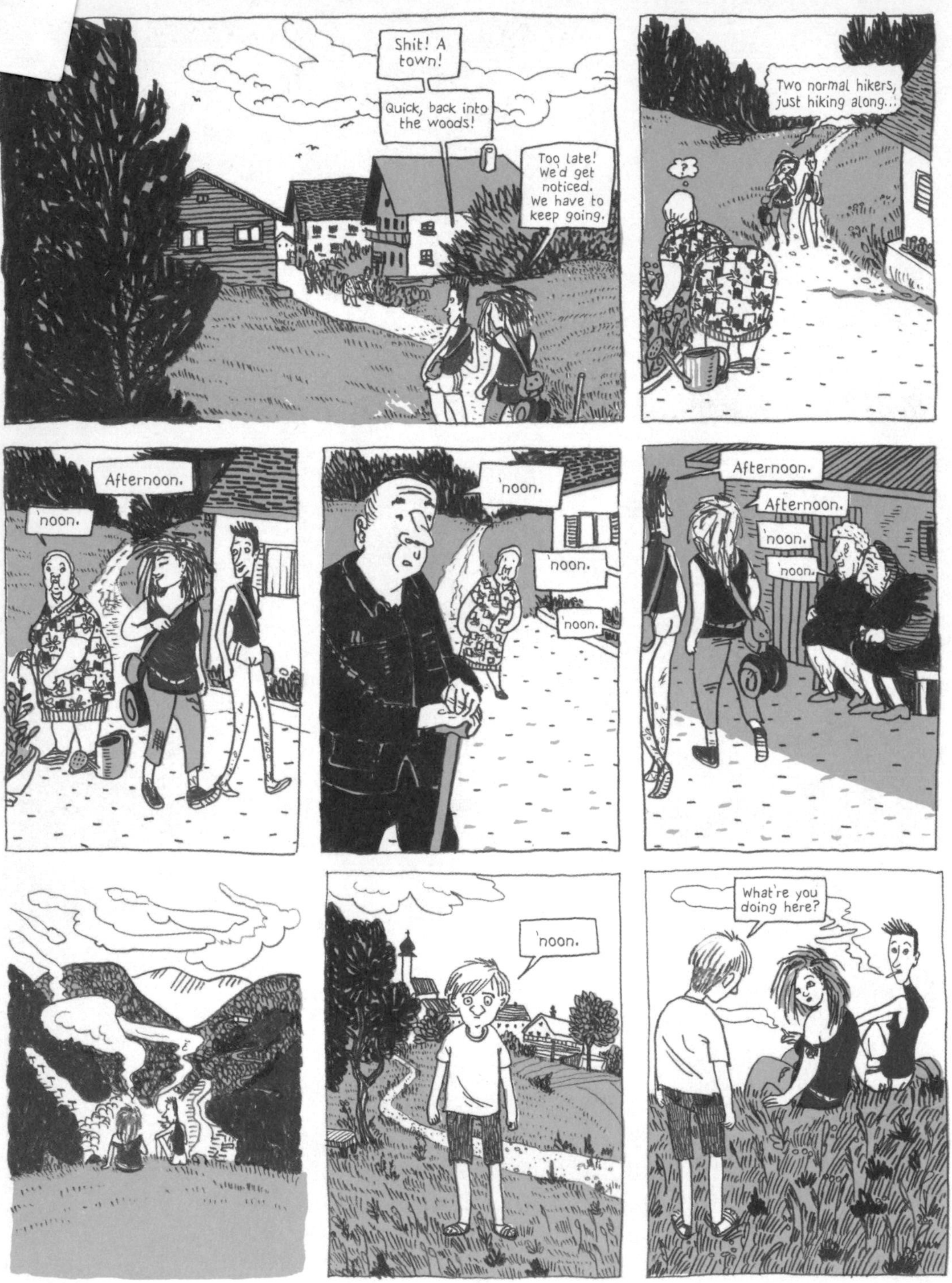
Shit! A town!
Quick, back into the woods!
Too late! We'd get noticed. We have to keep going.
Two normal hikers, just hiking along...
?
Afternoon.
'noon.
'noon.
'noon.
'noon.
Afternoon.
Afternoon.
'noon.
'noon.
'noon.
What're you doing here?

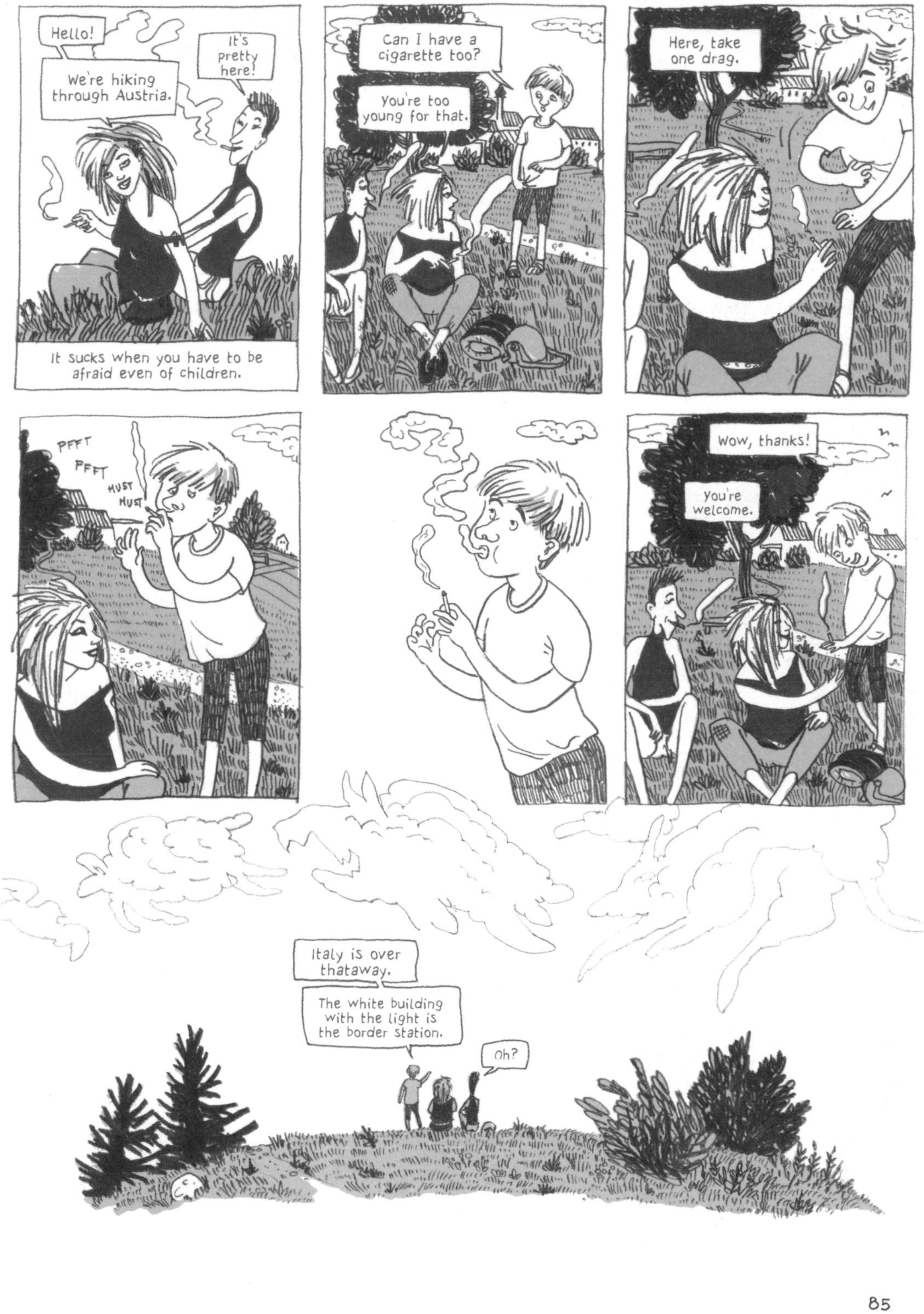
Hello!
We're hiking through Austria.
It's pretty here!
It sucks when you have to be afraid even of children.
Can I have a cigarette too?
You're too young for that.
Here, take one drag.
PFFT
PFFT
HUST
HUST
Wow, thanks!
You're welcome.
Italy is over thataway.
The white building with the light is the border station.
Oh?

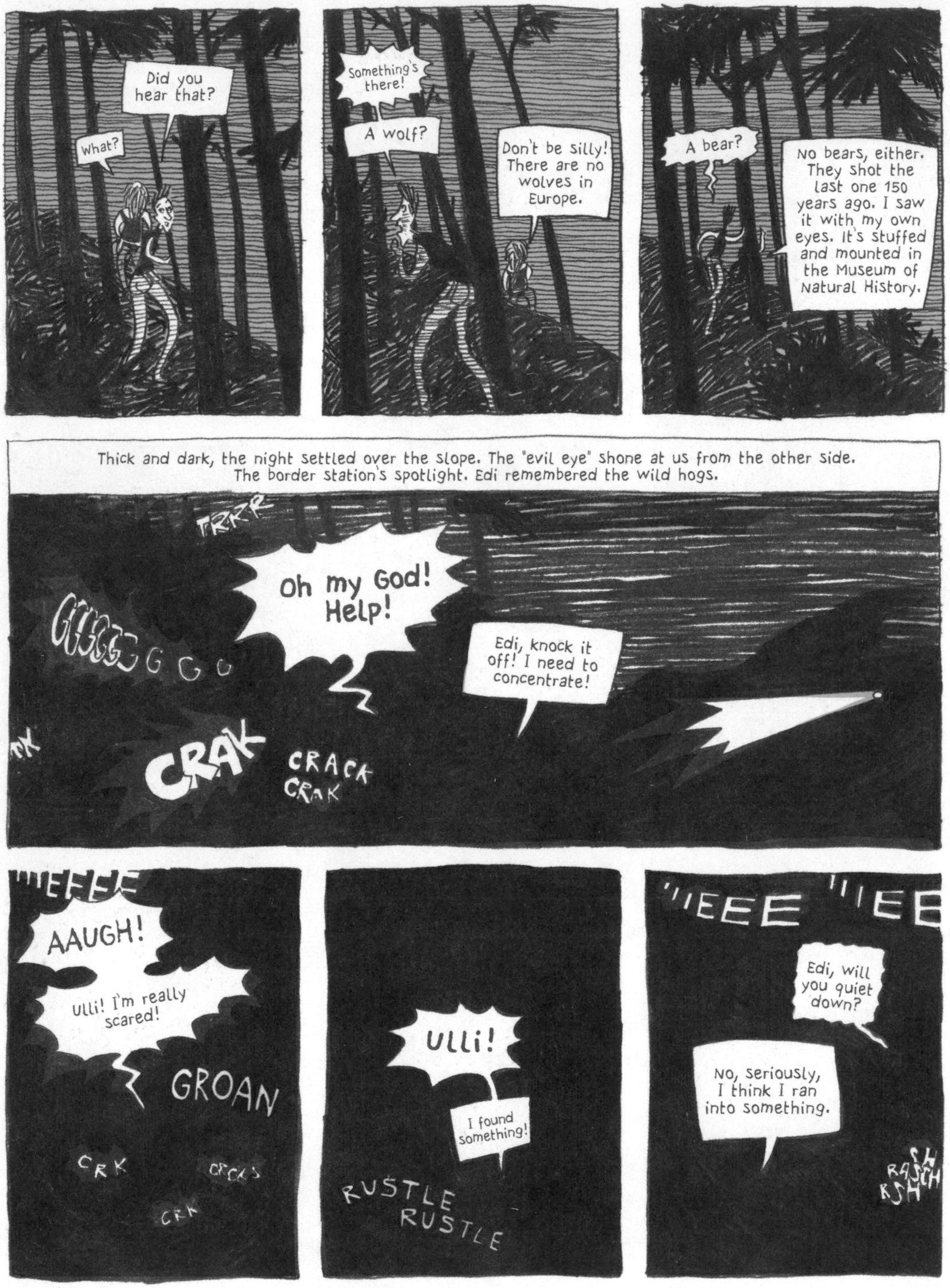
Did you hear that?
What?
Something's there!
A wolf?
Don't be silly! There are no wolves in Europe.
A bear?
No bears, either. They shot the last one 150 years ago. I saw it with my own eyes. It's stuffed and mounted in the Museum of Natural History.
Thick and dark, the night settled over the slope. The "evil eye" shone at us from the other side. The border station's spotlight. Edi remembered the wild hogs.
Oh my God! Help!
Edi, knock it off! I need to concentrate!
CRAK
CRACK
CRAK
AAUGH!
Ulli! I'm really scared!
GROAN
Ulli!
I found something!
RUSTLE
RUSTLE
Edi, will you quiet down?
No, seriously, I think I ran into something.

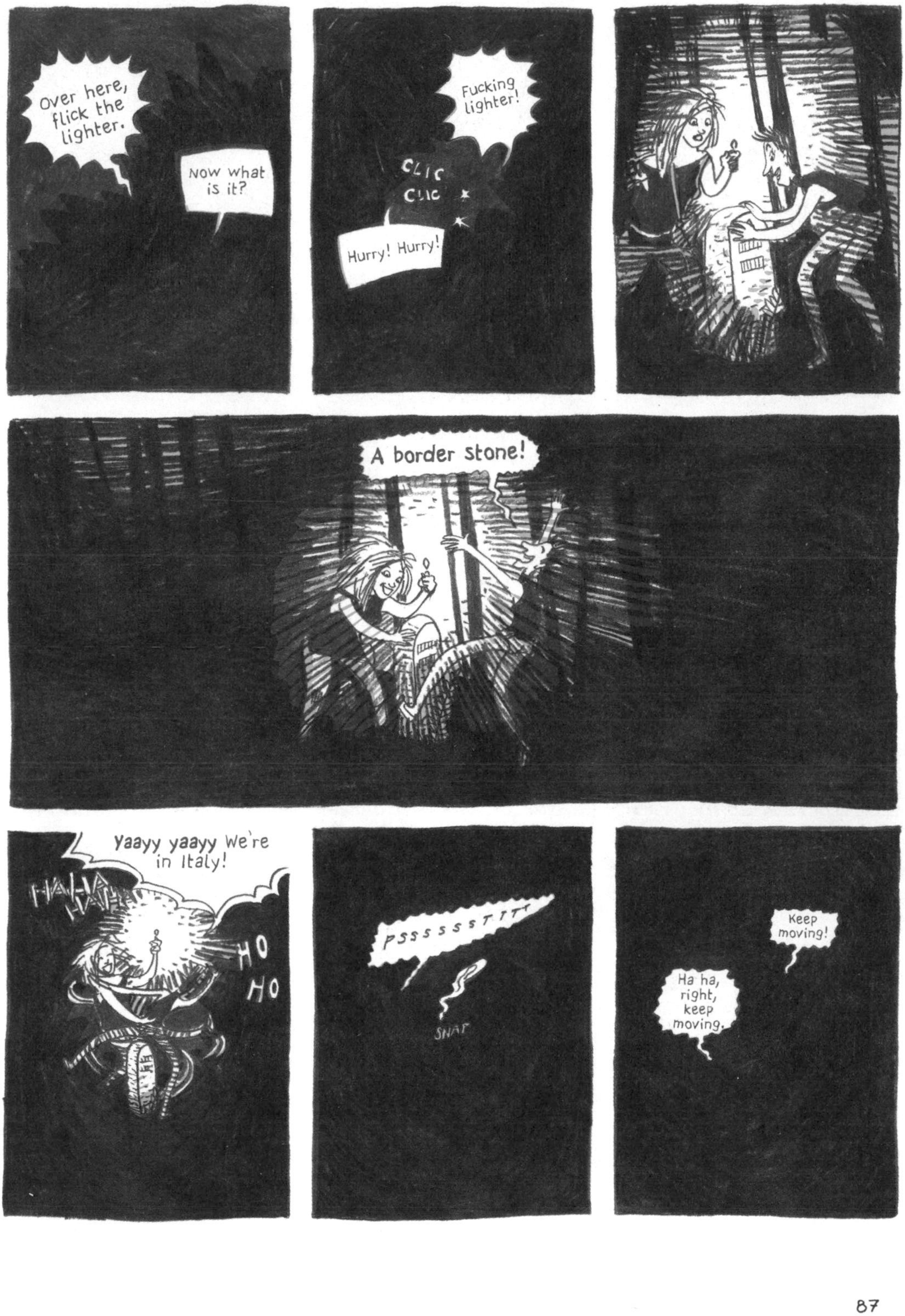
Over here, flick the lighter.
Now what is it?
Fucking lighter!
CLIC
CLIC
Hurry! Hurry!
A border stone!
yaayy yaayy We're in Italy!
HAHA HAHA
HO HO
PSSSSSSTTTT
SNAT
Keep moving!
Ha ha, right, keep moving.

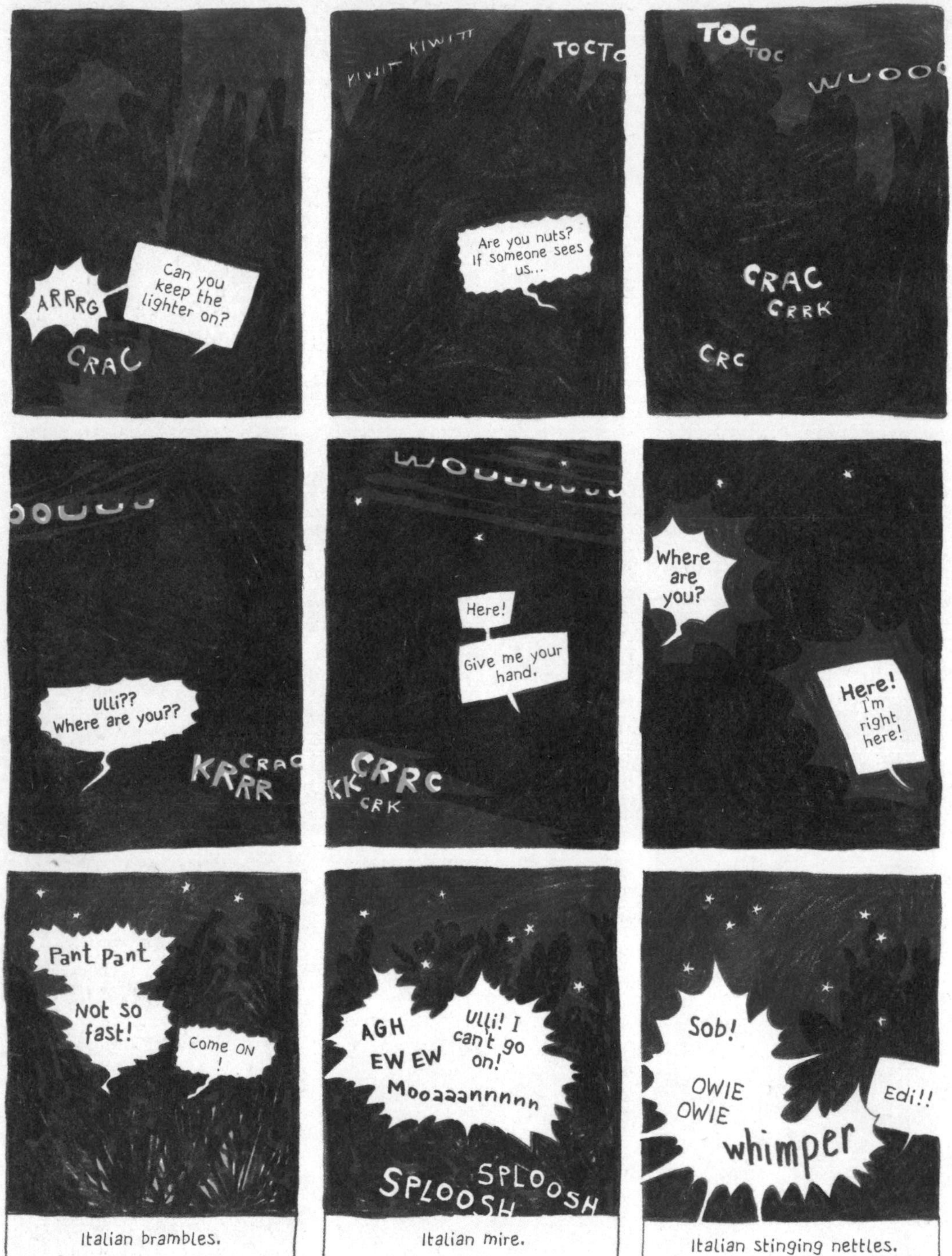
Can you keep the lighter on?
ARRRG
CRAC
KIWITT KIWITT
TOCTO
Are you nuts? If someone sees us...
TOC TOC
WUOOO
CRAC
CRRK
CRC
OOUUUU
Ulli?? Where are you??
KRRRR
CRAC
WOUUUUUUU
Here!
Give me your hand.
KK CRRC
CRK
Where are you?
Here! I'm right here!
Pant Pant
Not so fast!
Come ON !
AGH
EW EW
Ulli! I can't go on!
Mooaaannnnn
SPLOOSH
SPLOOSH
Sob!
OWIE OWIE
whimper
Edi!!

Italian brambles.

Italian mire.

Italian stinging nettles.

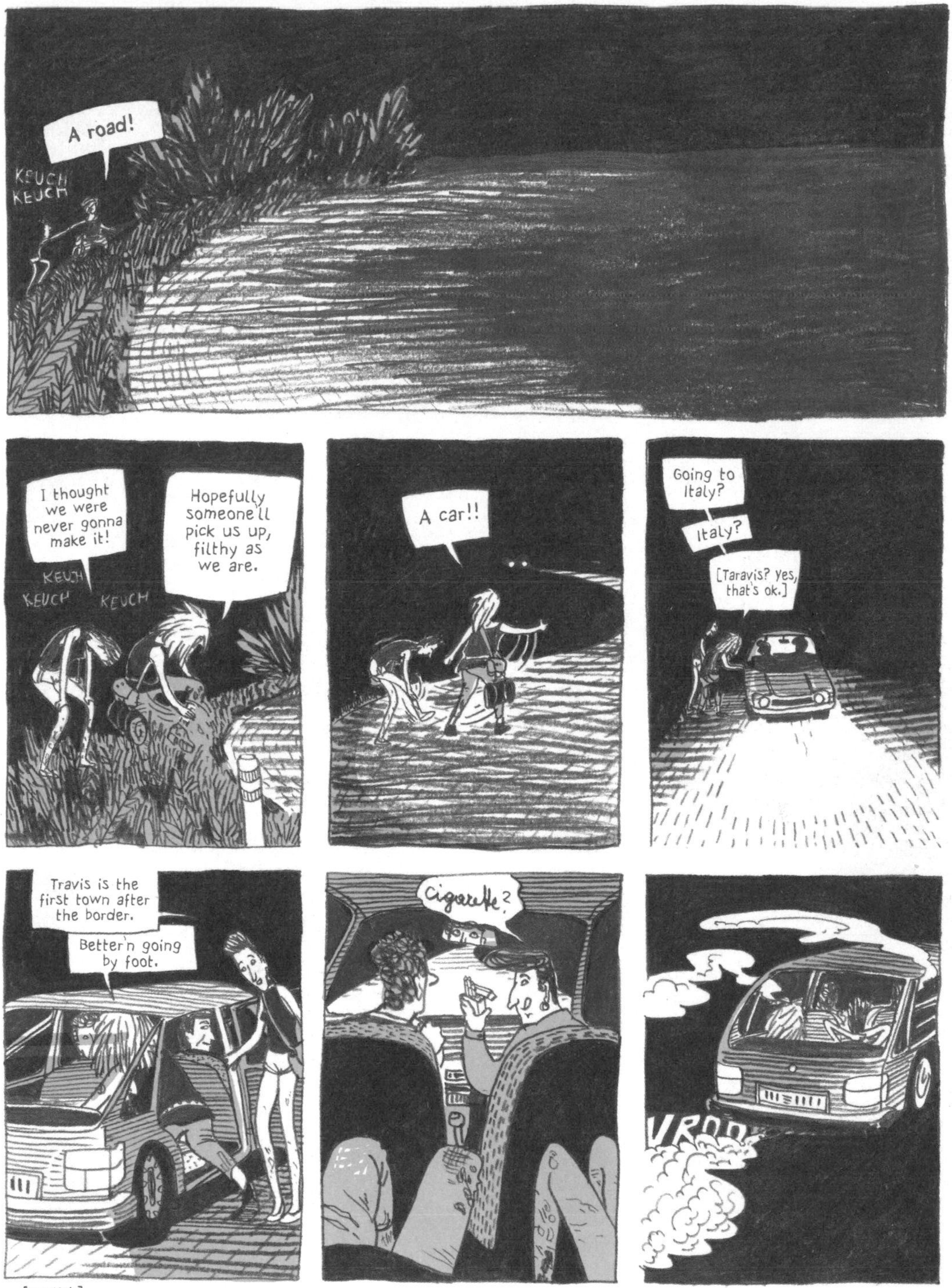
A road!
KEUCH KEUCH
I thought we were never gonna make it!
KEUCH KEUCH
Hopefully someone'll pick us up, filthy as we are.
KEUCH
A car!!
Going to Italy?
Italy?
[Taravis? yes, that's ok.]
Travis is the first town after the border.
Better'n going by foot.
Cigarette?
VROO

[English]

[What do you do in Italy?]
[We want to go to the sea.]
[Swim in the sea!]
AHHH Mare!
Mare bella Bella Italia!
[Yes!]
AHHHH Bella Italia!!
passaporto?
[Yes, yes.]
?
Passaporto??
[Your passports, please!]
[Passport?]
[Passport?]
[Yes, yes.]

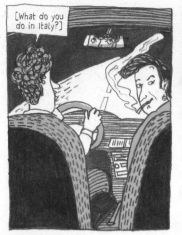

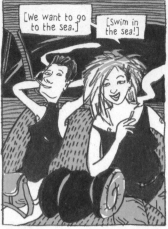

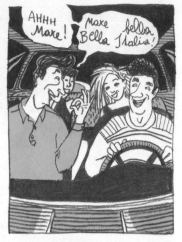

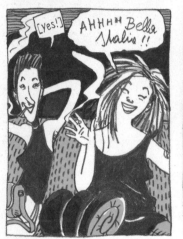

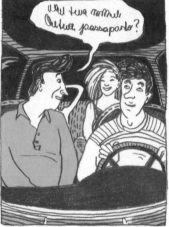

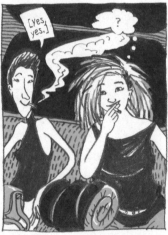

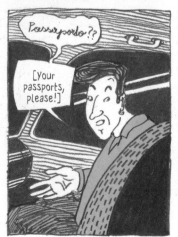

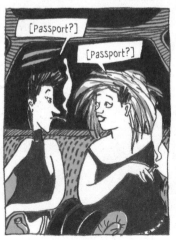

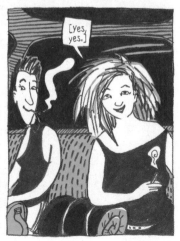

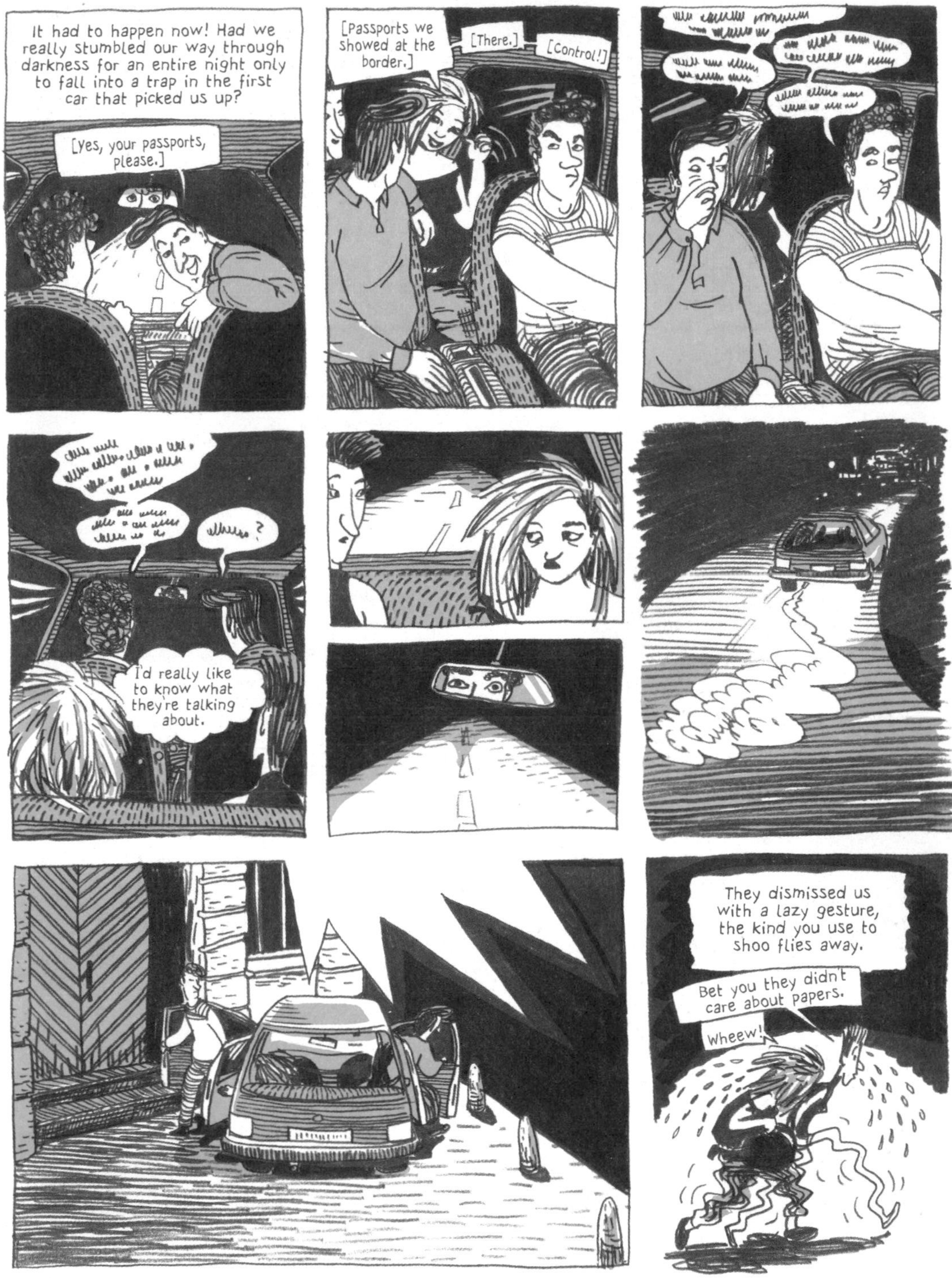

It had to happen now! Had we really stumbled our way through darkness for an entire night only to fall into a trap in the first car that picked us up?
[Yes, your passports, please.]
[Passports we showed at the border.]
[There.]
[Control!]
I'd really like to know what they're talking about.
They dismissed us with a lazy gesture, the kind you use to shoo flies away.
Bet you they didn't care about papers.
Wheew!

VI. the CONQUEST

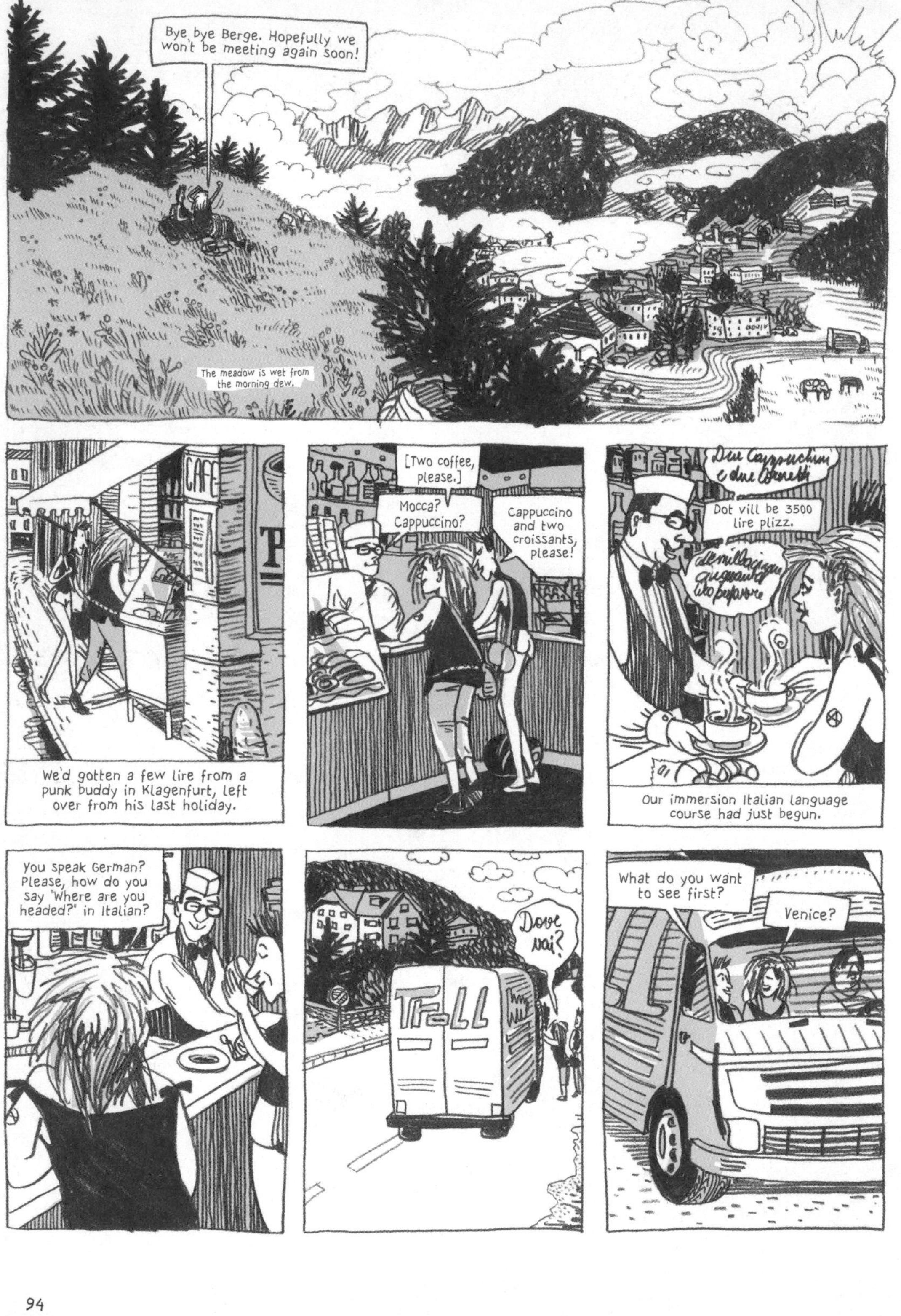
Bye bye Berge. Hopefully we won't be meeting again soon!
The meadow is wet from the morning dew.
We'd gotten a few lire from a punk buddy in Klagenfurt, left over from his last holiday.
CAFE
[Two coffee, please.]
Mocca? Cappuccino?
Cappuccino and two croissants, please!
Due Cappuccini e due Cornetti
Dot vill be 3500 lire plizz.
Our immersion Italian language course had just begun.
You speak German? Please, how do you say "Where are you headed?" in Italian?
Dove vai?
TRALL
What do you want to see first?
Venice?

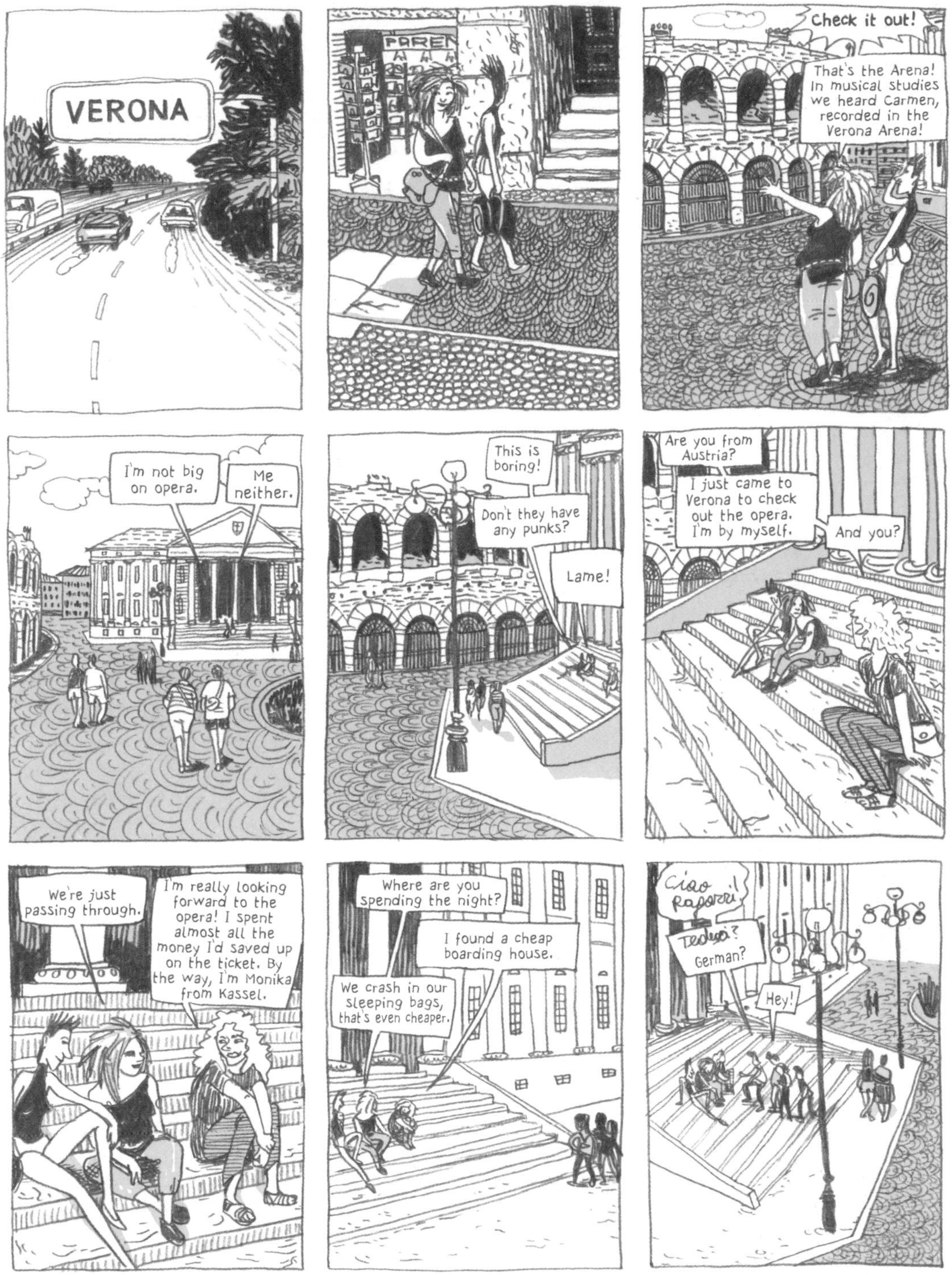

VERONA
PAREN
Check it out!
That's the Arena! In musical studies we heard Carmen, recorded in the Verona Arena!
I'm not big on opera.
Me neither.
This is boring!
Don't they have any punks?
Lame!
Are you from Austria?
I just came to Verona to check out the opera. I'm by myself.
And you?
We're just passing through.
I'm really looking forward to the opera! I spent almost all the money I'd saved up on the ticket. By the way, I'm Monika from Kassel.
Where are you spending the night?
I found a cheap boarding house.
We crash in our sleeping bags, that's even cheaper.
Ciao Ragazzi!
Tedesca? German?
Hey!

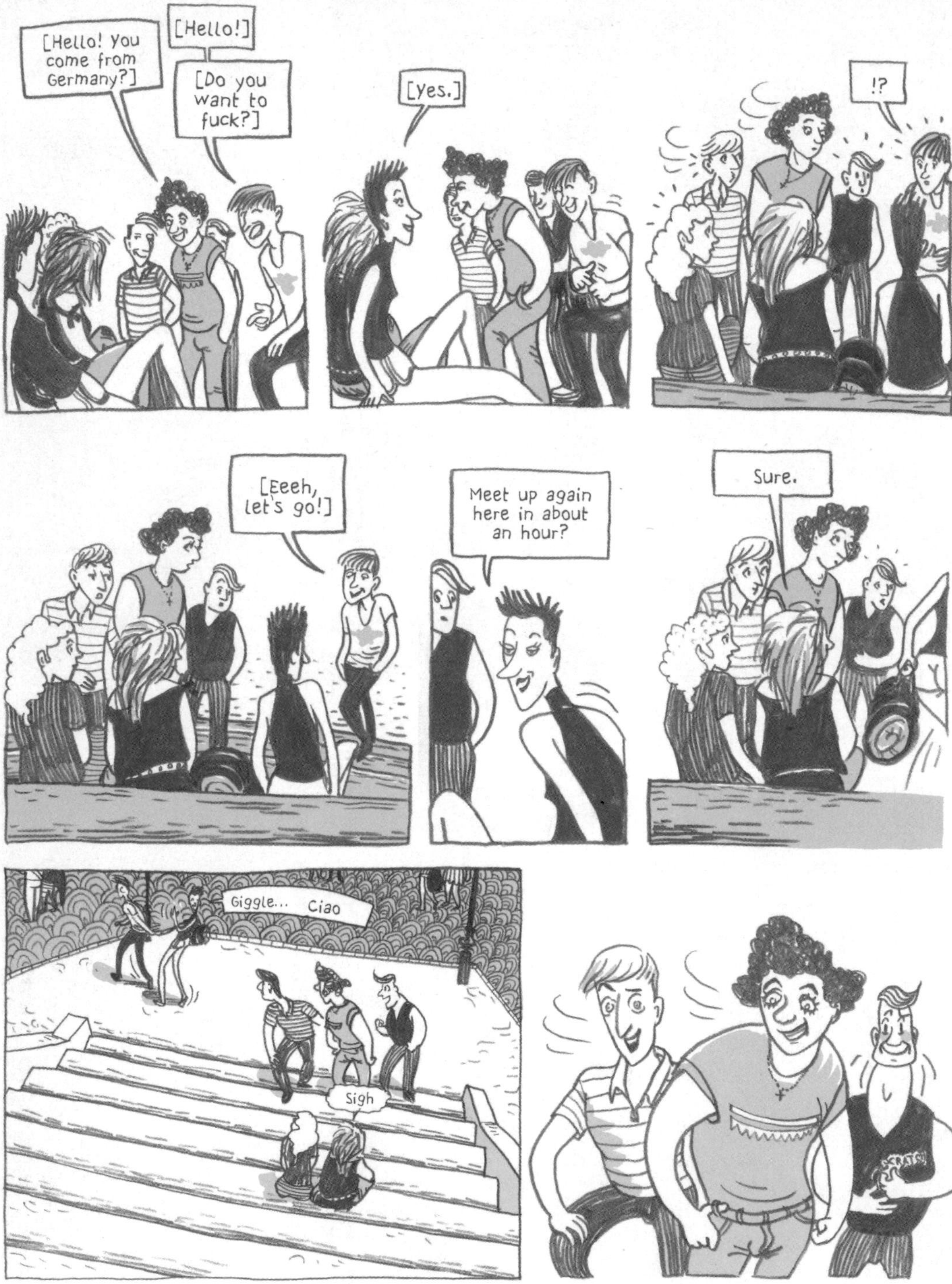
[Hello! You come from Germany?]
[Hello!]
[Do you want to fuck?]
[Yes.]
!?
[Eeeh, let's go!]
Meet up again here in about an hour?
Sure.
Giggle... Ciao
Sigh
SCRATCH

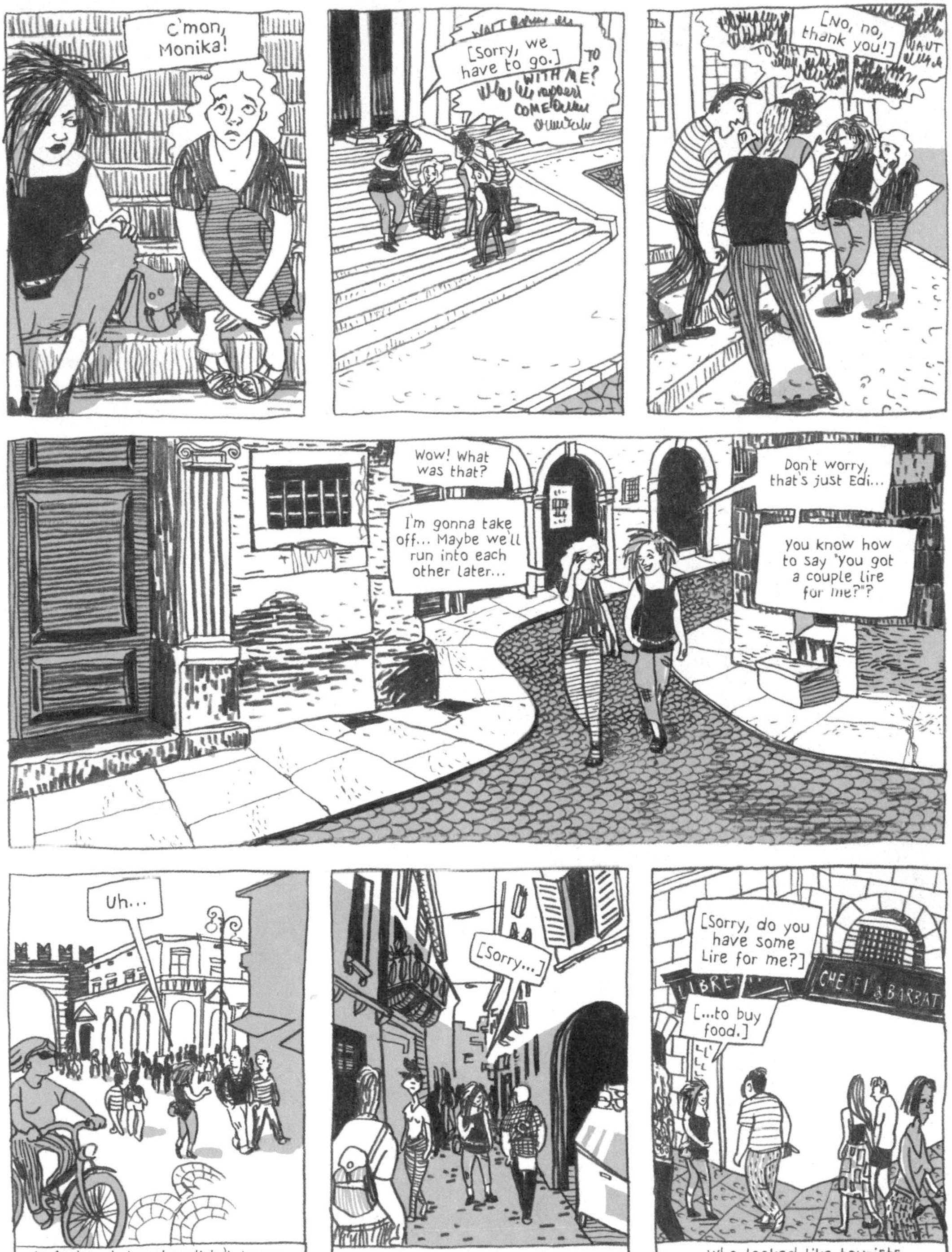
C'mon, Monika!
[Sorry, we have to go.]
[No, no, thank you!]
Wow! What was that?
I'm gonna take off... Maybe we'll run into each other later...
Don't worry, that's just Edi...
You know how to say "You got a couple lire for me?"?
Uh...
Unfortunately, she didn't know.
[Sorry...]
I approached people...
[Sorry, do you have some Lire for me?]
[...to buy food.]
...who looked like tourists.

Are you hungry?

yes.

Can I buy you a pizza?

So you just took off without any money?

Pretty bold!

I've never been to the sea. I just wanted to see it.

He talked about his own journeys. He said he also used to travel broke (he gave me 10,000 lire!), and he enjoyed having company after the death of his wife.

I know a painter. He's got a studio in Verona. You might be able to spend the night there.

That would be awesome! Can I get the rest of the pizza to go?

It's here.

Hey!

Let go!

C'mon, I was nice to you, be a little nice to me.

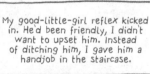

My good-little-girl reflex kicked in. He'd been friendly, I didn't want to upset him. Instead of ditching him, I gave him a handjob in the staircase.

SCHNAUF SCHNAUF

What if someone comes?

I hope!

Please don't stop!

He was the only one who came.

Blecchhh!

Gross!

98

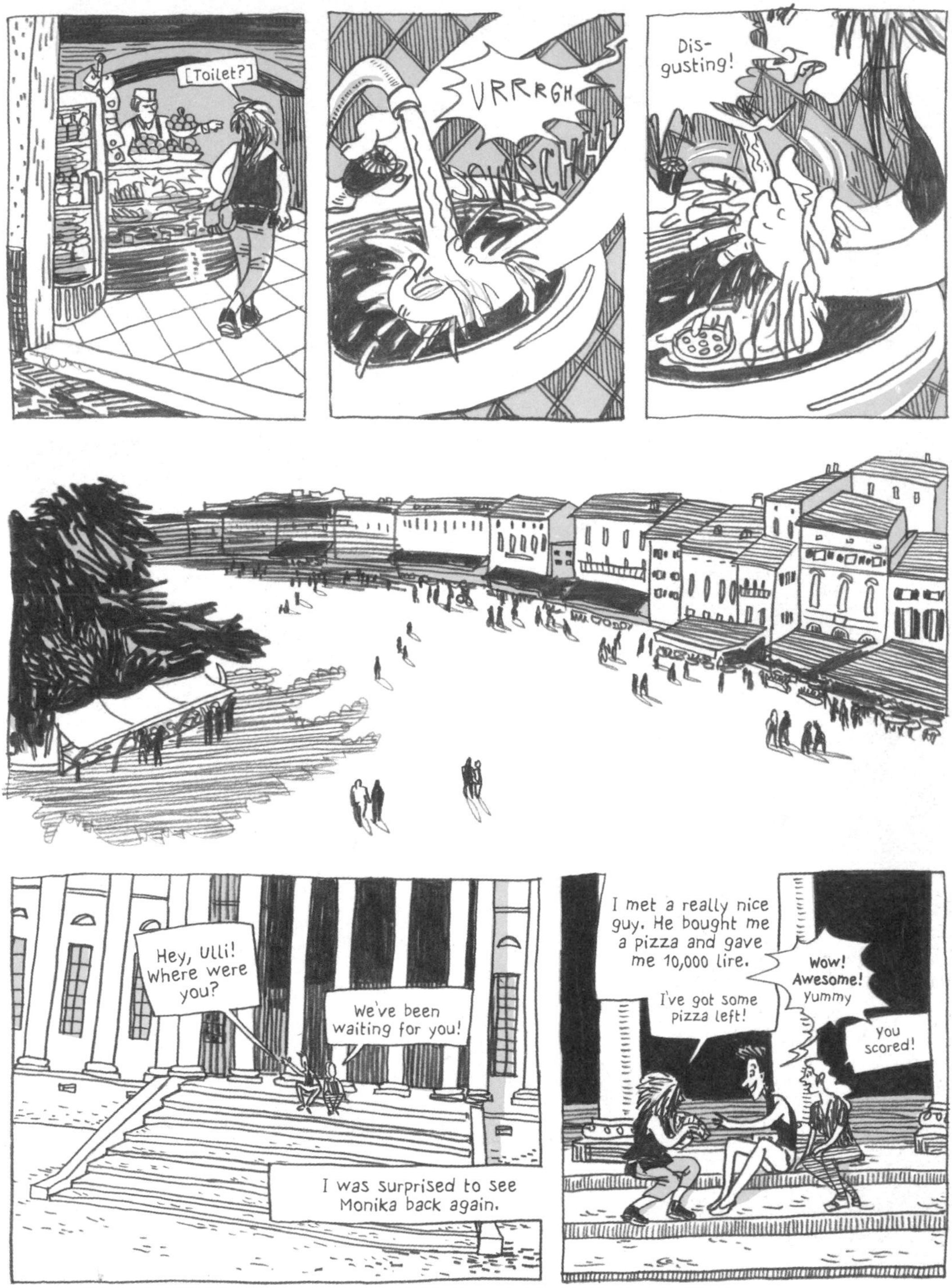

[Toilet?]
VRRRGH
SSWSCHH
Dis-gusting!
Hey, Ulli! Where were you?
We've been waiting for you!
I was surprised to see Monika back again.
I met a really nice guy. He bought me a pizza and gave me 10,000 lire.
Wow! Awesome! Yummy
I've got some pizza left!
You scored!

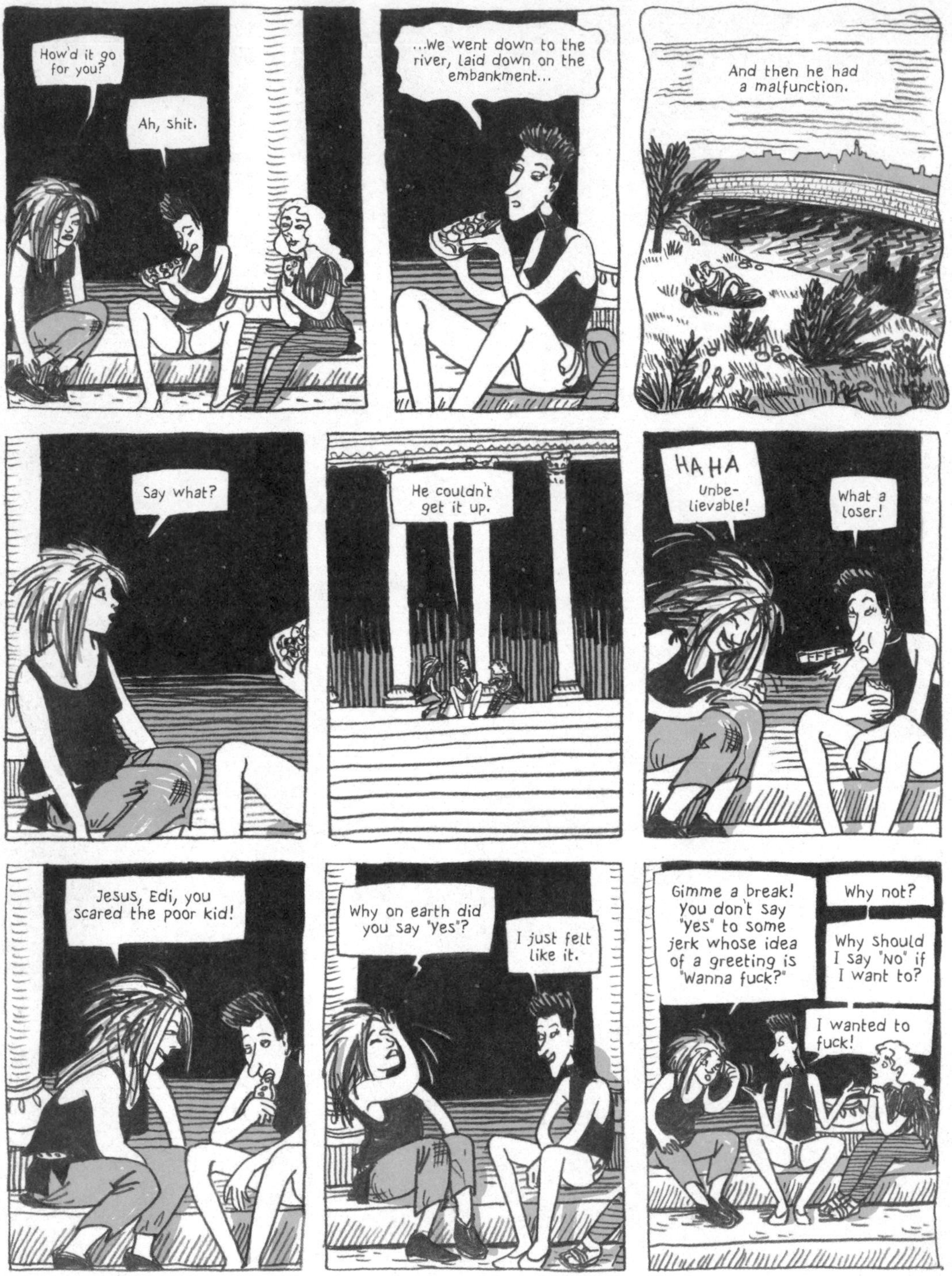
How'd it go for you?
Ah, shit.
...We went down to the river, laid down on the embankment...
And then he had a malfunction.
Say what?
He couldn't get it up.
HA HA
Unbe-lievable!
What a loser!
FFFFF
Jesus, Edi, you scared the poor kid!
Why on earth did you say "yes"?
I just felt like it.
Gimme a break! You don't say "yes" to some jerk whose idea of a greeting is "Wanna fuck?"
Why not?
Why should I say "No" if I want to?
I wanted to fuck!

You shoulda seen his buddies' eyes bugging out of their heads!

As soon as you left, they looked at Monika and me as if an orgy was about to erupt.

We said no, thanks.

HA HA HA HA HA HA HI HI HI

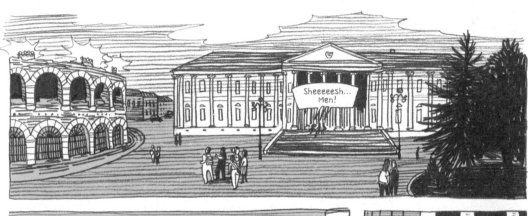

Sheeeeesh... Men!

I've gotta run, the opera's starting up!

Have fun!

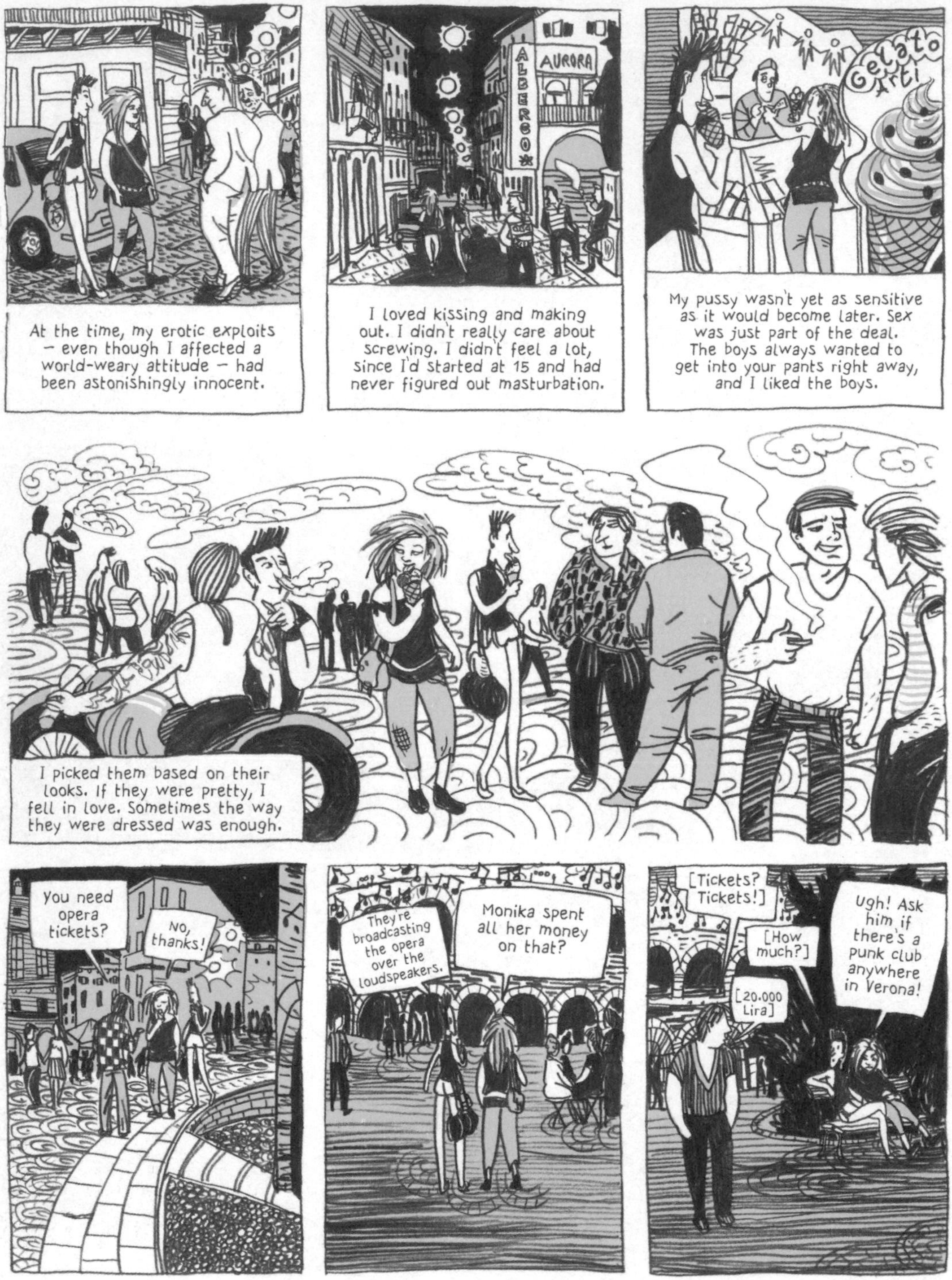
At the time, my erotic exploits – even though I affected a world-weary attitude – had been astonishingly innocent.
ALBERGO
AURORA
I loved kissing and making out. I didn't really care about screwing. I didn't feel a lot, since I'd started at 15 and had never figured out masturbation.
Gelato Arti
My pussy wasn't yet as sensitive as it would become later. Sex was just part of the deal. The boys always wanted to get into your pants right away, and I liked the boys.
I picked them based on their looks. If they were pretty, I fell in love. Sometimes the way they were dressed was enough.
You need opera tickets?
No, thanks!
They're broadcasting the opera over the loudspeakers.
Monika spent all her money on that?
[Tickets? Tickets!]
[How much?]
[20.000 Lira]
Ugh! Ask him if there's a punk club anywhere in Verona!

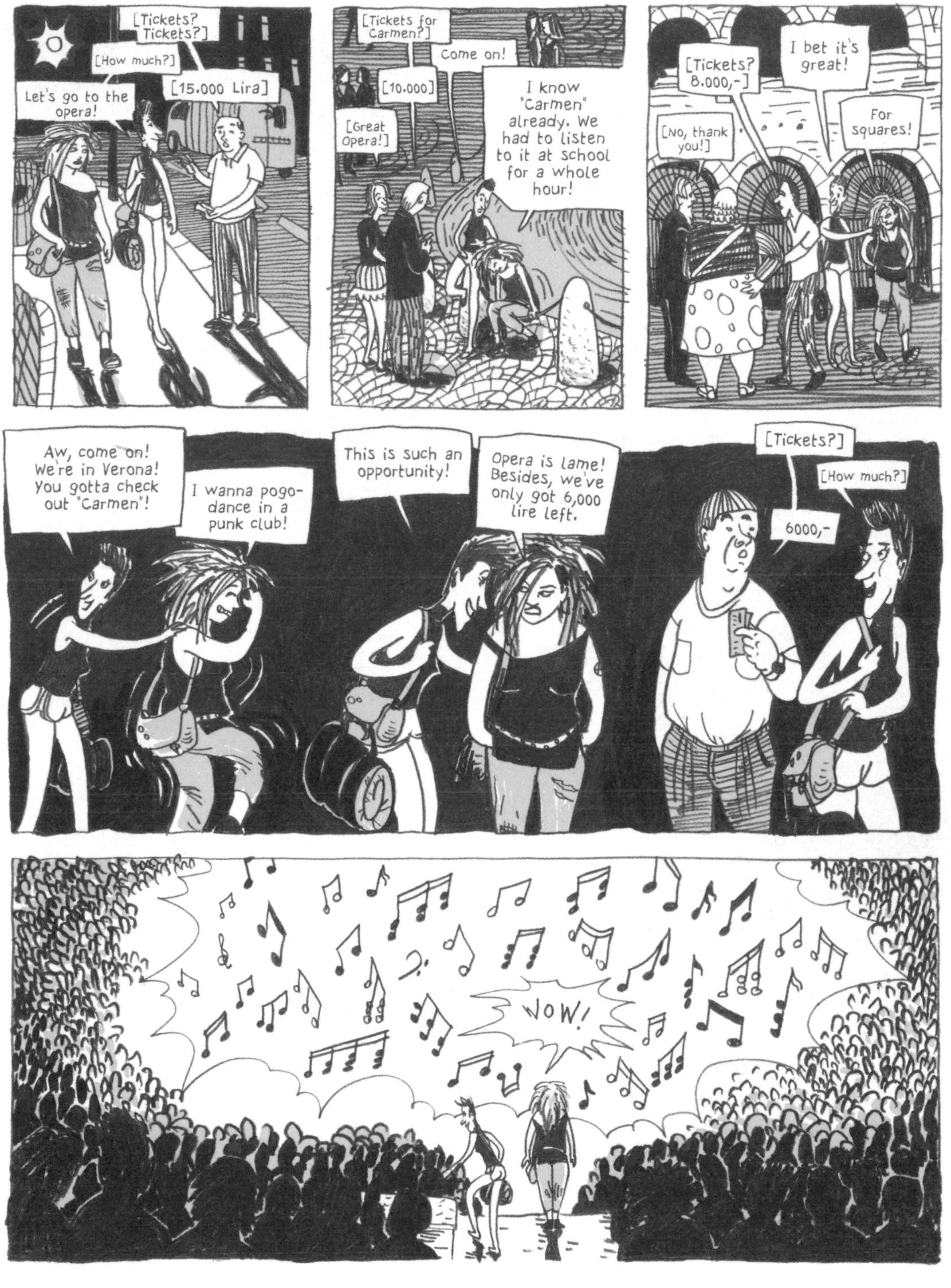
[Tickets? Tickets?]
[How much?]
Let's go to the opera!
[15.000 Lira]
[Tickets for Carmen?]
Come on!
[10.000]
[Great Opera!]
I know "Carmen" already. We had to listen to it at school for a whole hour!
[Tickets? 8.000,-]
I bet it's great!
[No, thank you!]
For squares!
Aw, come on! We're in Verona! You gotta check out "Carmen"!
I wanna pogo-dance in a punk club!
This is such an opportunity!
Opera is lame! Besides, we've only got 6,000 lire left.
[Tickets?]
[How much?]
6000,-
WOW!

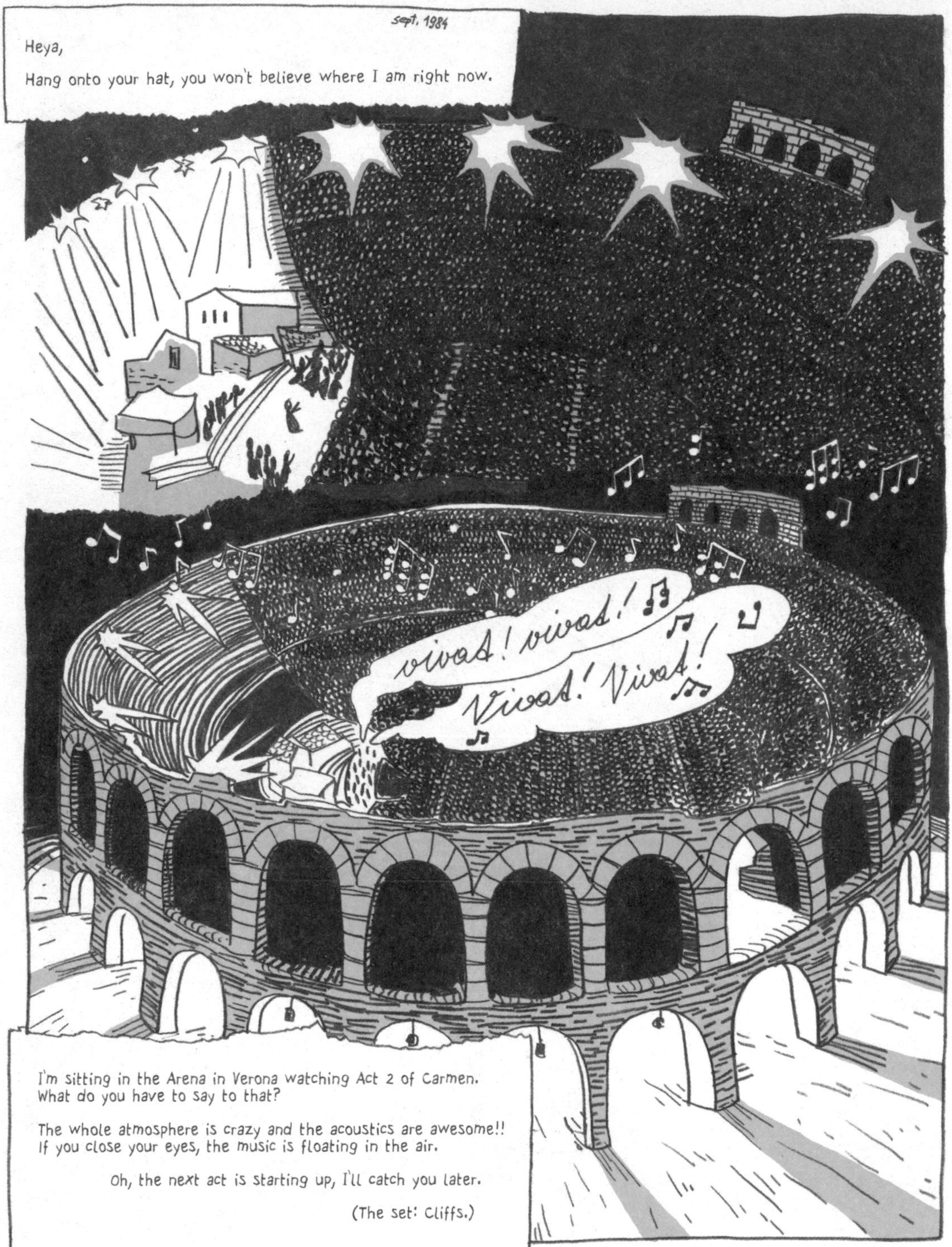
sept. 1984
Heya,
Hang onto your hat, you won't believe where I am right now.
vivat! vivat! Vivat! Vivat!
I'm sitting in the Arena in Verona watching Act 2 of Carmen. What do you have to say to that?
The whole atmosphere is crazy and the acoustics are awesome!! If you close your eyes, the music is floating in the air.
Oh, the next act is starting up, I'll catch you later.
(The set: Cliffs.)

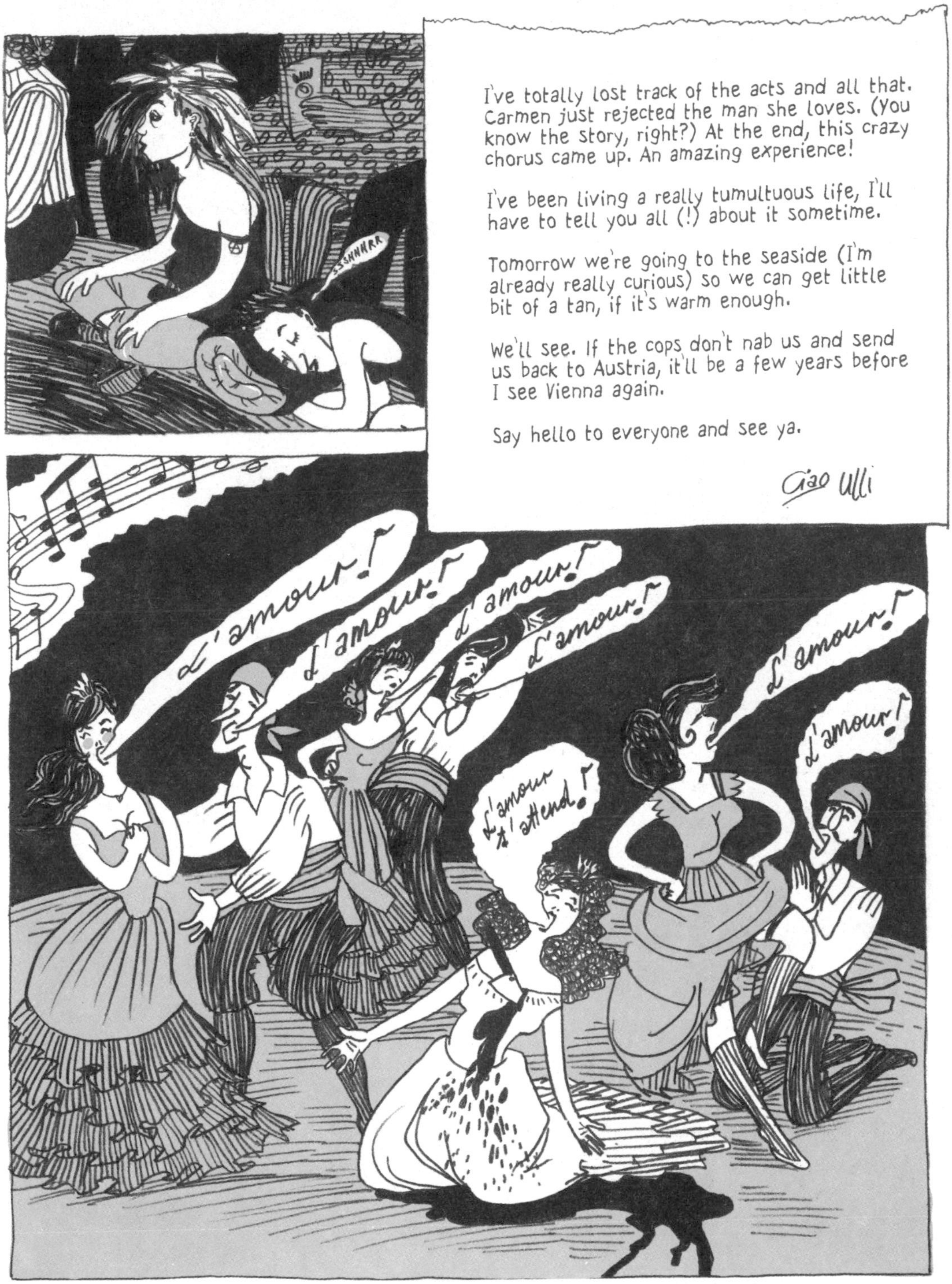
SSSHNHRR
I've totally lost track of the acts and all that. Carmen just rejected the man she loves. (You know the story, right?) At the end, this crazy chorus came up. An amazing experience!
I've been living a really tumultuous life, I'll have to tell you all (!) about it sometime.
Tomorrow we're going to the seaside (I'm already really curious) so we can get little bit of a tan, if it's warm enough.
We'll see. If the cops don't nab us and send us back to Austria, it'll be a few years before I see Vienna again.
Say hello to everyone and see ya.
Ciao Ulli
L'amour!
L'amour!
L'amour!
L'amour!
L'amour t'attend!
L'amour!
L'amour!

(Love... love... love... love is waiting for you!)

I'm so excited.

[You like Italy?]

[Yes!] [In Rimini we first have to go to the sea. She will see the sea first time in her life.]

[Ahhh, what a lucky girl!] [Ahh, you will love sea!]

[Really? First time?]

mare e belle bellissimo

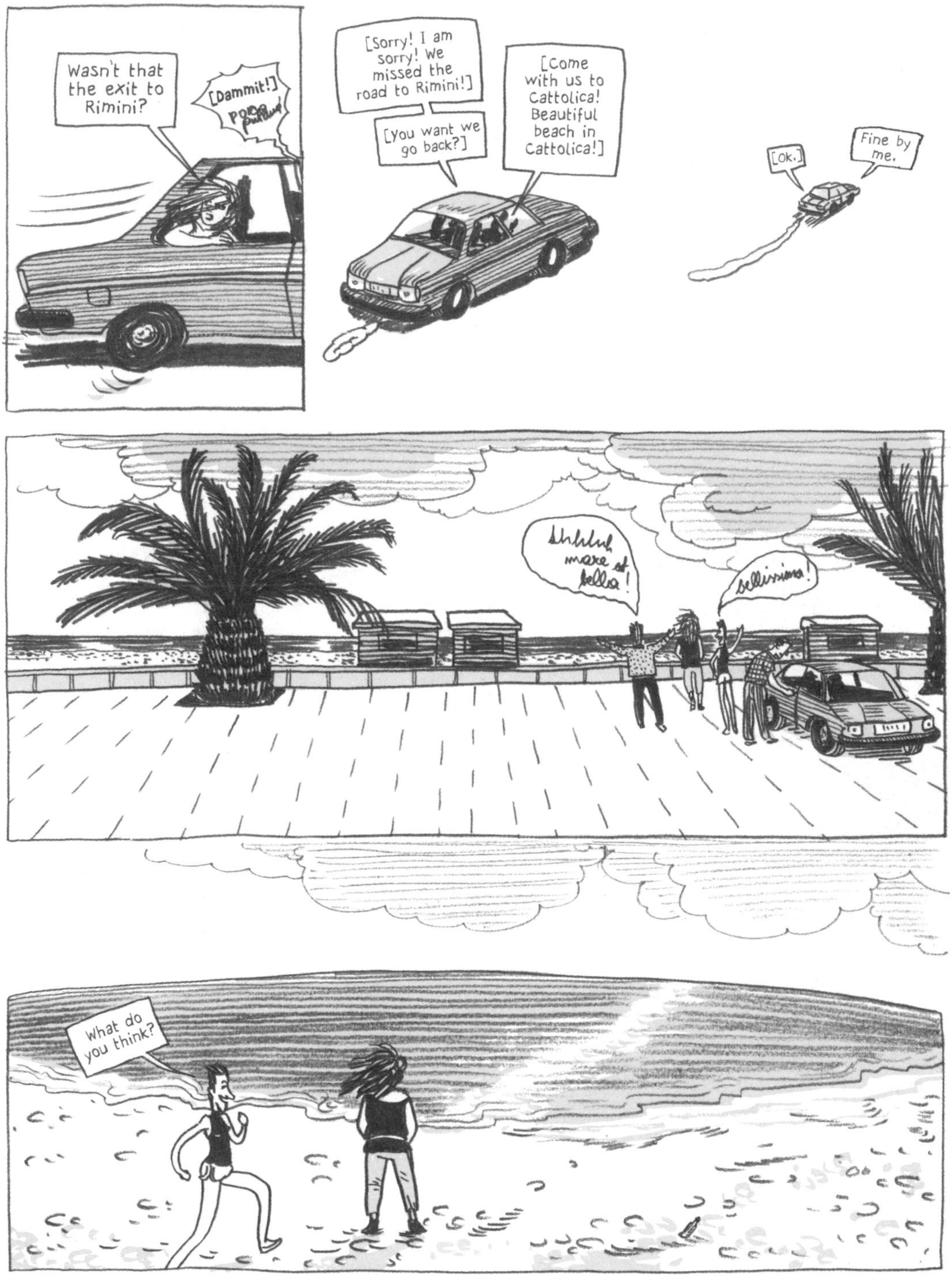
Wasn't that the exit to Rimini?
[Dammit!]
[Sorry! I am sorry! We missed the road to Rimini!]
[You want we go back?]
[Come with us to Cattolica! Beautiful beach in Cattolica!]
[Ok.]
Fine by me.
bellissima!
What do you think?

Worn-out waves were lapping at my feet. Sluggish gray water all the way out to the horizon.

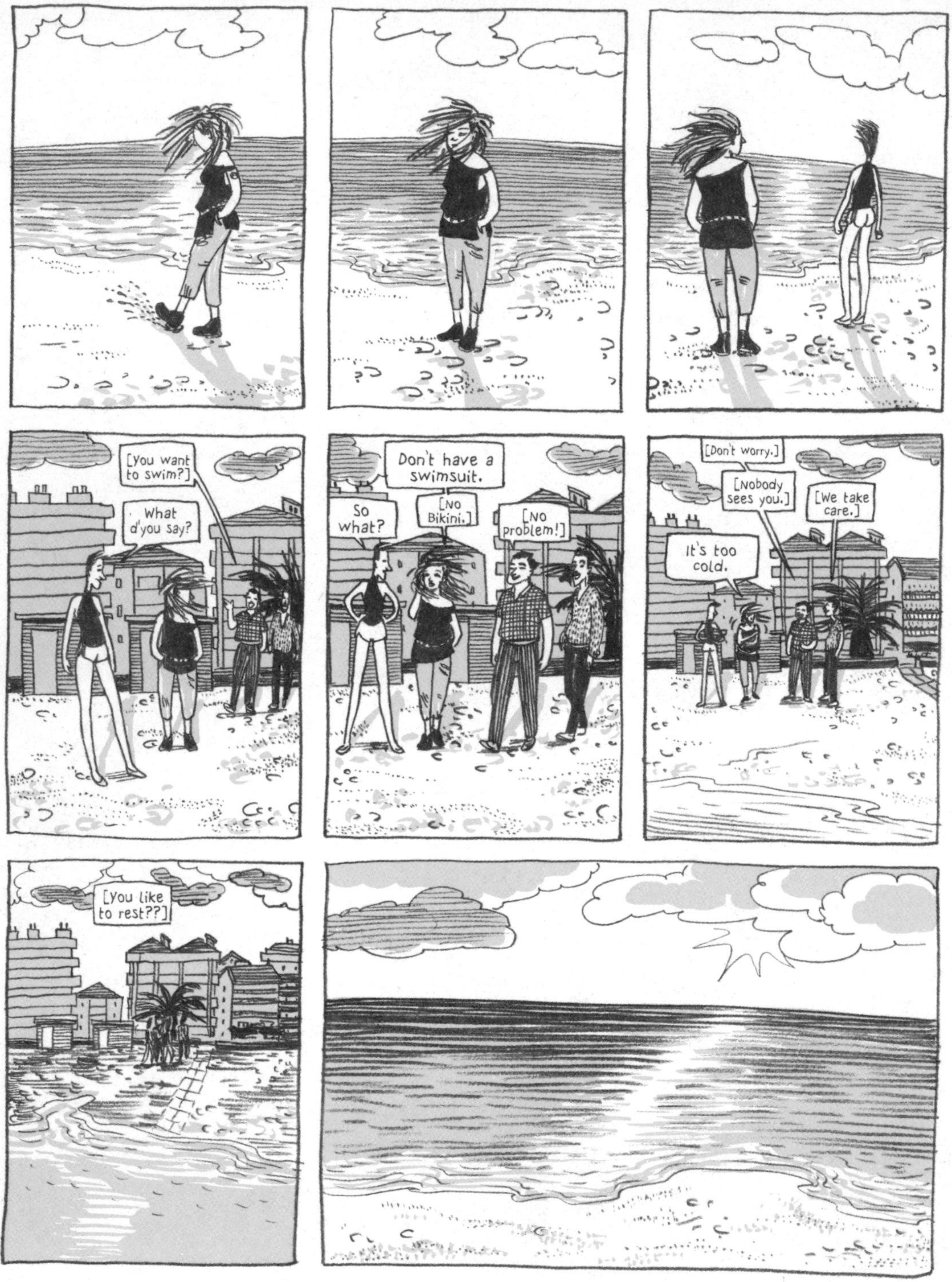
[You want to swim?]
What d'you say?
Don't have a swimsuit.
So what?
[No Bikini.]
[No problem!]
[Don't worry.]
[Nobody sees you.]
[We take care.]
It's too cold.
[You like to rest??]

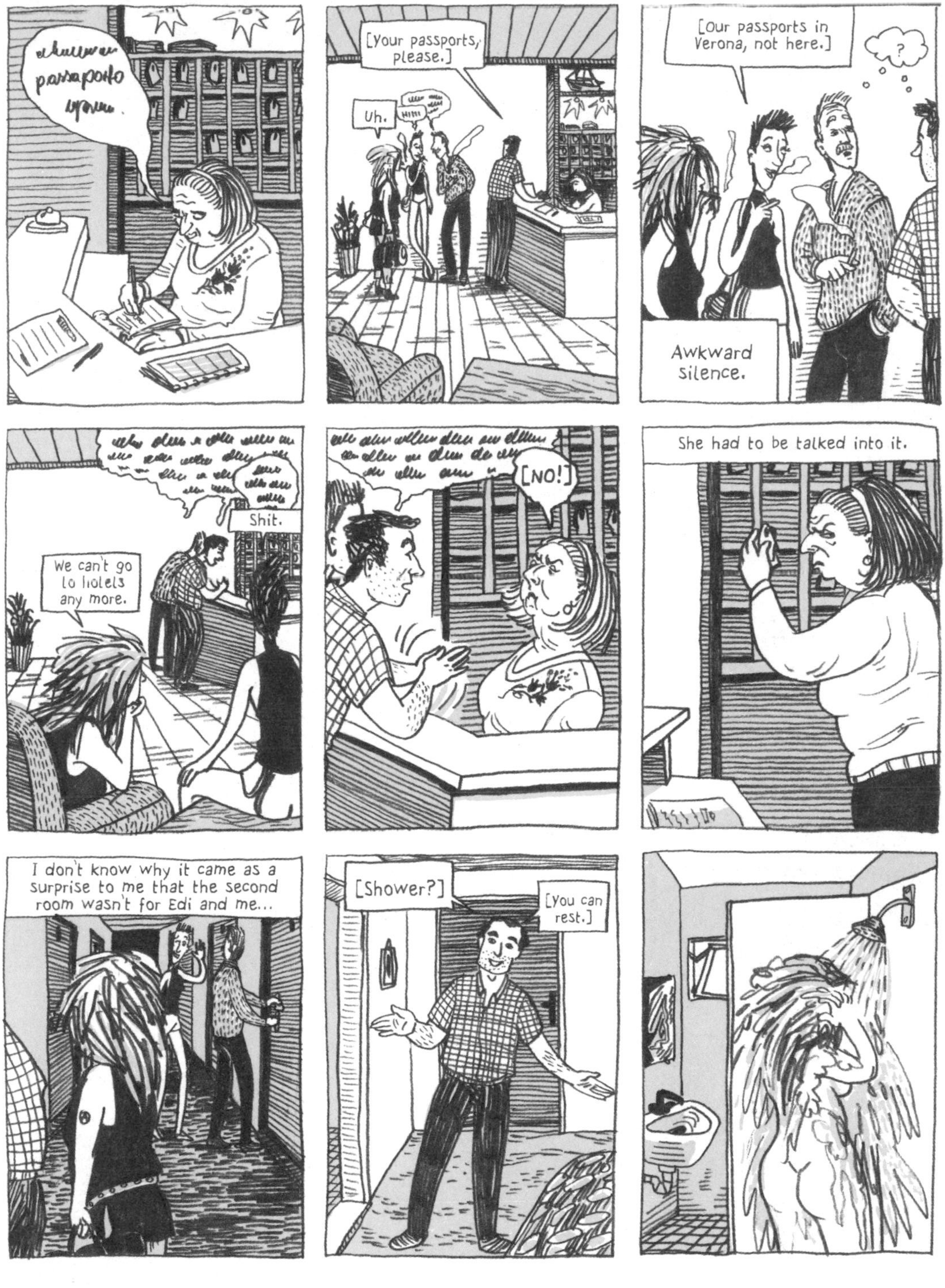
passaporto
[Your passports, please.]
Uh.
HI!!!
[Our passports in Verona, not here.]
?
Awkward silence.
Shit.
We can't go to hotels any more.
[NO!]
She had to be talked into it.
I don't know why it came as a surprise to me that the second room wasn't for Edi and me...
[Shower?]
[You can rest.]

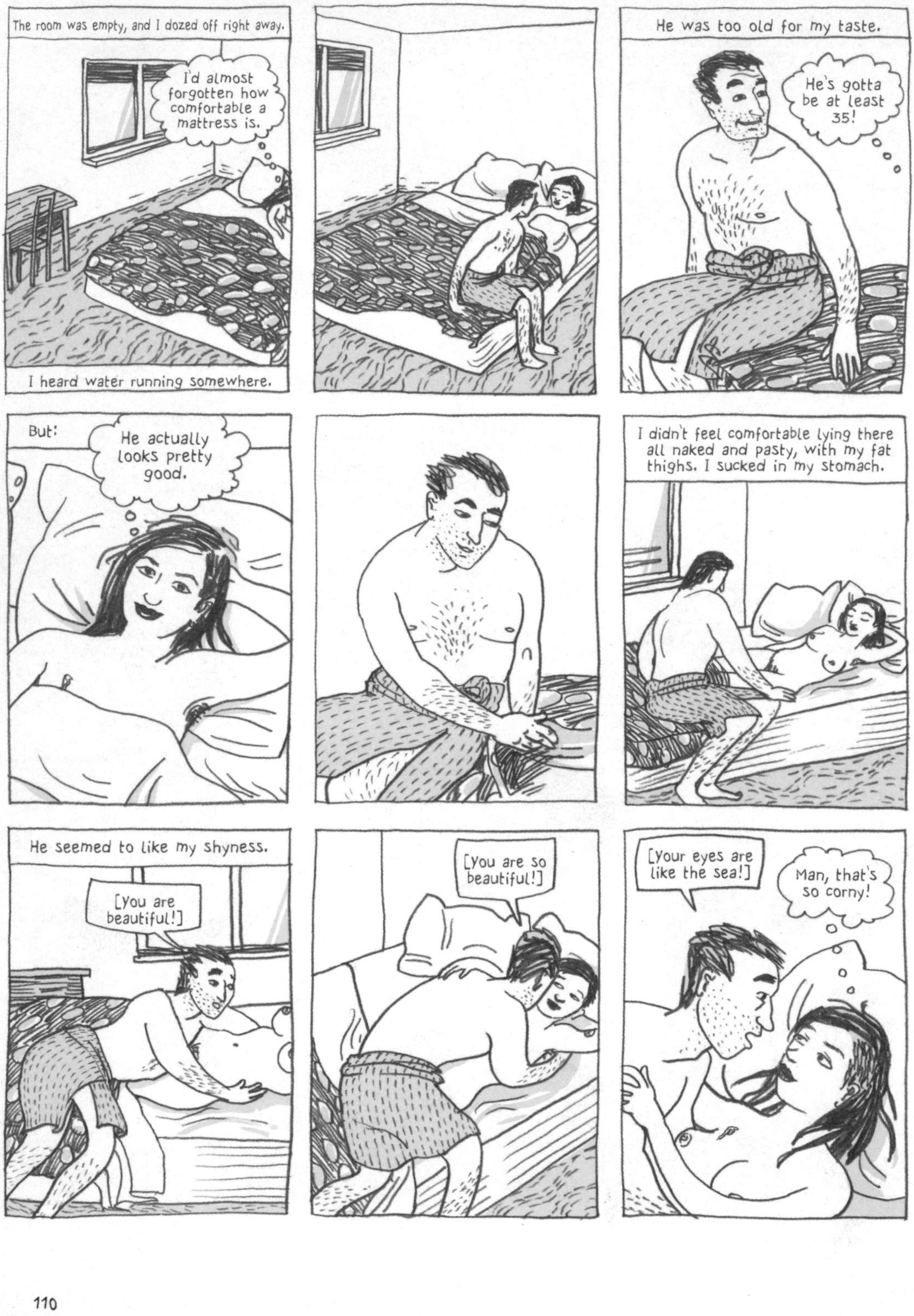
The room was empty, and I dozed off right away.
I'd almost forgotten how comfortable a mattress is.
I heard water running somewhere.
He was too old for my taste.
He's gotta be at least 35!
But:
He actually looks pretty good.
I didn't feel comfortable lying there all naked and pasty, with my fat thighs. I sucked in my stomach.
He seemed to like my shyness.
[You are beautiful!]
[You are so beautiful!]
[Your eyes are like the sea!]
Man, that's so corny!

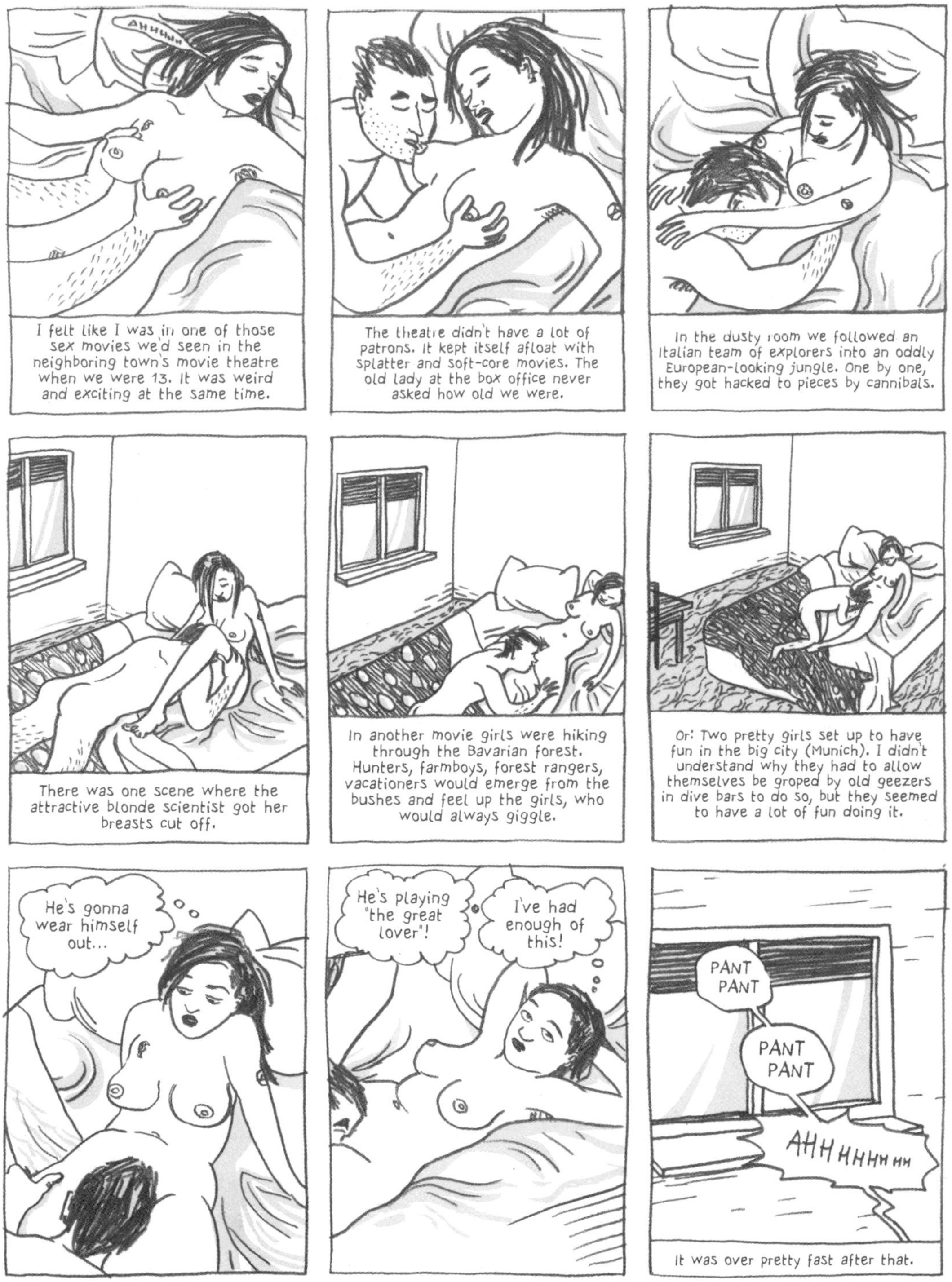
I felt like I was in one of those sex movies we'd seen in the neighboring town's movie theatre when we were 13. It was weird and exciting at the same time.
The theatre didn't have a lot of patrons. It kept itself afloat with splatter and soft-core movies. The old lady at the box office never asked how old we were.
In the dusty room we followed an Italian team of explorers into an oddly European-looking jungle. One by one, they got hacked to pieces by cannibals.
There was one scene where the attractive blonde scientist got her breasts cut off.
In another movie girls were hiking through the Bavarian forest. Hunters, farmboys, forest rangers, vacationers would emerge from the bushes and feel up the girls, who would always giggle.
Or: Two pretty girls set up to have fun in the big city (Munich). I didn't understand why they had to allow themselves be groped by old geezers in dive bars to do so, but they seemed to have a lot of fun doing it.
He's gonna wear himself out...
He's playing "the great lover"!
I've had enough of this!
PANT PANT
PANT PANT
AHHHHHHHH
It was over pretty fast after that.

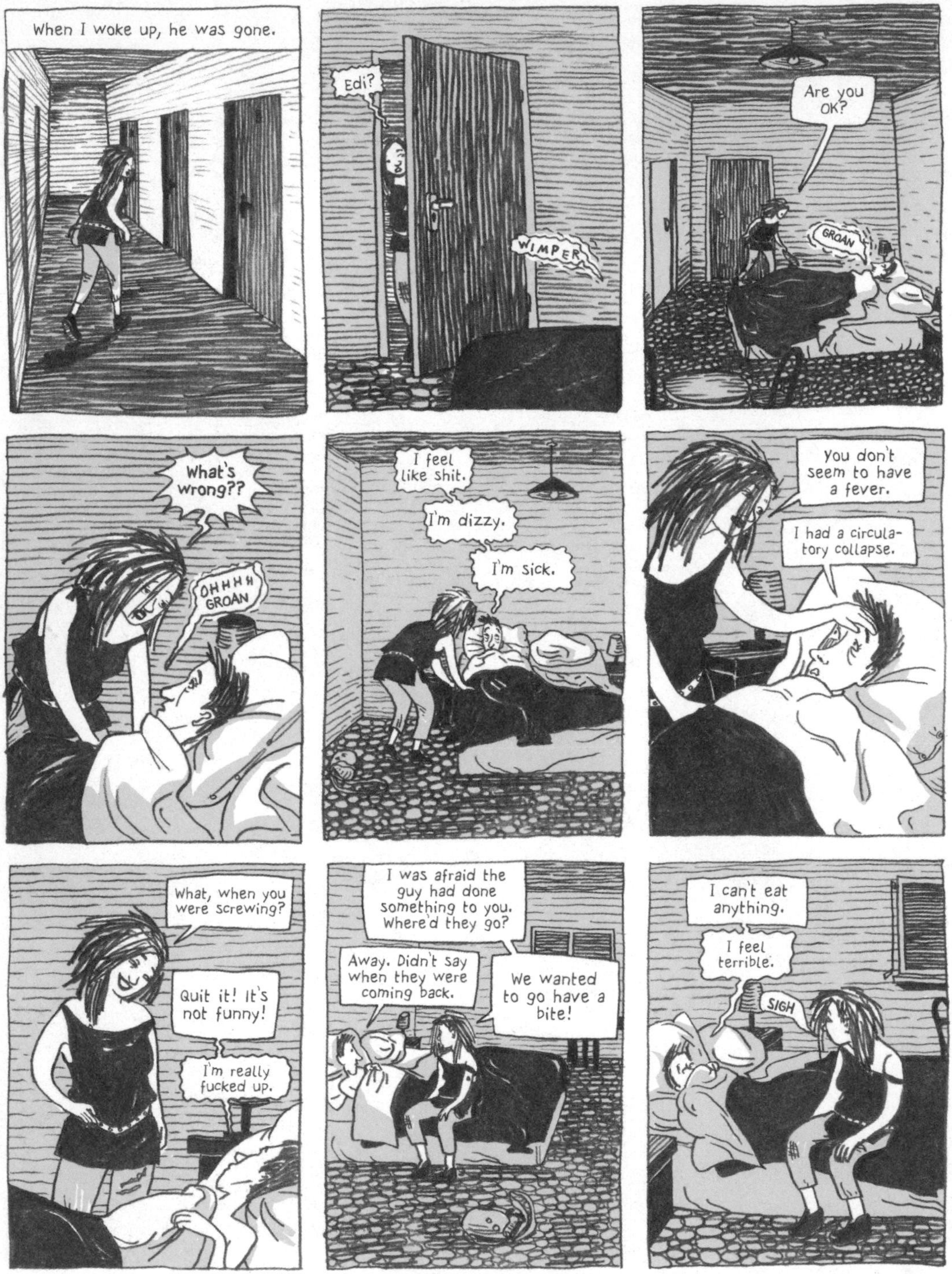
When I woke up, he was gone.
Edi?
WIMPER
Are you OK?
GROAN
What's wrong??
OHHHH GROAN
I feel like shit.
I'm dizzy.
I'm sick.
You don't seem to have a fever.
I had a circulatory collapse.
What, when you were screwing?
Quit it! It's not funny!
I'm really fucked up.
I was afraid the guy had done something to you. Where'd they go?
Away. Didn't say when they were coming back.
We wanted to go have a bite!
I can't eat anything.
I feel terrible.
SIGH

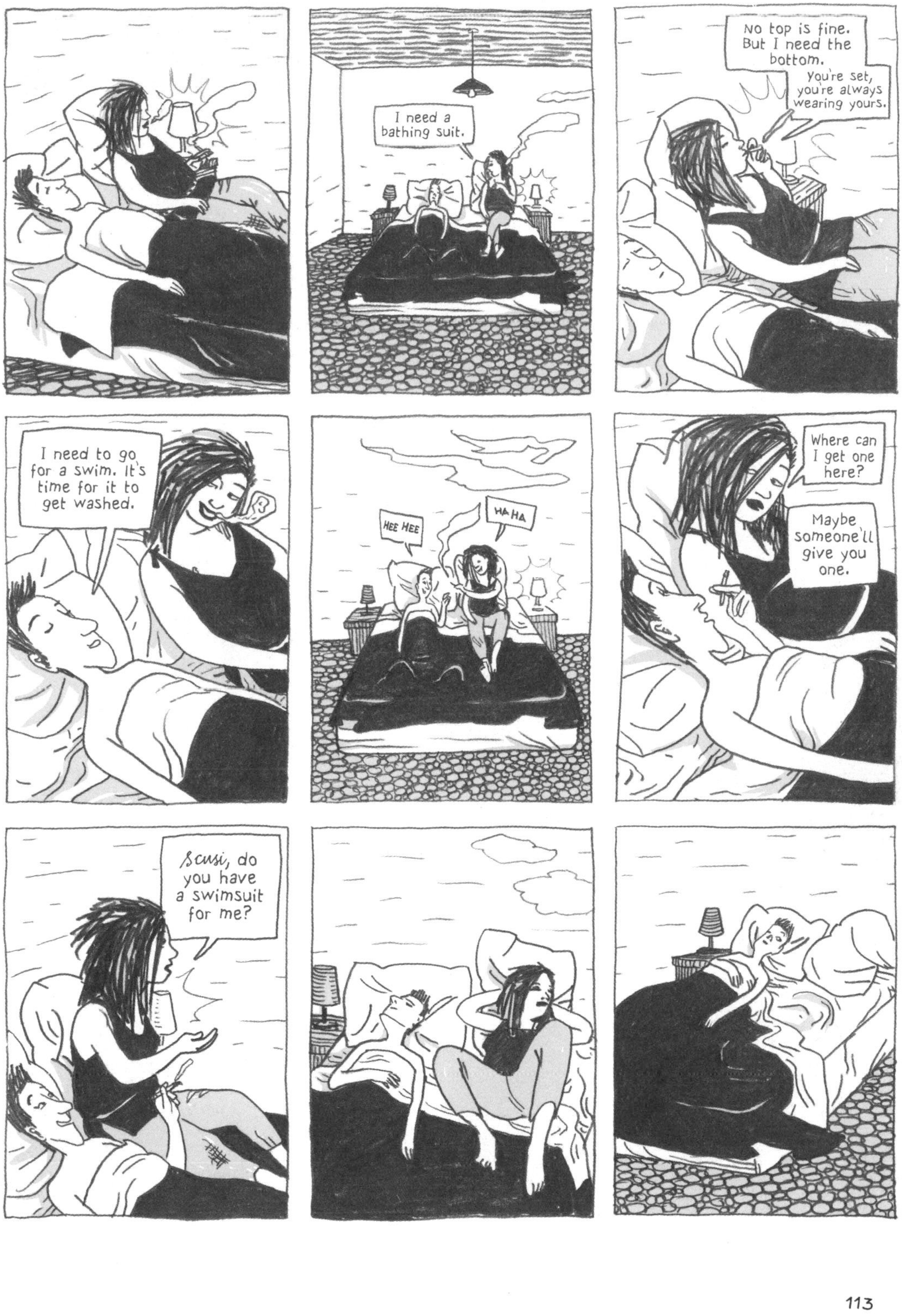
I need a bathing suit.
No top is fine. But I need the bottom.
You're set, you're always wearing yours.
I need to go for a swim. It's time for it to get washed.
HEE HEE
HA HA
Where can I get one here?
Maybe someone'll give you one.
Scusi, do you have a swimsuit for me?

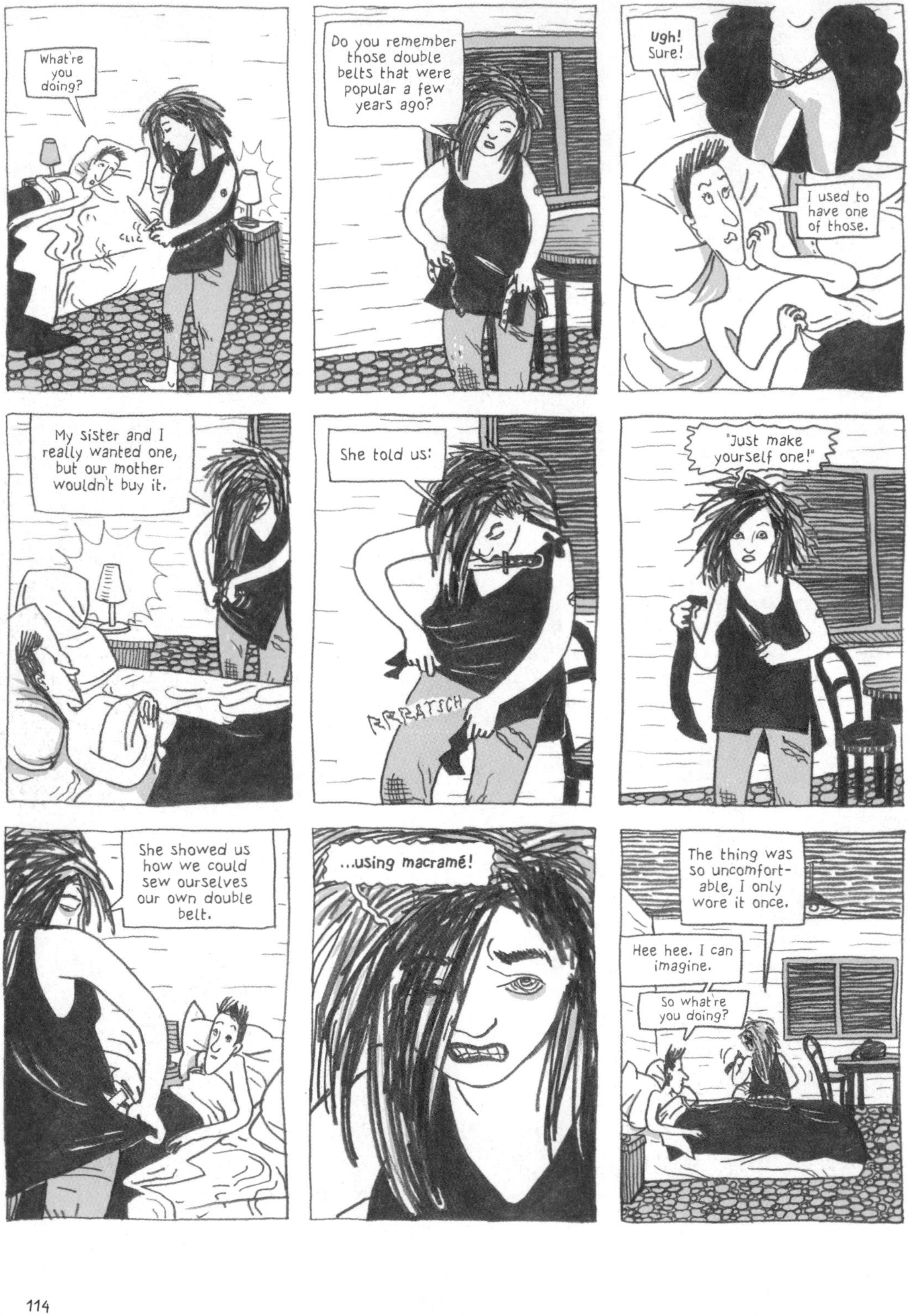
What're you doing?
Do you remember those double belts that were popular a few years ago?
Ugh! Sure!
I used to have one of those.
My sister and I really wanted one, but our mother wouldn't buy it.
She told us:
RRRATSCH
"Just make yourself one!"
She showed us how we could sew ourselves our own double belt.
...using macramé!
The thing was so uncomfort-able, I only wore it once.
Hee hee. I can imagine.
So what're you doing?

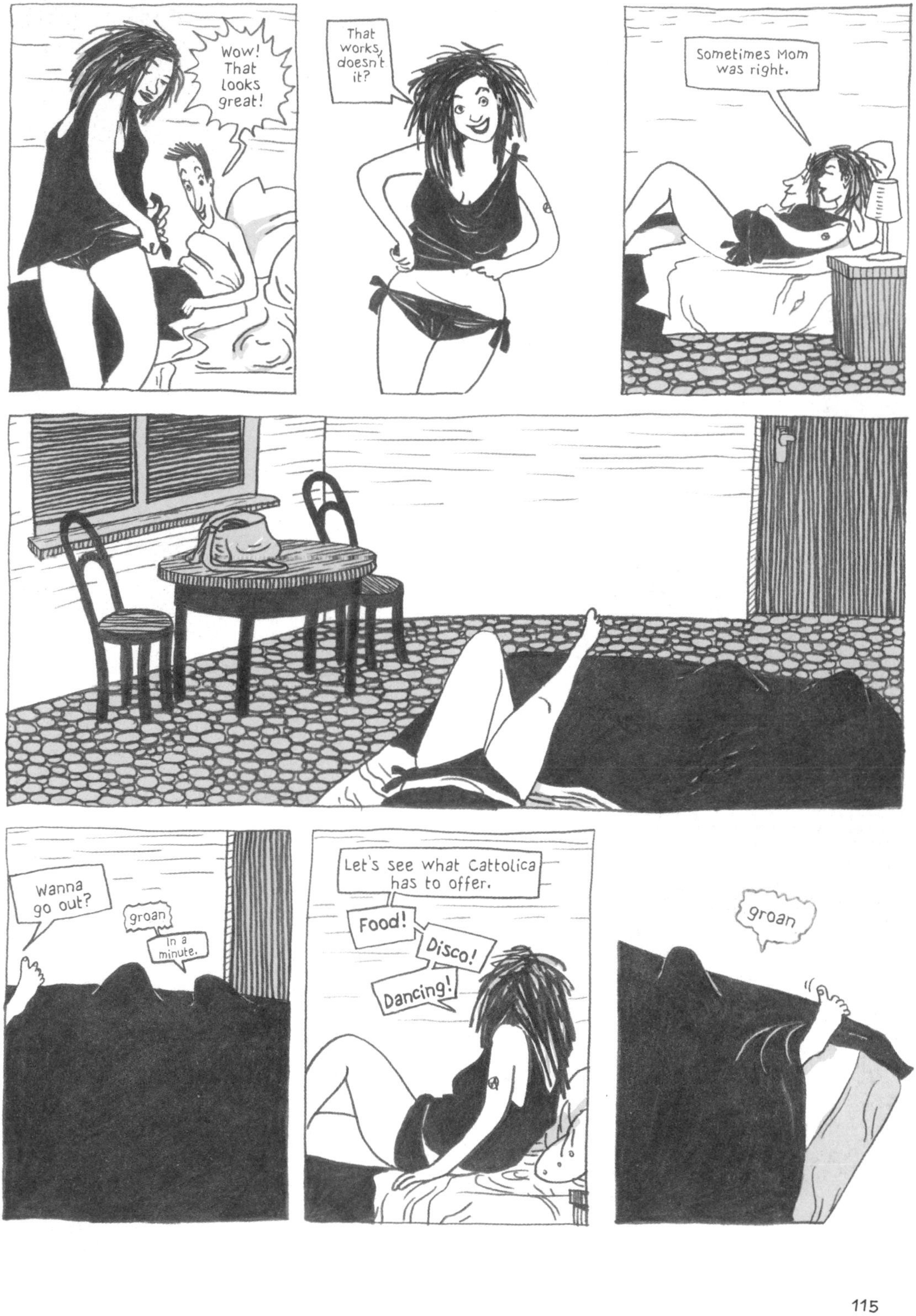
Wow! That looks great!
That works, doesn't it?
Sometimes Mom was right.
Wanna go out?
groan
In a minute.
Let's see what Cattolica has to offer.
Food!
Disco!
Dancing!
groan

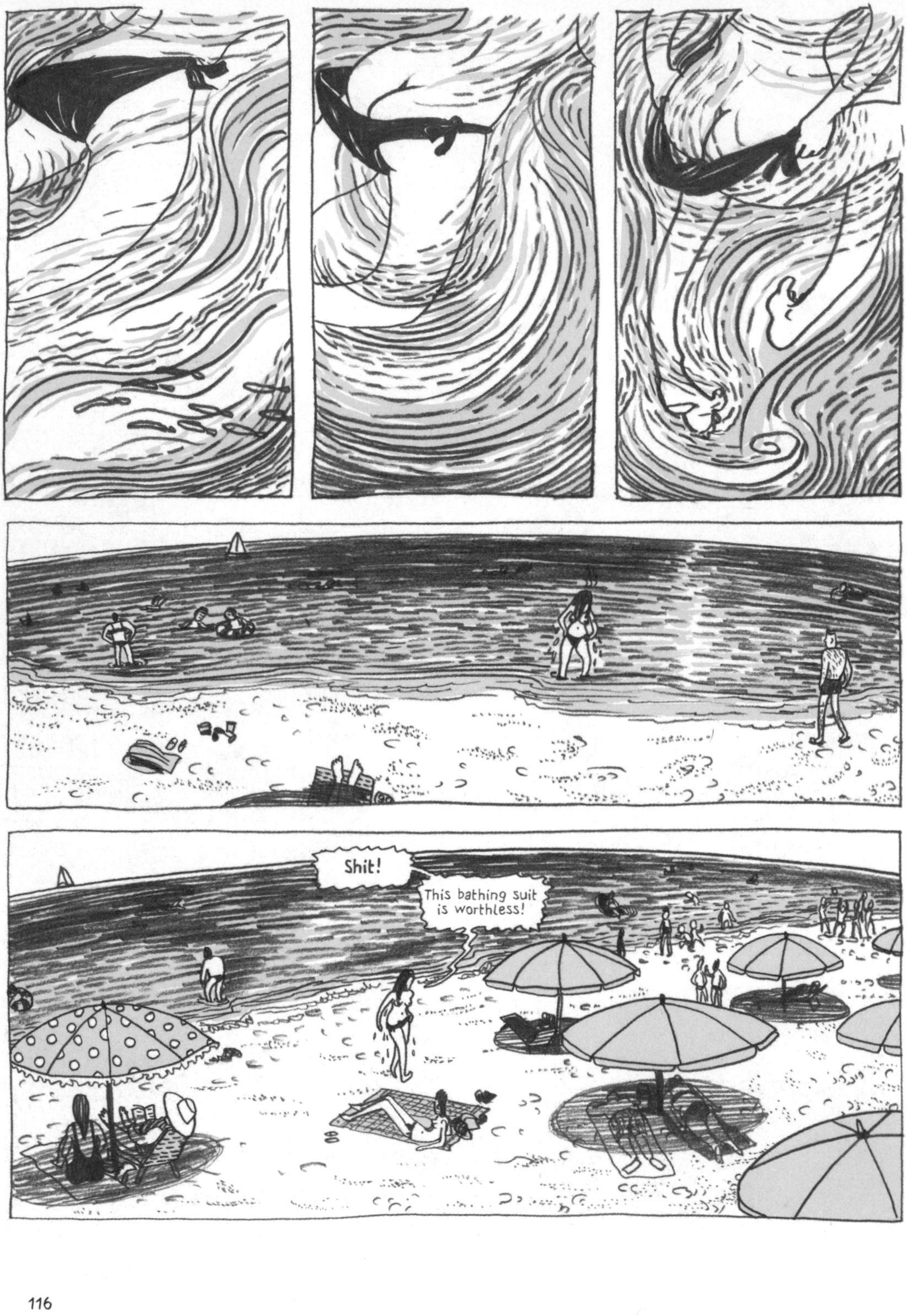
Shit!
This bathing suit is worthless!

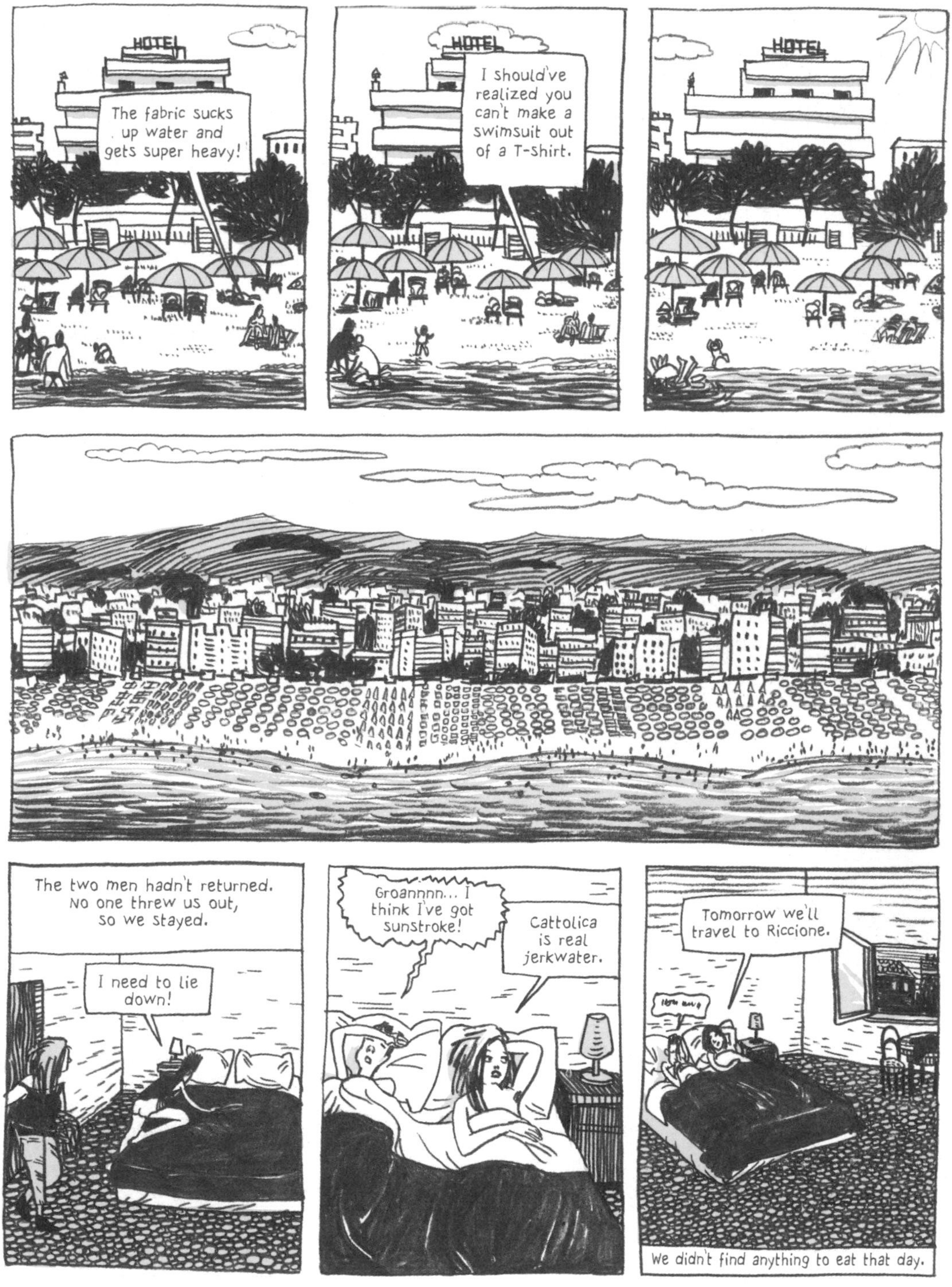

The fabric sucks up water and gets super heavy!
I should've realized you can't make a swimsuit out of a T-shirt.
The two men hadn't returned. No one threw us out, so we stayed.
I need to lie down!
Groannnn... I think I've got sunstroke!
Cattolica is real jerkwater.
Tomorrow we'll travel to Riccione.
We didn't find anything to eat that day.

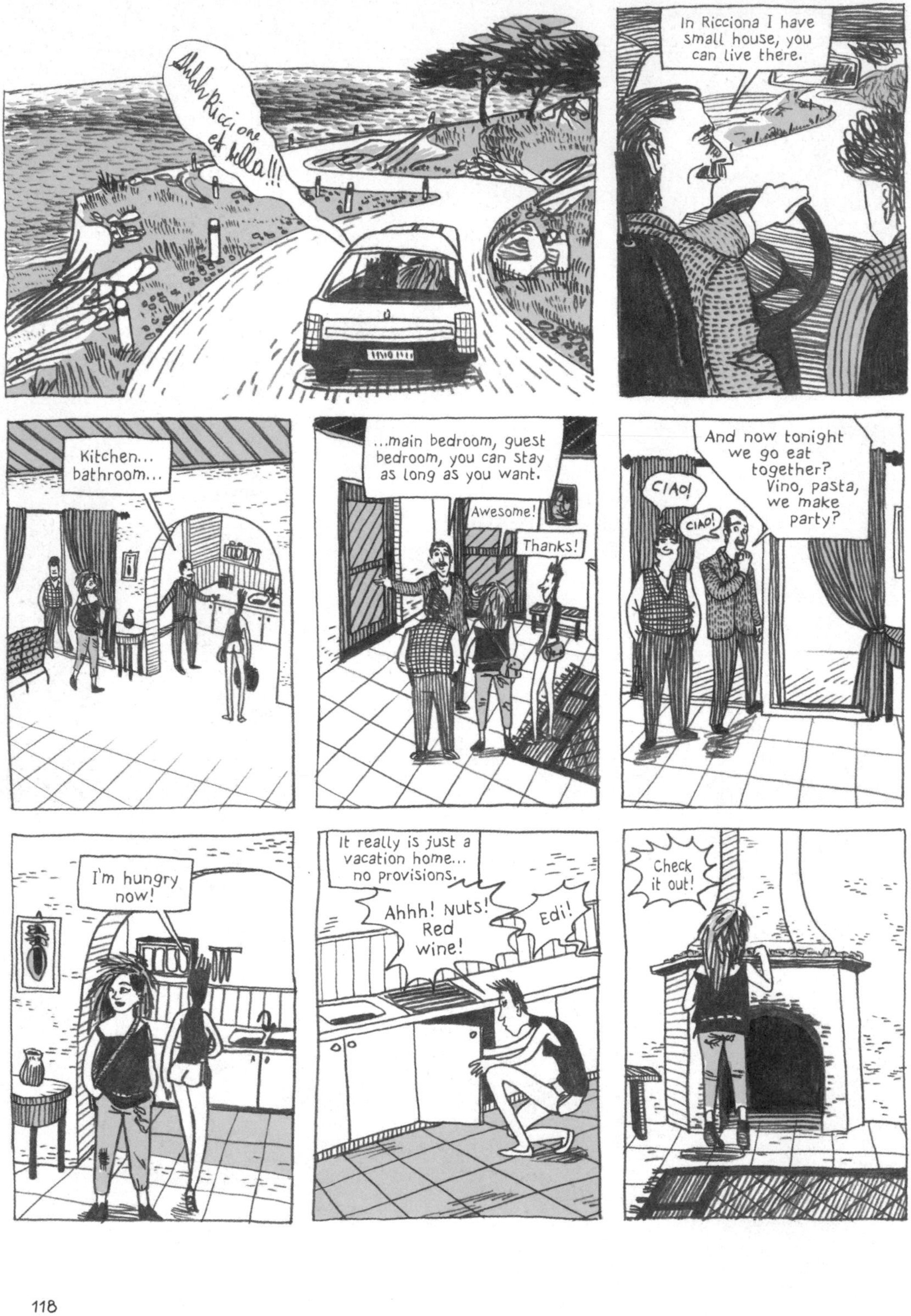
Ahhh Riccione et bella!!!
In Ricciona I have small house, you can live there.
Kitchen... bathroom...
...main bedroom, guest bedroom, you can stay as long as you want.
Awesome!
Thanks!
And now tonight we go eat together? Vino, pasta, we make party?
CIAO!
CIAO!
I'm hungry now!
It really is just a vacation home... no provisions.
Ahhh! Nuts! Red wine!
Edi!
Check it out!

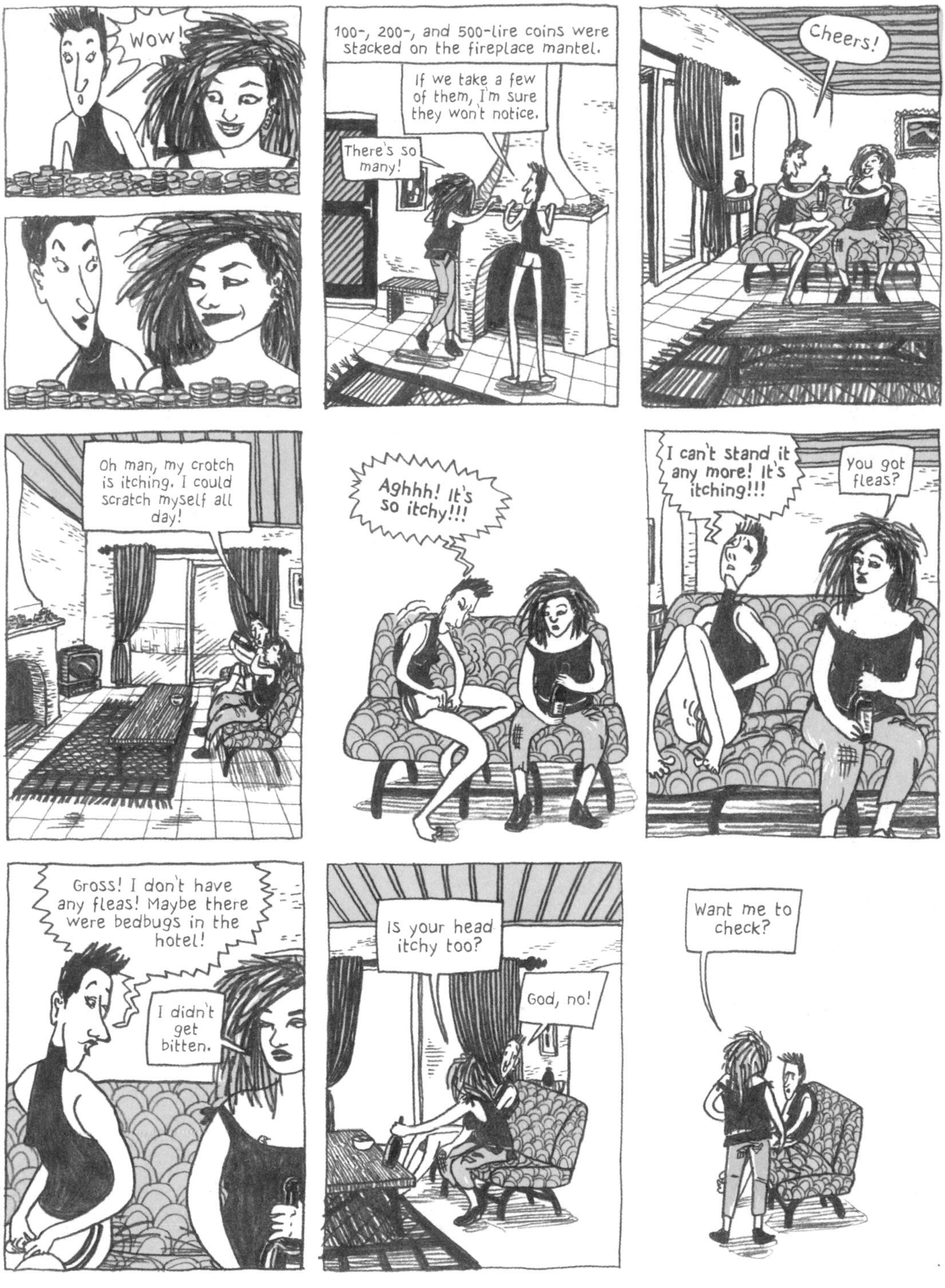
Wow!
100-, 200-, and 500-lire coins were stacked on the fireplace mantel.
If we take a few of them, I'm sure they won't notice.
There's so many!
Cheers!
Oh man, my crotch is itching. I could scratch myself all day!
Aghhh! It's so itchy!!!
I can't stand it any more! It's itching!!!
You got fleas?
Gross! I don't have any fleas! Maybe there were bedbugs in the hotel!
I didn't get bitten.
Is your head itchy too?
God, no!
Want me to check?

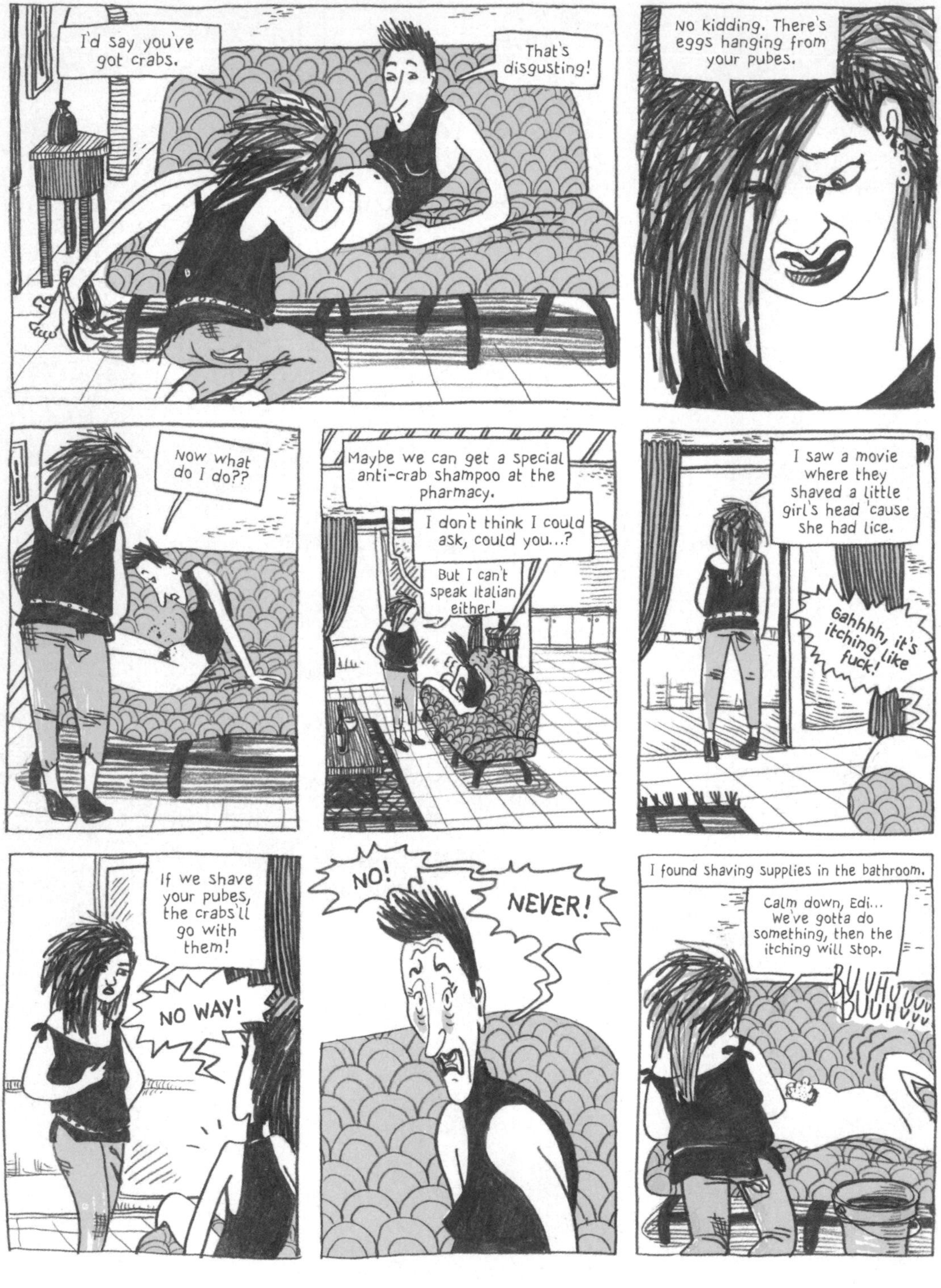
I'd say you've got crabs.
That's disgusting!
No kidding. There's eggs hanging from your pubes.
Now what do I do??
Maybe we can get a special anti-crab shampoo at the pharmacy.
I don't think I could ask, could you...?
But I can't speak Italian either!
I saw a movie where they shaved a little girl's head 'cause she had lice.
Gahhhh, it's itching like fuck!
If we shave your pubes, the crabs'll go with them!
NO WAY!
NO!
NEVER!
I found shaving supplies in the bathroom.
Calm down, Edi... We've gotta do something, then the itching will stop.
BUUHUUUU BUUHUUUU

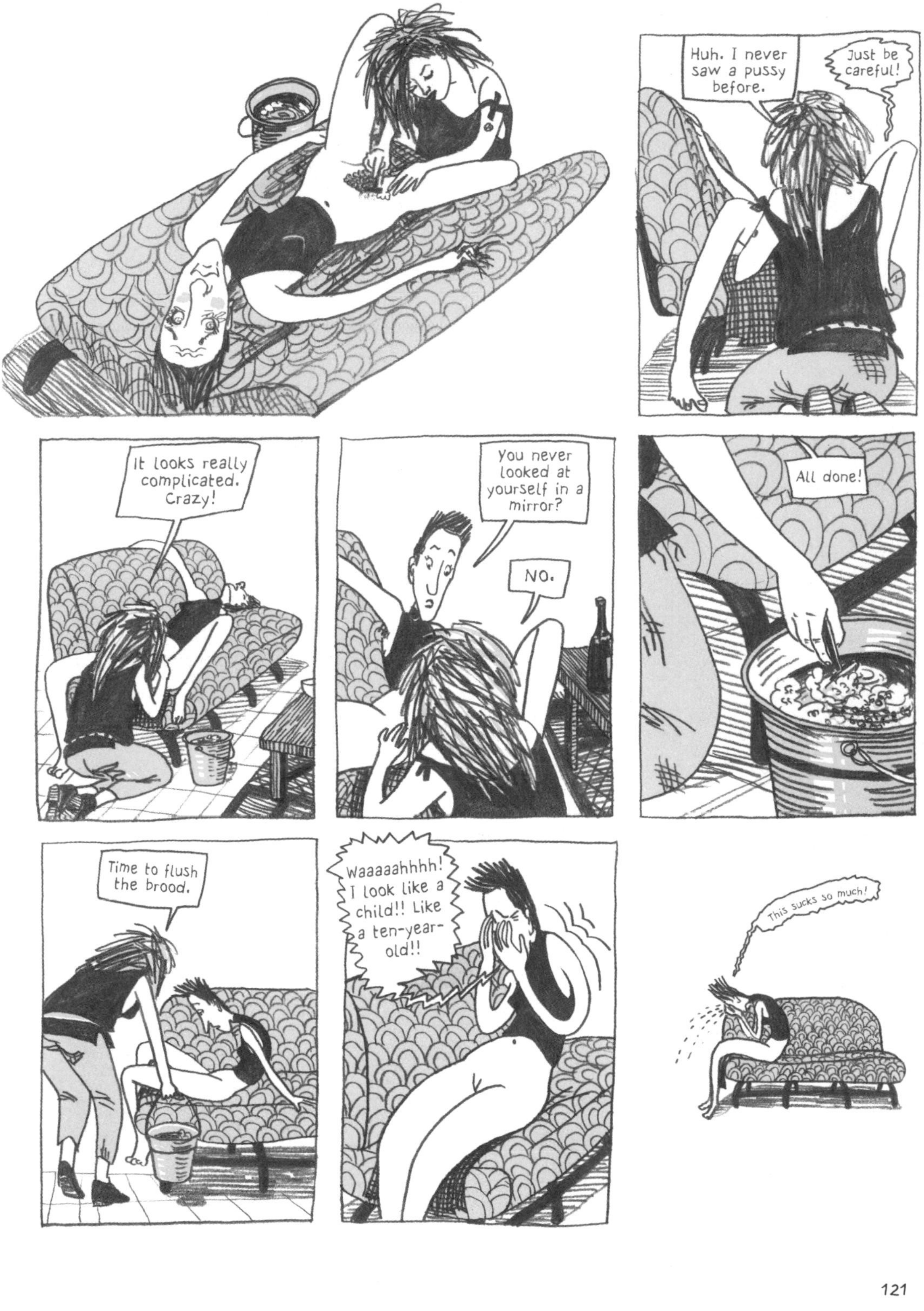

Huh. I never saw a pussy before.
Just be careful!
It looks really complicated. Crazy!
You never looked at yourself in a mirror?
NO.
All done!
Time to flush the brood.
Waaaaahhhh! I look like a child!! Like a ten-year-old!!
This sucks so much!

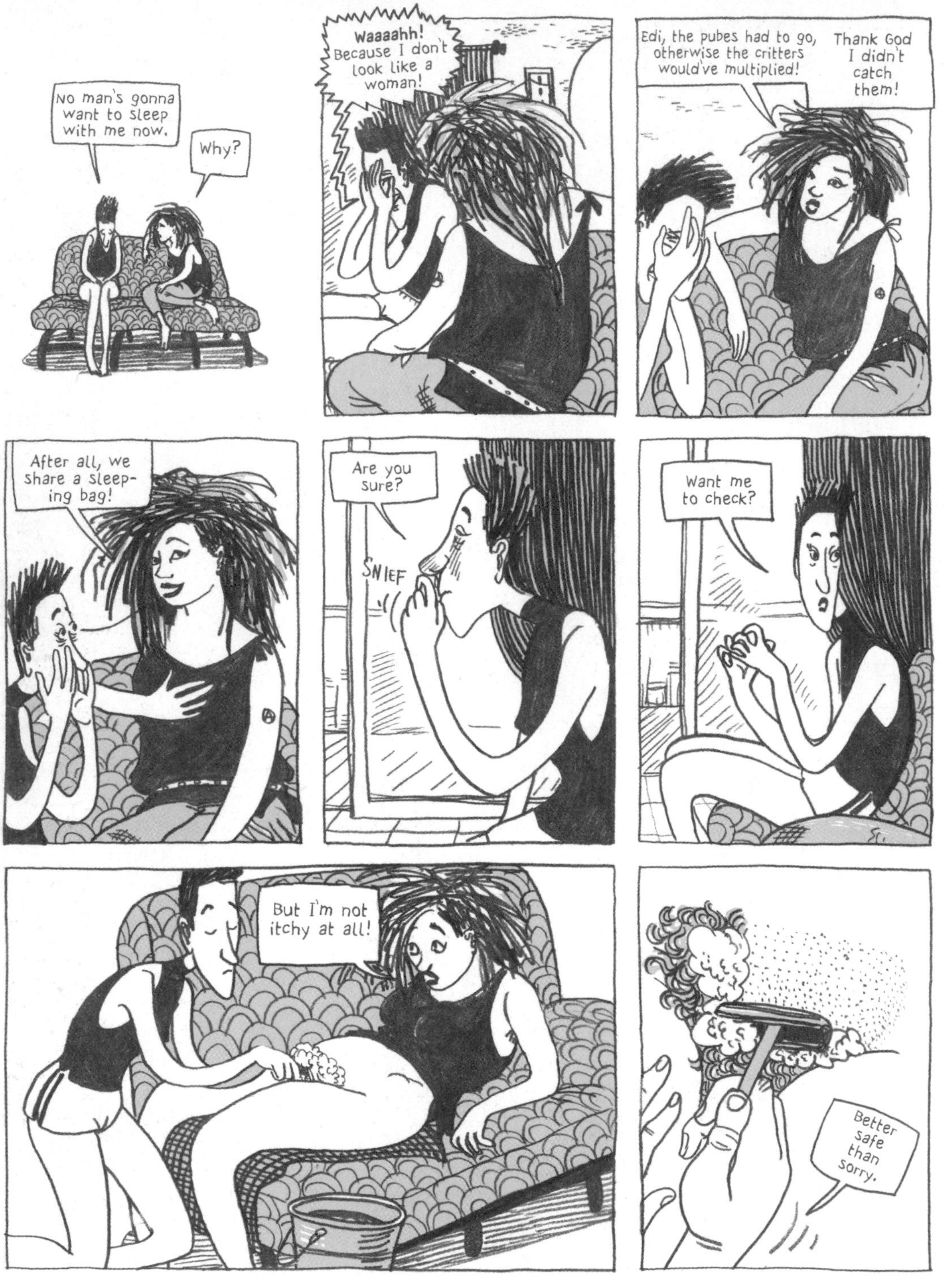
No man's gonna want to sleep with me now.
Why?
Waaaahh! Because I don't look like a woman!
Edi, the pubes had to go, otherwise the critters would've multiplied!
Thank God I didn't catch them!
After all, we share a sleeping bag!
Are you sure?
SNIEF
Want me to check?
But I'm not itchy at all!
Better safe than sorry.

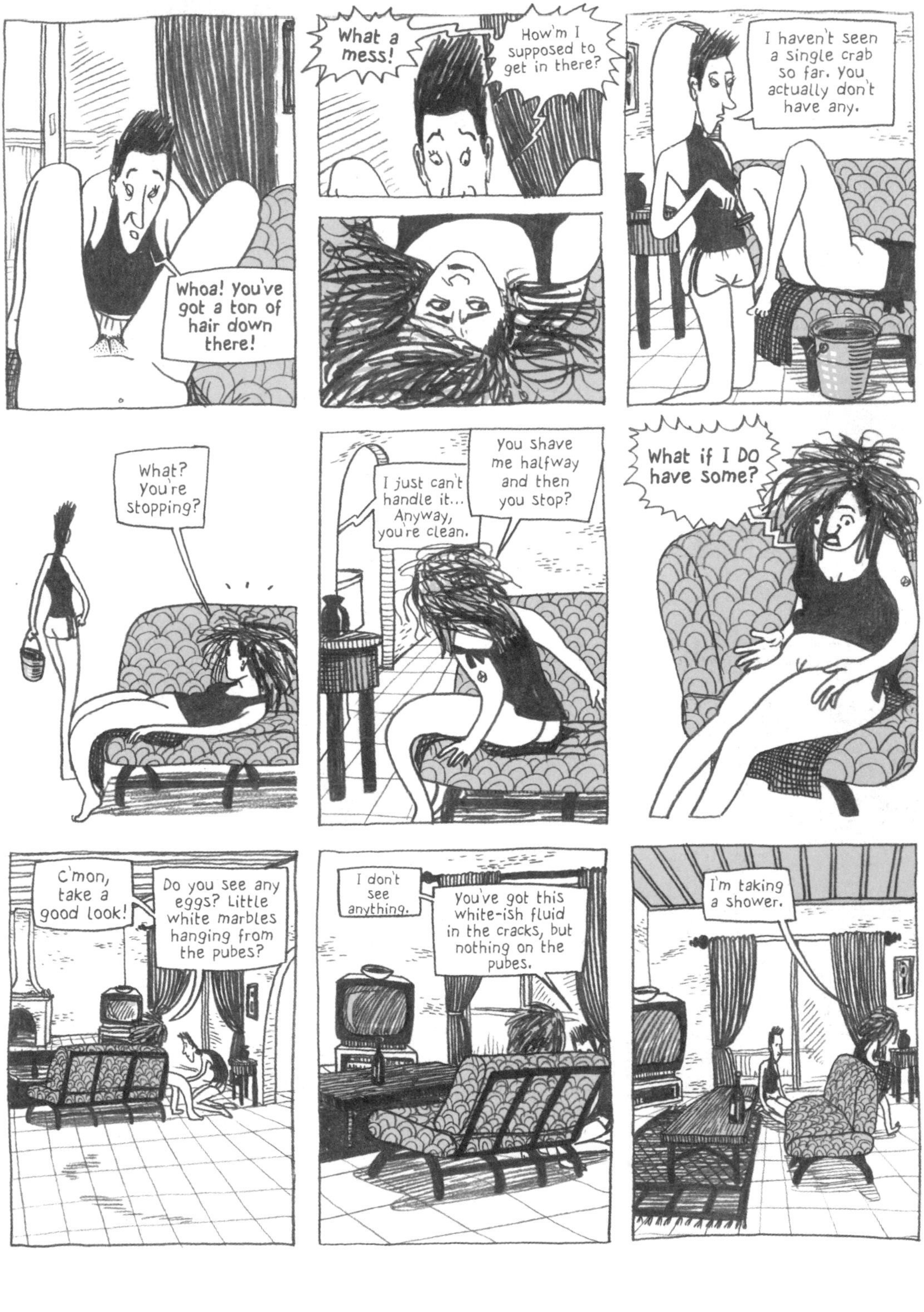
Whoa! You've got a ton of hair down there!
What a mess!
How'm I supposed to get in there?
I haven't seen a single crab so far. You actually don't have any.
What? You're stopping?
I just can't handle it... Anyway, you're clean.
You shave me halfway and then you stop?
What if I DO have some?
C'mon, take a good look!
Do you see any eggs? Little white marbles hanging from the pubes?
I don't see anything.
You've got this white-ish fluid in the cracks, but nothing on the pubes.
I'm taking a shower.

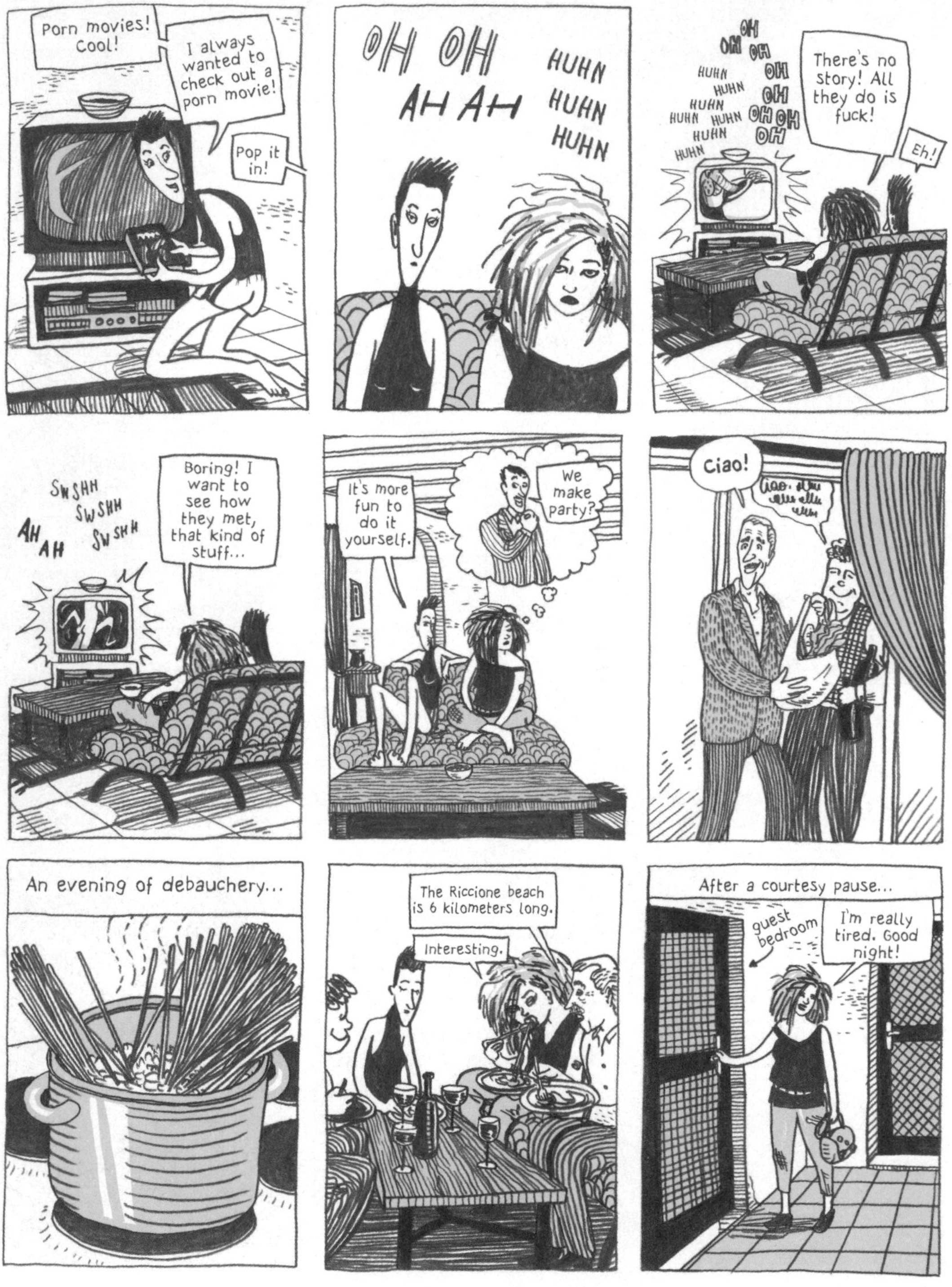
Porn movies! Cool!
I always wanted to check out a porn movie!
Pop it in!
OH OH
AH AH
HUHN HUHN HUHN
OH OH OH OH OH OH OH OH OH
HUHN HUHN HUHN HUHN HUHN HUHN HUHN
There's no story! All they do is fuck!
Eh!
SWSHH SWSHH SWSHH
AH AH
Boring! I want to see how they met, that kind of stuff...
It's more fun to do it yourself.
We make party?
Ciao!
An evening of debauchery...
The Riccione beach is 6 kilometers long.
Interesting.
After a courtesy pause...
guest bedroom
I'm really tired. Good night!

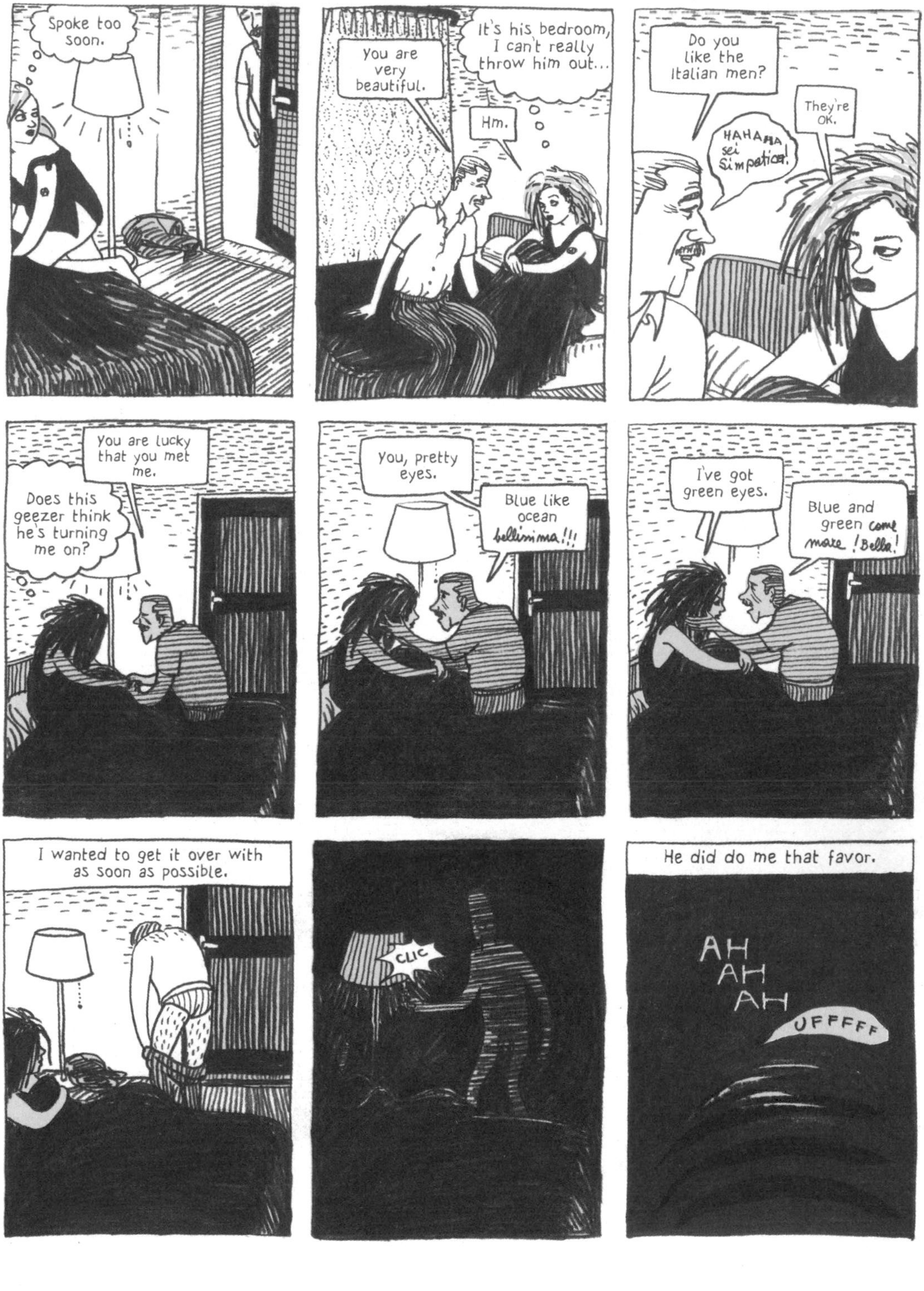
Spoke too soon.
You are very beautiful.
It's his bedroom, I can't really throw him out...
Hm.
Do you like the Italian men?
HAHAHA sei simpatica!
They're OK.
Does this geezer think he's turning me on?
You are lucky that you met me.
You, pretty eyes.
Blue like ocean bellissima!!!
I've got green eyes.
Blue and green come mare! Bella!
I wanted to get it over with as soon as possible.
CLIC
He did do me that favor.
AH
AH
AH
UFFFFF

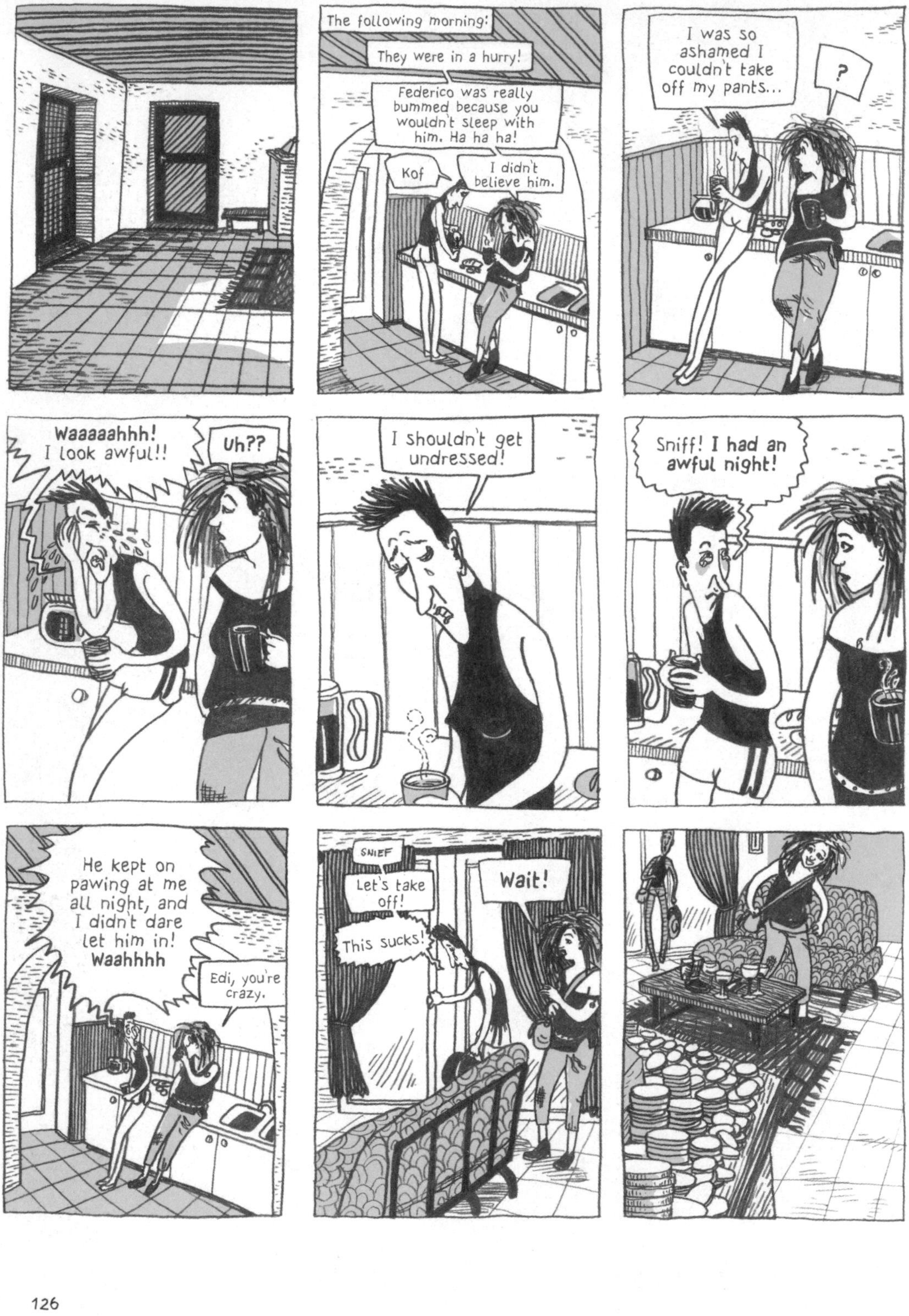
The following morning:
They were in a hurry!
Federico was really bummed because you wouldn't sleep with him. Ha ha ha!
Kof
I didn't believe him.
I was so ashamed I couldn't take off my pants...
?
Waaaaahhh! I look awful!!
Uh??
I shouldn't get undressed!
Sniff! I had an awful night!
He kept on pawing at me all night, and I didn't dare let him in! Waahhhh
Edi, you're crazy.
SNIFF
Let's take off!
This sucks!
Wait!

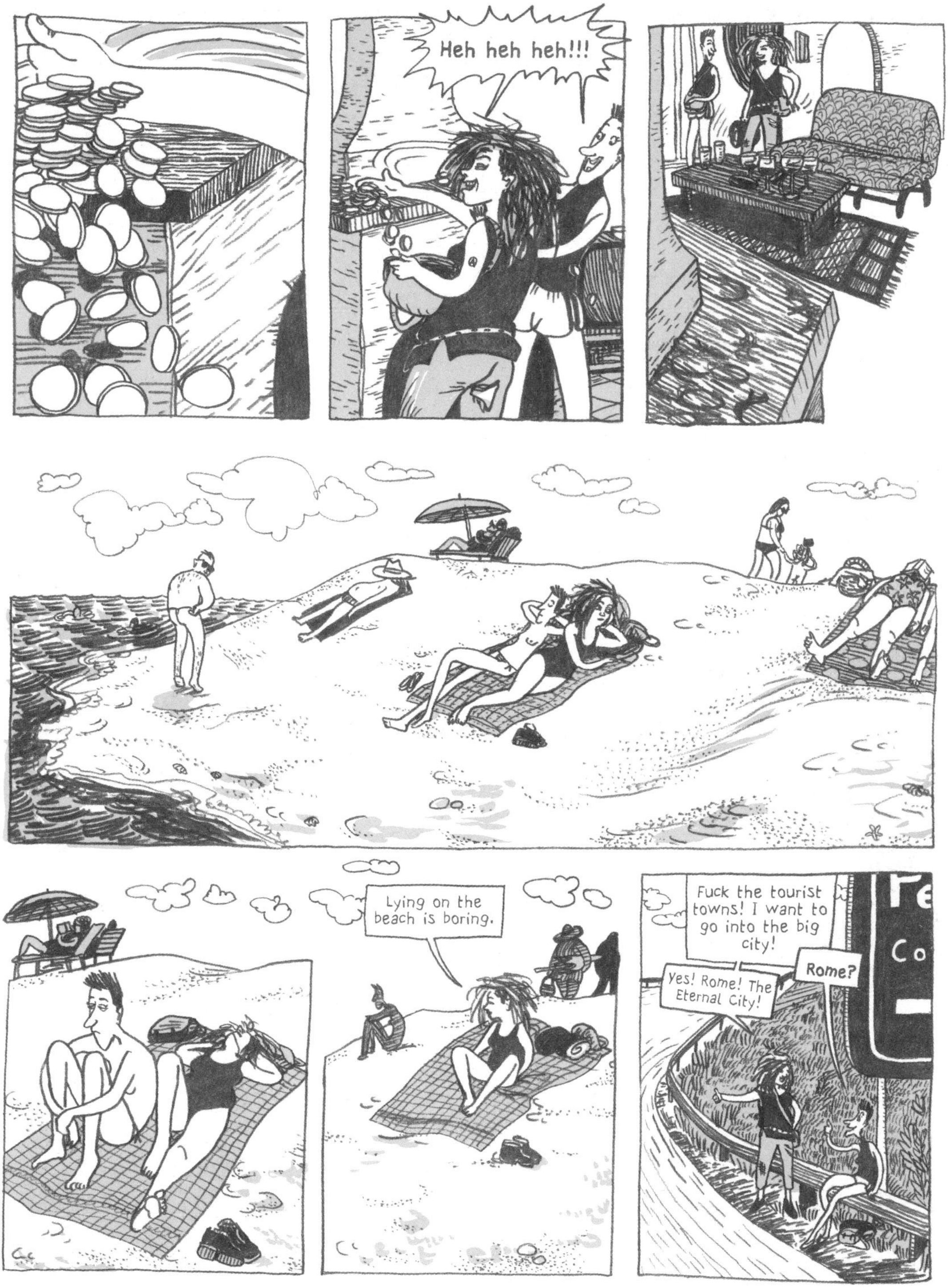
Heh heh heh!!!
Lying on the beach is boring.
Fuck the tourist towns! I want to go into the big city!
Rome?
Yes! Rome! The Eternal City!

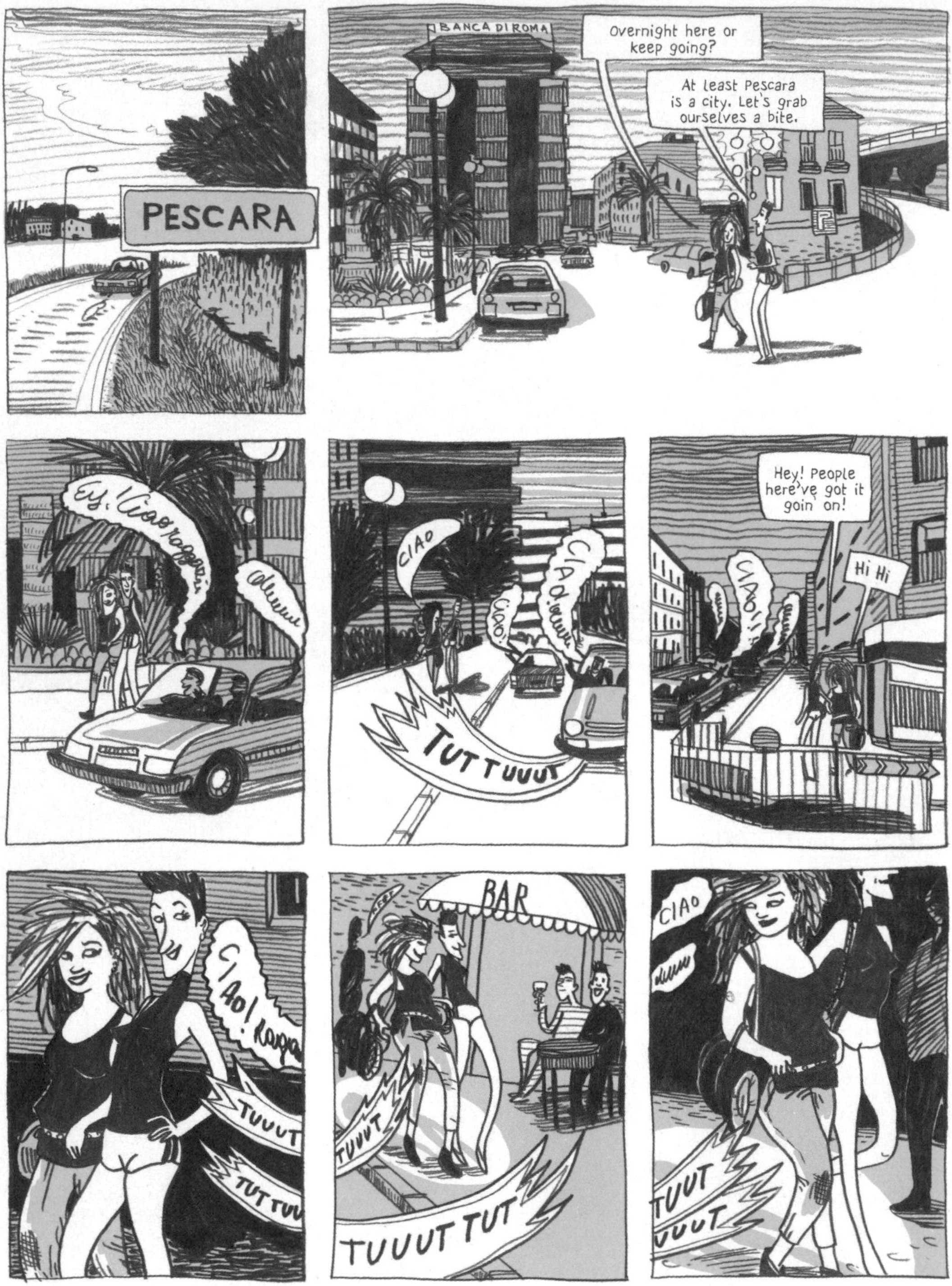
PESCARA
BANCA DI ROMA
Overnight here or keep going?
At least Pescara is a city. Let's grab ourselves a bite.
Ey! Ciao ragazzi
CIAO
CIAO!
TUT TUUUT
Hey! People here've got it goin' on!
Hi Hi
CIAO!
TUUUT
BAR
TUUUT
TUUUT TUT
CIAO
TUUT
UUUT

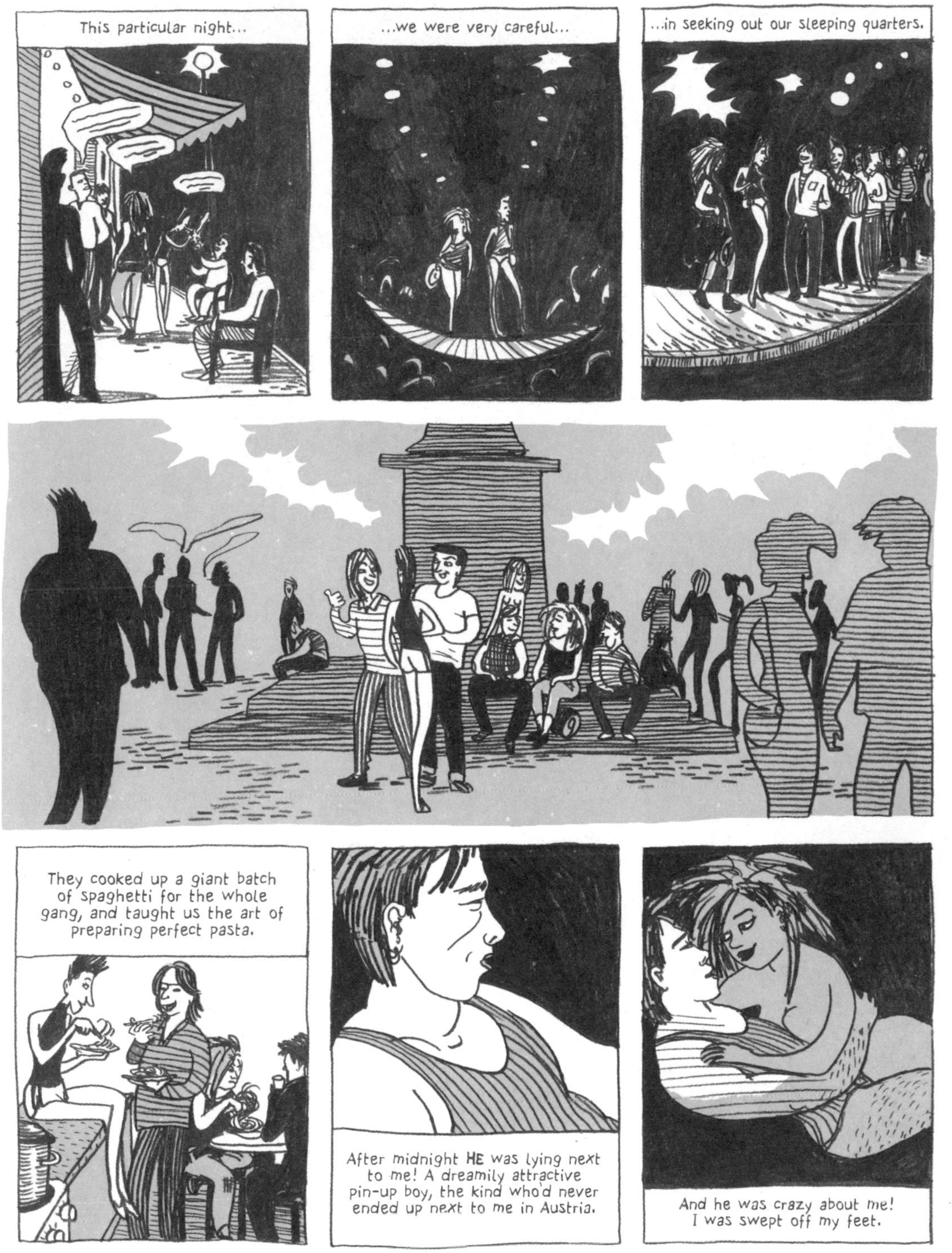
This particular night...
...we were very careful...
...in seeking out our sleeping quarters.
They cooked up a giant batch of spaghetti for the whole gang, and taught us the art of preparing perfect pasta.
After midnight HE was lying next to me! A dreamily attractive pin-up boy, the kind who'd never ended up next to me in Austria.
And he was crazy about me! I was swept off my feet.

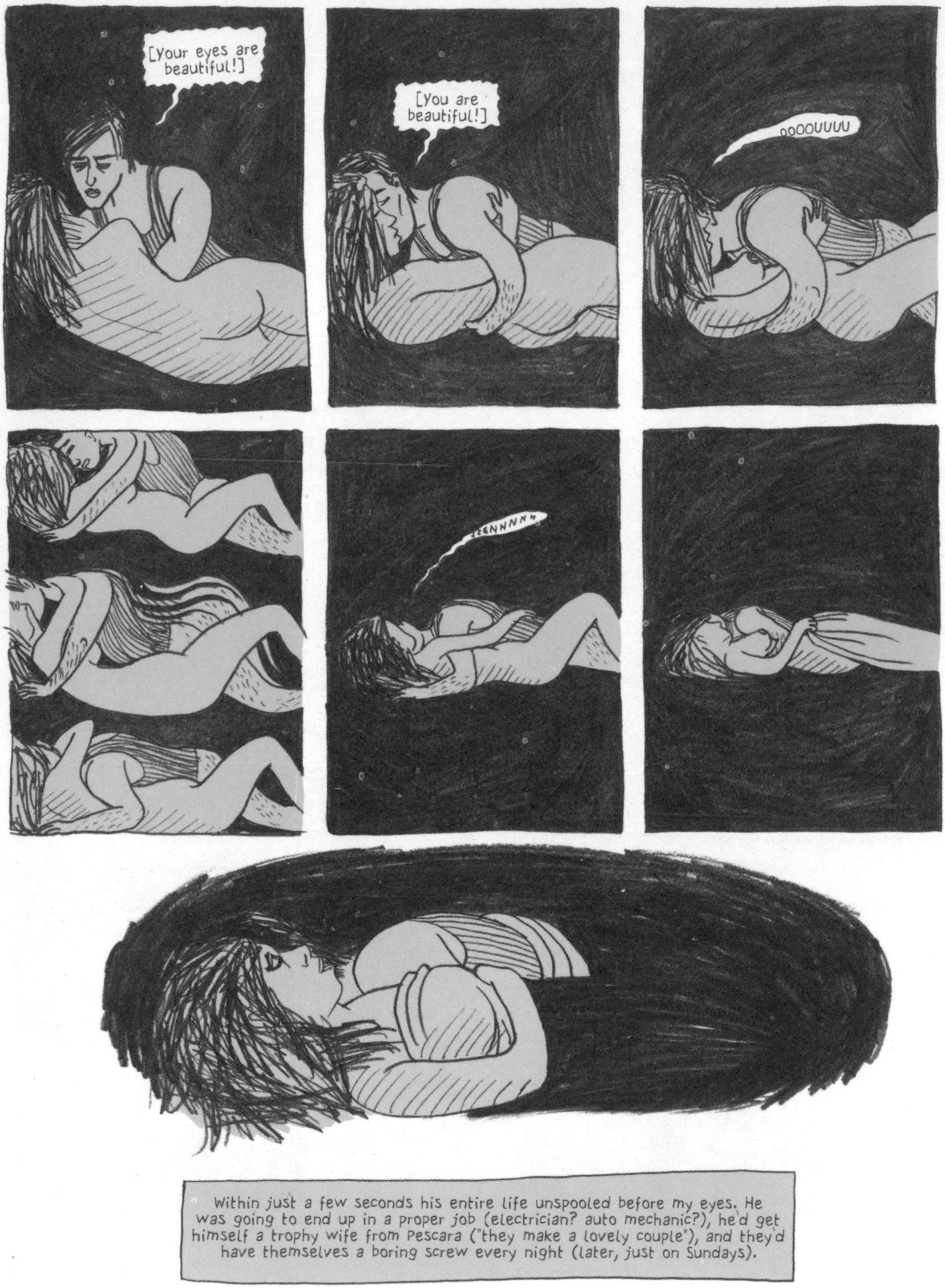
[Your eyes are beautiful!]
[You are beautiful!]
OOOOUUUU
EENNNNNN
Within just a few seconds his entire life unspooled before my eyes. He was going to end up in a proper job (electrician? auto mechanic?), he'd get himself a trophy wife from Pescara ("they make a lovely couple"), and they'd have themselves a boring screw every night (later, just on Sundays).

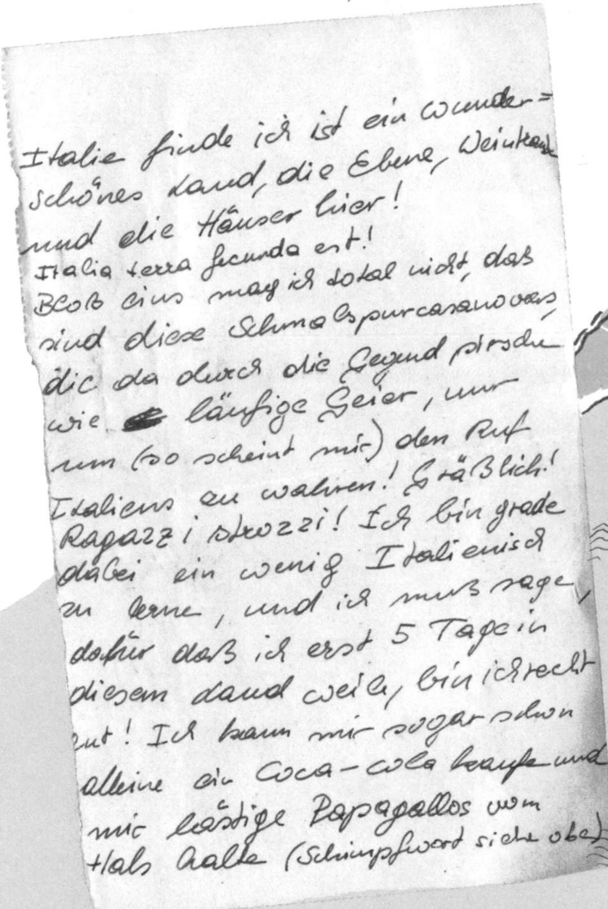
Italie finde ich ist ein wunder=
schönes Land, die Ebene, Weinkau
und die Häuser hier!
Italia terra fecunda est!
Bloß eins mag ich total nicht, das
sind diese Schmalspurcasanovas,
die da durch die Gegend pirsche
wie läufige Geier, um
um (so scheint mir) den Ruf
Italiens zu wahren! Gräßlich!
Ragazzi strozzi! Ich bin grade
dabei ein wenig Italienisch
zu lerne, und ich muß sage,
dafür daß ich erst 5 Tage in
diesem Land weile, bin ich recht
gut! Ich kann mir sogar schon
alleine ein Coca-cola kaufe und
mir lästige Papagallos vom
Hals halte (Schimpfwort siehe obe)

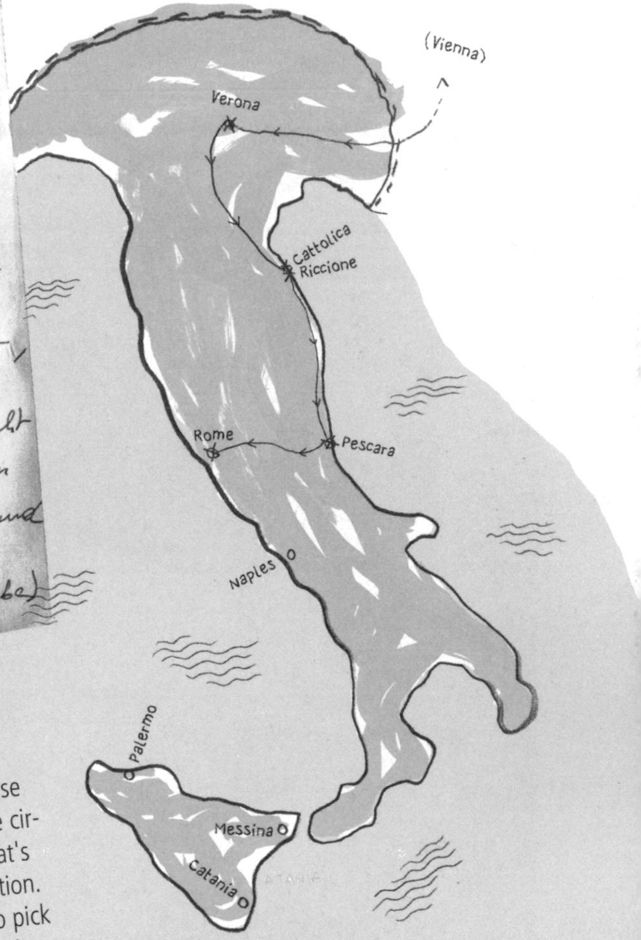
(Vienna)
Verona
Cattolica
Riccione
Rome
Pescara
Naples
Palermo
Messina
Catania

I find Italy a wondrously beautiful country: the plains, the vineyards, the houses!

Italia terra fecunda est! *

There's just one thing I really don't like: these penny-ante Casanovas who stalk the land like circling vultures, just for the sake of (at least that's how it seems to me) protecting Italy's reputation. Awful! Ragazzi strozzi! ** I've just started to pick up a little Italian, and I've got to say, considering I've only spent five days in this country, I'm doing pretty well! Why, I can already buy myself a Coca-Cola on my own, and keep annoying papagallos *** off my back (insult, see above).

* Italy is a fertile land! (Latin)
** Ragazzi stronzi (Italian) = Fucking assholes!
*** literally parrot (Italian) = slang for young men who hit on female tourists

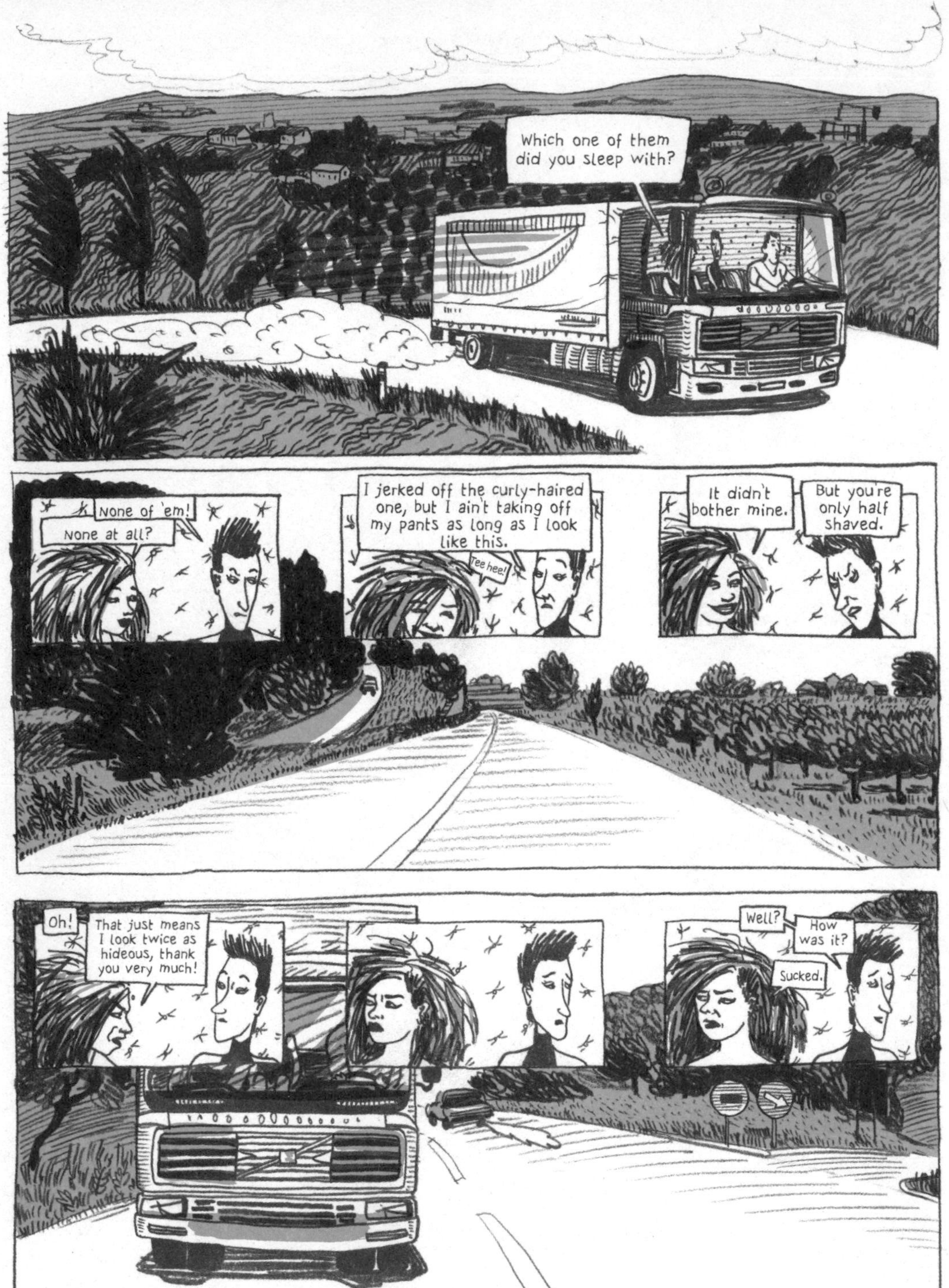
Which one of them did you sleep with?
None of 'em!
None at all?
I jerked off the curly-haired one, but I ain't taking off my pants as long as I look like this.
Tee hee!
It didn't bother mine.
But you're only half shaved.
Oh!
That just means I look twice as hideous, thank you very much!
Well?
How was it?
Sucked.

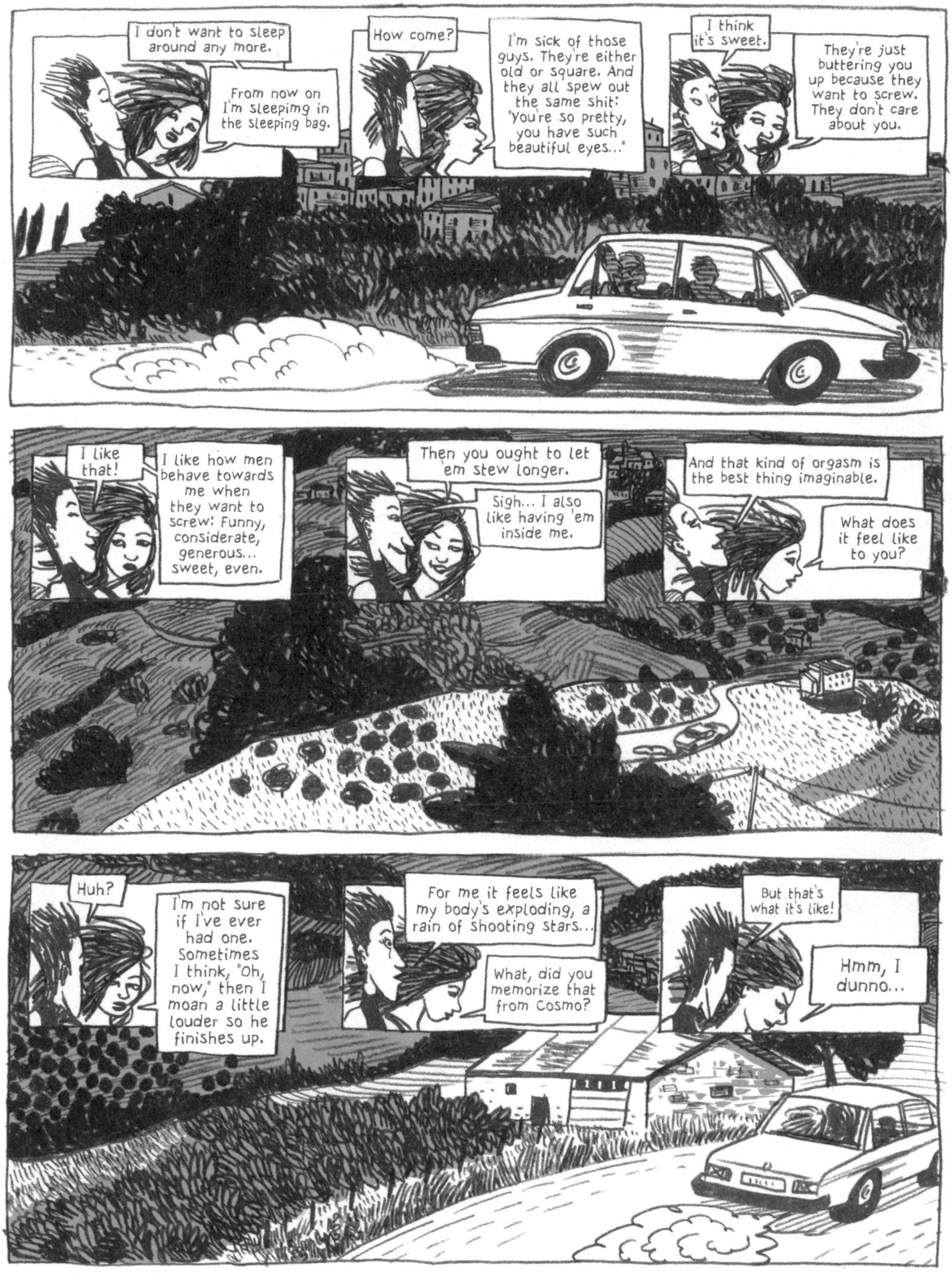

I don't want to sleep around any more.
From now on I'm sleepimg in the sleeping bag.
How come?
I'm sick of those guys. They're either old or square. And they all spew out the same shit: "You're so pretty, you have such beautiful eyes..."
I think it's sweet.
They're just buttering you up because they want to screw. They don't care about you.
I like that!
I like how men behave towards me when they want to screw: Funny, considerate, generous... sweet, even.
Then you ought to let 'em stew longer.
Sigh... I also like having 'em inside me.
And that kind of orgasm is the best thing imaginable.
What does it feel like to you?
Huh?
I'm not sure if I've ever had one. Sometimes I think, "Oh, now," then I moan a little louder so he finishes up.
For me it feels like my body's exploding, a rain of shooting stars...
What, did you memorize that from Cosmo?
But that's what it's like!
Hmm, I dunno...

VII. the INITIATION

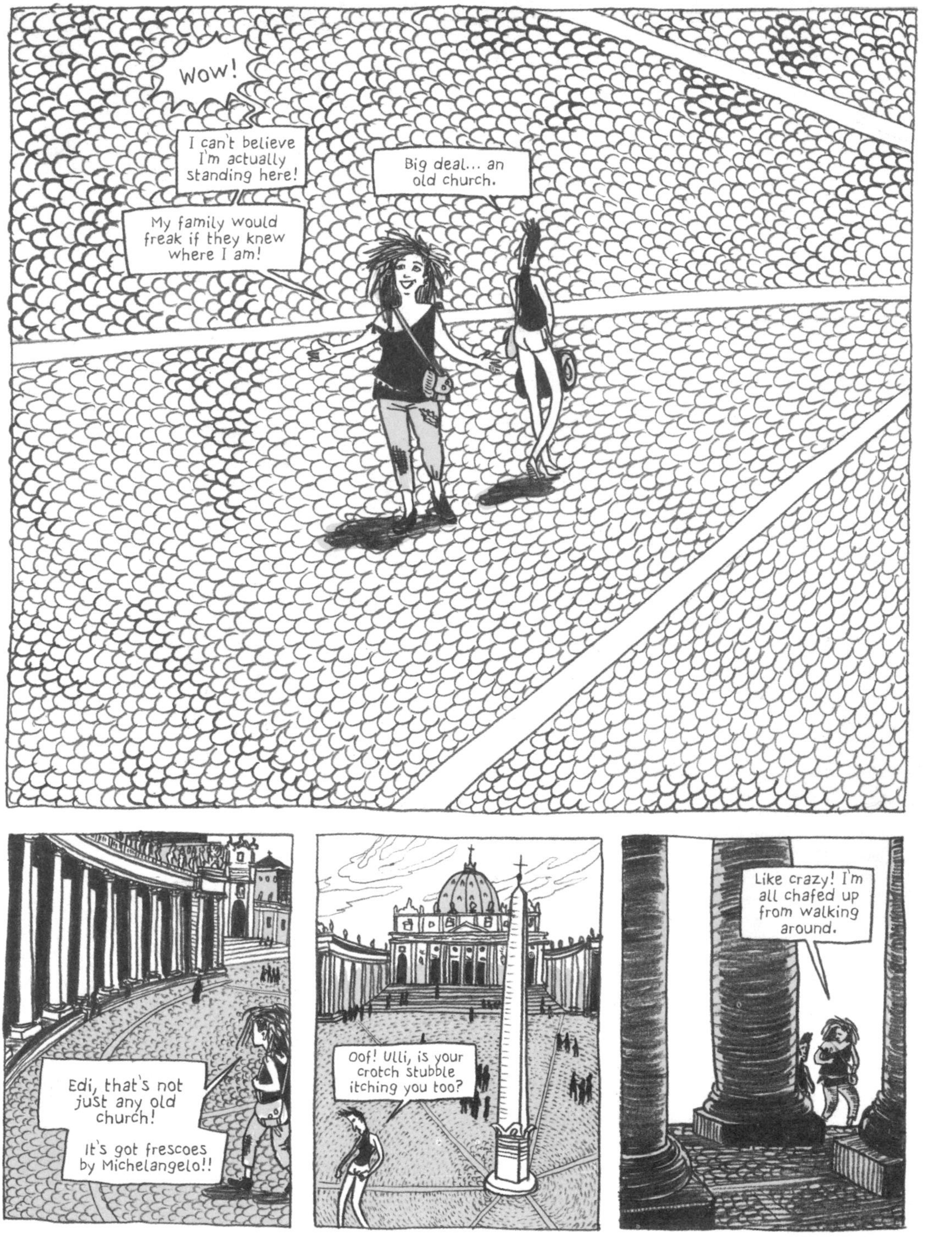
WOW!
I can't believe I'm actually standing here!
My family would freak if they knew where I am!
Big deal... an old church.
Edi, that's not just any old church!
It's got frescoes by Michelangelo!!
Oof! Ulli, is your crotch stubble itching you too?
Like crazy! I'm all chafed up from walking around.

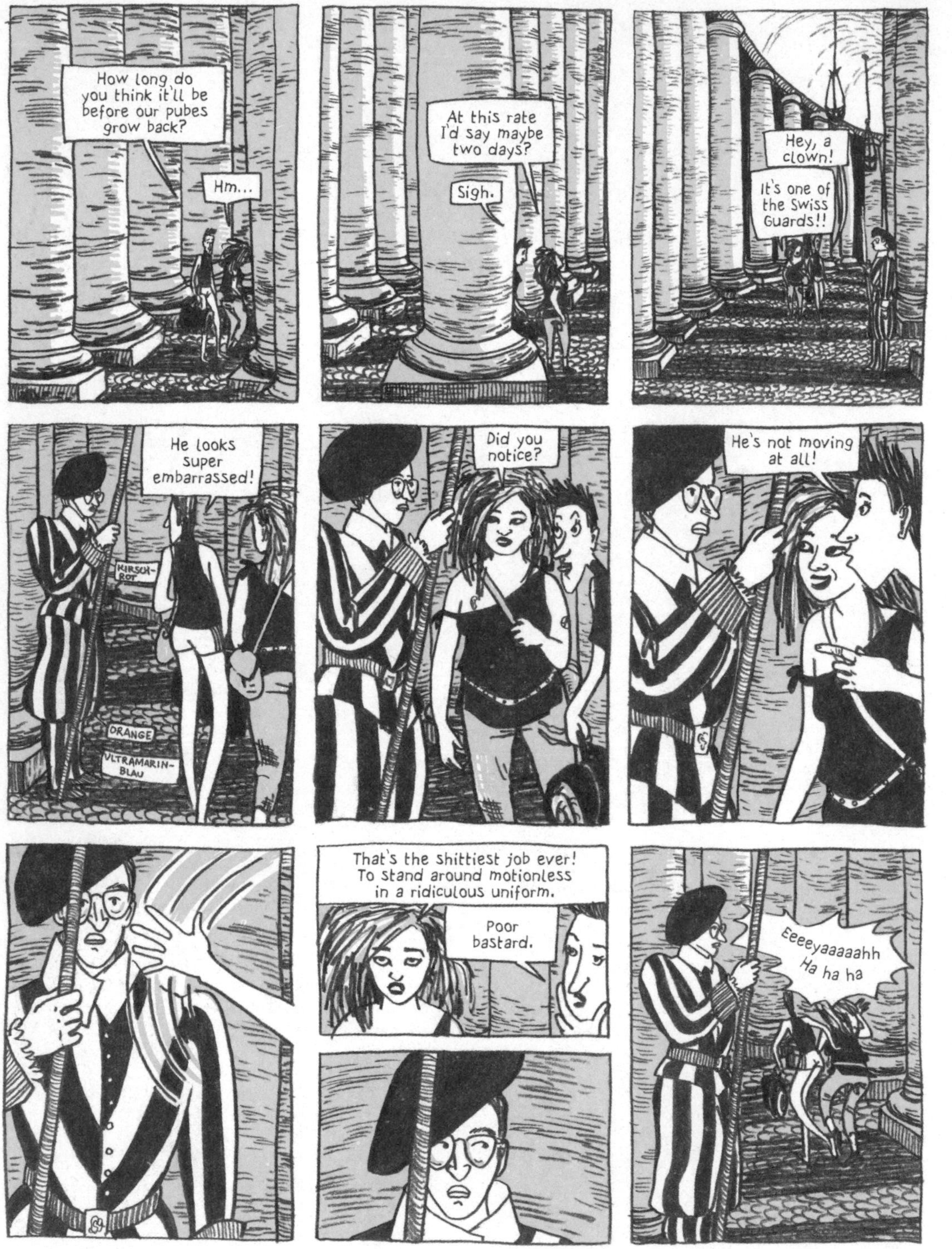
How long do you think it'll be before our pubes grow back?
Hm...
At this rate I'd say maybe two days?
Sigh.
Hey, a clown!
It's one of the Swiss Guards!!
He looks super embarrassed!
KIRSCH-ROT
ORANGE
ULTRAMARIN-BLAU
Did you notice?
He's not moving at all!
That's the shittiest job ever! To stand around motionless in a ridiculous uniform.
Poor bastard.
Eeeeyaaaaahh Ha ha ha

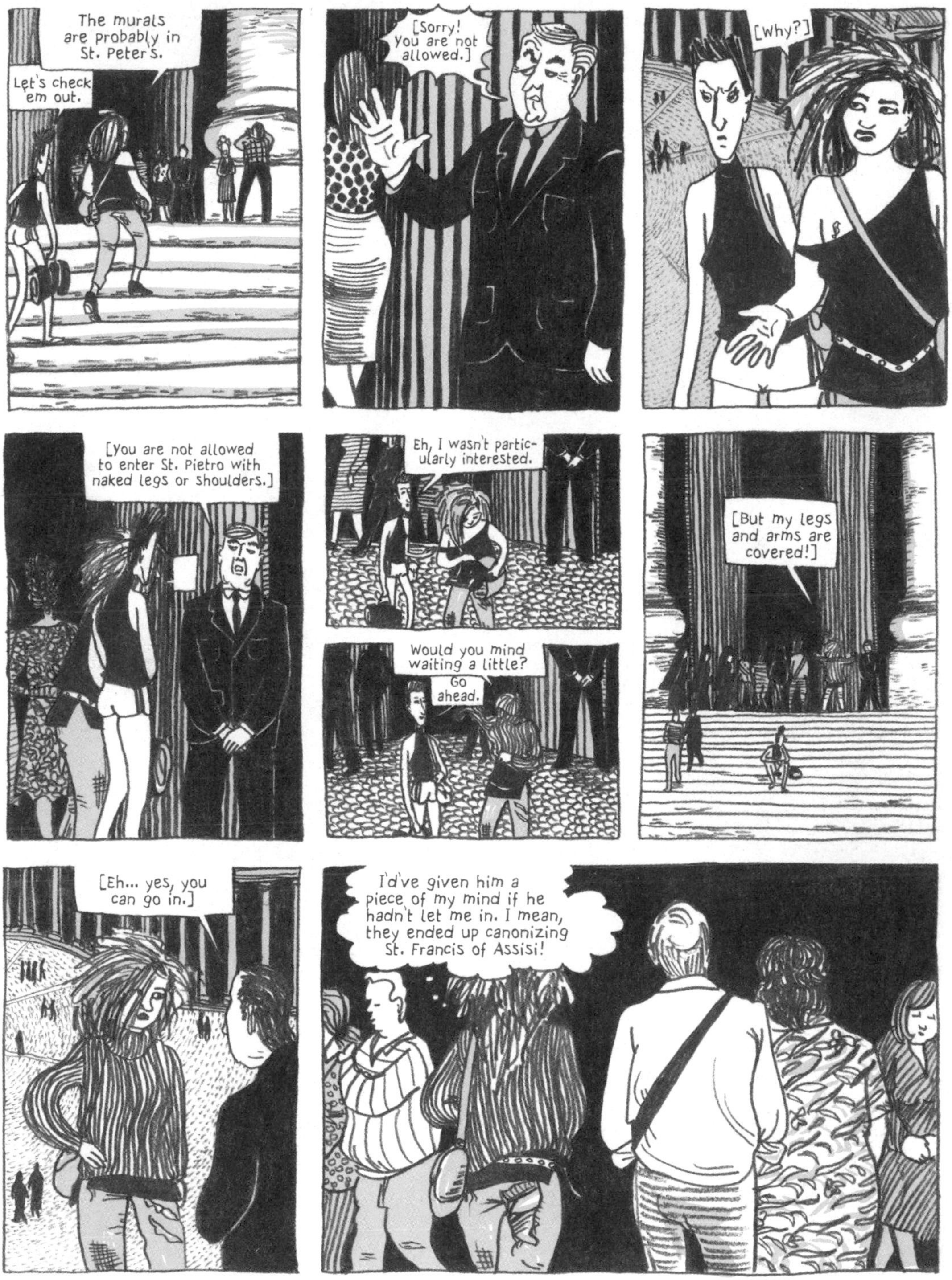
The murals are probably in St. Peter's.
Let's check em out.
[Sorry! You are not allowed.]
[Why?]
[You are not allowed to enter St. Pietro with naked legs or shoulders.]
Eh, I wasn't particularly interested.
Would you mind waiting a little?
Go ahead.
[But my legs and arms are covered!]
[Eh... yes, you can go in.]
I'd've given him a piece of my mind if he hadn't let me in. I mean, they ended up canonizing St. Francis of Assisi!

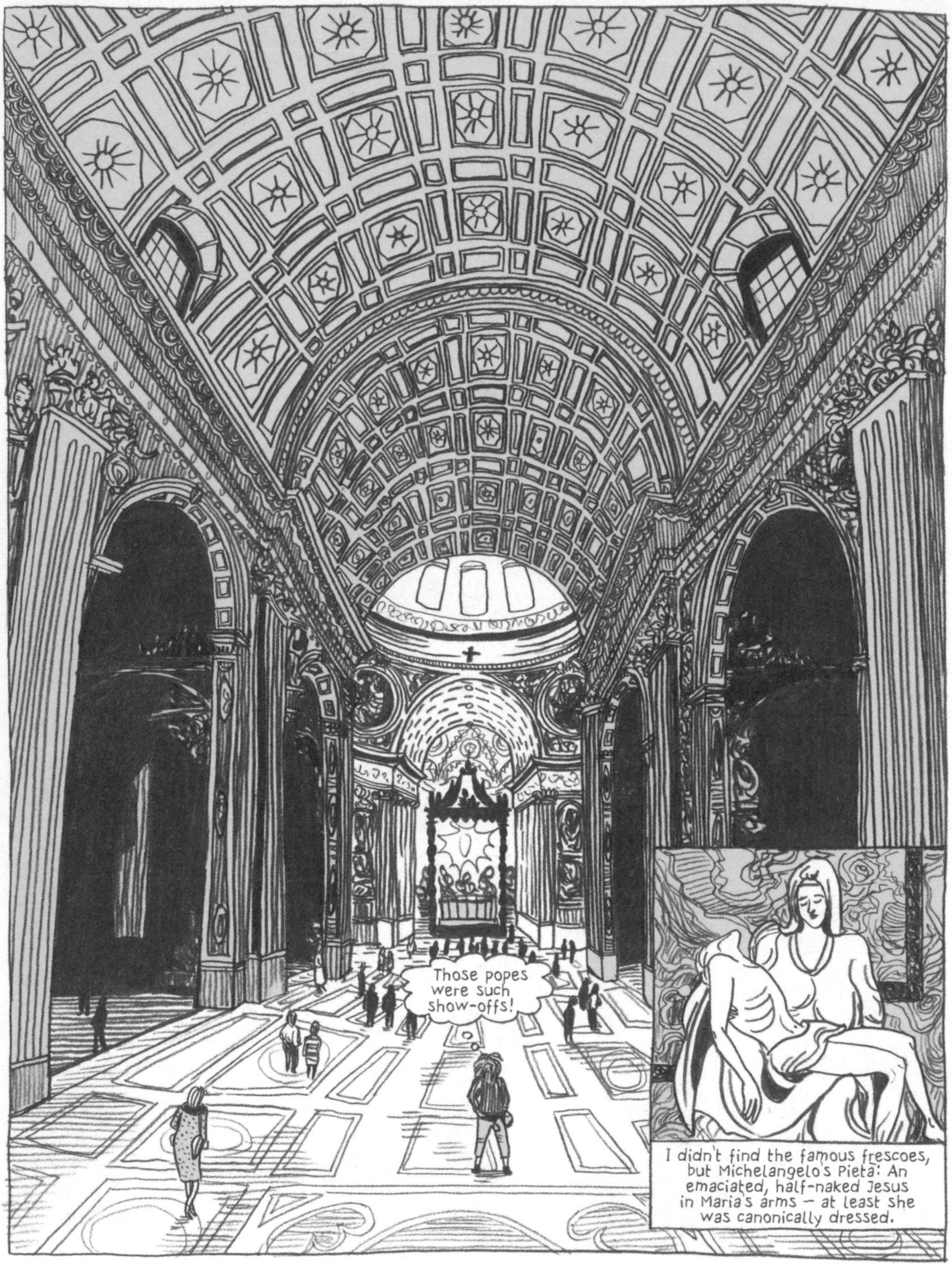
Those popes were such show-offs!
I didn't find the famous frescoes, but Michelangelo's Pieta: An emaciated, half-naked Jesus in Maria's arms – at least she was canonically dressed.

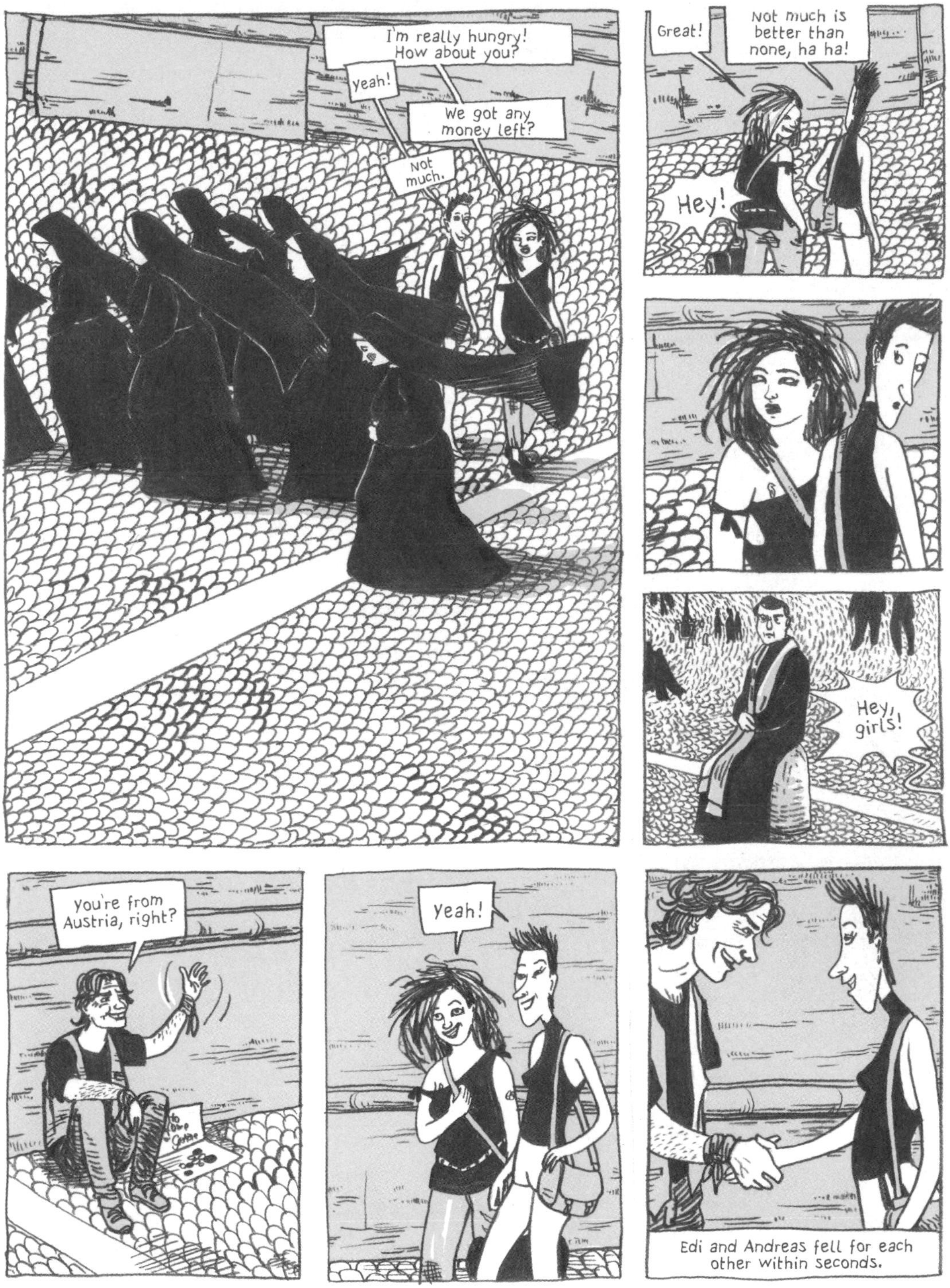
I'm really hungry! How about you?
Yeah!
We got any money left?
Not much.
Great!
Not much is better than none, ha ha!
Hey!
Hey, girls!
You're from Austria, right?
Yeah!
Edi and Andreas fell for each other within seconds.

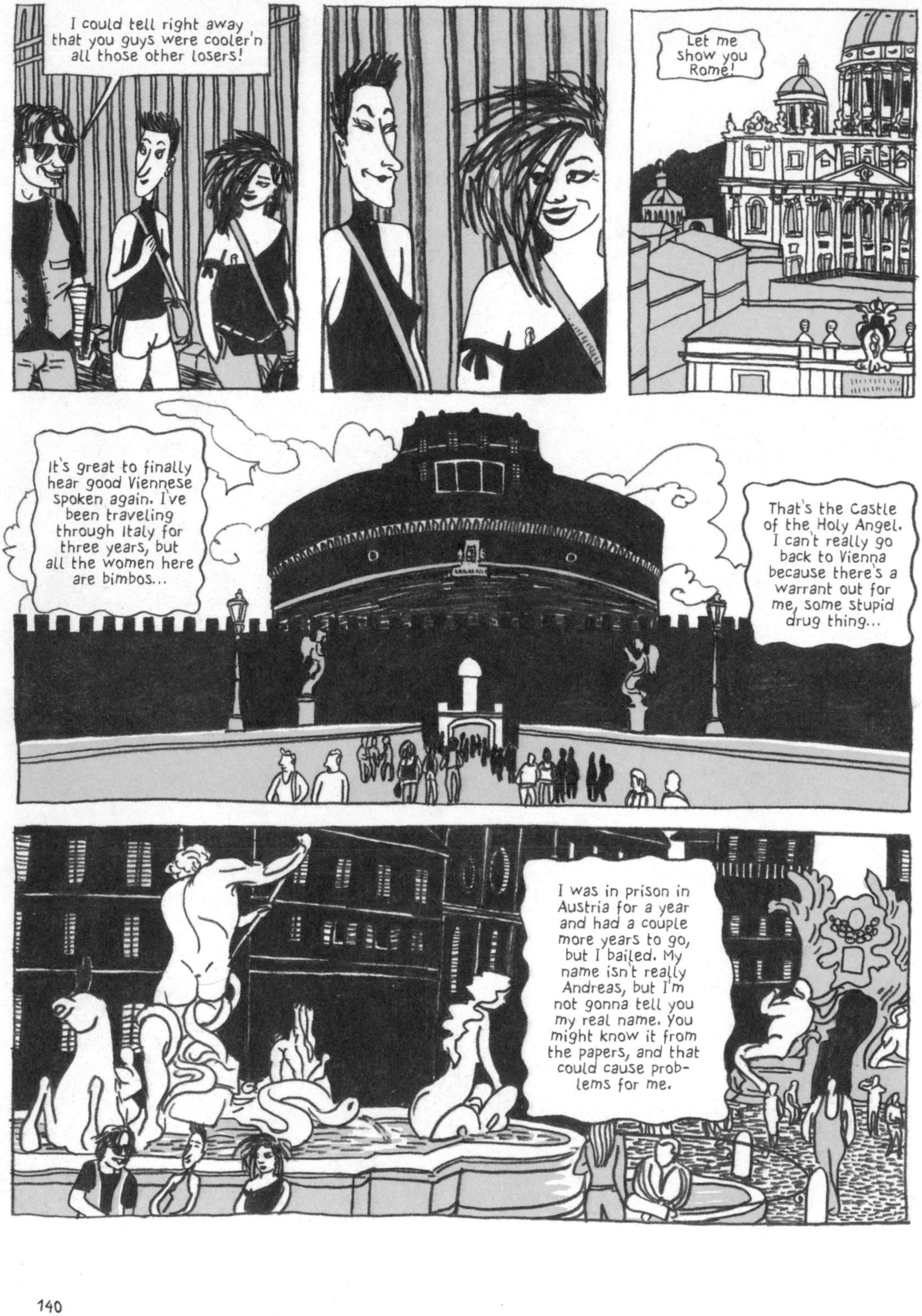
I could tell right away that you guys were cooler'n all those other losers!
Let me show you Rome!
It's great to finally hear good Viennese spoken again. I've been traveling through Italy for three years, but all the women here are bimbos...
That's the Castle of the Holy Angel. I can't really go back to Vienna because there's a warrant out for me, some stupid drug thing...
I was in prison in Austria for a year and had a couple more years to go, but I bailed. My name isn't really Andreas, but I'm not gonna tell you my real name. You might know it from the papers, and that could cause problems for me.

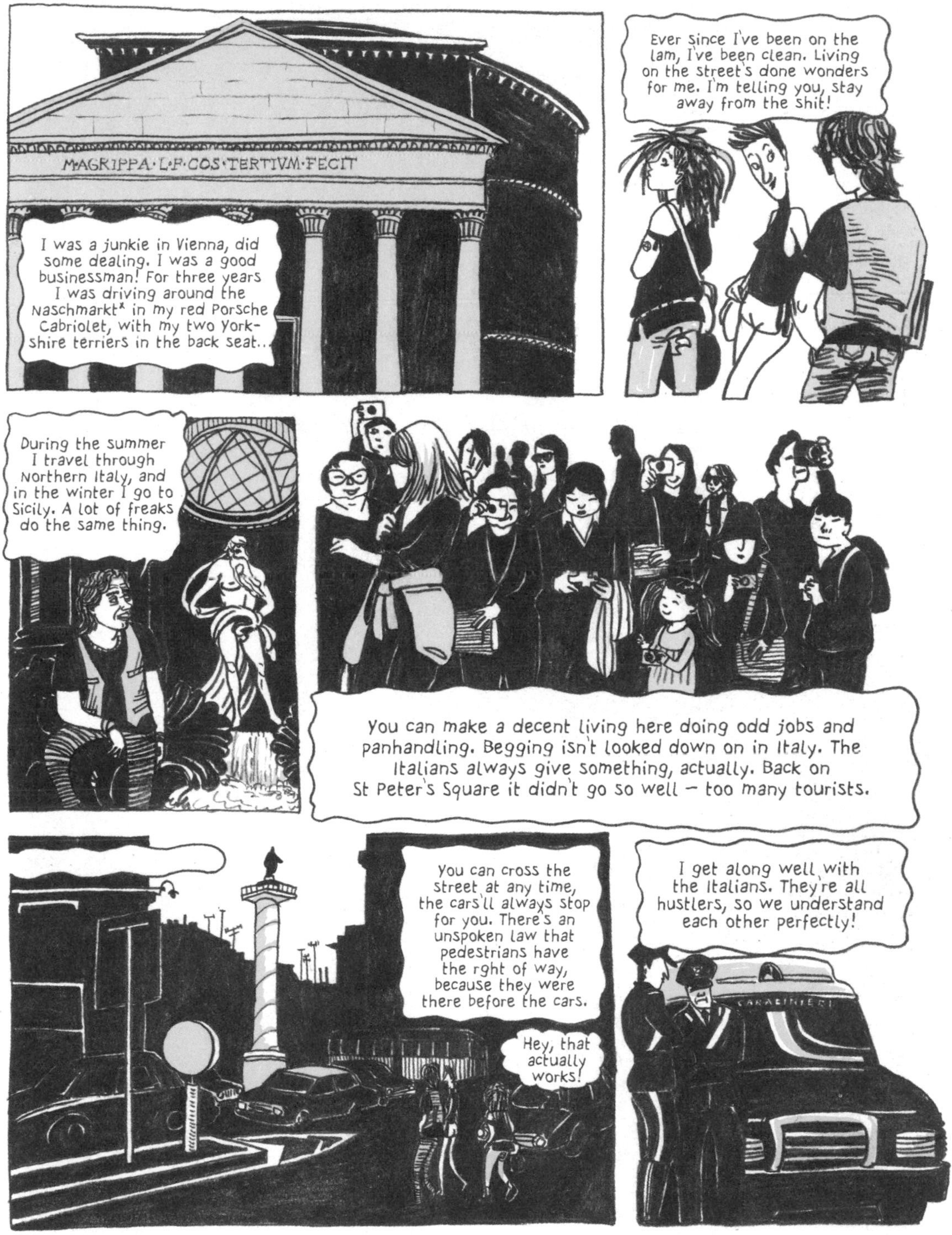
M·AGRIPPA·L·F·COS·TERTIVM·FECIT
I was a junkie in Vienna, did some dealing. I was a good businessman! For three years I was driving around the Naschmarkt* in my red Porsche Cabriolet, with my two Yorkshire terriers in the back seat...
Ever since I've been on the lam, I've been clean. Living on the street's done wonders for me. I'm telling you, stay away from the shit!
During the summer I travel through Northern Italy, and in the winter I go to Sicily. A lot of freaks do the same thing.
You can make a decent living here doing odd jobs and panhandling. Begging isn't looked down on in Italy. The Italians always give something, actually. Back on St Peter's Square it didn't go so well – too many tourists.
You can cross the street at any time, the cars'll always stop for you. There's an unspoken law that pedestrians have the rght of way, because they were there before the cars.
Hey, that actually works!
I get along well with the Italians. They're all hustlers, so we understand each other perfectly!

* Famous Viennese open-air market.

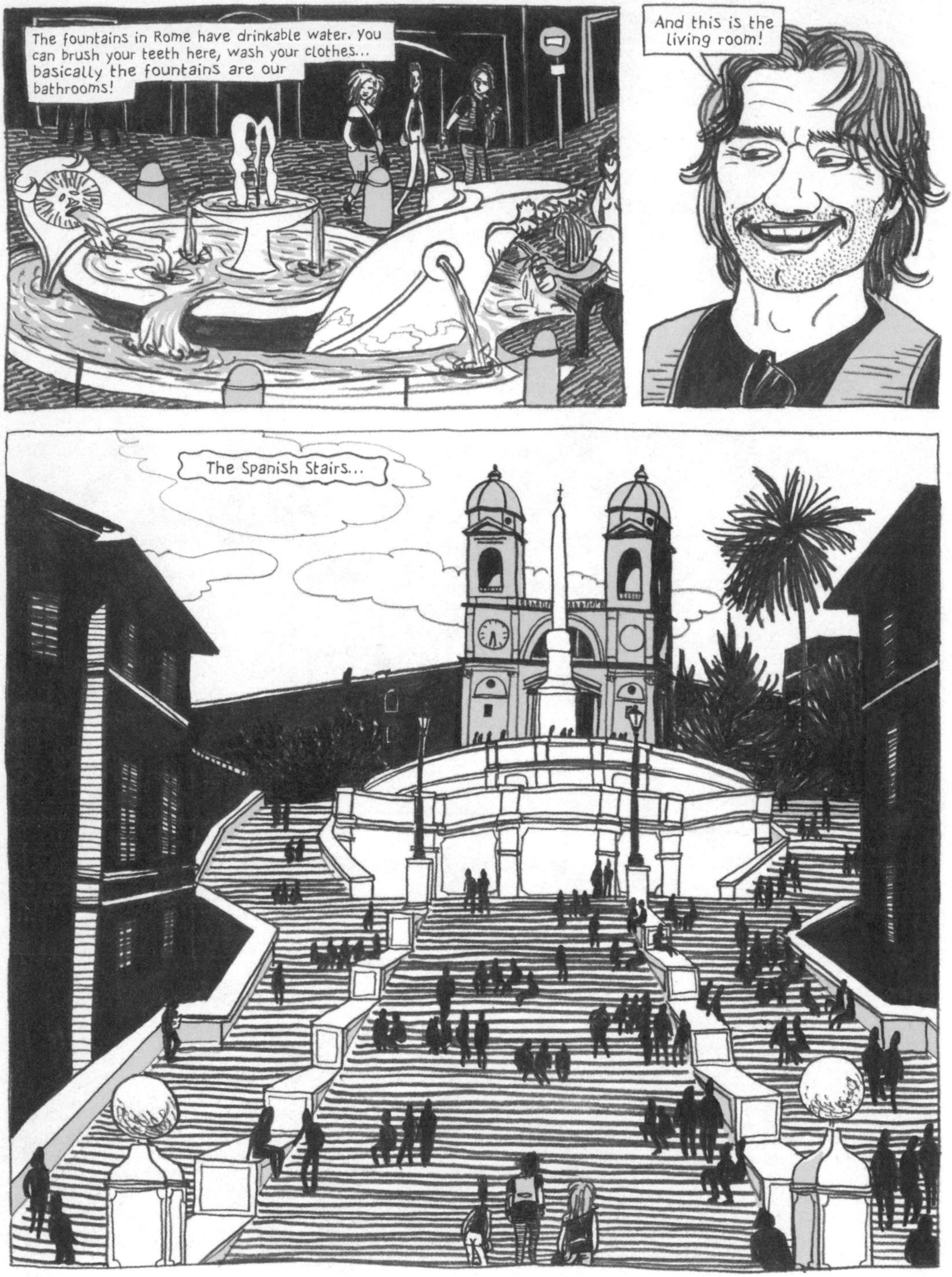
The fountains in Rome have drinkable water. You can brush your teeth here, wash your clothes... basically the fountains are our bathrooms!
And this is the living room!
The Spanish Stairs...

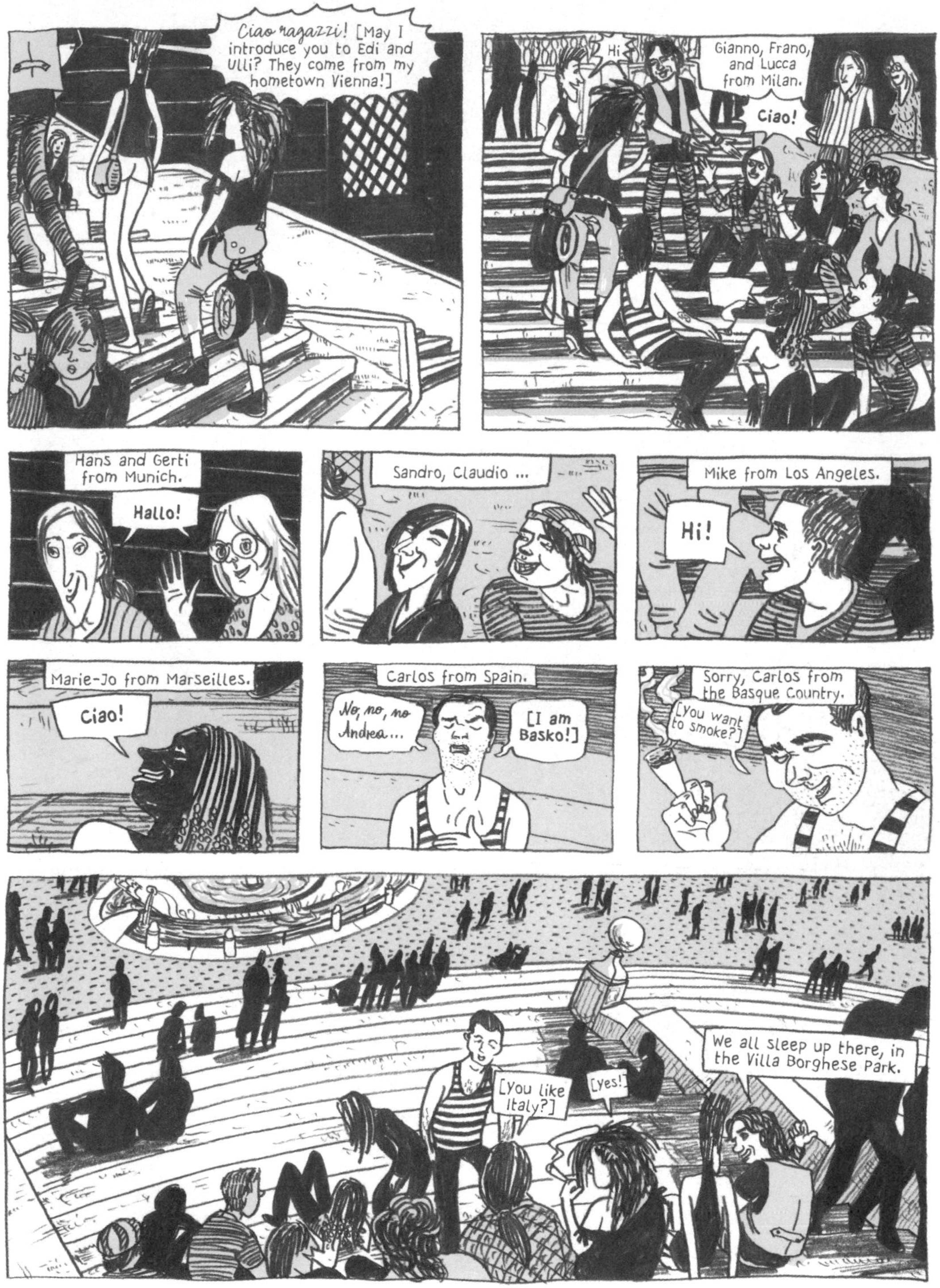
Ciao ragazzi! [May I introduce you to Edi and Ulli? They come from my hometown Vienna!]
Hi
Gianno, Frano, and Lucca from Milan.
Ciao!
Hans and Gerti from Munich.
Hallo!
Sandro, Claudio ...
Mike from Los Angeles.
Hi!
Marie-Jo from Marseilles.
Ciao!
Carlos from Spain.
No, no, no Andrea...
[I am Basko!]
Sorry, Carlos from the Basque Country.
[You want to smoke?]
We all sleep up there, in the Villa Borghese Park.
[You like Italy?]
[Yes!]

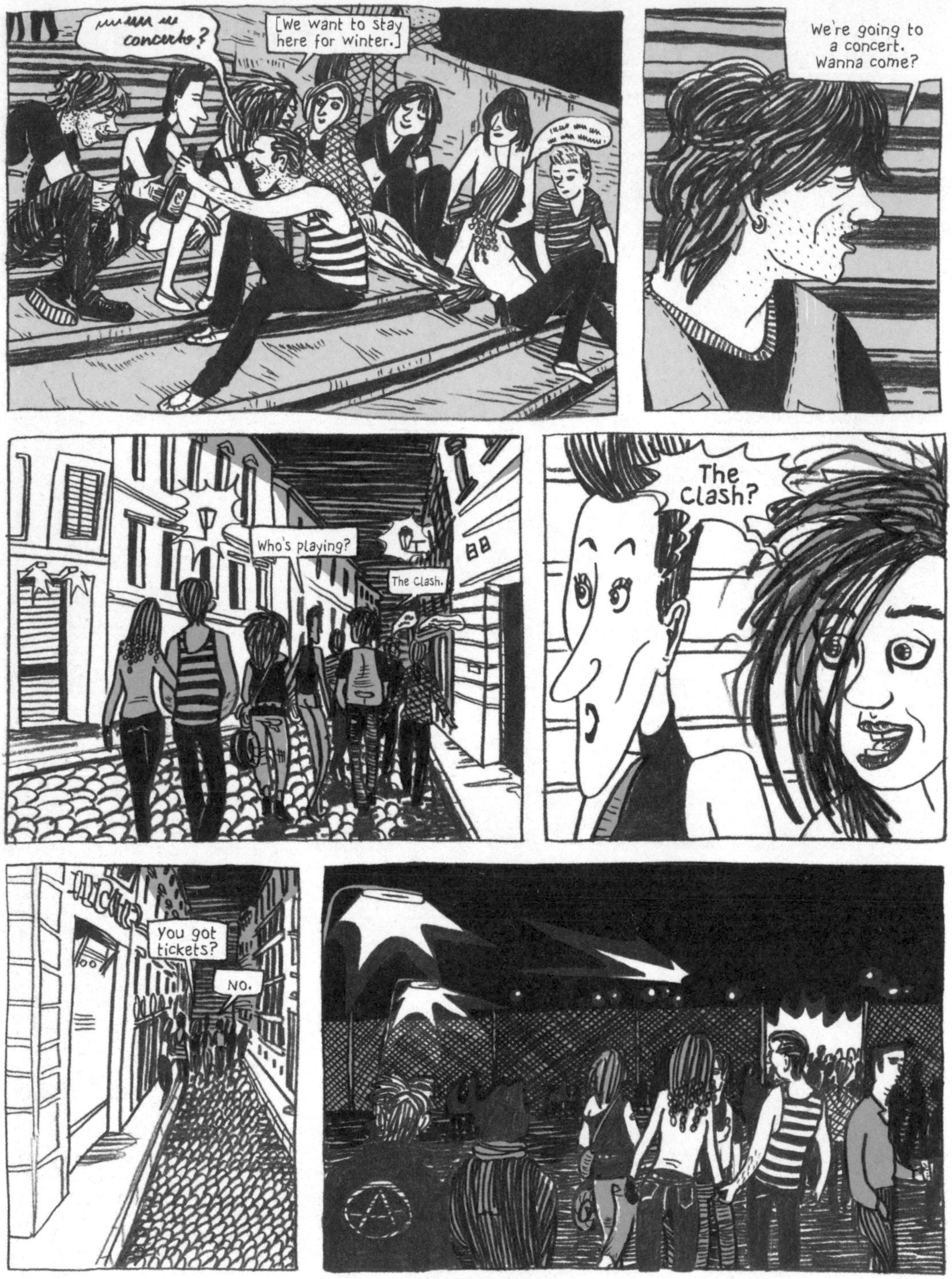
concerto?
[We want to stay here for winter.]
We're going to a concert. Wanna come?
Who's playing?
The Clash.
The Clash?
You got tickets?
No.

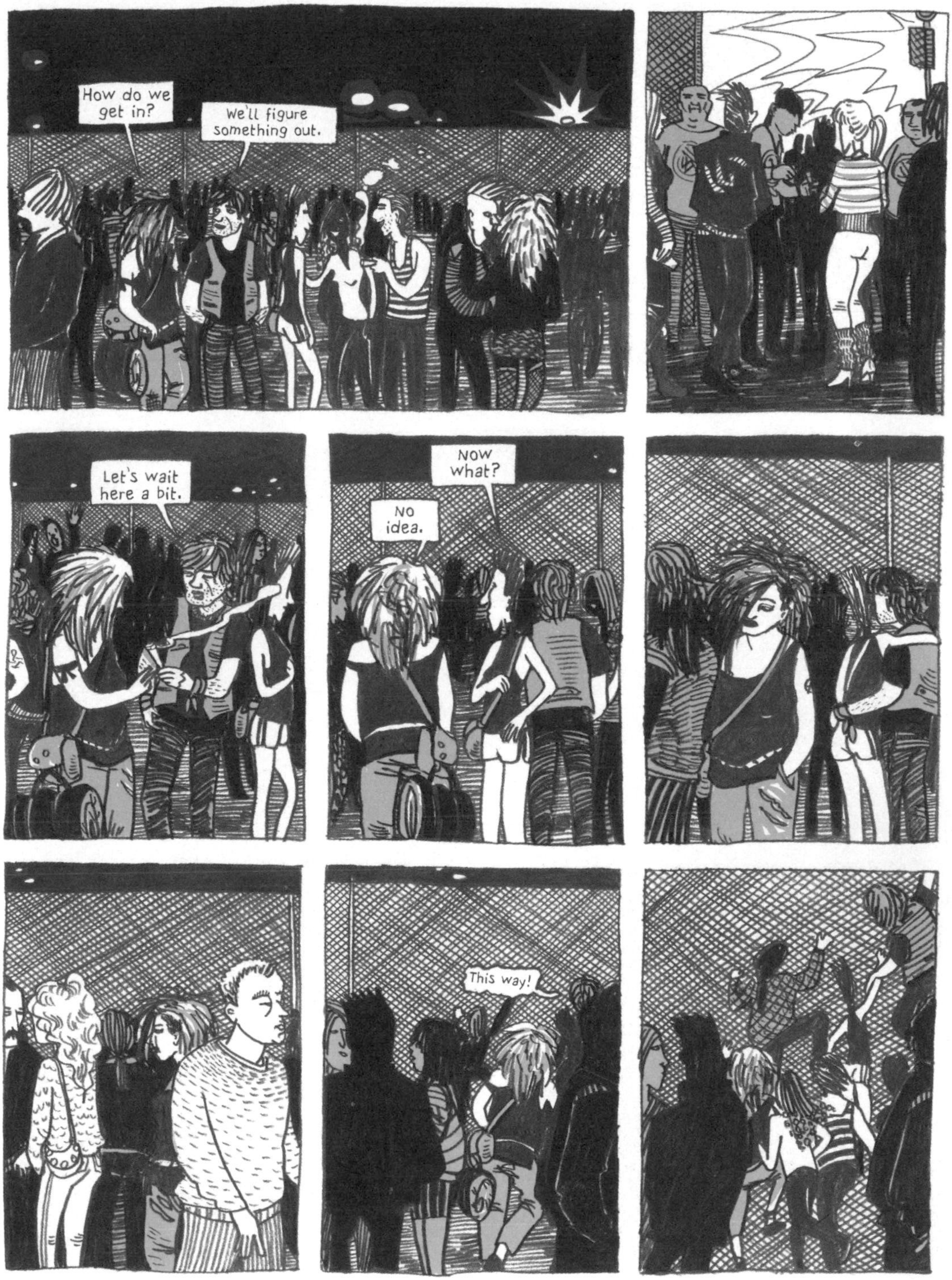
How do we get in?
We'll figure something out.
Let's wait here a bit.
Now what?
No idea.
This way!

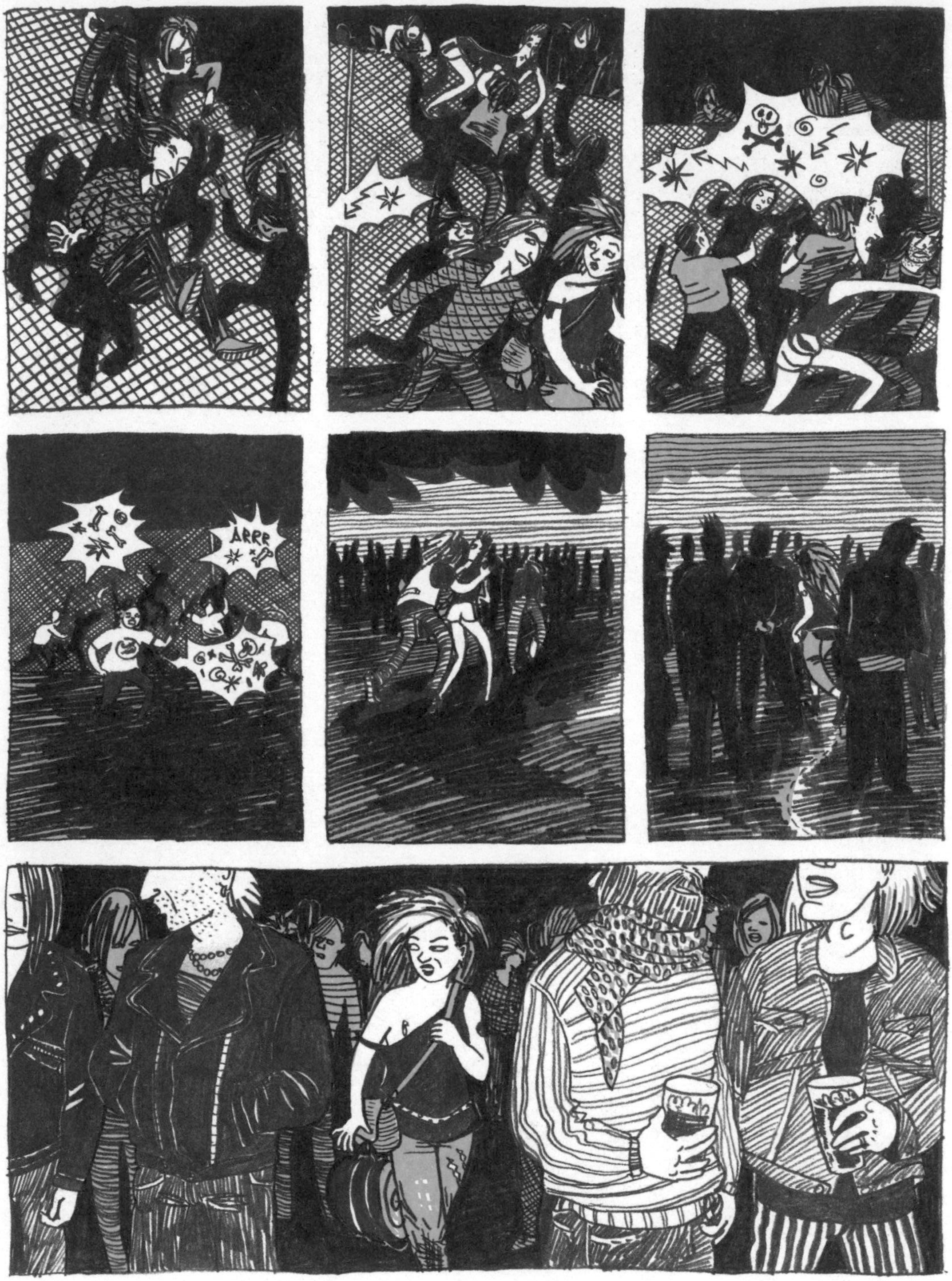
ÅRRR

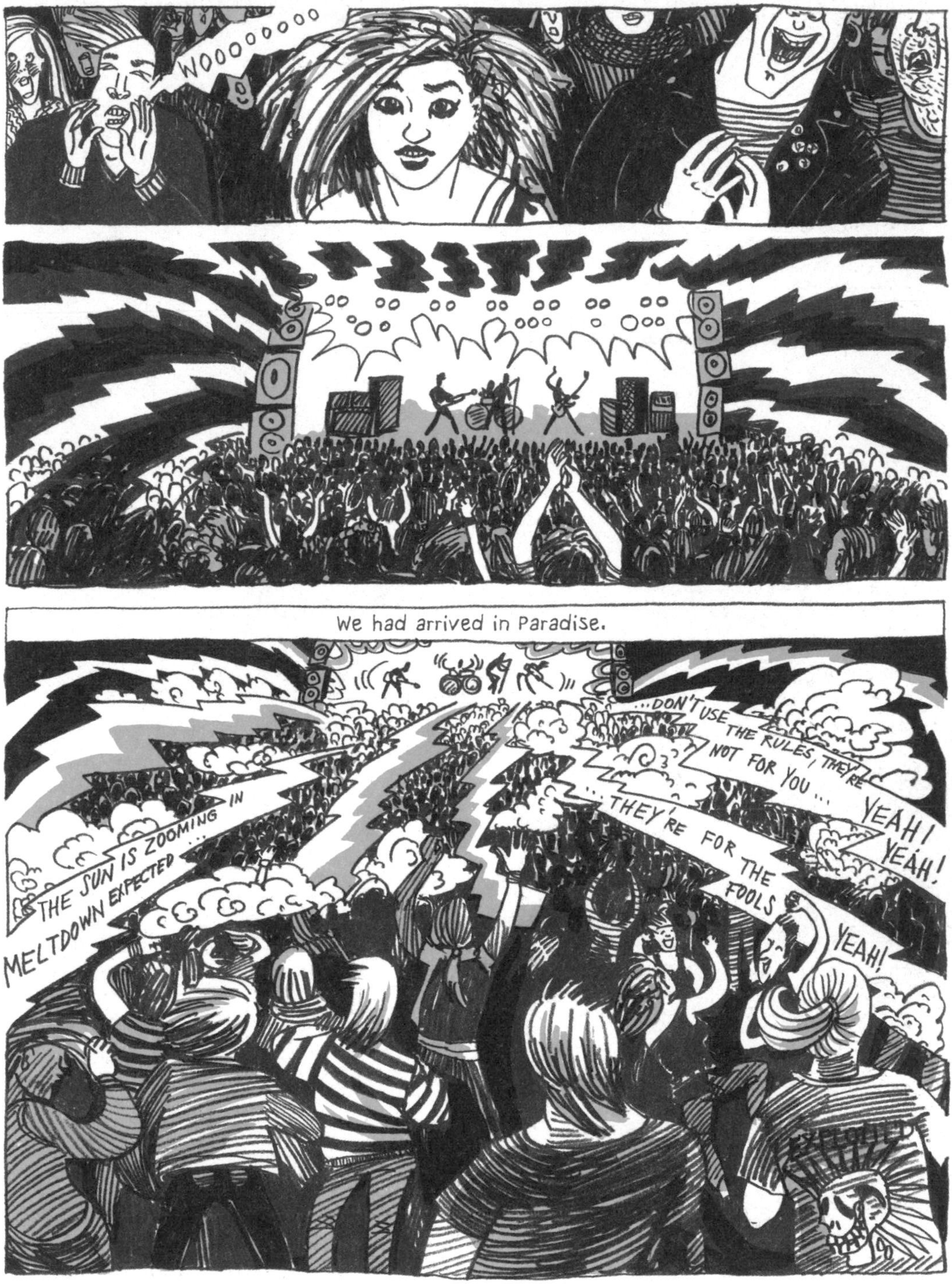
WOOOOOOOO
We had arrived in Paradise.
THE SUN IS ZOOMING IN
MELTDOWN EXPECTED ...
... DON'T USE THE RULES, THEY'RE NOT FOR YOU ...
... THEY'RE FOR THE FOOLS
YEAH! YEAH!
YEAH!
EXPLOITED

In the park above
the Spanish Steps...

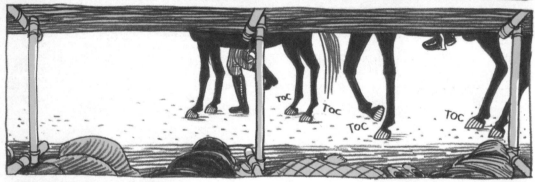

TOC TOC TOC

TOC TOC

TOC

TOC

He ordered us to get out
of the park by 10 o'clock.

I soon got used to the
morning wake-up ritual,
announced by soft
hoof beats.

They only asked the
sleepers to leave
sometimes.

You need
papers.

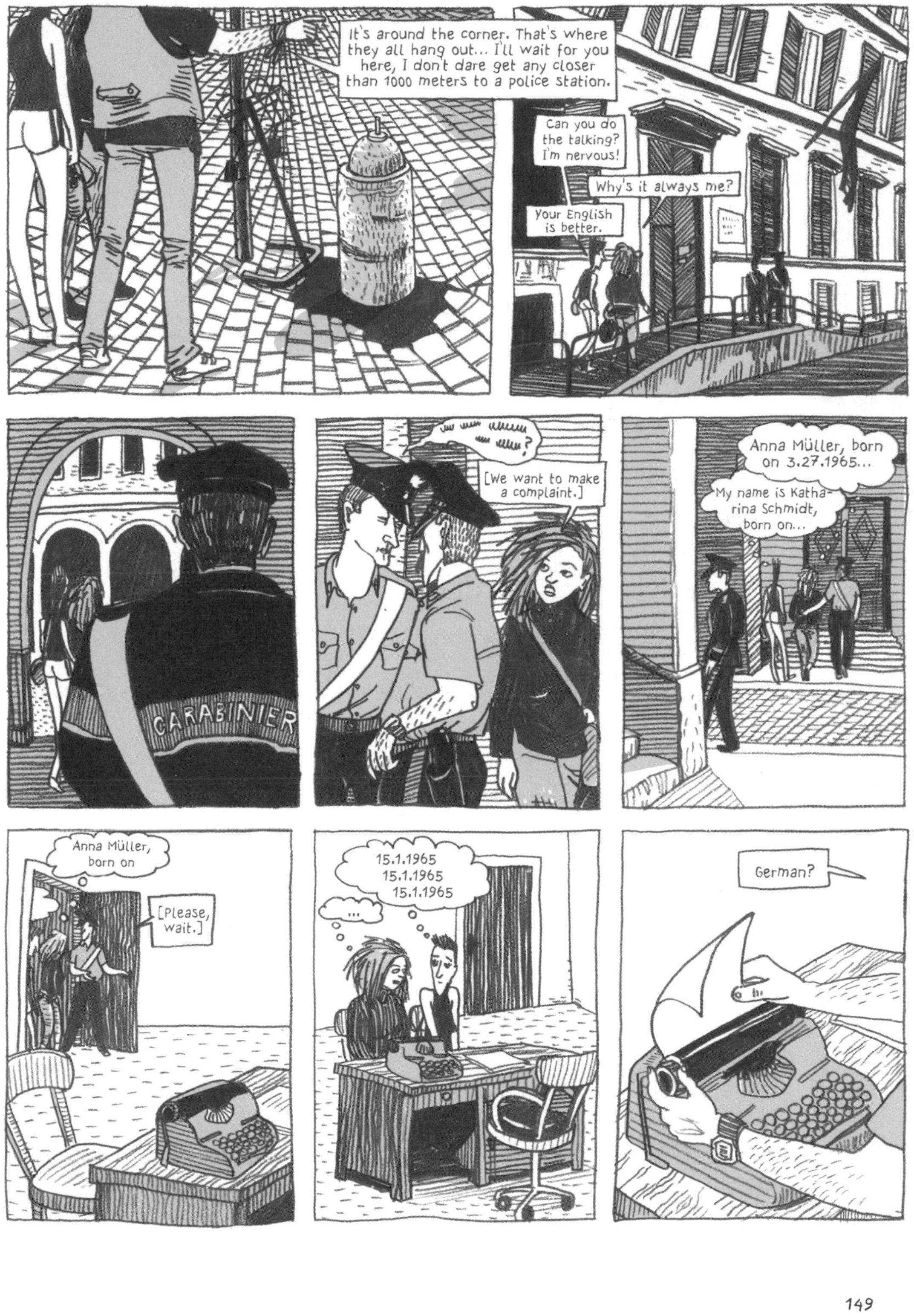
It's around the corner. That's where they all hang out... I'll wait for you here, I don't dare get any closer than 1000 meters to a police station.
Can you do the talking? I'm nervous!
Why's it always me?
Your English is better.
CARABINIER
[We want to make a complaint.]
Anna Müller, born on 3.27.1965...
My name is Katharina Schmidt, born on...
Anna Müller, born on
[Please, wait.]
15.1.1965
15.1.1965
15.1.1965
...
German?

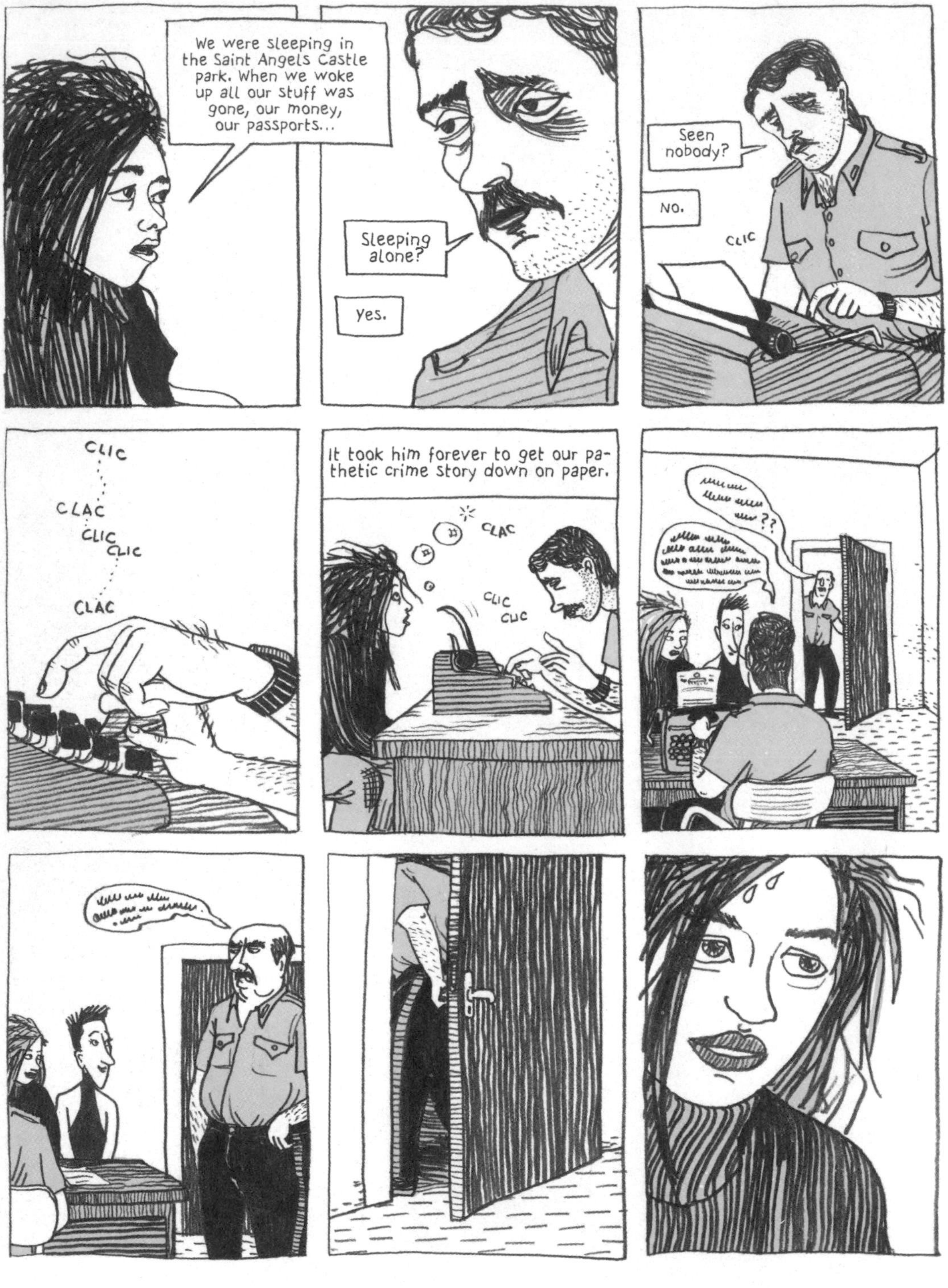

We were sleeping in the Saint Angels Castle park. When we woke up all our stuff was gone, our money, our passports...
Sleeping alone?
yes.
Seen nobody?
No.
CLIC
CLIC
CLAC
CLIC
CLIC
CLAC
It took him forever to get our pathetic crime story down on paper.
CLAC
CLIC
CLIC
??

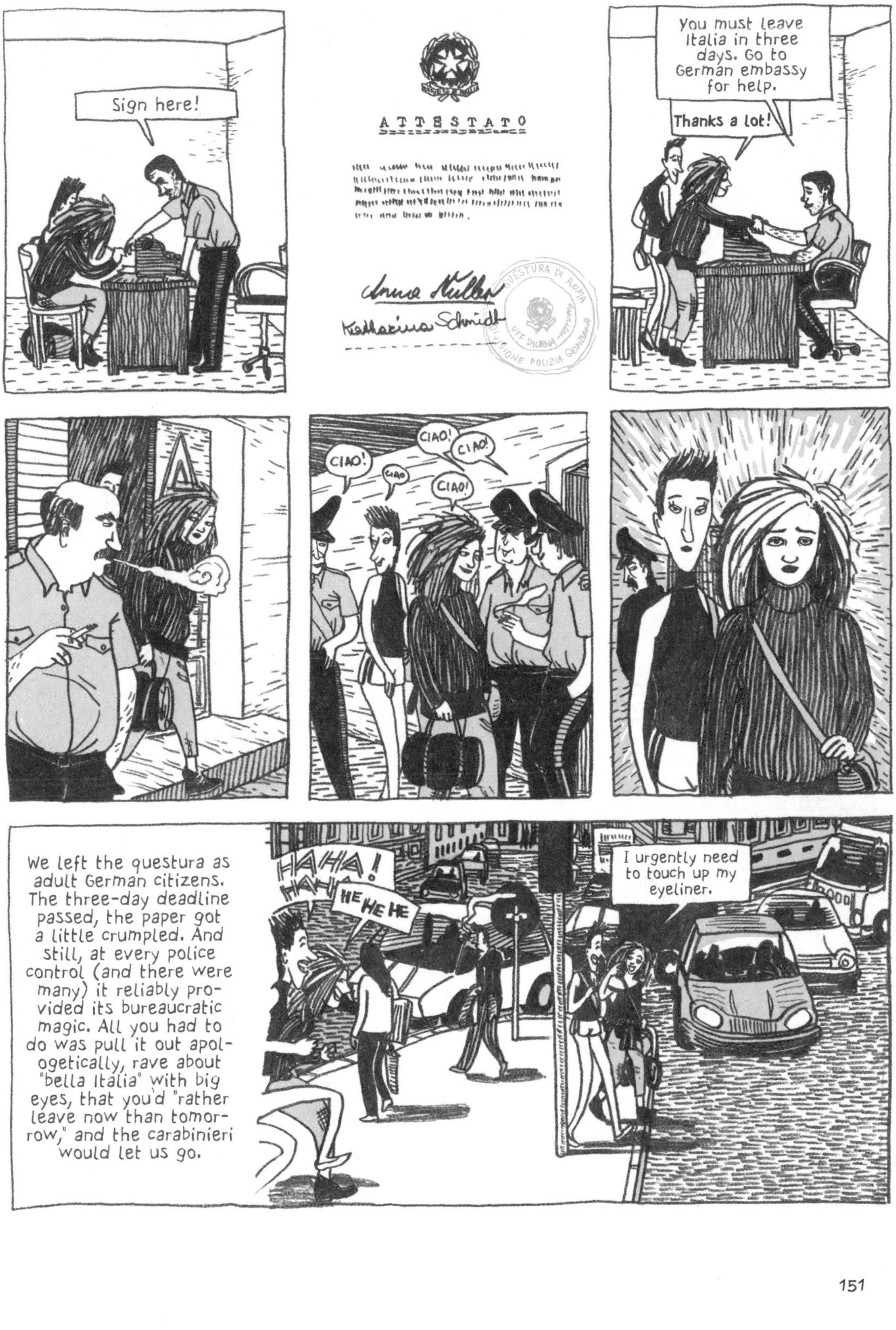
Sign here!
ATTESTATO
QUESTURA DI ROMA
You must leave Italia in three days. Go to German embassy for help.
Thanks a lot!
CIAO!
CIAO
CIAO!
CIAO!
CIAO!
We left the questura as adult German citizens. The three-day deadline passed, the paper got a little crumpled. And still, at every police control (and there were many) it reliably provided its bureaucratic magic. All you had to do was pull it out apologetically, rave about "bella Italia" with big eyes, that you'd "rather leave now than tomorrow," and the carabinieri would let us go.
HAHA!
HAHA
HE HE HE
I urgently need to touch up my eyeliner.

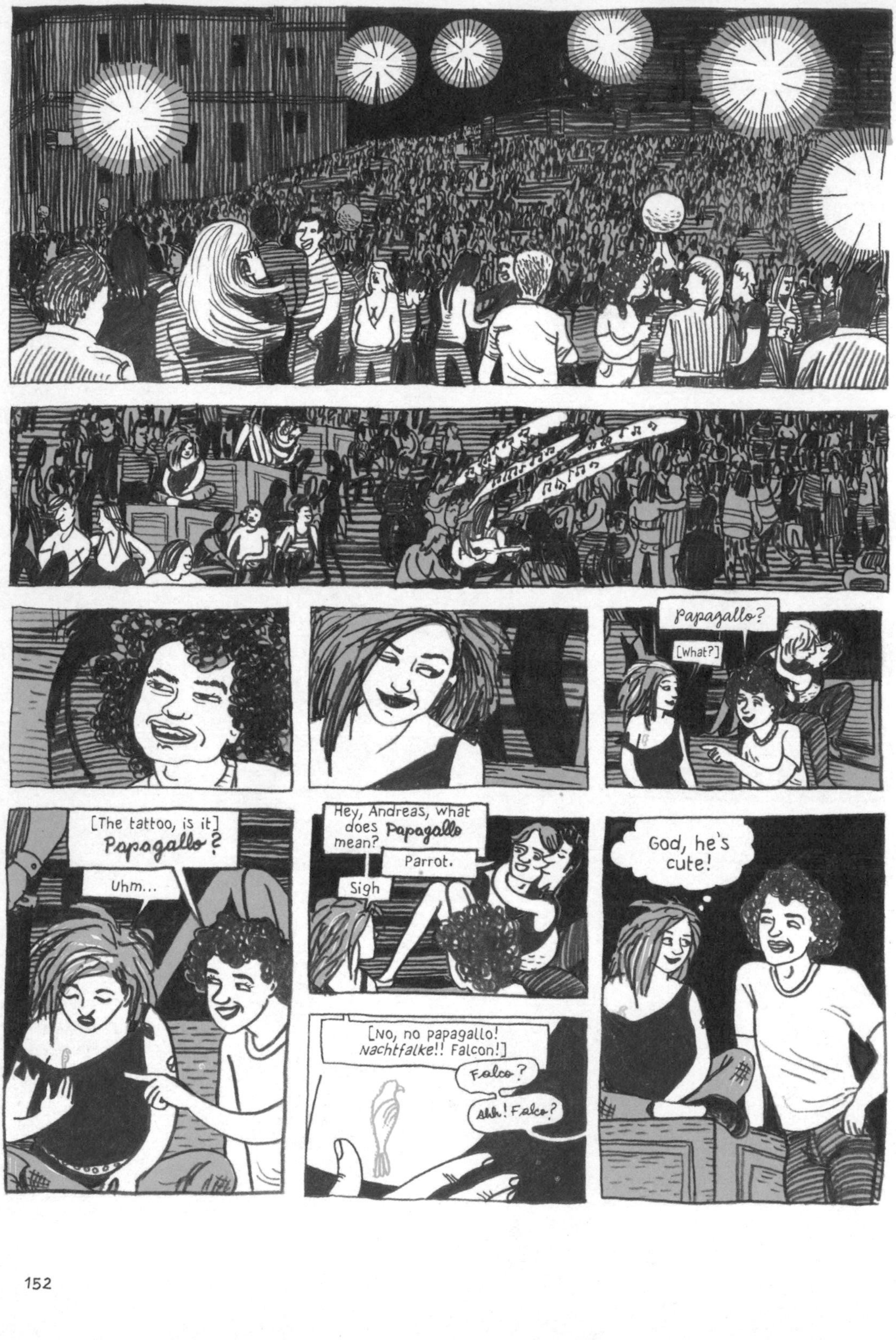
Papagallo?
[What?]
[The tattoo, is it] Papagallo?
Uhm...
Hey, Andreas, what does Papagallo mean?
Parrot.
Sigh
[No, no papagallo! Nachtfalke!! Falcon!]
Falco?
Ahh! Falco?
God, he's cute!

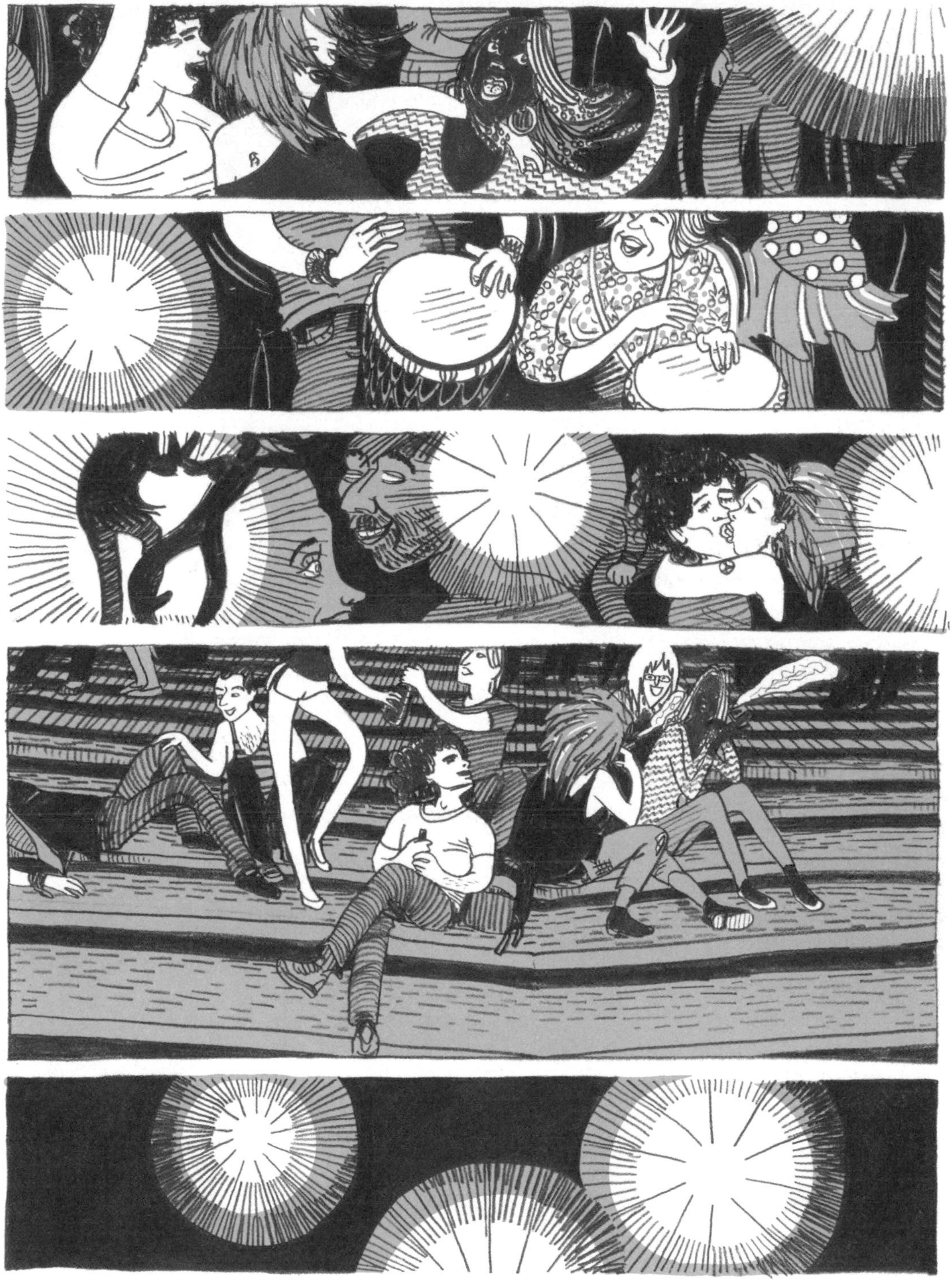

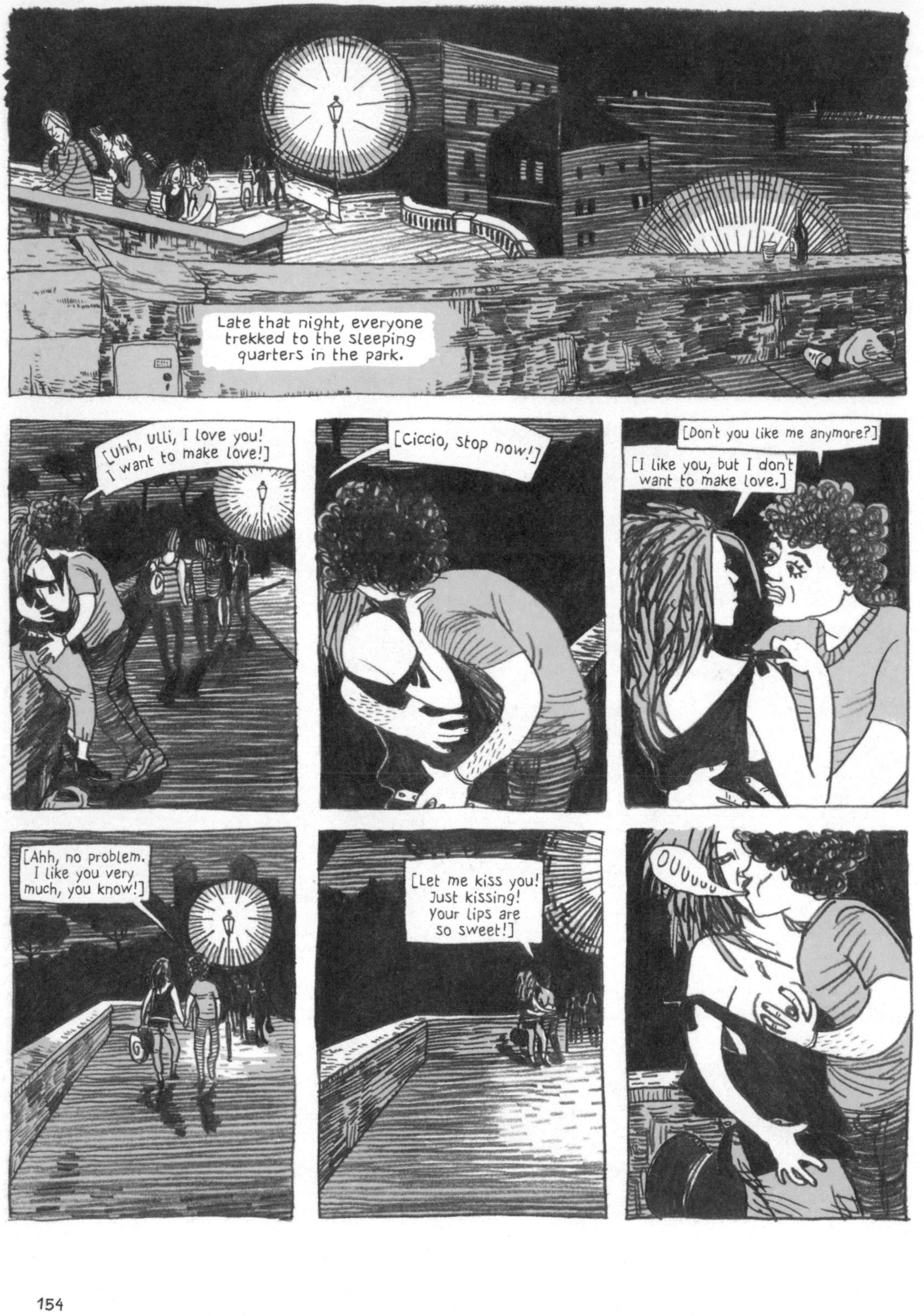
Late that night, everyone trekked to the sleeping quarters in the park.
[Uhh, Ulli, I love you! I want to make love!]
[Ciccio, stop now!]
[Don't you like me anymore?]
[I like you, but I don't want to make love.]
[Ahh, no problem. I like you very much, you know!]
[Let me kiss you! Just kissing! Your lips are so sweet!]
OUuuuu

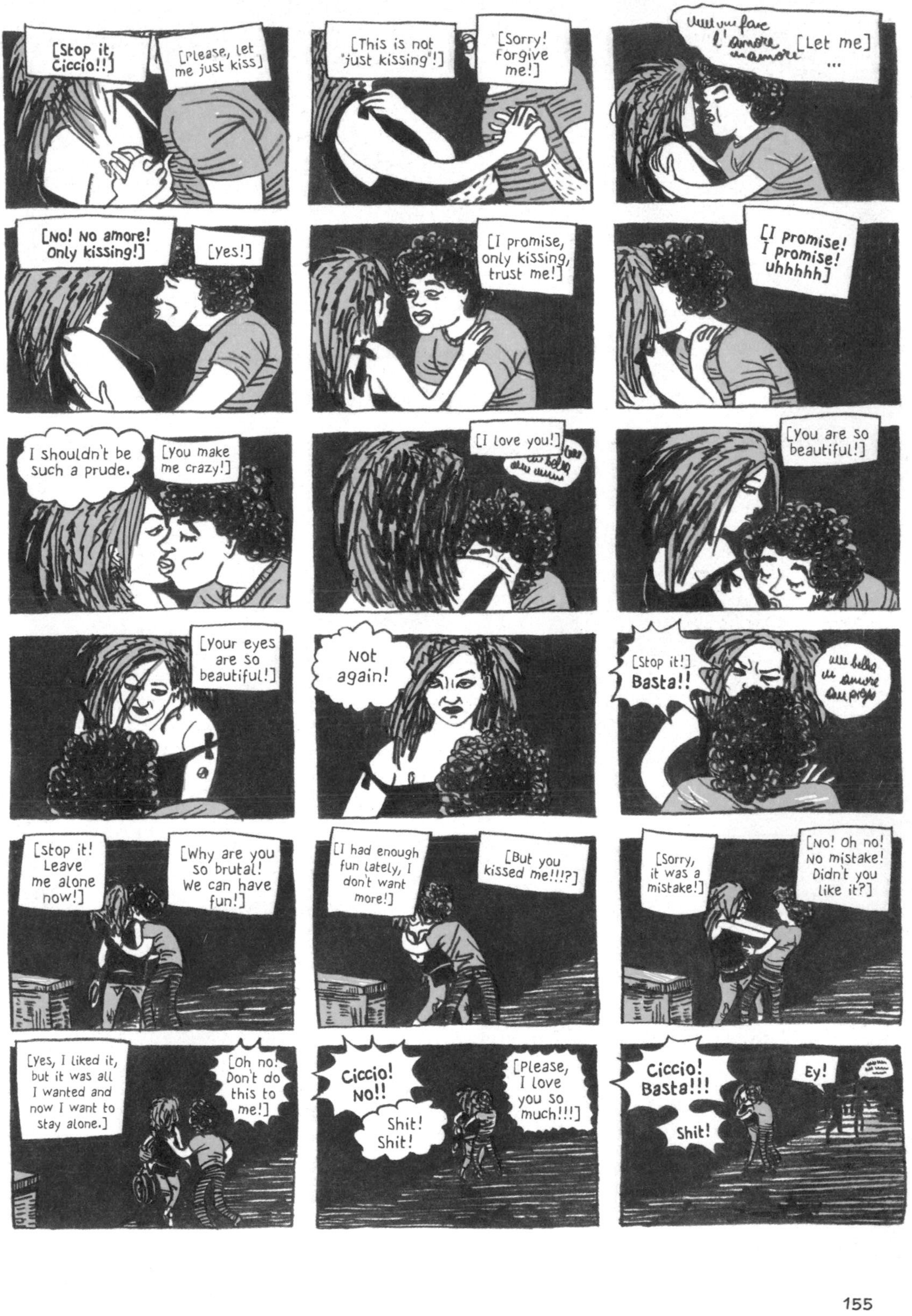
[Stop it, Ciccio!!]
[Please, let me just kiss]
[This is not "just kissing"!]
[Sorry! Forgive me!]
l'amore
[Let me] ...
[No! No amore! Only kissing!]
[Yes!]
[I promise, only kissing, trust me!]
[I promise! I promise! uhhhhh]
I shouldn't be such a prude.
[You make me crazy!]
[I love you!]
[You are so beautiful!]
[Your eyes are so beautiful!]
Not again!
[Stop it!] Basta!!
[Stop it! Leave me alone now!]
[Why are you so brutal! We can have fun!]
[I had enough fun lately, I don't want more!]
[But you kissed me!!!?]
[Sorry, it was a mistake!]
[No! Oh no! No mistake! Didn't you like it?]
[Yes, I liked it, but it was all I wanted and now I want to stay alone.]
[Oh no! Don't do this to me!]
Ciccio! No!!
Shit! Shit!
[Please, I love you so much!!!]
Ciccio! Basta!!!
Shit!
Ey!

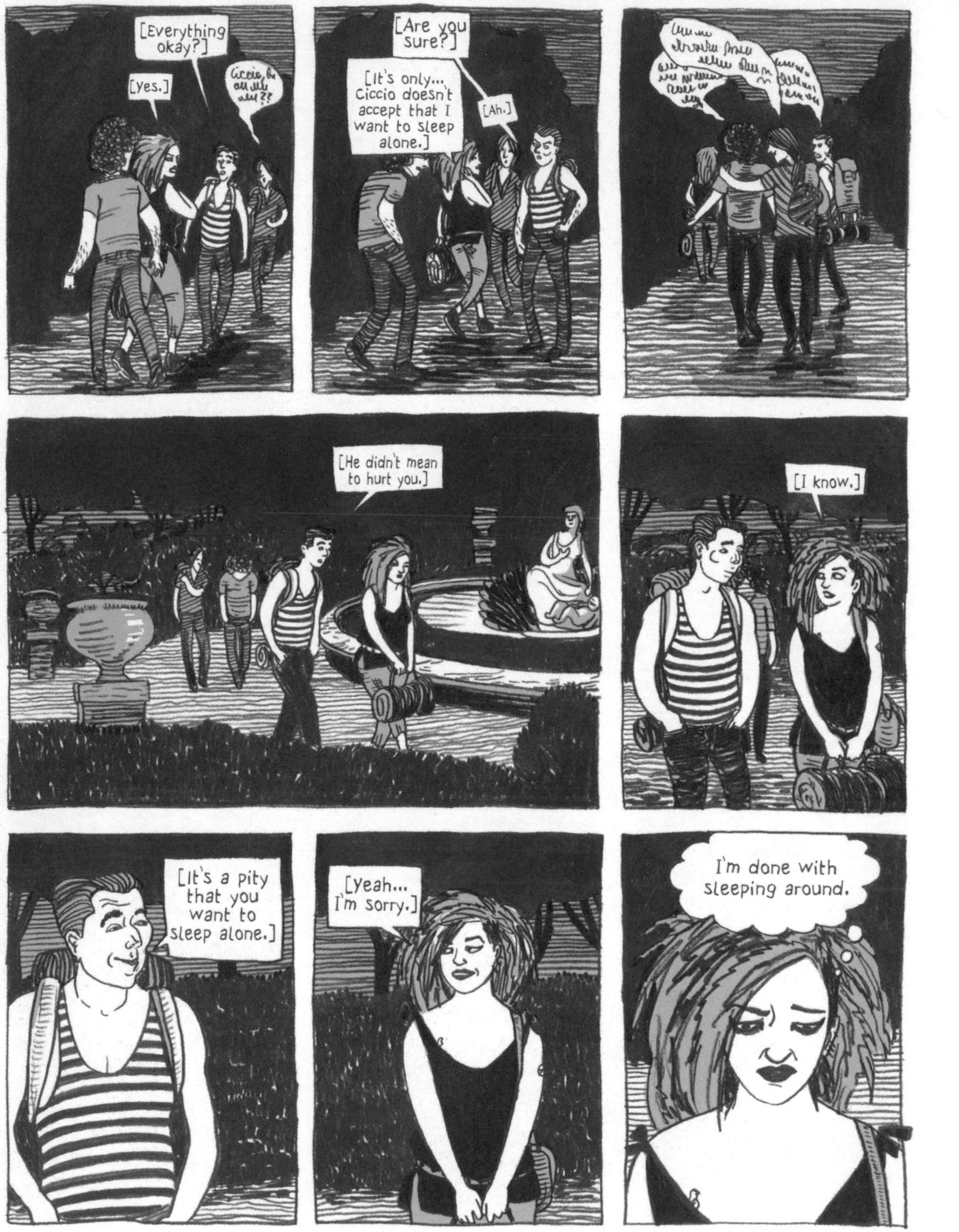
[Everything okay?]
[Yes.]
[Are you sure?]
[It's only... Ciccio doesn't accept that I want to sleep alone.]
[Ah.]
[He didn't mean to hurt you.]
[I know.]
[It's a pity that you want to sleep alone.]
[Yeah... I'm sorry.]
I'm done with sleeping around.

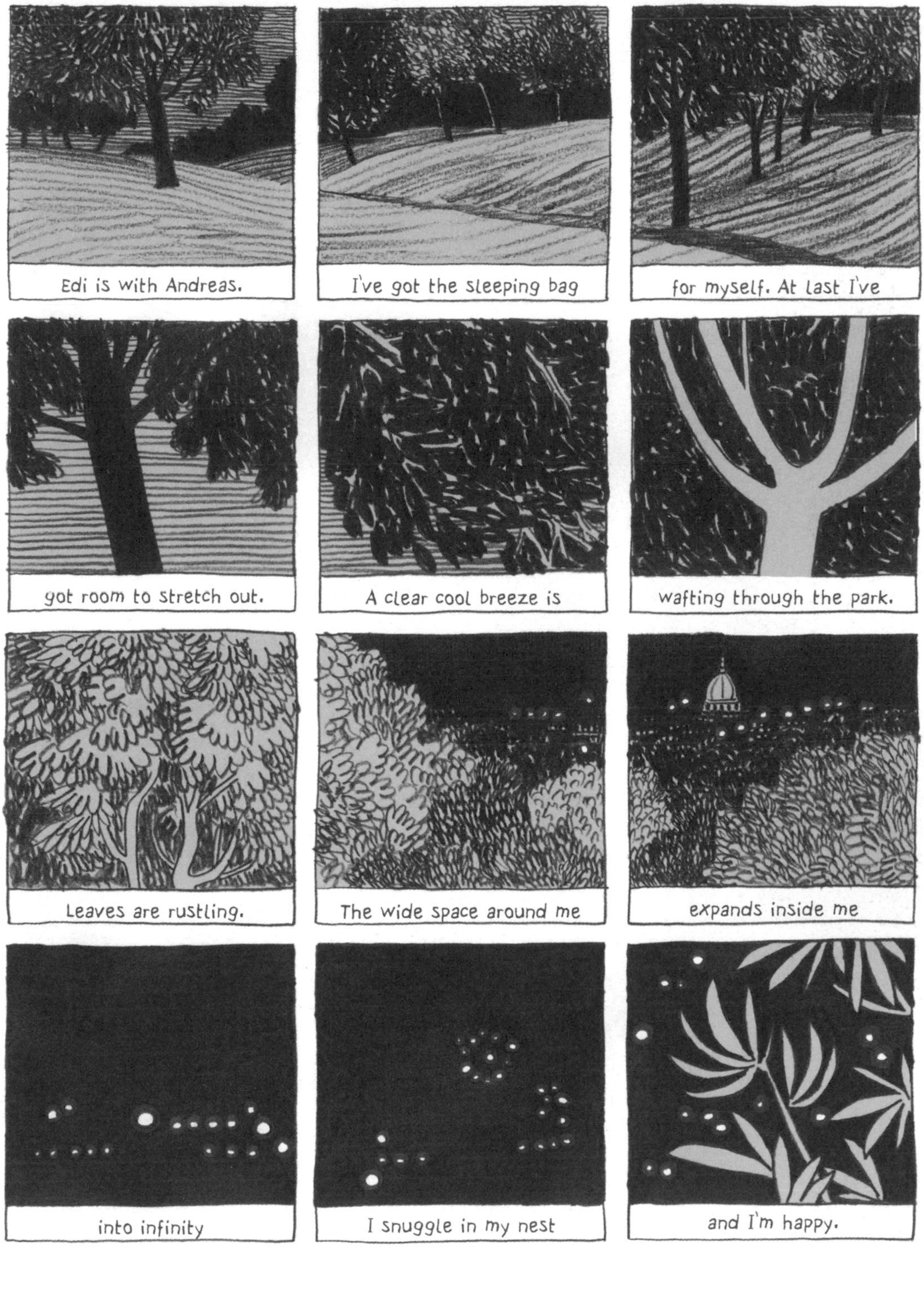
Edi is with Andreas.
I've got the sleeping bag
for myself. At last I've
got room to stretch out.
A clear cool breeze is
wafting through the park.
Leaves are rustling.
The wide space around me
expands inside me
into infinity
I snuggle in my nest
and I'm happy.

VIII. the COMMUNITY

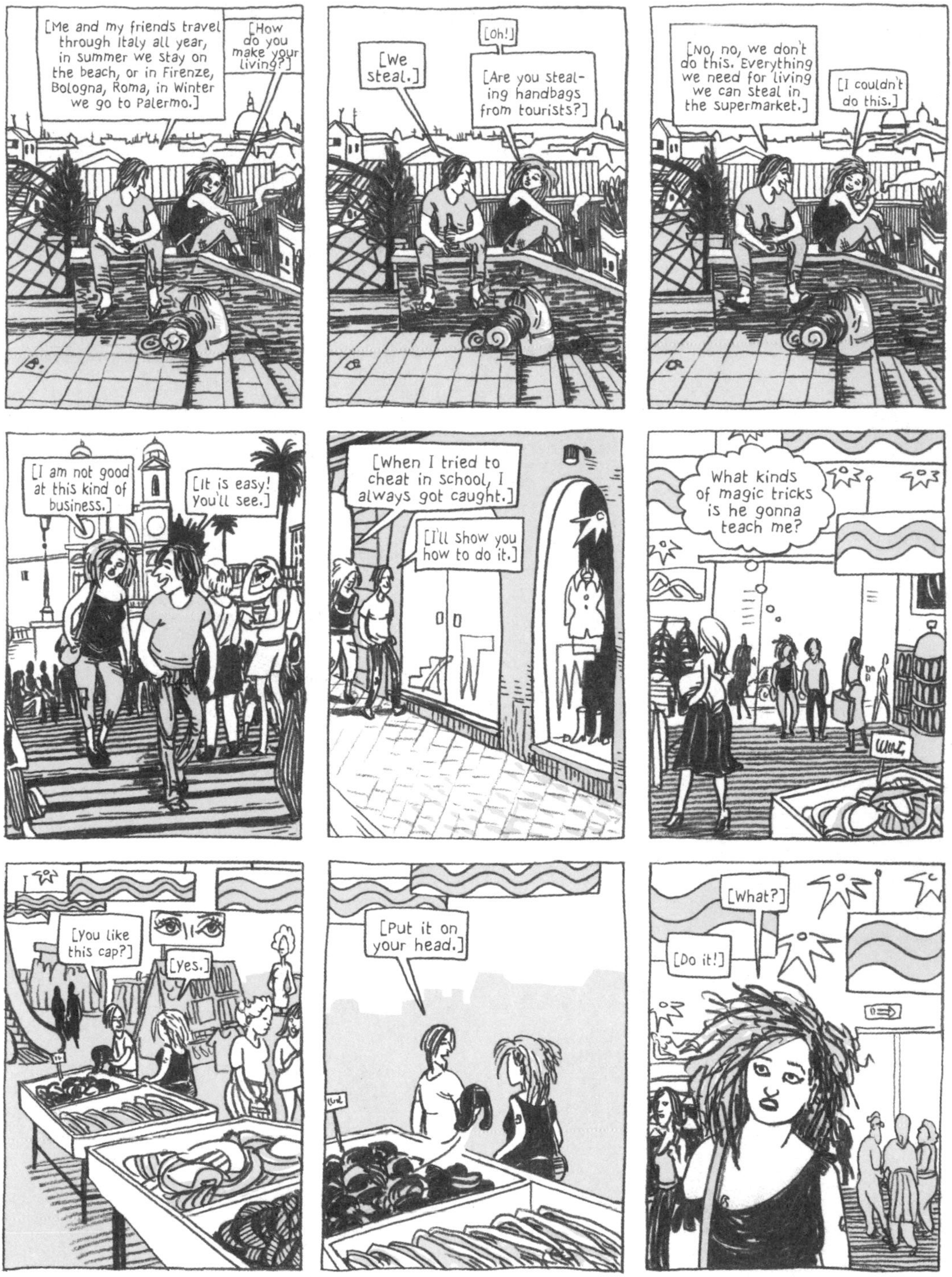
[Me and my friends travel through Italy all year, in summer we stay on the beach, or in Firenze, Bologna, Roma, in Winter we go to Palermo.]
[How do you make your living?]
[We steal.]
[Oh!]
[Are you stealing handbags from tourists?]
[No, no, we don't do this. Everything we need for living we can steal in the supermarket.]
[I couldn't do this.]
[I am not good at this kind of business.]
[It is easy! You'll see.]
[When I tried to cheat in school, I always got caught.]
[I'll show you how to do it.]
What kinds of magic tricks is he gonna teach me?
[You like this cap?]
[Yes.]
[Put it on your head.]
[What?]
[Do it!]

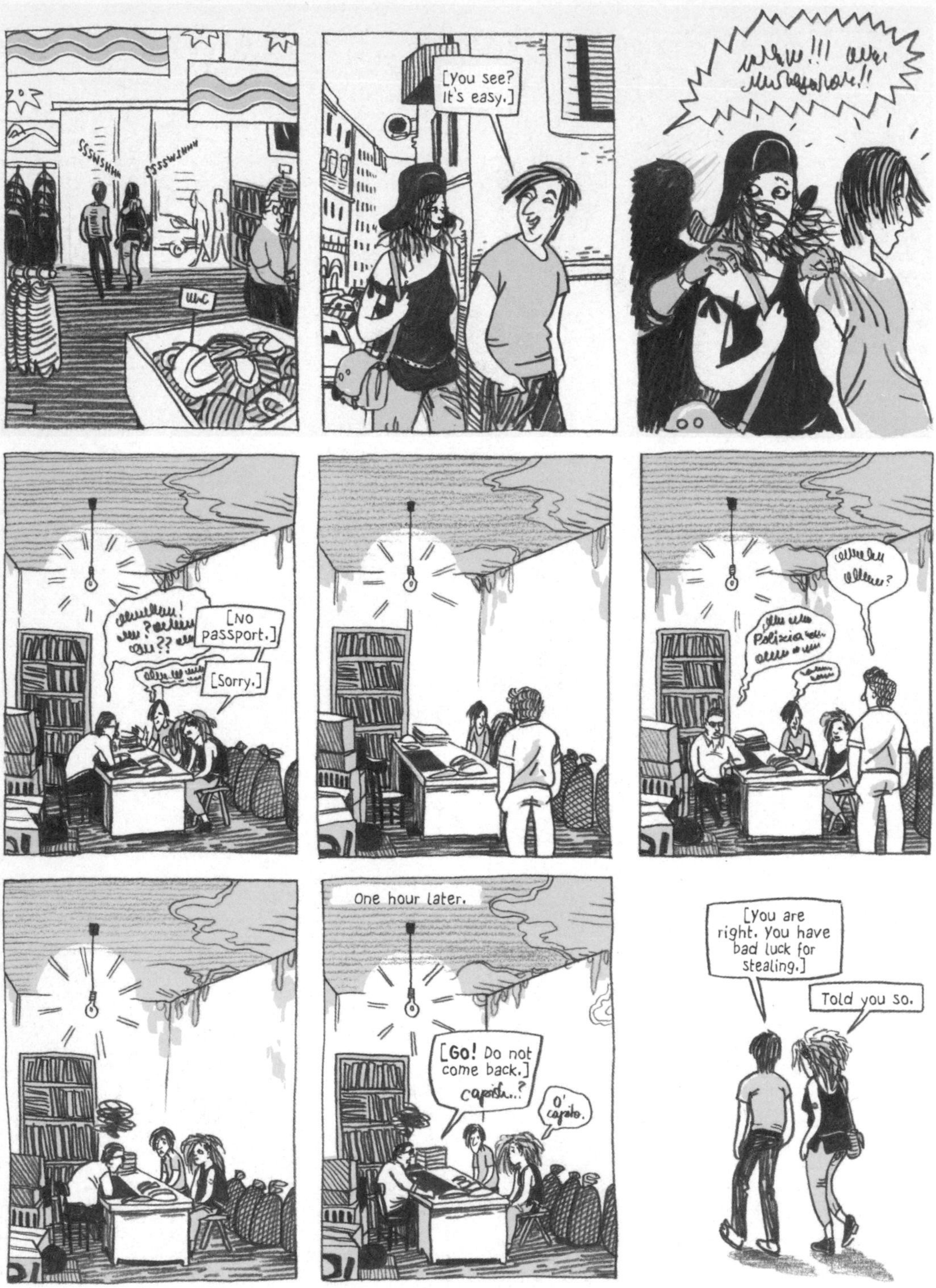
[You see? It's easy.]
[No passport.]
[Sorry.]
Polizia
One hour later.
[GO! Do not come back.]
capish...?
O' capito.
[You are right. You have bad luck for stealing.]
Told you so.

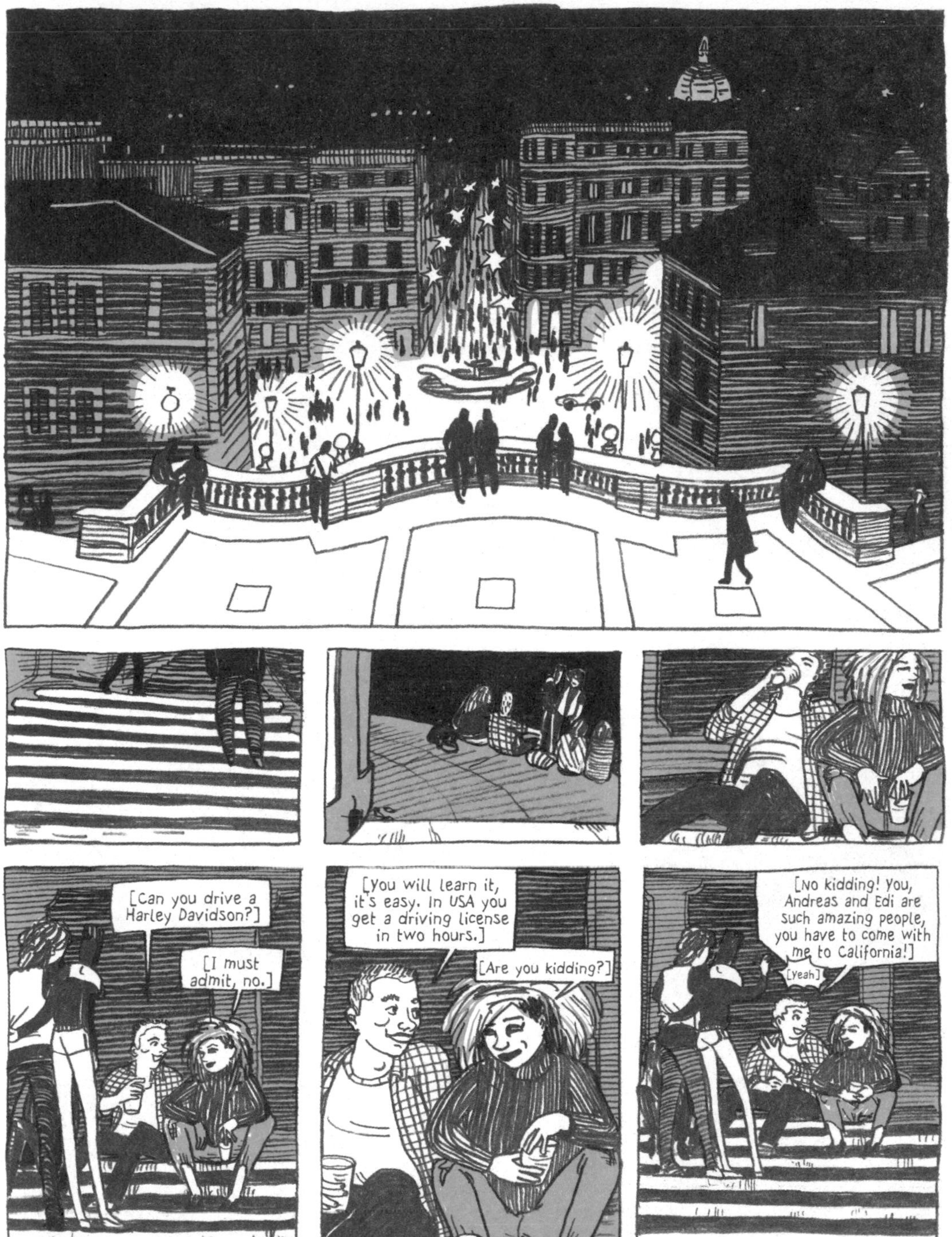

[Can you drive a Harley Davidson?]
[I must admit, no.]
[You will learn it, it's easy. In USA you get a driving license in two hours.]
[Are you kidding?]
[No kidding! You, Andreas and Edi are such amazing people, you have to come with me to California!]
[Yeah]

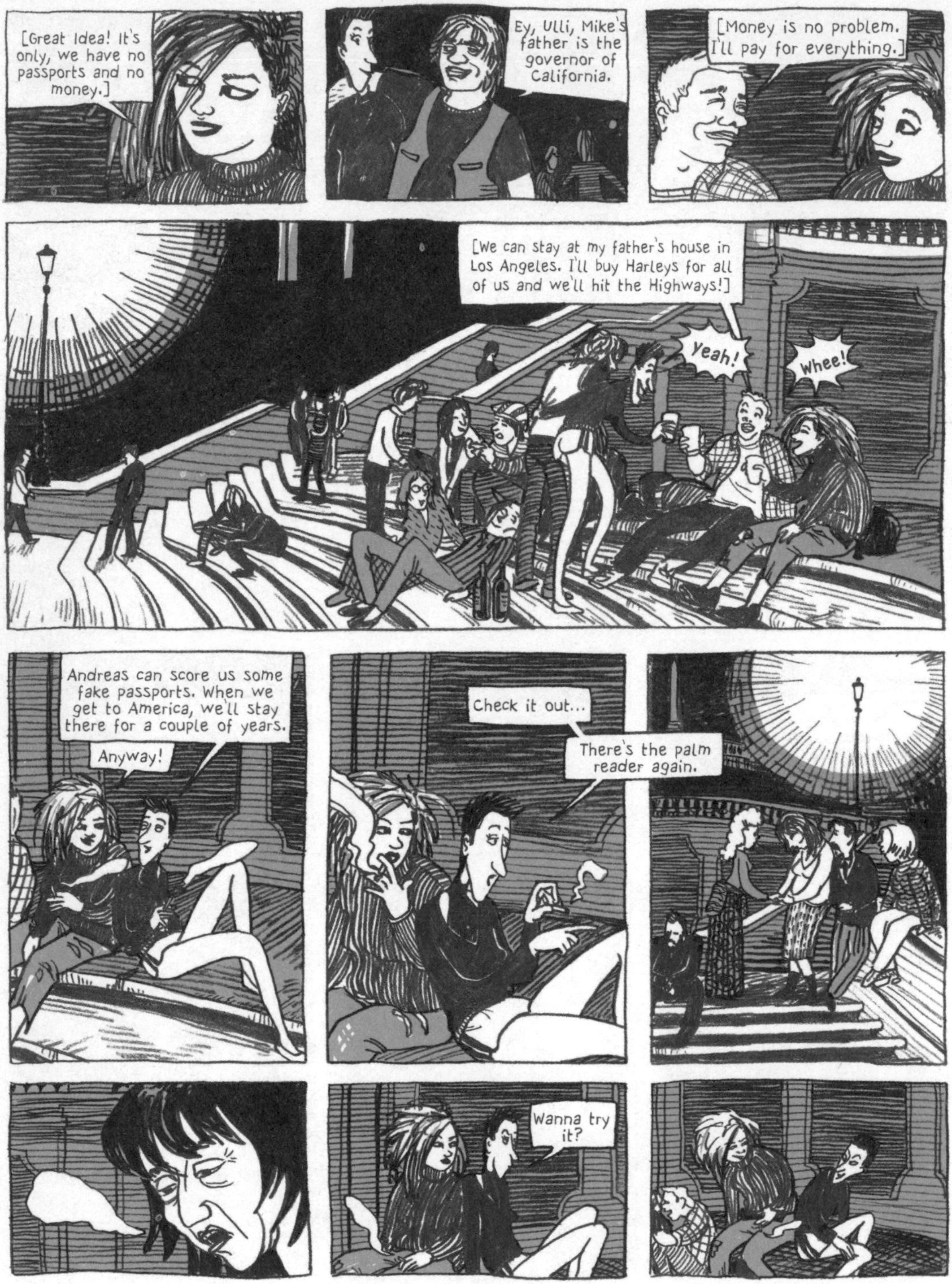

[Great Idea! It's only, we have no passports and no money.]
Ey, Ulli, Mike's father is the governor of California.
[Money is no problem. I'll pay for everything.]
[We can stay at my father's house in Los Angeles. I'll buy Harleys for all of us and we'll hit the Highways!]
Yeah!
Whee!
Andreas can score us some fake passports. When we get to America, we'll stay there for a couple of years.
Anyway!
Check it out...
There's the palm reader again.
Wanna try it?

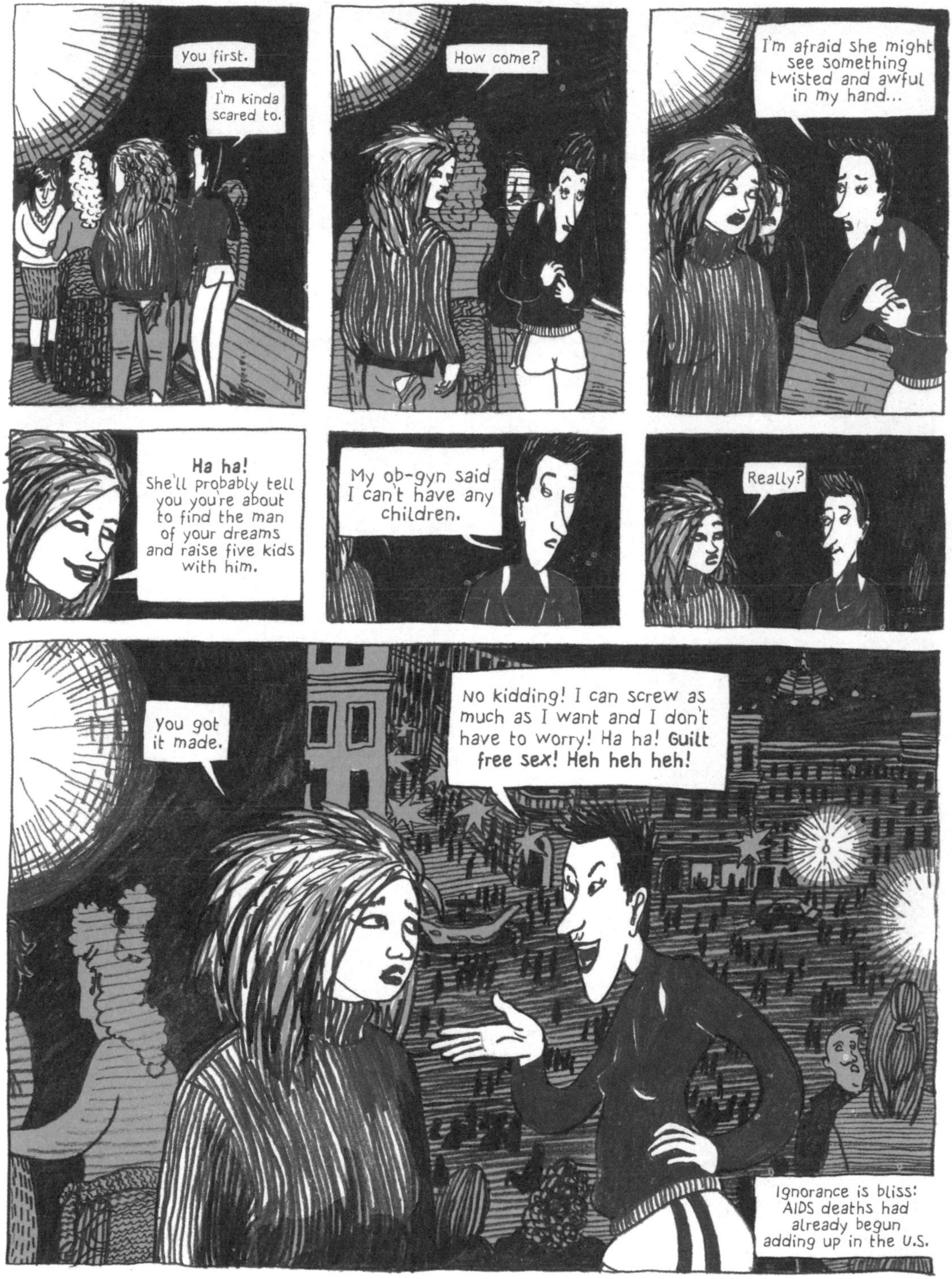

You first.
I'm kinda scared to.
How come?
I'm afraid she might see something twisted and awful in my hand...
Ha ha! She'll probably tell you you're about to find the man of your dreams and raise five kids with him.
My ob-gyn said I can't have any children.
Really?
You got it made.
No kidding! I can screw as much as I want and I don't have to worry! Ha ha! **Guilt free sex! Heh heh heh!**
Ignorance is bliss: AIDS deaths had already begun adding up in the U.S.

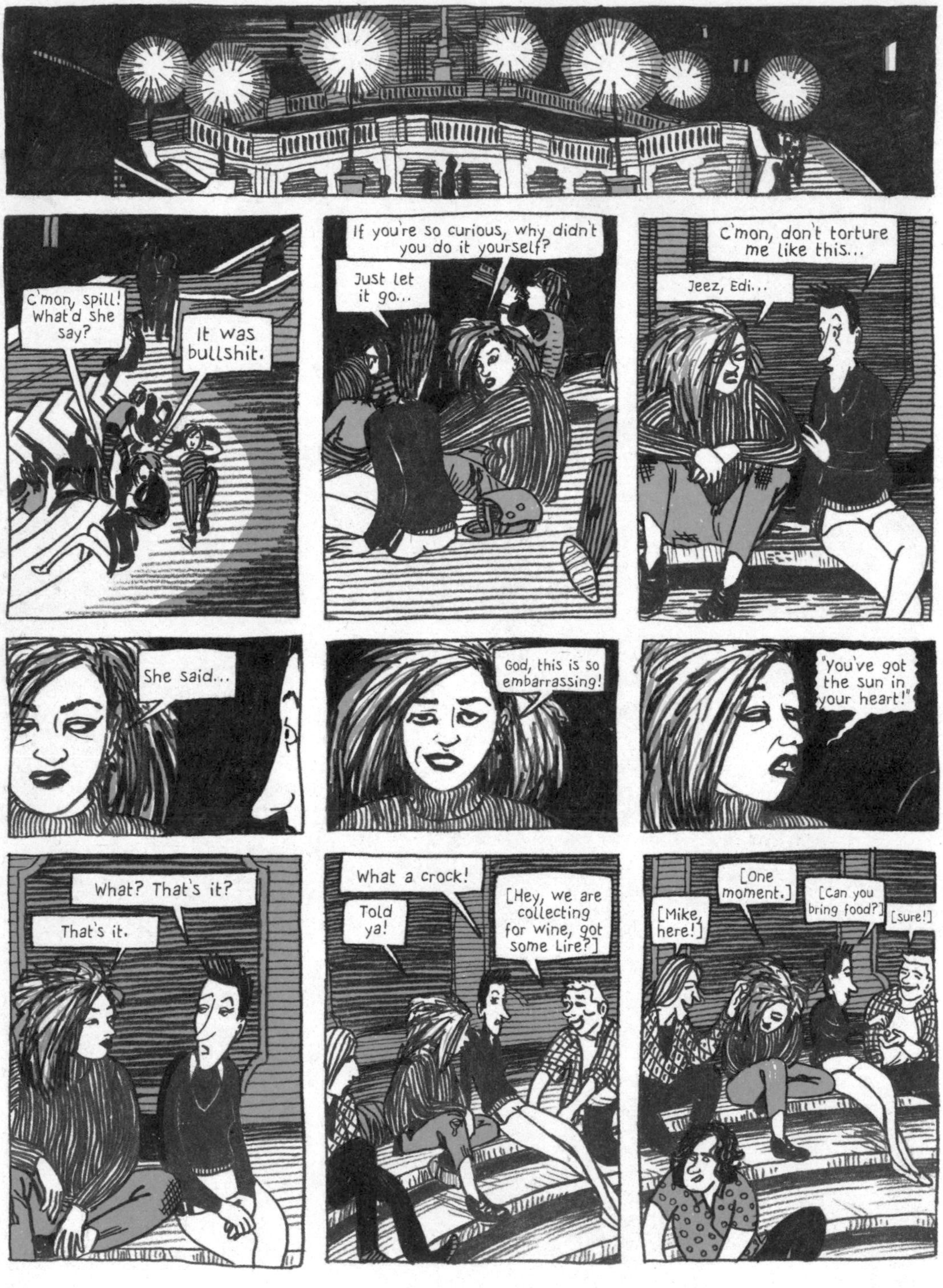

C'mon, spill! What'd she say?
It was bullshit.
If you're so curious, why didn't you do it yourself?
Just let it go...
C'mon, don't torture me like this...
Jeez, Edi...
She said...
God, this is so embarrassing!
"You've got the sun in your heart!"
What? That's it?
That's it.
What a crock!
Told ya!
[Hey, we are collecting for wine, got some Lire?]
[One moment.]
[Mike, here!]
[Can you bring food?]
[sure!]

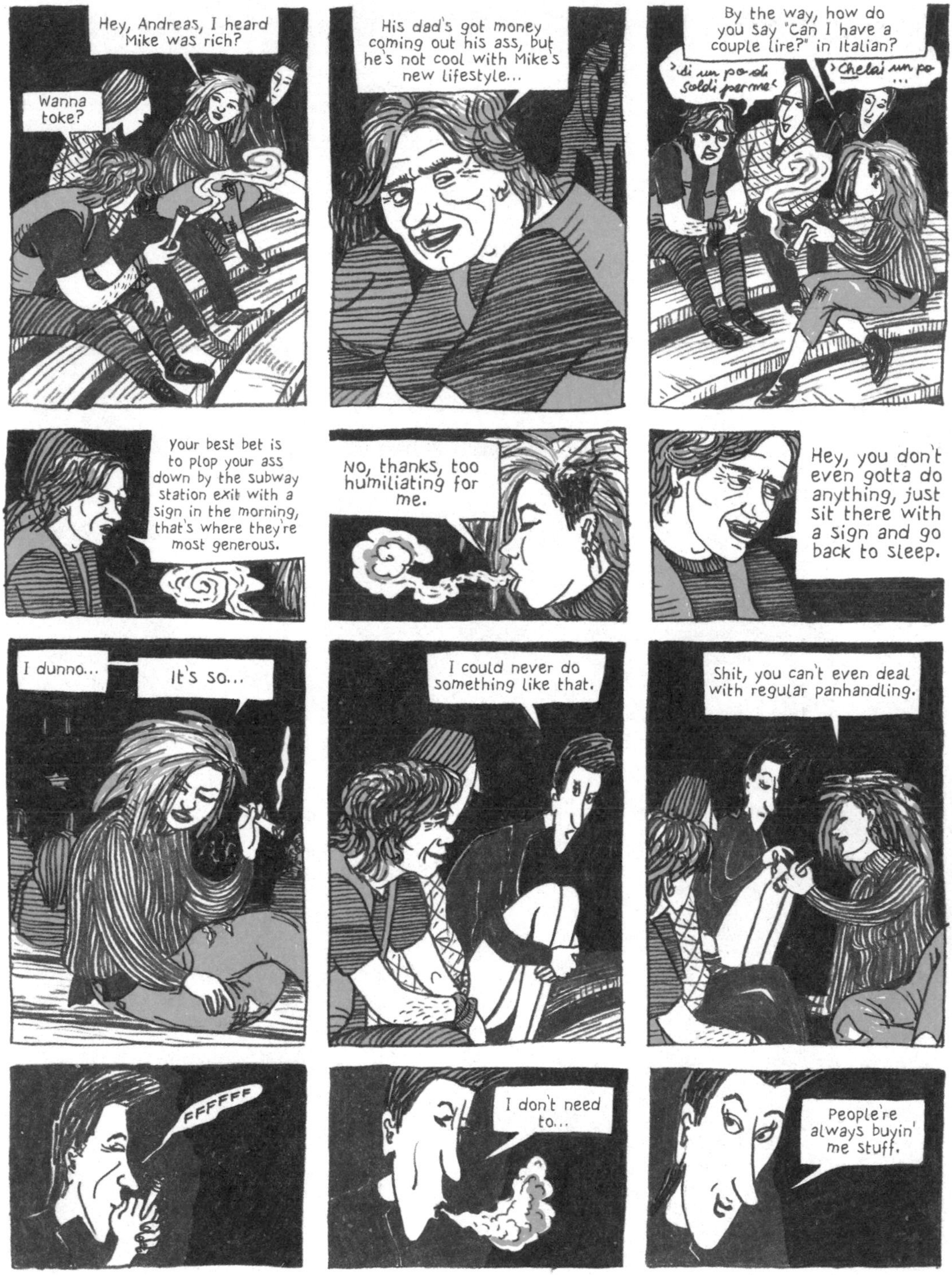
Hey, Andreas, I heard Mike was rich?
Wanna toke?
His dad's got money coming out his ass, but he's not cool with Mike's new lifestyle...
By the way, how do you say "Can I have a couple lire?" in Italian?
>di un po di soldi per me<
>Chelai un po ...
Your best bet is to plop your ass down by the subway station exit with a sign in the morning, that's where they're most generous.
No, thanks, too humiliating for me.
Hey, you don't even gotta do anything, just sit there with a sign and go back to sleep.
I dunno...
It's so...
I could never do something like that.
Shit, you can't even deal with regular panhandling.
FFFFFF
I don't need to...
People're always buyin' me stuff.

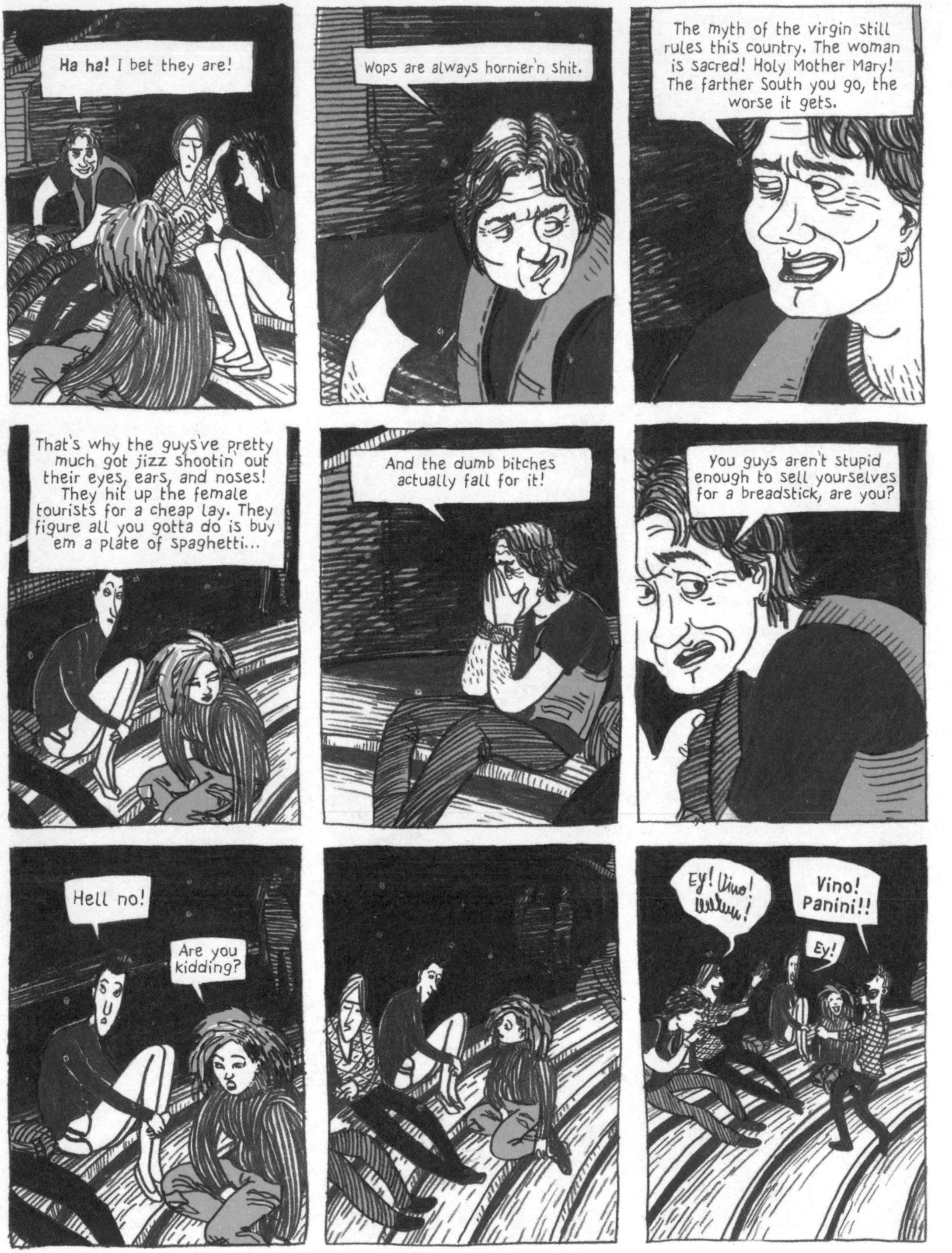
Ha ha! I bet they are!
Wops are always hornier'n shit.
The myth of the virgin still rules this country. The woman is sacred! Holy Mother Mary! The farther South you go, the worse it gets.
That's why the guys've pretty much got jizz shootin' out their eyes, ears, and noses! They hit up the female tourists for a cheap lay. They figure all you gotta do is buy em a plate of spaghetti...
And the dumb bitches actually fall for it!
You guys aren't stupid enough to sell yourselves for a breadstick, are you?
Hell no!
Are you kidding?
Ey! Vino!
Vino! Panini!!
Ey!

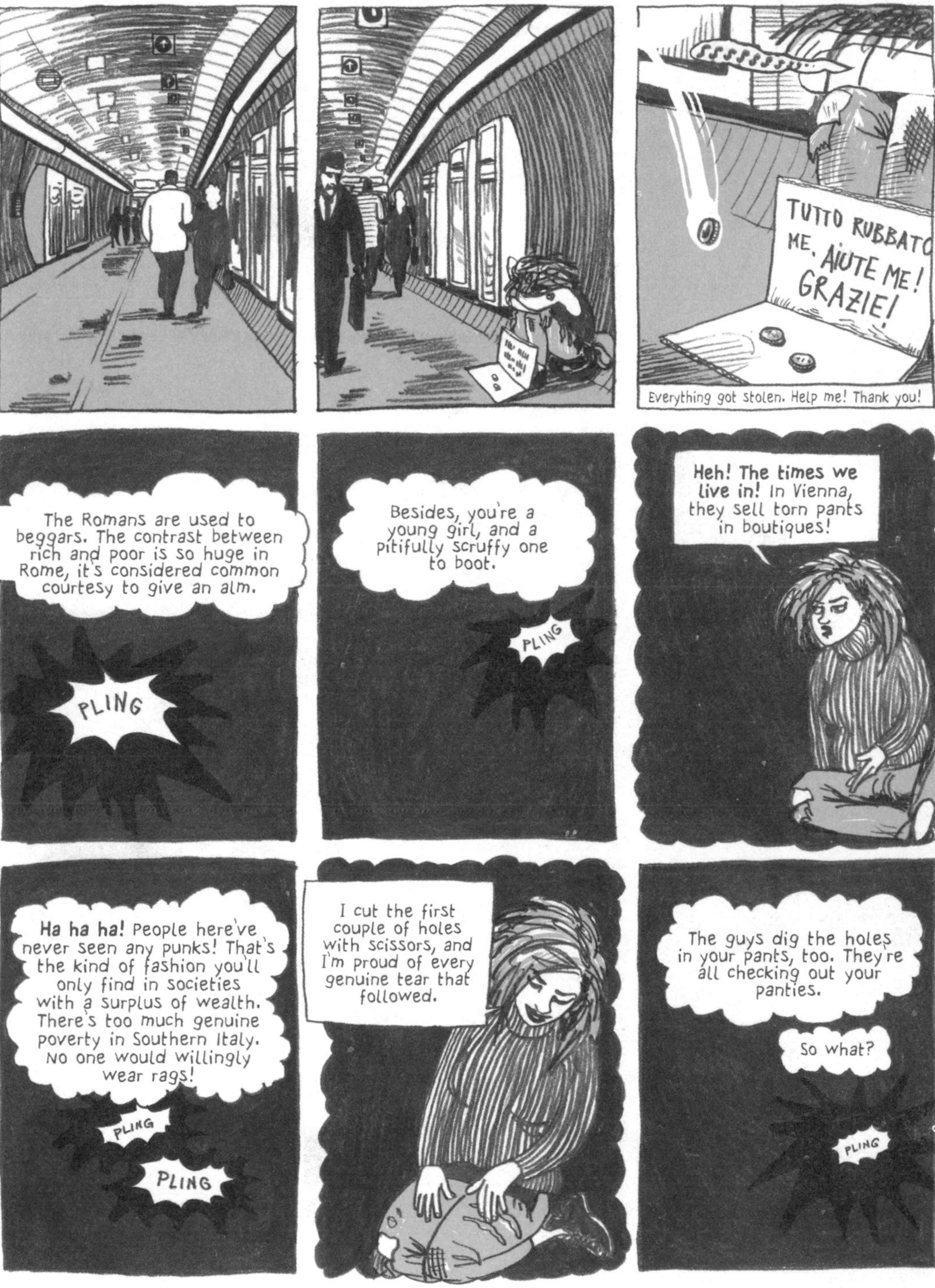

SSSSSSSSS
TUTTO RUBBATO ME. AIUTE ME! GRAZIE!
Everything got stolen. Help me! Thank you!
The Romans are used to beggars. The contrast between rich and poor is so huge in Rome, it's considered common courtesy to give an alm.
PLING
Besides, you're a young girl, and a pitifully scruffy one to boot.
PLING
Heh! The times we live in! In Vienna, they sell torn pants in boutiques!
Ha ha ha! People here've never seen any punks! That's the kind of fashion you'll only find in societies with a surplus of wealth. There's too much genuine poverty in Southern Italy. No one would willingly wear rags!
PLING
PLING
I cut the first couple of holes with scissors, and I'm proud of every genuine tear that followed.
The guys dig the holes in your pants, too. They're all checking out your panties.
So what?
PLING

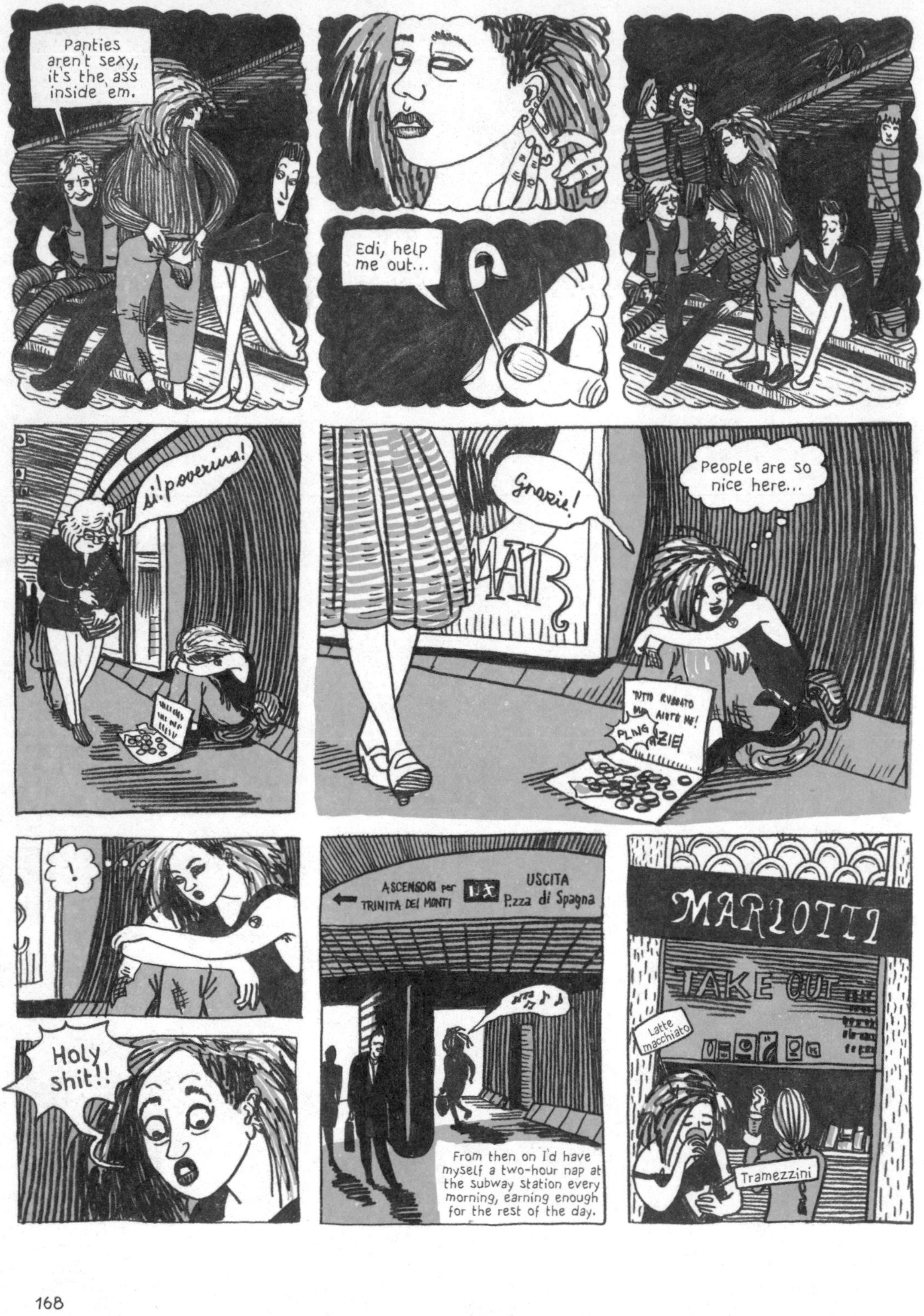
Panties aren't sexy, it's the ass inside 'em.
Edi, help me out...
Sì! poverina!
Grazie!
People are so nice here...
TUTTO RUBATO
AIUTO ME!
!
Holy shit!!
ASCENSORI per TRINITA DEI MONTI
USCITA P.zza di Spagna
From then on I'd have myself a two-hour nap at the subway station every morning, earning enough for the rest of the day.
MARIOTTI
TAKE OUT
Latte macchiato
Tramezzini

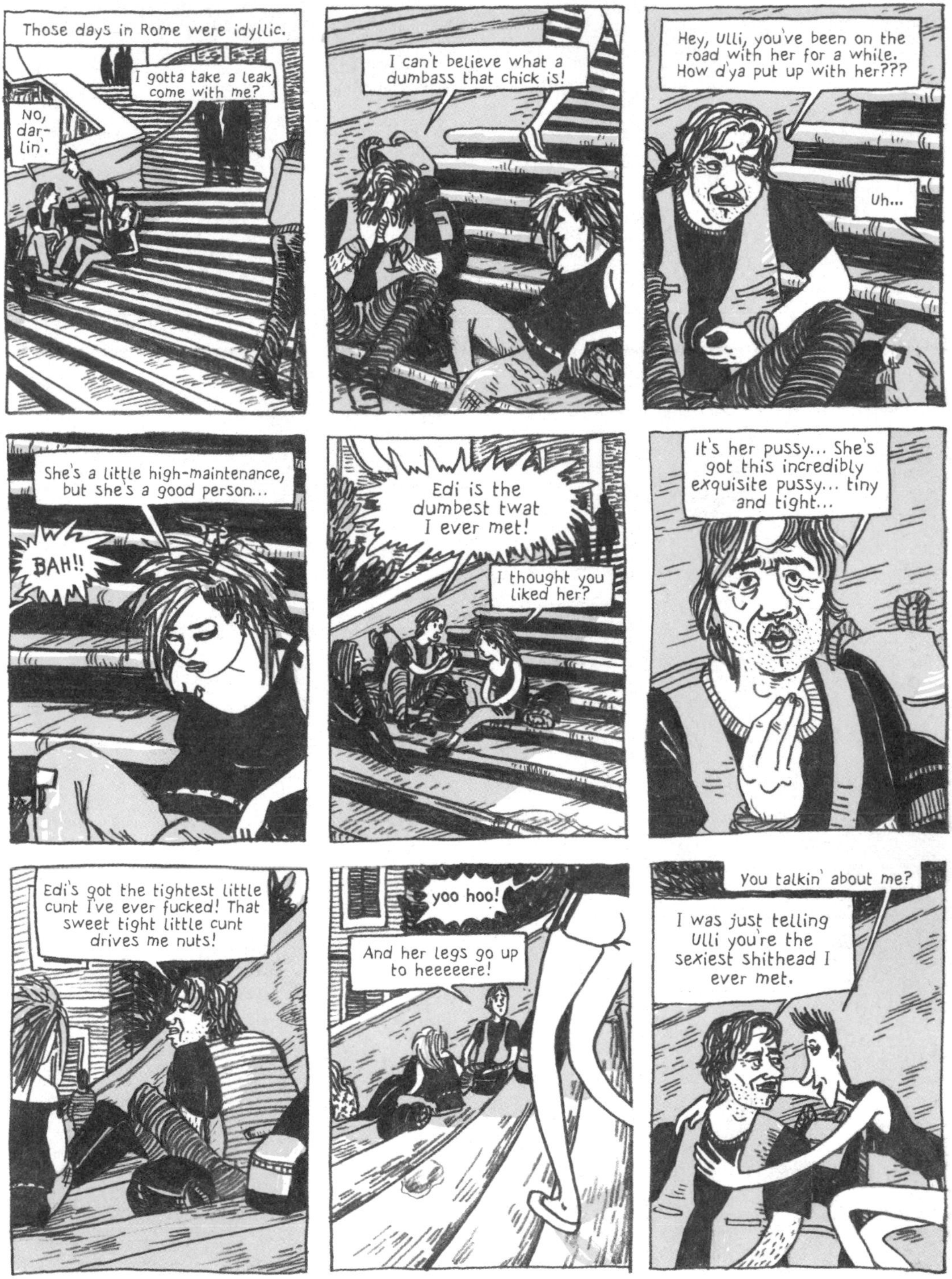

Those days in Rome were idyllic.
I gotta take a leak, come with me?
No, darlin'.
I can't believe what a dumbass that chick is!
Hey, Ulli, you've been on the road with her for a while. How d'ya put up with her???
Uh...
She's a little high-maintenance, but she's a good person...
BAH!!
Edi is the dumbest twat I ever met!
I thought you liked her?
It's her pussy... She's got this incredibly exquisite pussy... tiny and tight...
Edi's got the tightest little cunt I've ever fucked! That sweet tight little cunt drives me nuts!
yoo hoo!
And her legs go up to heeeeere!
You talkin' about me?
I was just telling Ulli you're the sexiest shithead I ever met.

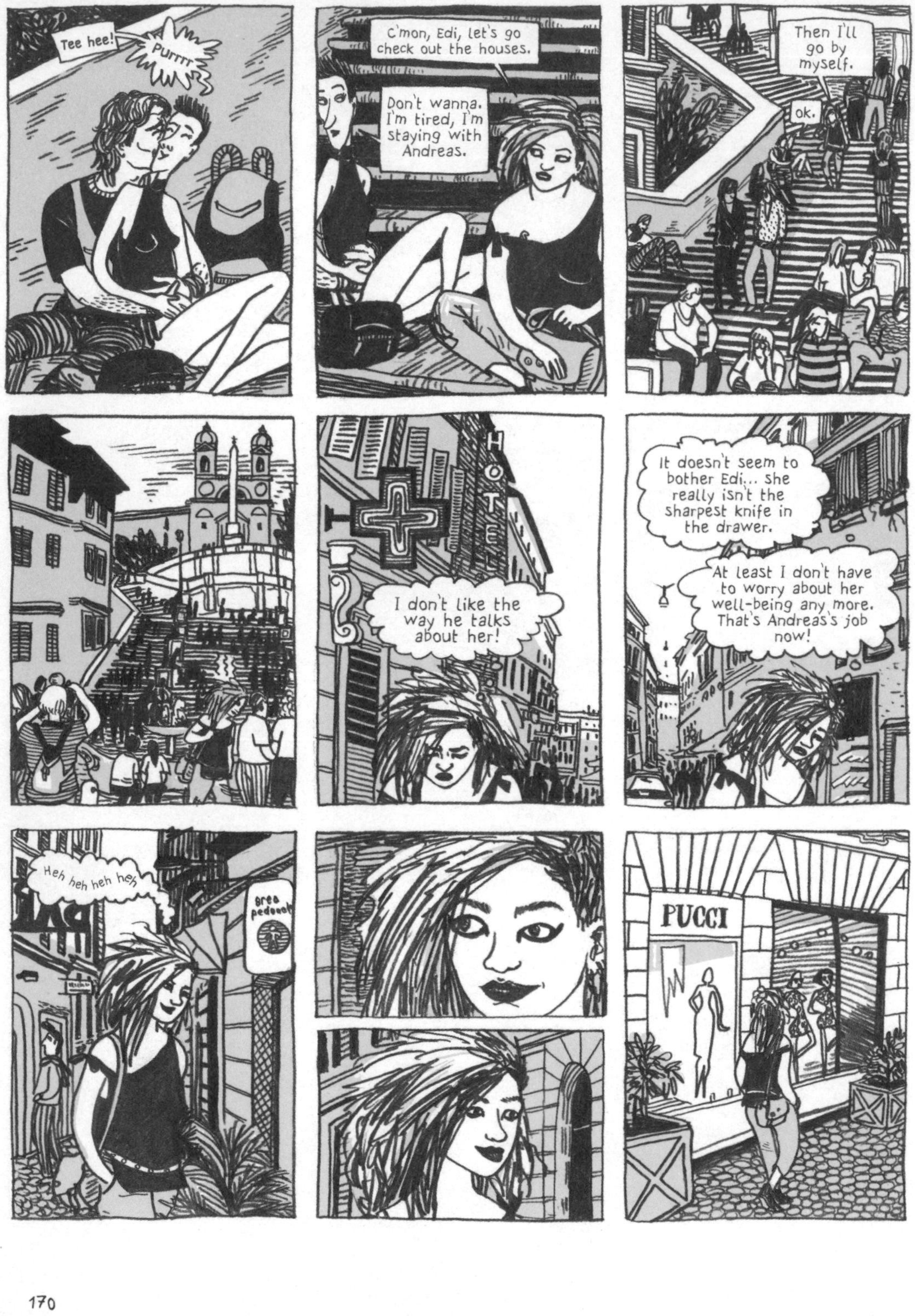
Tee hee!
Purrrr
C'mon, Edi, let's go check out the houses.
Don't wanna. I'm tired, I'm staying with Andreas.
Then I'll go by myself.
ok.
I don't like the way he talks about her!
It doesn't seem to bother Edi... she really isn't the sharpest knife in the drawer.
At least I don't have to worry about her well-being any more. That's Andreas's job now!
Heh heh heh heh
PUCCI

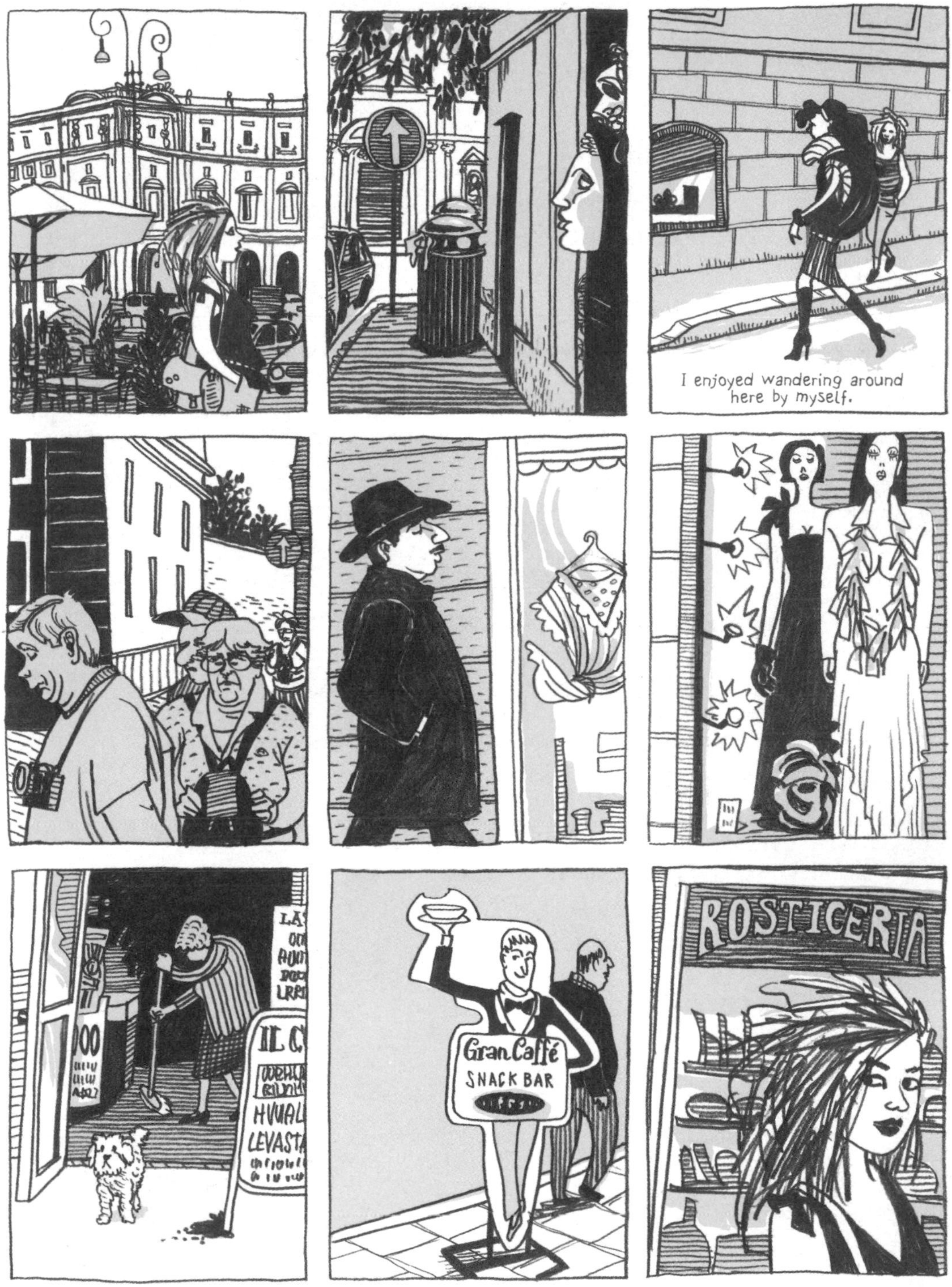
I enjoyed wandering around here by myself.
Gran Caffé
SNACK BAR
ROSTICERIA

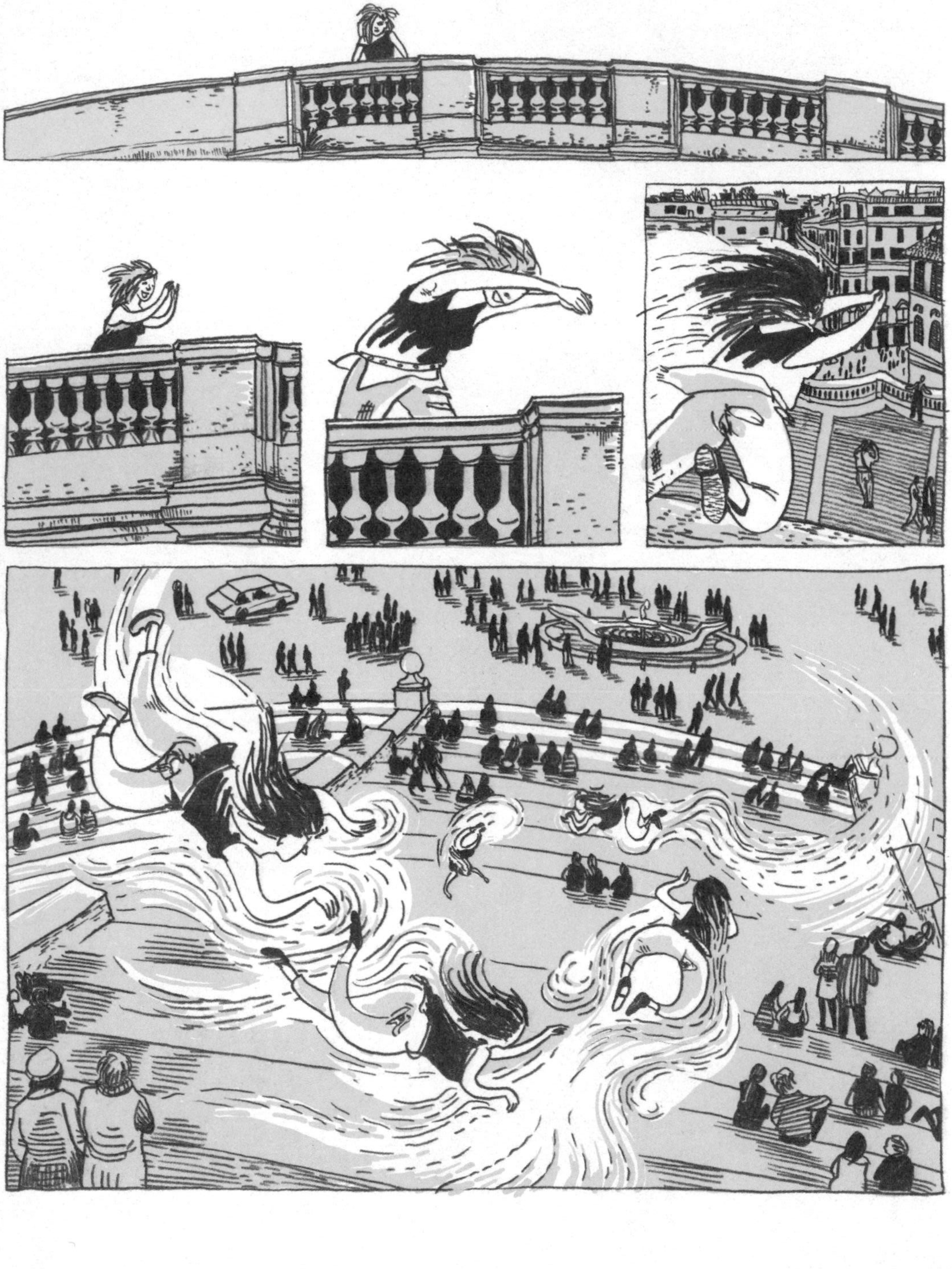

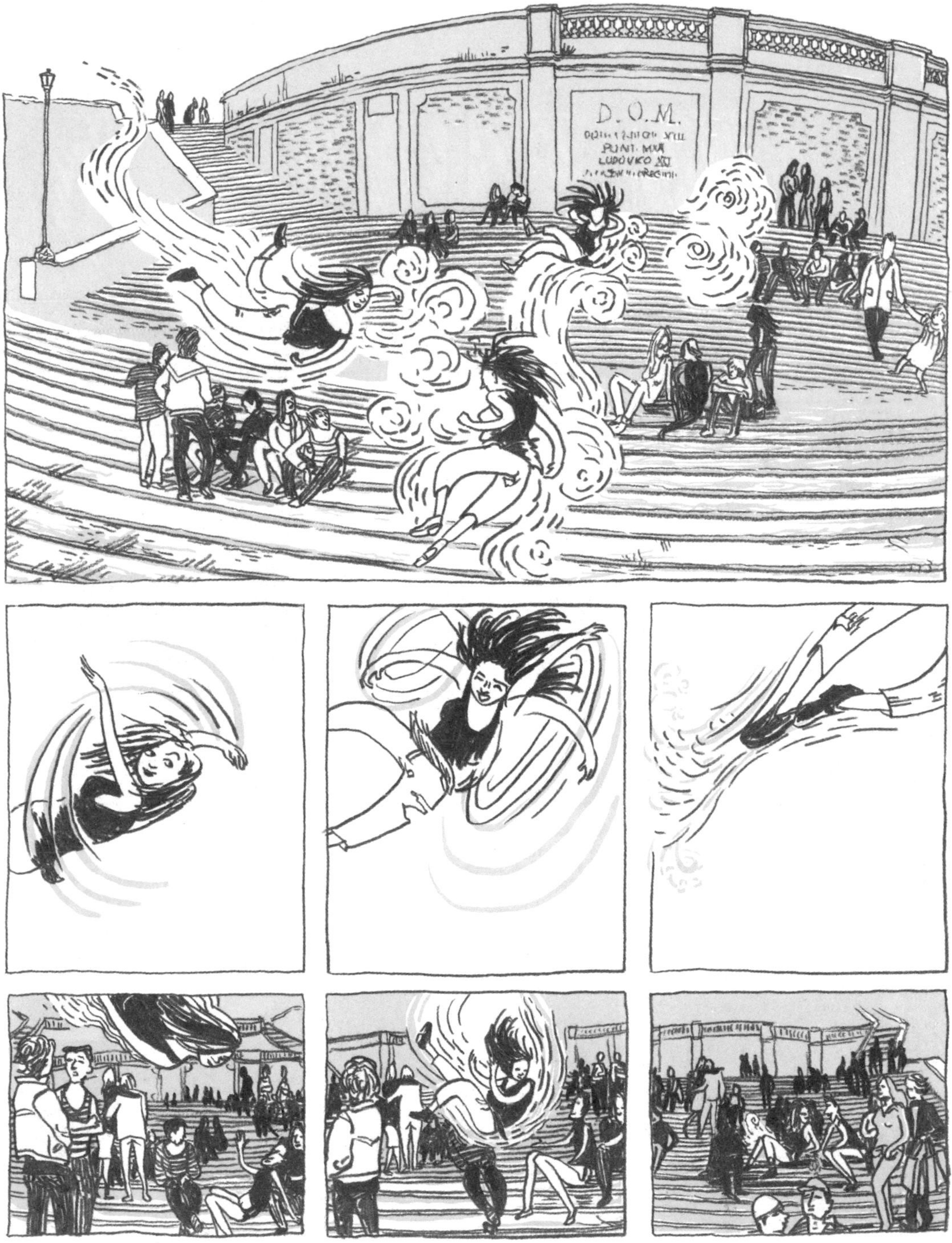
D.O.M.

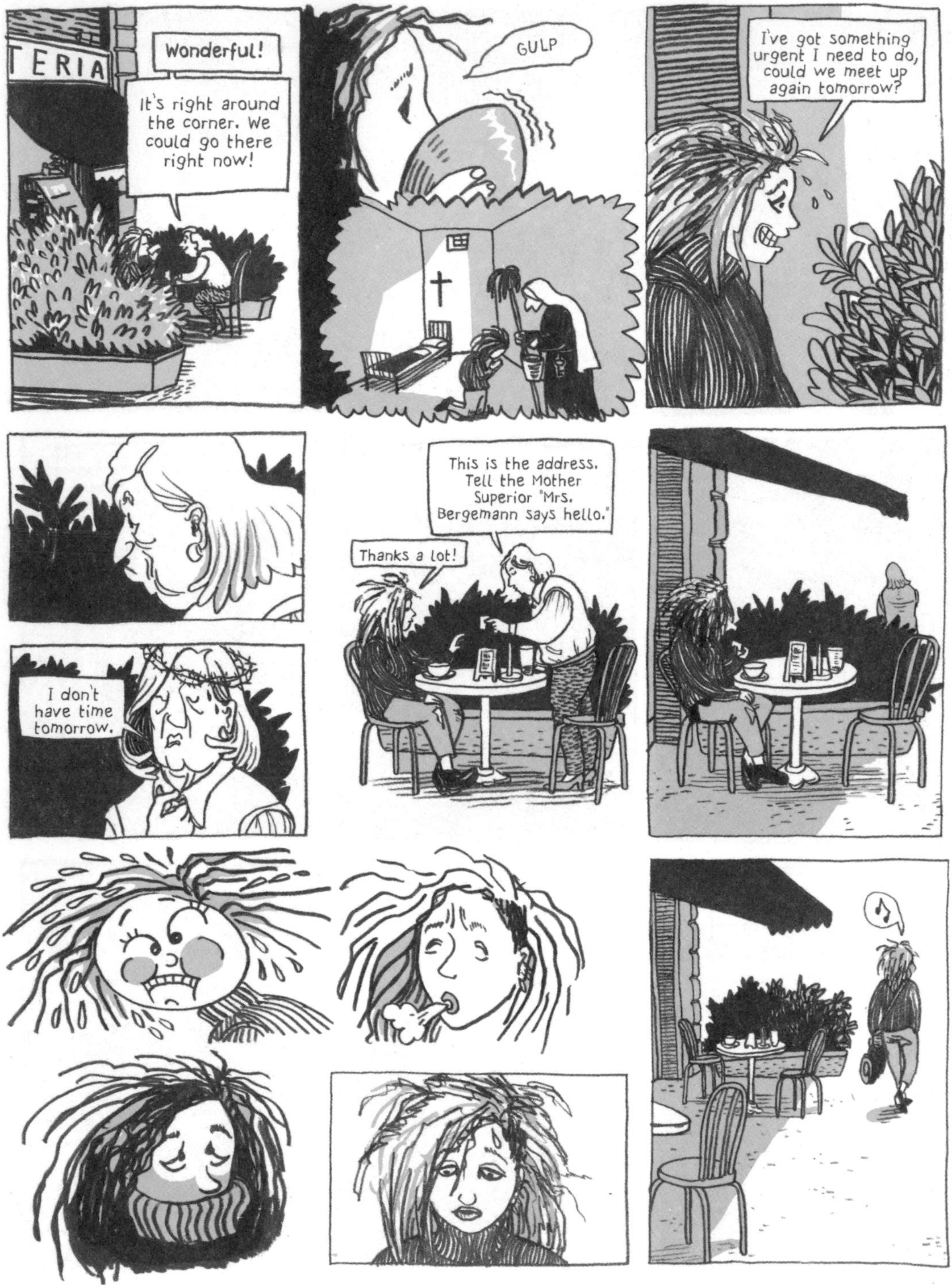

TERIA
Wonderful!
It's right around the corner. We could go there right now!
GULP
I've got something urgent I need to do, could we meet up again tomorrow?
I don't have time tomorrow.
This is the address. Tell the Mother Superior "Mrs. Bergemann says hello."
Thanks a lot!
♪

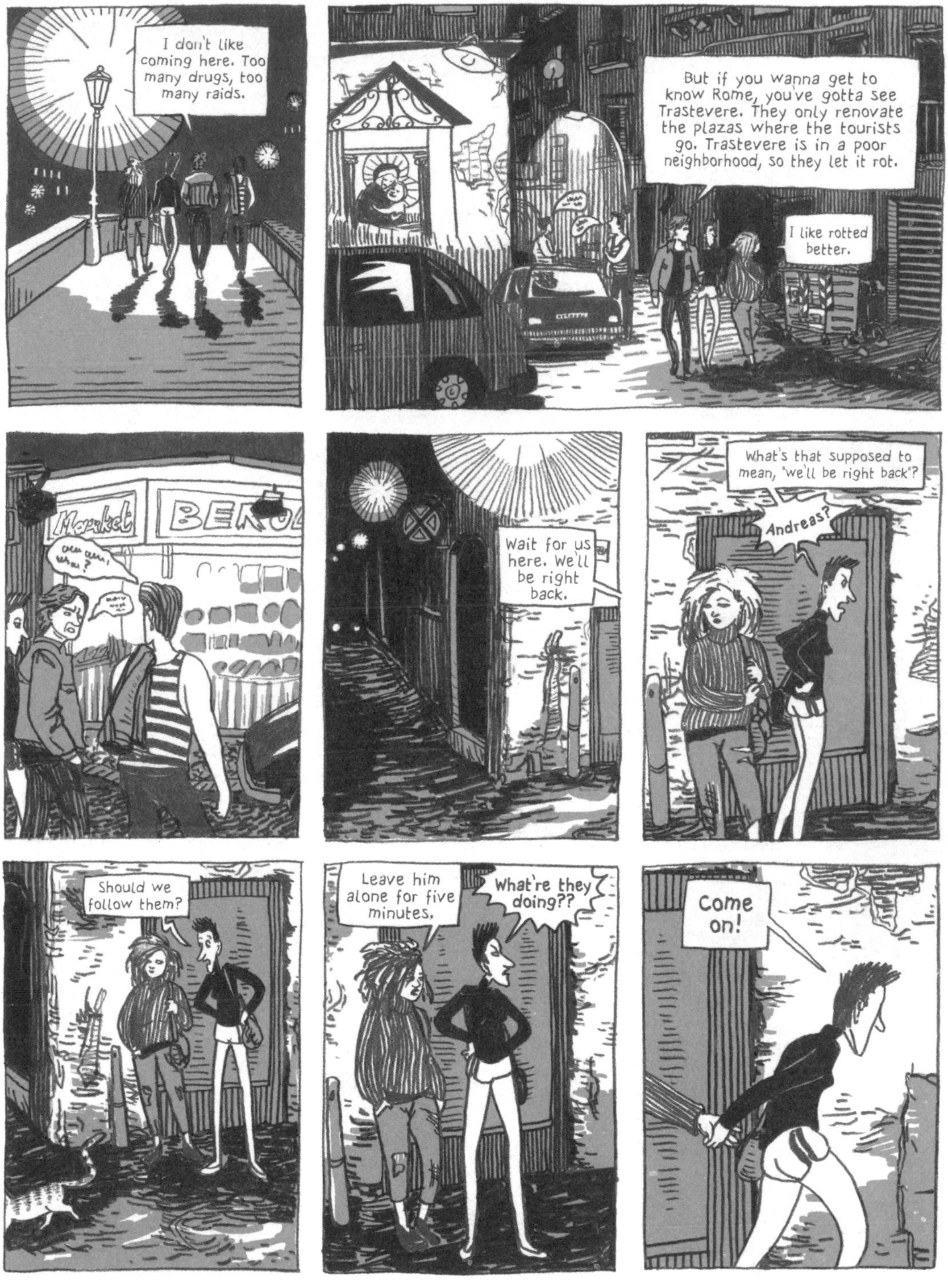
I don't like coming here. Too many drugs, too many raids.
But if you wanna get to know Rome, you've gotta see Trastevere. They only renovate the plazas where the tourists go. Trastevere is in a poor neighborhood, so they let it rot.
I like rotted better.
Market
Wait for us here. We'll be right back.
What's that supposed to mean, "we'll be right back"?
Andreas?
Should we follow them?
Leave him alone for five minutes.
What're they doing??
Come on!

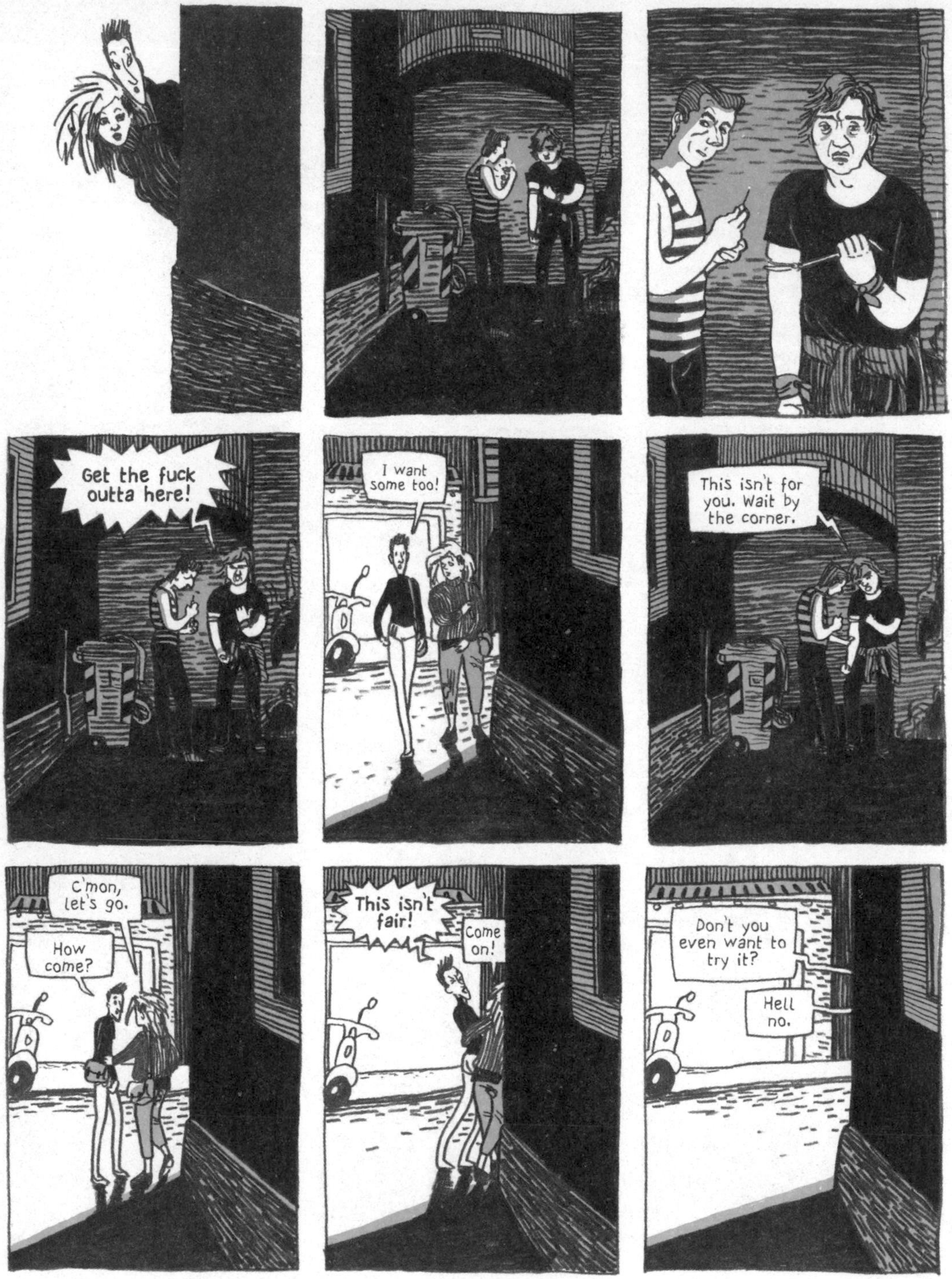
Get the fuck outta here!
I want some too!
This isn't for you. Wait by the corner.
C'mon, let's go.
How come?
This isn't fair!
Come on!
Don't you even want to try it?
Hell no.

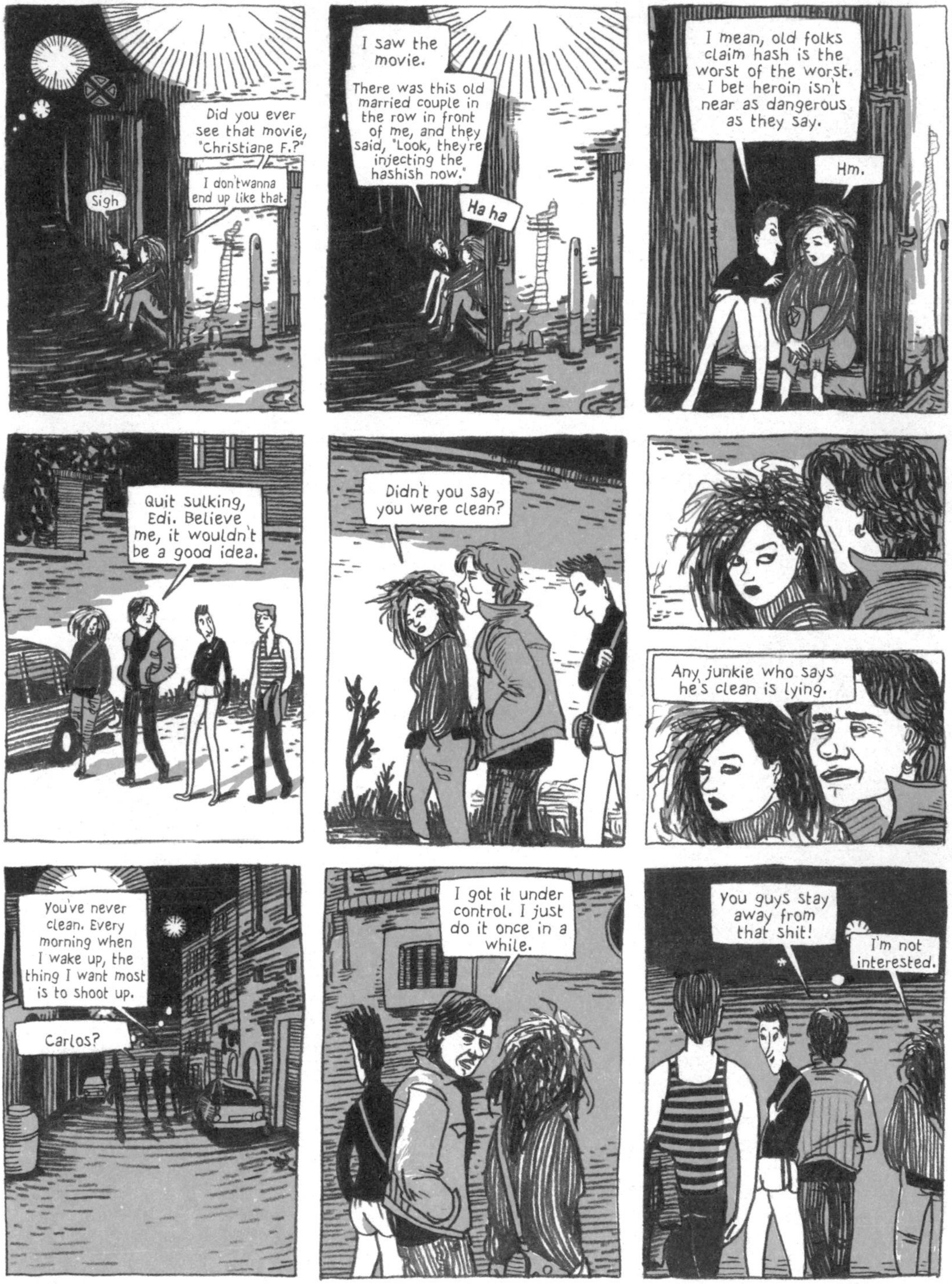

Did you ever see that movie, "Christiane F.?"
Sigh
I don'twanna end up like that.
I saw the movie.
There was this old married couple in the row in front of me, and they said, "Look, they're injecting the hashish now."
Ha ha
I mean, old folks claim hash is the worst of the worst. I bet heroin isn't near as dangerous as they say.
Hm.
Quit sulking, Edi. Believe me, it wouldn't be a good idea.
Didn't you say you were clean?
Any junkie who says he's clean is lying.
You've never clean. Every morning when I wake up, the thing I want most is to shoot up.
Carlos?
I got it under control. I just do it once in a while.
You guys stay away from that shit!
I'm not interested.

IX. the TRAP

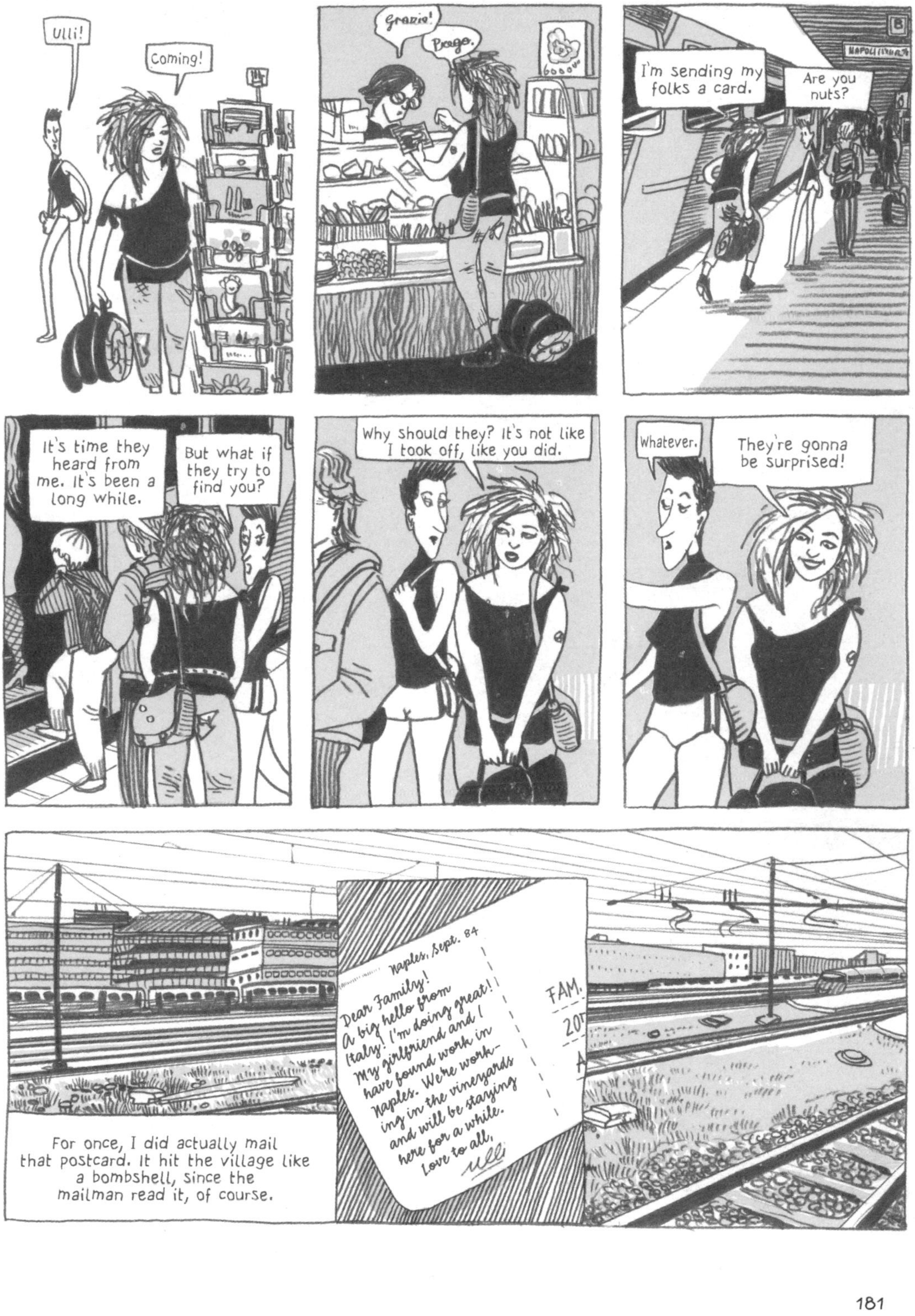
Ulli!
Coming!
Grazie!
Prego.
I'm sending my folks a card.
Are you nuts?
It's time they heard from me. It's been a long while.
But what if they try to find you?
Why should they? It's not like I took off, like you did.
Whatever.
They're gonna be surprised!
For once, I did actually mail that postcard. It hit the village like a bombshell, since the mailman read it, of course.
Naples, Sept. 84
Dear Family!
A big hello from Italy! I'm doing great! My girlfriend and I have found work in Naples. We're working in the vineyards and will be staying here for a while.
Love to all,
Ulli
FAM.

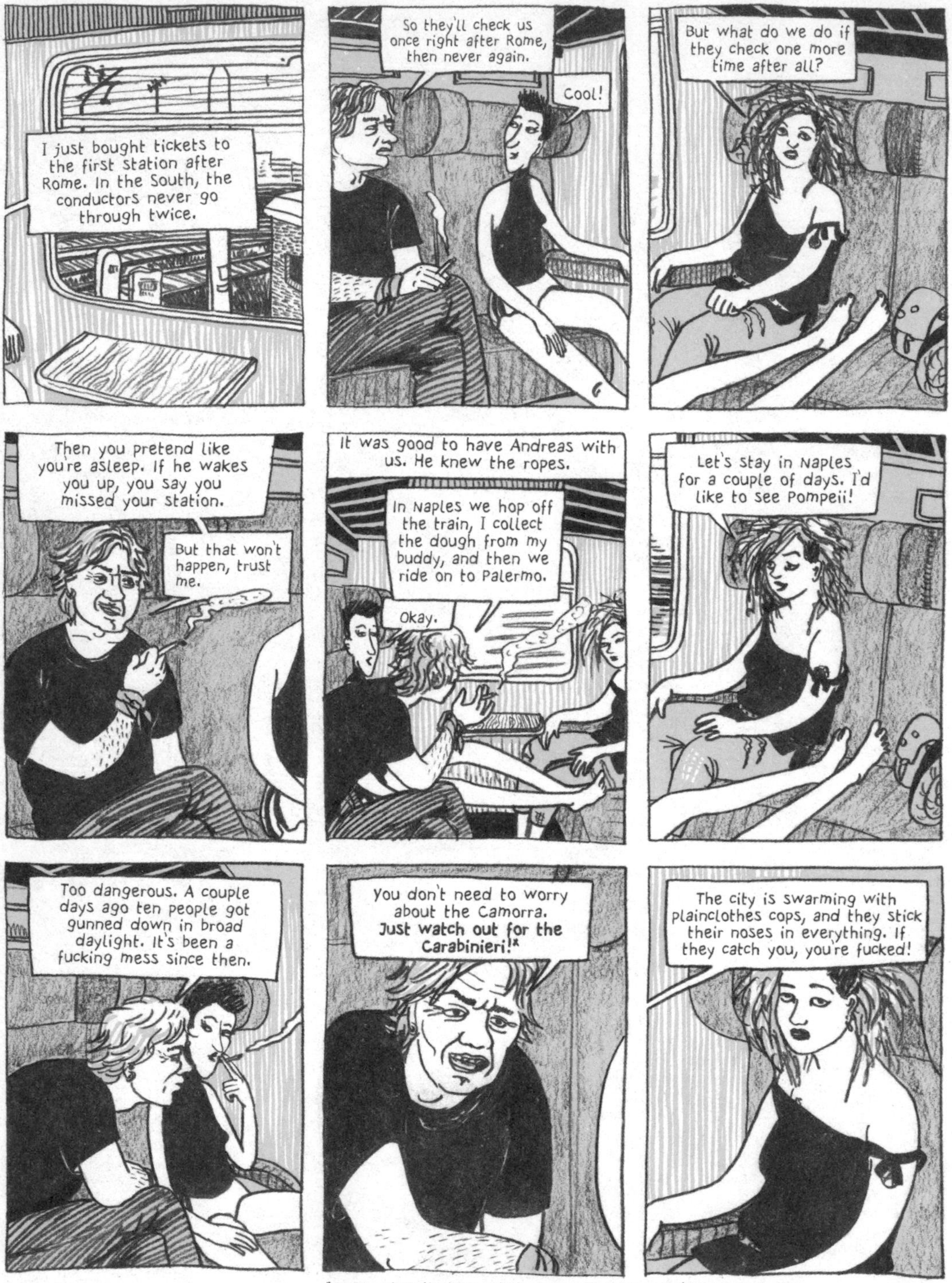
I just bought tickets to the first station after Rome. In the South, the conductors never go through twice.
So they'll check us once right after Rome, then never again.
Cool!
But what do we do if they check one more time after all?
Then you pretend like you're asleep. If he wakes you up, you say you missed your station.
But that won't happen, trust me.
It was good to have Andreas with us. He knew the ropes.
In Naples we hop off the train, I collect the dough from my buddy, and then we ride on to Palermo.
Okay.
Let's stay in Naples for a couple of days. I'd like to see Pompeii!
Too dangerous. A couple days ago ten people got gunned down in broad daylight. It's been a fucking mess since then.
You don't need to worry about the Camorra. Just watch out for the Carabinieri!*
The city is swarming with plainclothes cops, and they stick their noses in everything. If they catch you, you're fucked!

*Camorra: Mafia-type criminal organization. Carabinieri: Policemen.

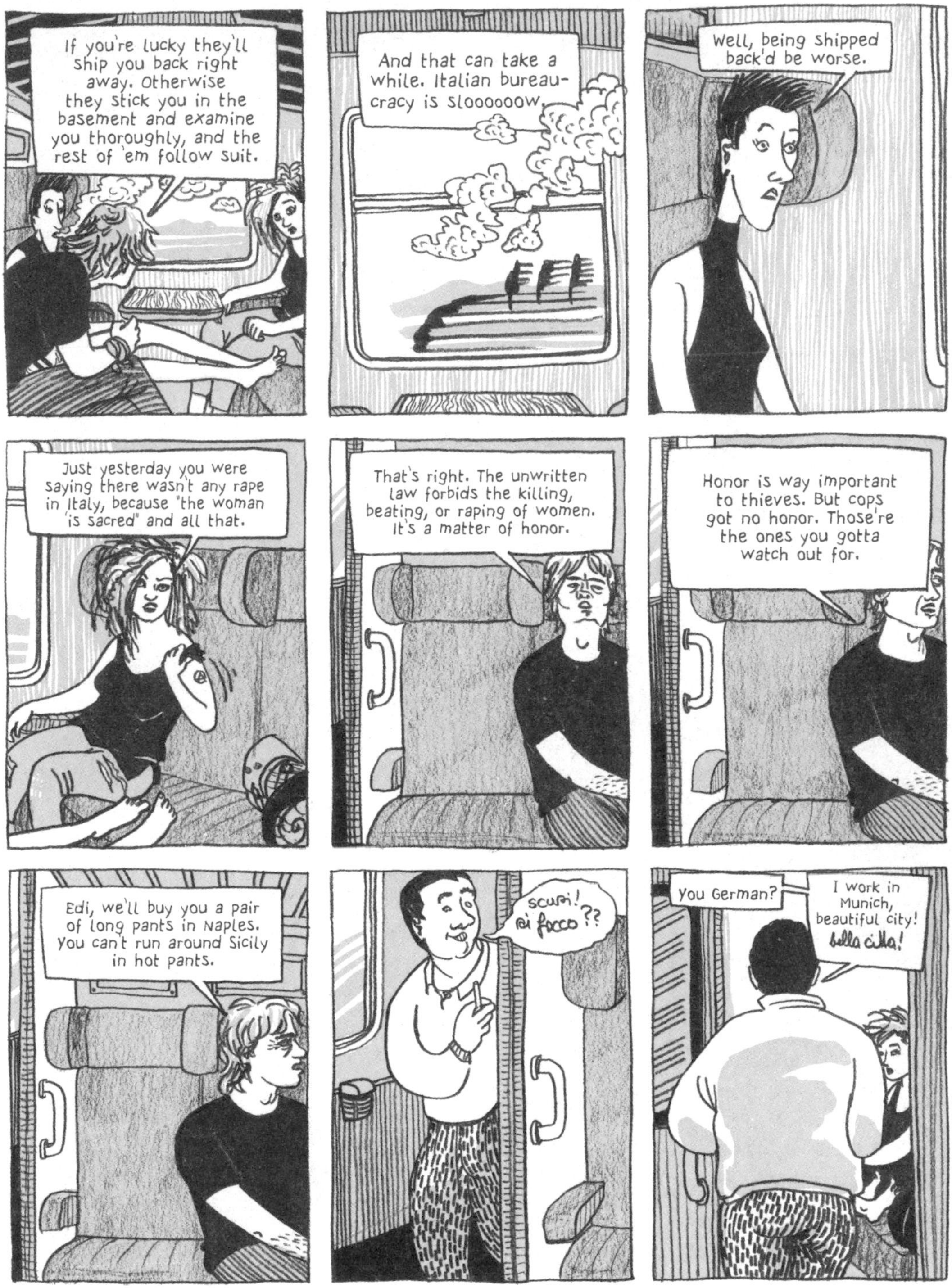
If you're lucky they'll ship you back right away. Otherwise they stick you in the basement and examine you thoroughly, and the rest of 'em follow suit.
And that can take a while. Italian bureaucracy is slooooow.
Well, being shipped back'd be worse.
Just yesterday you were saying there wasn't any rape in Italy, because "the woman is sacred" and all that.
That's right. The unwritten law forbids the killing, beating, or raping of women. It's a matter of honor.
Honor is way important to thieves. But cops got no honor. Those're the ones you gotta watch out for.
Edi, we'll buy you a pair of long pants in Naples. You can't run around Sicily in hot pants.
scusi! ci fosse??
You German?
I work in Munich, beautiful city! bella citta!

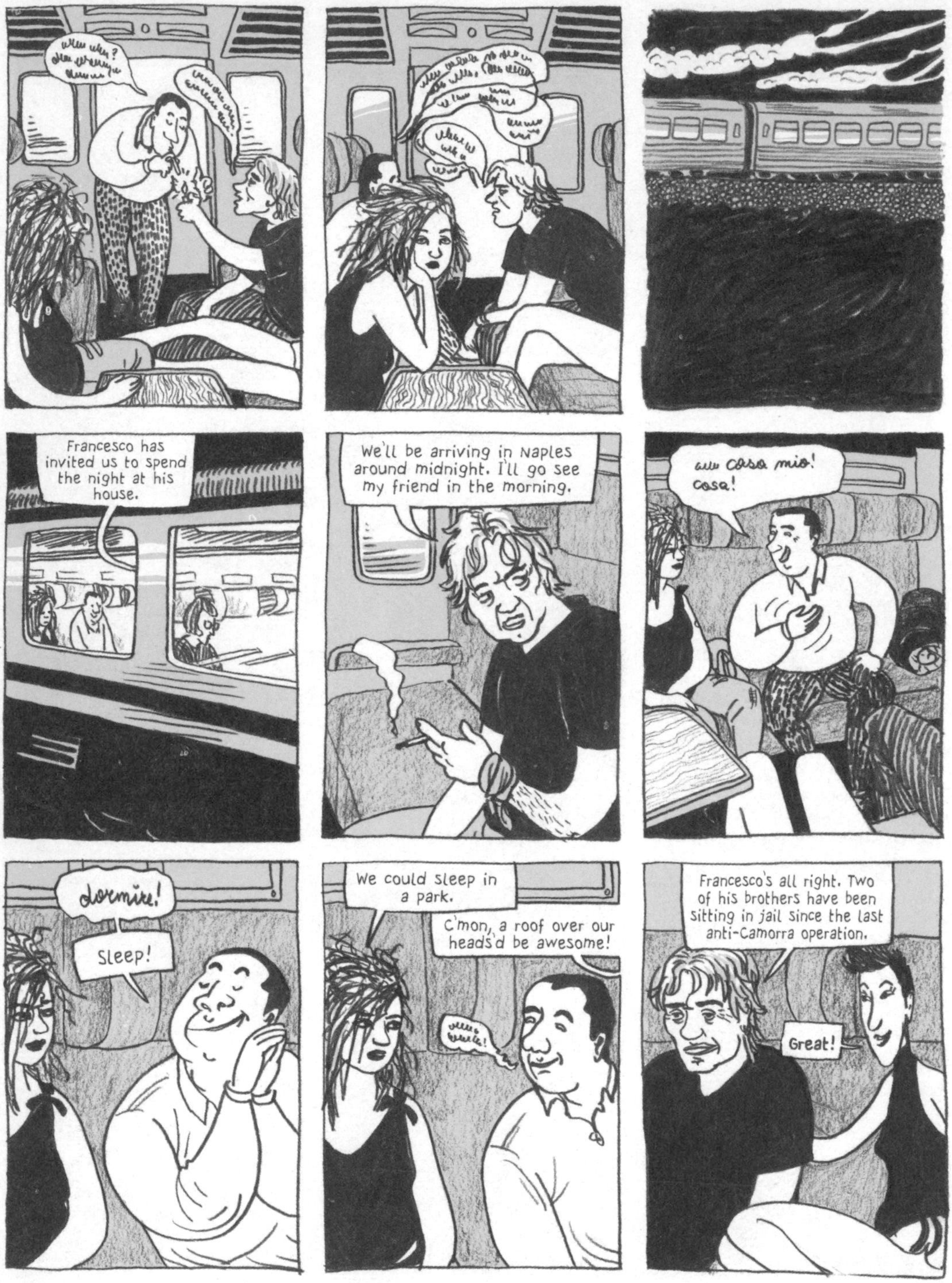
Francesco has invited us to spend the night at his house.
We'll be arriving in Naples around midnight. I'll go see my friend in the morning.
casa mia! casa!
dormire!
Sleep!
We could sleep in a park.
C'mon, a roof over our heads'd be awesome!
Francesco's all right. Two of his brothers have been sitting in jail since the last anti-Camorra operation.
Great!

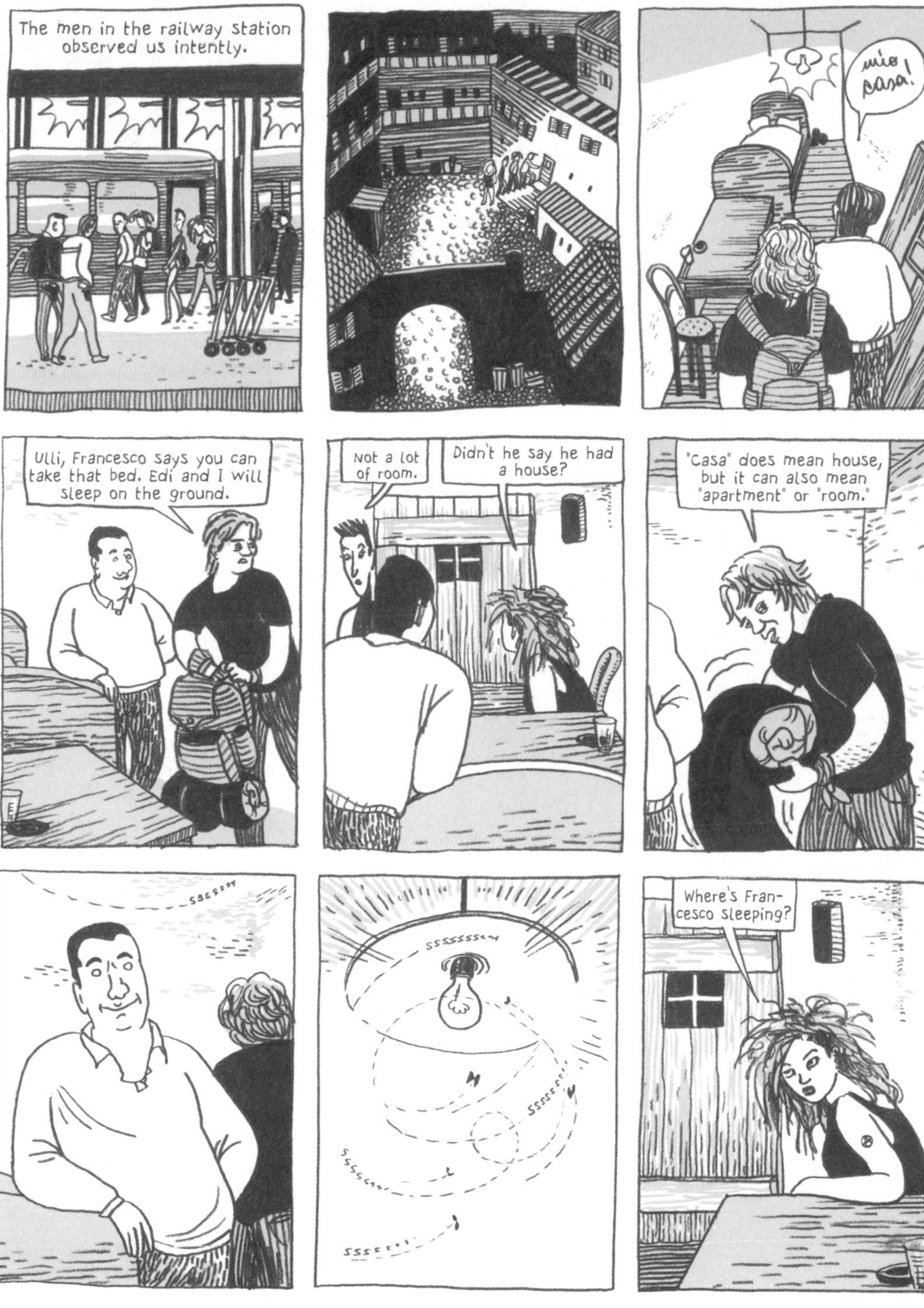
The men in the railway station observed us intently.
mia casa!
Ulli, Francesco says you can take that bed. Edi and I will sleep on the ground.
Not a lot of room.
Didn't he say he had a house?
"Casa" does mean house, but it can also mean "apartment" or "room."
Where's Francesco sleeping?

I want to sleep!

I'll go sleep on the floor.

No, no, stay!

Sleep!

Half asleep, I heard Andreas say, "Ulli, I'm gonna go collect the money with Edi. You can keep on sleeping, I set up a rendezvous with Francesco."

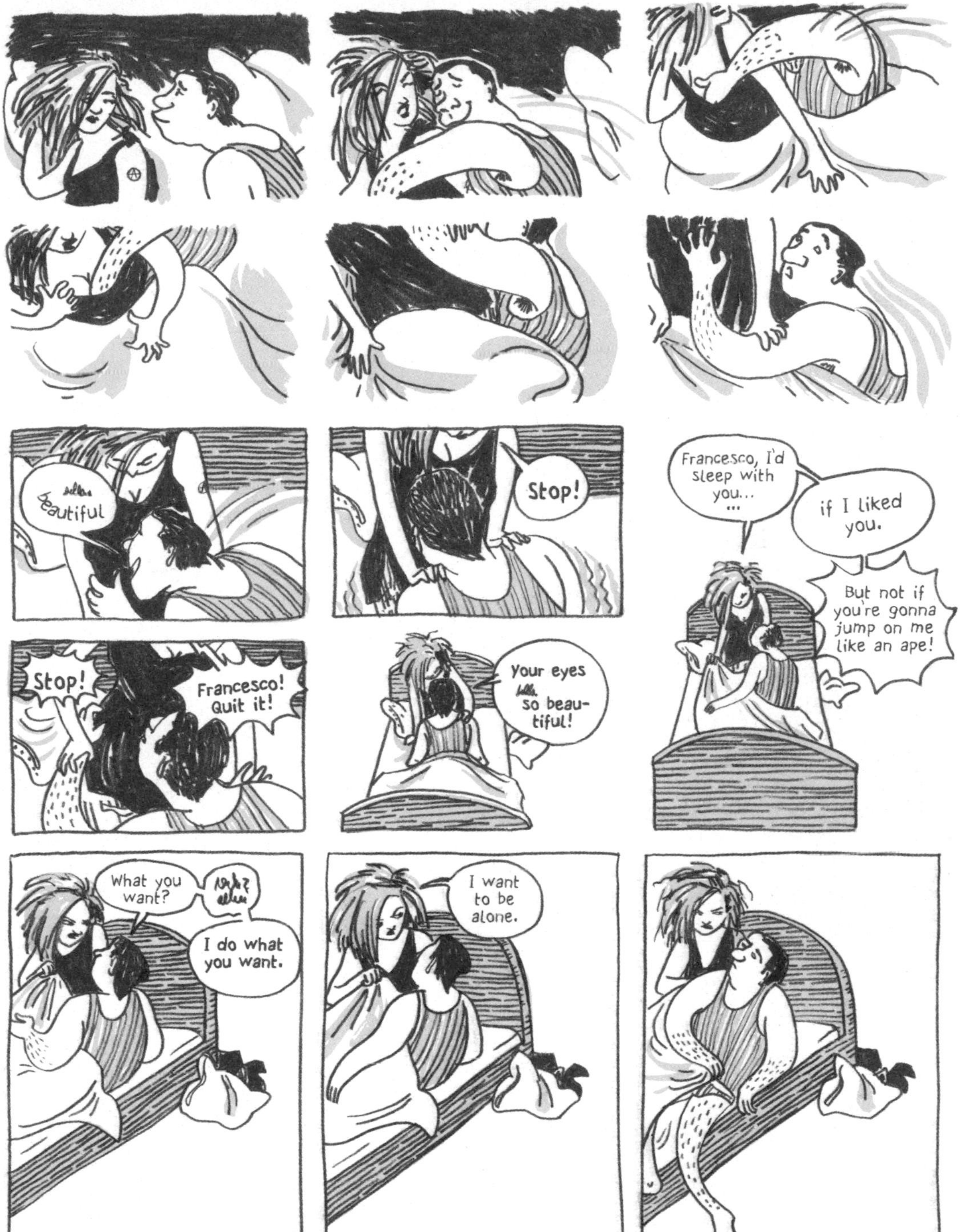
beautiful
Stop!
Francesco, I'd sleep with you... ...
if I liked you.
But not if you're gonna jump on me like an ape!
Stop!
Francesco! Quit it!
Your eyes so beau-tiful!
What you want?
I do what you want.
I want to be alone.

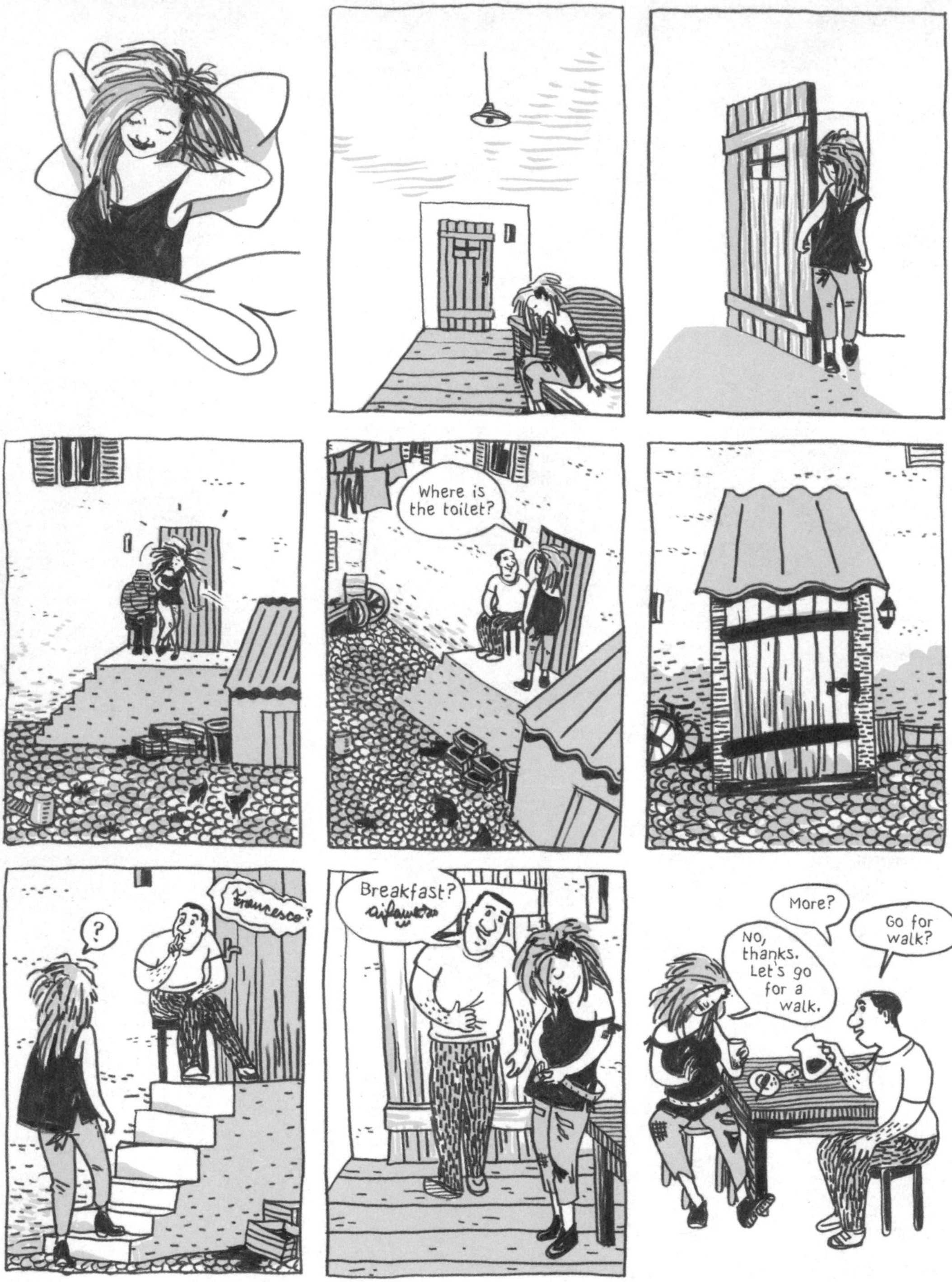
Where is the toilet?
?
Francesco?
Breakfast?
More?
No, thanks. Let's go for a walk.
Go for walk?

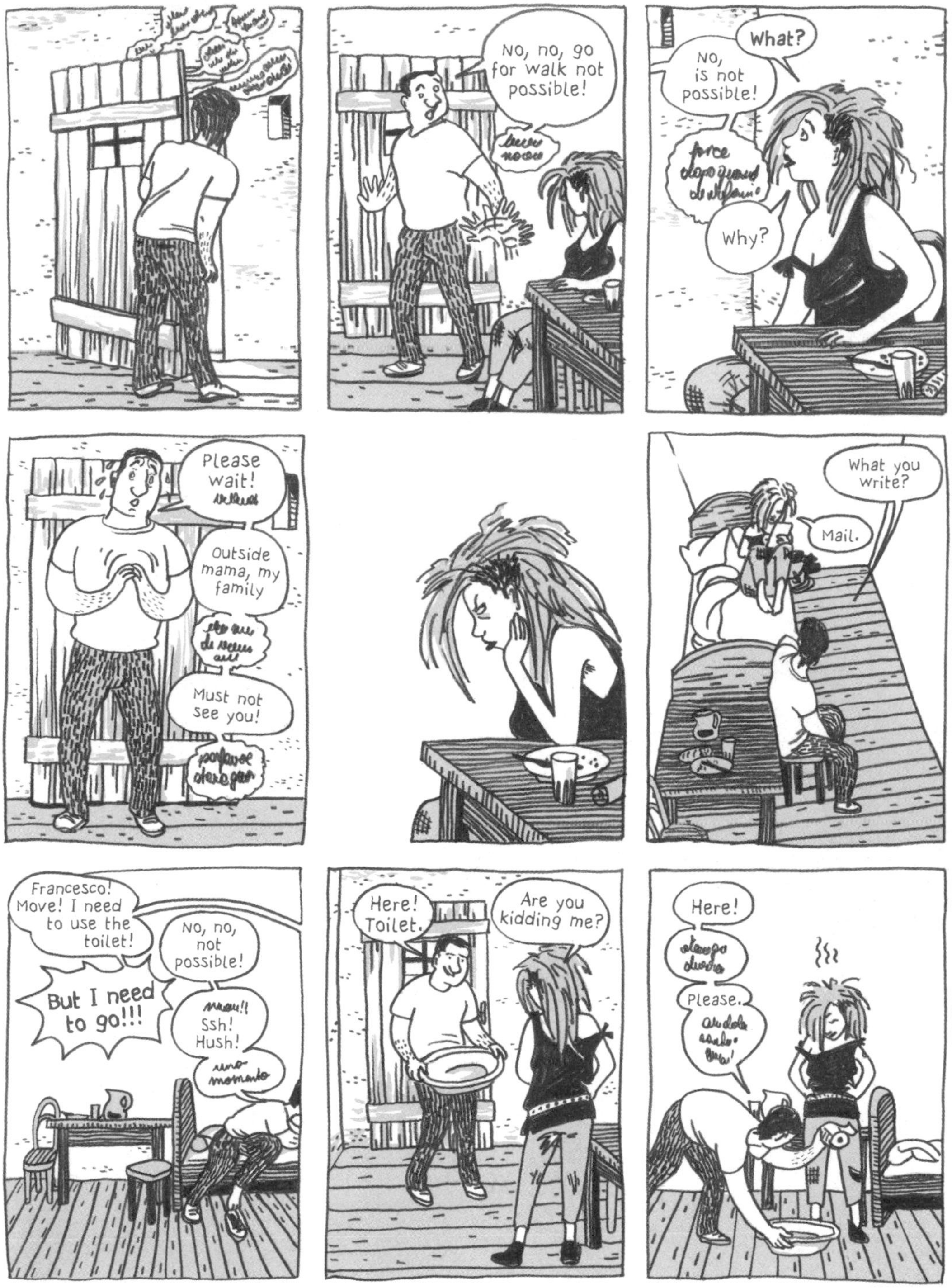
No, no, go for walk not possible!
What?
No, is not possible!
Why?
Please wait!
Outside mama, my family
Must not see you!
What you write?
Mail.
Francesco! Move! I need to use the toilet!
No, no, not possible!
But I need to go!!!
Ssh! Hush!
Here! Toilet.
Are you kidding me?
Here!
Please.

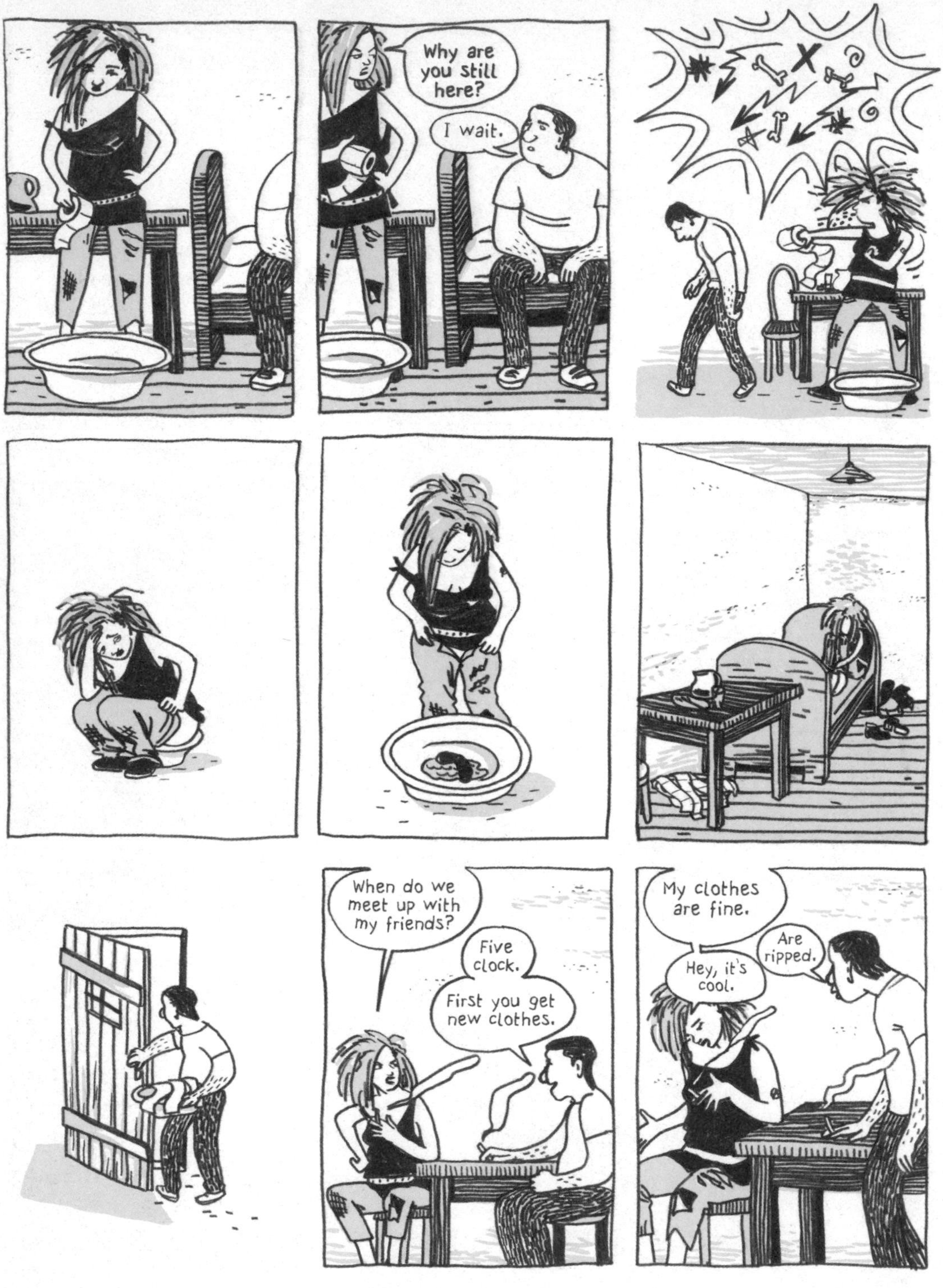
Why are you still here?
I wait.
When do we meet up with my friends?
Five clock.
First you get new clothes.
My clothes are fine.
Hey, it's cool.
Are ripped.

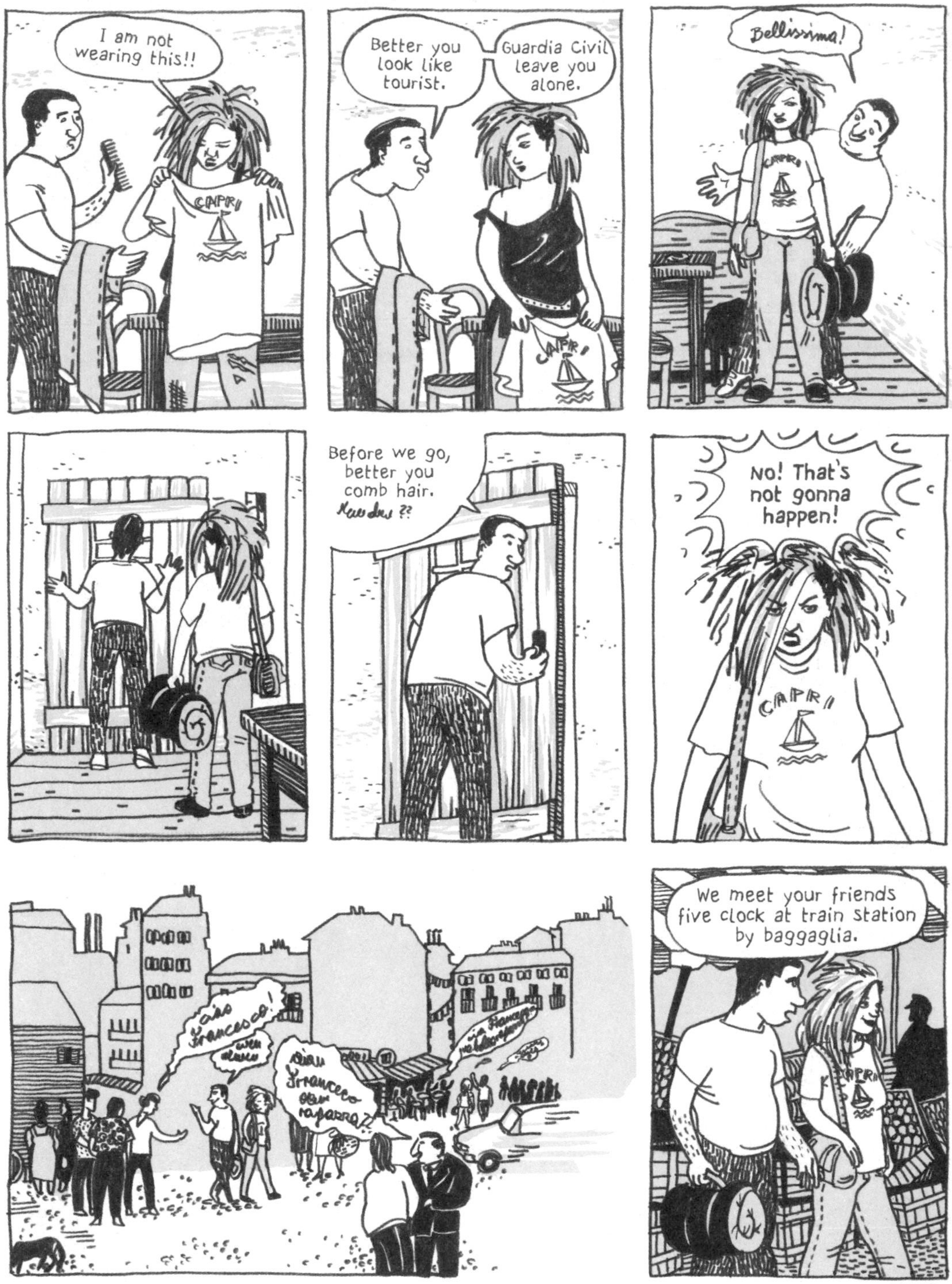
I am not wearing this!!
Better you look like tourist.
Guardia Civil leave you alone.
CAPRI
Bellissima!
Before we go, better you comb hair.
No! That's not gonna happen!
CAPRI
Ciao Francesco!
We meet your friends five clock at train station by baggaglia.

BAGGAGLIA
BAGGAGLIA
I look outside for your friends.
Wait here.
5 o'clock.
BAGGAGLIA
I hope nothing happened to them.

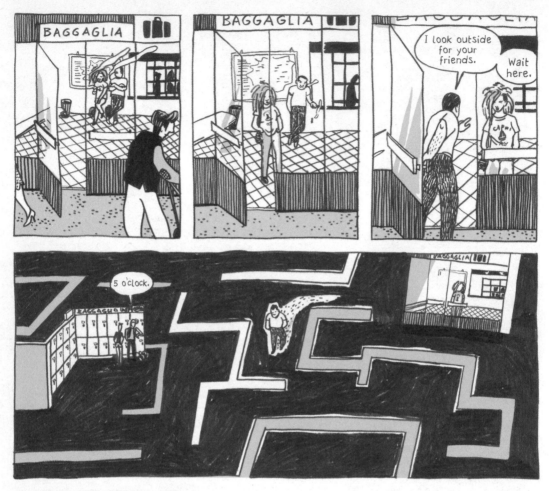

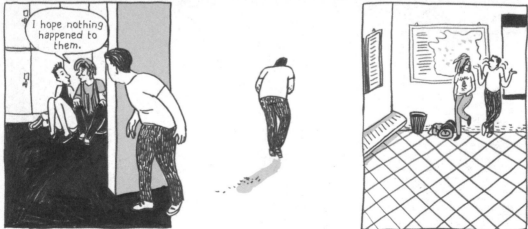

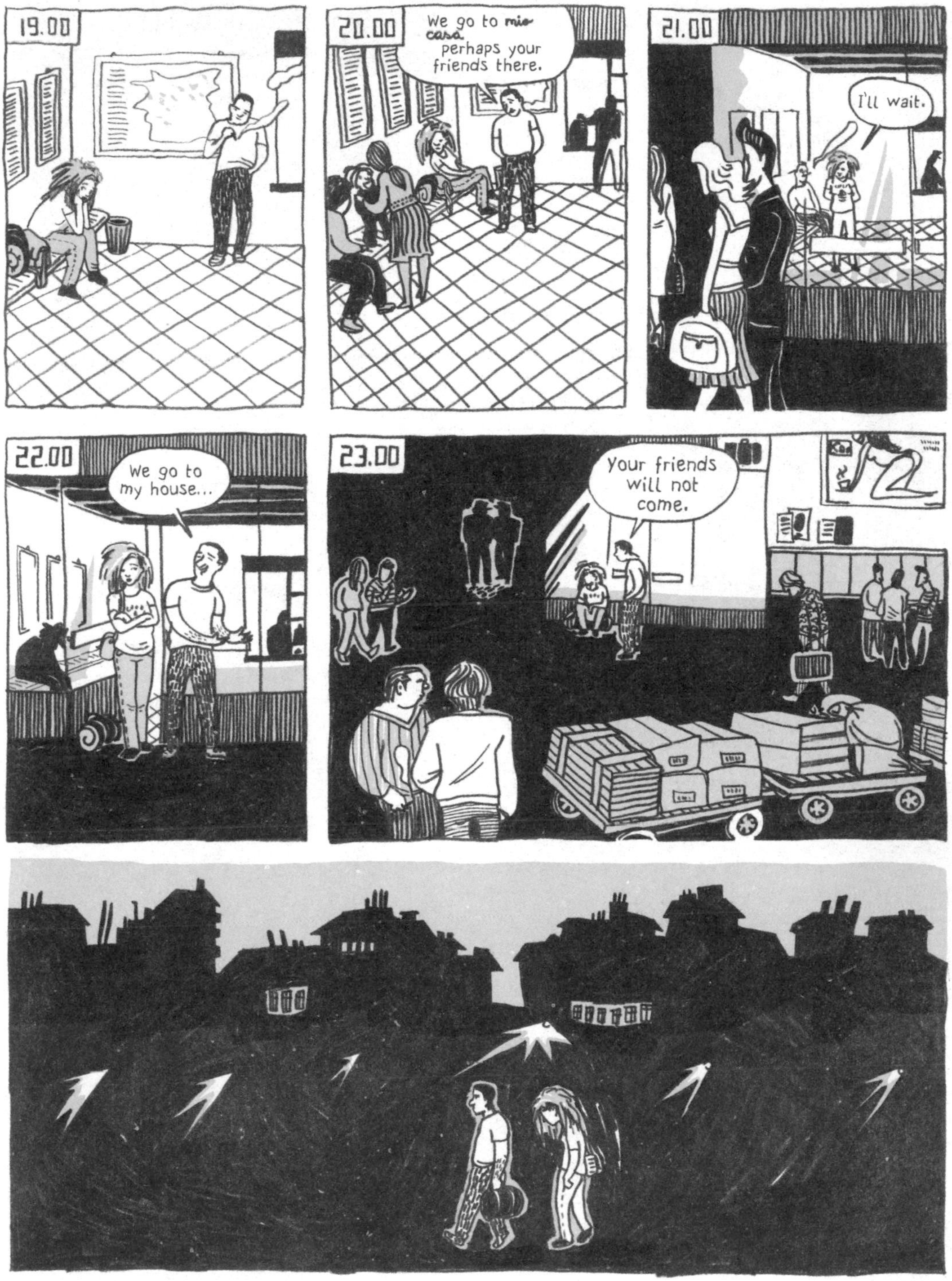
19.00
20.00
We go to mio casa perhaps your friends there.
21.00
I'll wait.
22.00
We go to my house...
23.00
Your friends will not come.

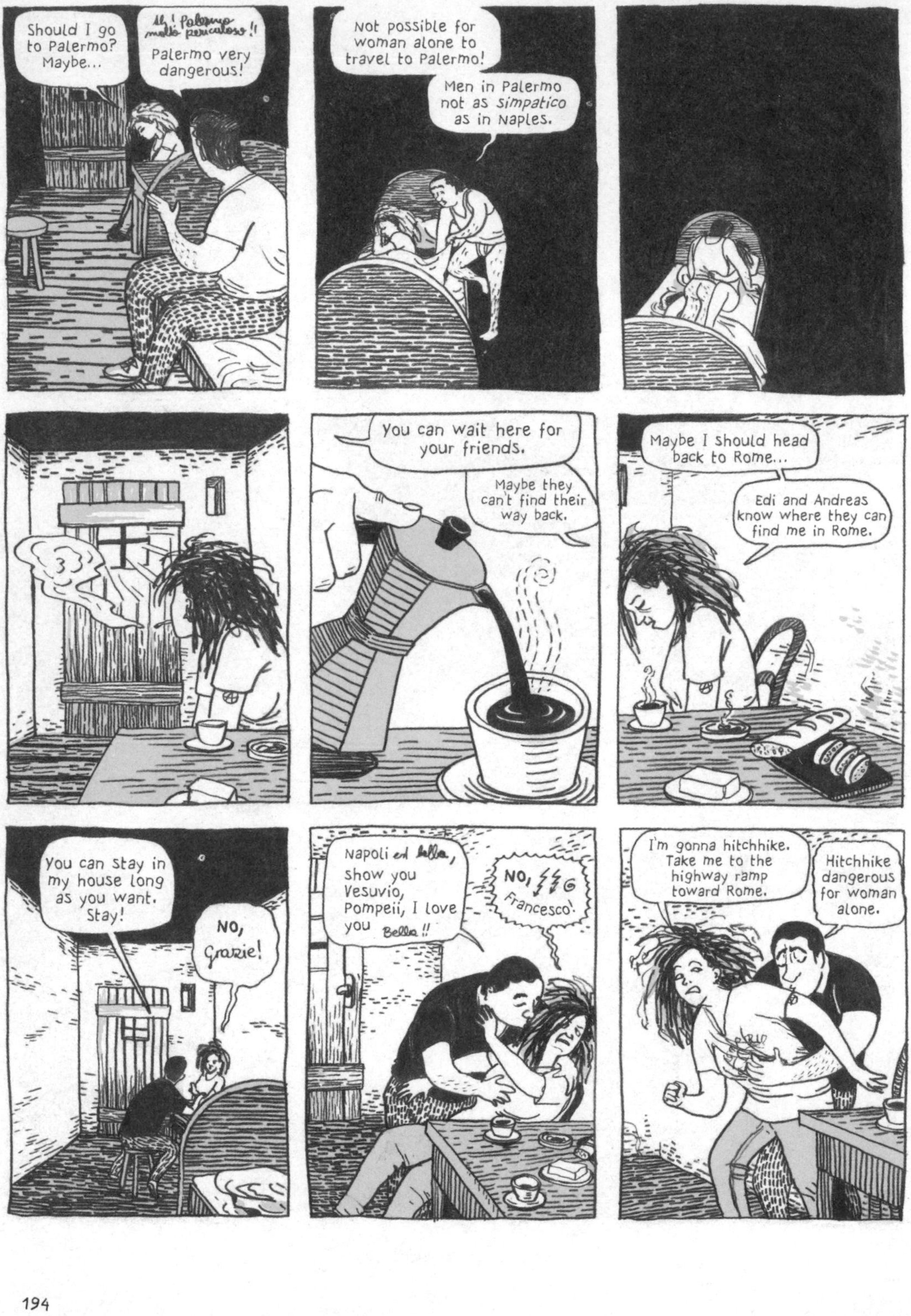
Should I go to Palermo? Maybe...
Ah! Palermo moltò pericoloso!!
Palermo very dangerous!
Not possible for woman alone to travel to Palermo!
Men in Palermo not as *simpatico* as in Naples.
You can wait here for your friends.
Maybe they can't find their way back.
Maybe I should head back to Rome...
Edi and Andreas know where they can find me in Rome.
You can stay in my house long as you want. Stay!
NO, Grazie!
Napoli ed bella, show you Vesuvio, Pompeii, I love you Bella!!
NO, Francesco!
I'm gonna hitchhike. Take me to the highway ramp toward Rome.
Hitchhike dangerous for woman alone.

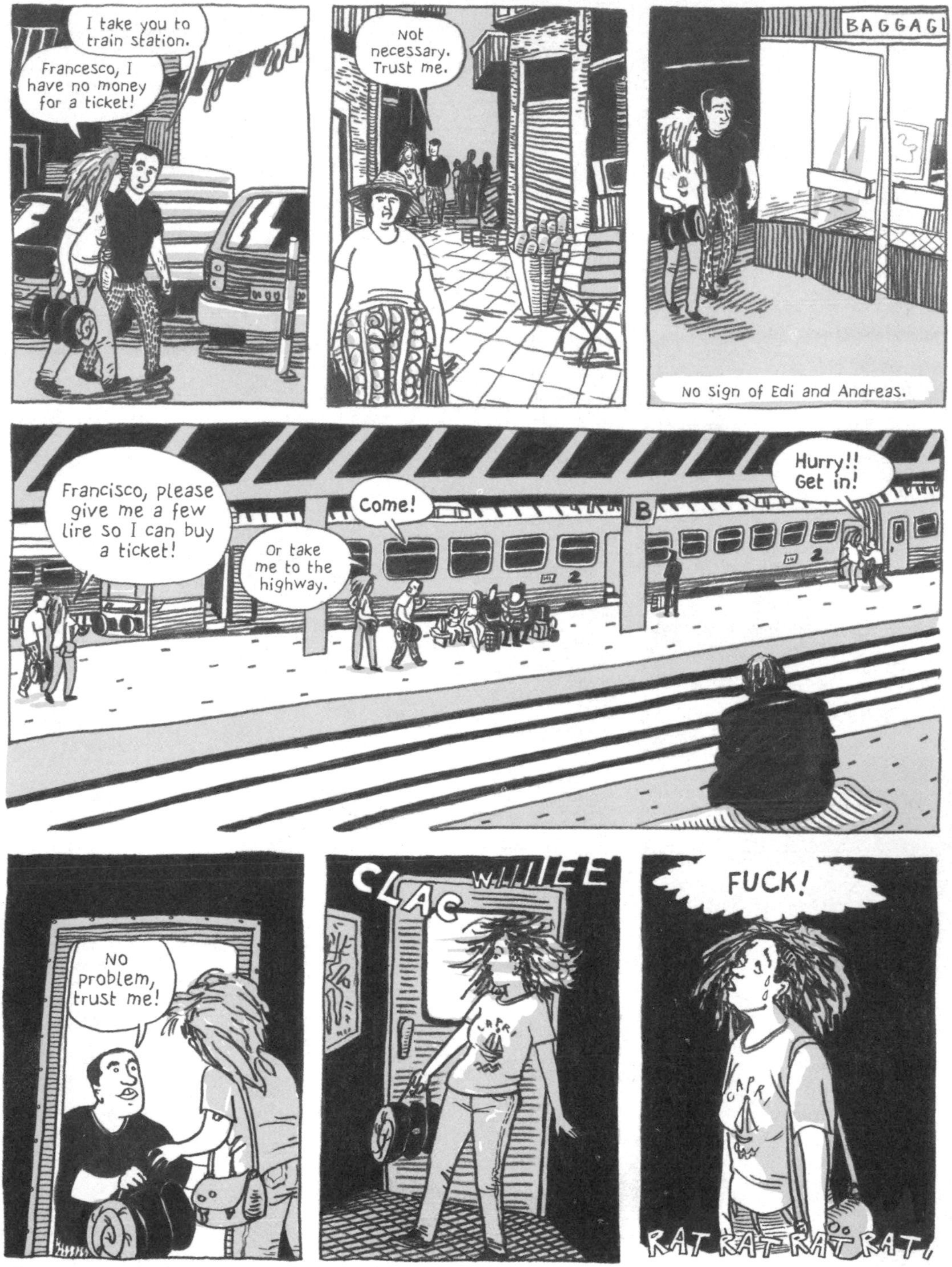
I take you to train station.
Francesco, I have no money for a ticket!
Not necessary. Trust me.
BAGGAGL
No sign of Edi and Andreas.
Francisco, please give me a few lire so I can buy a ticket!
Or take me to the highway.
Come!
B
Hurry!! Get in!
No problem, trust me!
CLAC
WIIIEE
FUCK!
RAT RAT RAT RAT

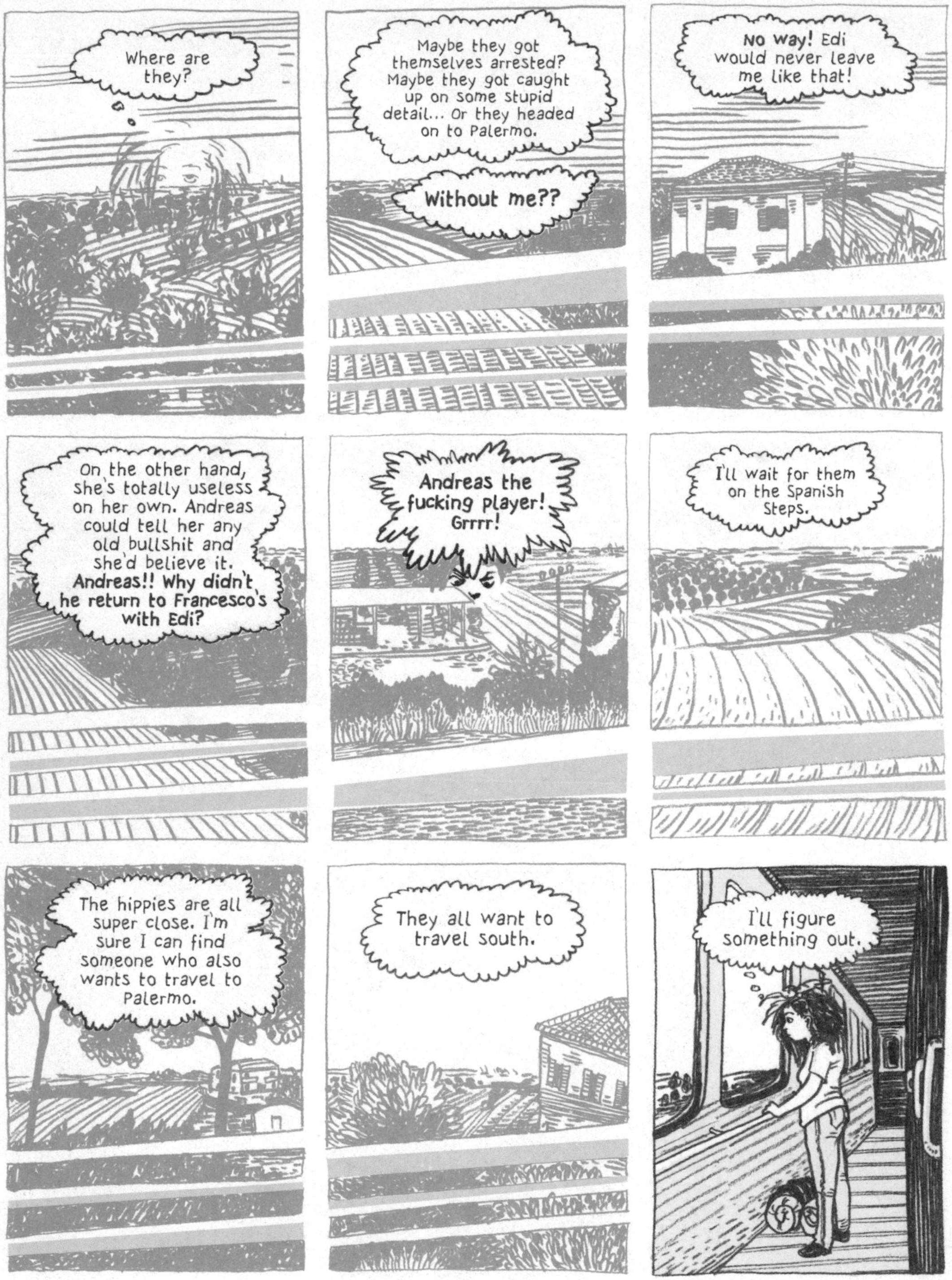
Where are they?
Maybe they got themselves arrested? Maybe they got caught up on some stupid detail... Or they headed on to Palermo.
Without me??
No way! Edi would never leave me like that!
On the other hand, she's totally useless on her own. Andreas could tell her any old bullshit and she'd believe it. Andreas!! Why didn't he return to Francesco's with Edi?
Andreas the fucking player! Grrrr!
I'll wait for them on the Spanish Steps.
The hippies are all super close. I'm sure I can find someone who also wants to travel to Palermo.
They all want to travel south.
I'll figure something out.

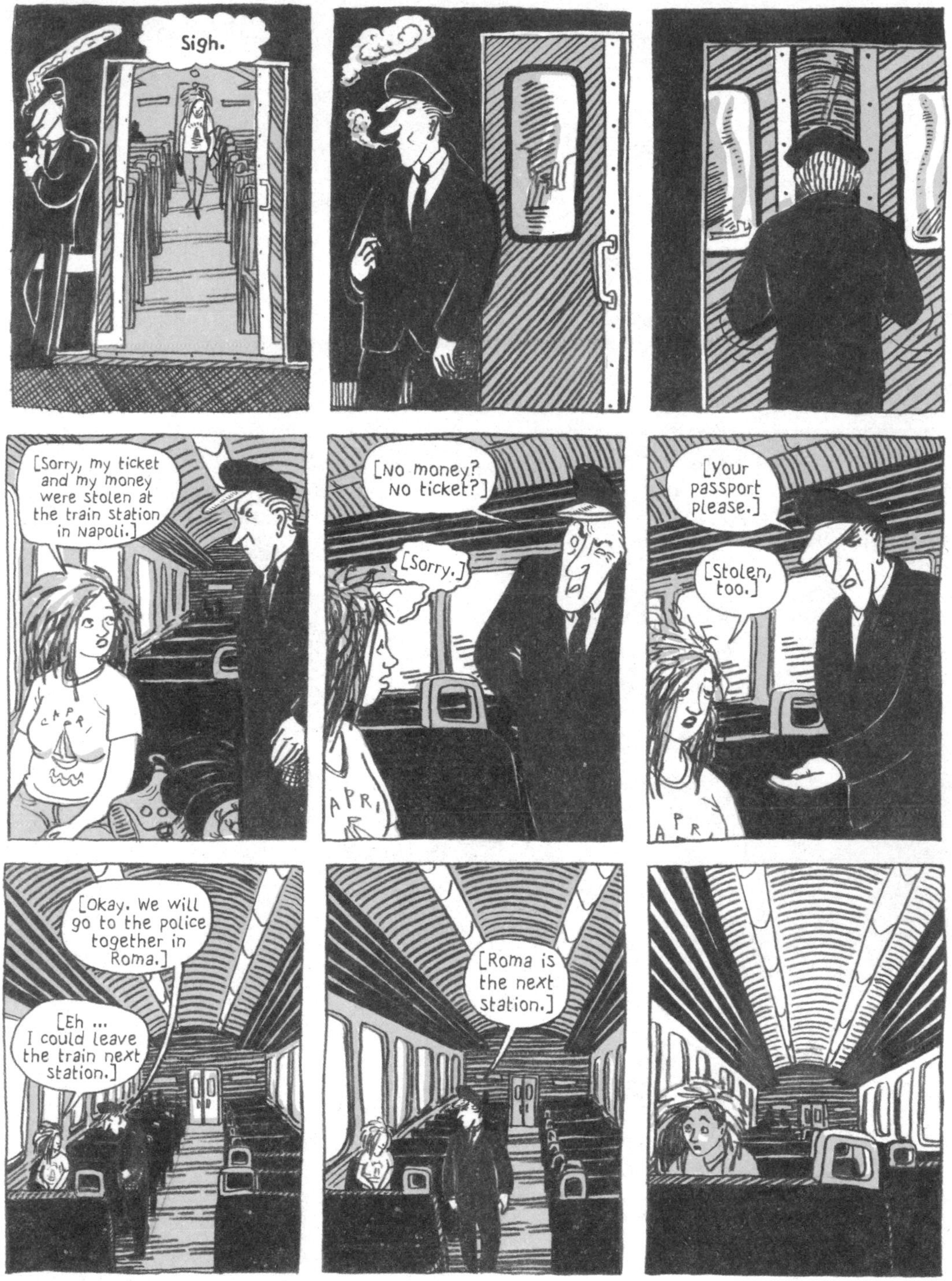
Sigh.
[Sorry, my ticket and my money were stolen at the train station in Napoli.]
[No money? No ticket?]
[Sorry.]
[Your passport please.]
[Stolen, too.]
[Okay. We will go to the police together in Roma.]
[Eh ... I could leave the train next station.]
[Roma is the next station.]

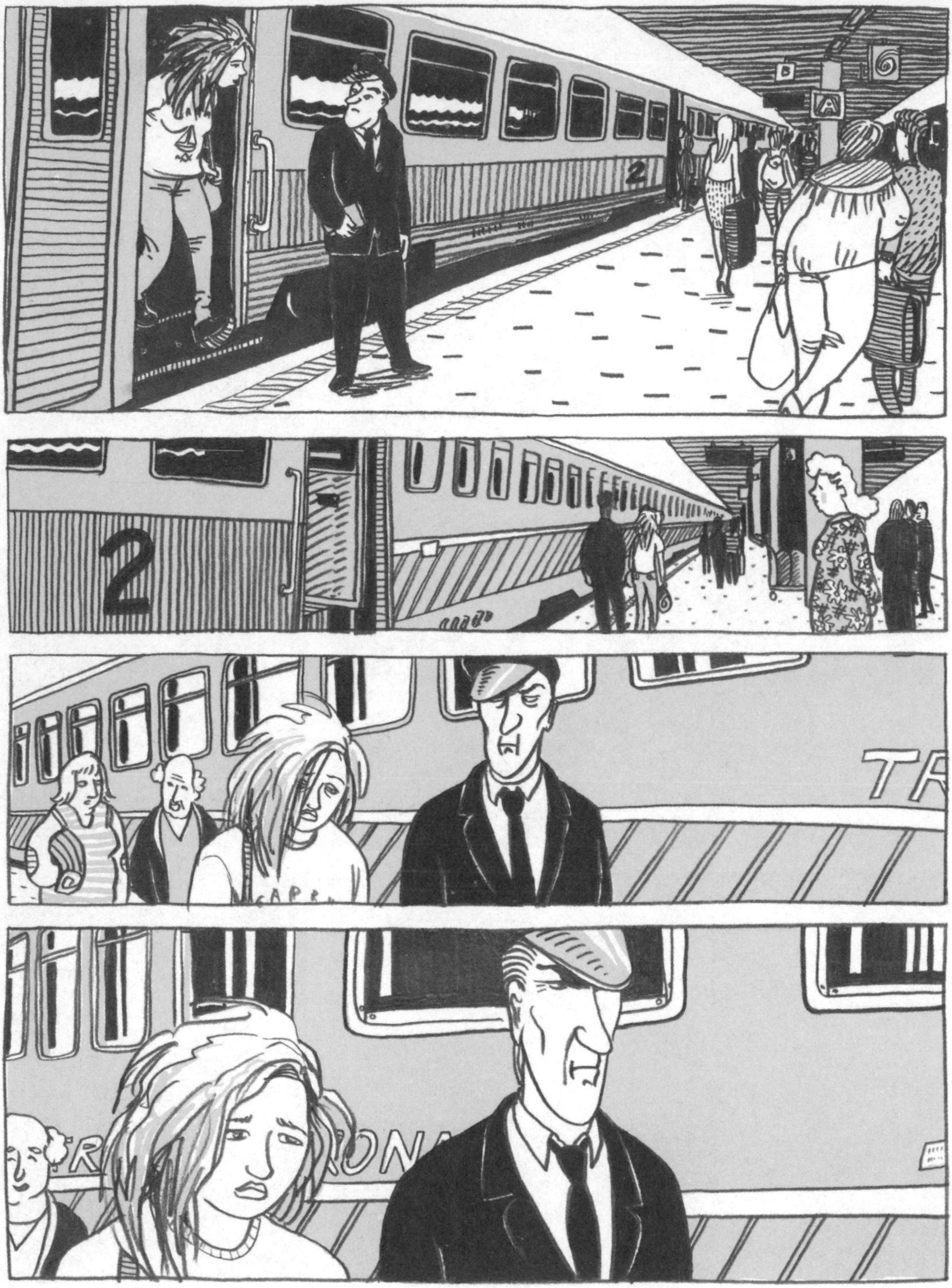
2

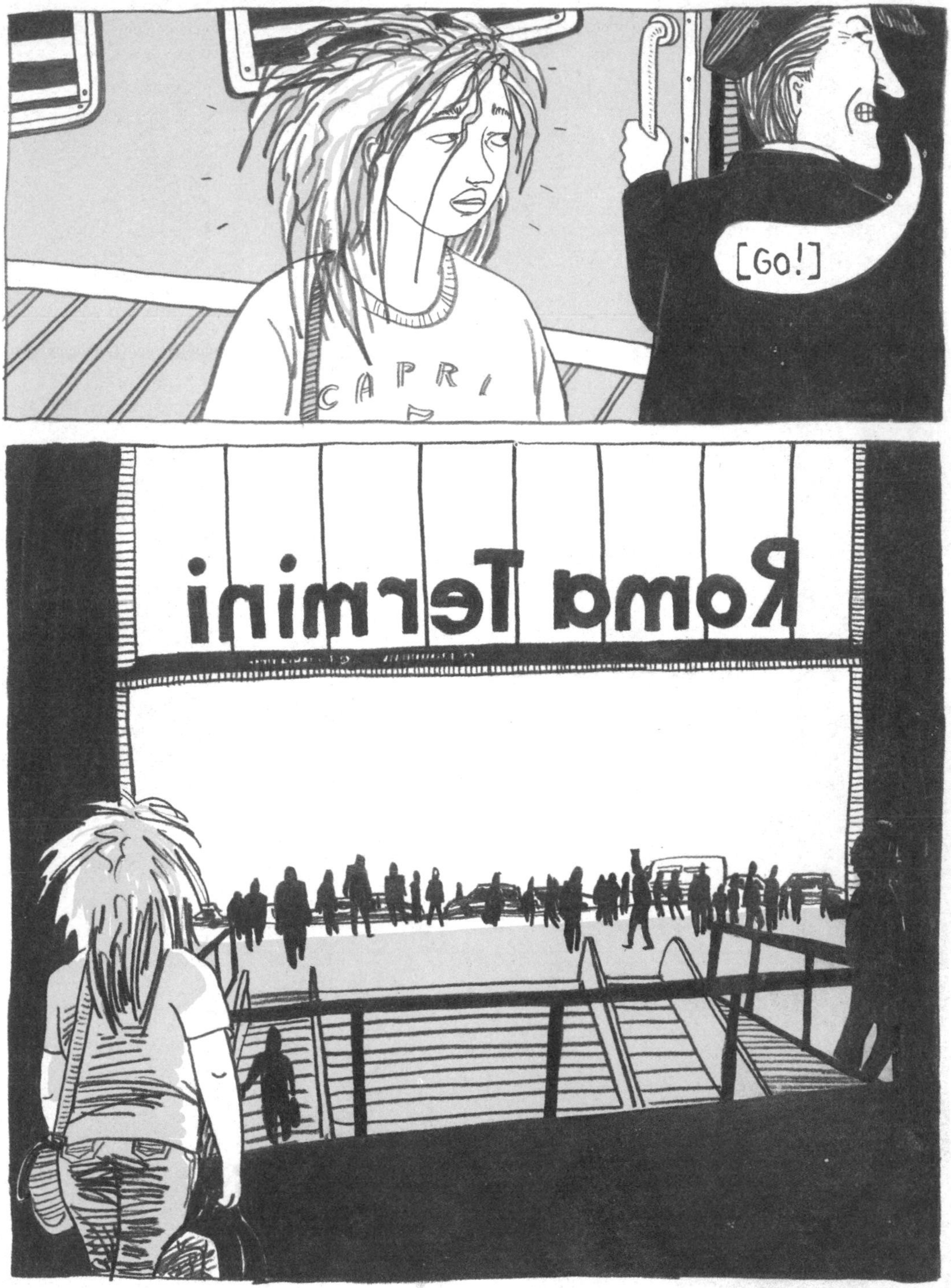
CAPRI
[Go!]
Roma Termini

X. the MIGRATORS

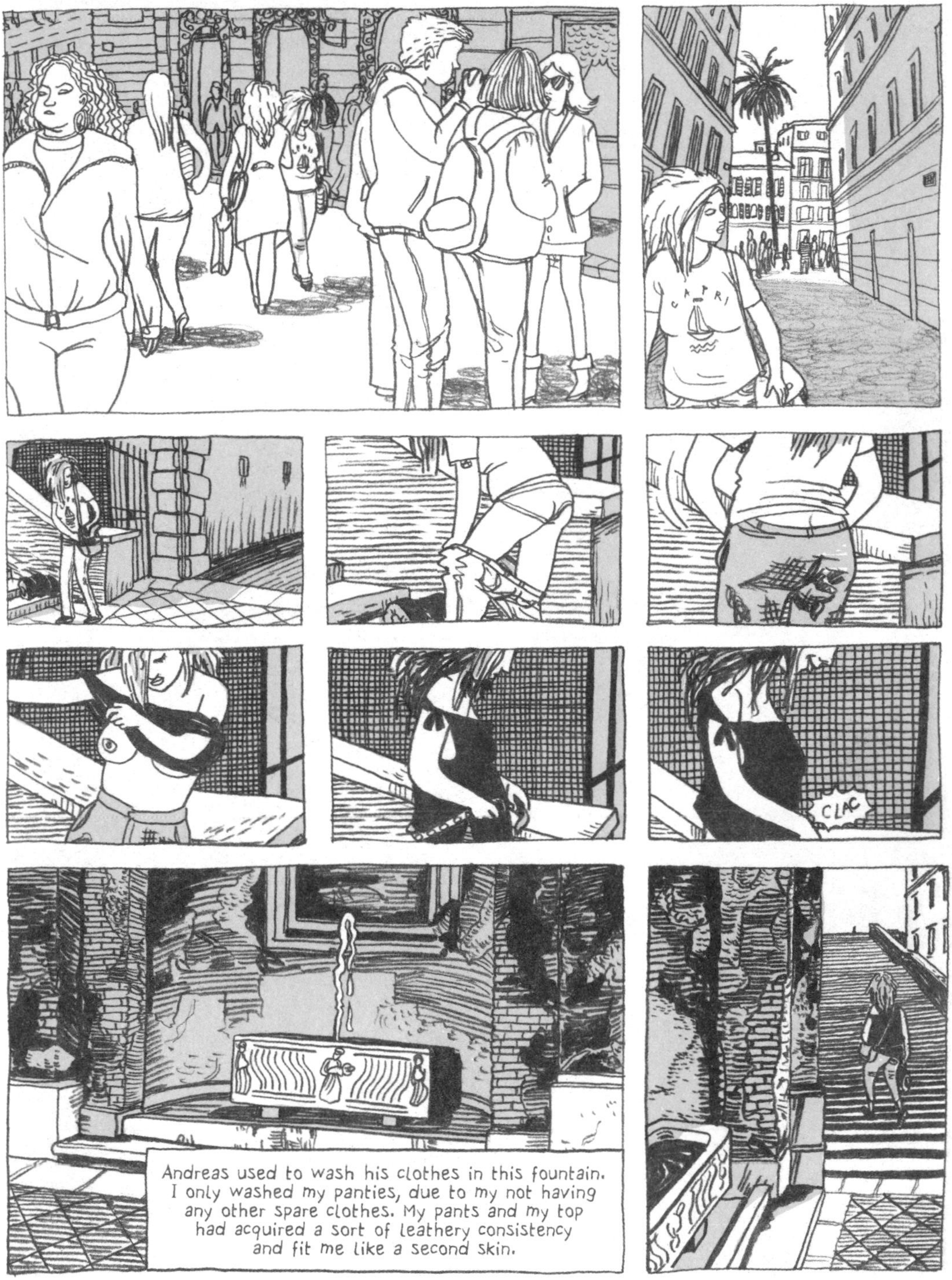
CAPRI
CLAC
Andreas used to wash his clothes in this fountain. I only washed my panties, due to my not having any other spare clothes. My pants and my top had acquired a sort of leathery consistency and fit me like a second skin.

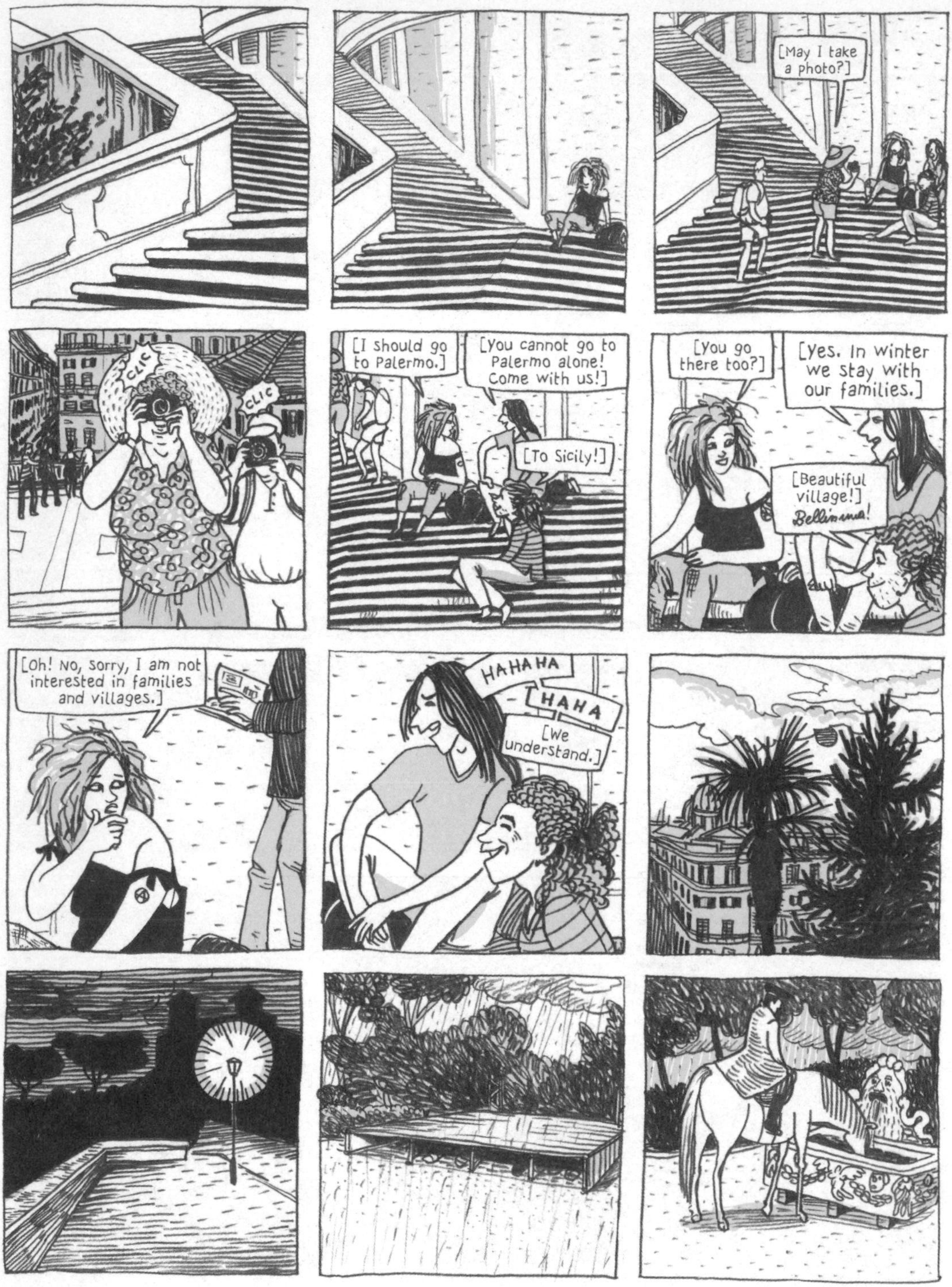
[May I take a photo?]
CLIC
CLIC
[I should go to Palermo.]
[You cannot go to Palermo alone! Come with us!]
[To Sicily!]
[You go there too?]
[Yes. In winter we stay with our families.]
[Beautiful village!]
Bellissima!
[Oh! No, sorry, I am not interested in families and villages.]
HAHAHA
HAHA
[We understand.]

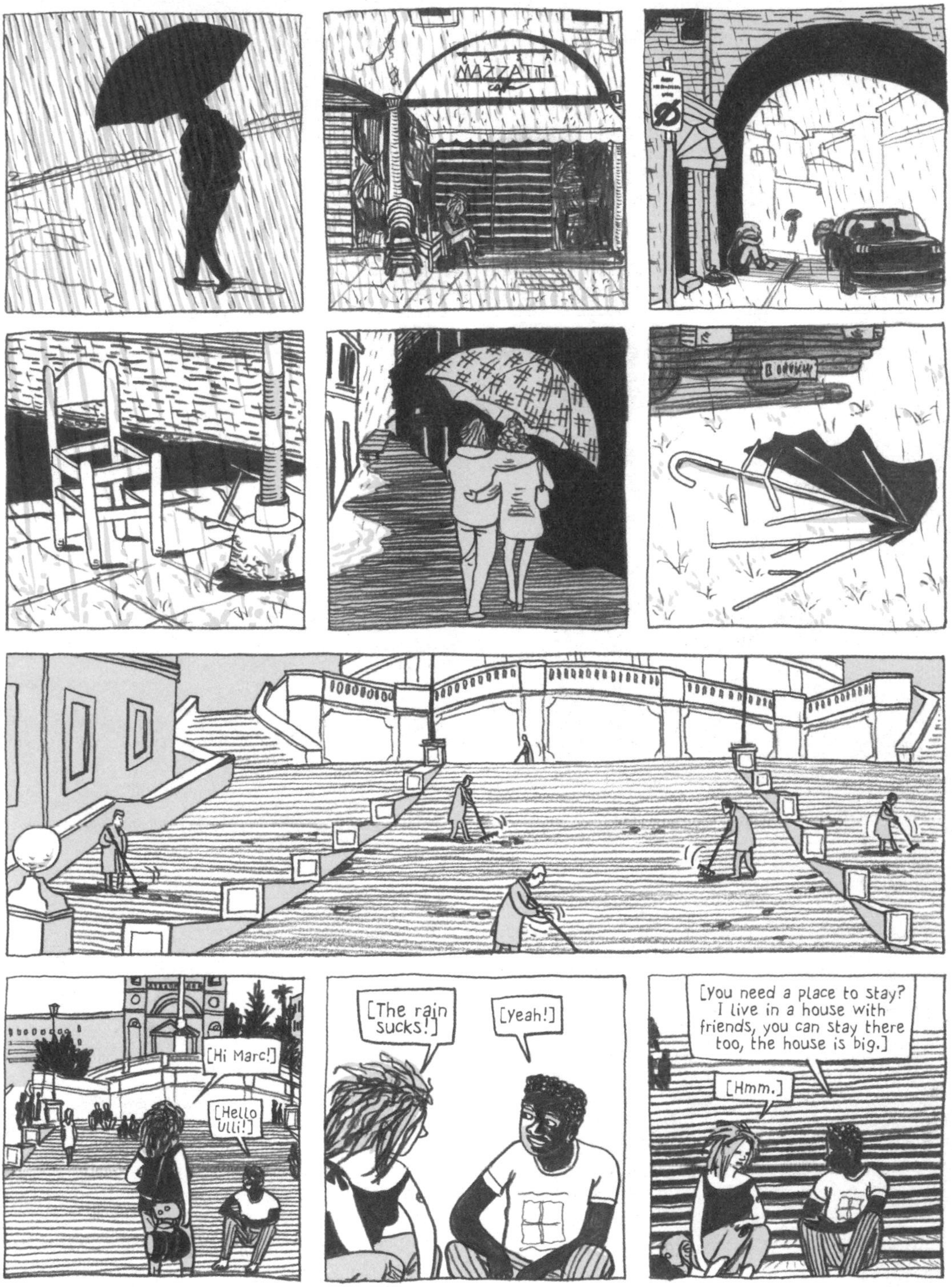
CASA
MAZZATTI
[Hi Marc!]
[Hello Ulli!]
[The rain sucks!]
[Yeah!]
[You need a place to stay? I live in a house with friends, you can stay there too, the house is big.]
[Hmm.]

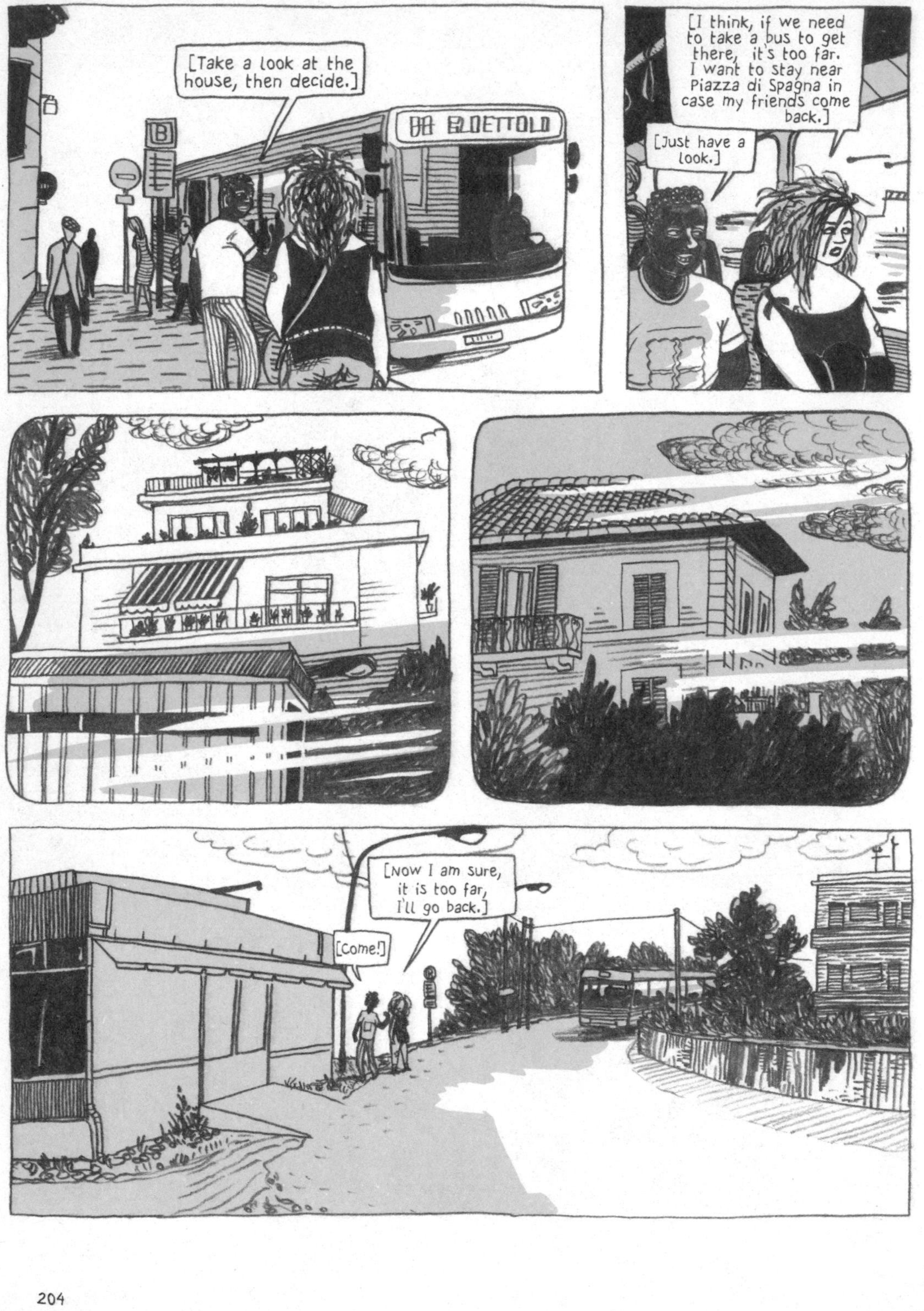
[Take a look at the house, then decide.]
[I think, if we need to take a bus to get there, it's too far. I want to stay near Piazza di Spagna in case my friends come back.]
[Just have a look.]
[Come!]
[Now I am sure, it is too far, I'll go back.]

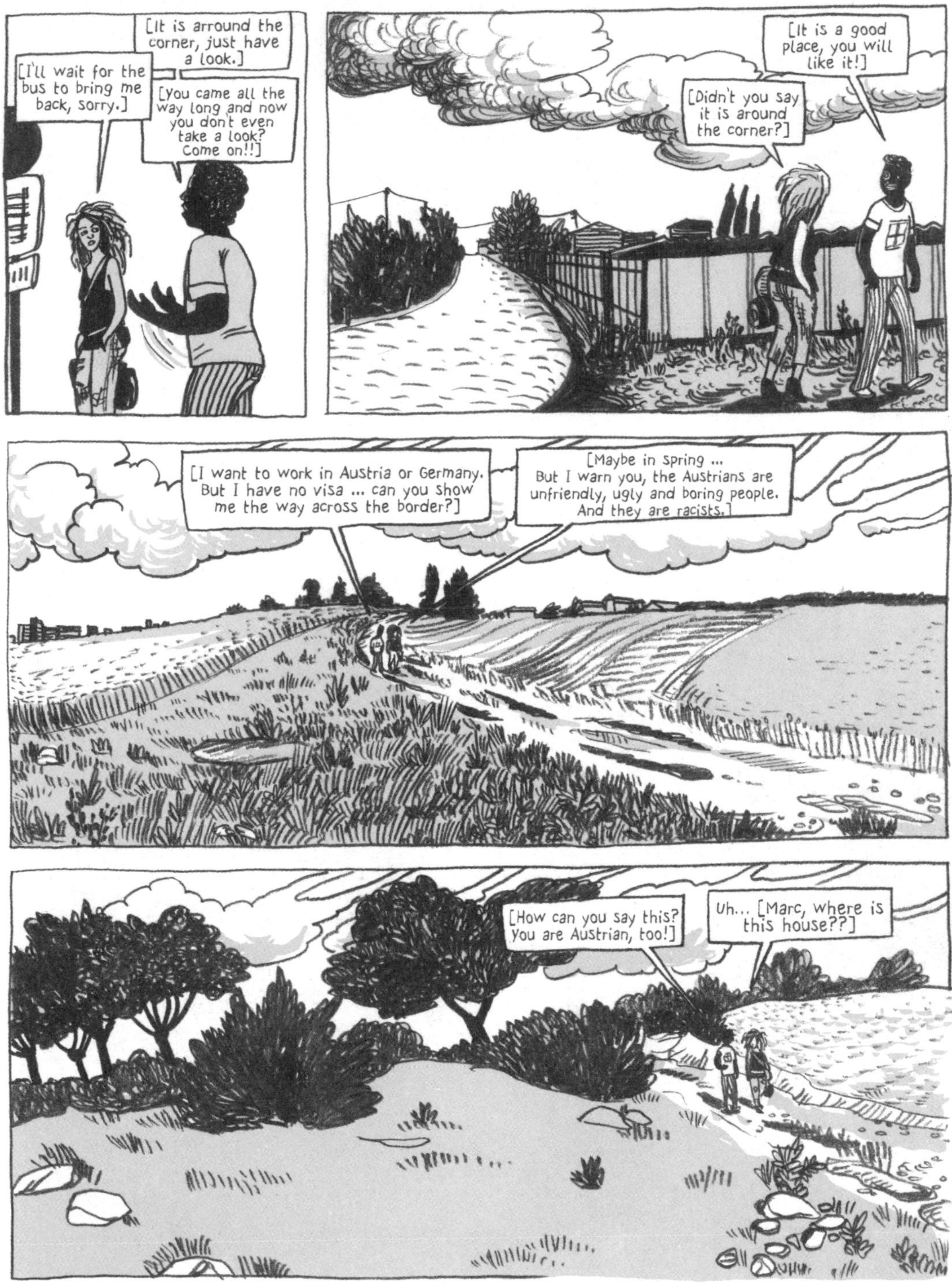
[It is arround the corner, just have a look.]
[I'll wait for the bus to bring me back, sorry.]
[You came all the way long and now you don't even take a look? Come on!!]
[It is a good place, you will like it!]
[Didn't you say it is around the corner?]
[I want to work in Austria or Germany. But I have no visa ... can you show me the way across the border?]
[Maybe in spring ... But I warn you, the Austrians are unfriendly, ugly and boring people. And they are racists.]
[How can you say this? You are Austrian, too!]
Uh... [Marc, where is this house??]

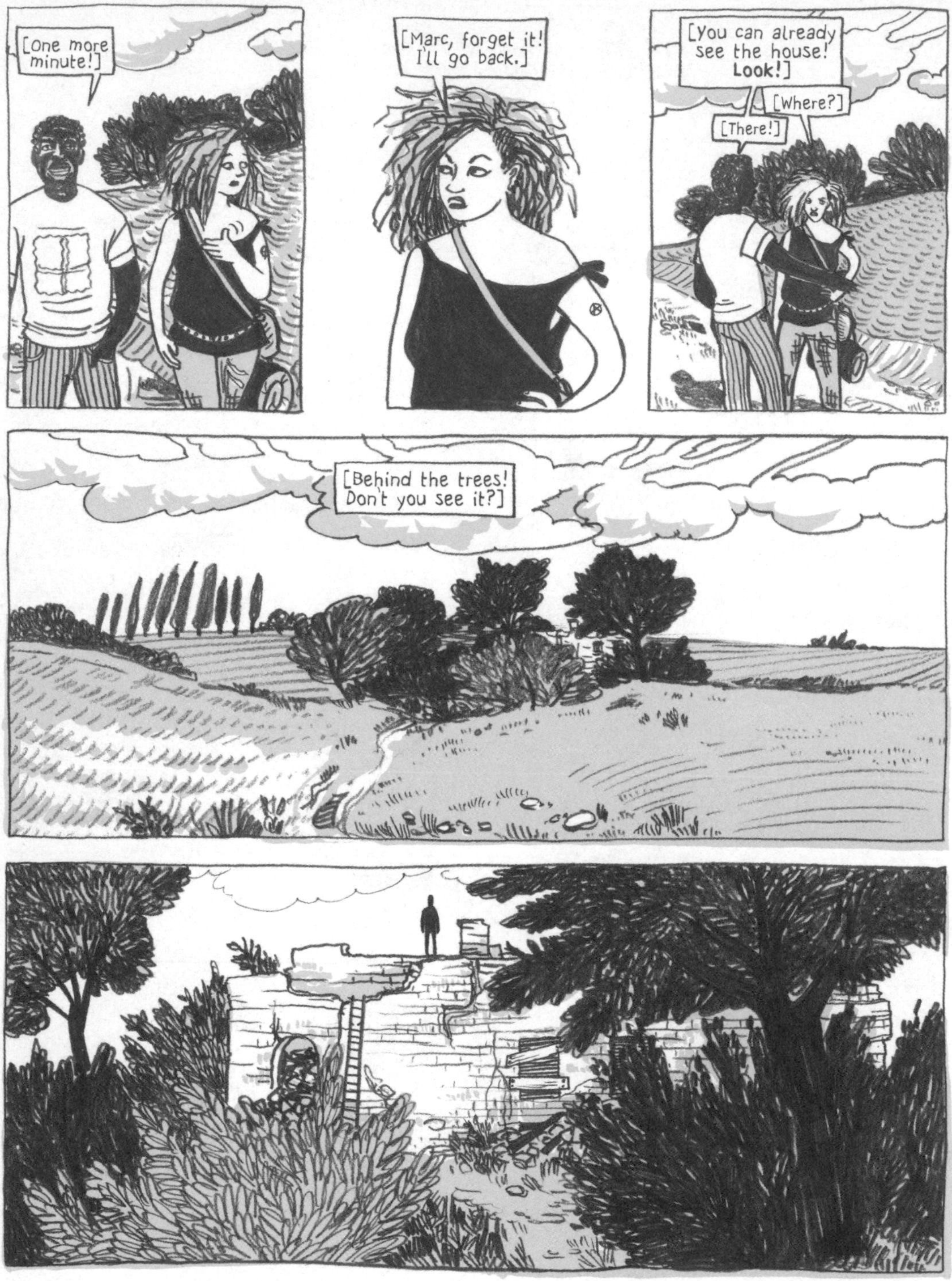
[One more minute!]
[Marc, forget it! I'll go back.]
[You can already see the house! **Look!**]
[Where?]
[There!]
[Behind the trees! Don't you see it?]

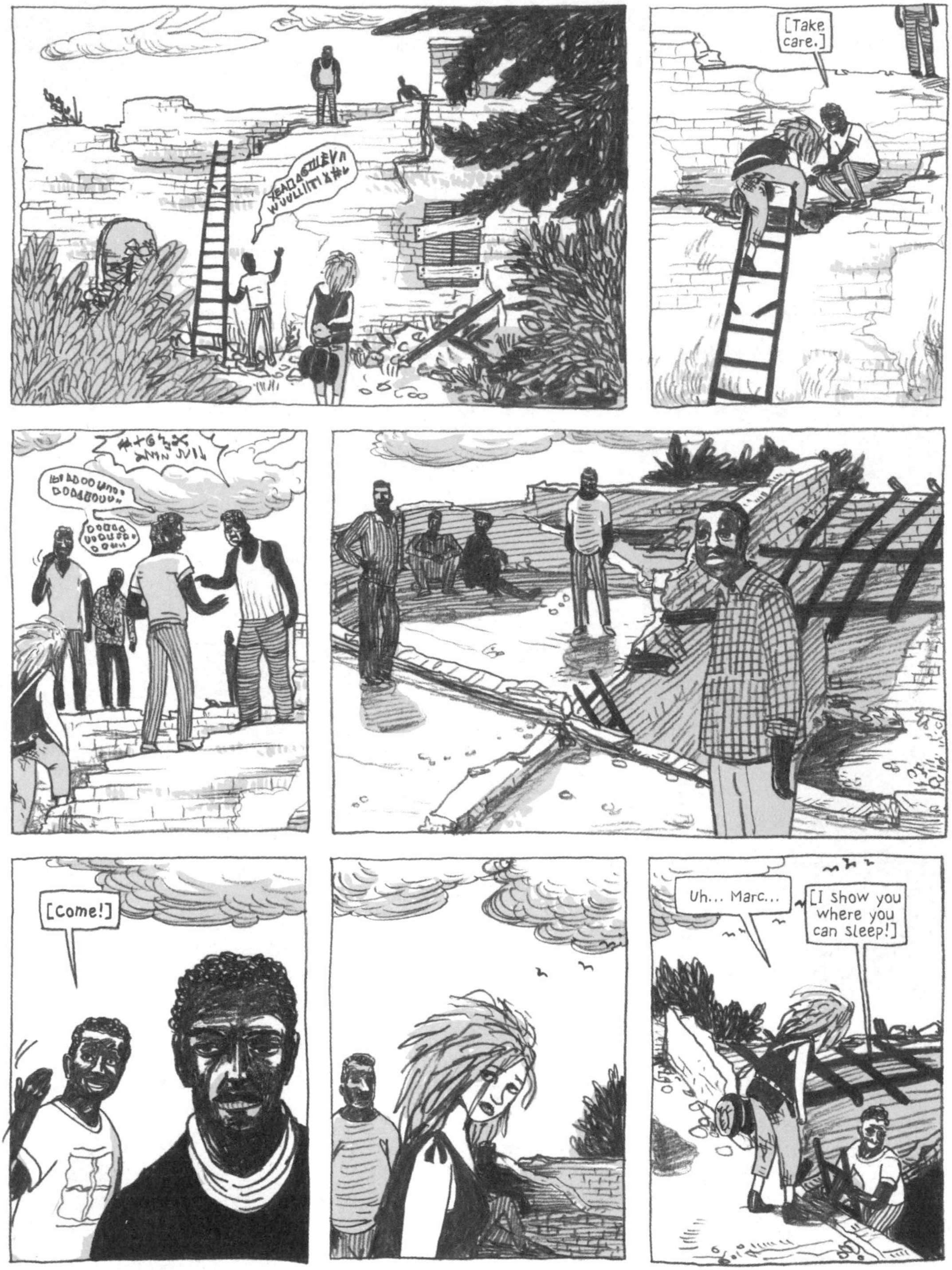
[Take care.]
[Come!]
Uh... Marc...
[I show you where you can sleep!]

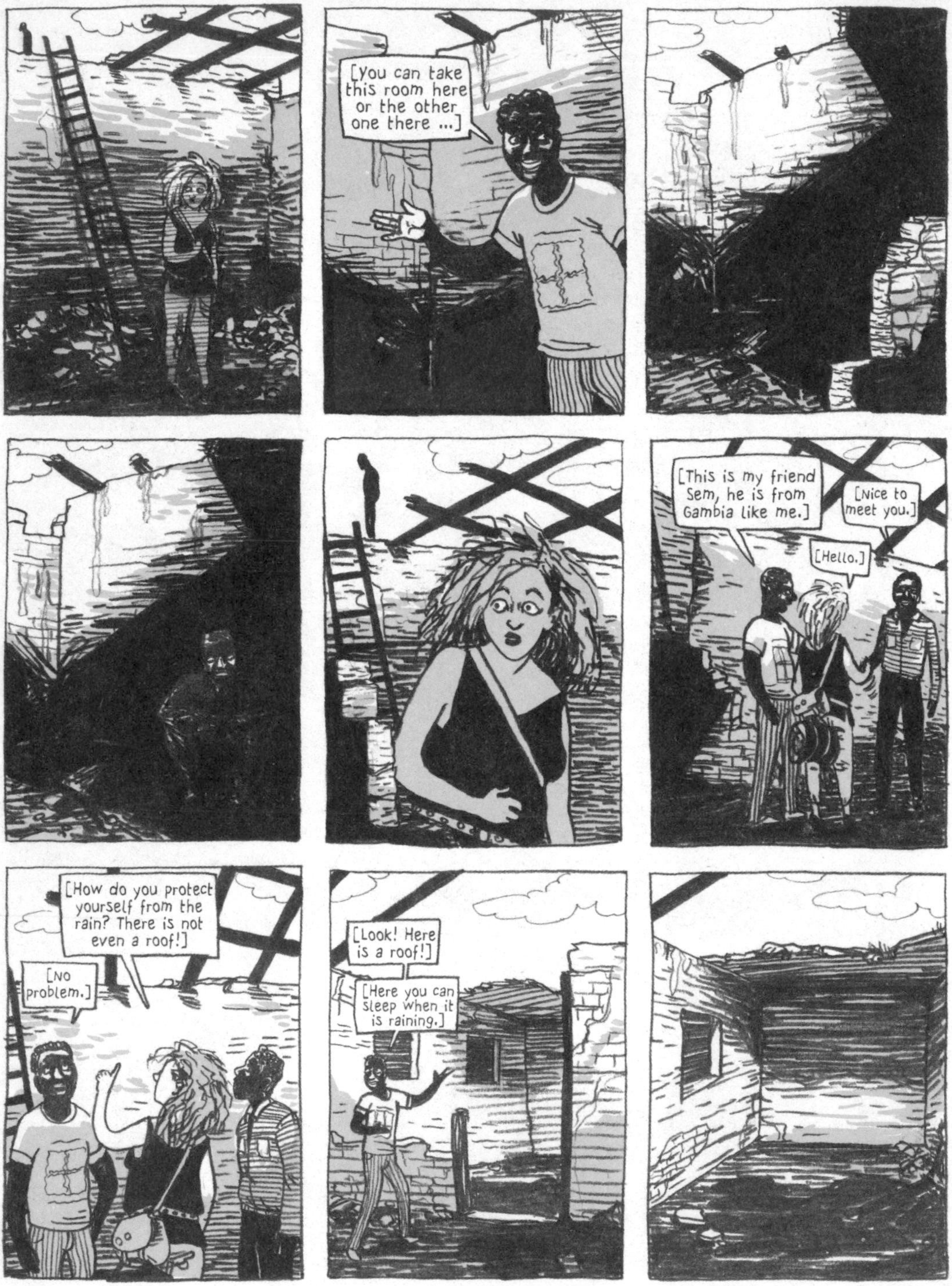
[You can take this room here or the other one there ...]
[This is my friend Sem, he is from Gambia like me.]
[Nice to meet you.]
[Hello.]
[How do you protect yourself from the rain? There is not even a roof!]
[No problem.]
[Look! Here is a roof!]
[Here you can sleep when it is raining.]

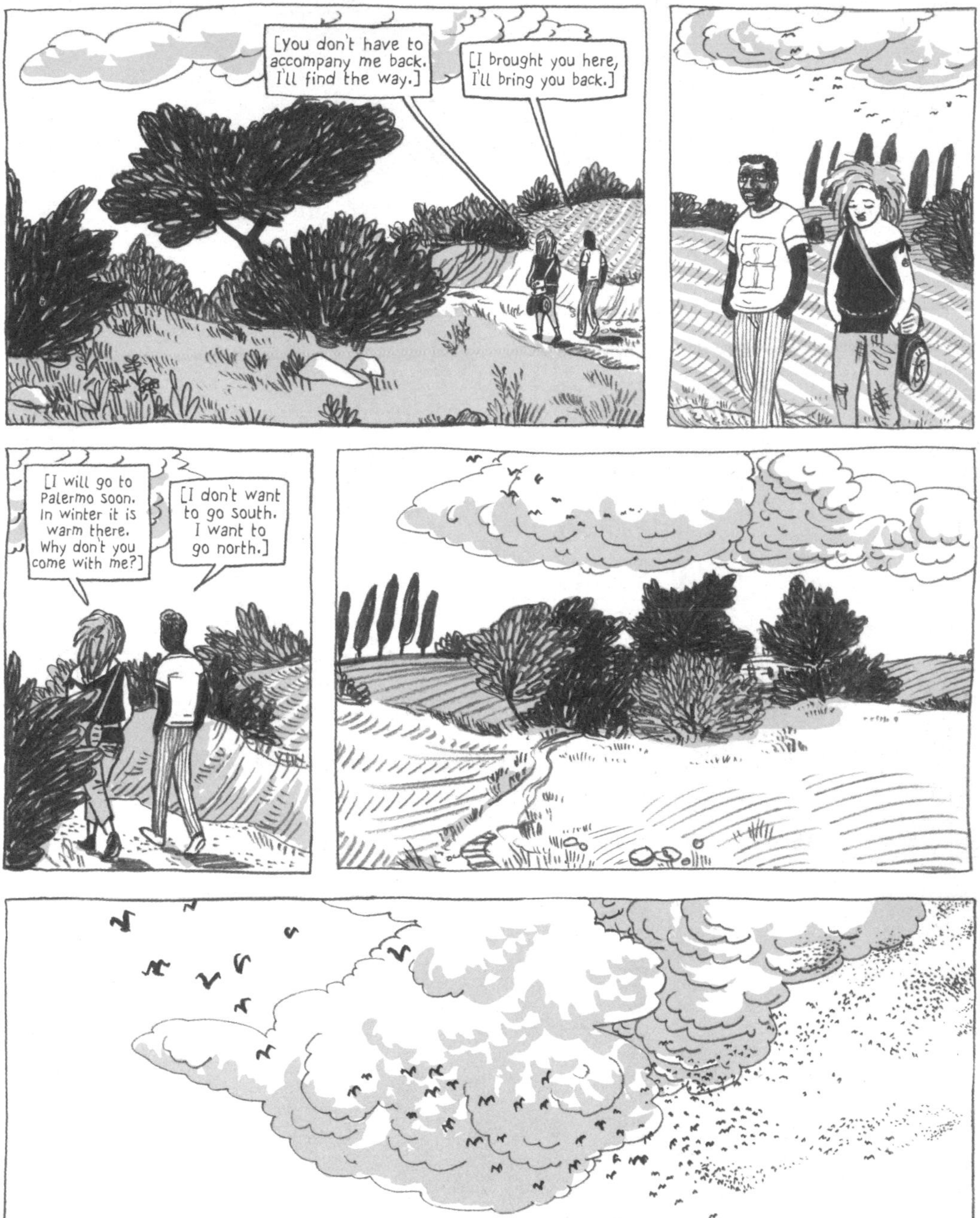
[You don't have to accompany me back. I'll find the way.]
[I brought you here, I'll bring you back.]
[I will go to Palermo soon. In winter it is warm there. Why don't you come with me?]
[I don't want to go south. I want to go north.]

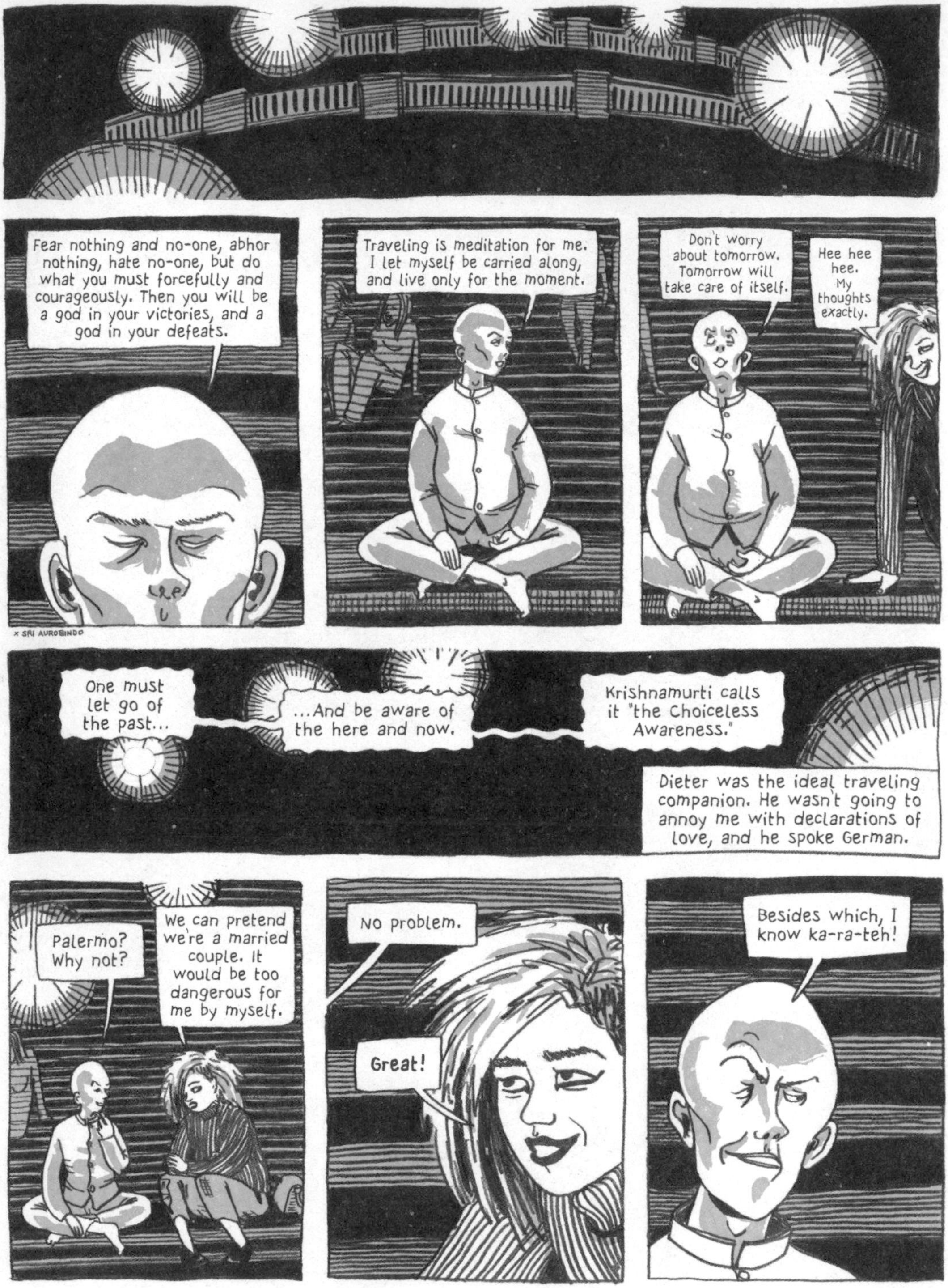
Fear nothing and no-one, abhor nothing, hate no-one, but do what you must forcefully and courageously. Then you will be a god in your victories, and a god in your defeats.
x SRI AUROBINDO
Traveling is meditation for me. I let myself be carried along, and live only for the moment.
Don't worry about tomorrow. Tomorrow will take care of itself.
Hee hee hee. My thoughts exactly.
One must let go of the past...
...And be aware of the here and now.
Krishnamurti calls it "the Choiceless Awareness."
Dieter was the ideal traveling companion. He wasn't going to annoy me with declarations of love, and he spoke German.
Palermo? Why not?
We can pretend we're a married couple. It would be too dangerous for me by myself.
No problem.
Great!
Besides which, I know ka-ra-teh!

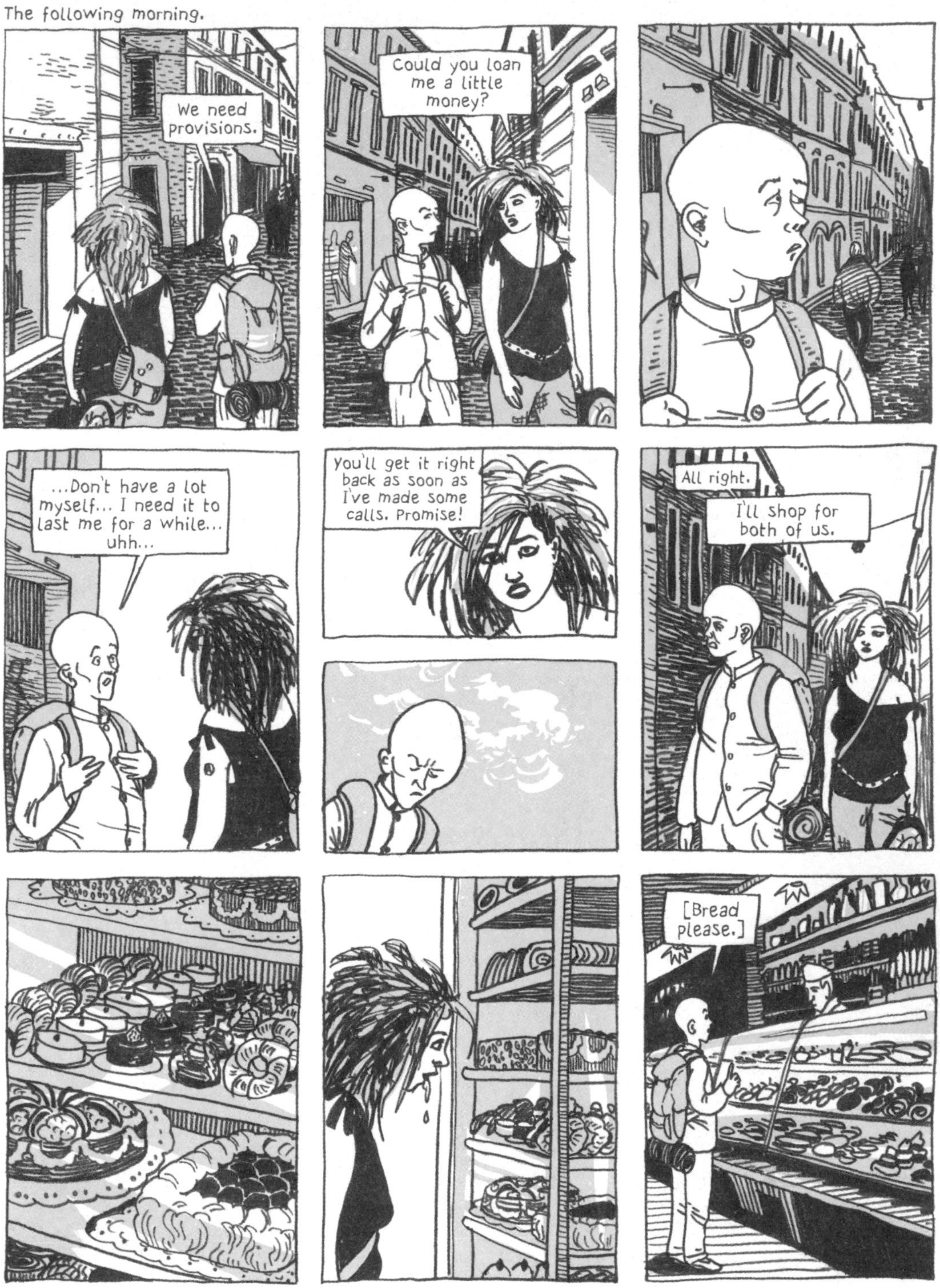
The following morning.
We need provisions.
Could you loan me a little money?
...Don't have a lot myself... I need it to last me for a while... uhh...
You'll get it right back as soon as I've made some calls. Promise!
All right.
I'll shop for both of us.
[Bread please.]

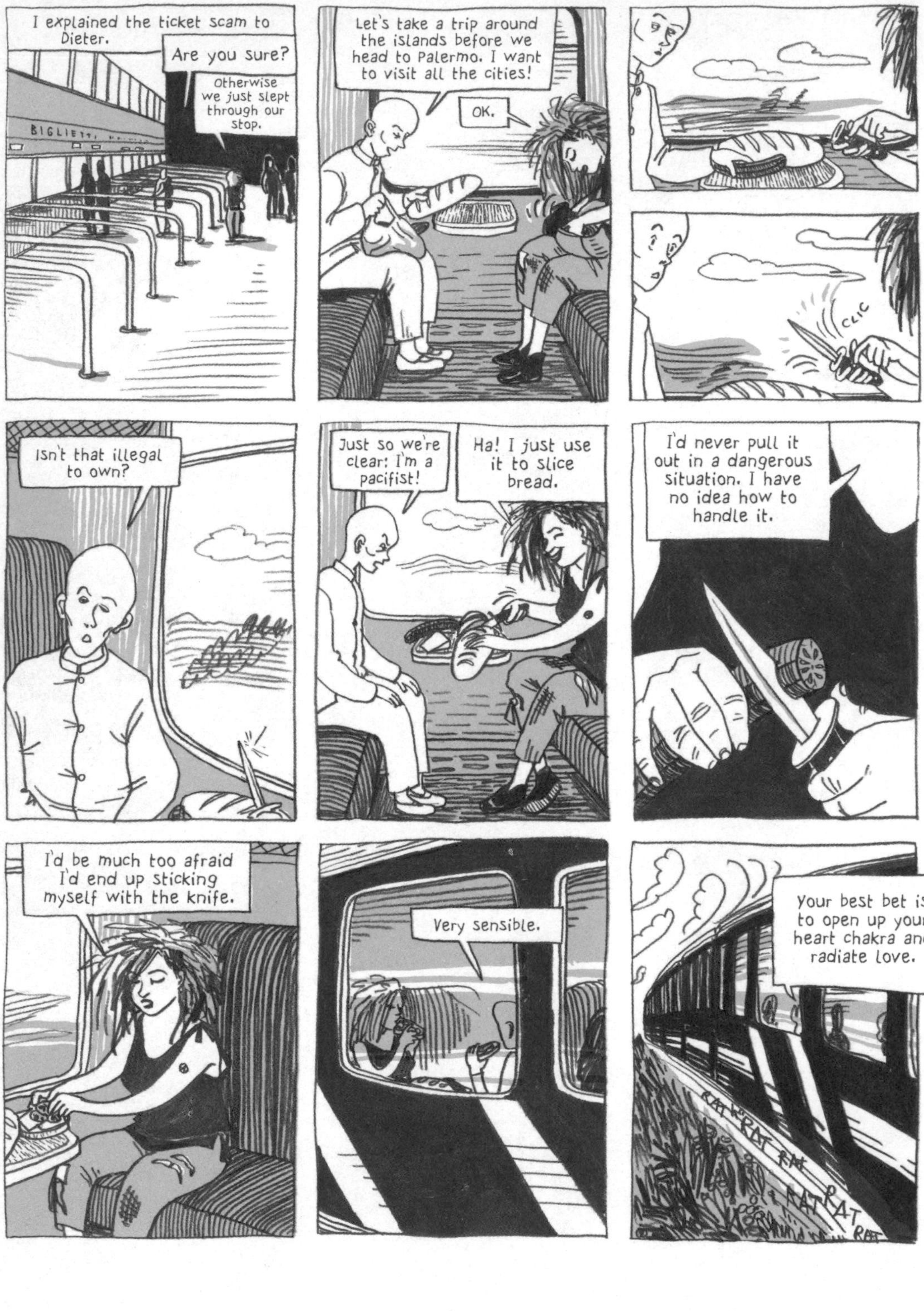

I explained the ticket scam to Dieter.
Are you sure?
Otherwise we just slept through our stop.
BIGLIETTI
Let's take a trip around the islands before we head to Palermo. I want to visit all the cities!
OK.
CLIC
Isn't that illegal to own?
Just so we're clear: I'm a pacifist!
Ha! I just use it to slice bread.
I'd never pull it out in a dangerous situation. I have no idea how to handle it.
I'd be much too afraid I'd end up sticking myself with the knife.
Very sensible.
Your best bet is to open up your heart chakra and radiate love.
RAT RAT RAT RAT RAT RAT

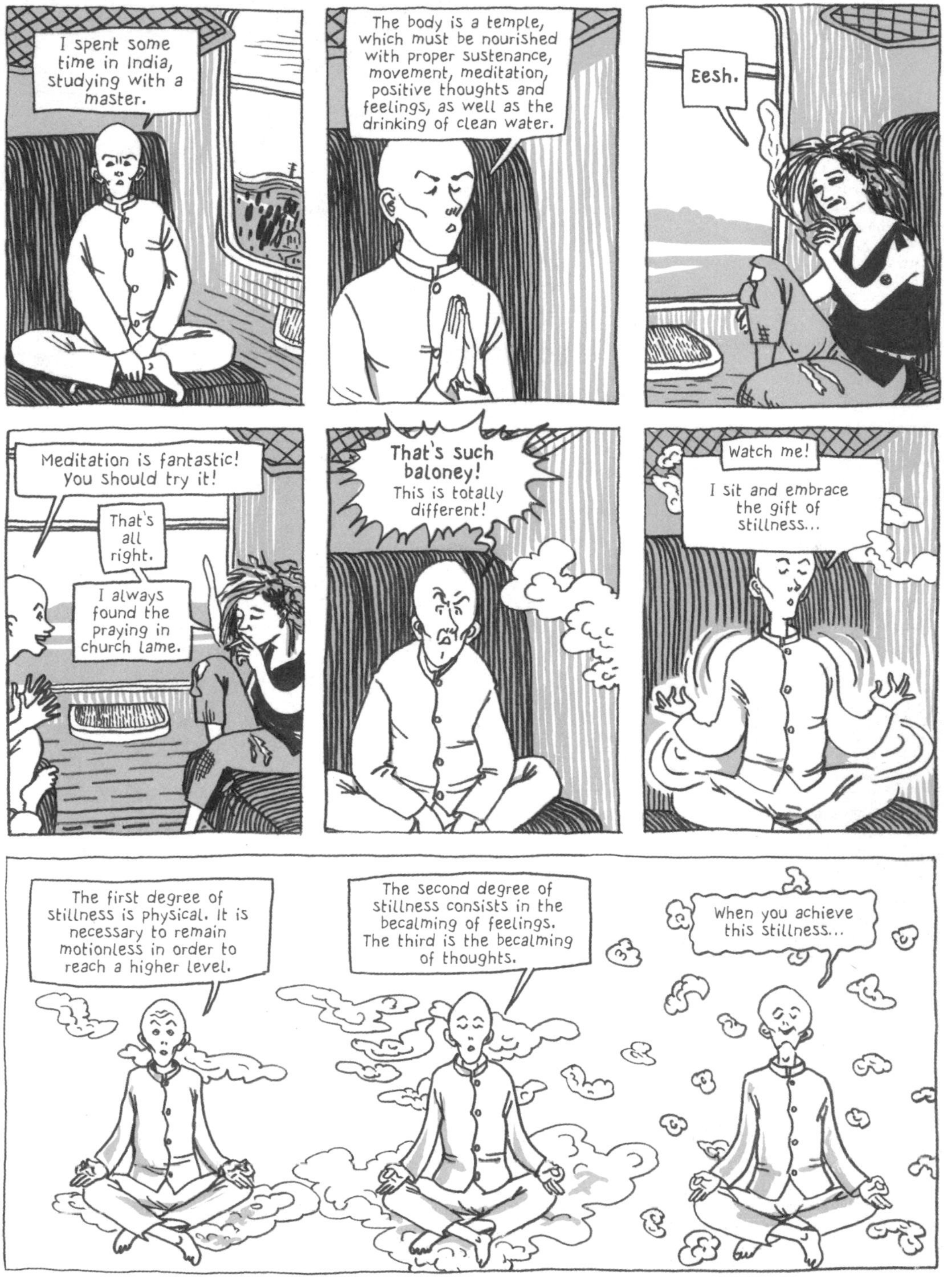
I spent some time in India, studying with a master.
The body is a temple, which must be nourished with proper sustenance, movement, meditation, positive thoughts and feelings, as well as the drinking of clean water.
Eesh.
Meditation is fantastic! You should try it!
That's all right.
I always found the praying in church lame.
That's such baloney!
This is totally different!
Watch me!
I sit and embrace the gift of stillness...
The first degree of stillness is physical. It is necessary to remain motionless in order to reach a higher level.
The second degree of stillness consists in the becalming of feelings. The third is the becalming of thoughts.
When you achieve this stillness...

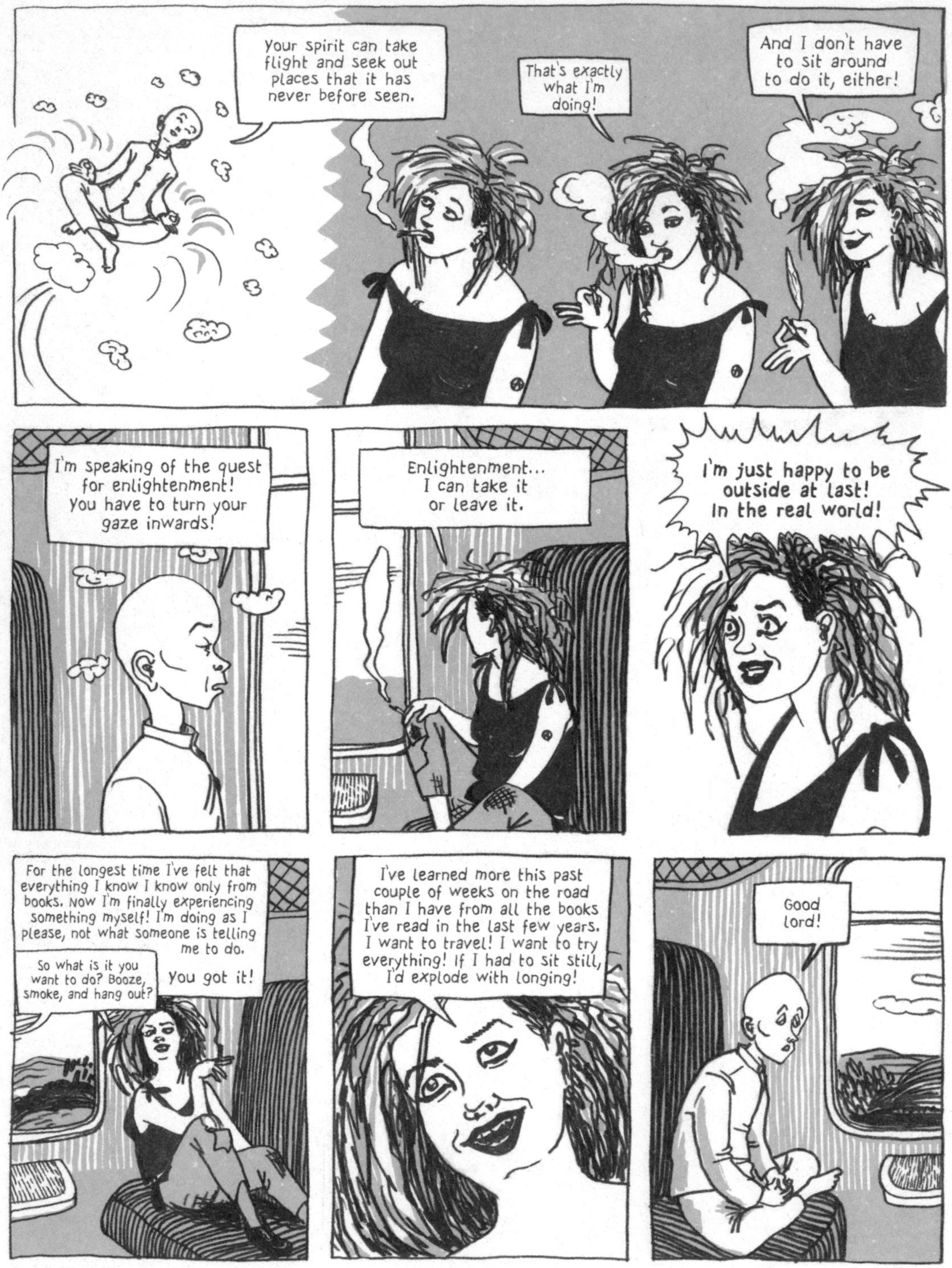

Your spirit can take flight and seek out places that it has never before seen.
That's exactly what I'm doing!
And I don't have to sit around to do it, either!
I'm speaking of the quest for enlightenment! You have to turn your gaze inwards!
Enlightenment... I can take it or leave it.
I'm just happy to be outside at last! In the real world!
For the longest time I've felt that everything I know I know only from books. Now I'm finally experiencing something myself! I'm doing as I please, not what someone is telling me to do.
So what is it you want to do? Booze, smoke, and hang out?
You got it!
I've learned more this past couple of weeks on the road than I have from all the books I've read in the last few years. I want to travel! I want to try everything! If I had to sit still, I'd explode with longing!
Good lord!

XI. the BEAST

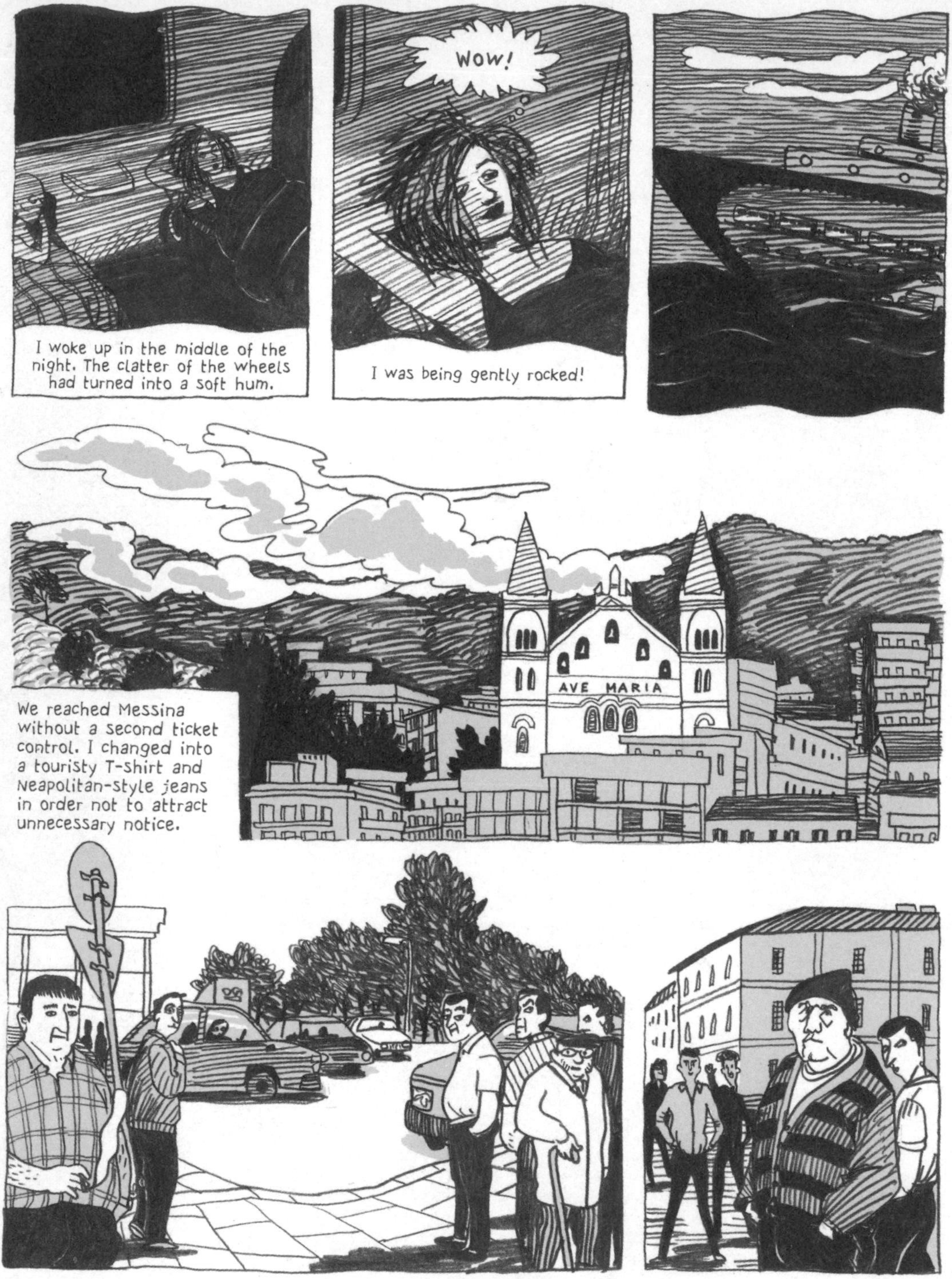
I woke up in the middle of the night. The clatter of the wheels had turned into a soft hum.
WOW!
I was being gently rocked!
AVE MARIA
We reached Messina without a second ticket control. I changed into a touristy T-shirt and Neapolitan-style jeans in order not to attract unnecessary notice.

[Hello.]
What's going on?
?
Come on, keep moving.
[Sorry, I don't speak Italian.]

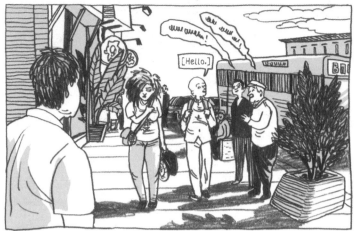

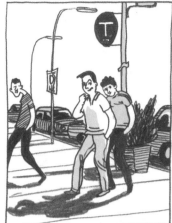

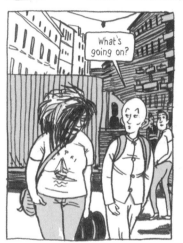

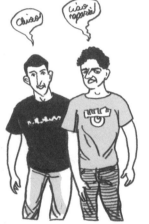

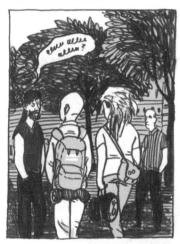

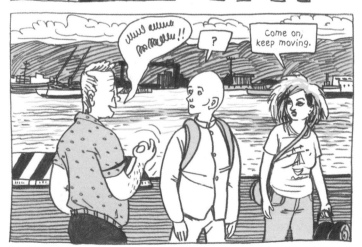

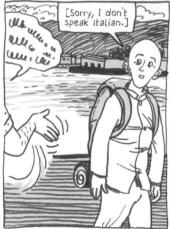

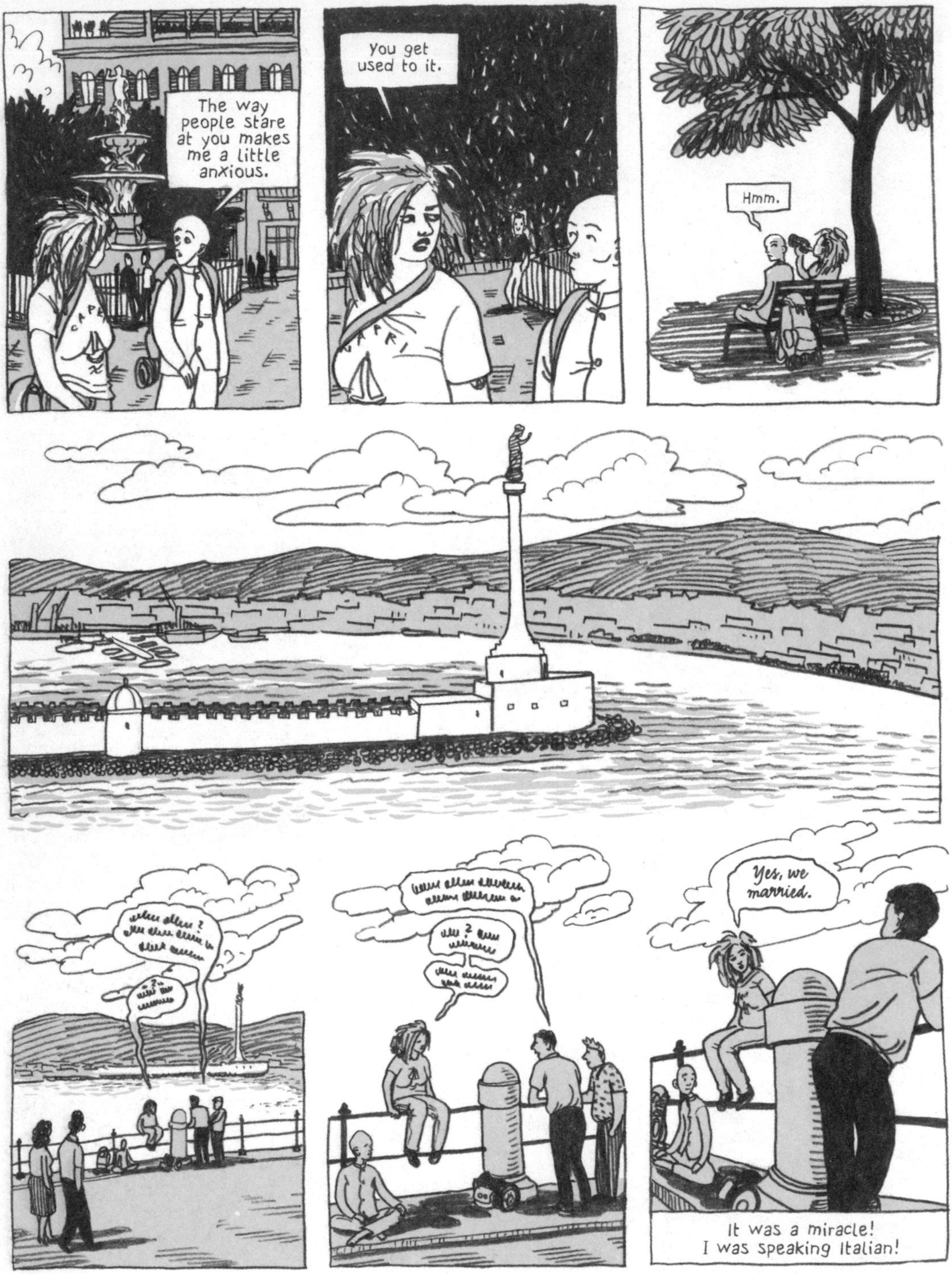
The way people stare at you makes me a little anxious.
You get used to it.
CAPRI
Hmm.
Yes, we married.
It was a miracle! I was speaking Italian!

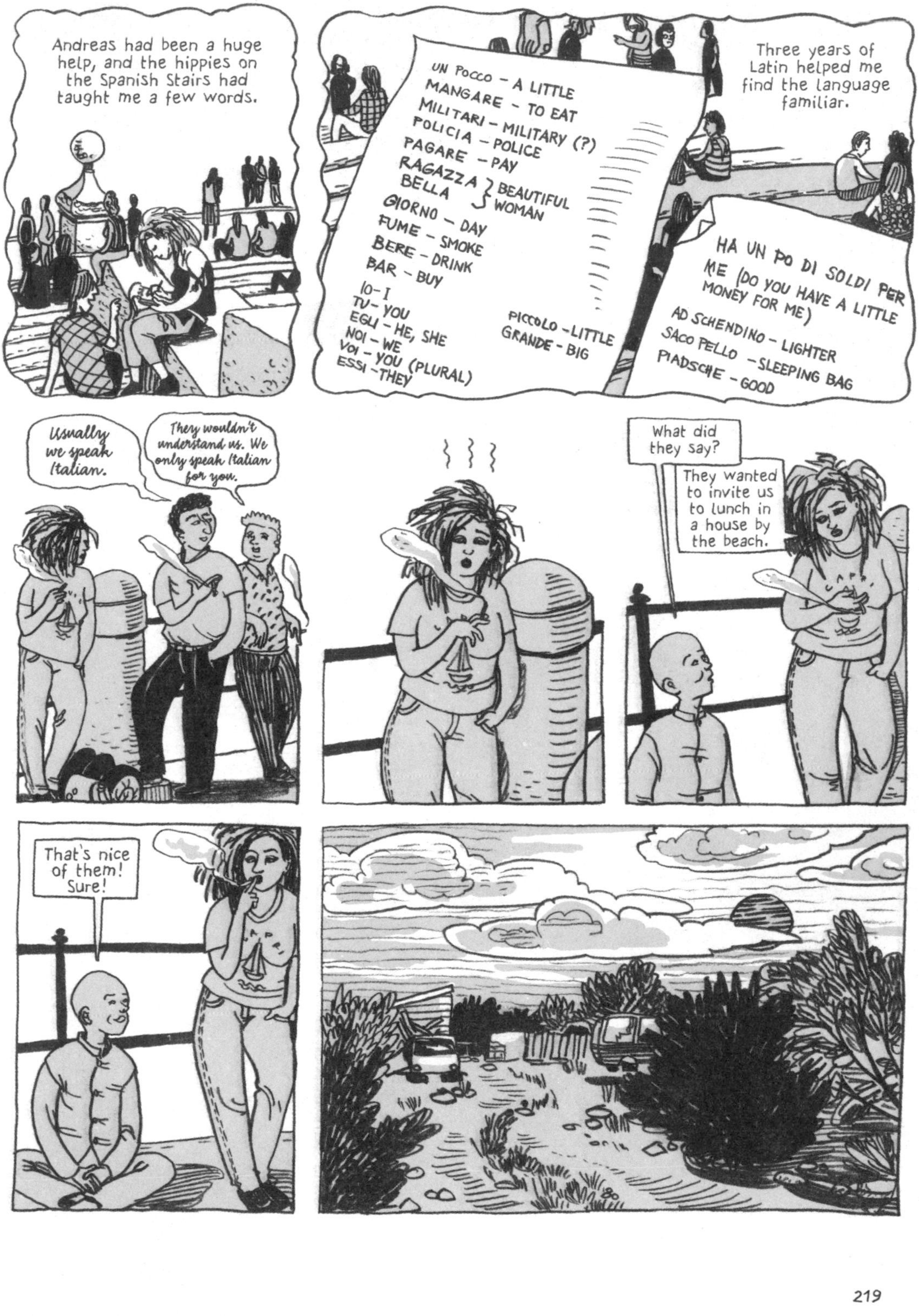

Andreas had been a huge help, and the hippies on the Spanish Stairs had taught me a few words.
UN POCCO – A LITTLE
MANGARE – TO EAT
MILITARI – MILITARY (?)
POLICIA – POLICE
PAGARE – PAY
RAGAZZA BELLA } BEAUTIFUL WOMAN
GIORNO – DAY
FUME – SMOKE
BERE – DRINK
BAR – BUY
IO – I
TU – YOU
EGLI – HE, SHE
NOI – WE
VOI – YOU (PLURAL)
ESSI – THEY
PICCOLO – LITTLE
GRANDE – BIG
Three years of Latin helped me find the language familiar.
HA UN PO DI SOLDI PER ME (DO YOU HAVE A LITTLE MONEY FOR ME)
AD SCHENDINO – LIGHTER
SACO PELLO – SLEEPING BAG
PIADSCHE – GOOD
Usually we speak Italian.
They wouldn't understand us. We only speak Italian for you.
What did they say?
They wanted to invite us to lunch in a house by the beach.
That's nice of them! Sure!

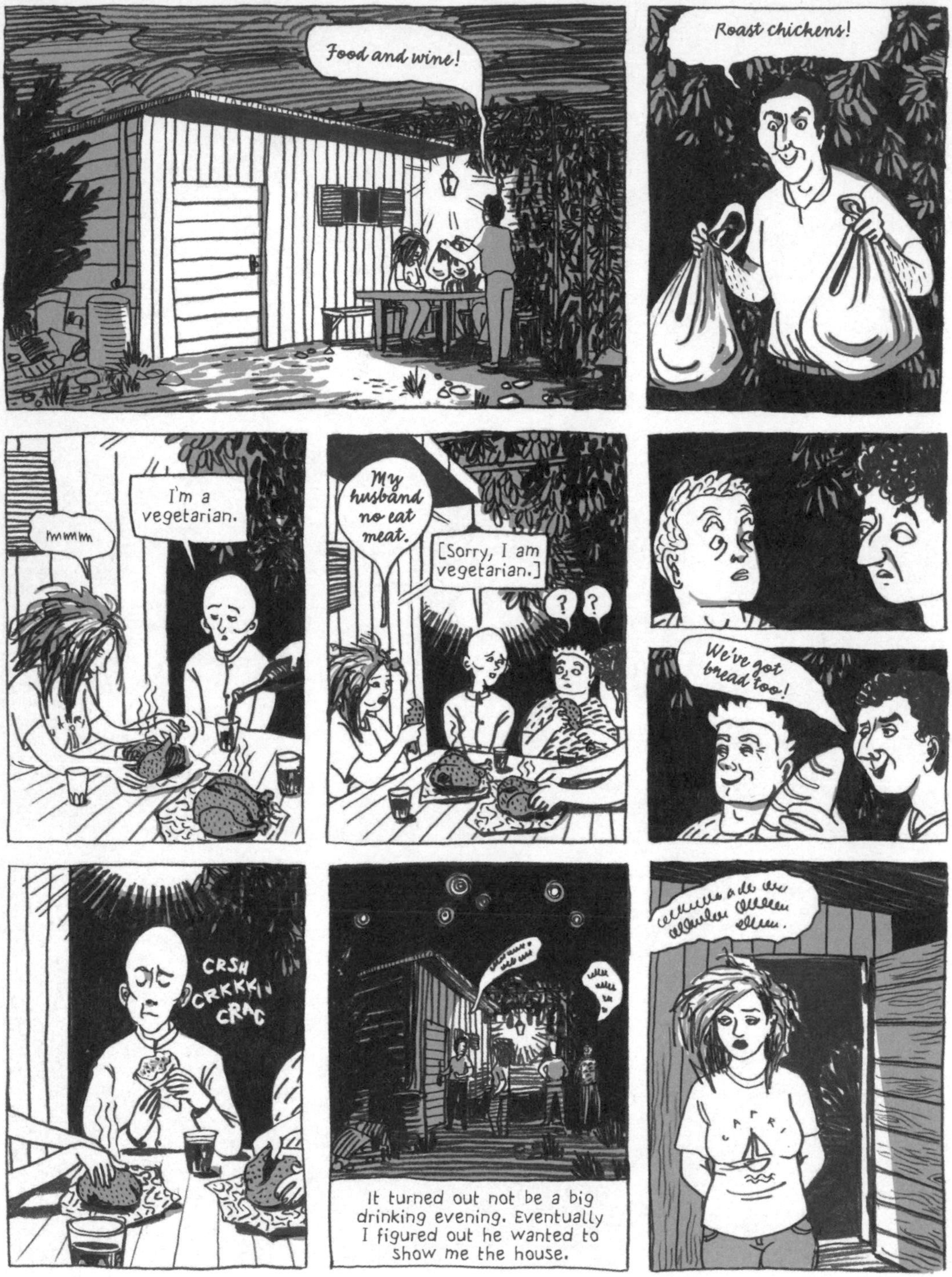
Food and wine!
Roast chickens!
mmmm
I'm a vegetarian.
My husband no eat meat.
[Sorry, I am vegetarian.]
? ?
We've got bread too!
CRSH CRKKKK CRAC
It turned out not be a big drinking evening. Eventually I figured out he wanted to show me the house.

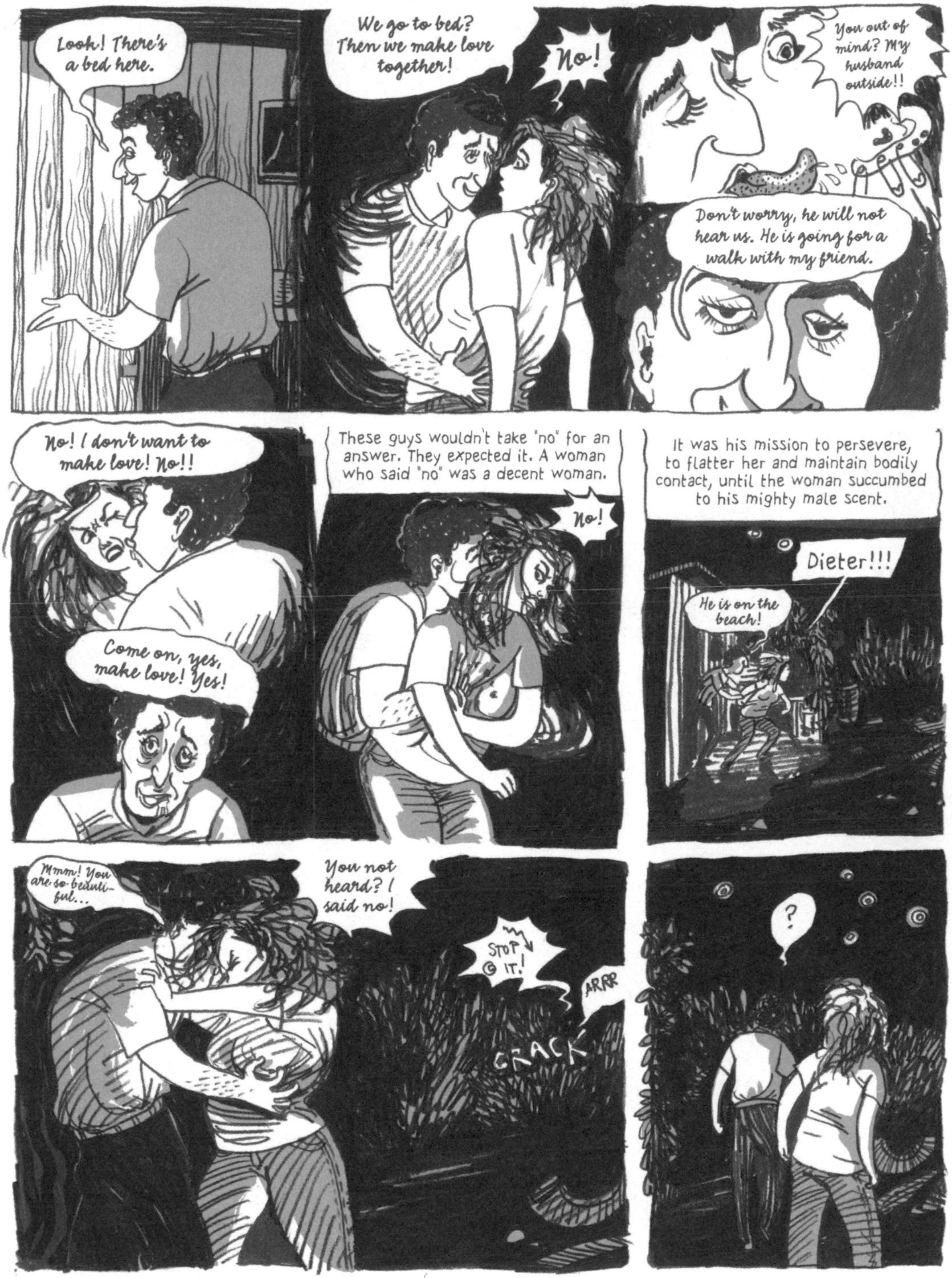

Look! There's a bed here.
We go to bed? Then we make love together!
No!
You out of mind? My husband outside!!
Don't worry, he will not hear us. He is going for a walk with my friend.
No! I don't want to make love! No!!
Come on, yes, make love! Yes!
These guys wouldn't take "no" for an answer. They expected it. A woman who said "no" was a decent woman.
No!
It was his mission to persevere, to flatter her and maintain bodily contact, until the woman succumbed to his mighty male scent.
Dieter!!!
He is on the beach!
Mmm! You are so beautiful...
You not heard? I said no!
STOP IT!
ARRR
CRACK
?

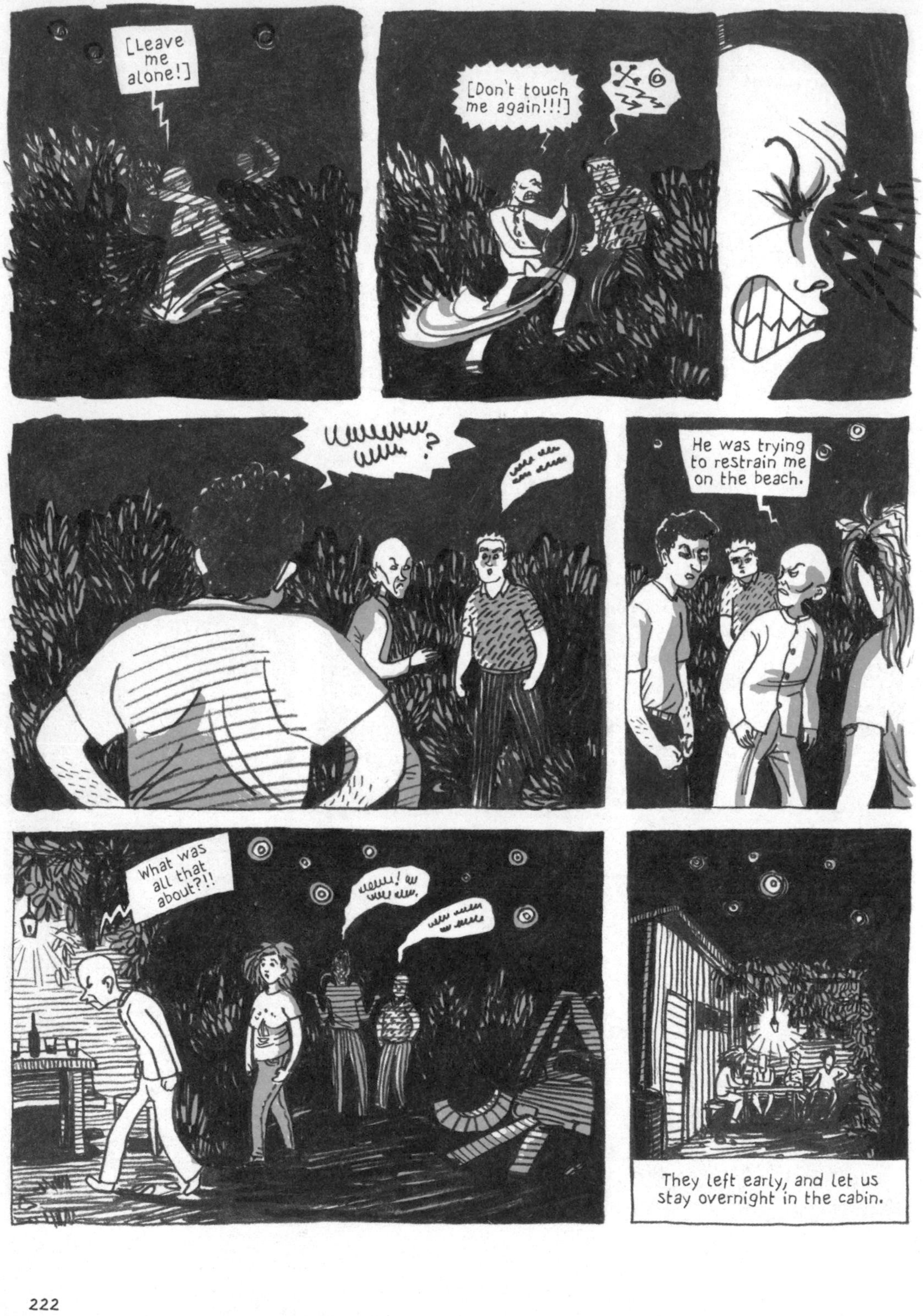
[Leave me alone!]
[Don't touch me again!!!]
He was trying to restrain me on the beach.
What was all that about?!!
They left early, and let us stay overnight in the cabin.

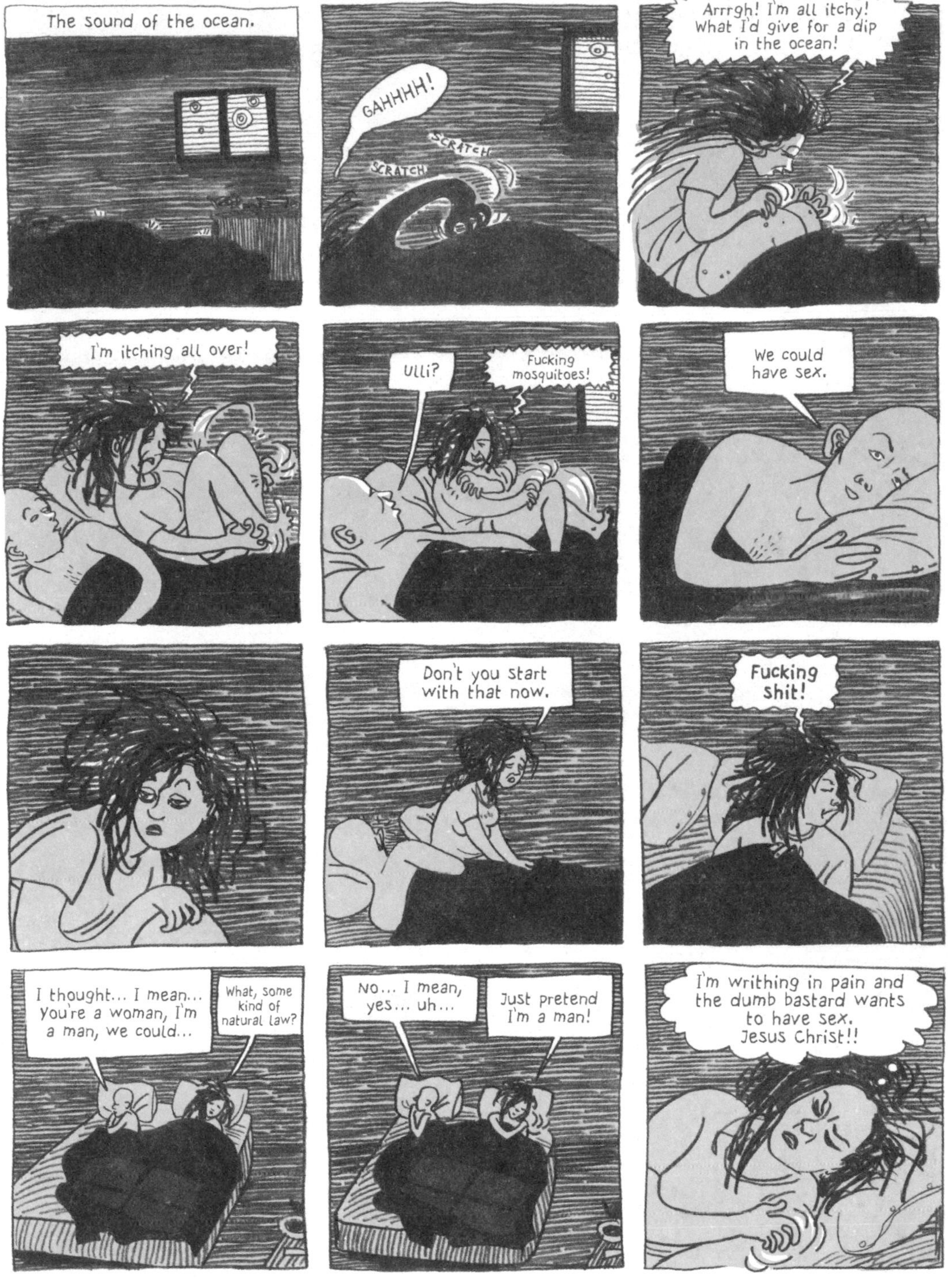
The sound of the ocean.
GAHHHH!
SCRATCH
SCRATCH
Arrrgh! I'm all itchy! What I'd give for a dip in the ocean!
I'm itching all over!
Ulli?
Fucking mosquitoes!
We could have sex.
Don't you start with that now.
Fucking shit!
I thought... I mean... You're a woman, I'm a man, we could...
What, some kind of natural law?
No... I mean, yes... uh...
Just pretend I'm a man!
I'm writhing in pain and the dumb bastard wants to have sex. Jesus Christ!!

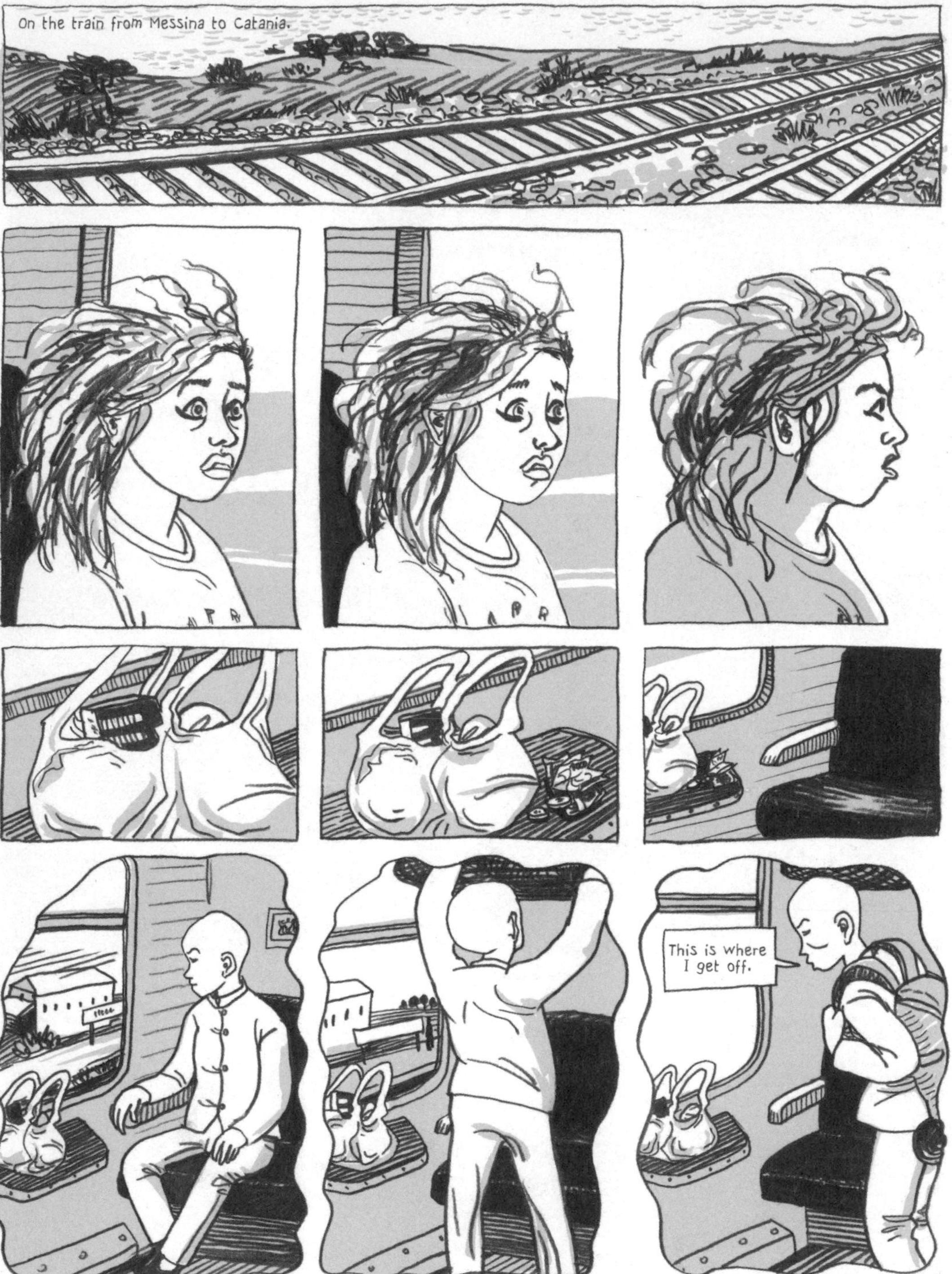
On the train from Messina to Catania.
This is where I get off.

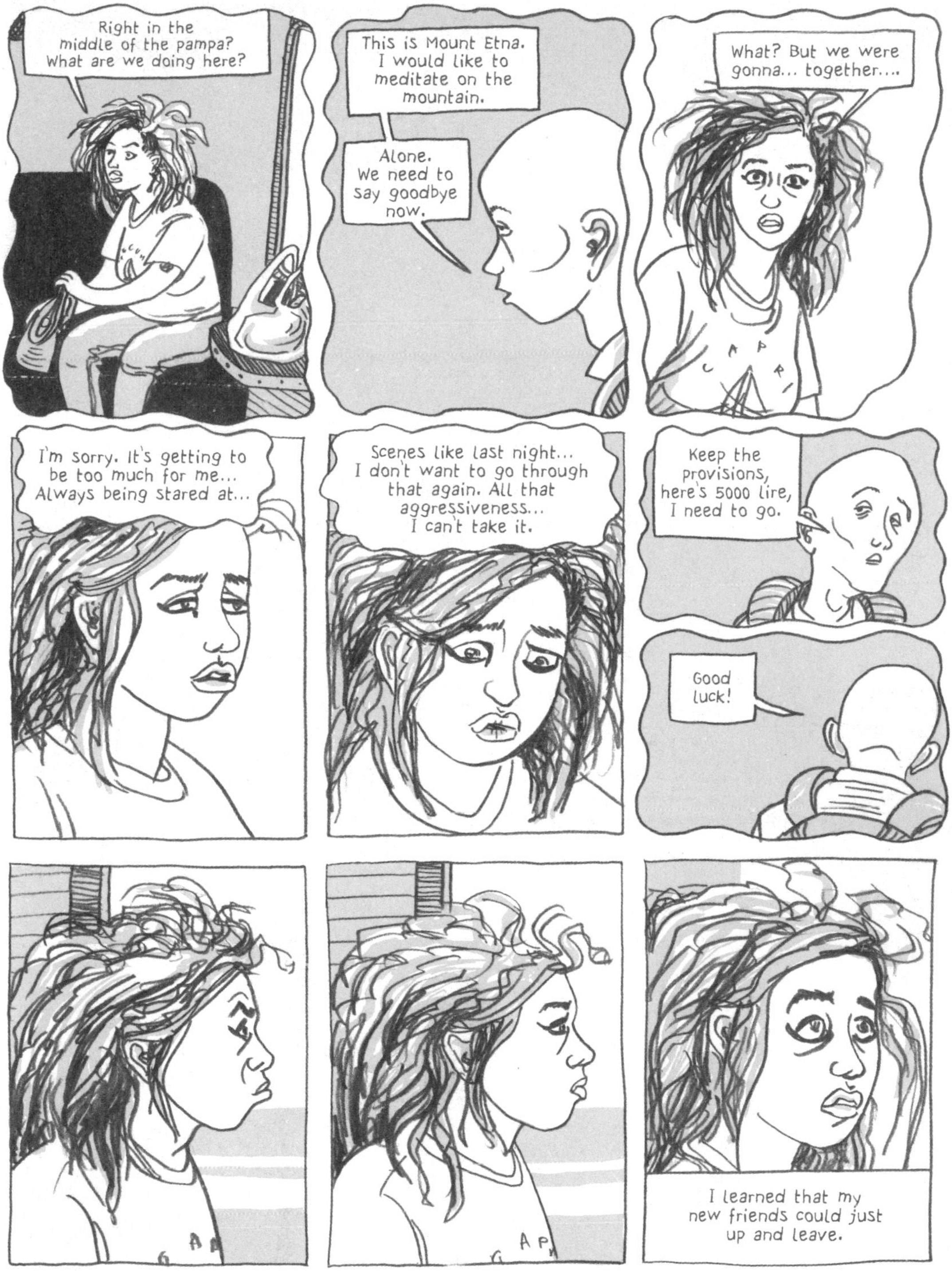
Right in the middle of the pampa? What are we doing here?
This is Mount Etna. I would like to meditate on the mountain.
Alone. We need to say goodbye now.
What? But we were gonna... together....
I'm sorry. It's getting to be too much for me... Always being stared at...
Scenes like last night... I don't want to go through that again. All that aggressiveness... I can't take it.
Keep the provisions, here's 5000 lire, I need to go.
Good luck!
I learned that my new friends could just up and leave.

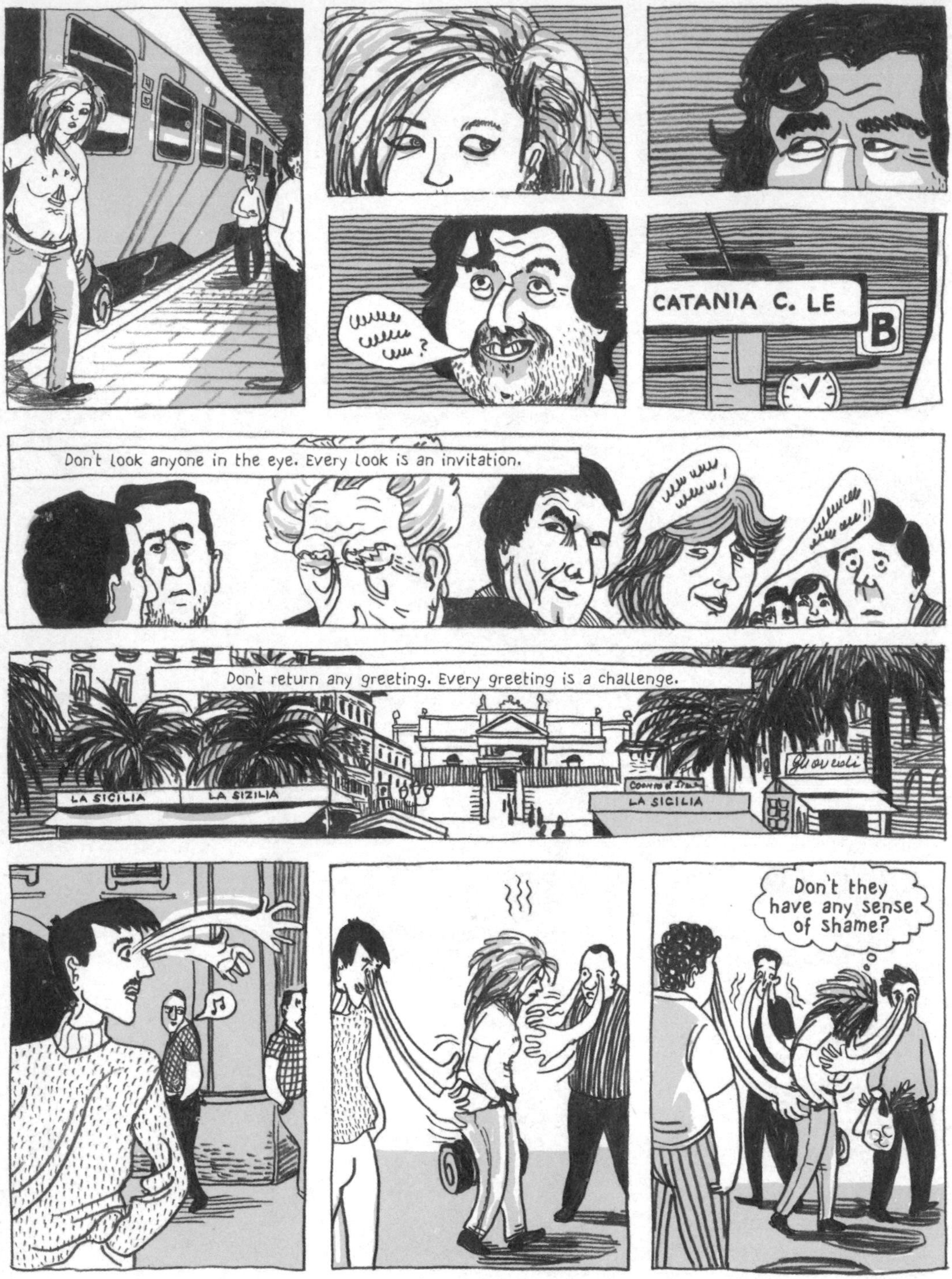
CATANIA C. LE
B
Don't look anyone in the eye. Every look is an invitation.
Don't return any greeting. Every greeting is a challenge.
LA SICILIA
LA SIZILIA
LA SICILIA
Don't they have any sense of shame?

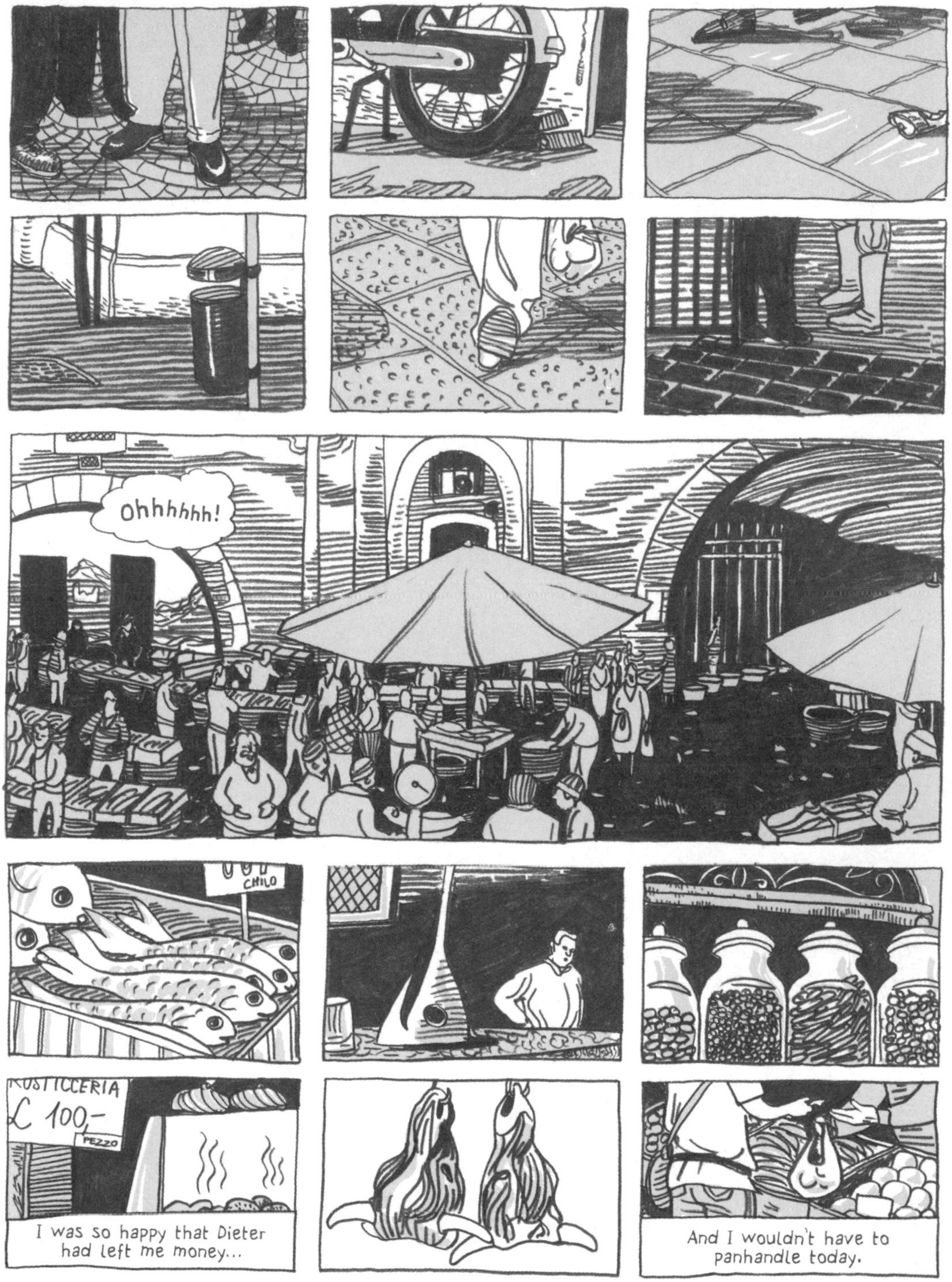
Ohhhhhh!
CHILO
ROSTICCERIA
L 100,-
PEZZO
I was so happy that Dieter had left me money...
And I wouldn't have to panhandle today.

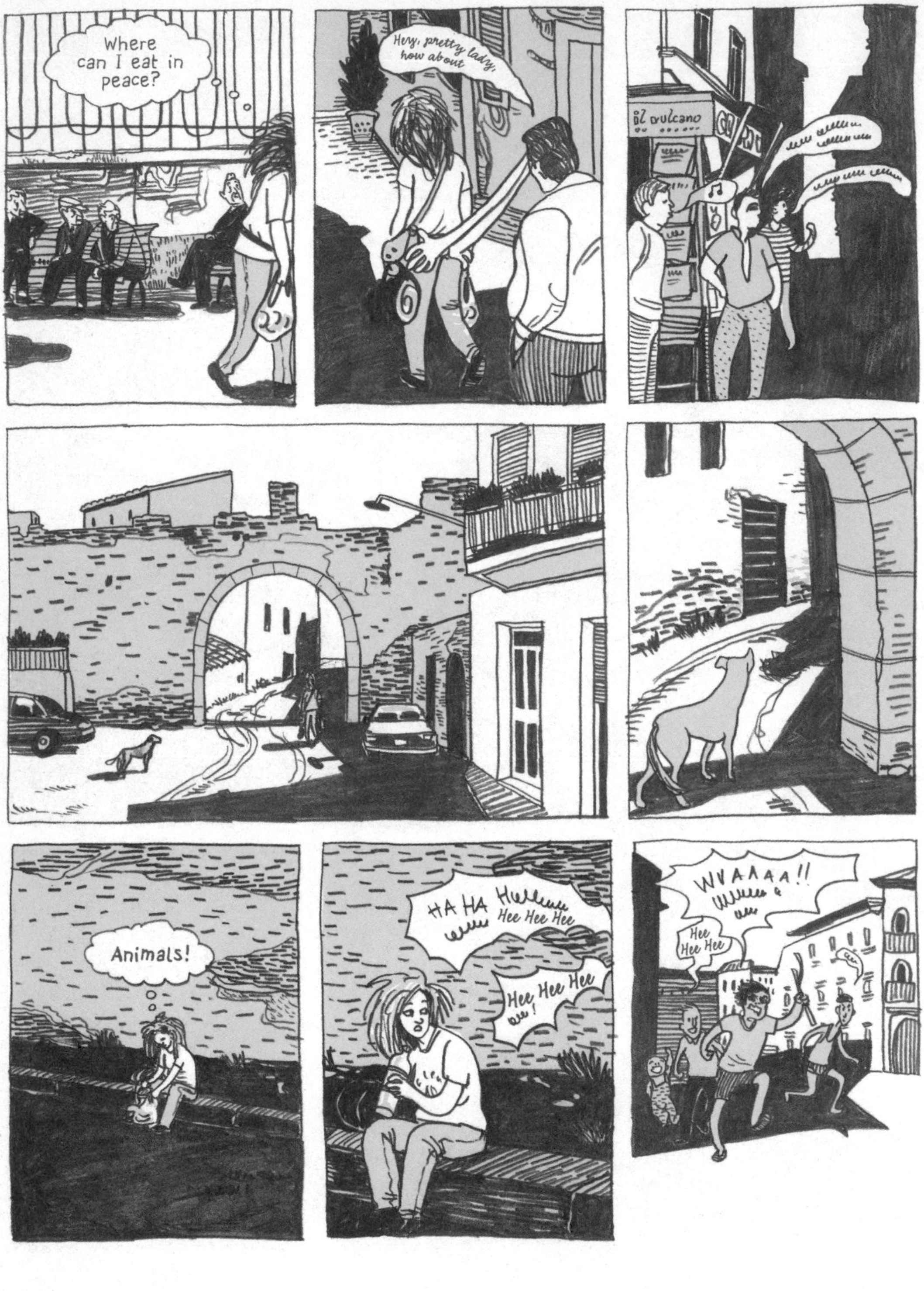
Where can I eat in peace?
Hey, pretty lady, how about
il vulcano
Animals!
HA HA H
Hee Hee Hee
Hee Hee Hee
WVAAAA!!
Hee Hee Hee

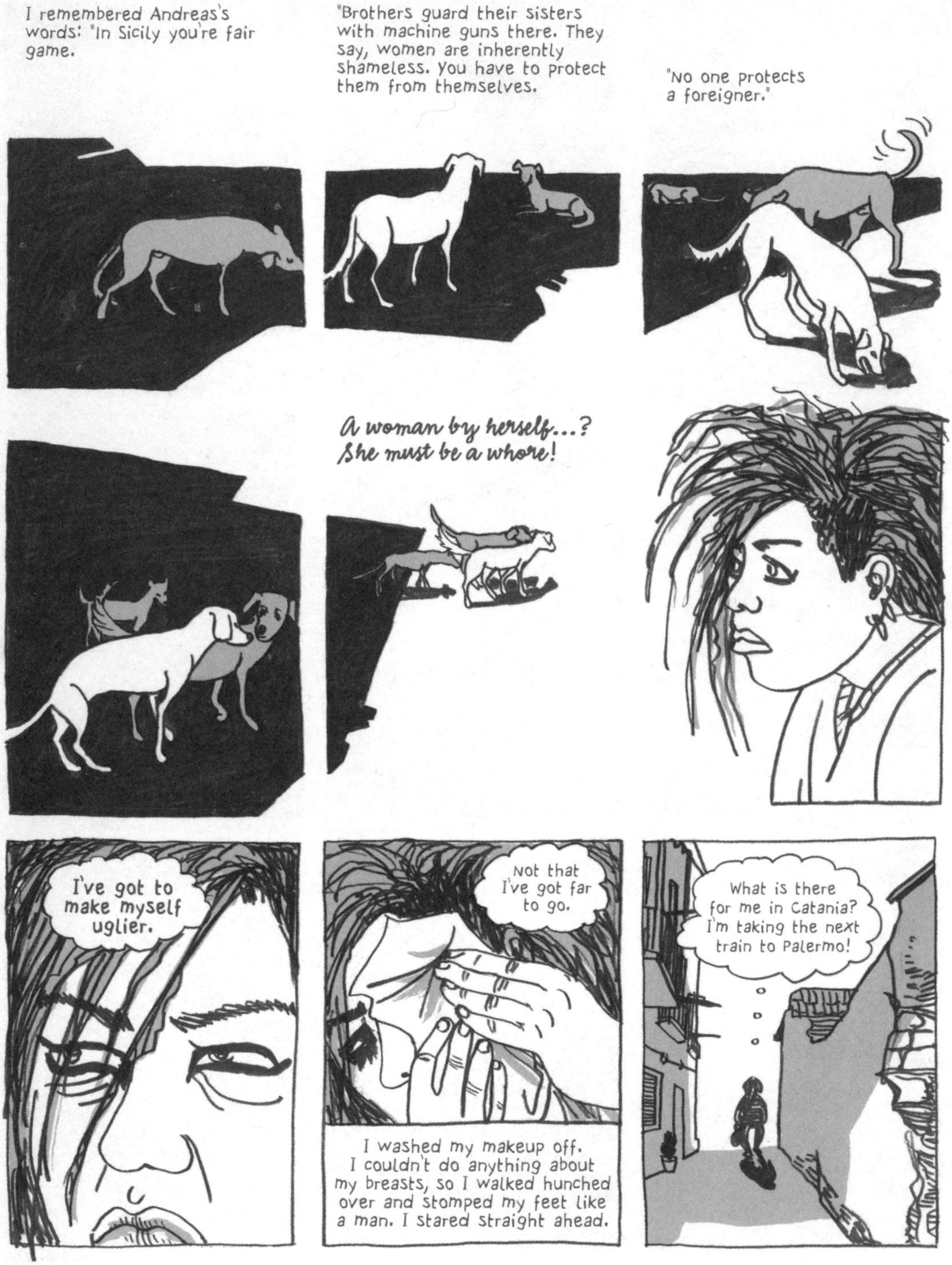
I remembered Andreas's words: "In Sicily you're fair game.
"Brothers guard their sisters with machine guns there. They say, women are inherently shameless. You have to protect them from themselves.
"No one protects a foreigner."
A woman by herself...? She must be a whore!
I've got to make myself uglier.
Not that I've got far to go.
I washed my makeup off. I couldn't do anything about my breasts, so I walked hunched over and stomped my feet like a man. I stared straight ahead.
What is there for me in Catania? I'm taking the next train to Palermo!

XII. the SPOILS

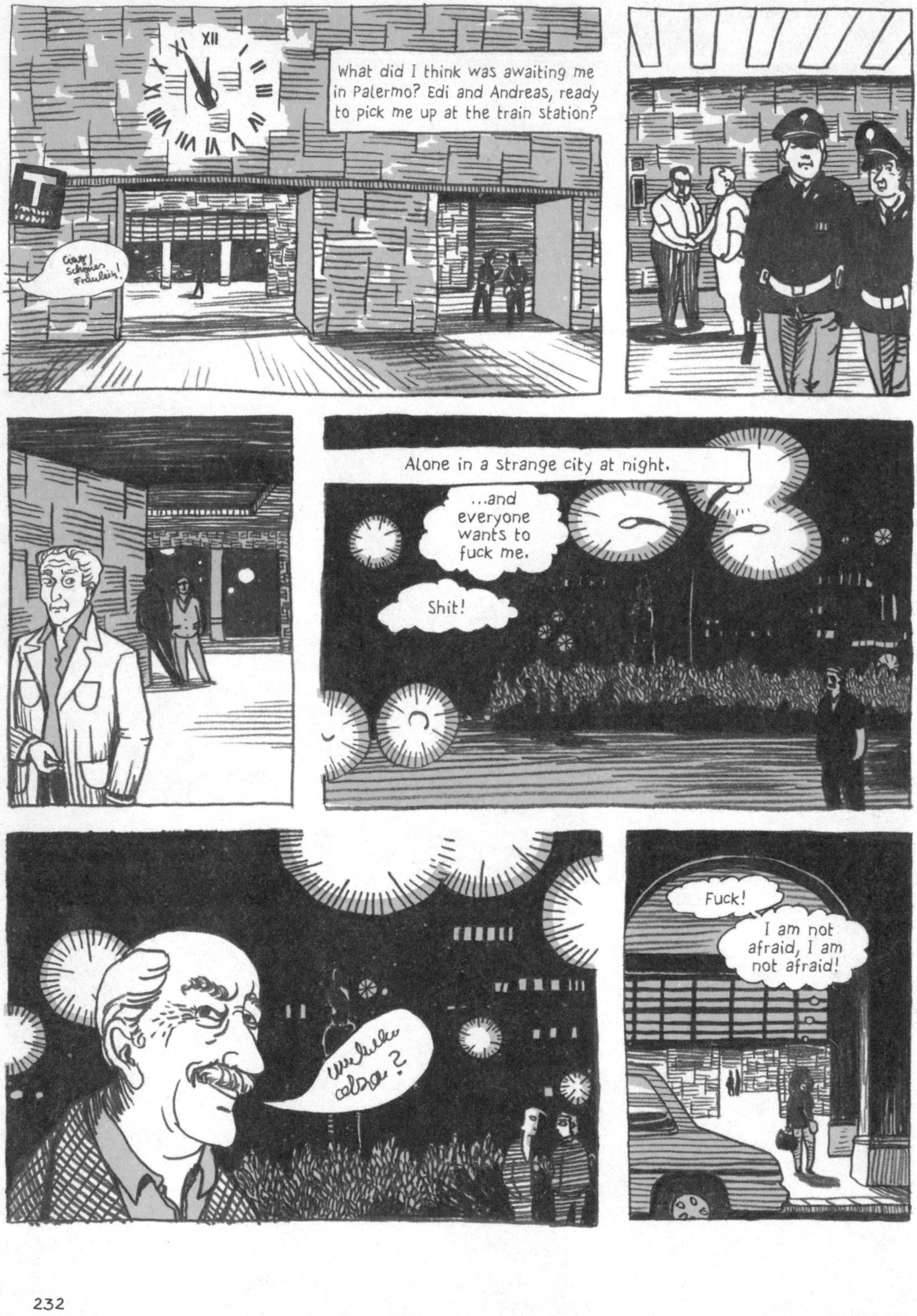
What did I think was awaiting me in Palermo? Edi and Andreas, ready to pick me up at the train station?
Ciao! schönes Fräulein!
Alone in a strange city at night.
...and everyone wants to fuck me.
Shit!
Fuck!
I am not afraid, I am not afraid!

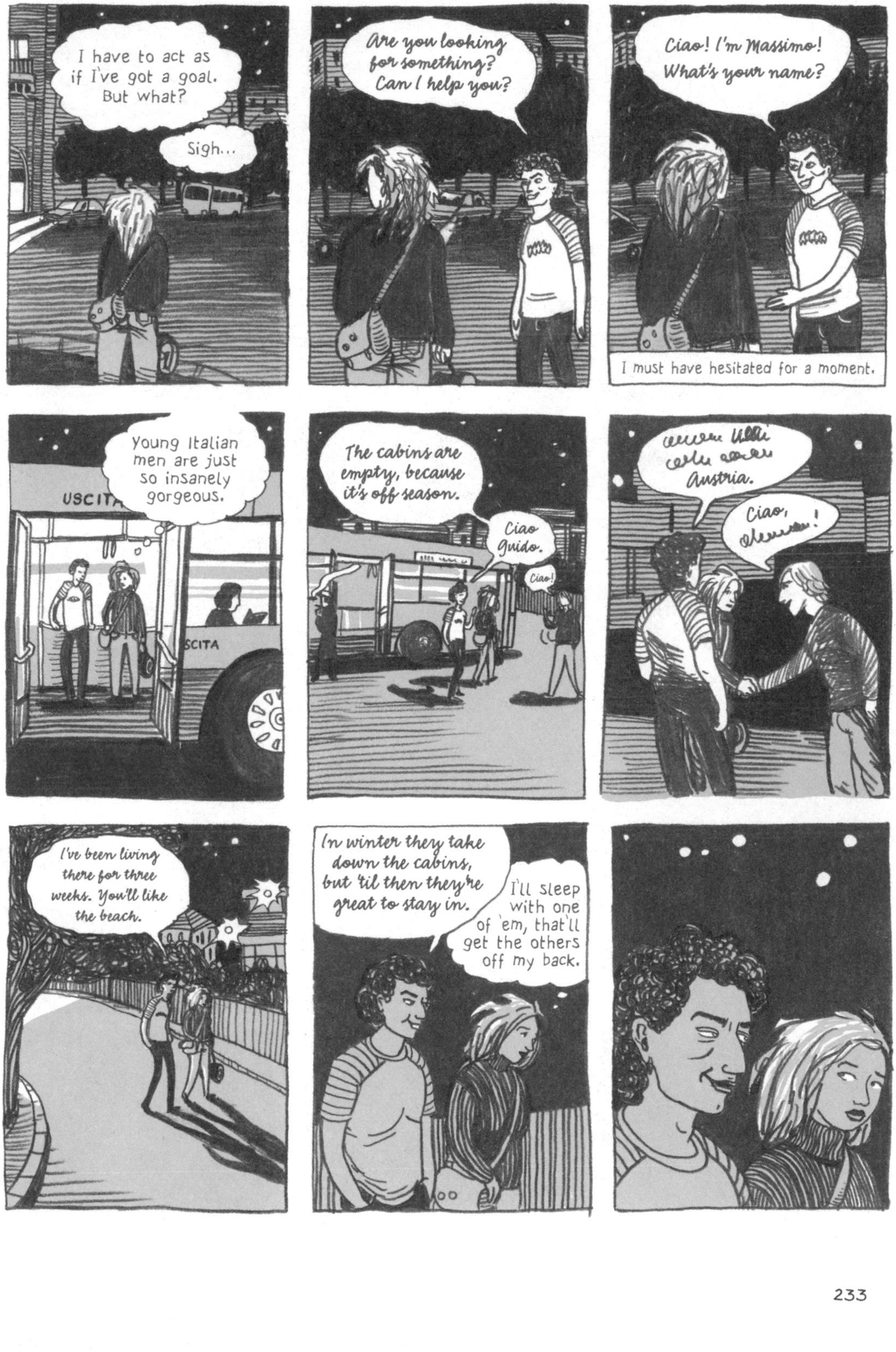
I have to act as if I've got a goal. But what?
Sigh...
Are you looking for something? Can I help you?
Ciao! I'm Massimo! What's your name?
I must have hesitated for a moment.
Young Italian men are just so insanely gorgeous.
USCITA
USCITA
The cabins are empty, because it's off season.
Ciao Guido.
Ciao!
Austria.
Ciao,
I've been living there for three weeks. You'll like the beach.
In winter they take down the cabins, but 'til then they're great to stay in.
I'll sleep with one of 'em, that'll get the others off my back.

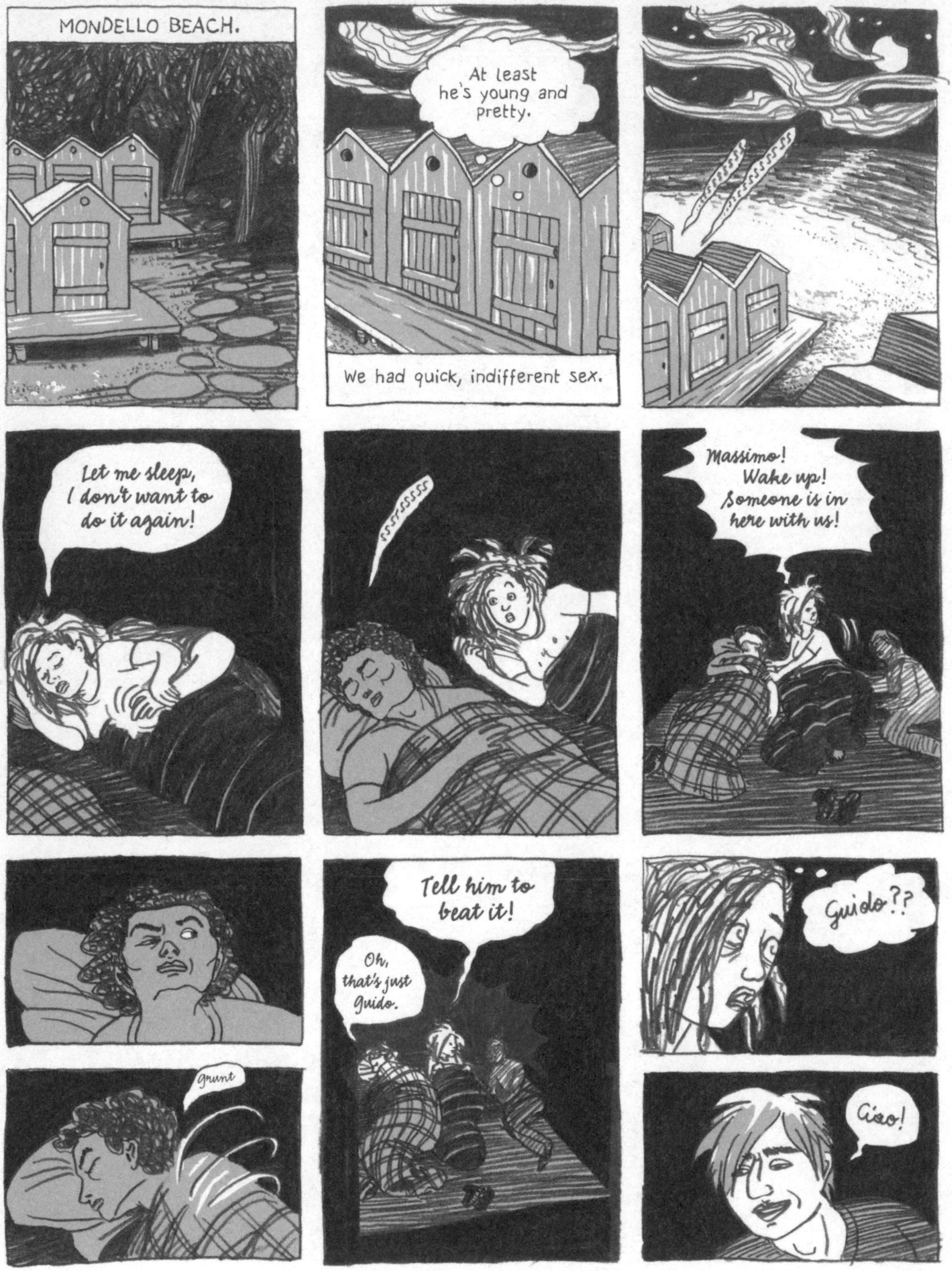
MONDELLO BEACH.
At least he's young and pretty.
We had quick, indifferent sex.
Let me sleep, I don't want to do it again!
Massimo! Wake up! Someone is in here with us!
Tell him to beat it!
Oh, that's just Guido.
Guido??
Grunt
Ciao!

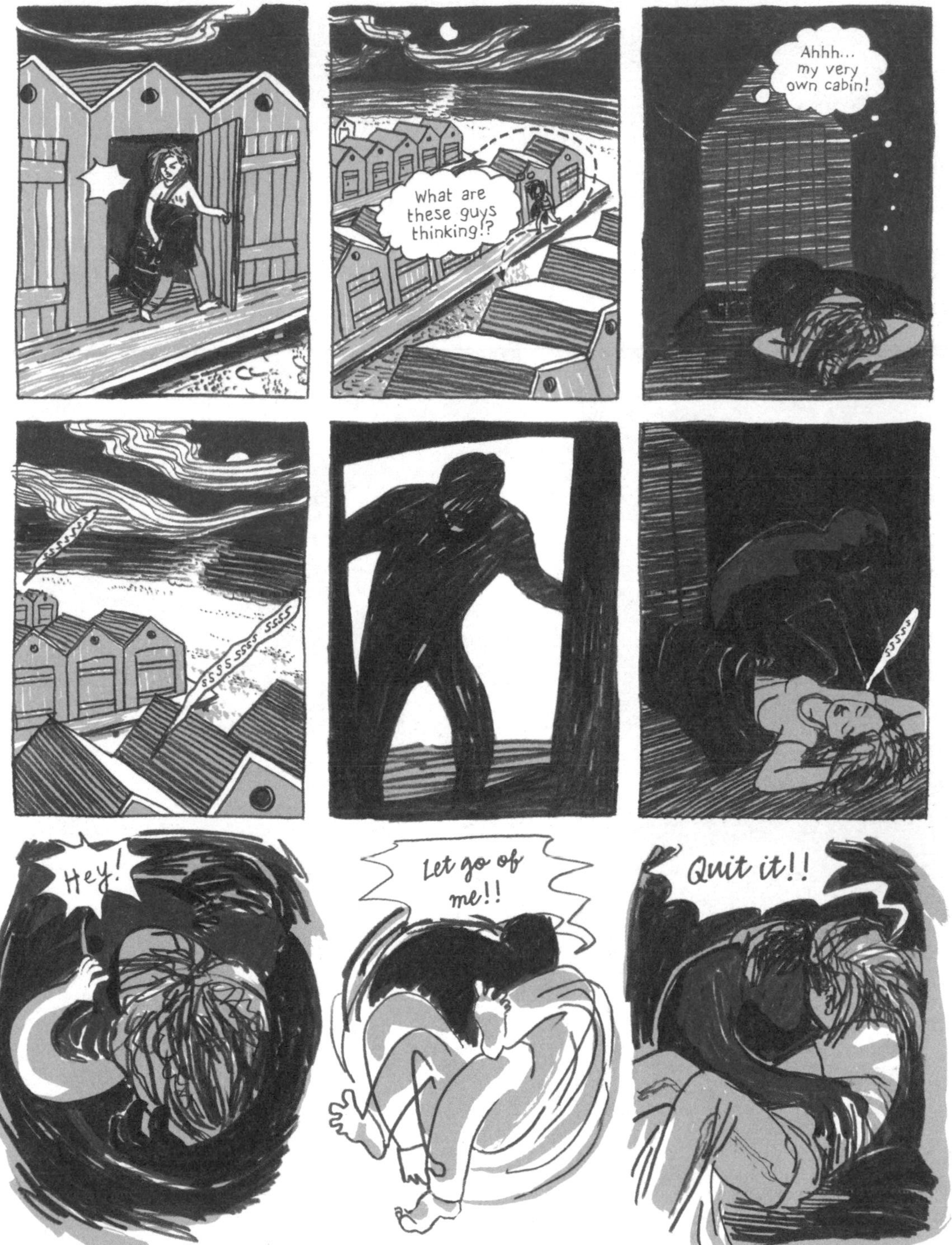
What are these guys thinking!?
Ahhh... my very own cabin!
Hey!
Let go of me!!
Quit it!!

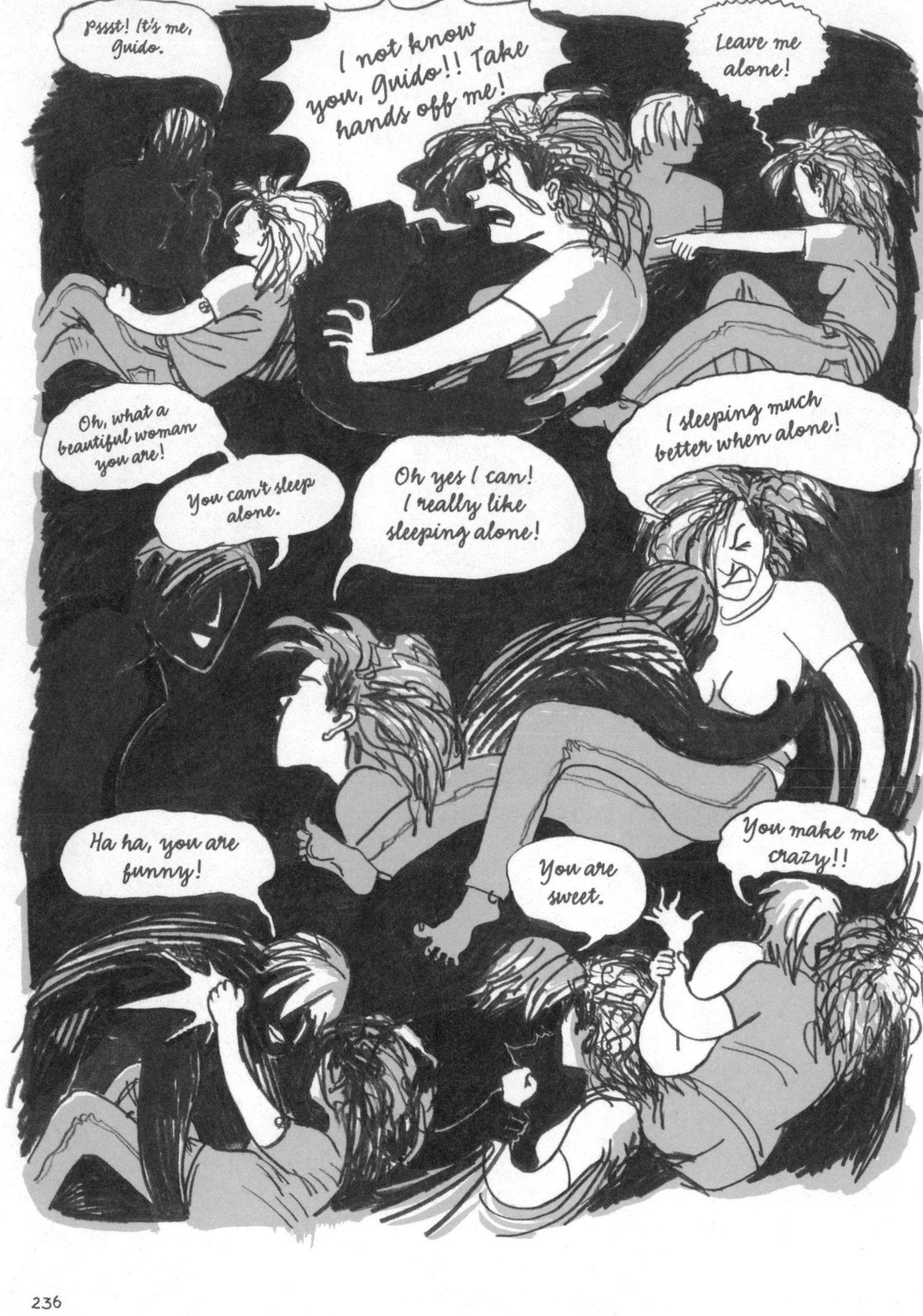
Pssst! It's me, Guido.
I not know you, Guido!! Take hands off me!
Leave me alone!
Oh, what a beautiful woman you are!
You can't sleep alone.
Oh yes I can! I really like sleeping alone!
I sleeping much better when alone!
Ha ha, you are funny!
You are sweet.
You make me crazy!!

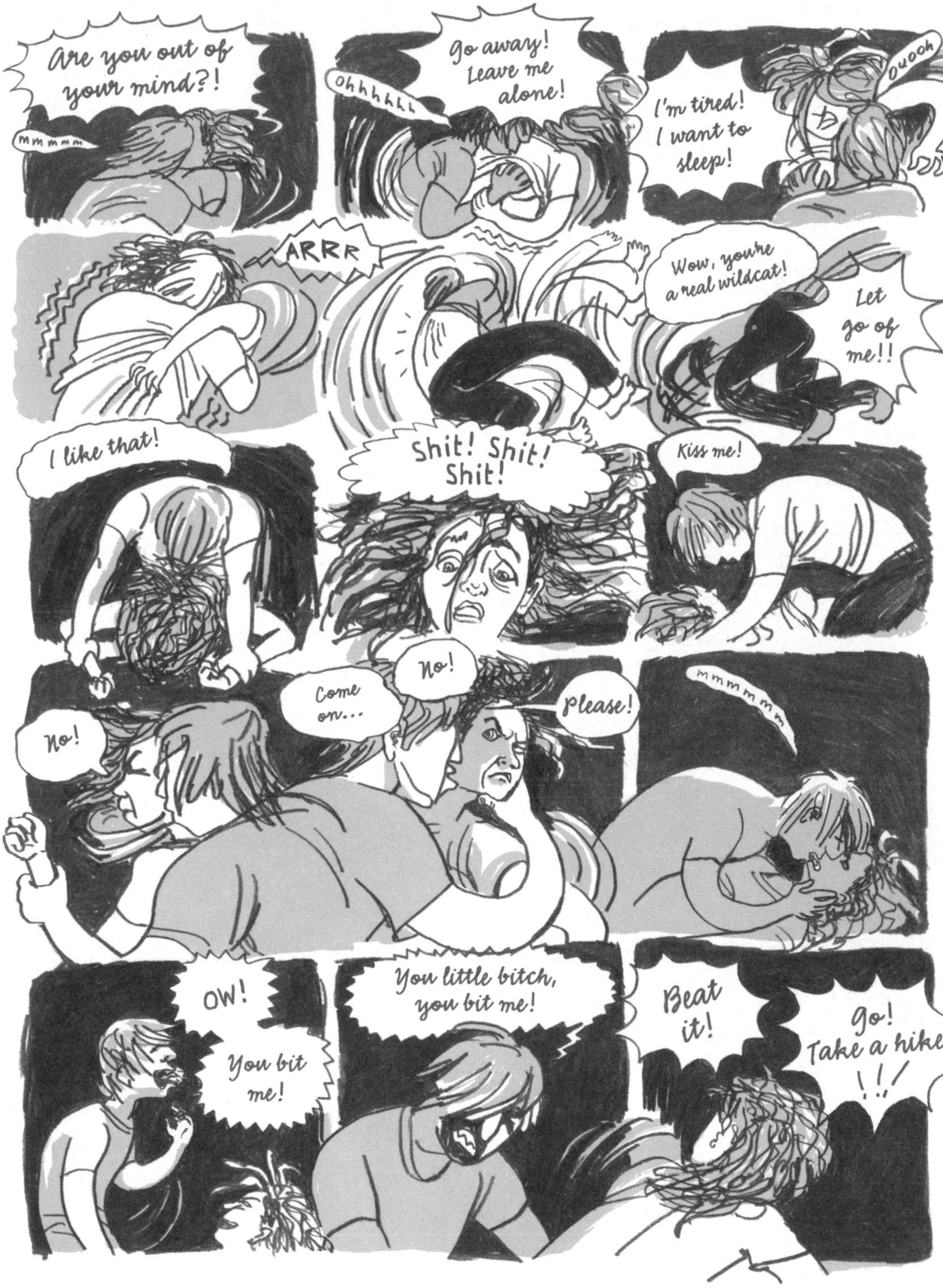
Are you out of your mind?!
mmmmm
Go away! Leave me alone!
Ohhhhhh
I'm tired! I want to sleep!
Ouooh
ARRR
Wow, you're a real wildcat!
Let go of me!!
I like that!
Shit! Shit! Shit!
Kiss me!
No!
Come on...
No!
please!
mmmmmm
OW!
You bit me!
You little bitch, you bit me!
Beat it!
Go! Take a hike!!!

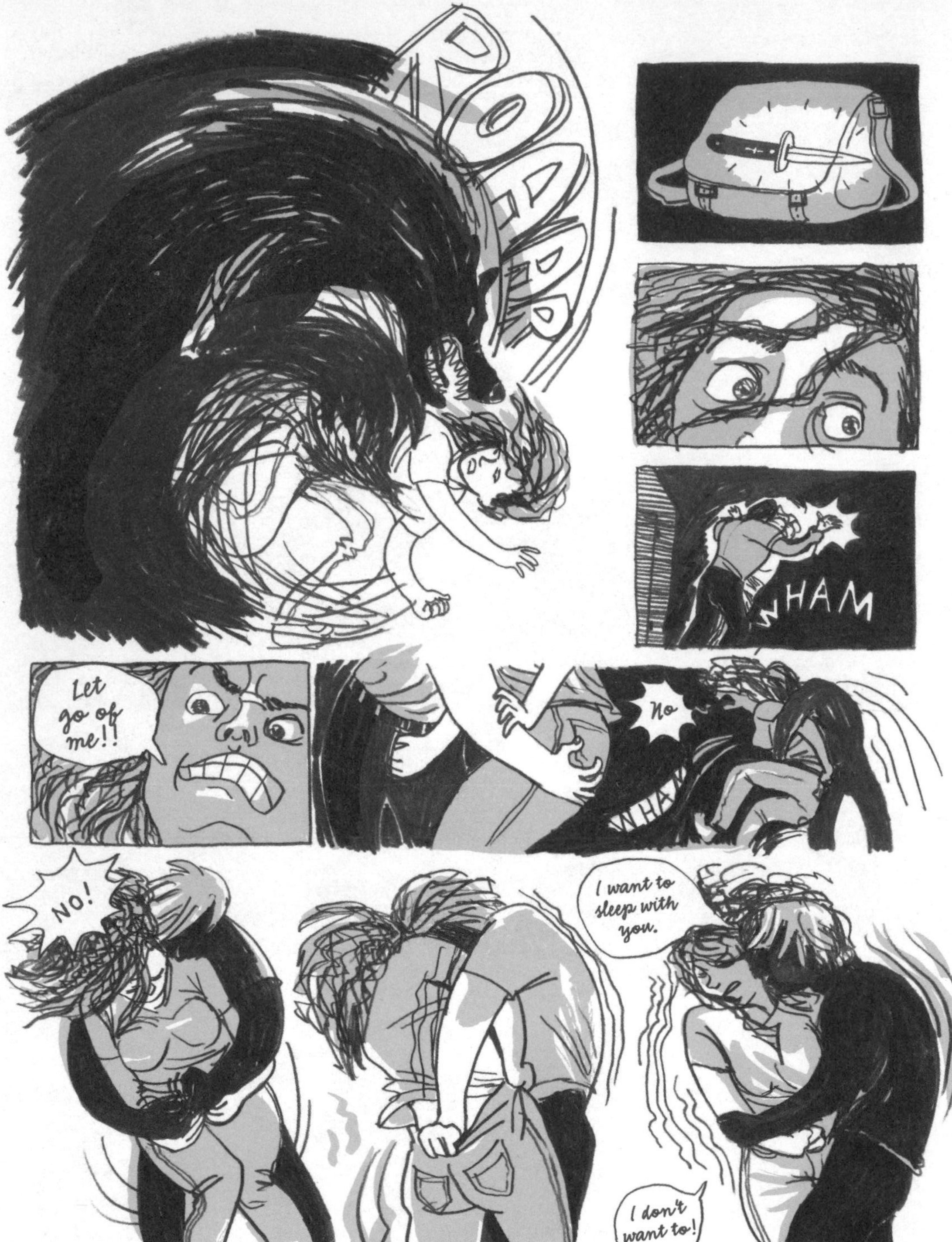
ROAAARR
WHAM
Let go of me!!
No
WHAM
NO!
I want to sleep with you.
I don't want to!

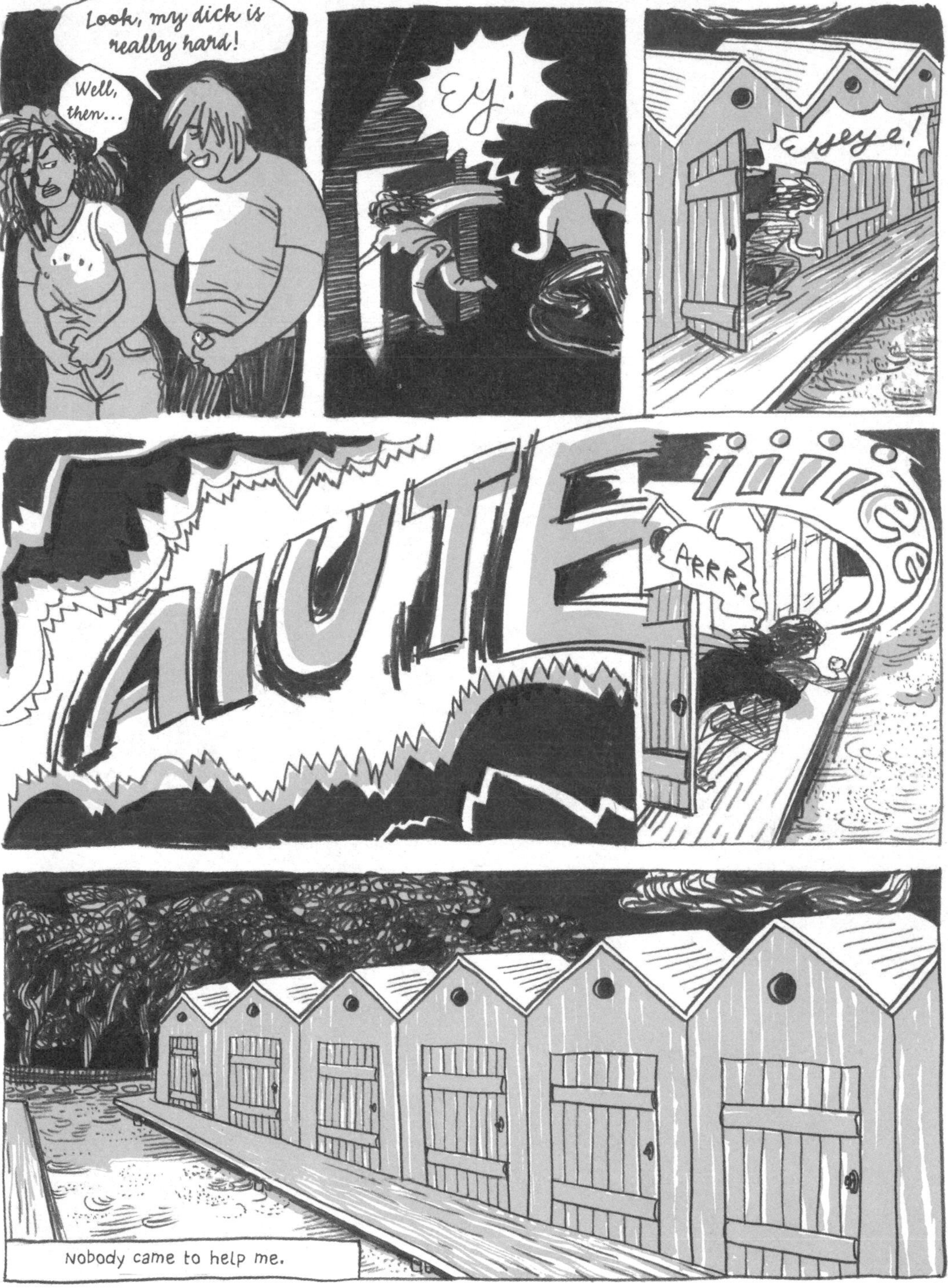
Look, my dick is really hard!
Well, then…
Ey!
Eyeye!
AIUTEiiiie
ARRRR
Nobody came to help me.

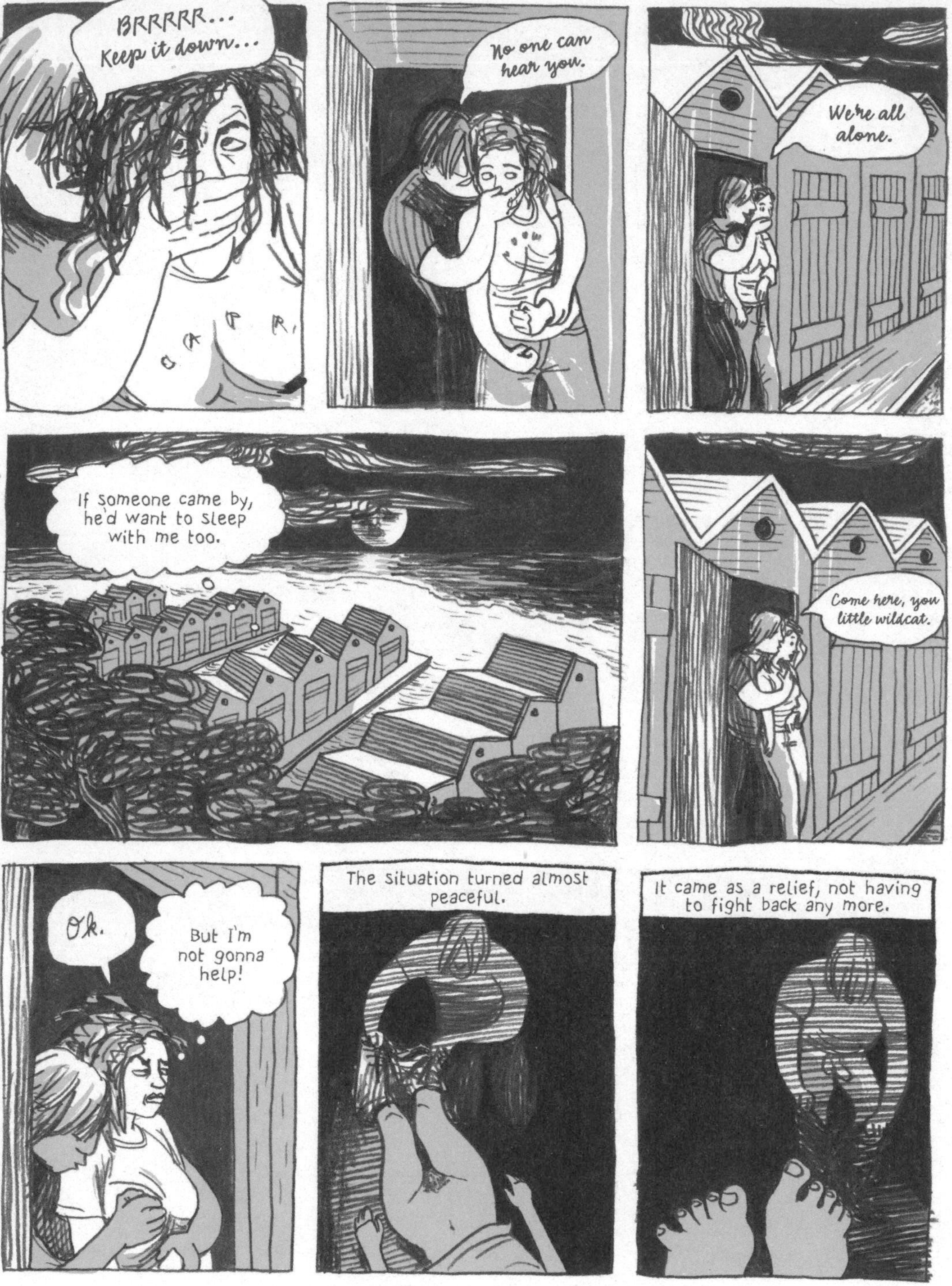
BRRRRR...
Keep it down...
No one can hear you.
We're all alone.
If someone came by, he'd want to sleep with me too.
Come here, you little wildcat.
Ok.
But I'm not gonna help!
The situation turned almost peaceful.
It came as a relief, not having to fight back any more.

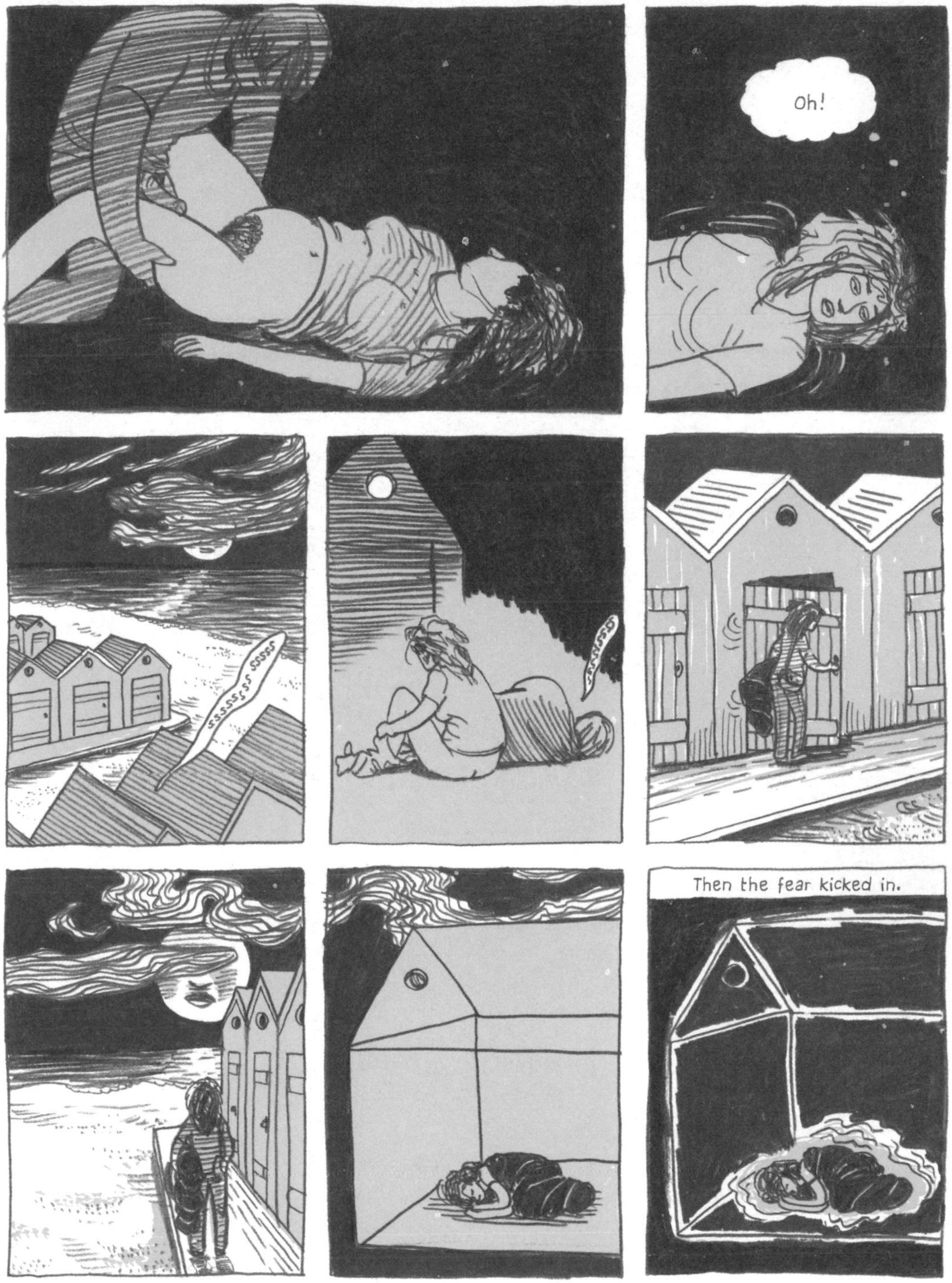
Oh!
Then the fear kicked in.

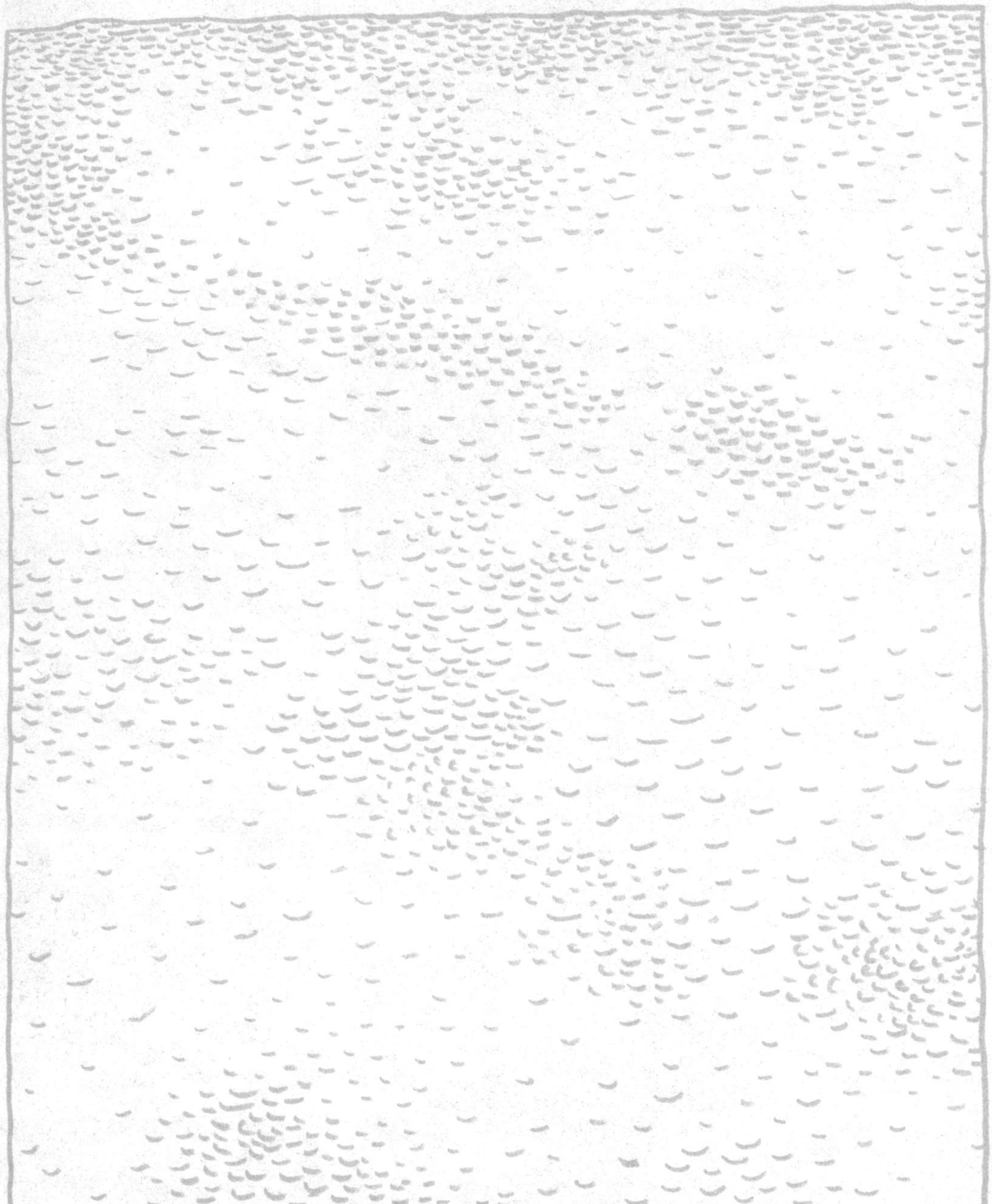

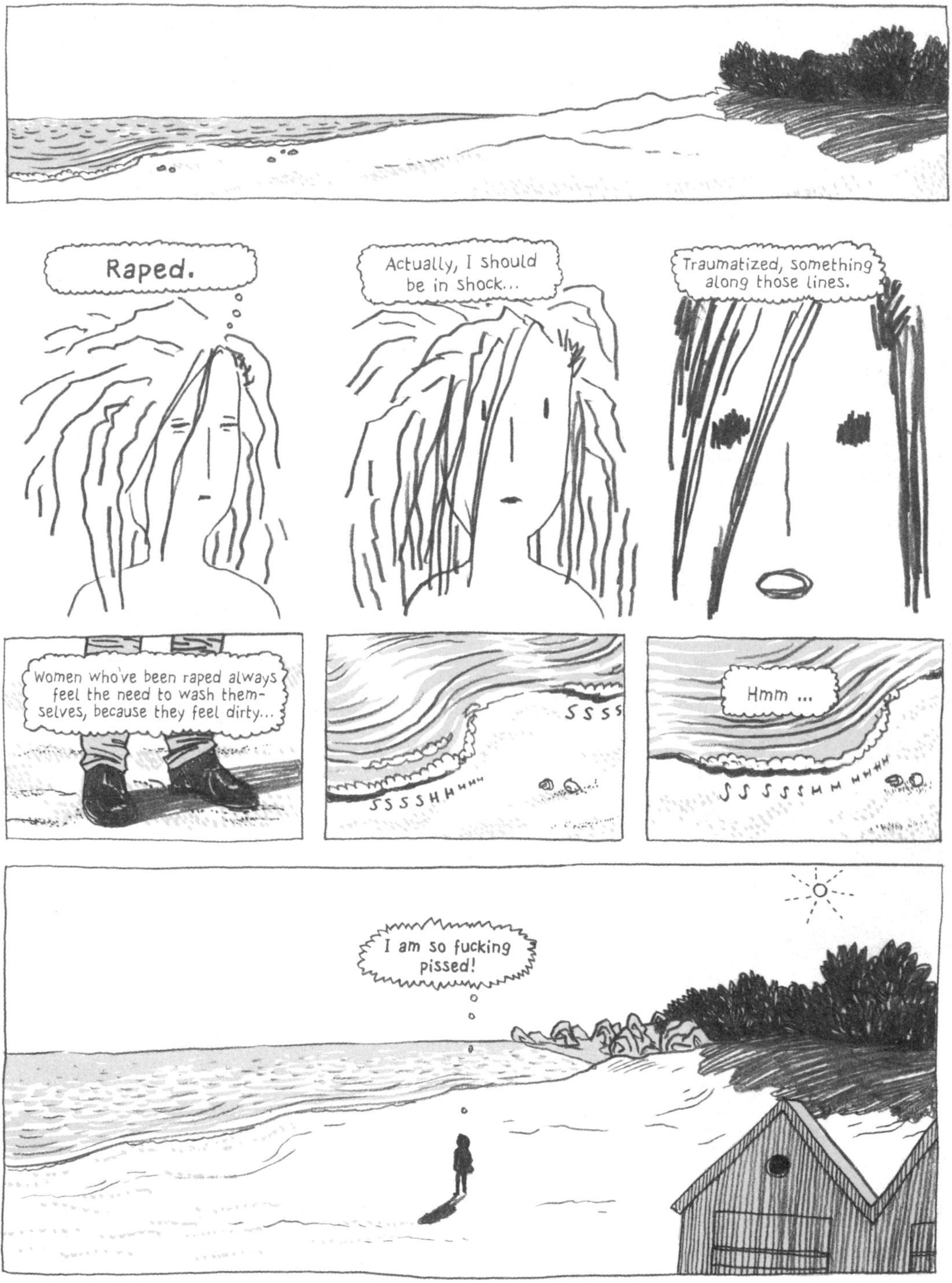
Raped.
Actually, I should be in shock...
Traumatized, something along those lines.
Women who've been raped always feel the need to wash themselves, because they feel dirty...
SSSS
SSSSHHHHH
Hmm ...
SSSSSHHHHHH
I am so fucking pissed!

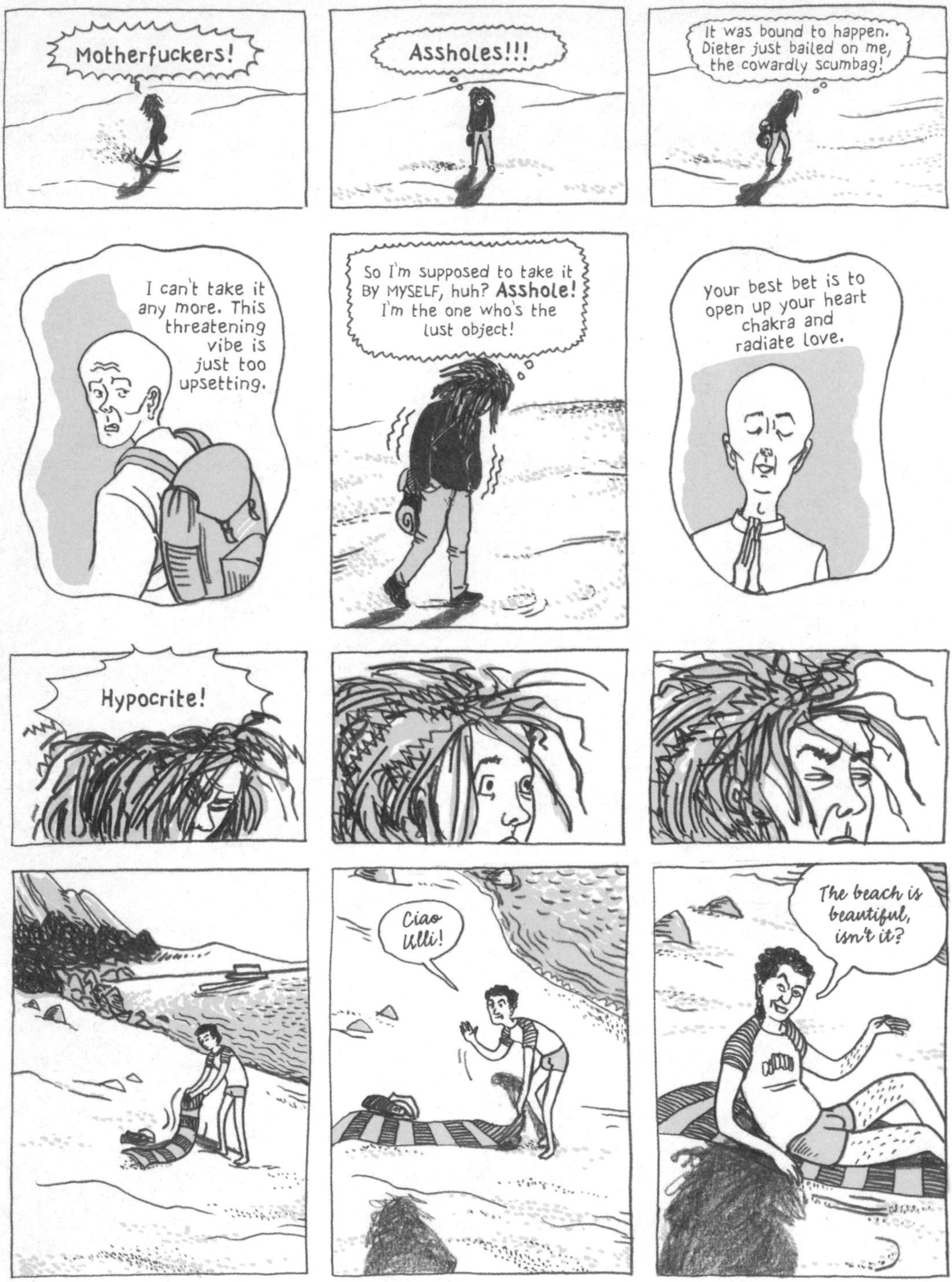
Motherfuckers!
Assholes!!!
It was bound to happen. Dieter just bailed on me, the cowardly scumbag!
I can't take it any more. This threatening vibe is just too upsetting.
So I'm supposed to take it BY MYSELF, huh? Asshole! I'm the one who's the lust object!
Your best bet is to open up your heart chakra and radiate love.
Hypocrite!
Ciao Ulli!
The beach is beautiful, isn't it?

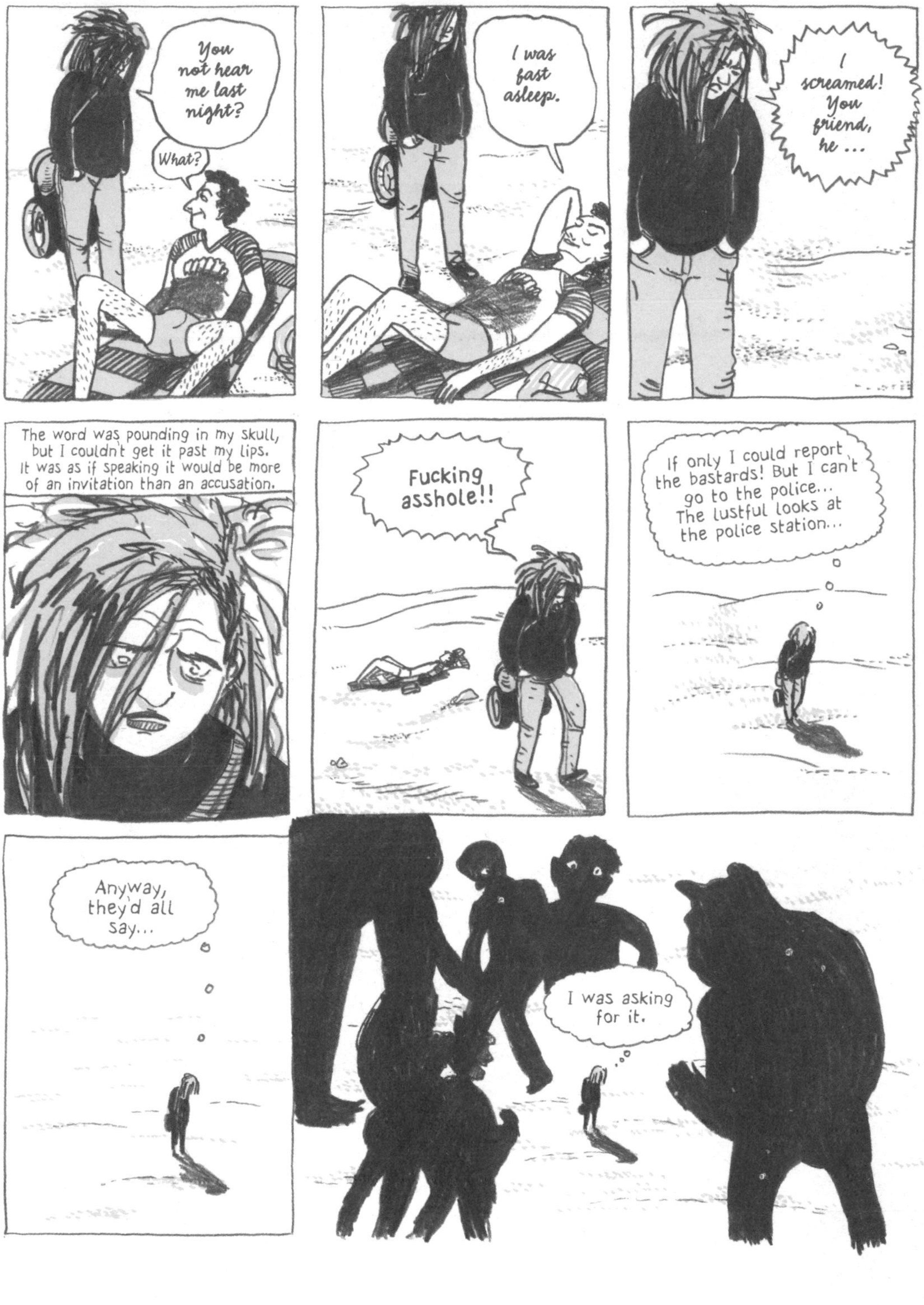

You not hear me last night?
What?
I was fast asleep.
I screamed! You friend, he ...
The word was pounding in my skull, but I couldn't get it past my lips. It was as if speaking it would be more of an invitation than an accusation.
Fucking asshole!!
If only I could report the bastards! But I can't go to the police... The lustful looks at the police station...
Anyway, they'd all say...
I was asking for it.

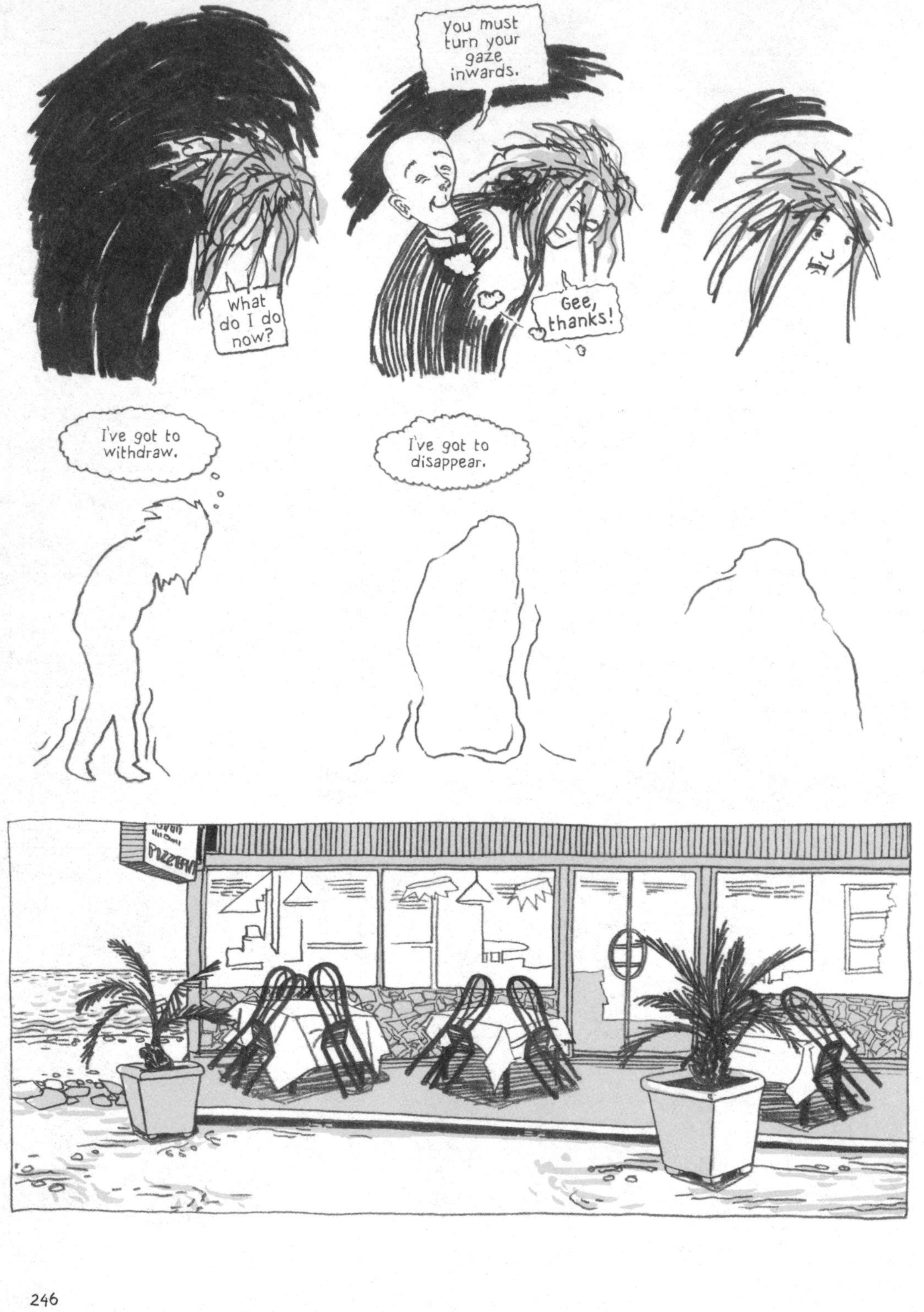
What do I do now?
You must turn your gaze inwards.
Gee, thanks!
I've got to withdraw.
I've got to disappear.

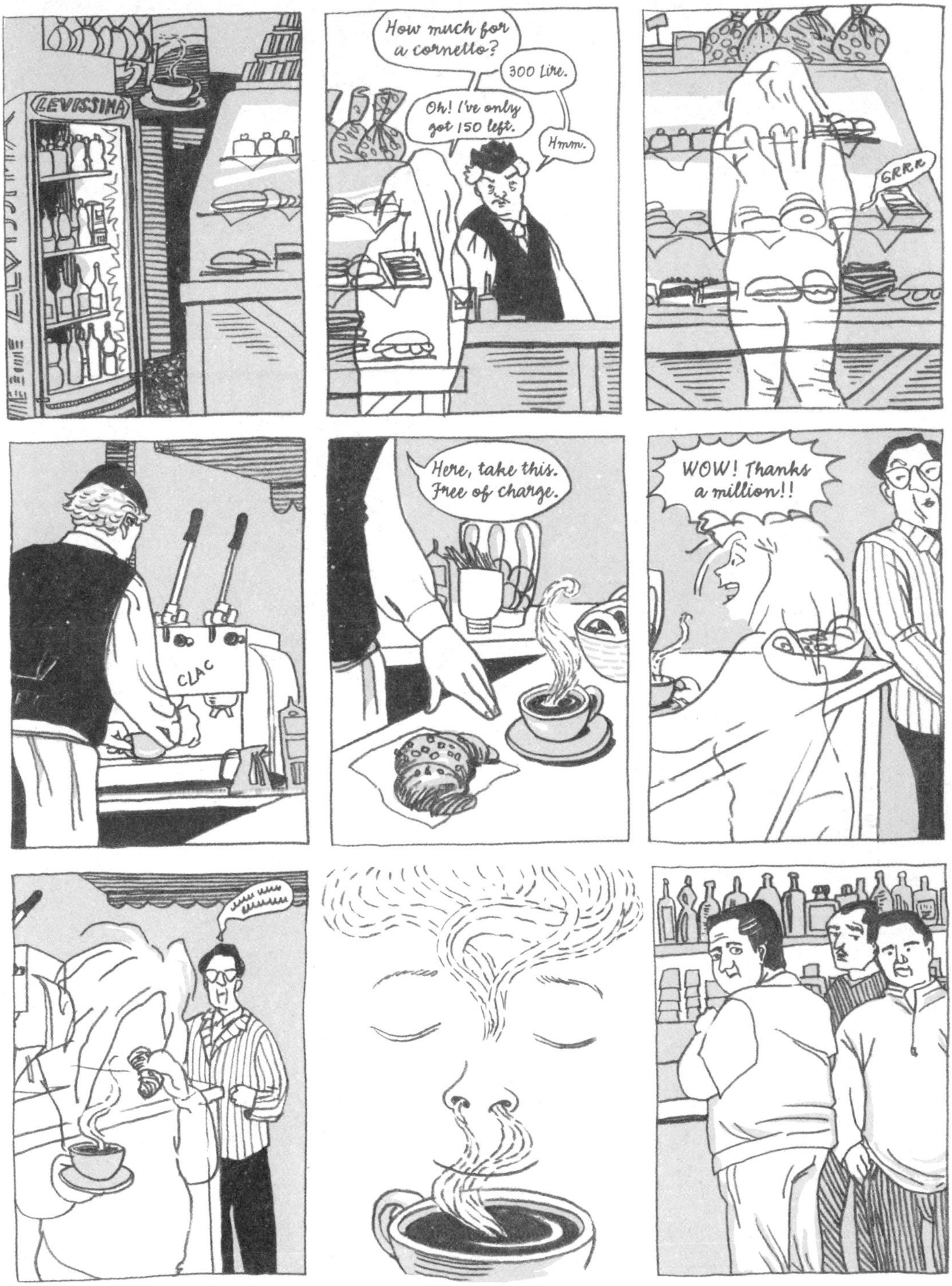
LEVISSINA
How much for a cornello?
300 Lire.
Oh! I've only got 150 left.
Hmm.
GRRR
CLAC
Here, take this. Free of charge.
WOW! Thanks a million!!

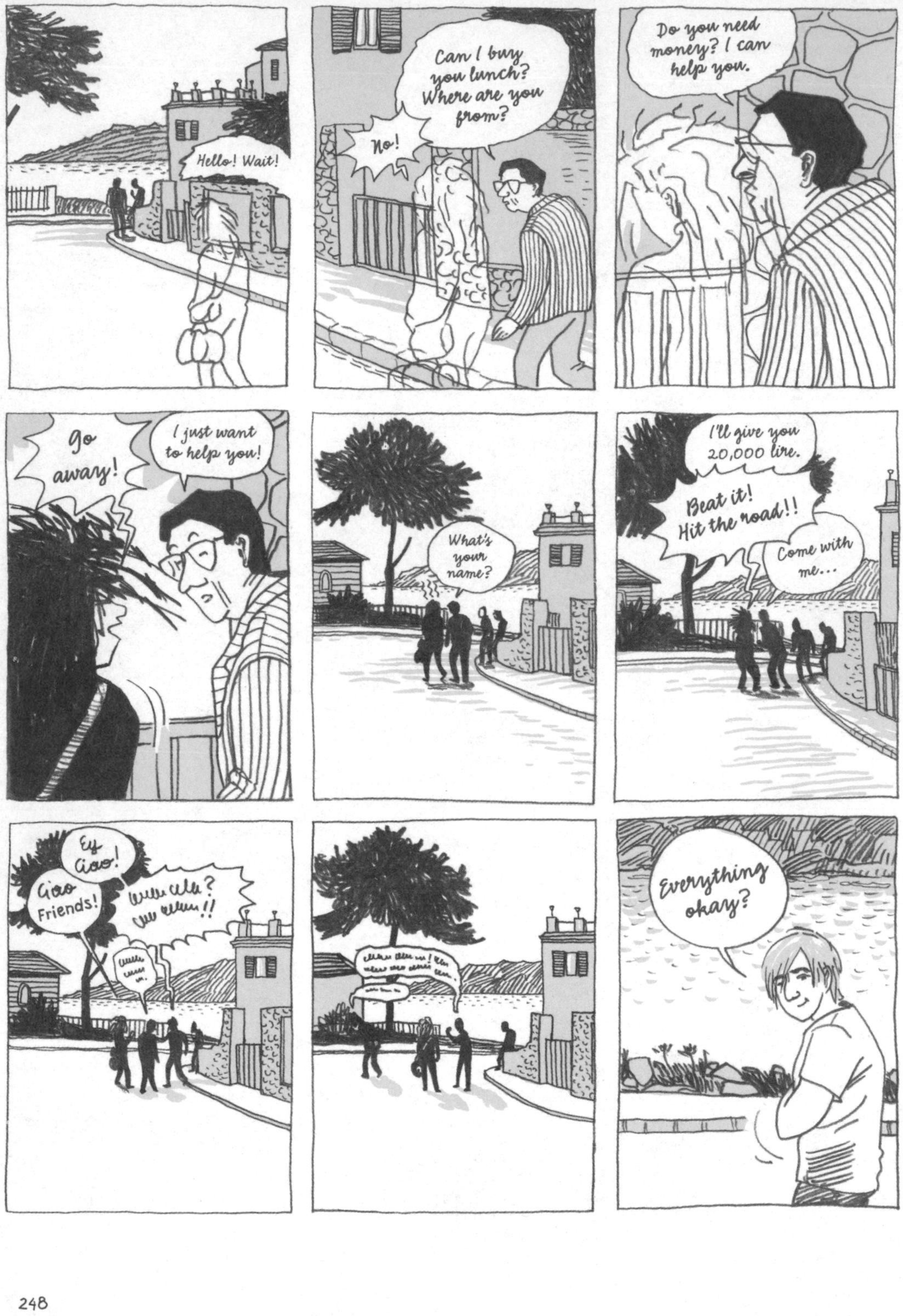
Hello! Wait!
Can I buy you lunch? Where are you from?
No!
Do you need money? I can help you.
Go away!
I just want to help you!
What's your name?
I'll give you 20,000 lire.
Beat it! Hit the road!!
Come with me...
Ey Ciao!
Ciao Friends!
Everything okay?

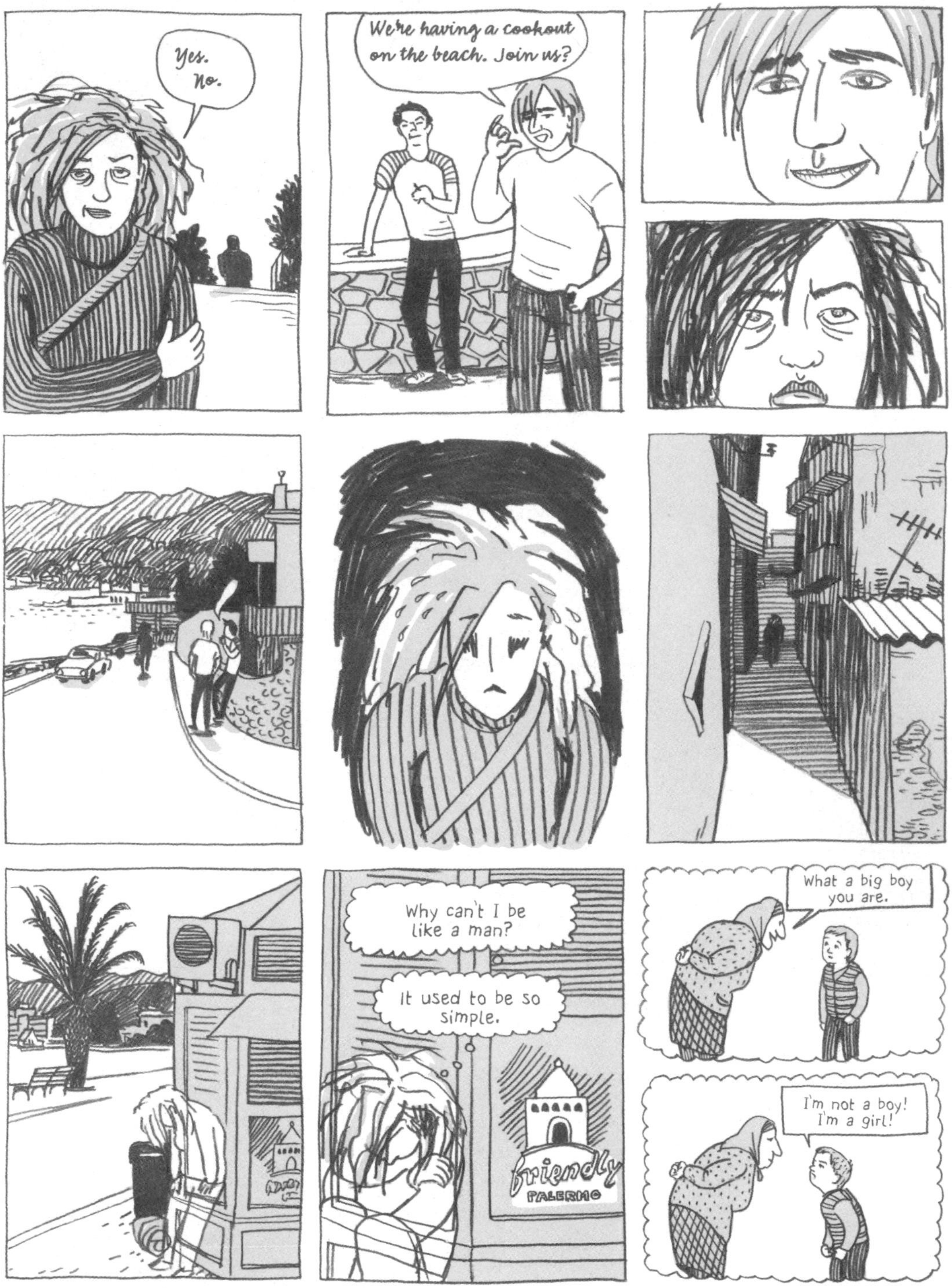
Yes.
No.
We're having a cookout on the beach. Join us?
Why can't I be like a man?
It used to be so simple.
friendly
PALERMO
What a big boy you are.
I'm not a boy! I'm a girl!

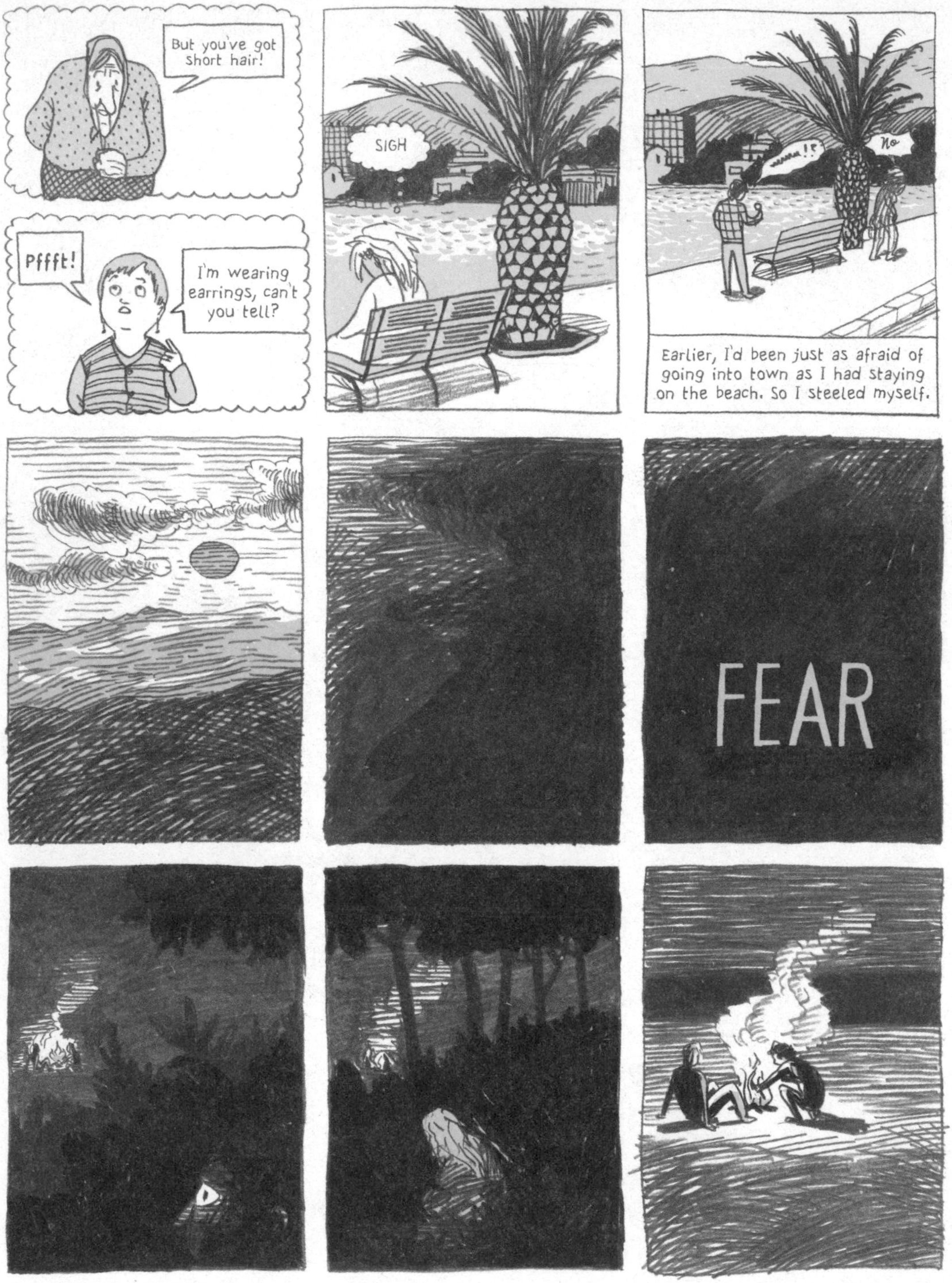

But you've got short hair!
Pffft!
I'm wearing earrings, can't you tell?
SIGH
No
Earlier, I'd been just as afraid of going into town as I had staying on the beach. So I steeled myself.
FEAR

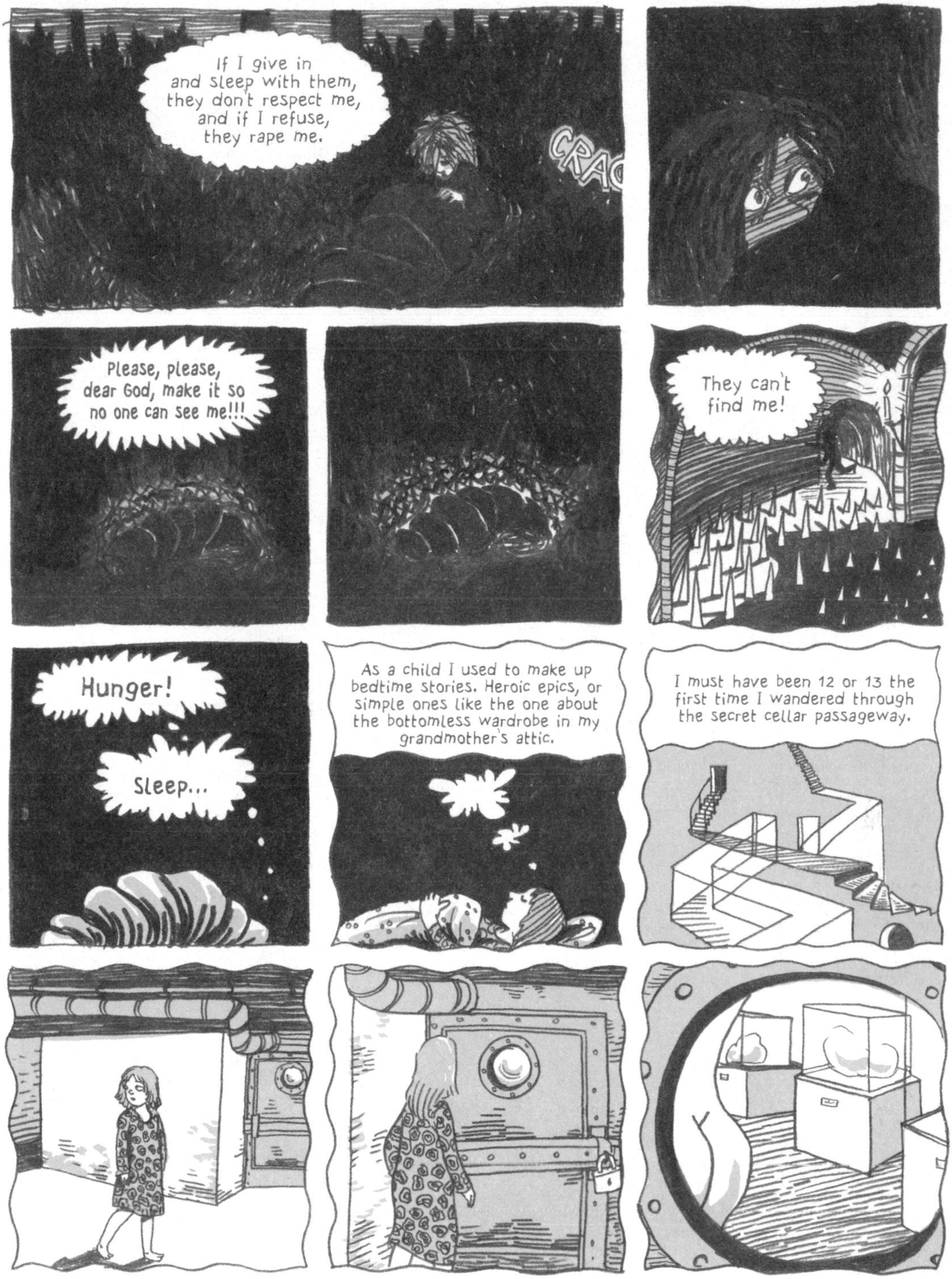
If I give in and sleep with them, they don't respect me, and if I refuse, they rape me.
CRAC
Please, please, dear God, make it so no one can see me!!!
They can't find me!
Hunger!
Sleep...
As a child I used to make up bedtime stories. Heroic epics, or simple ones like the one about the bottomless wardrobe in my grandmother's attic.
I must have been 12 or 13 the first time I wandered through the secret cellar passageway.

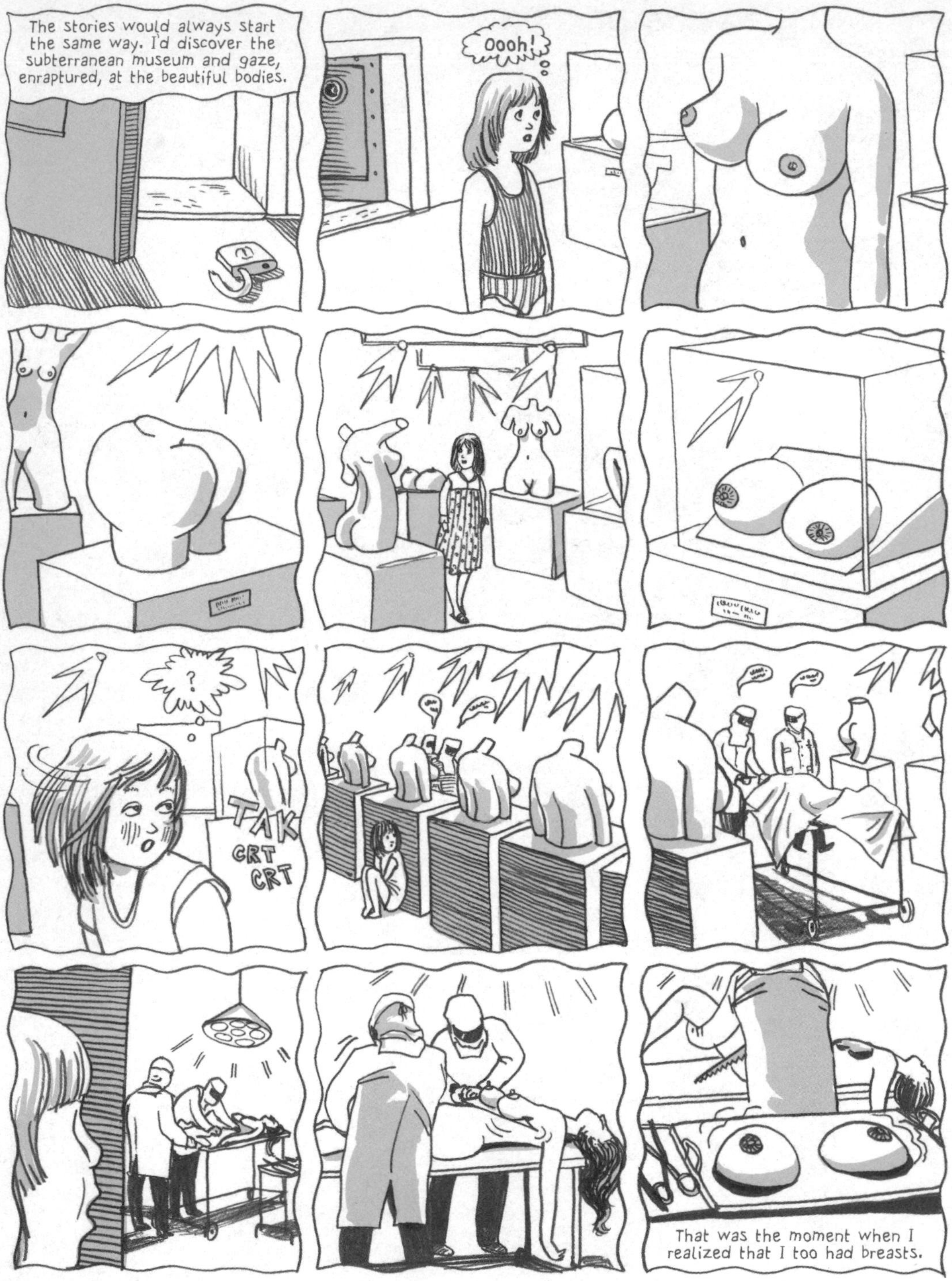
The stories would always start the same way. I'd discover the subterranean museum and gaze, enraptured, at the beautiful bodies.
Oooh!
?
TAK
CRT
CRT
That was the moment when I realized that I too had breasts.

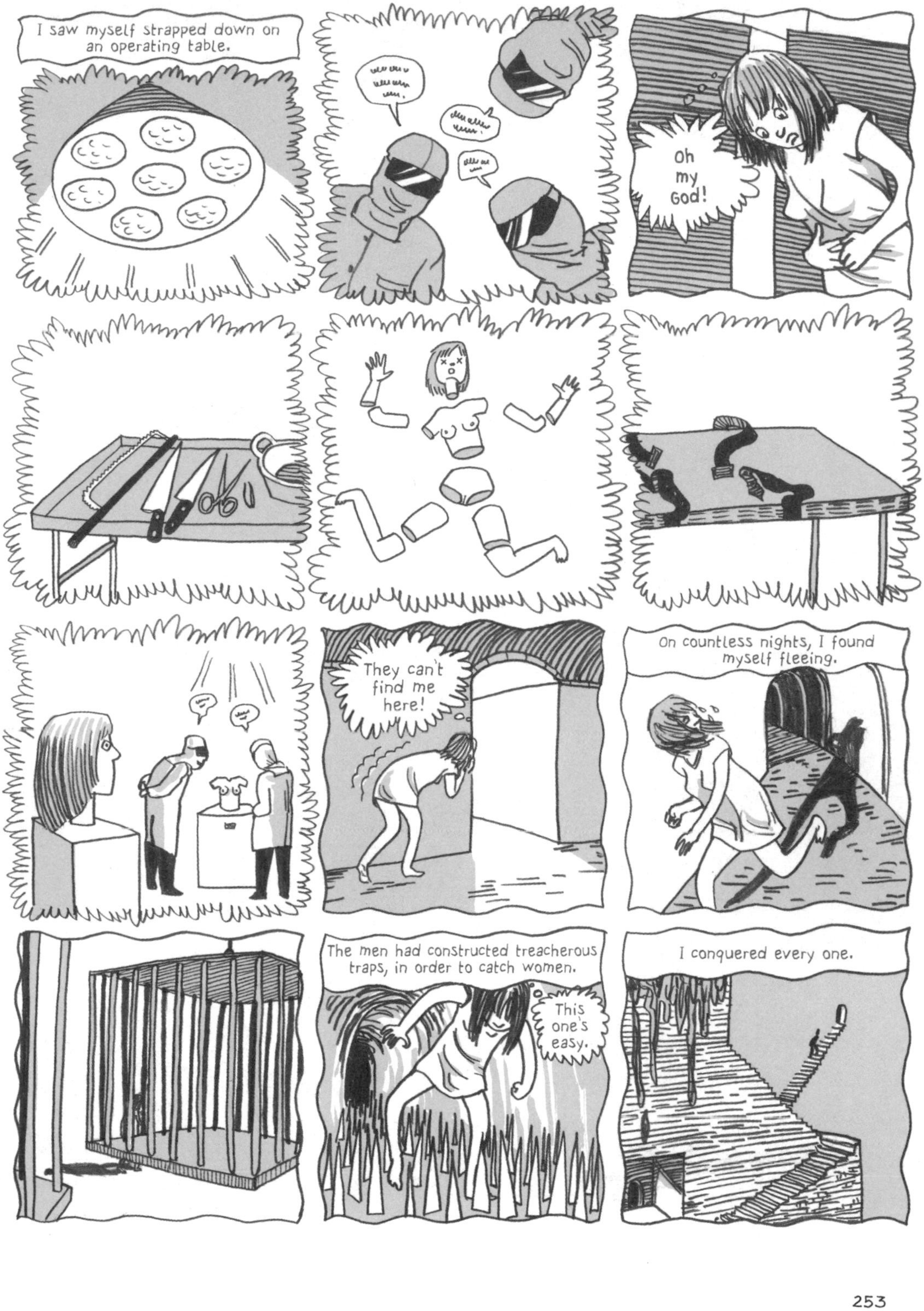
I saw myself strapped down on an operating table.
Oh my God!
They can't find me here!
On countless nights, I found myself fleeing.
The men had constructed treacherous traps, in order to catch women.
This one's easy.
I conquered every one.

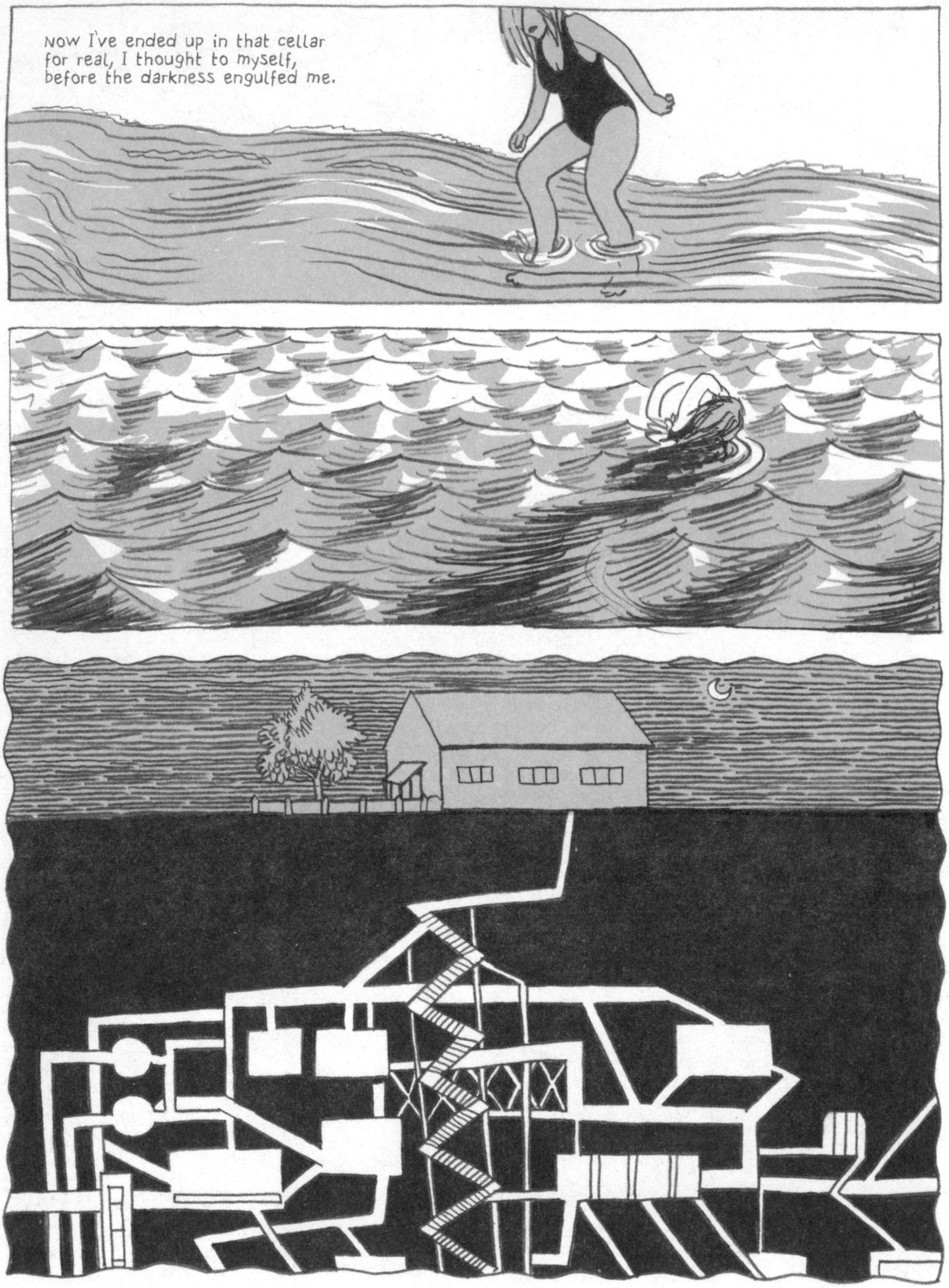
Now I've ended up in that cellar for real, I thought to myself, before the darkness engulfed me.

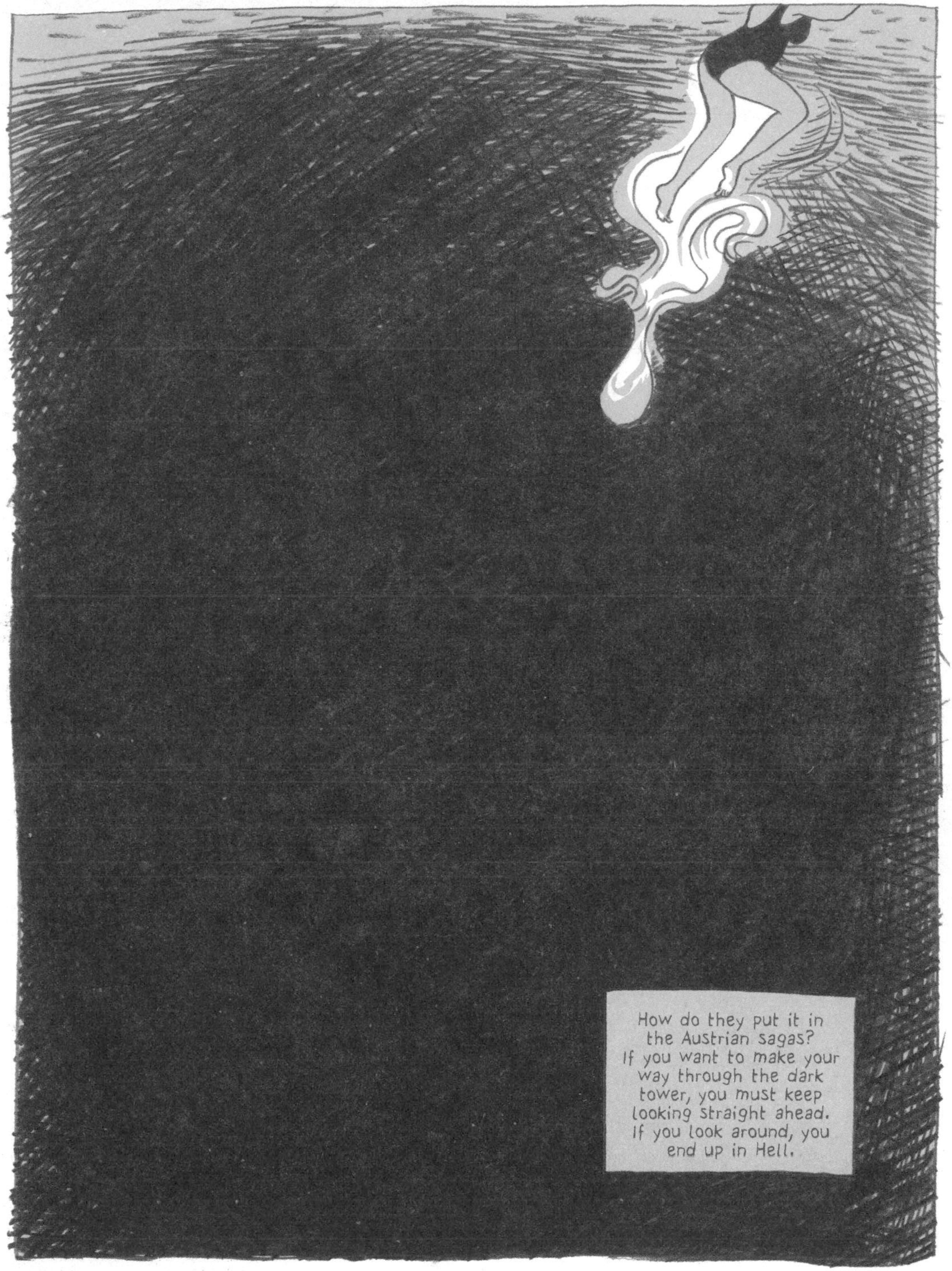
How do they put it in the Austrian sagas? If you want to make your way through the dark tower, you must keep looking straight ahead. If you look around, you end up in Hell.

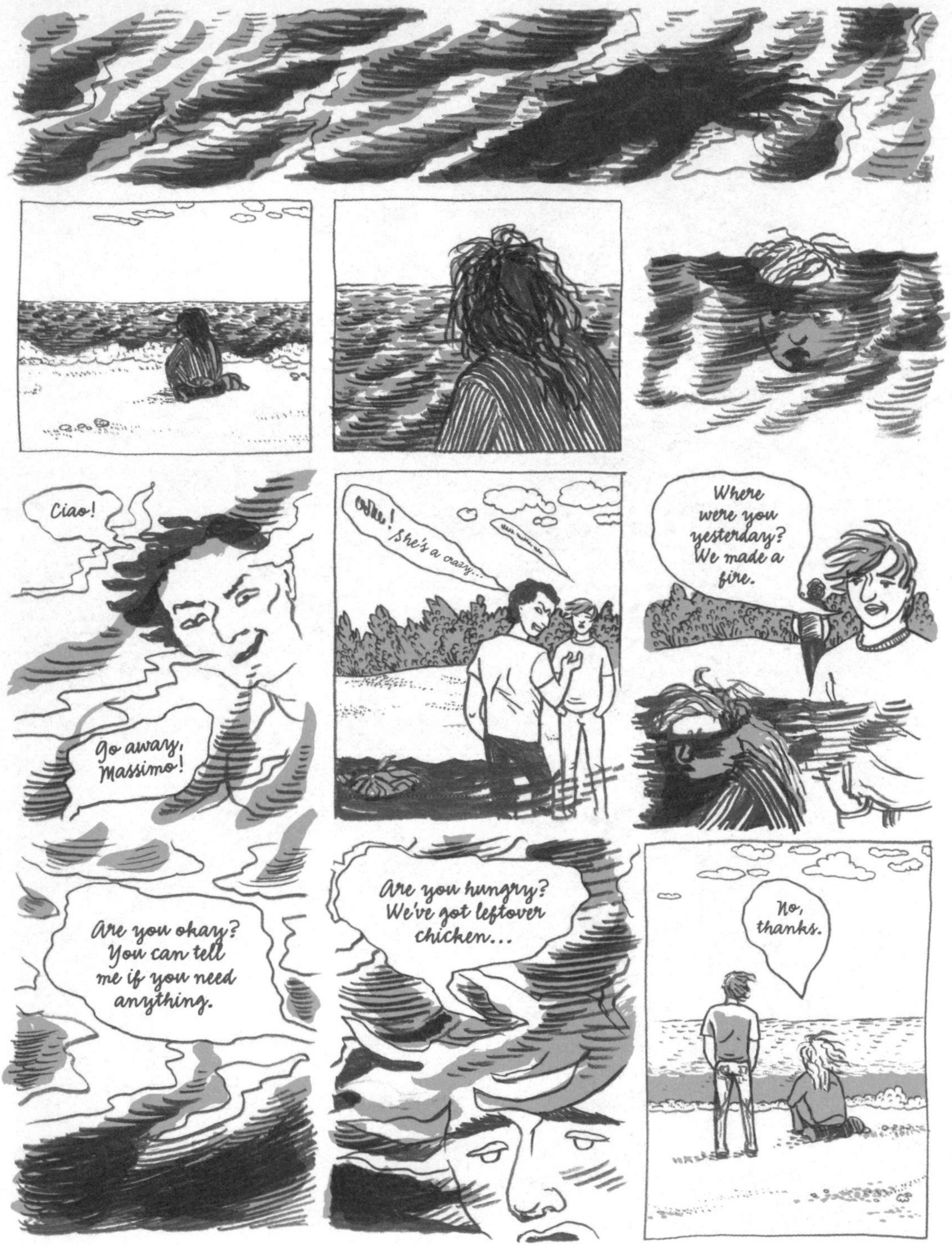
Ciao!
Go away, Massimo!
She's a crazy...
Where were you yesterday? We made a fire.
Are you okay? You can tell me if you need anything.
Are you hungry? We've got leftover chicken...
No, thanks.

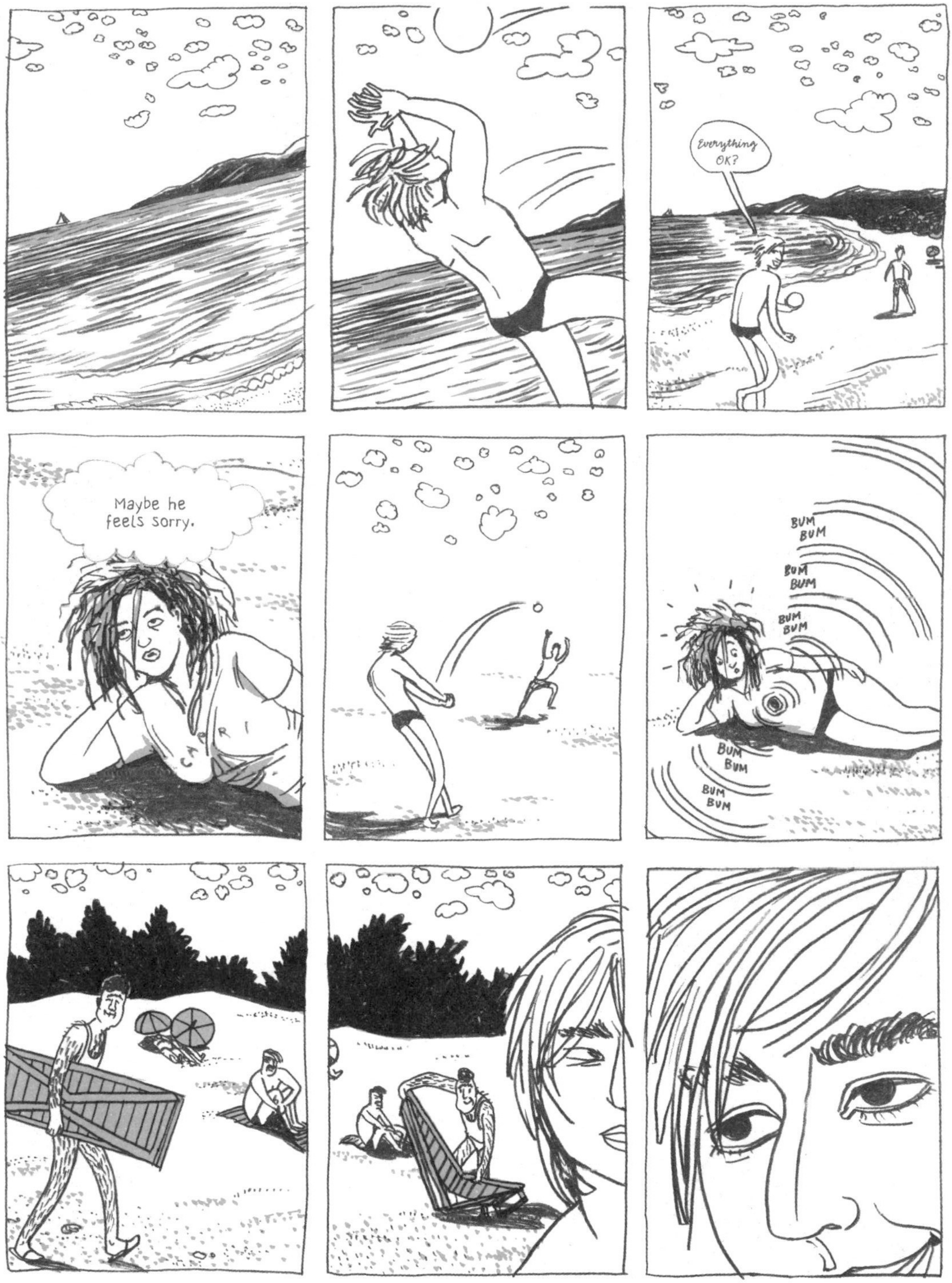
Everything OK?
Maybe he feels sorry.
BUM BUM
BUM BUM
BUM BUM
BUM BUM
BUM BUM

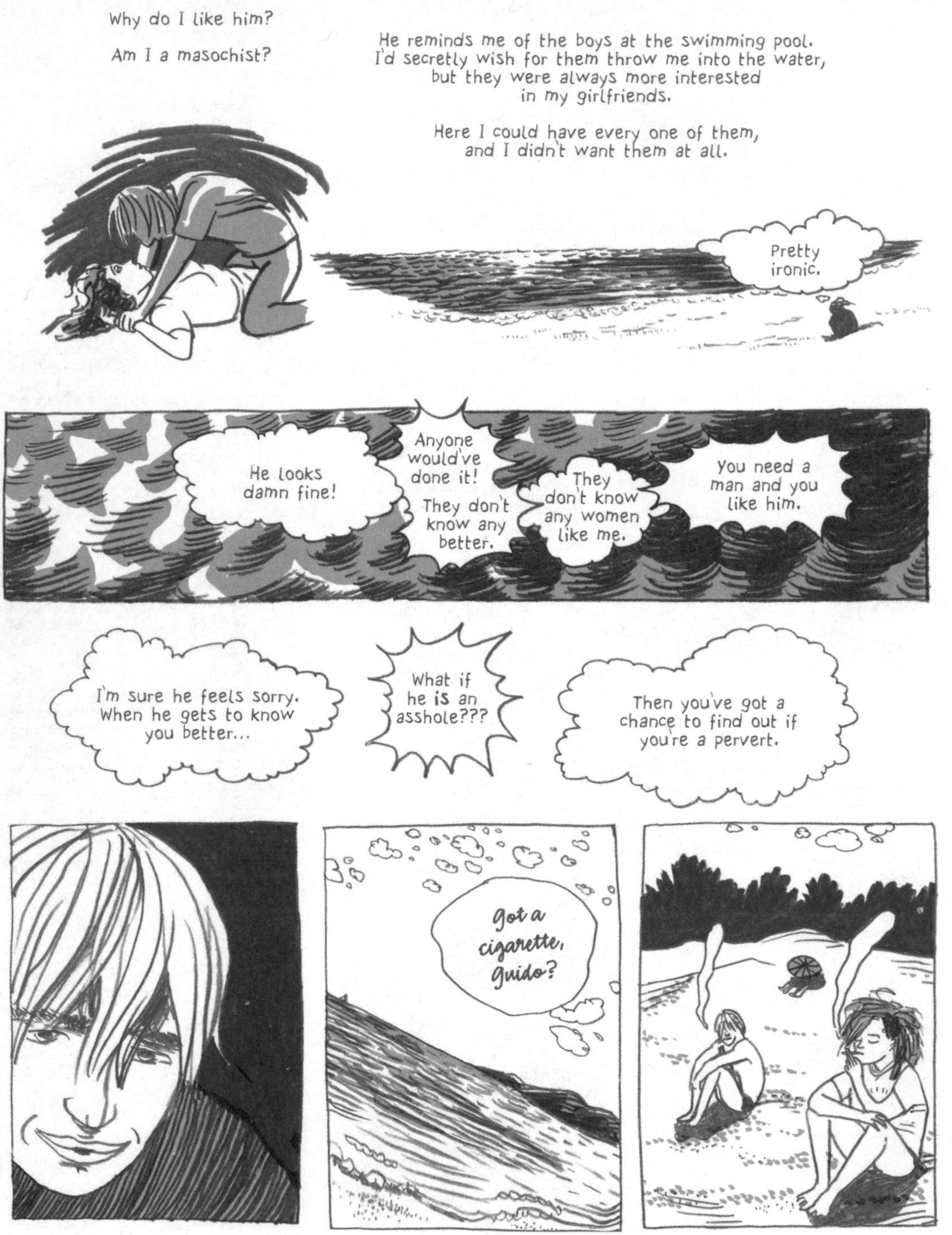
Why do I like him?
Am I a masochist?
He reminds me of the boys at the swimming pool. I'd secretly wish for them throw me into the water, but they were always more interested in my girlfriends.
Here I could have every one of them, and I didn't want them at all.
Pretty ironic.
He looks damn fine!
Anyone would've done it!
They don't know any better.
They don't know any women like me.
You need a man and you like him.
I'm sure he feels sorry. When he gets to know you better...
What if he **is** an asshole???
Then you've got a chance to find out if you're a pervert.
Got a cigarette, Guido?

XIII. the BRIDEGROOM

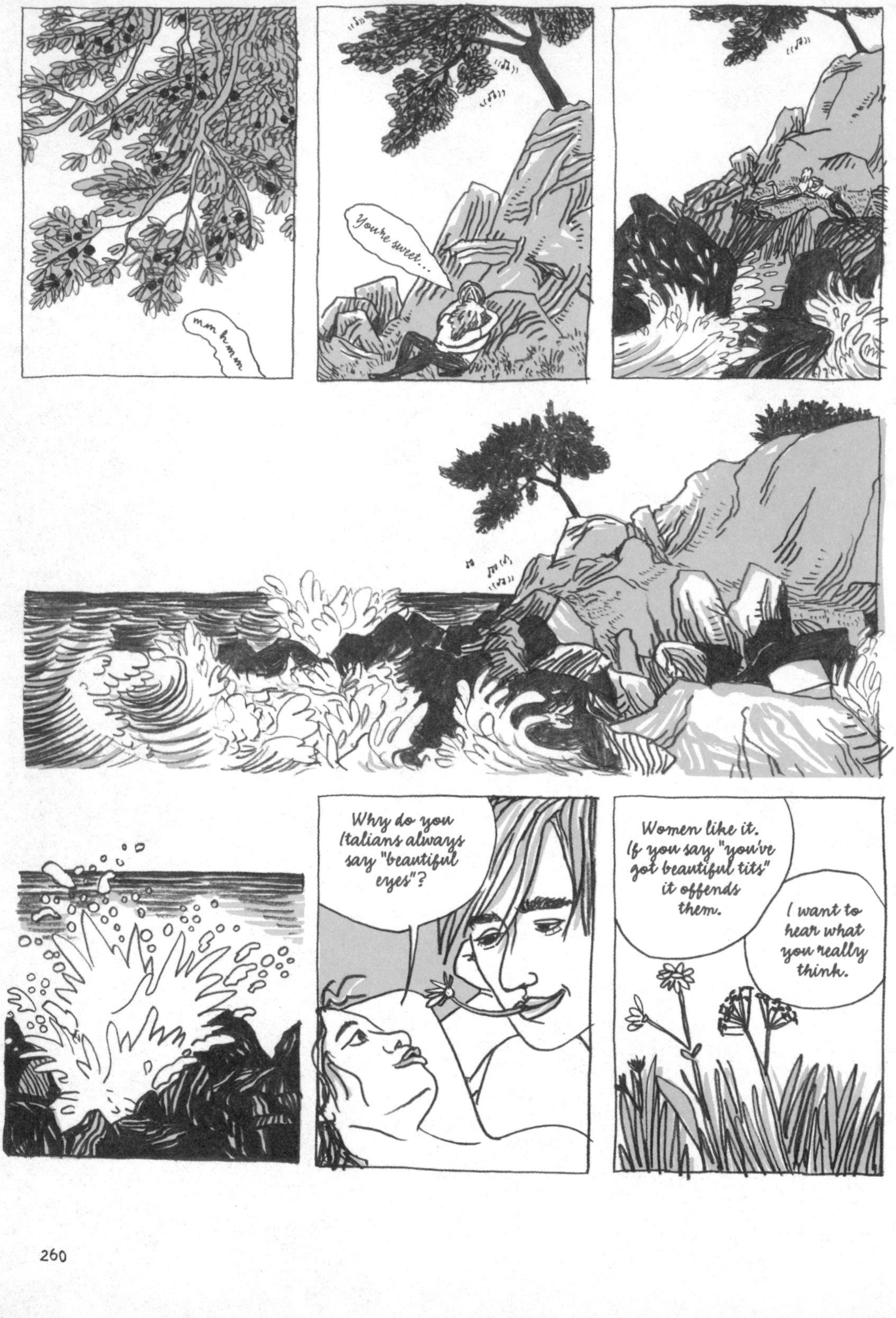
mm hmm
You're sweet...
Why do you Italians always say "beautiful eyes"?
Women like it. If you say "you've got beautiful tits" it offends them.
I want to hear what you really think.

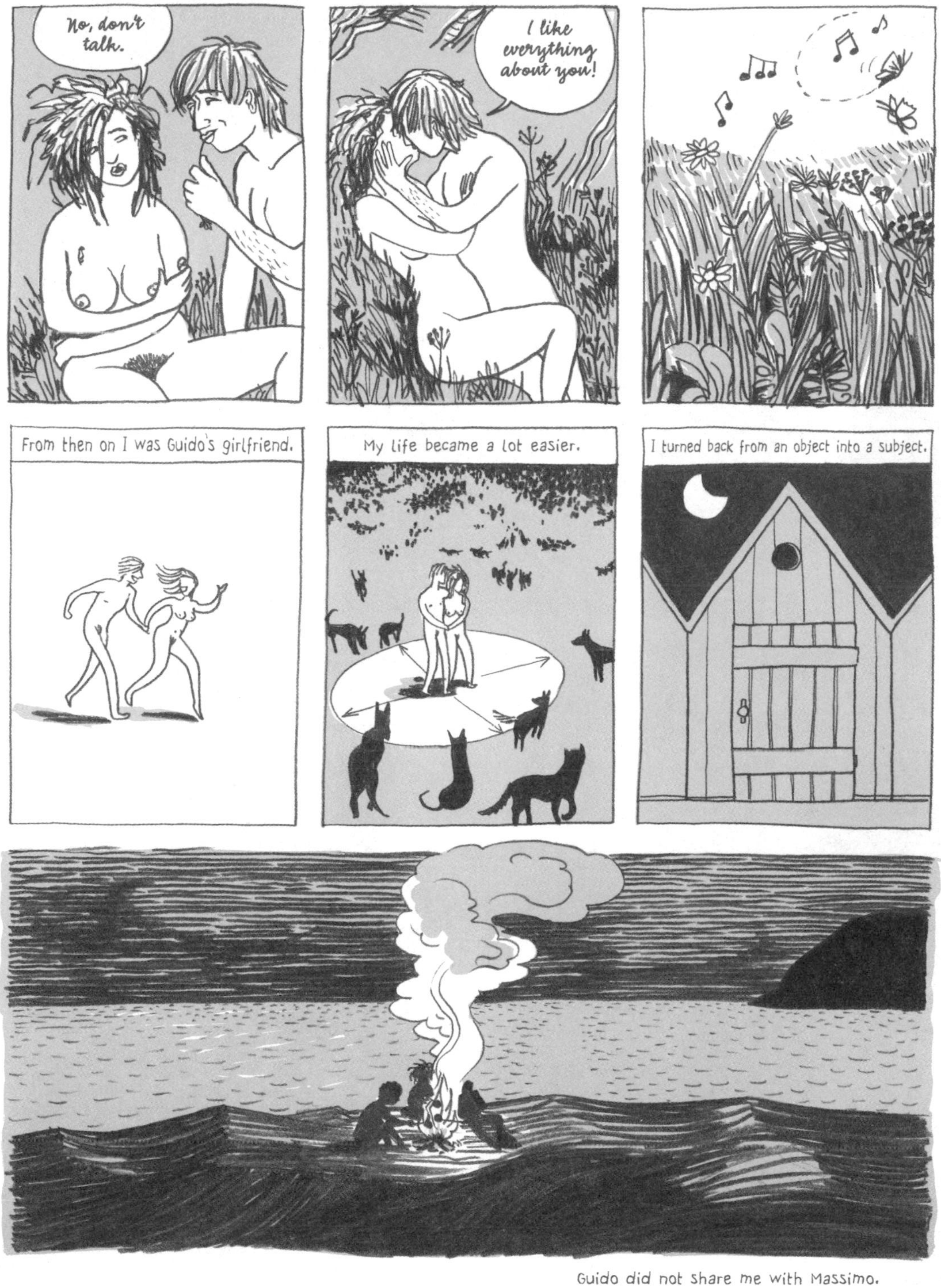

No, don't talk.
I like everything about you!
From then on I was Guido's girlfriend.
My life became a lot easier.
I turned back from an object into a subject.
Guido did not share me with Massimo.

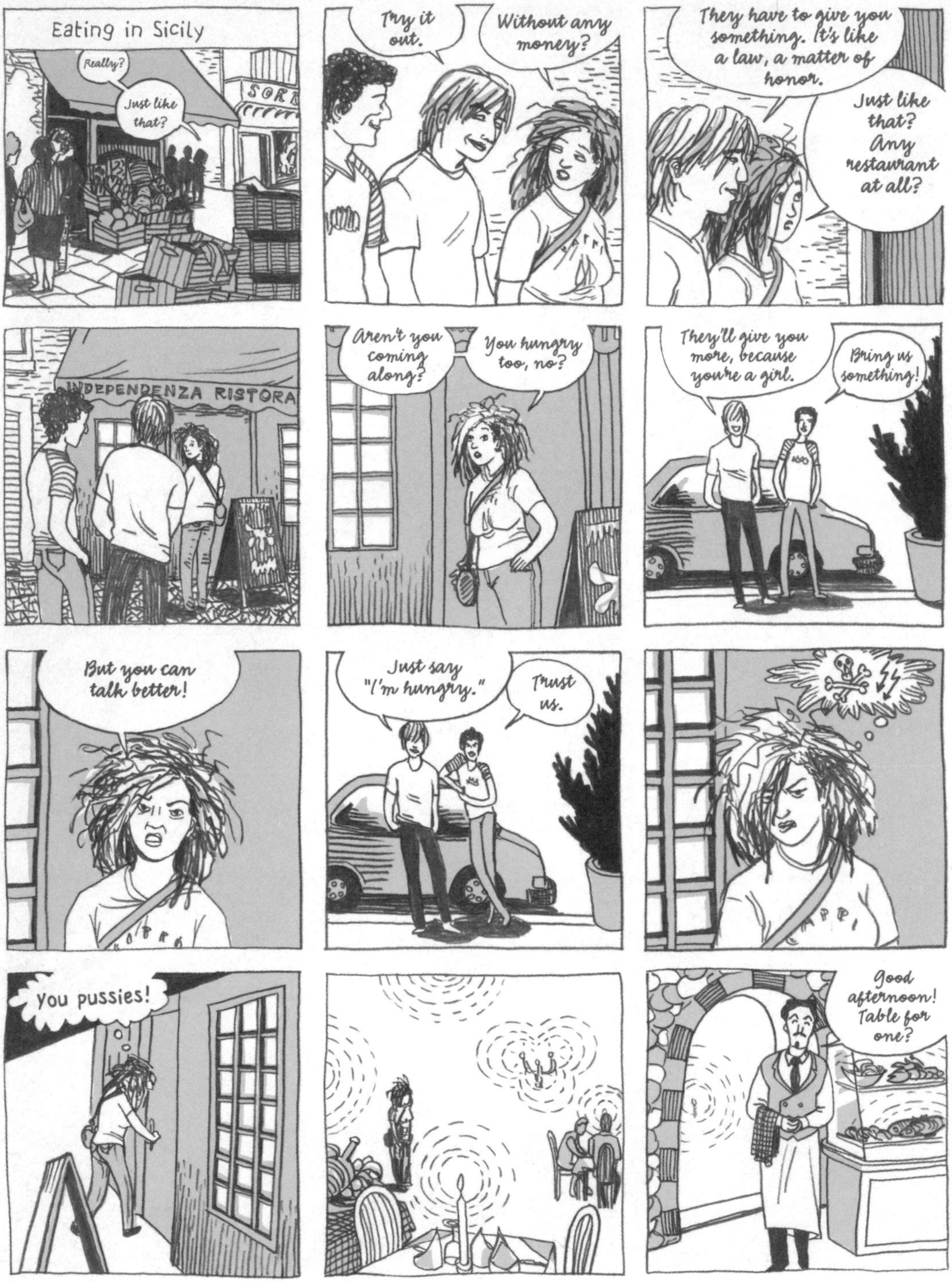

Eating in Sicily
Really?
Just like that?
Try it out.
Without any money?
They have to give you something. It's like a law, a matter of honor.
Just like that? Any restaurant at all?
INDEPENDENZA RISTORA
Aren't you coming along?
You hungry too, no?
They'll give you more, because you're a girl.
Bring us something!
But you can talk better!
Just say "I'm hungry."
Trust us.
You pussies!
Good afternoon! Table for one?

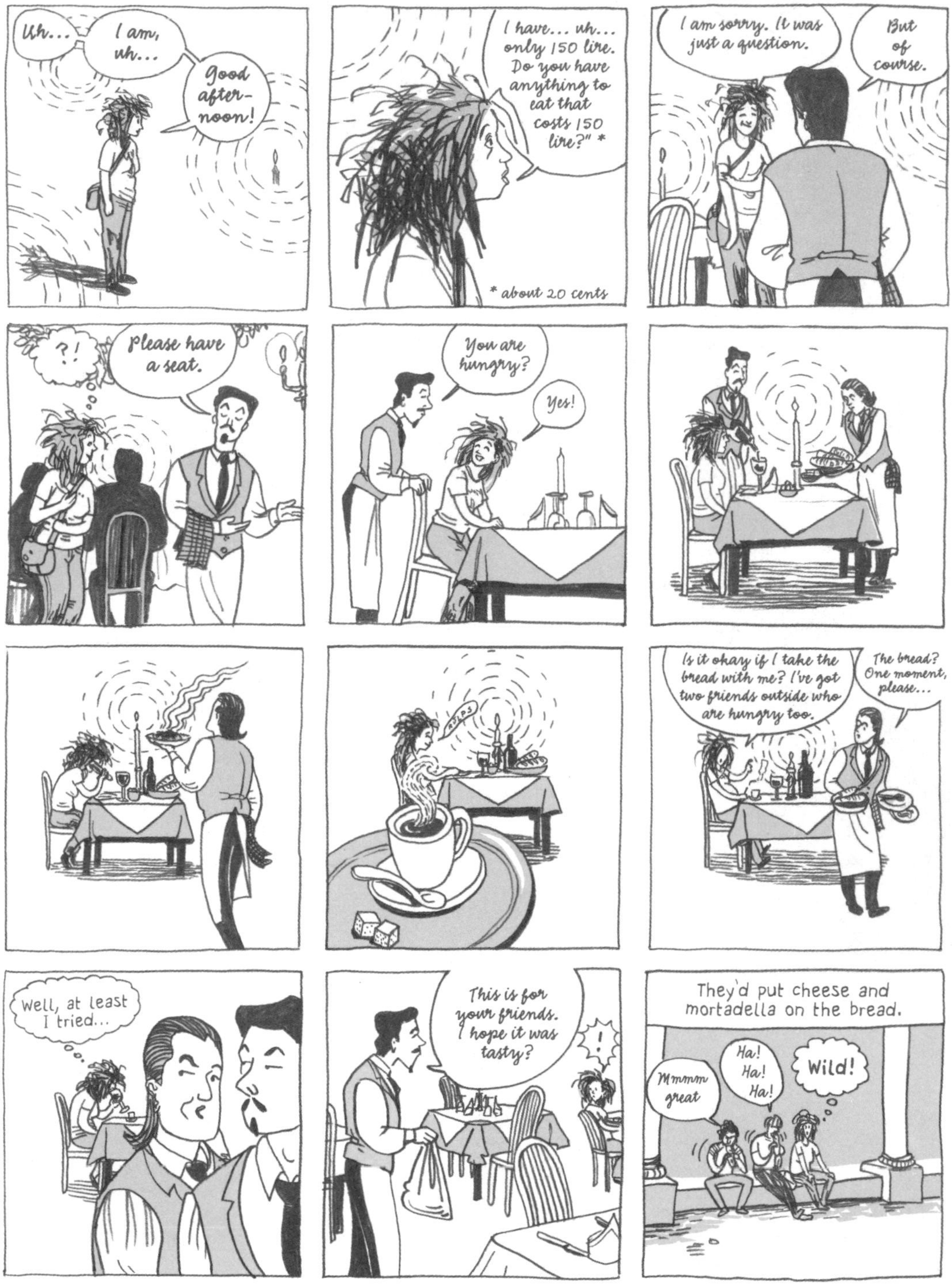
Uh...
I am, uh...
Good after-noon!
I have... uh... only 150 lire. Do you have anything to eat that costs 150 lire?" *
* about 20 cents
I am sorry. It was just a question.
But of course.
?!
Please have a seat.
You are hungry?
Yes!
Is it okay if I take the bread with me? I've got two friends outside who are hungry too.
The bread? One moment, please...
Well, at least I tried...
This is for your friends. I hope it was tasty?
!
They'd put cheese and mortadella on the bread.
Mmmm great
Ha! Ha! Ha!
Wild!

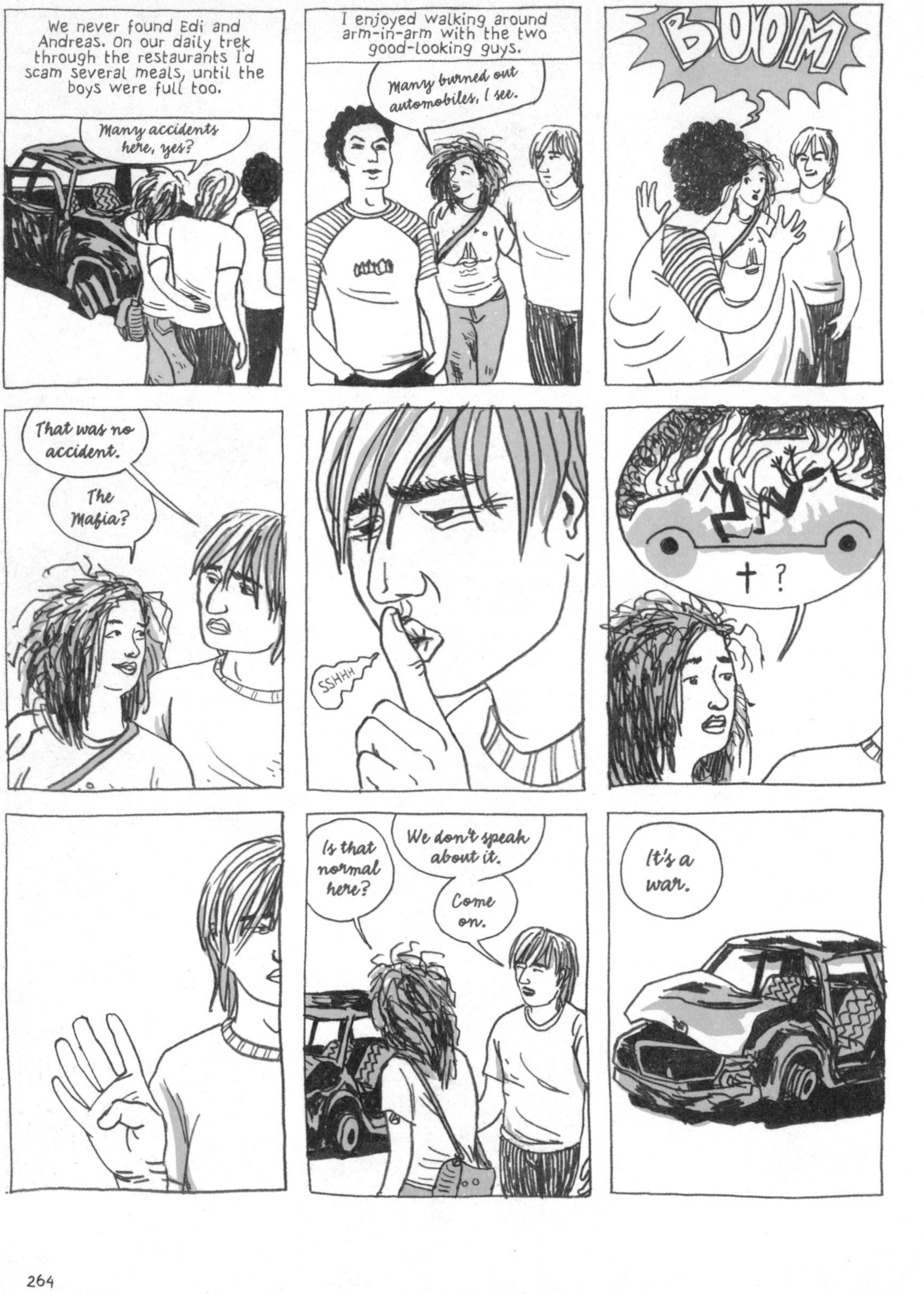
We never found Edi and Andreas. On our daily trek through the restaurants I'd scam several meals, until the boys were full too.
Many accidents here, yes?
I enjoyed walking around arm-in-arm with the two good-looking guys.
Many burned out automobiles, I see.
BOOM
That was no accident.
The Mafia?
SSHHH
† ?
Is that normal here?
We don't speak about it.
Come on.
It's a war.

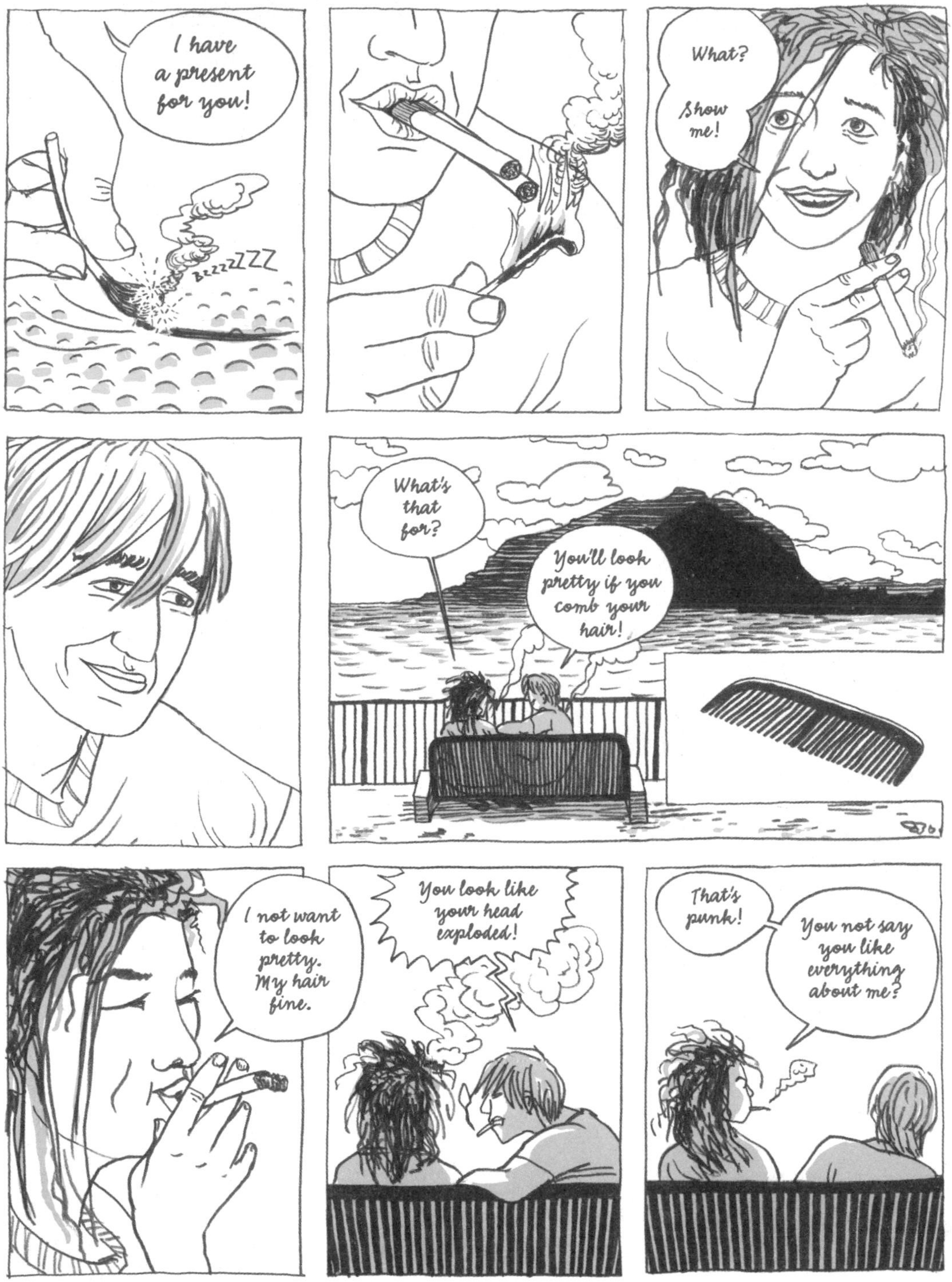
I have a present for you!
BzzzzZZZ
What?
Show me!
What's that for?
You'll look pretty if you comb your hair!
I not want to look pretty. My hair fine.
You look like your head exploded!
That's punk!
You not say you like everything about me?

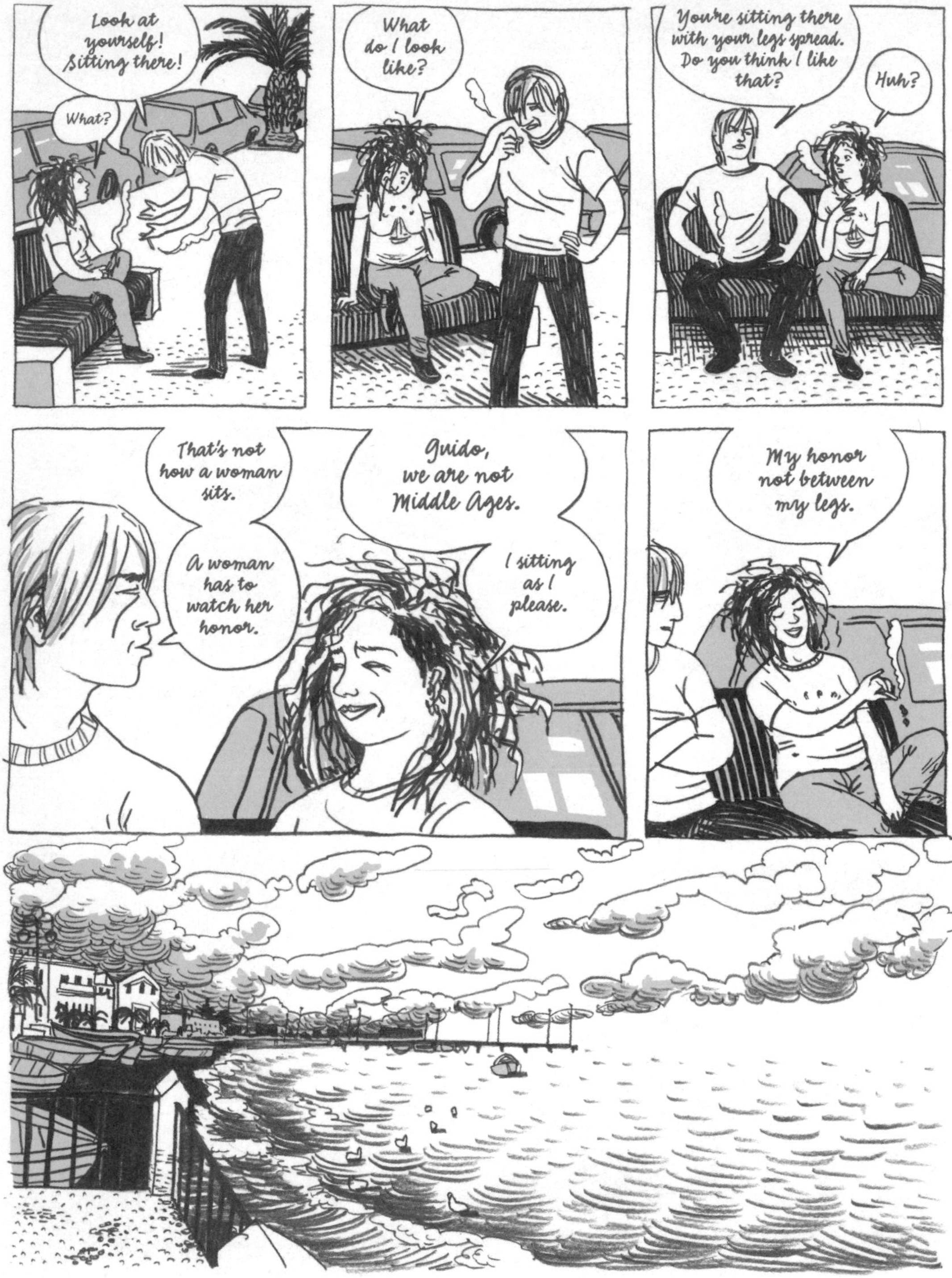

Look at yourself! Sitting there!
What?
What do I look like?
You're sitting there with your legs spread. Do you think I like that?
Huh?
That's not how a woman sits.
A woman has to watch her honor.
Guido, we are not Middle Ages.
I sitting as I please.
My honor not between my legs.

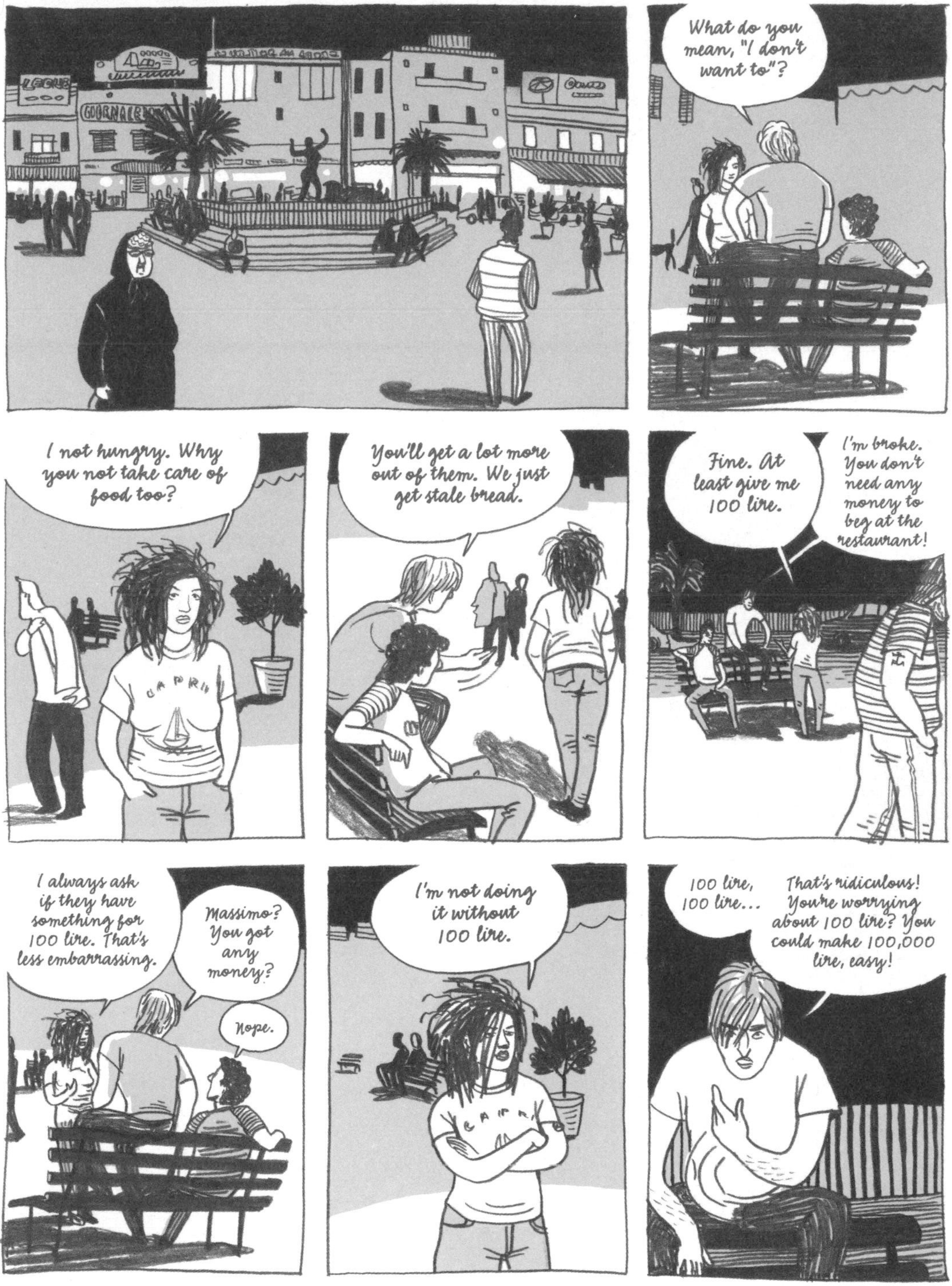
What do you mean, "I don't want to"?
I not hungry. Why you not take care of food too?
CAPRI
You'll get a lot more out of them. We just get stale bread.
Fine. At least give me 100 lire.
I'm broke. You don't need any money to beg at the restaurant!
I always ask if they have something for 100 lire. That's less embarrassing.
Massimo? You got any money?
Nope.
I'm not doing it without 100 lire.
100 lire, 100 lire...
That's ridiculous! You're worrying about 100 lire? You could make 100,000 lire, easy!

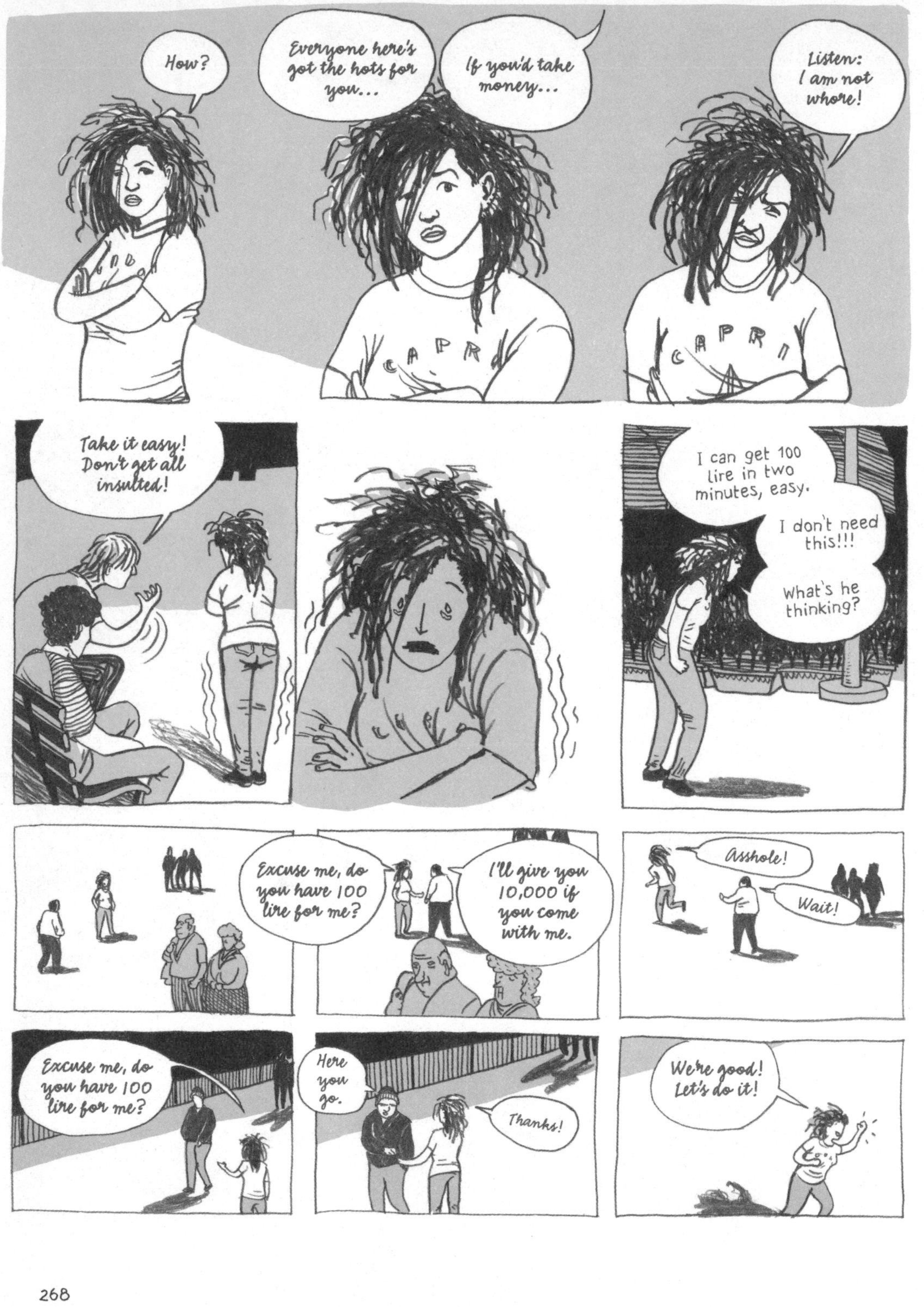
How?
Everyone here's got the hots for you...
If you'd take money...
Listen: I am not whore!
CAPRI
Take it easy! Don't get all insulted!
I can get 100 lire in two minutes, easy.
I don't need this!!!
What's he thinking?
Excuse me, do you have 100 lire for me?
I'll give you 10,000 if you come with me.
Asshole!
Wait!
Excuse me, do you have 100 lire for me?
Here you go.
Thanks!
We're good! Let's do it!

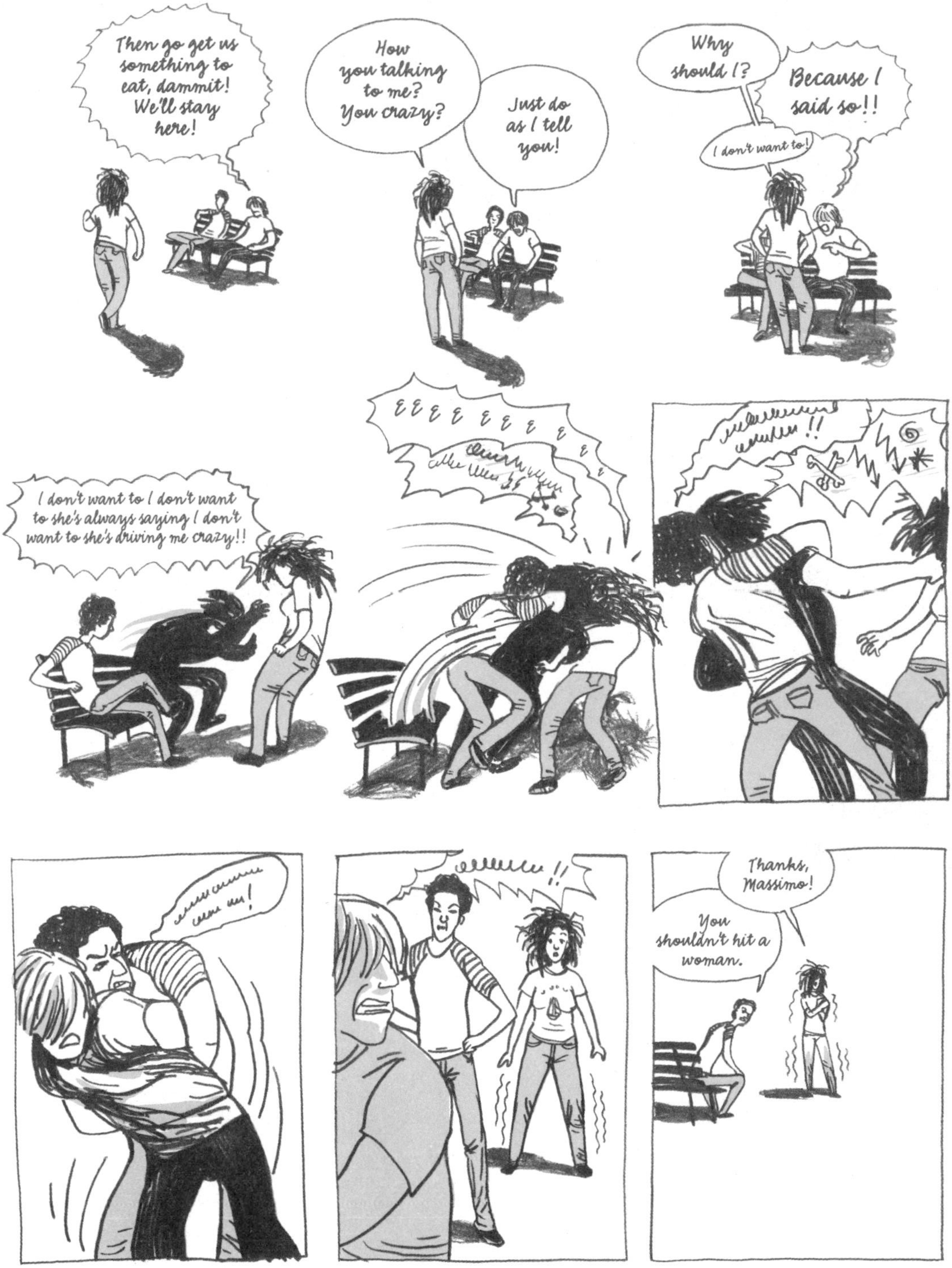
Then go get us something to eat, dammit! We'll stay here!
How you talking to me? You crazy?
Just do as I tell you!
Why should I?
Because I said so!!
I don't want to!
I don't want to I don't want to she's always saying I don't want to she's driving me crazy!!
Thanks, Massimo!
You shouldn't hit a woman.

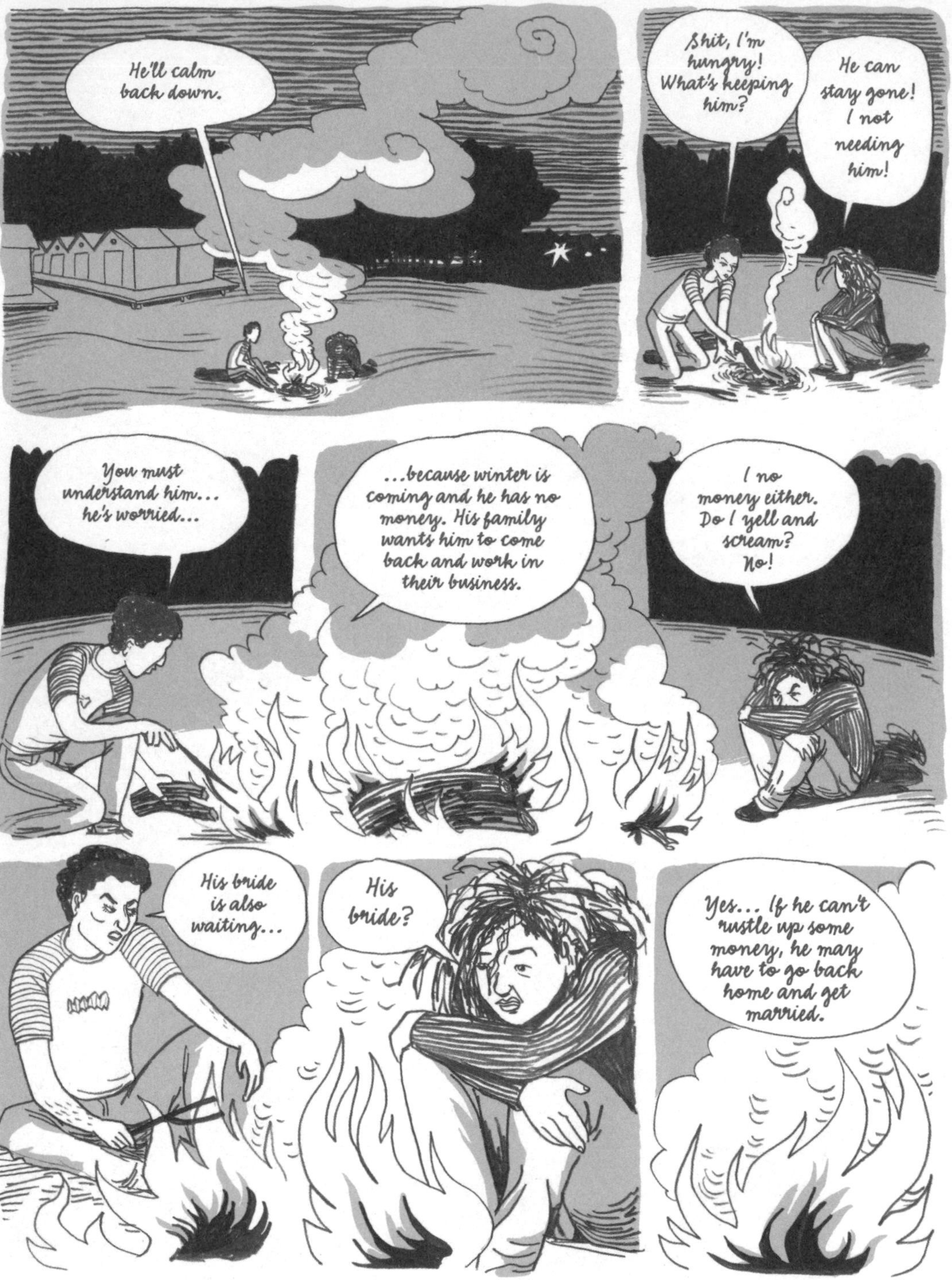
He'll calm back down.
Shit, I'm hungry! What's keeping him?
He can stay gone! I not needing him!
You must understand him... he's worried...
...because winter is coming and he has no money. His family wants him to come back and work in their business.
I no money either. Do I yell and scream? No!
His bride is also waiting...
His bride?
Yes... If he can't rustle up some money, he may have to go back home and get married.

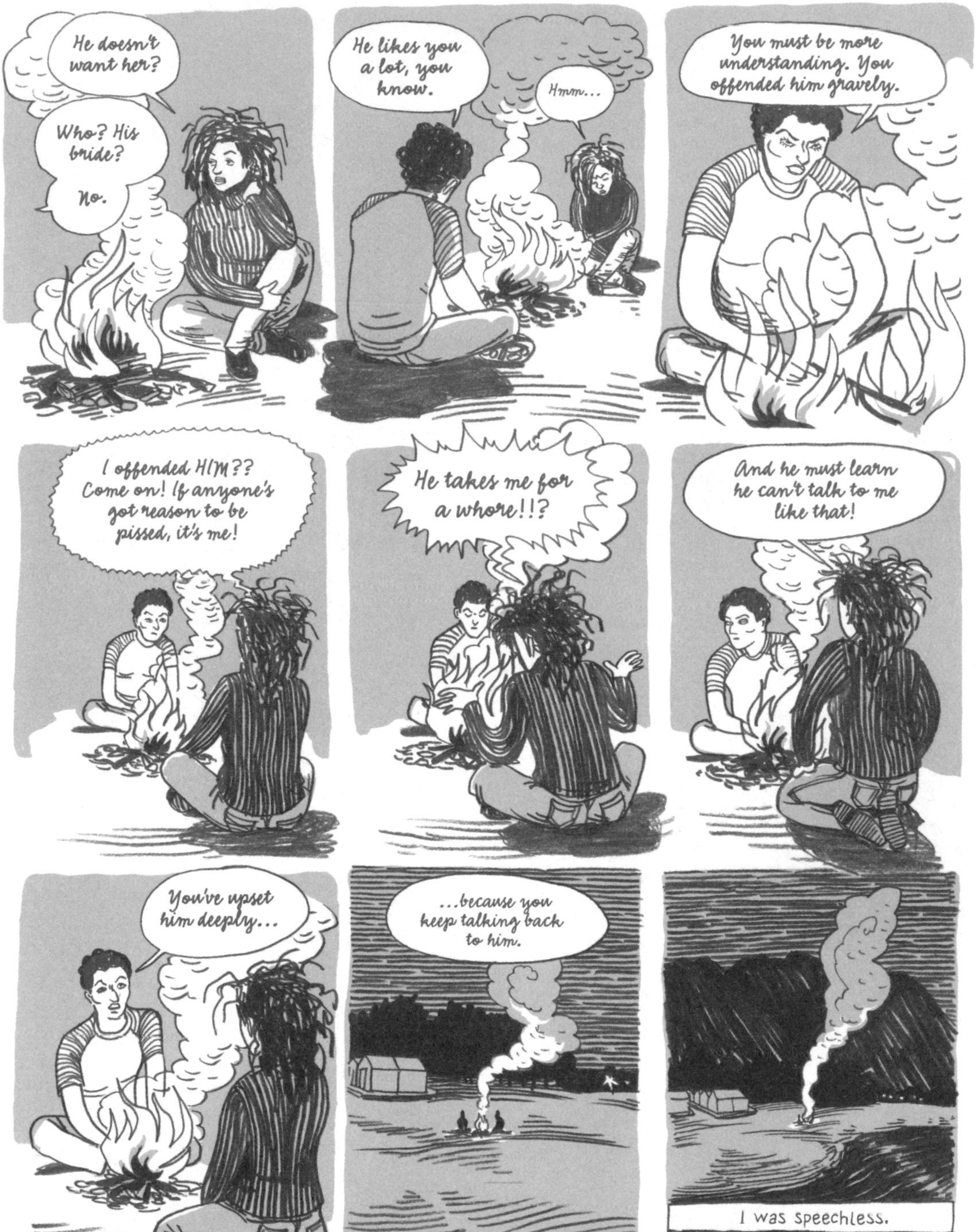
He doesn't want her?
Who? His bride?
No.
He likes you a lot, you know.
Hmm...
You must be more understanding. You offended him gravely.
I offended HIM?? Come on! If anyone's got reason to be pissed, it's me!
He takes me for a whore!!?
And he must learn he can't talk to me like that!
You've upset him deeply...
...because you keep talking back to him.
I was speechless.

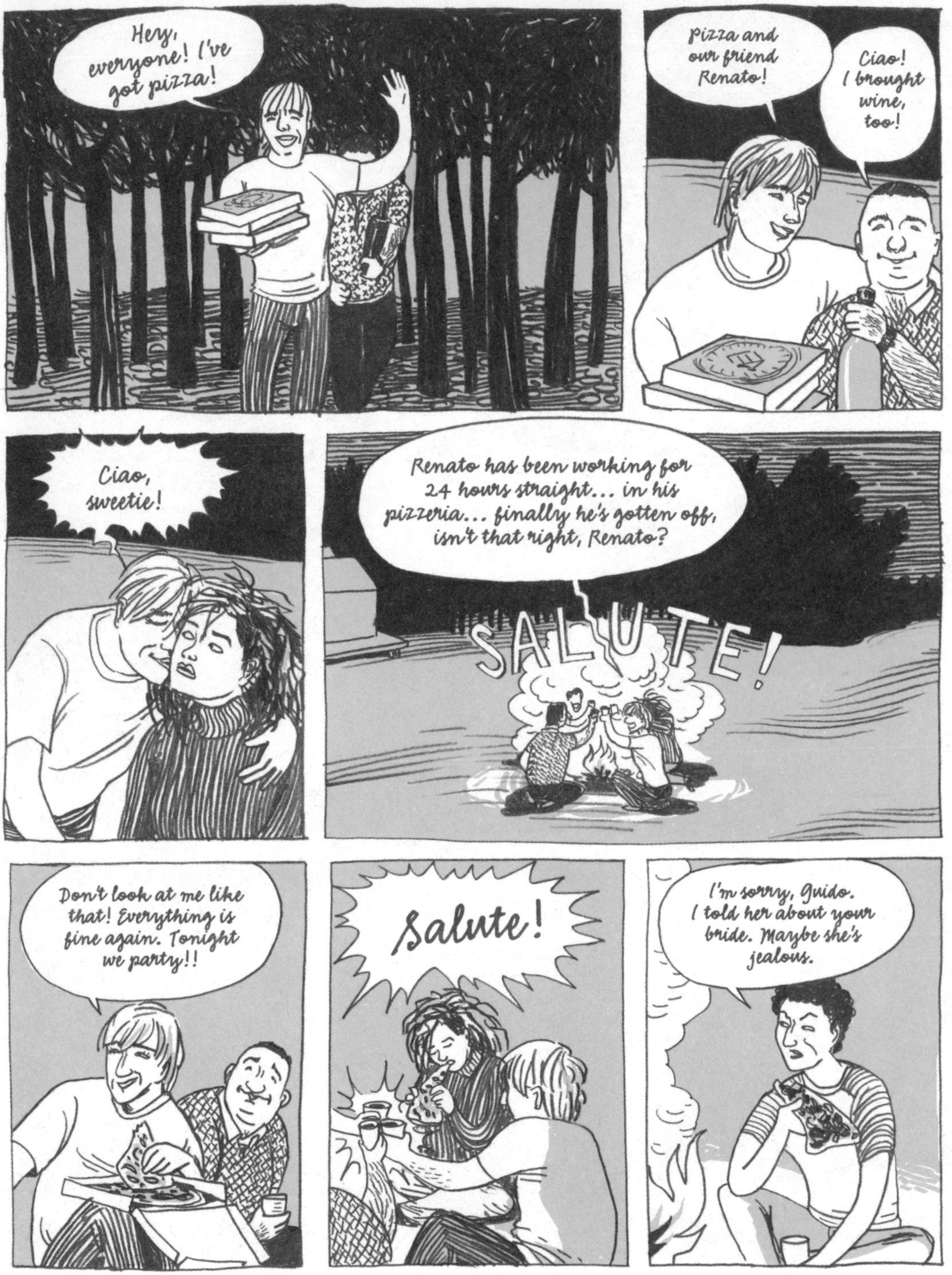
Hey, everyone! I've got pizza!
Pizza and our friend Renato!
Ciao! I brought wine, too!
Ciao, sweetie!
Renato has been working for 24 hours straight... in his pizzeria... finally he's gotten off, isn't that right, Renato?
SALUTE!
Don't look at me like that! Everything is fine again. Tonight we party!!
Salute!
I'm sorry, Guido. I told her about your bride. Maybe she's jealous.

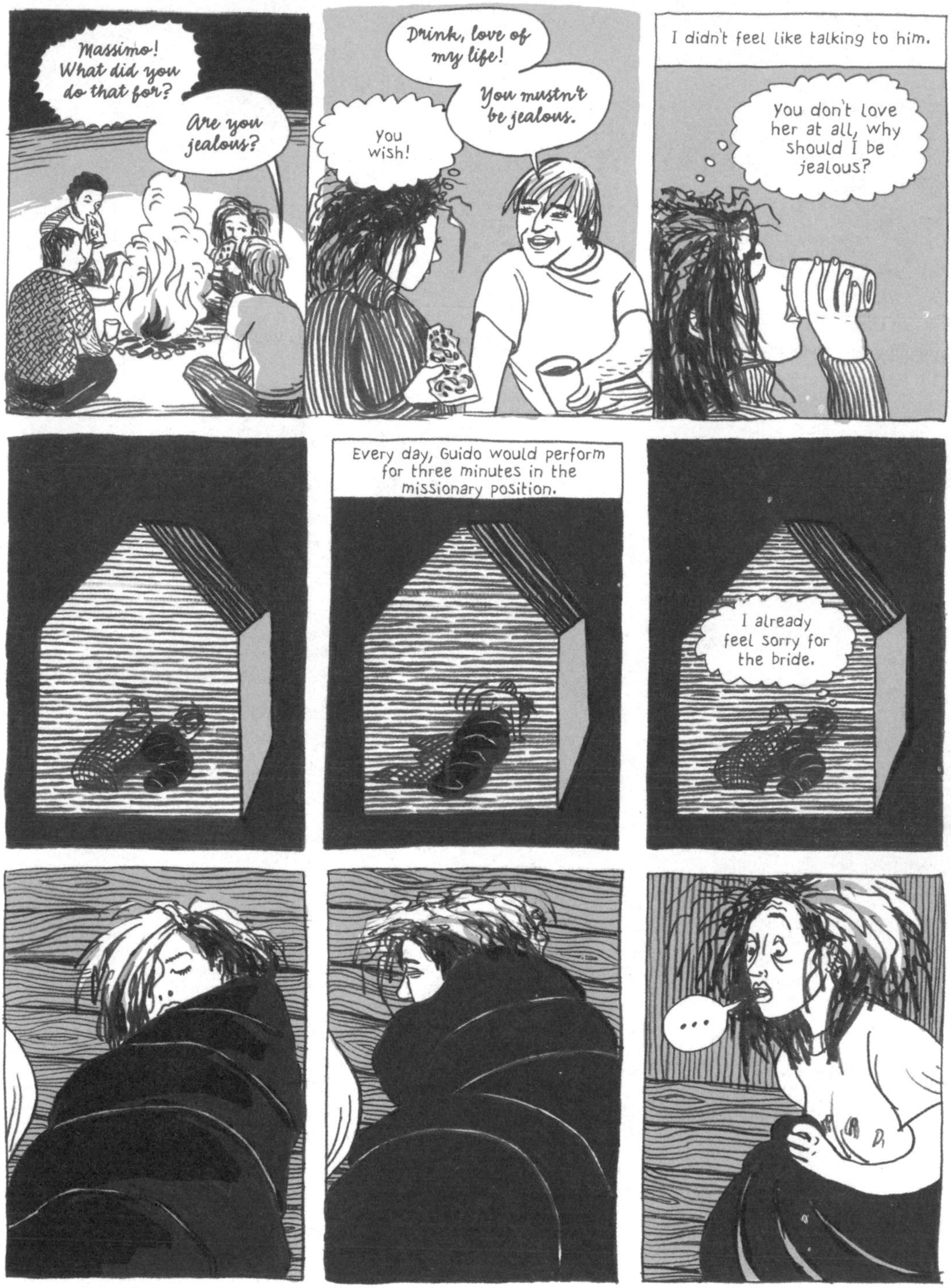
Massimo! What did you do that for?
Are you jealous?
Drink, love of my life!
You wish!
You mustn't be jealous.
I didn't feel like talking to him.
You don't love her at all, why should I be jealous?
Every day, Guido would perform for three minutes in the missionary position.
I already feel sorry for the bride.
...

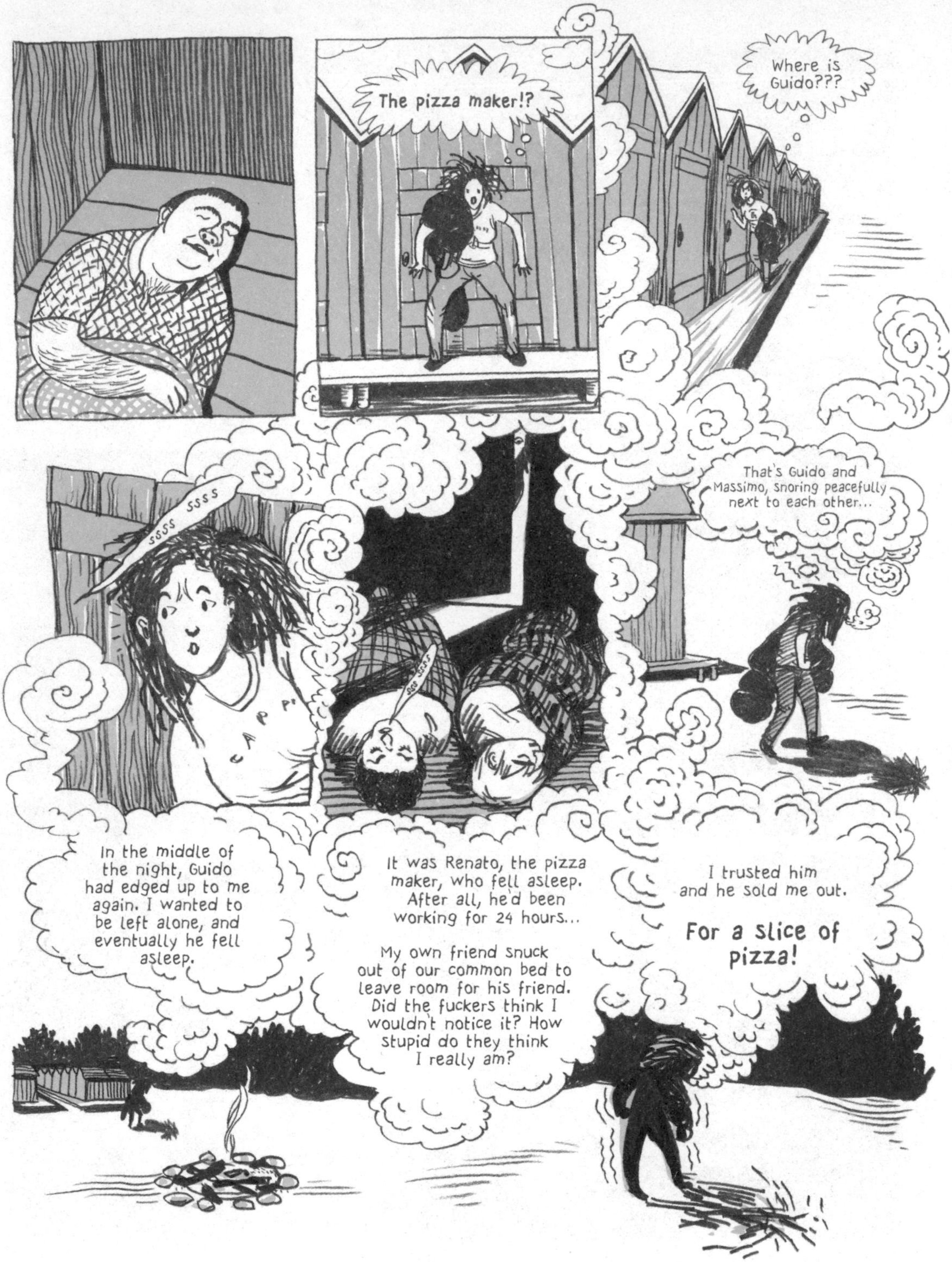
The pizza maker!?
Where is Guido???
That's Guido and Massimo, snoring peacefully next to each other...
SSSS SSSS
In the middle of the night, Guido had edged up to me again. I wanted to be left alone, and eventually he fell asleep.
It was Renato, the pizza maker, who fell asleep. After all, he'd been working for 24 hours...
My own friend snuck out of our common bed to leave room for his friend. Did the fuckers think I wouldn't notice it? How stupid do they think I really am?
I trusted him and he sold me out.
For a slice of pizza!

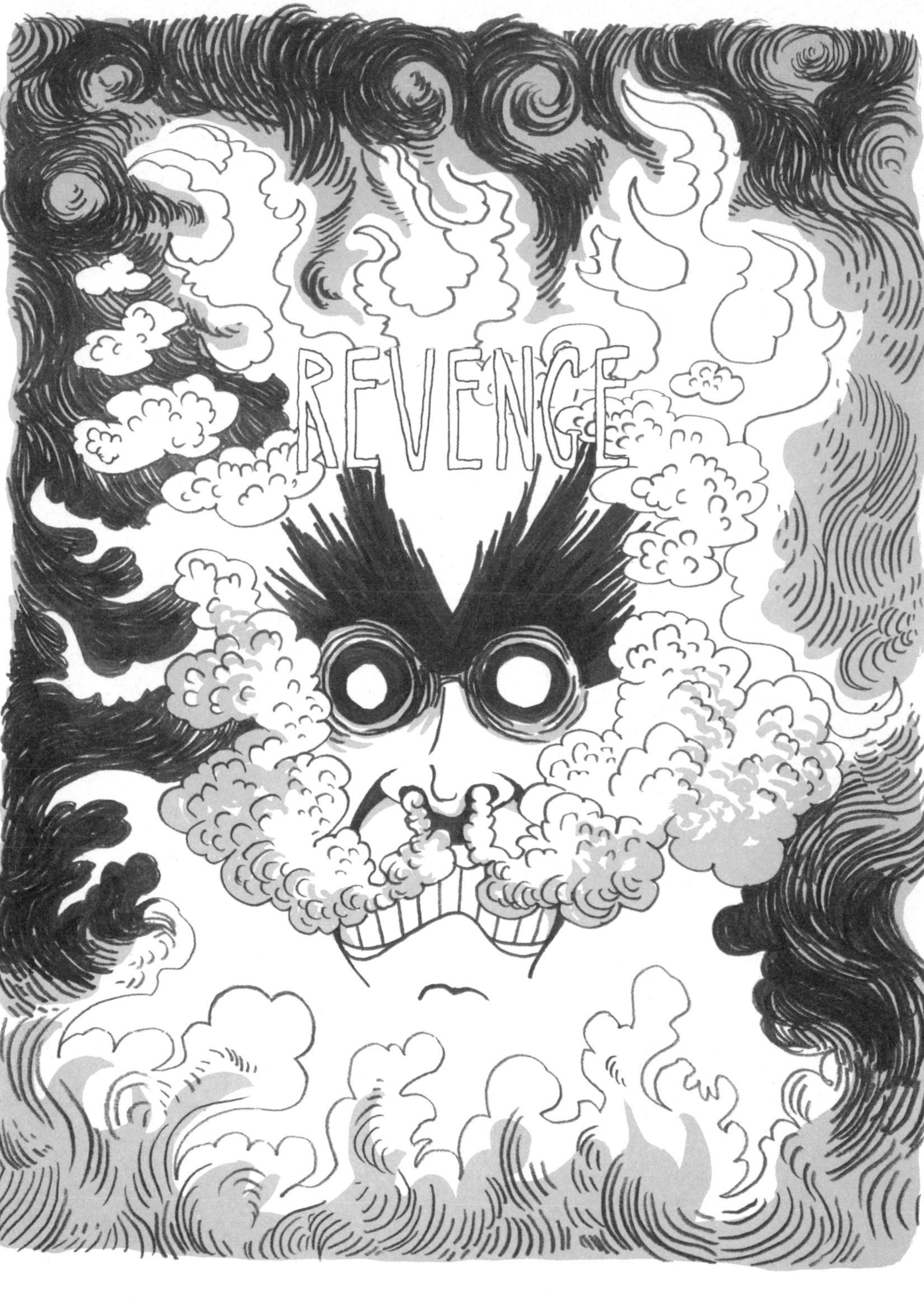
REVENGE

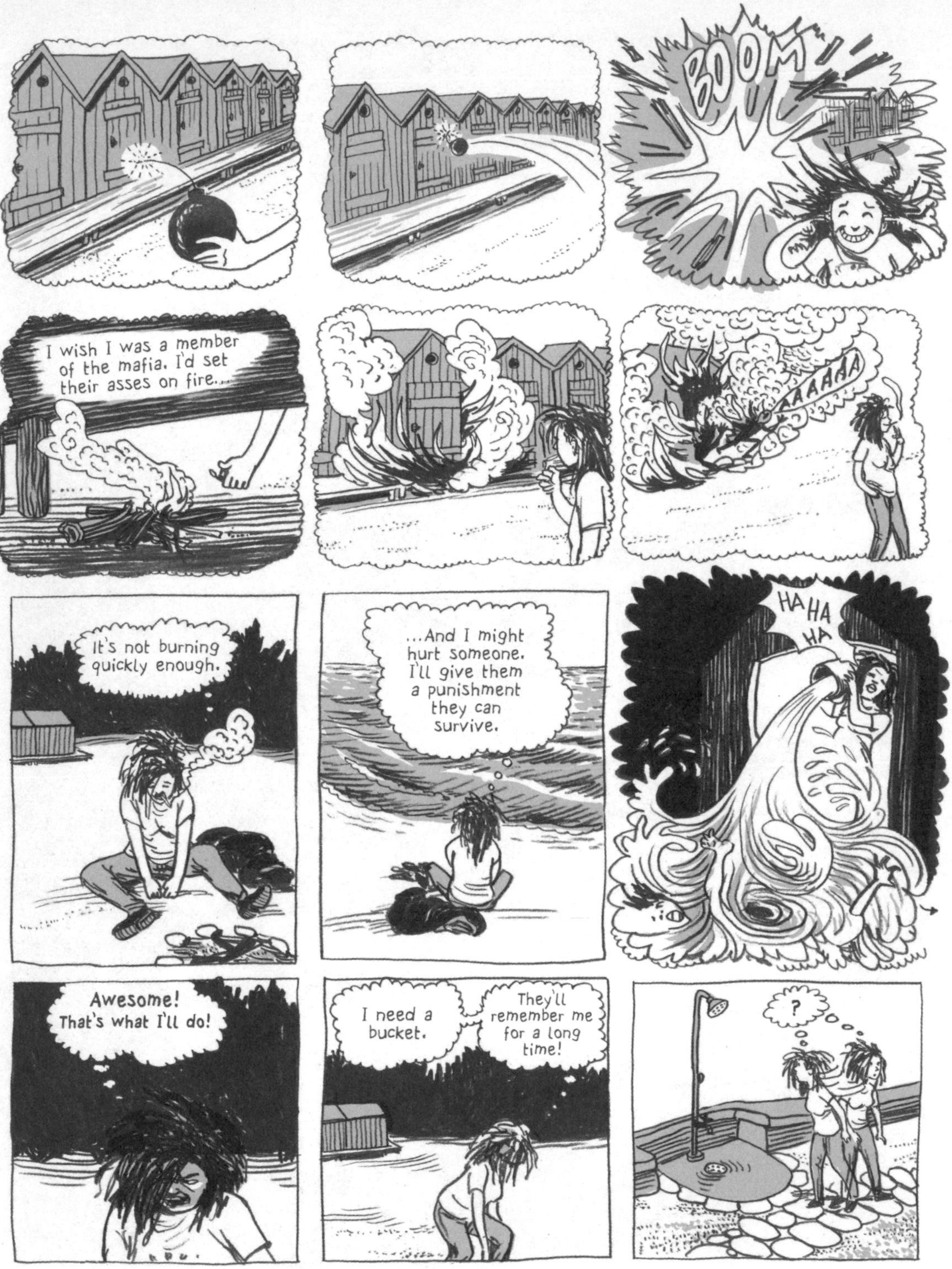
BOOM!
I wish I was a member of the mafia. I'd set their asses on fire...
AAAAAA
It's not burning quickly enough.
...And I might hurt someone. I'll give them a punishment they can survive.
HA HA HA
Awesome! That's what I'll do!
I need a bucket.
They'll remember me for a long time!
?

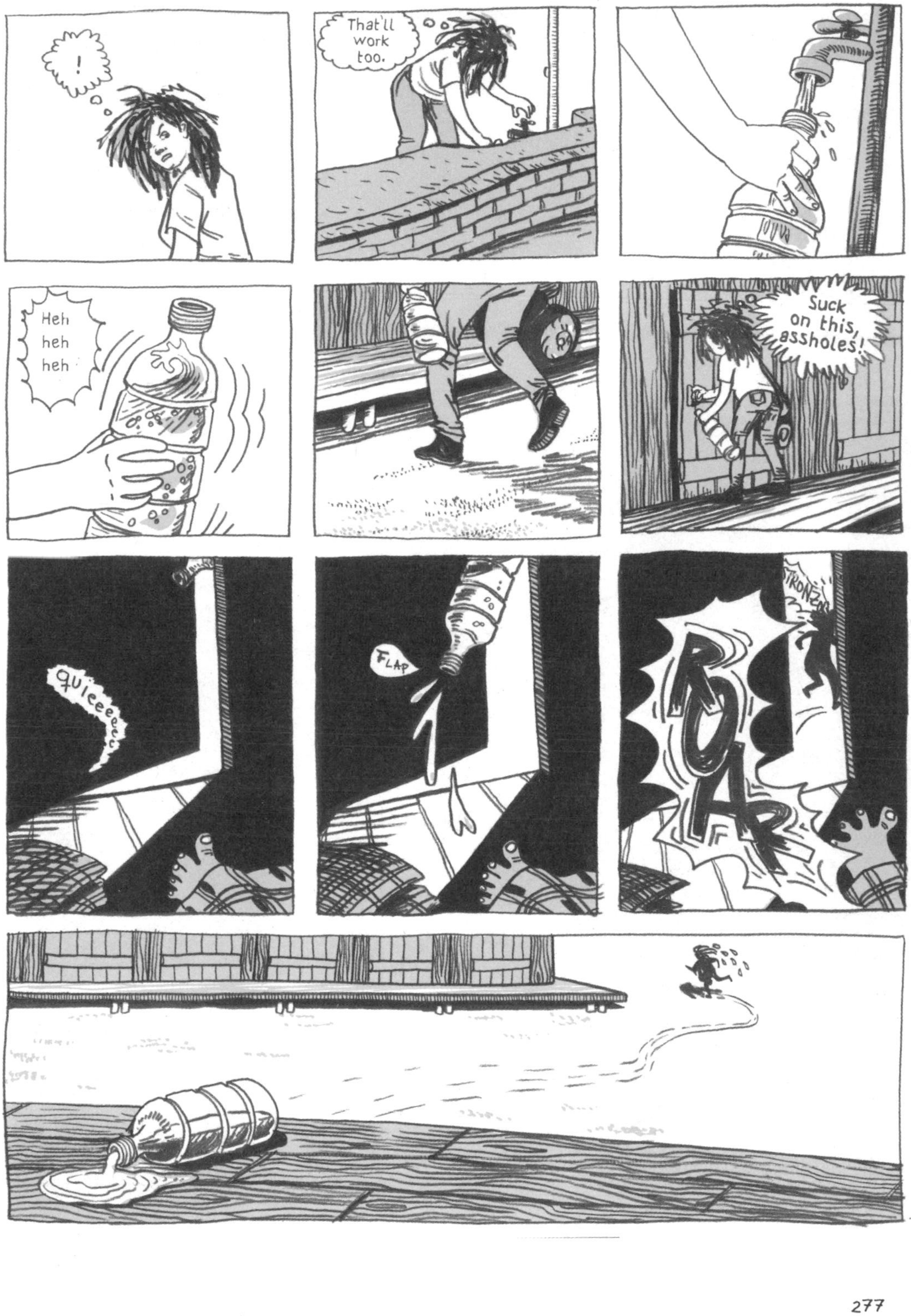
!
That'll work too.
Heh heh heh
Suck on this, assholes!
quiceeeeet
FLAP
ROAR

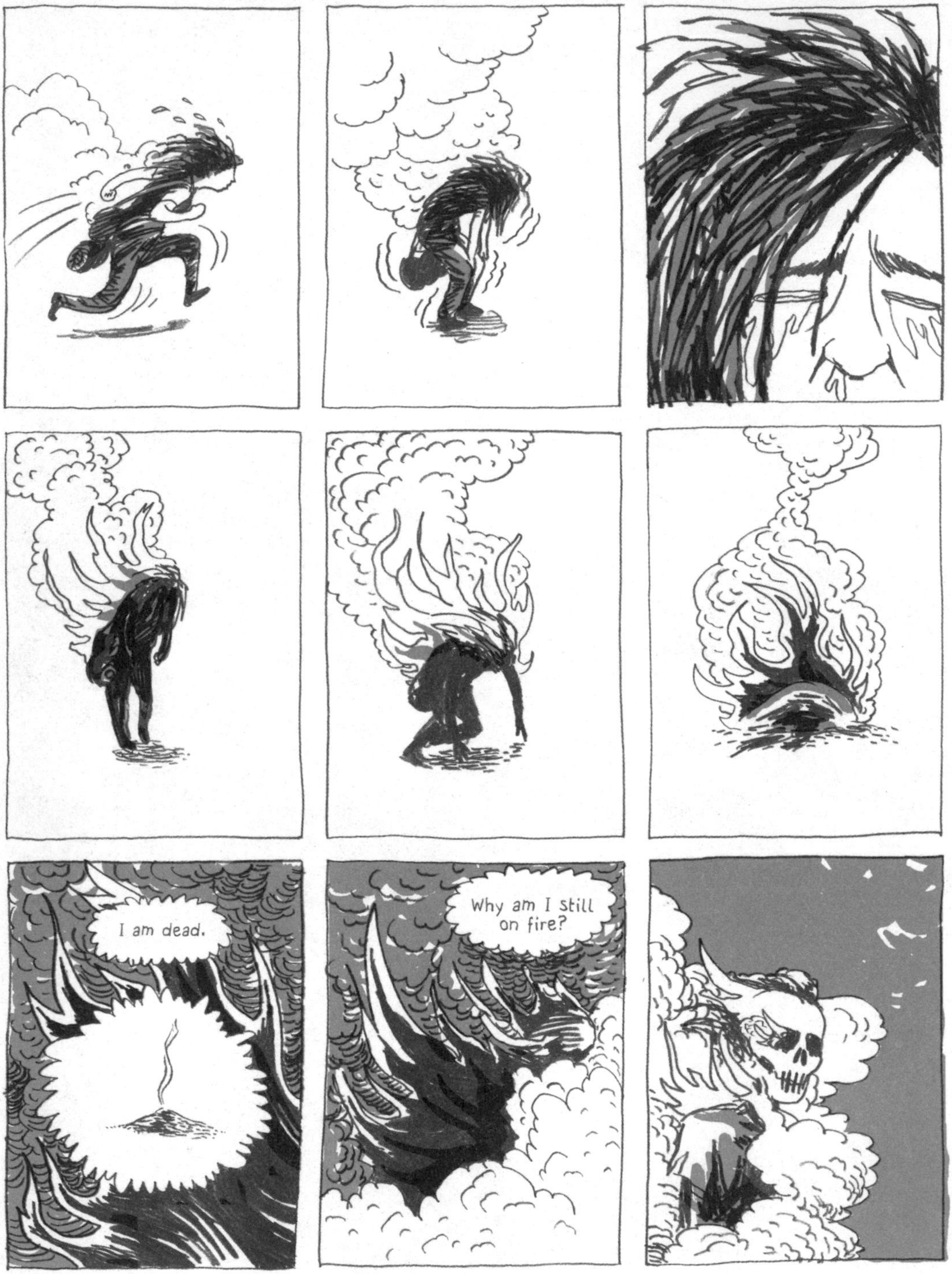
I am dead.
Why am I still on fire?

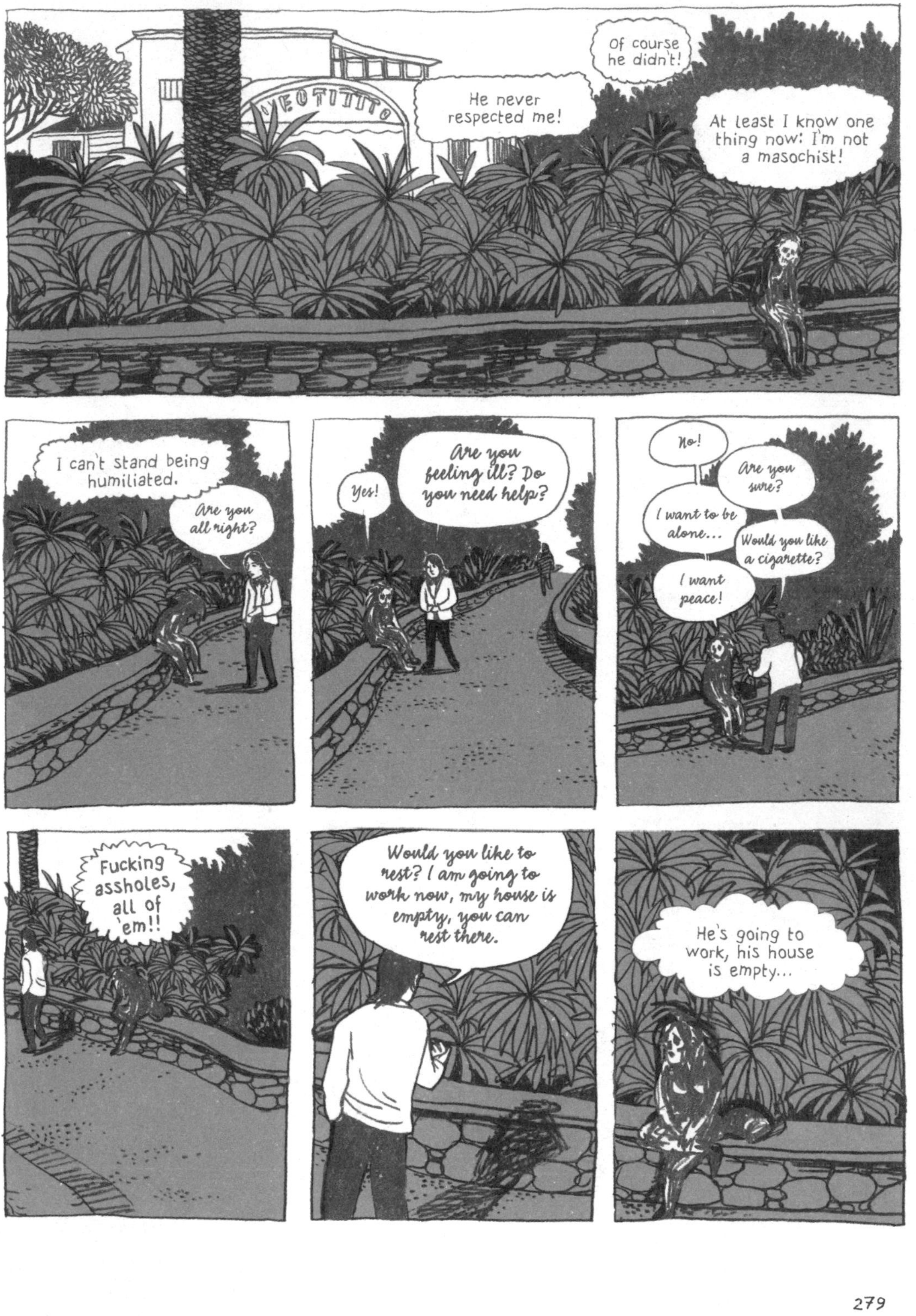
He never respected me!
Of course he didn't!
At least I know one thing now: I'm not a masochist!
I can't stand being humiliated.
Are you all right?
Yes!
Are you feeling ill? Do you need help?
No!
Are you sure?
I want to be alone...
Would you like a cigarette?
I want peace!
Fucking assholes, all of 'em!!
Would you like to rest? I am going to work now, my house is empty, you can rest there.
He's going to work, his house is empty...

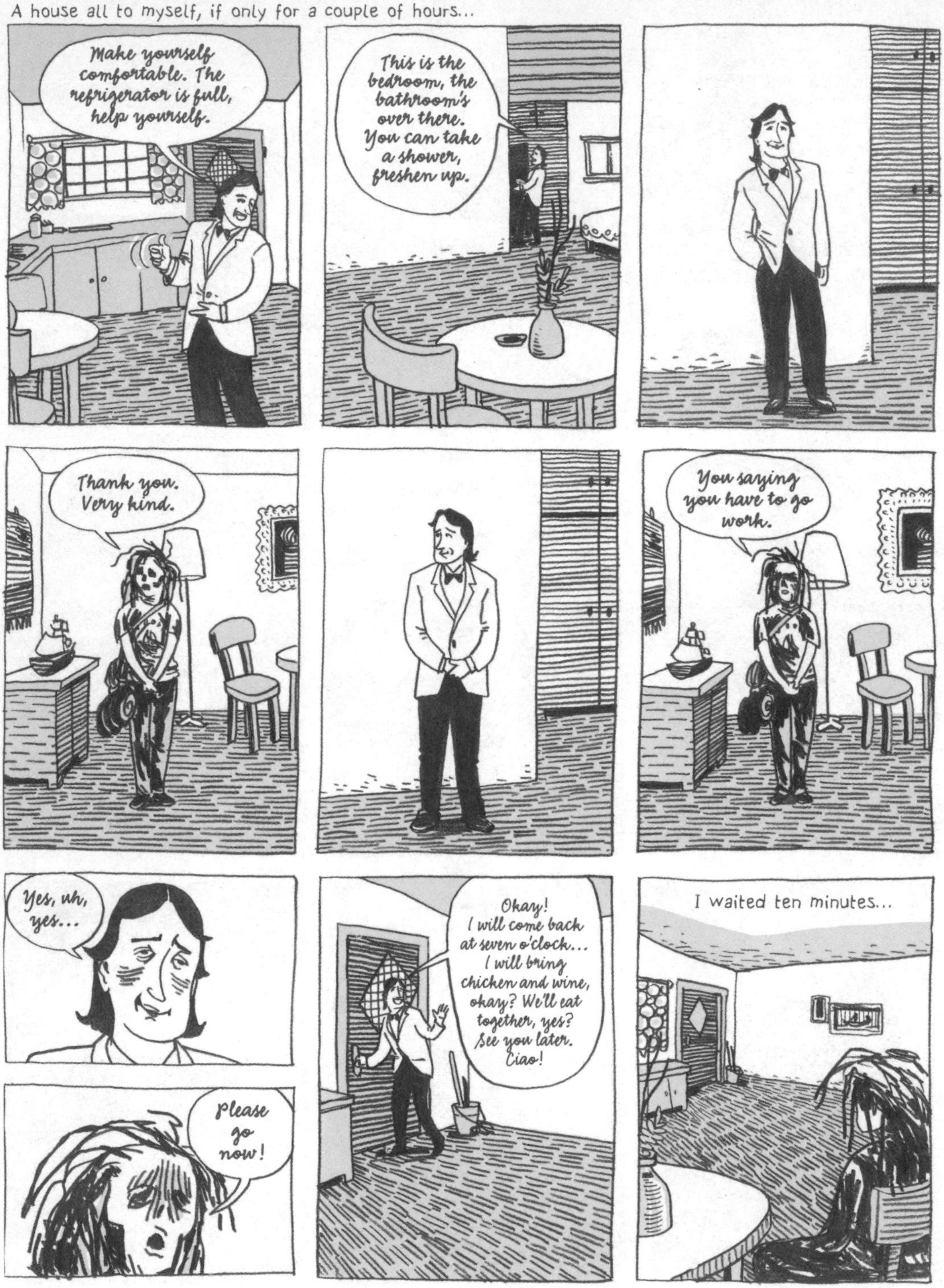
A house all to myself, if only for a couple of hours...
Make yourself comfortable. The refrigerator is full, help yourself.
This is the bedroom, the bathroom's over there. You can take a shower, freshen up.
Thank you. Very kind.
You saying you have to go work.
Yes, uh, yes...
Please go now!
Okay! I will come back at seven o'clock... I will bring chicken and wine, okay? We'll eat together, yes? See you later. Ciao!
I waited ten minutes...

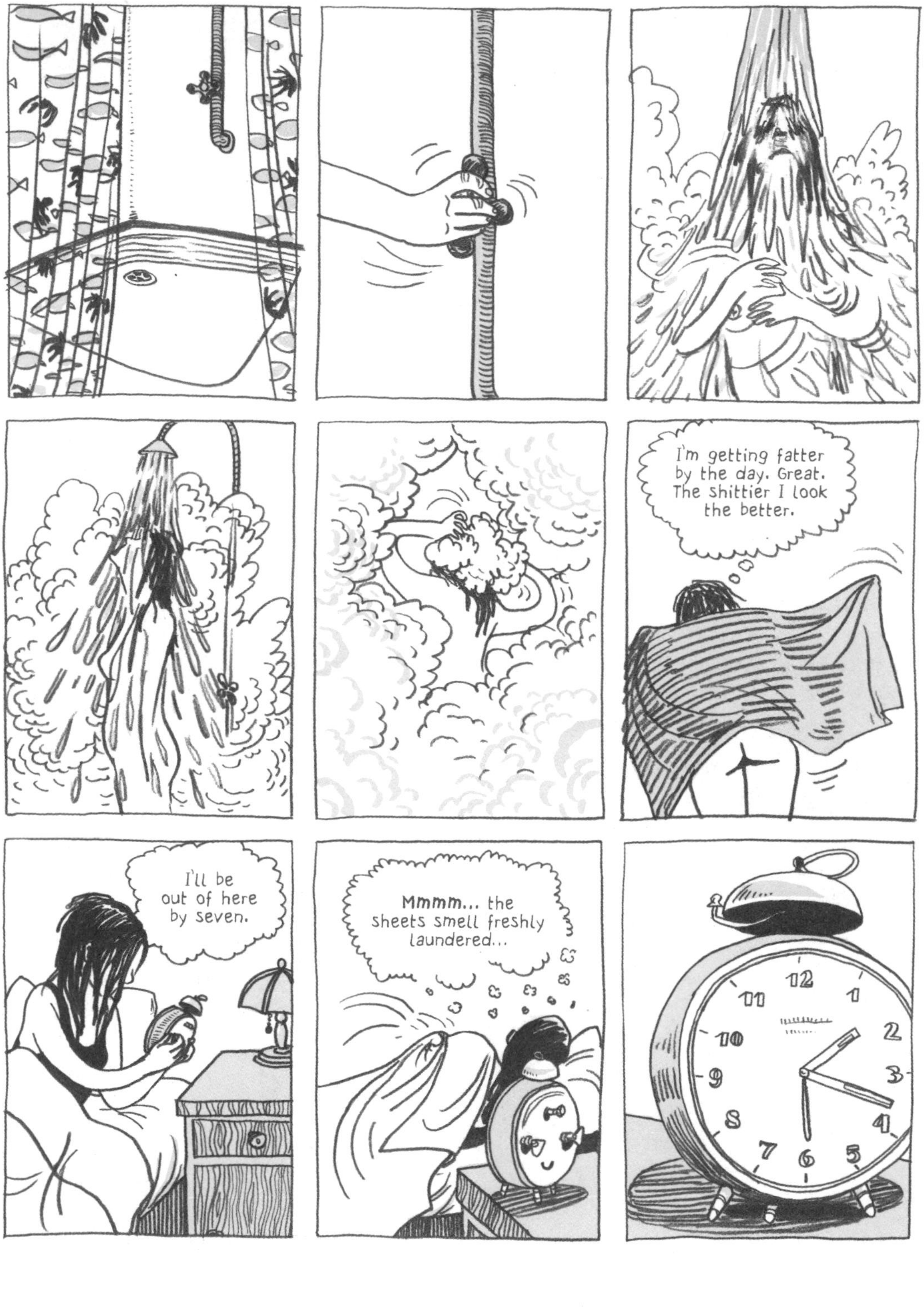
I'm getting fatter by the day. Great. The shittier I look the better.
I'll be out of here by seven.
Mmmm... the sheets smell freshly laundered...

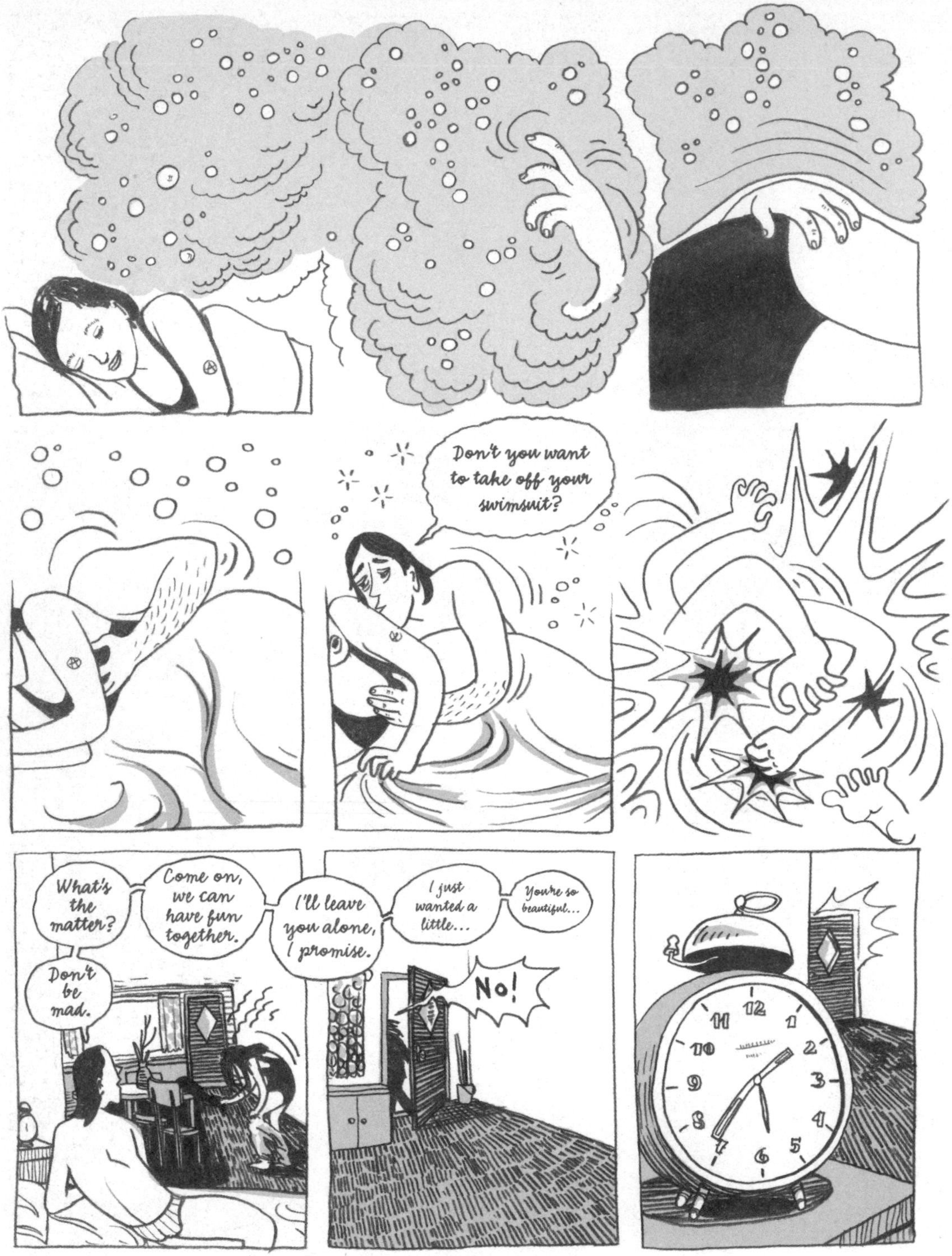
Don't you want to take off your swimsuit?
What's the matter?
Don't be mad.
Come on, we can have fun together.
I'll leave you alone, I promise.
I just wanted a little...
You're so beautiful...
No!

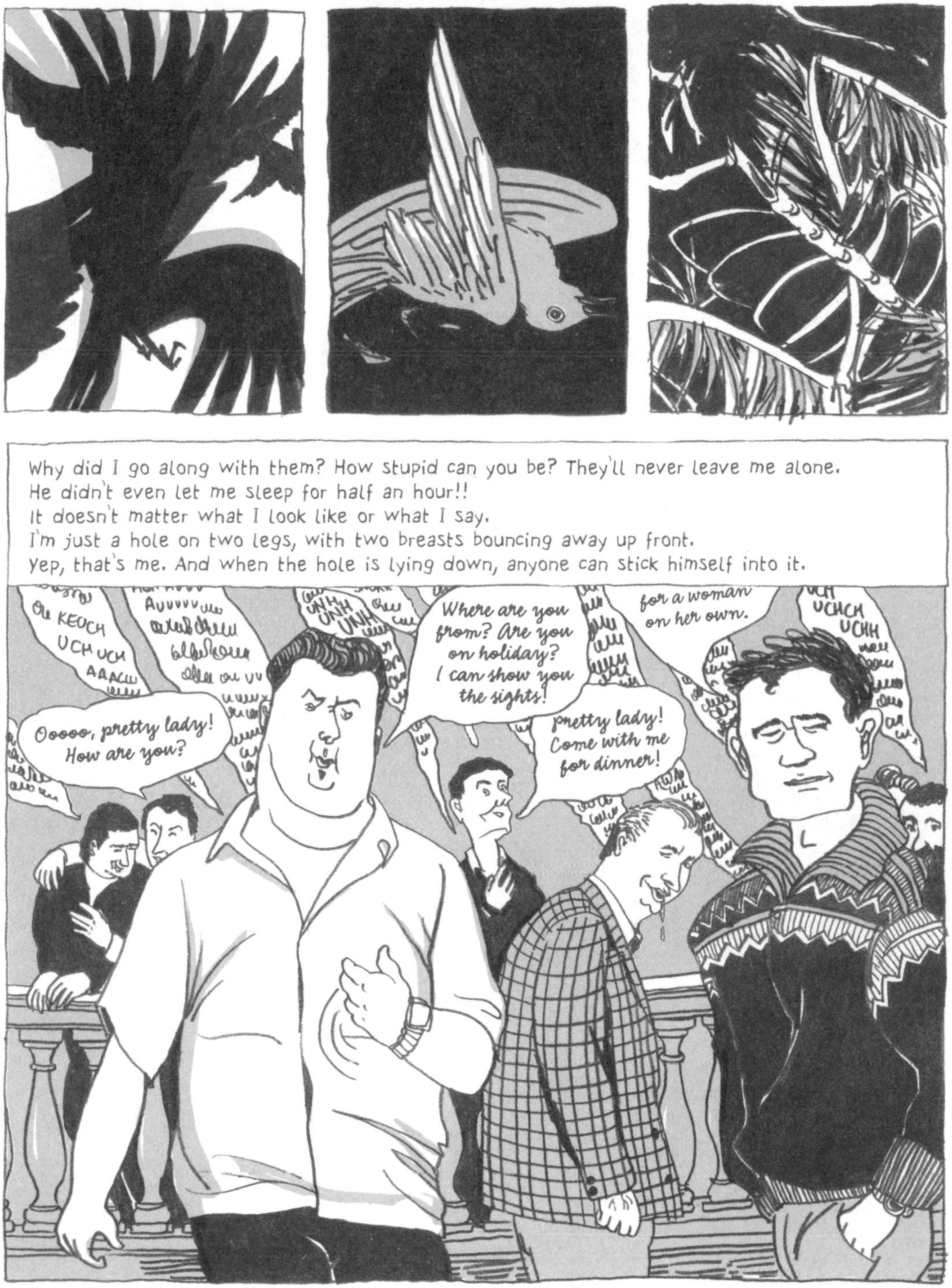
Why did I go along with them? How stupid can you be? They'll never leave me alone.
He didn't even let me sleep for half an hour!!
It doesn't matter what I look like or what I say.
I'm just a hole on two legs, with two breasts bouncing away up front.
Yep, that's me. And when the hole is lying down, anyone can stick himself into it.
Ooooo, pretty lady! How are you?
Where are you from? Are you on holiday? I can show you the sights!
pretty lady! Come with me for dinner!
for a woman on her own.

Should I climb into the next train and go home? I could claim that I lost my passport at the border.

What would I do there? I've changed so much, I won't fit into my old skin. I'd go crazy. There's no way back.

I refuse to surrender, to let the Philistines believe they were right.

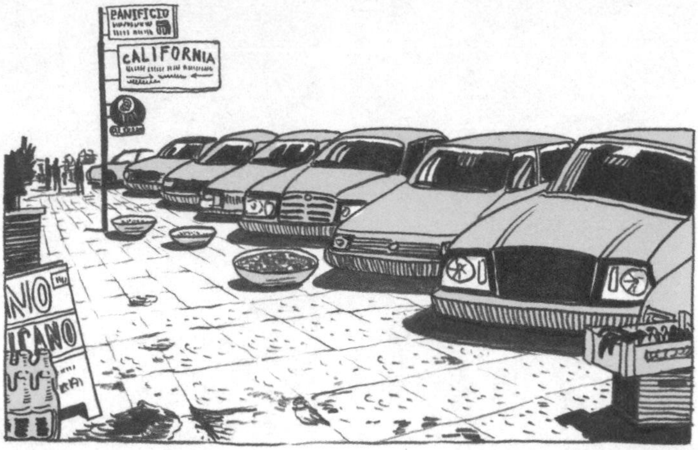
PANIFICIO
CALIFORNIA

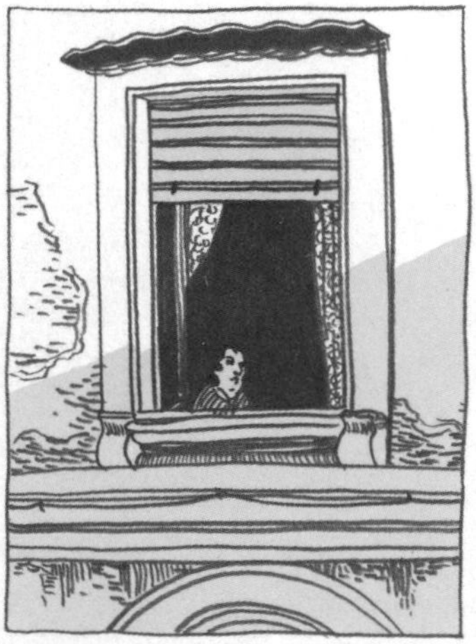

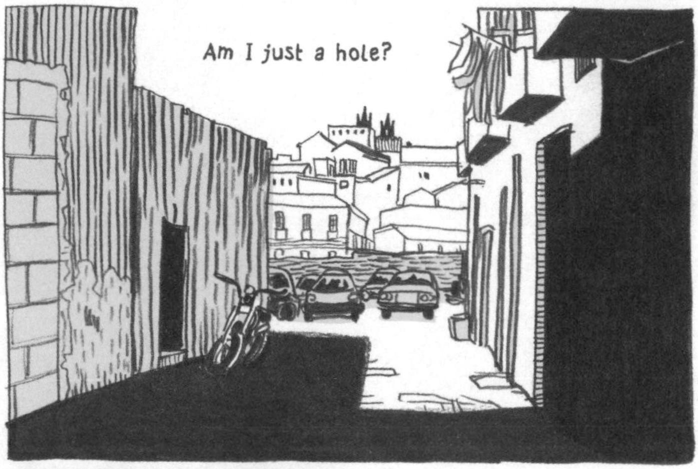
Am I just a hole?

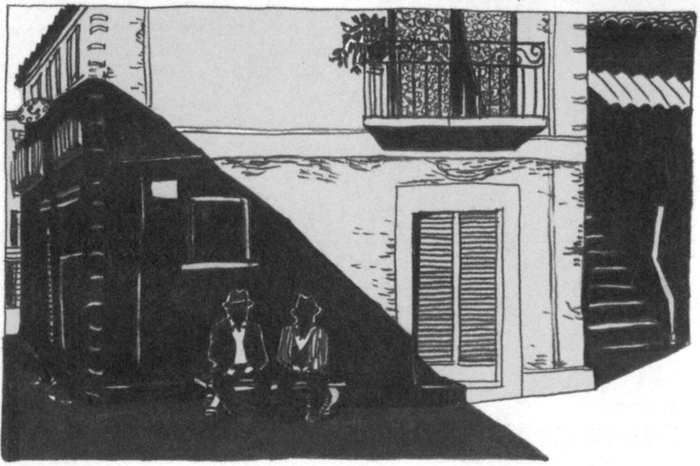

I'm a black hole, a hole that doesn't accept your rules.

So you don't know any women like me? Well, watch and learn! I've come here from the future.

I can do anything a man can. My eyes are looking straight ahead, not at the ground!

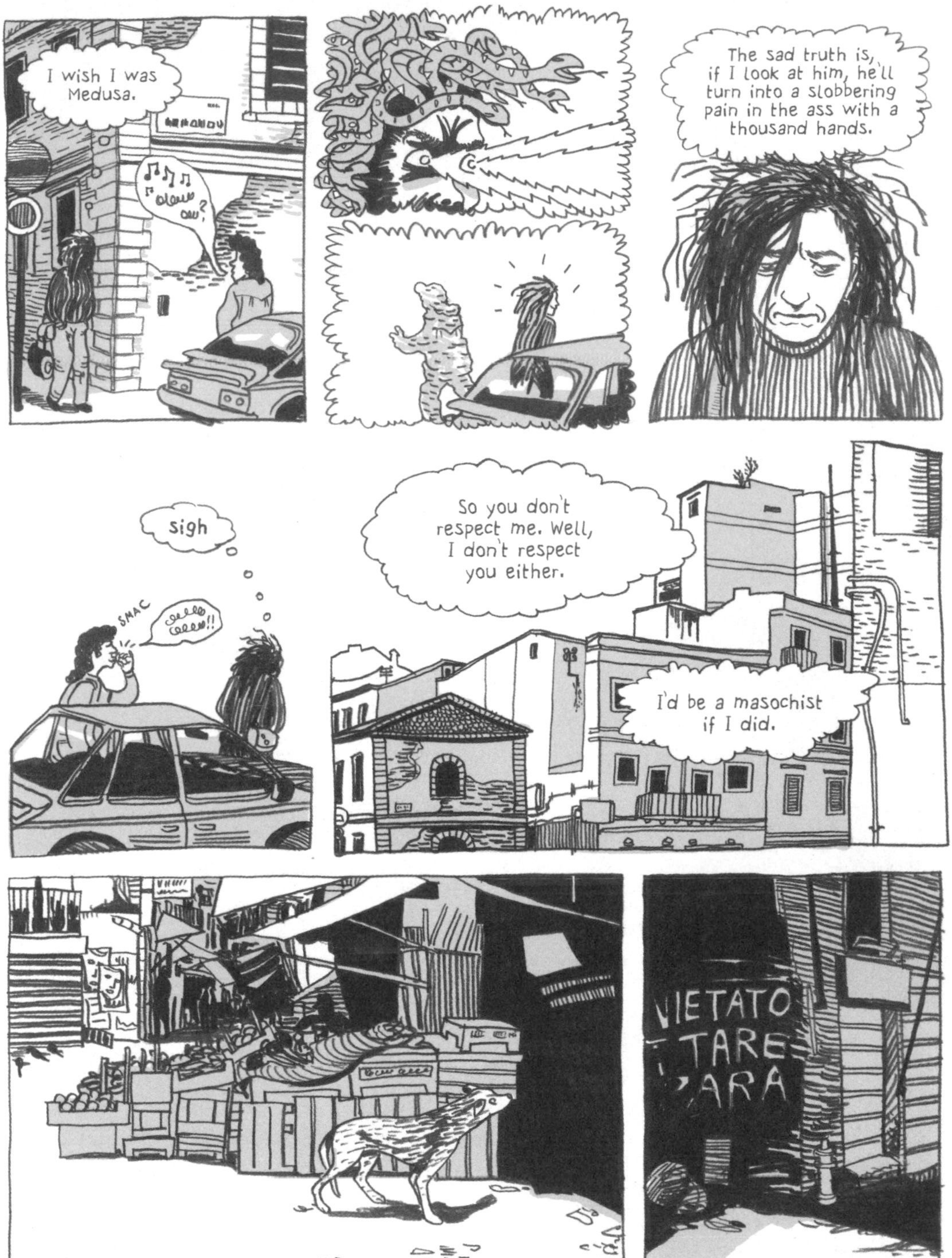

I wish I was Medusa.
The sad truth is, if I look at him, he'll turn into a slobbering pain in the ass with a thousand hands.
sigh
SMAC
So you don't respect me. Well, I don't respect you either.
I'd be a masochist if I did.
VIETATO
TARE
ARA

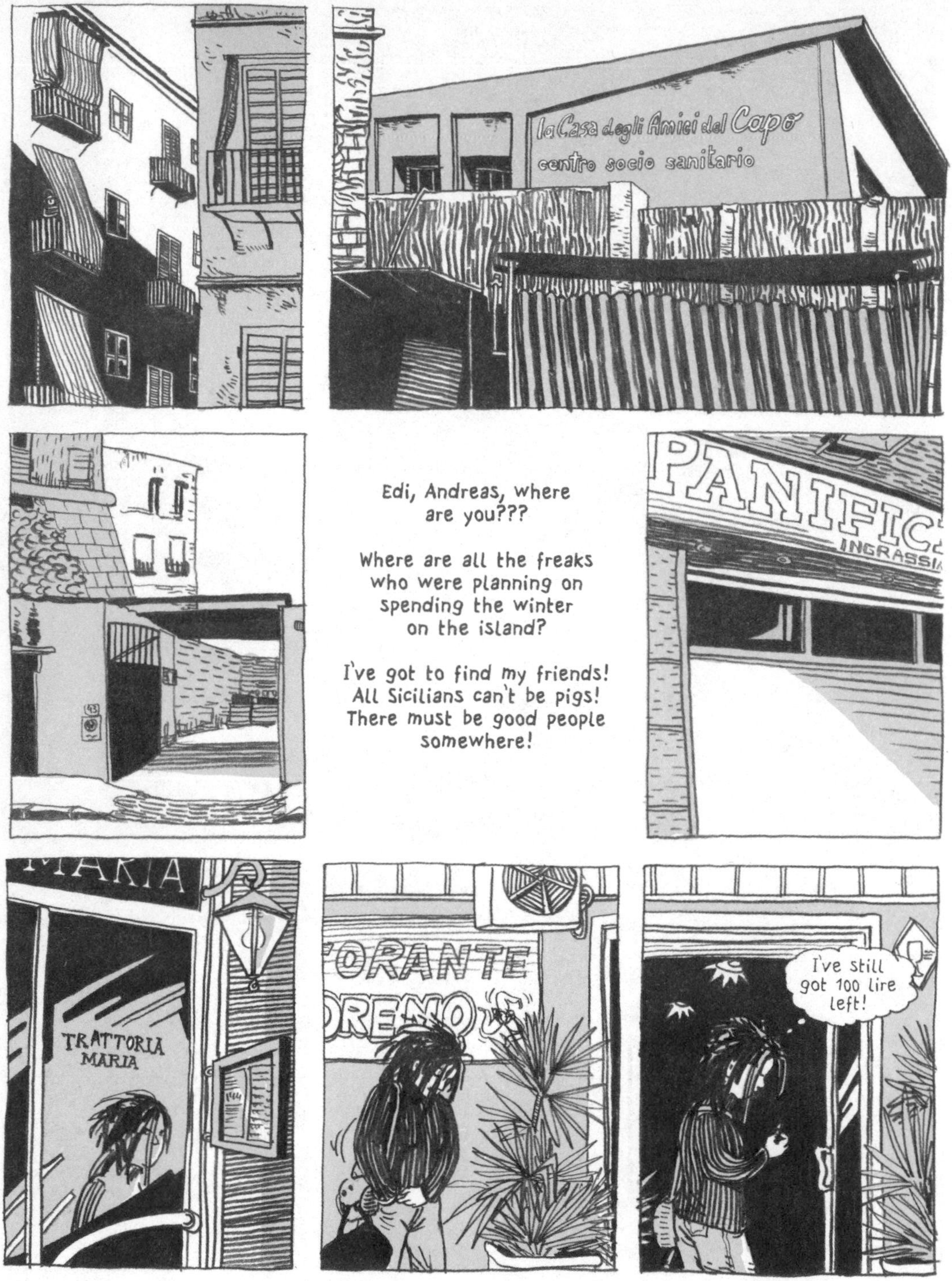
la Casa degli Amici del Capo
centro socio sanitario
Edi, Andreas, where are you???
Where are all the freaks who were planning on spending the winter on the island?
I've got to find my friends! All Sicilians can't be pigs! There must be good people somewhere!
PANIFIC
INGRASSIA
MARIA
TRATTORIA MARIA
TORANTE
I've still got 100 lire left!

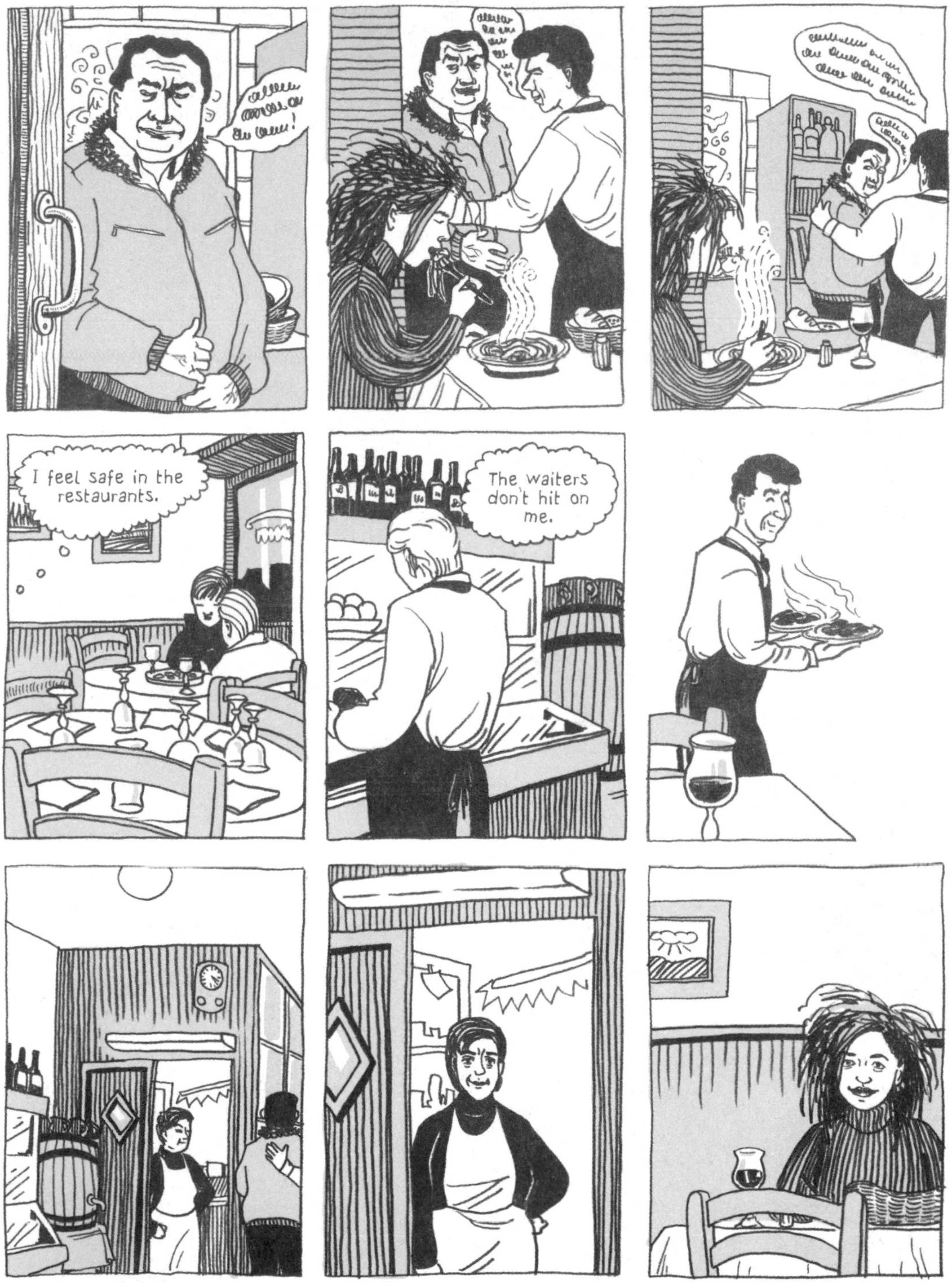
I feel safe in the restaurants.
The waiters don't hit on me.

XIV. the WRATH of Santa Rosalia

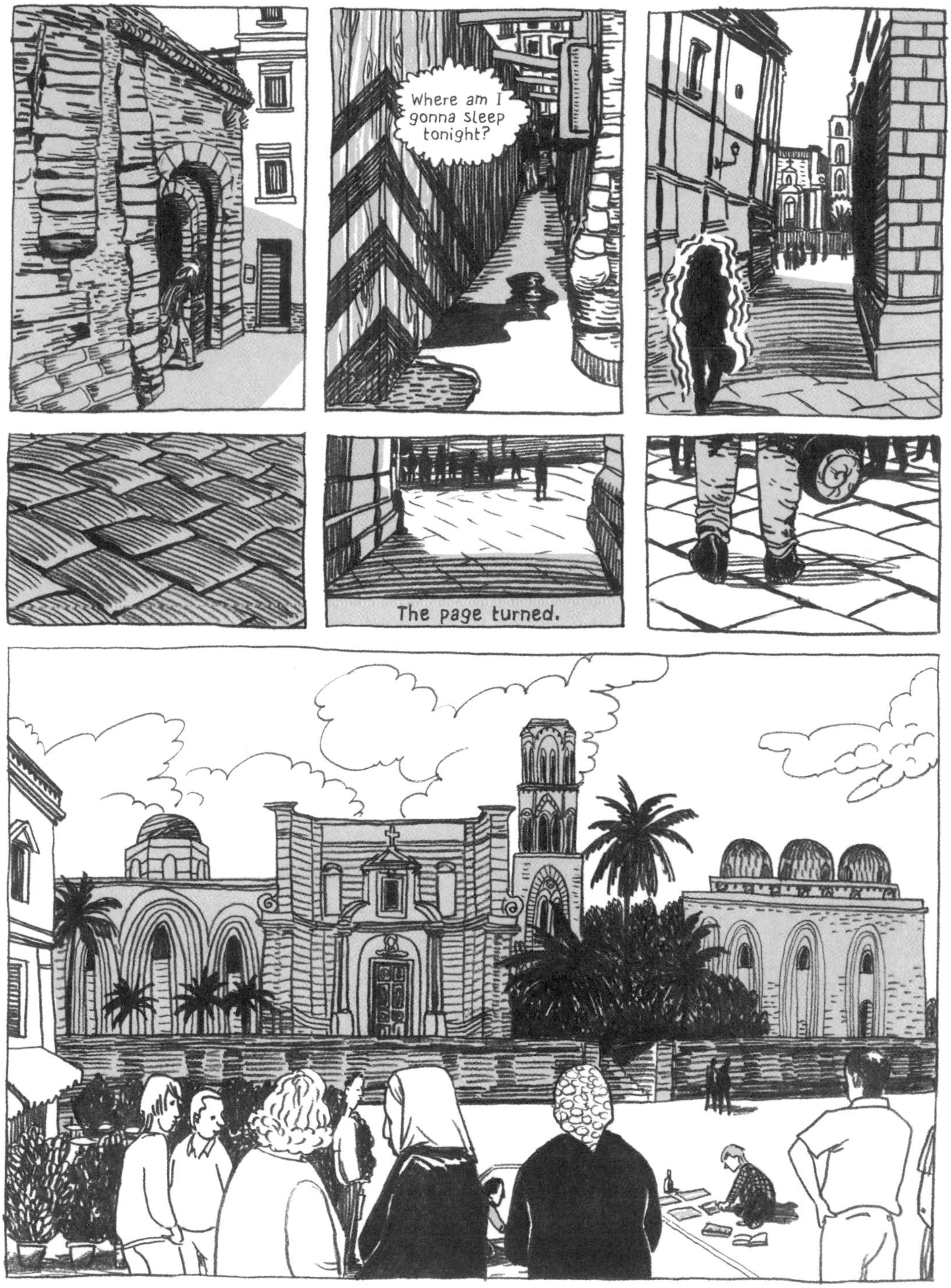
Where am I gonna sleep tonight?
The page turned.

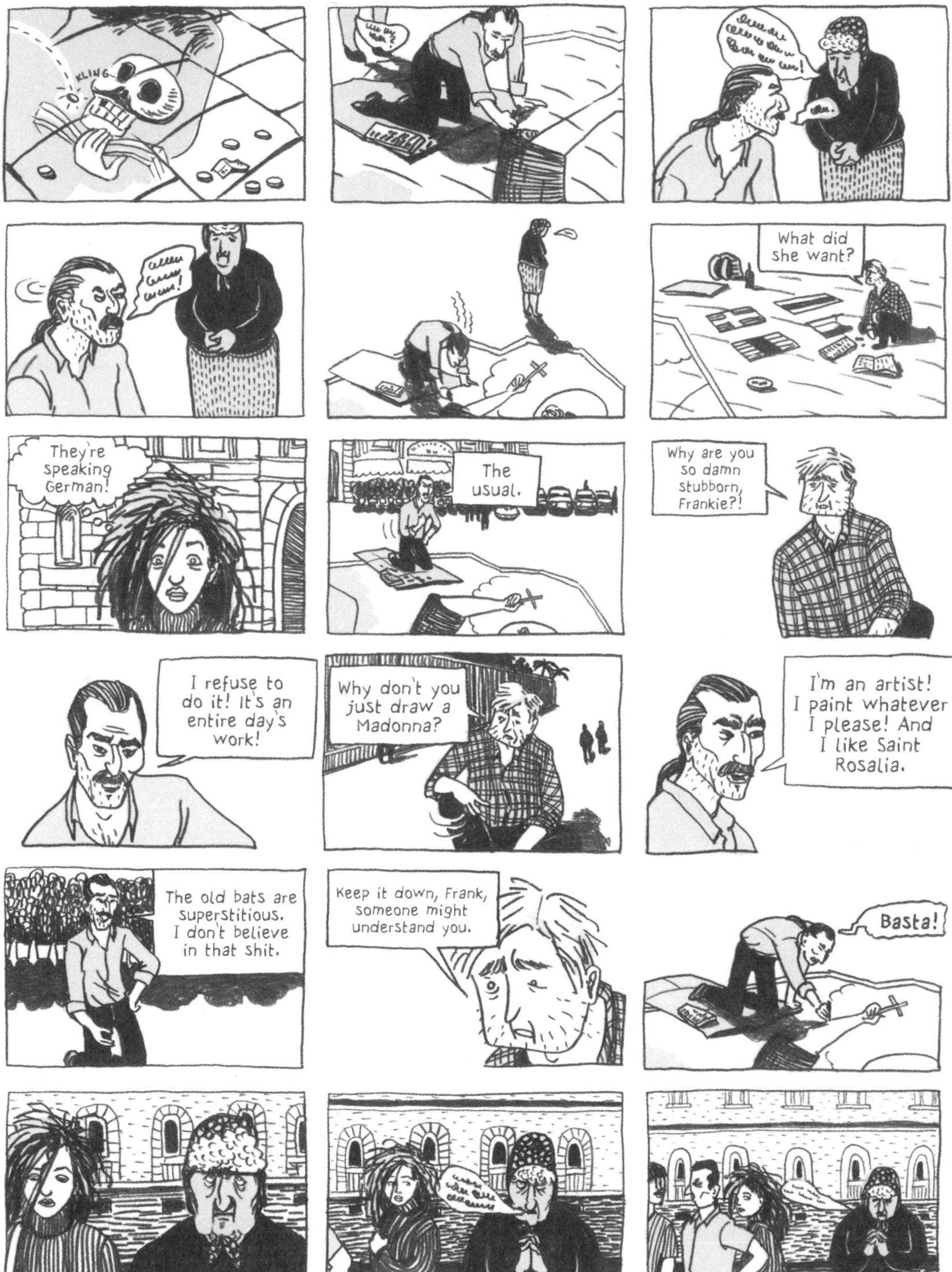
KLING
What did she want?
They're speaking German!
The usual.
Why are you so damn stubborn, Frankie?!
I refuse to do it! It's an entire day's work!
Why don't you just draw a Madonna?
I'm an artist! I paint whatever I please! And I like Saint Rosalia.
The old bats are superstitious. I don't believe in that shit.
Keep it down, Frank, someone might understand you.
Basta!

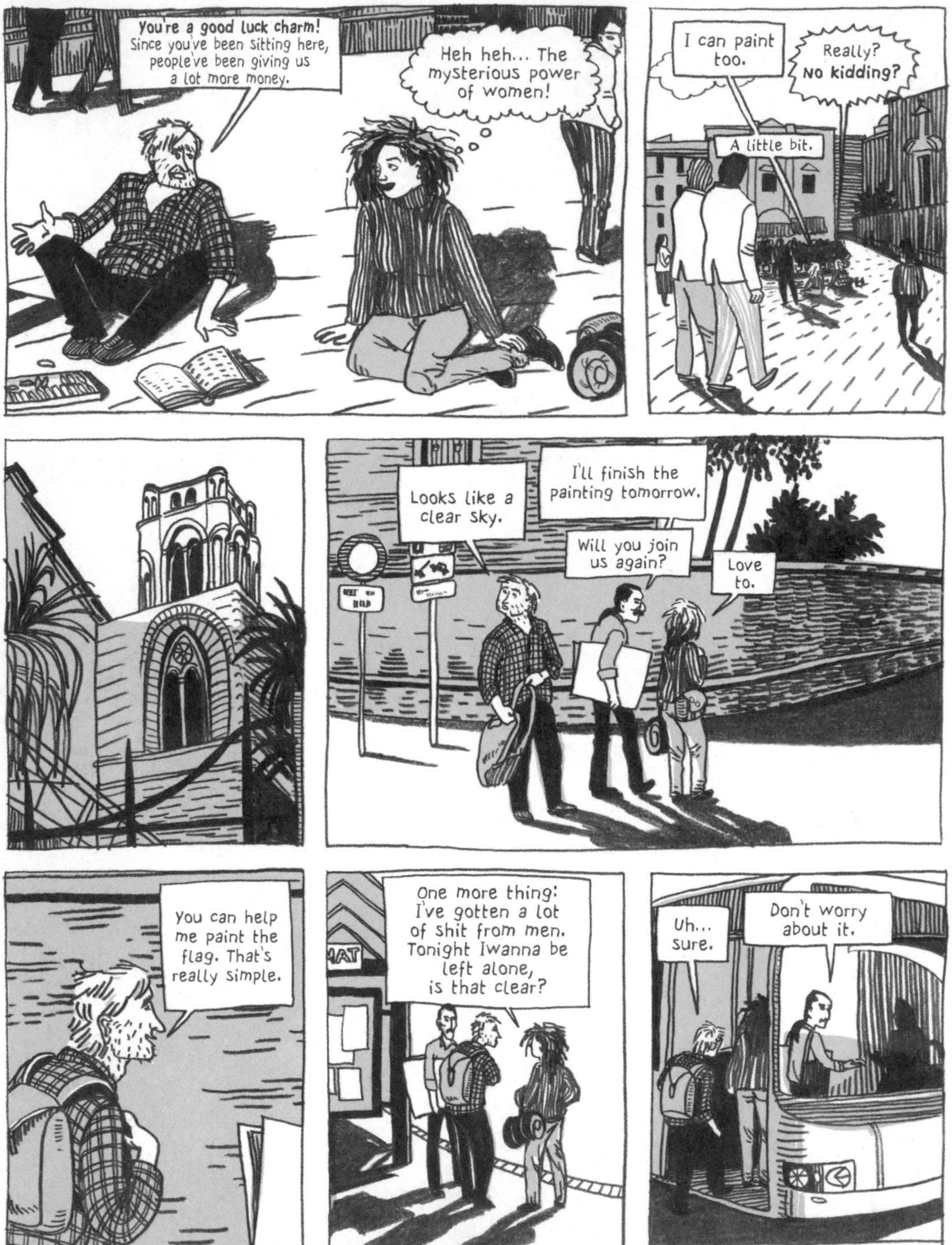

You're a good luck charm! Since you've been sitting here, people've been giving us a lot more money.
Heh heh... The mysterious power of women!
I can paint too.
Really? No kidding?
A little bit.
Looks like a clear sky.
I'll finish the painting tomorrow.
Will you join us again?
Love to.
You can help me paint the flag. That's really simple.
One more thing: I've gotten a lot of shit from men. Tonight Iwanna be left alone, is that clear?
Uh... sure.
Don't worry about it.
I thought, "That's what they all say!"

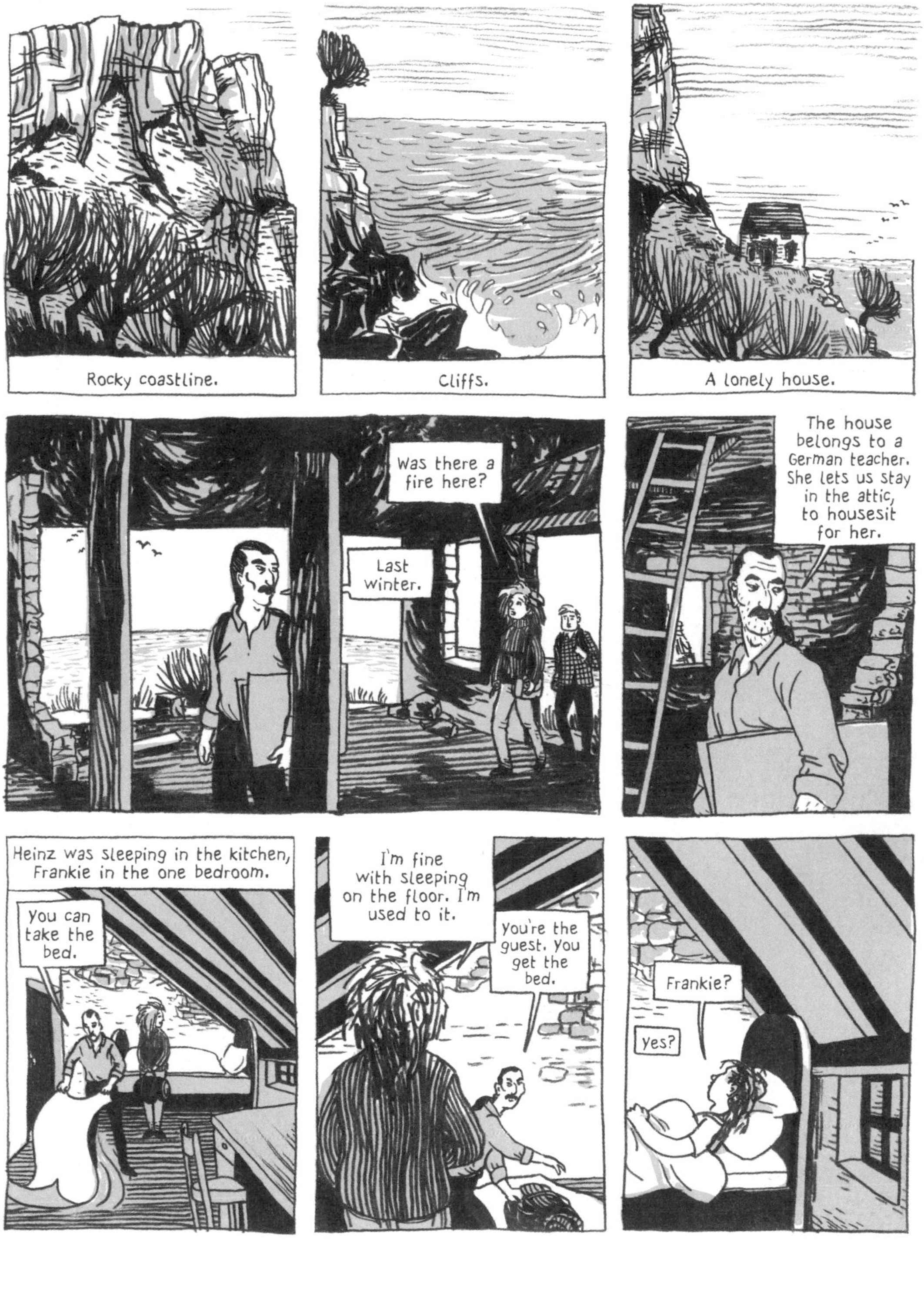
Rocky coastline.
Cliffs.
A lonely house.
Was there a fire here?
Last winter.
The house belongs to a German teacher. She lets us stay in the attic, to housesit for her.
Heinz was sleeping in the kitchen, Frankie in the one bedroom.
You can take the bed.
I'm fine with sleeping on the floor. I'm used to it.
You're the guest. You get the bed.
Frankie?
yes?

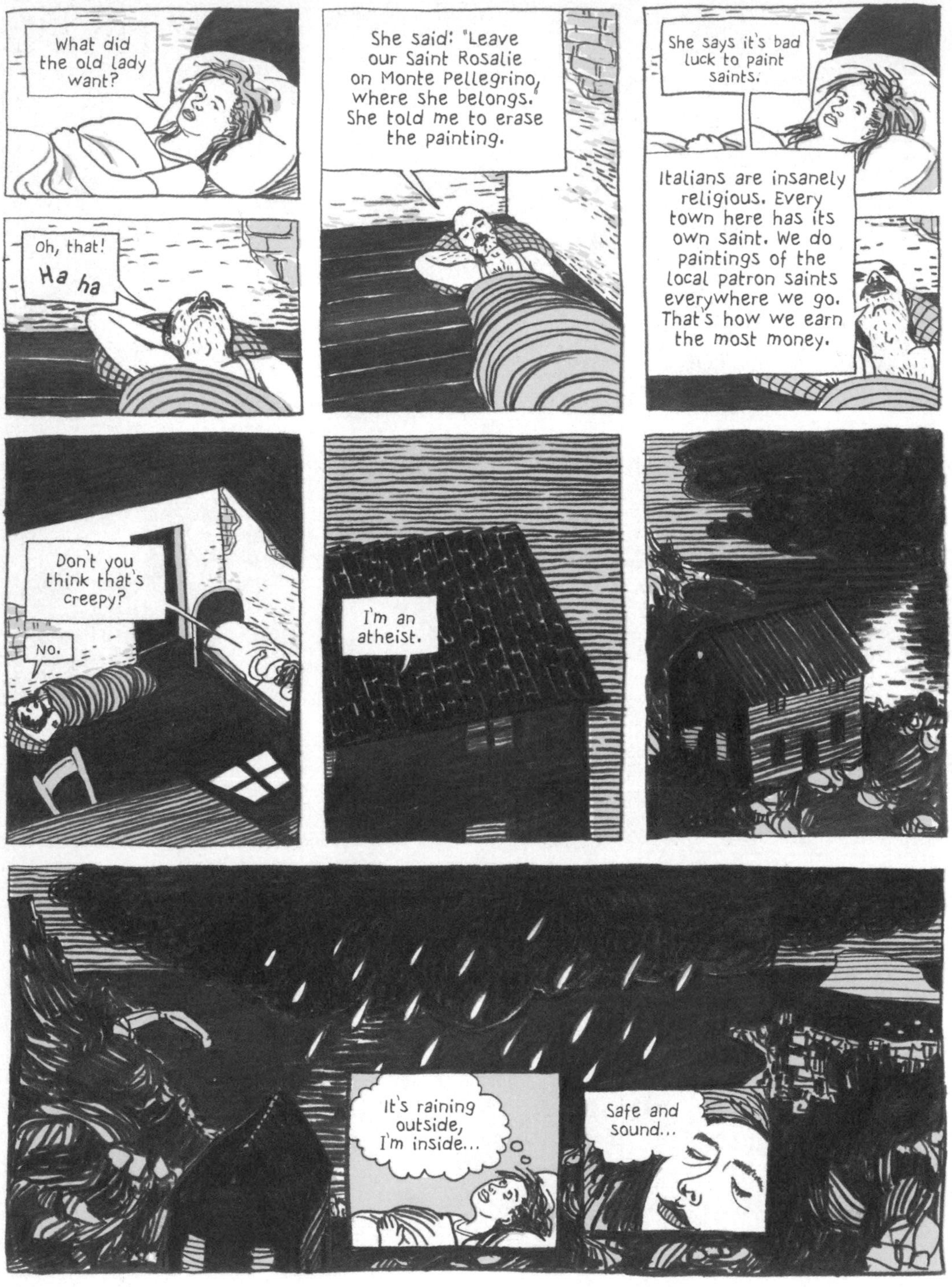
What did the old lady want?
She said: "Leave our Saint Rosalie on Monte Pellegrino, where she belongs." She told me to erase the painting.
She says it's bad luck to paint saints.
Oh, that! Ha ha
Italians are insanely religious. Every town here has its own saint. We do paintings of the local patron saints everywhere we go. That's how we earn the most money.
Don't you think that's creepy?
No.
I'm an atheist.
It's raining outside, I'm inside...
Safe and sound...

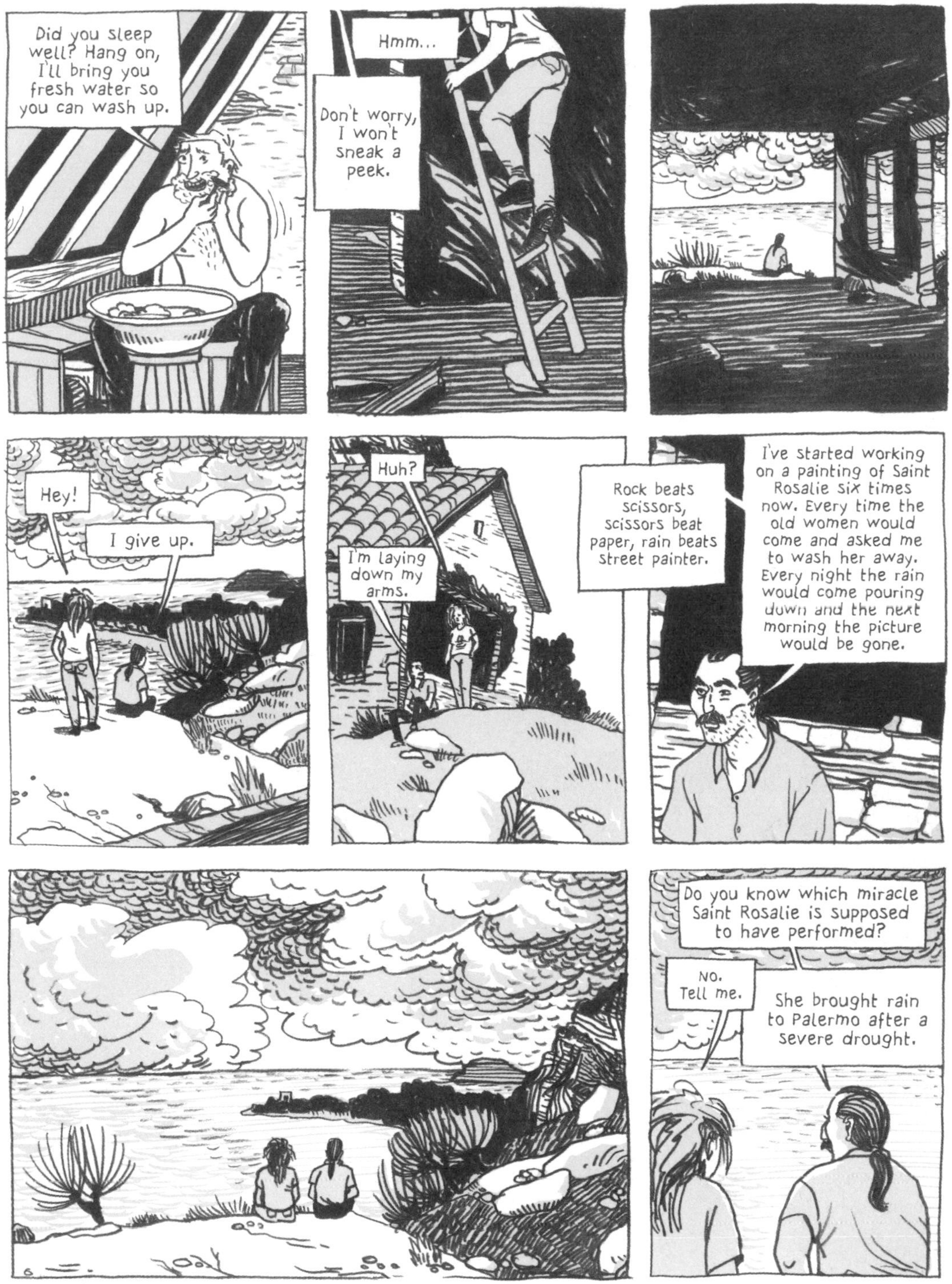

Did you sleep well? Hang on, I'll bring you fresh water so you can wash up.
Hmm...
Don't worry, I won't sneak a peek.
Hey!
I give up.
Huh?
I'm laying down my arms.
Rock beats scissors, scissors beat paper, rain beats street painter.
I've started working on a painting of Saint Rosalie six times now. Every time the old women would come and asked me to wash her away. Every night the rain would come pouring down and the next morning the picture would be gone.
Do you know which miracle Saint Rosalie is supposed to have performed?
No. Tell me.
She brought rain to Palermo after a severe drought.

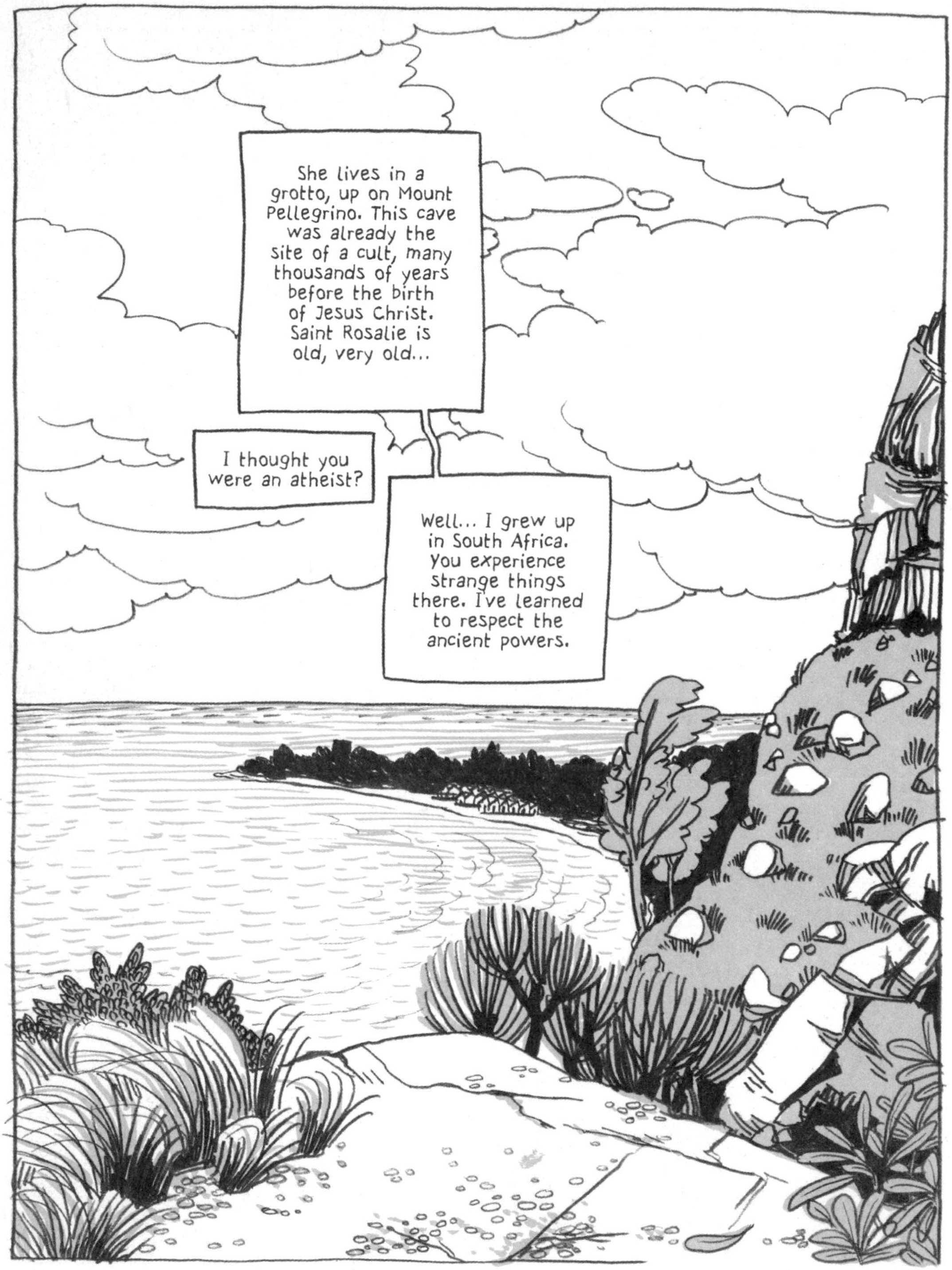
She lives in a grotto, up on Mount Pellegrino. This cave was already the site of a cult, many thousands of years before the birth of Jesus Christ. Saint Rosalie is old, very old...
I thought you were an atheist?
Well... I grew up in South Africa. You experience strange things there. I've learned to respect the ancient powers.

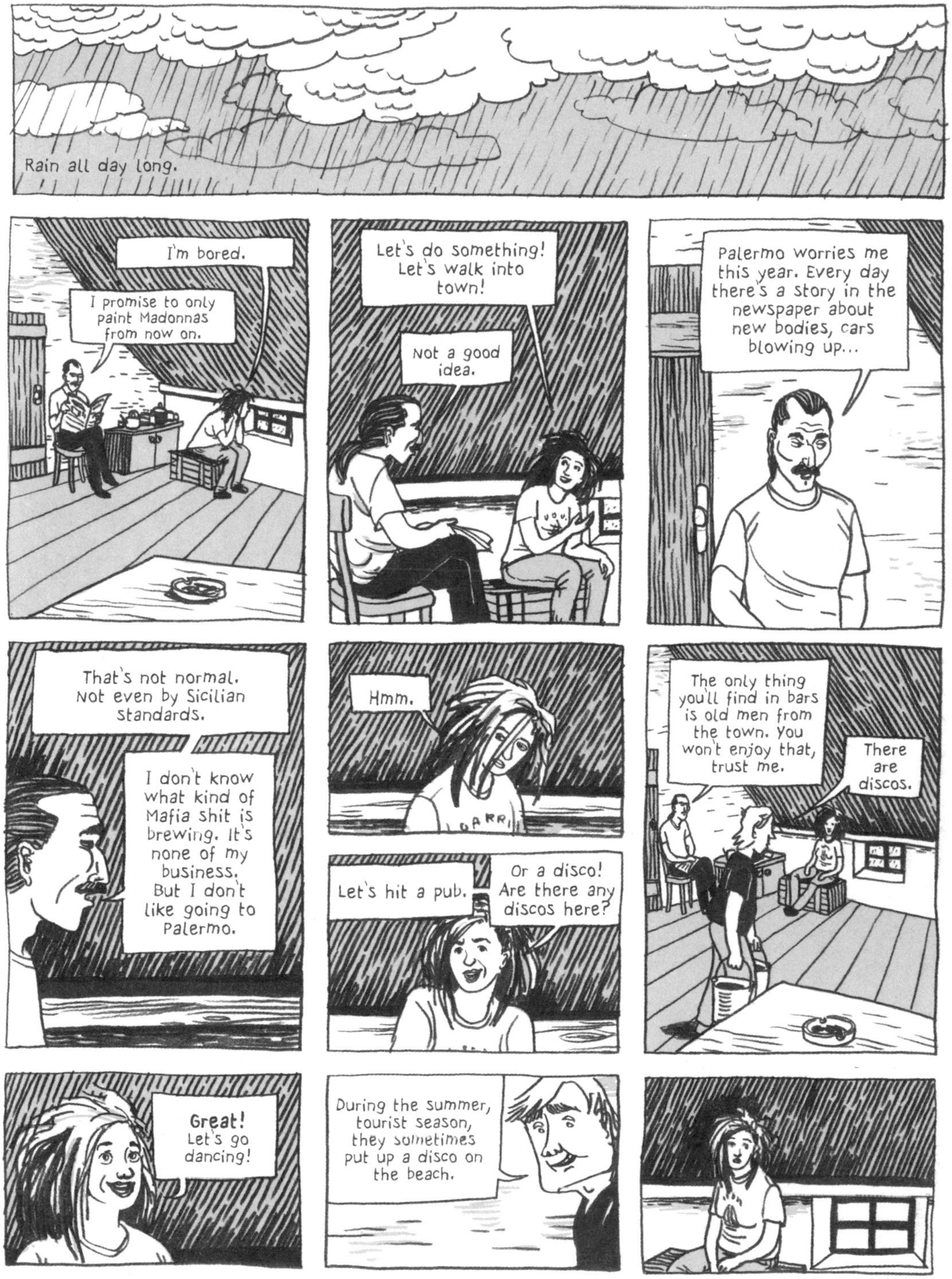
Rain all day long.
I'm bored.
I promise to only paint Madonnas from now on.
Let's do something! Let's walk into town!
Not a good idea.
Palermo worries me this year. Every day there's a story in the newspaper about new bodies, cars blowing up...
That's not normal. Not even by Sicilian standards.
I don't know what kind of Mafia shit is brewing. It's none of my business. But I don't like going to Palermo.
Hmm.
Let's hit a pub.
Or a disco! Are there any discos here?
The only thing you'll find in bars is old men from the town. You won't enjoy that, trust me.
There are discos.
Great! Let's go dancing!
During the summer, tourist season, they sometimes put up a disco on the beach.

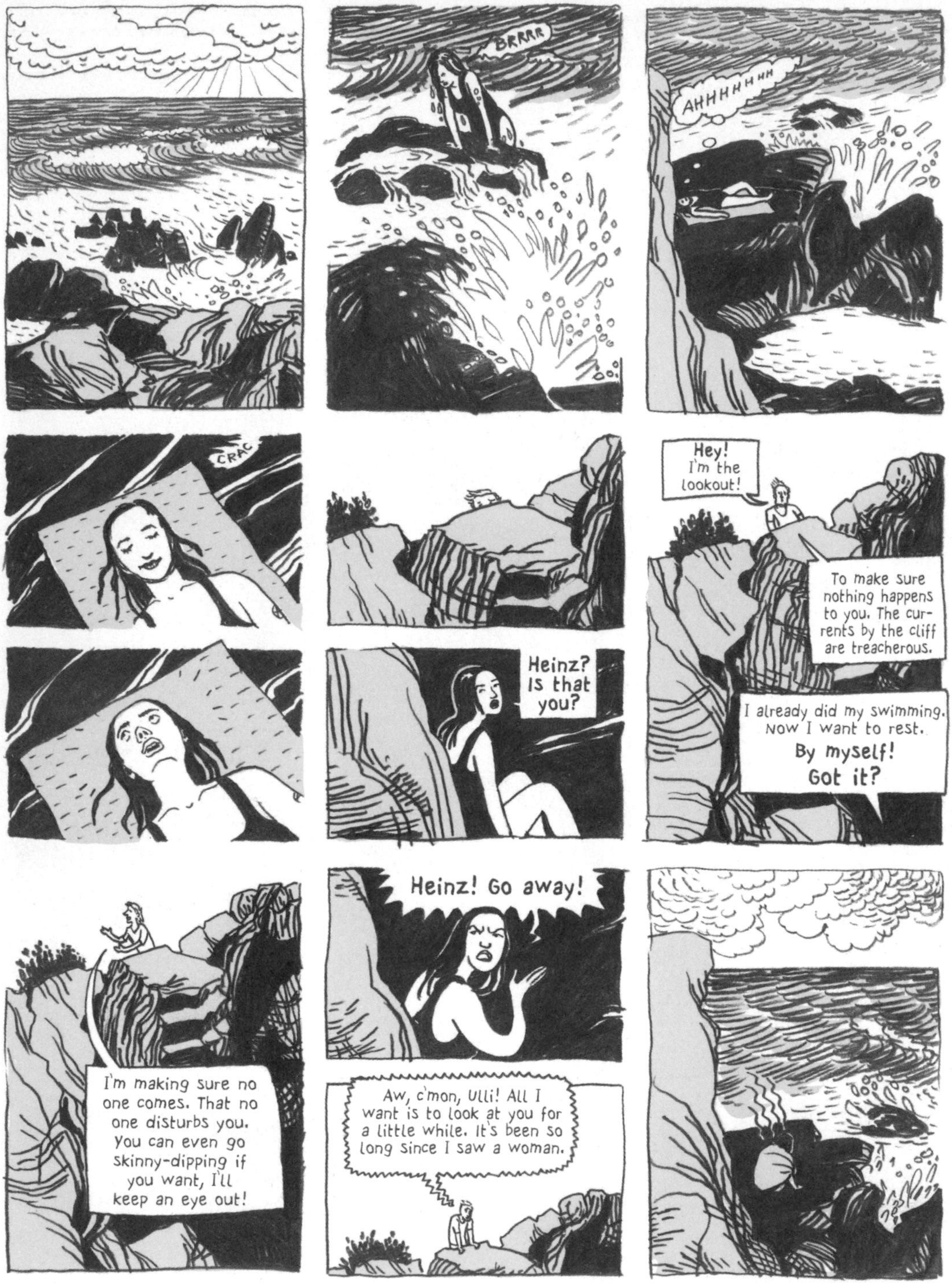
BRRRR
AHHHHHHHH
CRAC
Hey! I'm the lookout!
To make sure nothing happens to you. The currents by the cliff are treacherous.
Heinz? Is that you?
I already did my swimming. Now I want to rest. By myself! Got it?
I'm making sure no one comes. That no one disturbs you. You can even go skinny-dipping if you want, I'll keep an eye out!
Heinz! Go away!
Aw, c'mon, Ulli! All I want is to look at you for a little while. It's been so long since I saw a woman.

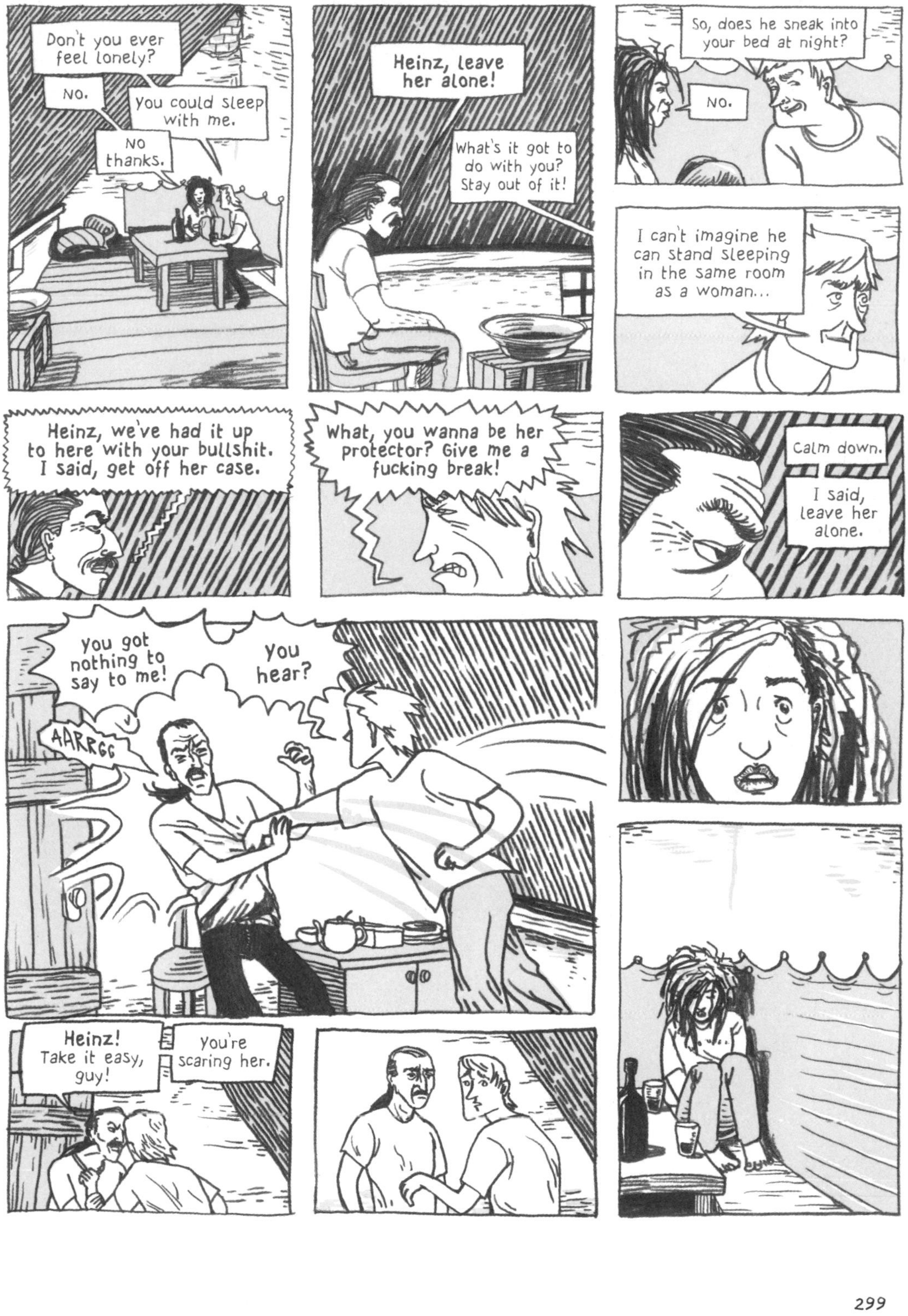
Don't you ever feel lonely?
No.
You could sleep with me.
No thanks.
Heinz, leave her alone!
What's it got to do with you? Stay out of it!
So, does he sneak into your bed at night?
No.
I can't imagine he can stand sleeping in the same room as a woman...
Heinz, we've had it up to here with your bullshit. I said, get off her case.
What, you wanna be her protector? Give me a fucking break!
Calm down.
I said, leave her alone.
You got nothing to say to me!
You hear?
AARRGG
Heinz! Take it easy, guy!
You're scaring her.

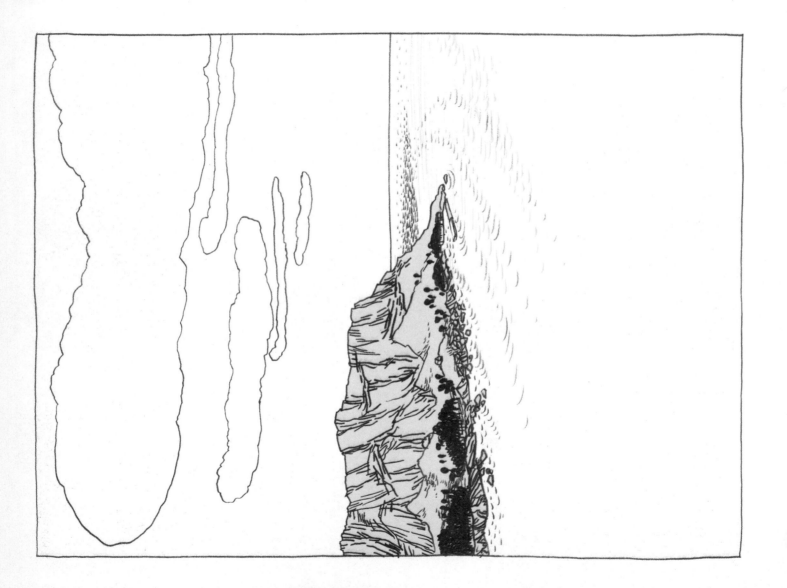

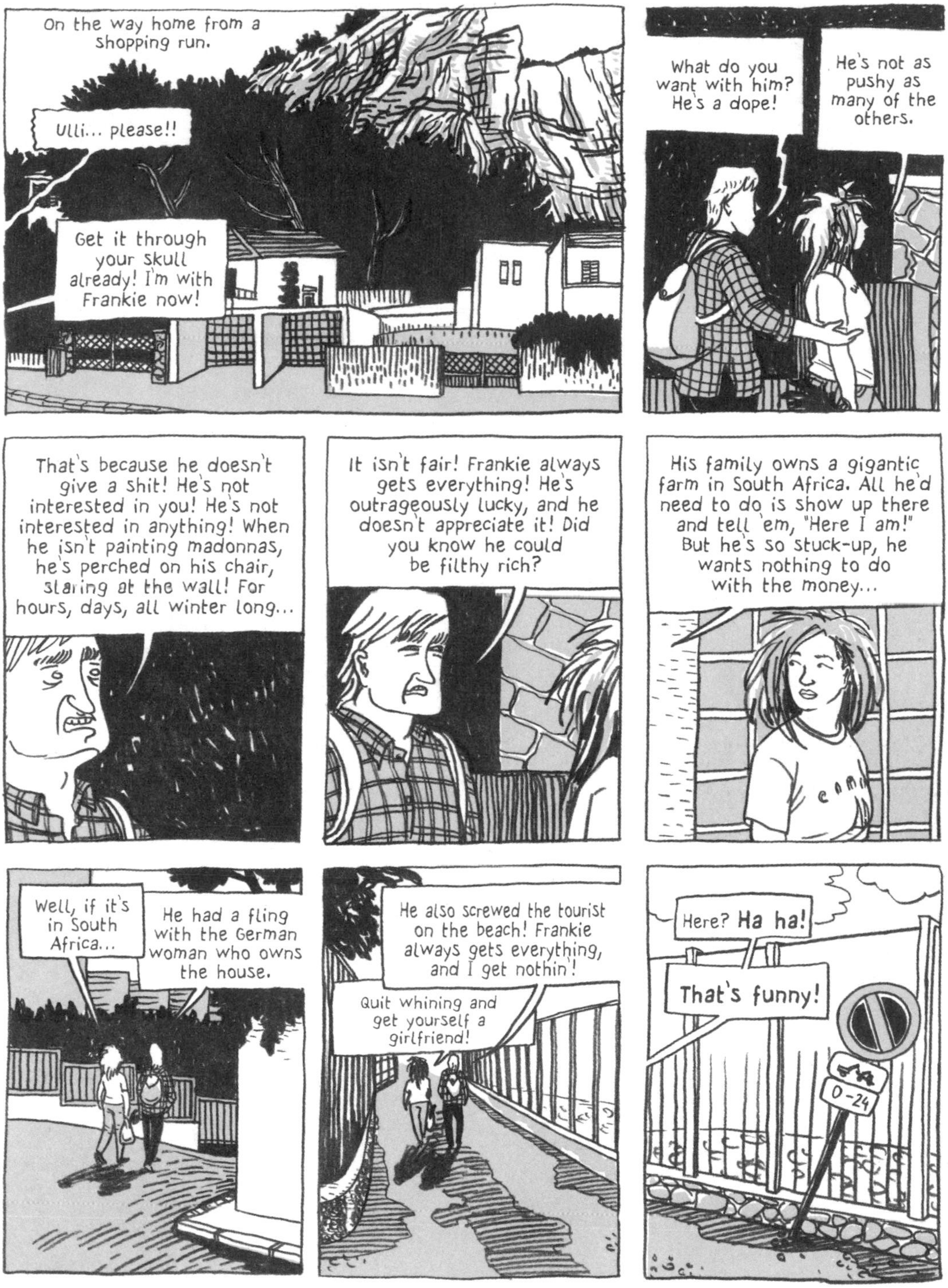
On the way home from a shopping run.
Ulli... please!!
Get it through your skull already! I'm with Frankie now!
What do you want with him? He's a dope!
He's not as pushy as many of the others.
That's because he doesn't give a shit! He's not interested in you! He's not interested in anything! When he isn't painting madonnas, he's perched on his chair, staring at the wall! For hours, days, all winter long...
It isn't fair! Frankie always gets everything! He's outrageously lucky, and he doesn't appreciate it! Did you know he could be filthy rich?
His family owns a gigantic farm in South Africa. All he'd need to do is show up there and tell 'em, "Here I am!" But he's so stuck-up, he wants nothing to do with the money...
Well, if it's in South Africa...
He had a fling with the German woman who owns the house.
He also screwed the tourist on the beach! Frankie always gets everything, and I get nothin'!
Quit whining and get yourself a girlfriend!
Here? Ha ha!
That's funny!
0-24

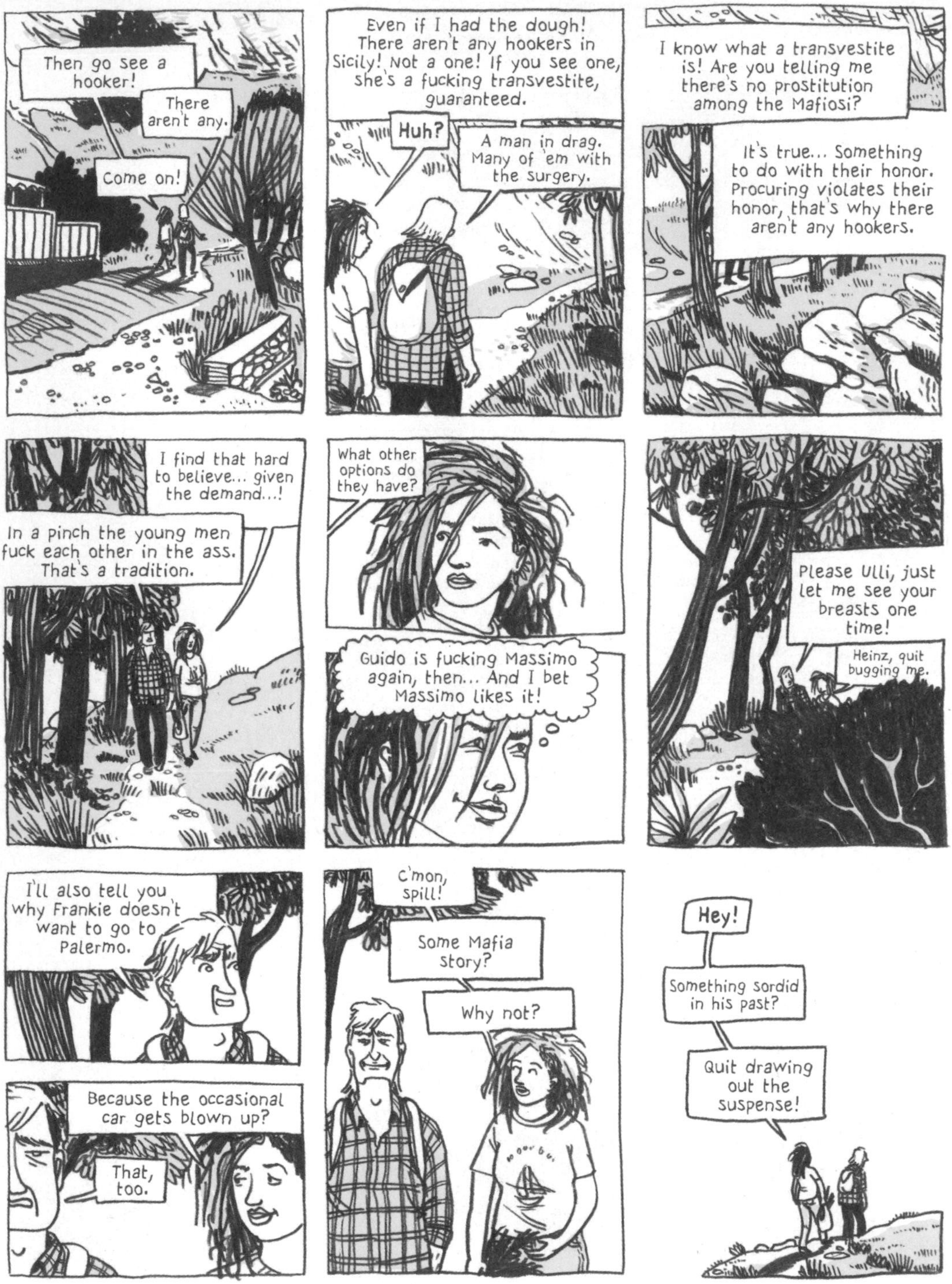
Then go see a hooker!
There aren't any.
Come on!
Even if I had the dough! There aren't any hookers in Sicily! Not a one! If you see one, she's a fucking transvestite, guaranteed.
Huh?
A man in drag. Many of 'em with the surgery.
I know what a transvestite is! Are you telling me there's no prostitution among the Mafiosi?
It's true... Something to do with their honor. Procuring violates their honor, that's why there aren't any hookers.
I find that hard to believe... given the demand...!
In a pinch the young men fuck each other in the ass. That's a tradition.
What other options do they have?
Guido is fucking Massimo again, then... And I bet Massimo likes it!
Please Ulli, just let me see your breasts one time!
Heinz, quit bugging me.
I'll also tell you why Frankie doesn't want to go to Palermo.
Because the occasional car gets blown up?
That, too.
C'mon, spill!
Some Mafia story?
Why not?
Hey!
Something sordid in his past?
Quit drawing out the suspense!

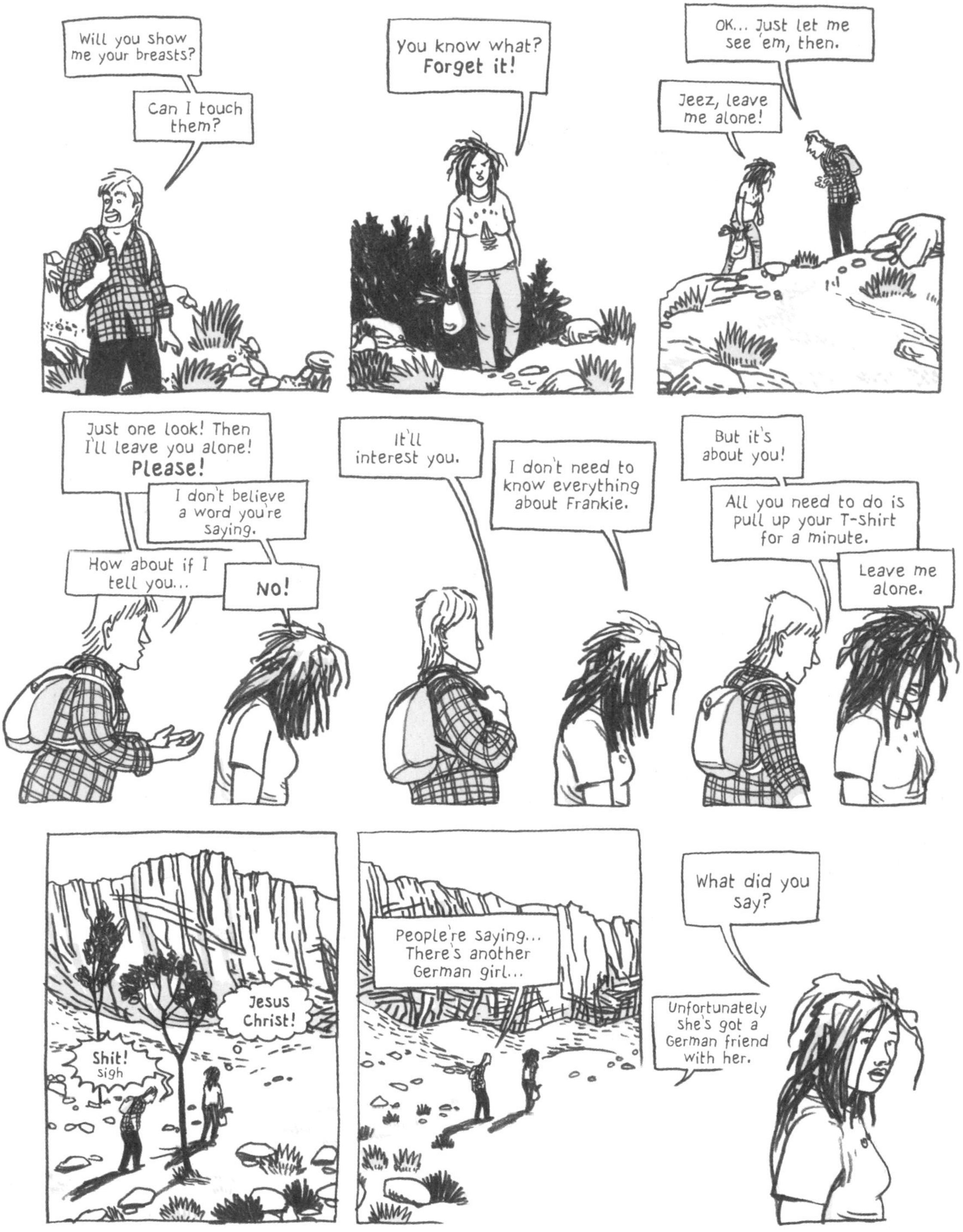

Will you show me your breasts?
Can I touch them?
You know what? **Forget it!**
OK... Just let me see 'em, then.
Jeez, leave me alone!
Just one look! Then I'll leave you alone! **Please!**
I don't believe a word you're saying.
How about if I tell you...
No!
It'll interest you.
I don't need to know everything about Frankie.
But it's about you!
All you need to do is pull up your T-Shirt for a minute.
Leave me alone.
Jesus Christ!
Shit! sigh
People're saying... There's another German girl...
Unfortunately she's got a German friend with her.
What did you say?

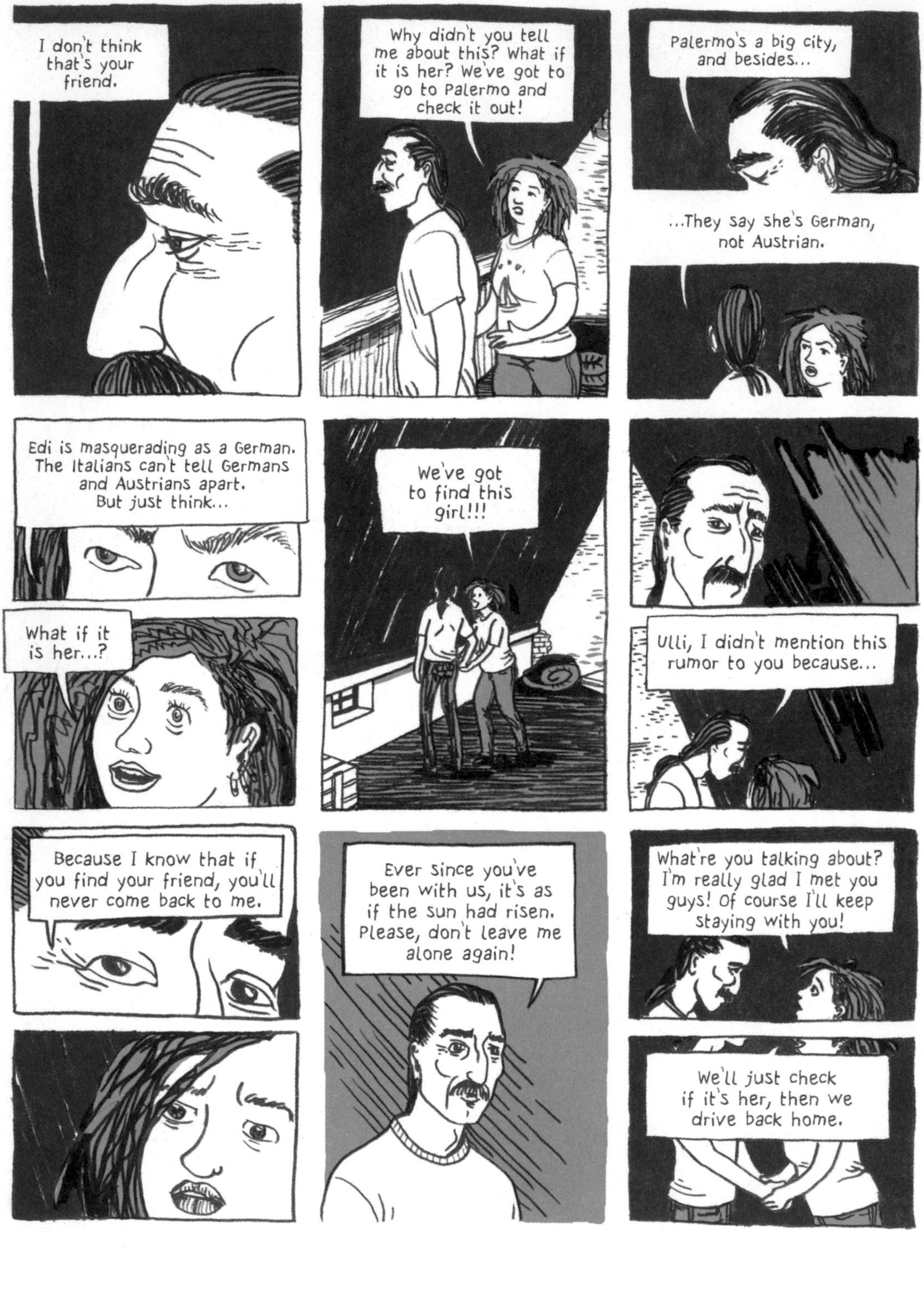
I don't think that's your friend.
Why didn't you tell me about this? What if it is her? We've got to go to Palermo and check it out!
Palermo's a big city, and besides...
...They say she's German, not Austrian.
Edi is masquerading as a German. The Italians can't tell Germans and Austrians apart. But just think...
What if it is her...?
We've got to find this girl!!!
Ulli, I didn't mention this rumor to you because...
Because I know that if you find your friend, you'll never come back to me.
Ever since you've been with us, it's as if the sun had risen. Please, don't leave me alone again!
What're you talking about? I'm really glad I met you guys! Of course I'll keep staying with you!
We'll just check if it's her, then we drive back home.

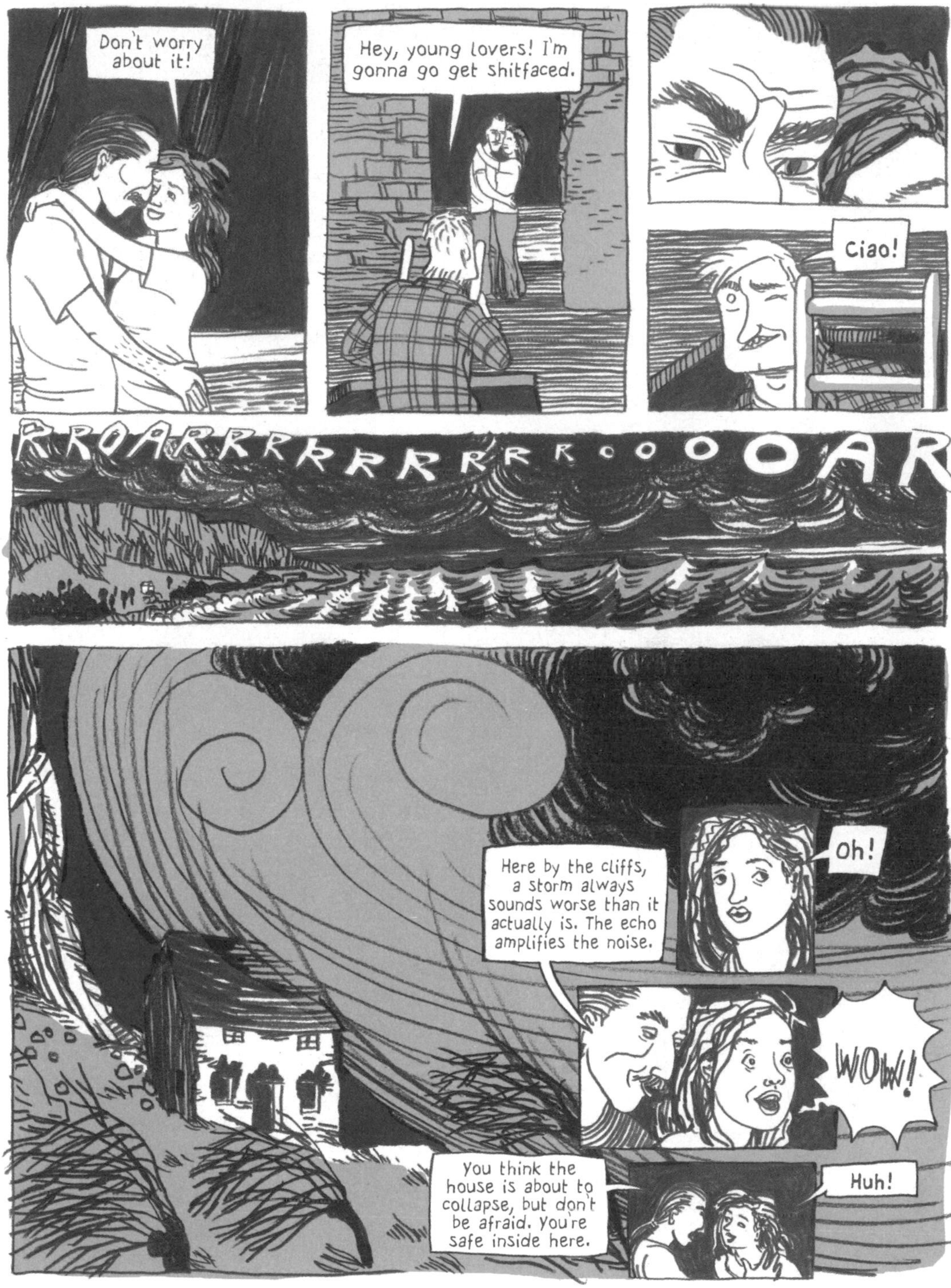
Don't worry about it!
Hey, young lovers! I'm gonna go get shitfaced.
Ciao!
RROARRRRRRRRRRrooOOOAR
Here by the cliffs, a storm always sounds worse than it actually is. The echo amplifies the noise.
Oh!
WOW!
You think the house is about to collapse, but don't be afraid. You're safe inside here.
Huh!

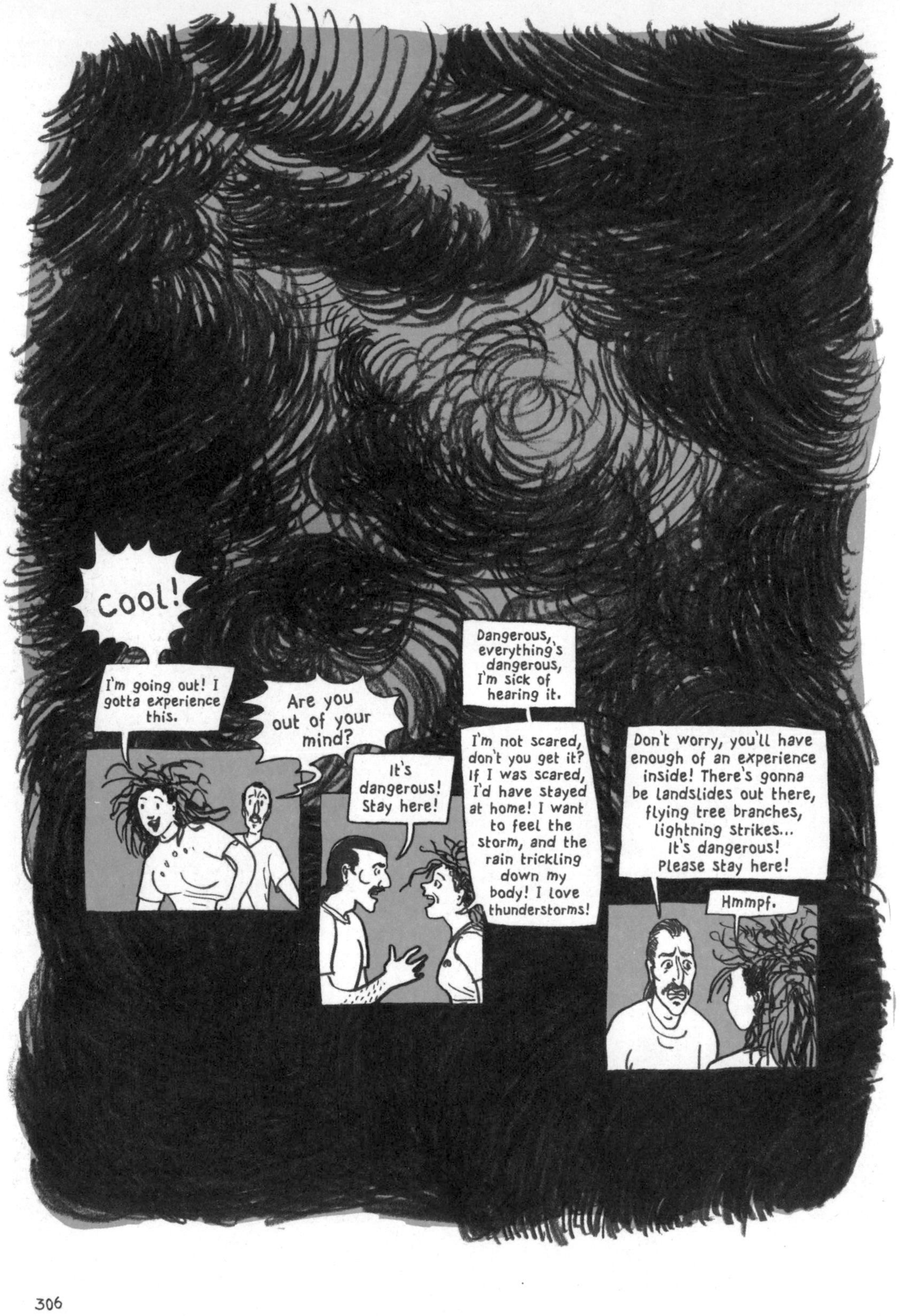
Cool!
I'm going out! I gotta experience this.
Are you out of your mind?
It's dangerous! Stay here!
Dangerous, everything's dangerous, I'm sick of hearing it.
I'm not scared, don't you get it? If I was scared, I'd have stayed at home! I want to feel the storm, and the rain trickling down my body! I love thunderstorms!
Don't worry, you'll have enough of an experience inside! There's gonna be landslides out there, flying tree branches, lightning strikes... It's dangerous! Please stay here!
Hmmpf.

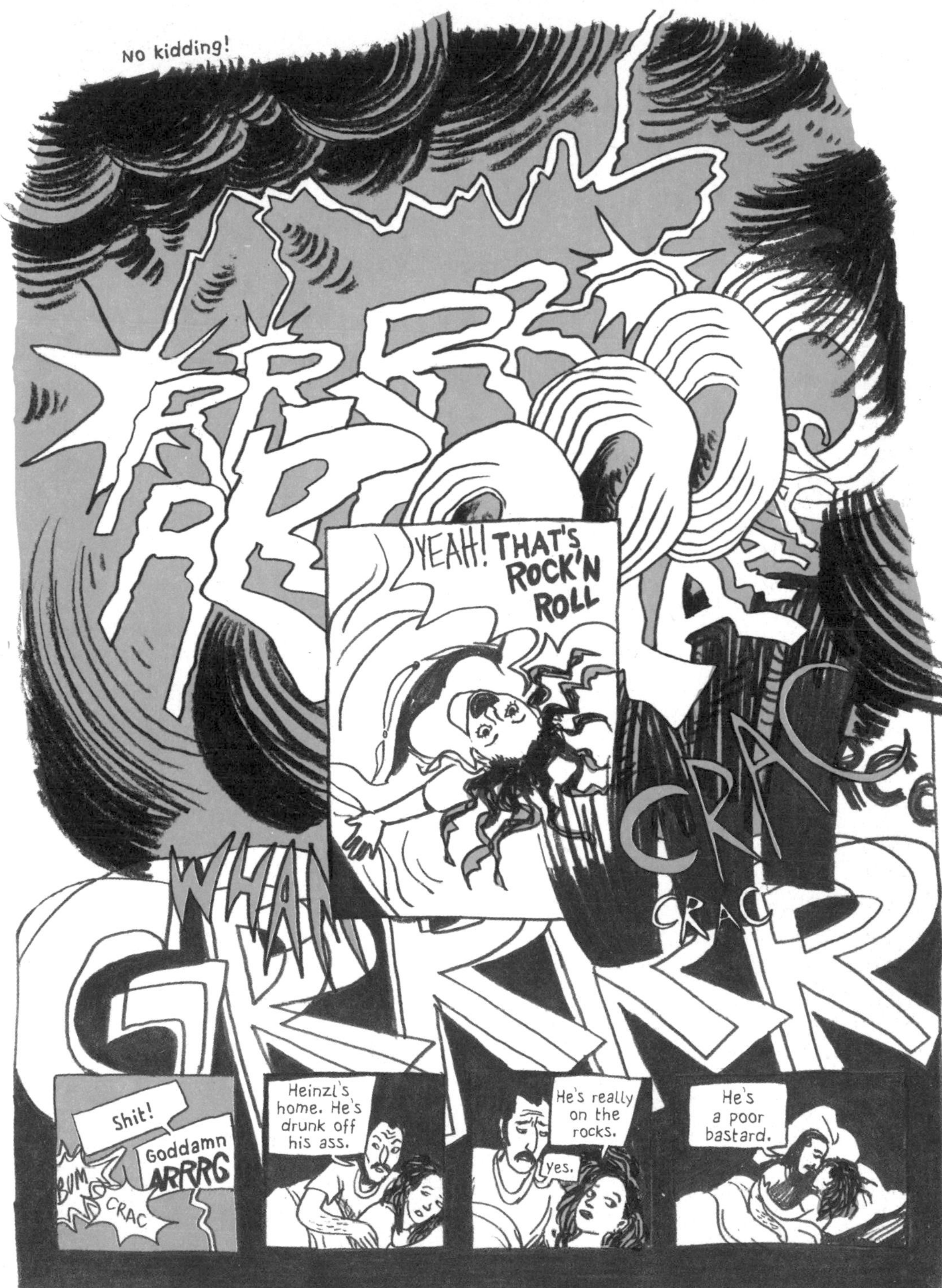
No kidding!
YEAH! THAT'S ROCK'N ROLL
WHAM
CRAC
CRAC
Shit!
Goddamn
ARRRG
BUM
CRAC
Heinzl's home. He's drunk off his ass.
He's really on the rocks.
Yes.
He's a poor bastard.

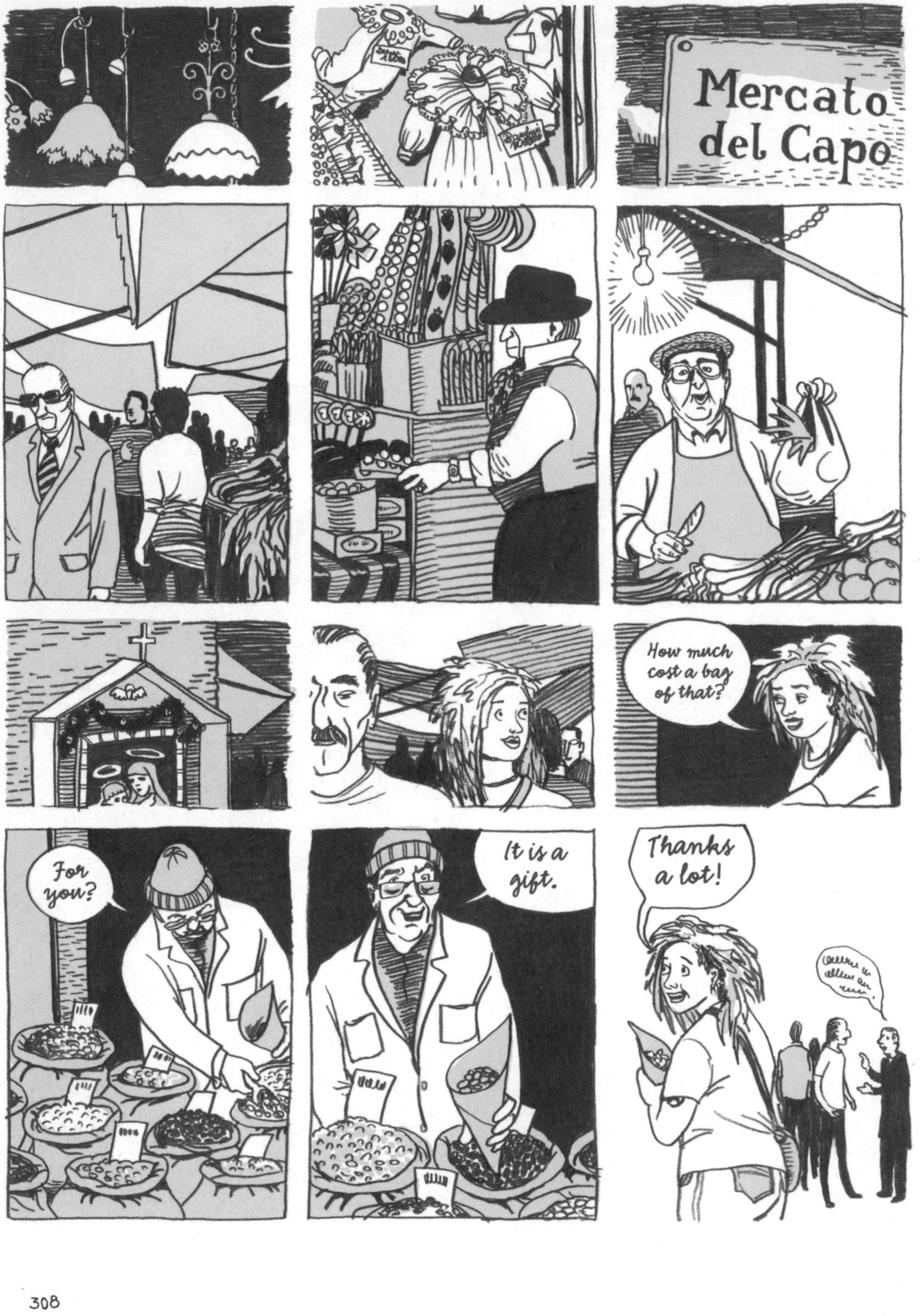
Mercato del Capo
How much cost a bag of that?
For you?
It is a gift.
Thanks a lot!

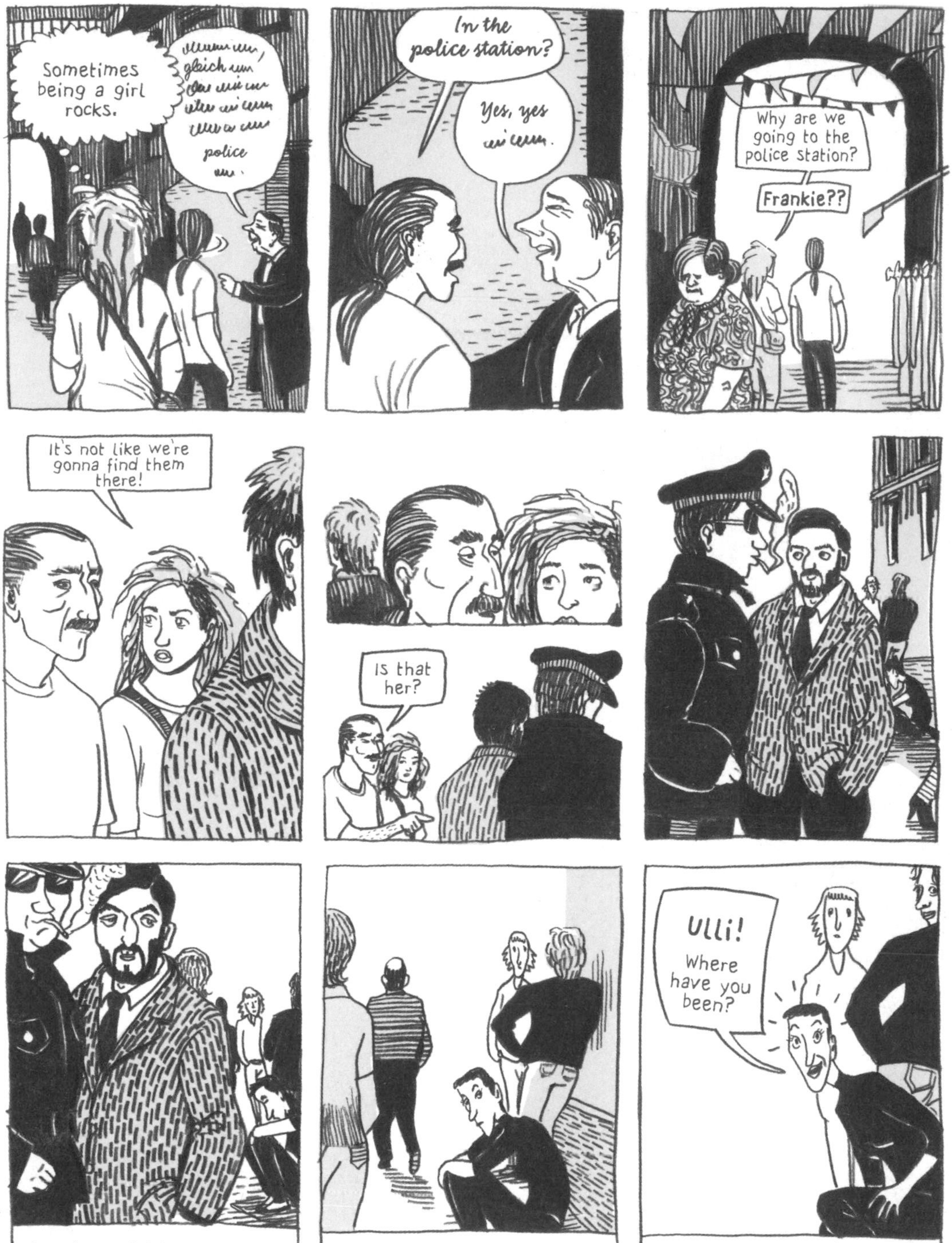
Sometimes being a girl rocks.
gleich
police
In the police station?
Yes, yes
Why are we going to the police station?
Frankie??
It's not like we're gonna find them there!
Is that her?
The wheel of fate took a spin.
A huge one.
Ulli!
Where have you been?
And luck was ascendant again.

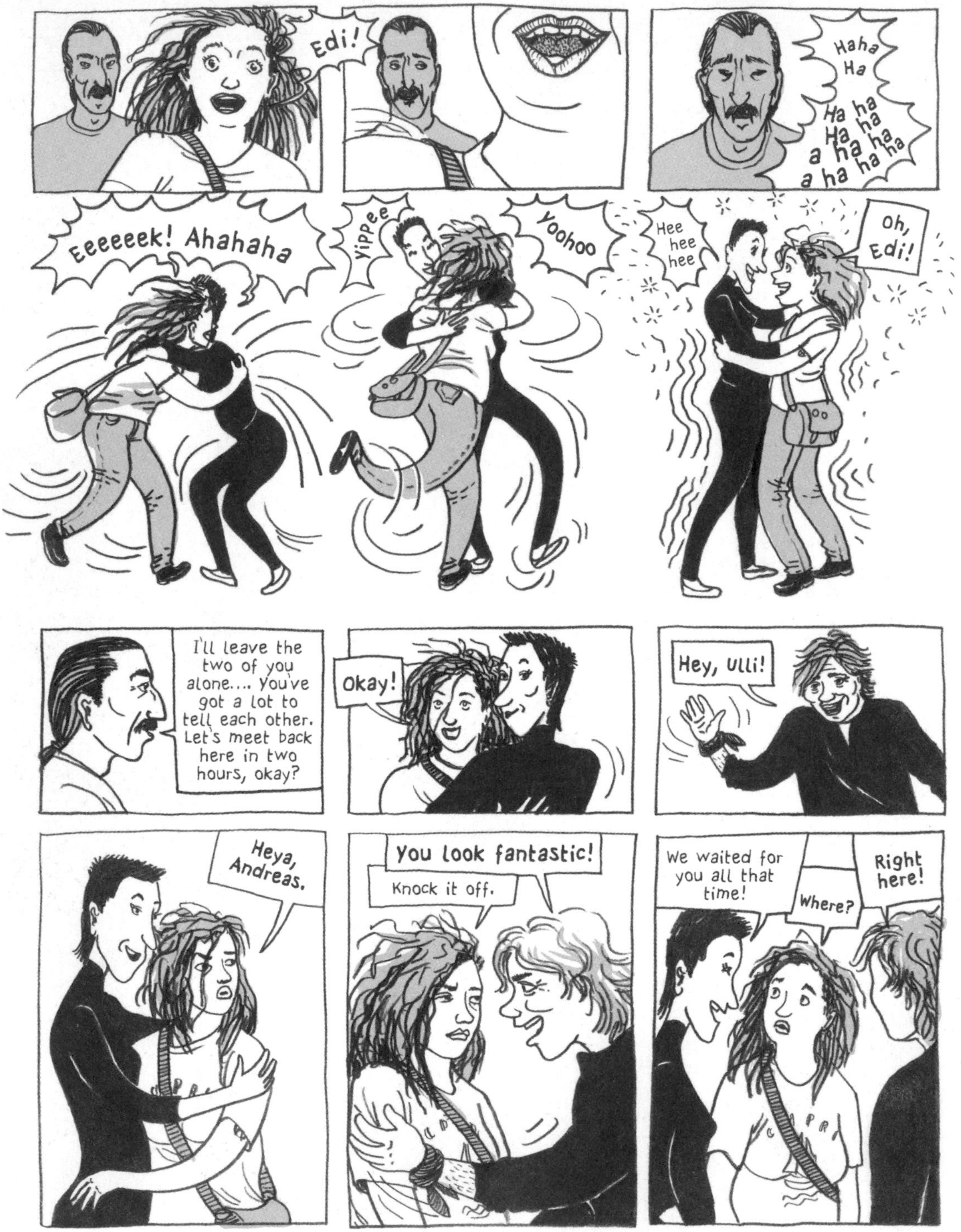
Edi!
Haha Ha Ha ha Ha ha a ha ha a ha ha ha
Eeeeeek! Ahahaha
Yippee
Yoohoo
Hee hee hee
Oh, Edi!
I'll leave the two of you alone.... You've got a lot to tell each other. Let's meet back here in two hours, okay?
Okay!
Hey, Ulli!
Heya, Andreas.
You look fantastic!
Knock it off.
We waited for you all that time!
Where?
Right here!

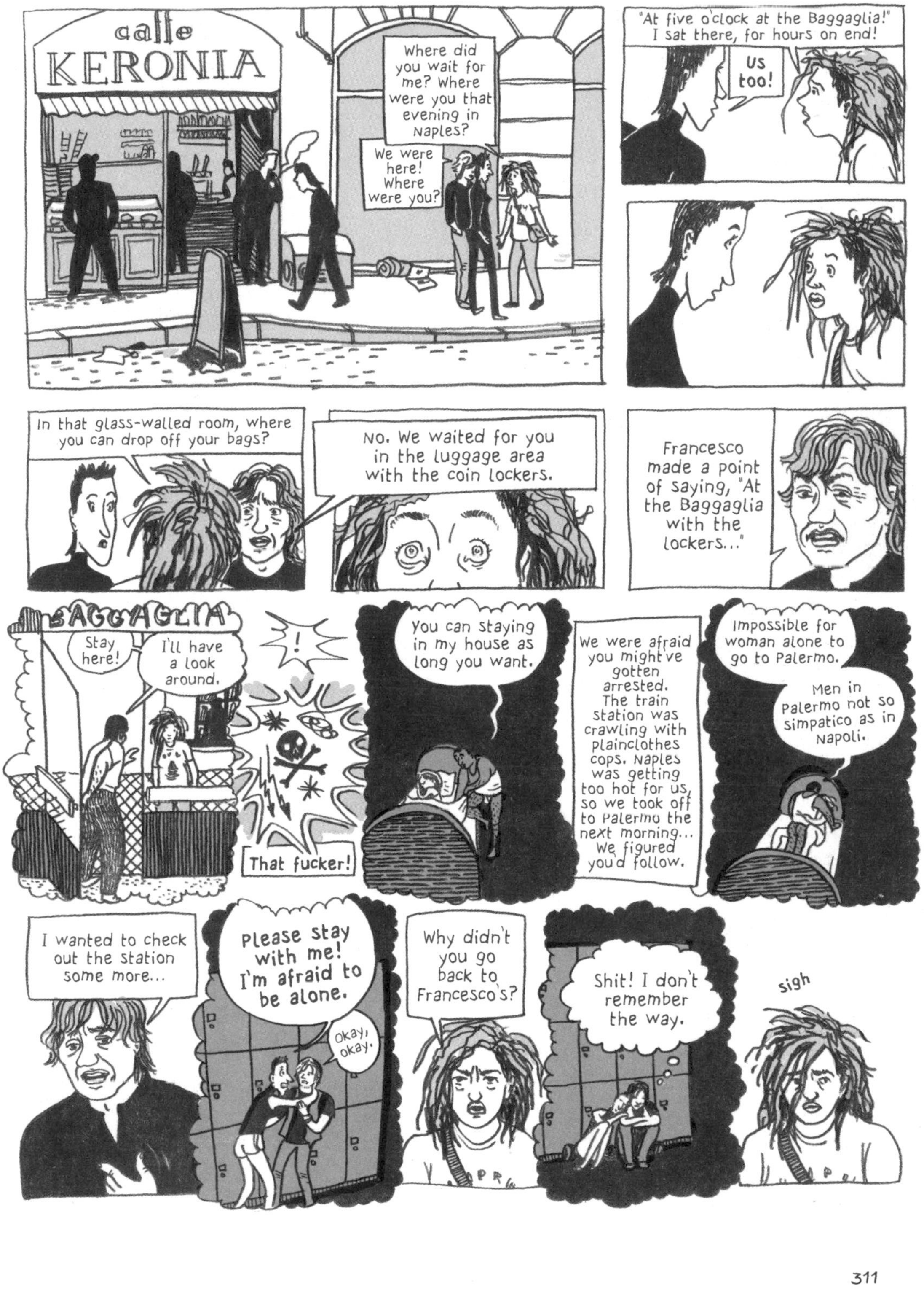
caffe
KERONIA
Where did you wait for me? Where were you that evening in Naples?
We were here! Where were you?
"At five o'clock at the Baggaglia!" I sat there, for hours on end!
Us too!
In that glass-walled room, where you can drop off your bags?
No. We waited for you in the luggage area with the coin lockers.
Francesco made a point of saying, "At the Baggaglia with the lockers..."
BAGGAGLIA
Stay here!
I'll have a look around.
!
That fucker!
You can staying in my house as long you want.
We were afraid you might've gotten arrested. The train station was crawling with plainclothes cops. Naples was getting too hot for us, so we took off to Palermo the next morning... We figured you'd follow.
Impossible for woman alone to go to Palermo.
Men in Palermo not so simpatico as in Napoli.
I wanted to check out the station some more...
Please stay with me! I'm afraid to be alone.
Okay, okay.
Why didn't you go back to Francesco's?
Shit! I don't remember the way.
sigh

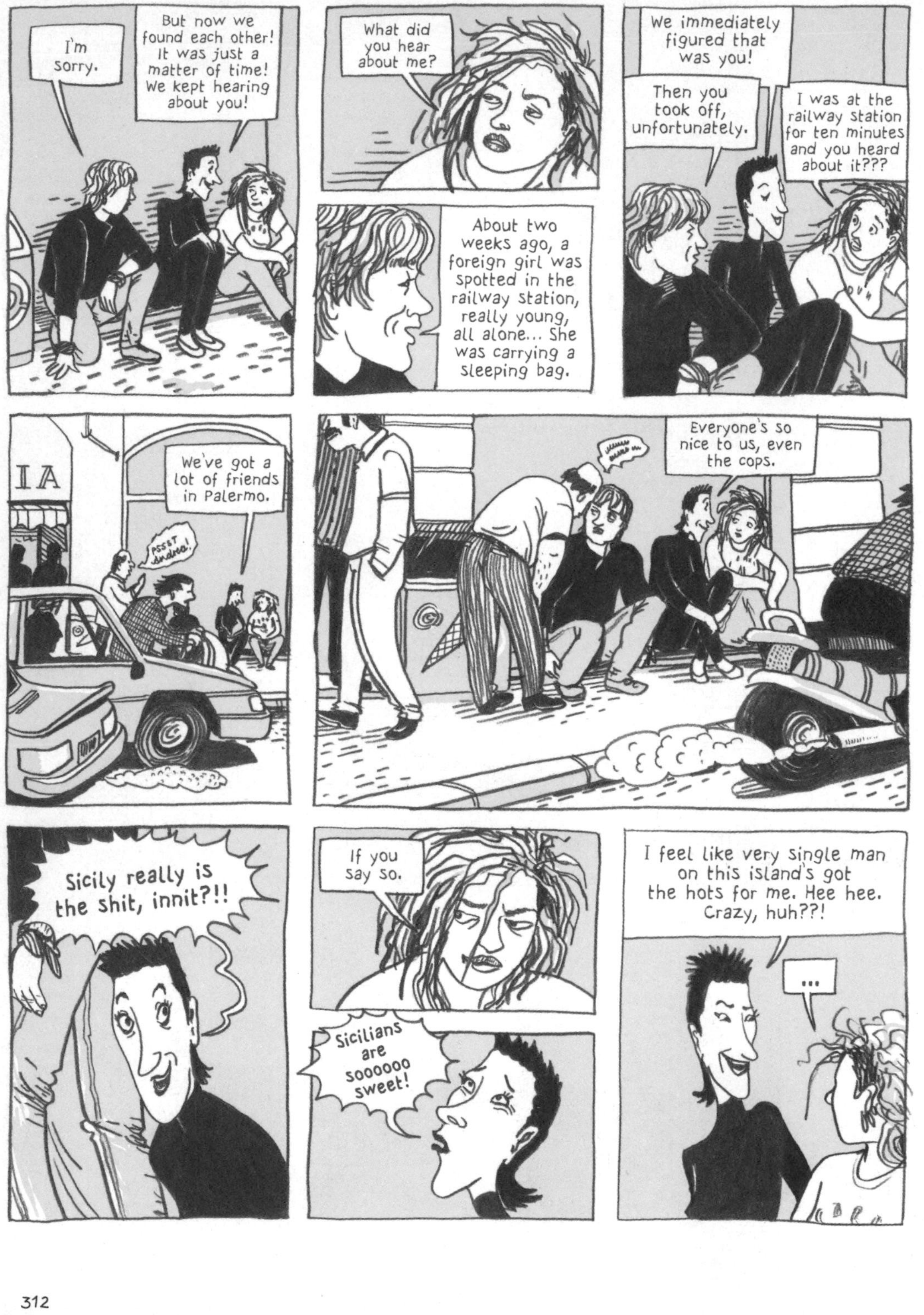
I'm sorry.
But now we found each other! It was just a matter of time! We kept hearing about you!
What did you hear about me?
About two weeks ago, a foreign girl was spotted in the railway station, really young, all alone... She was carrying a sleeping bag.
We immediately figured that was you!
Then you took off, unfortunately.
I was at the railway station for ten minutes and you heard about it???
We've got a lot of friends in Palermo.
PSSST Andrea!
Everyone's so nice to us, even the cops.
Sicily really is the shit, innit?!!
If you say so.
Sicilians are soooooo sweet!
I feel like very single man on this island's got the hots for me. Hee hee. Crazy, huh??!
...

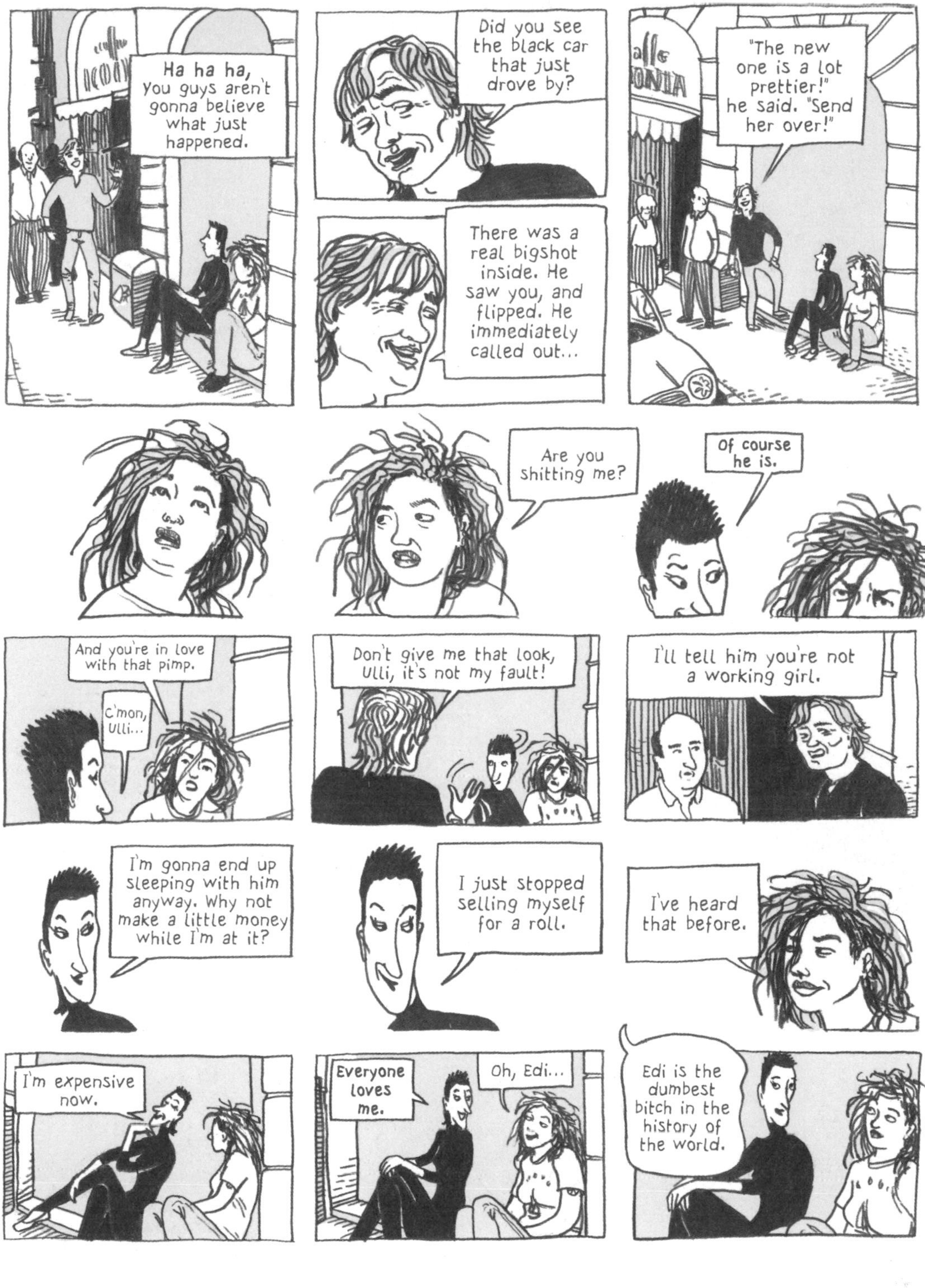
Ha ha ha, you guys aren't gonna believe what just happened.
Did you see the black car that just drove by?
There was a real bigshot inside. He saw you, and flipped. He immediately called out...
"The new one is a lot prettier!" he said. "Send her over!"
Are you shitting me?
Of course he is.
And you're in love with that pimp.
C'mon, Ulli...
Don't give me that look, Ulli, it's not my fault!
I'll tell him you're not a working girl.
I'm gonna end up sleeping with him anyway. Why not make a little money while I'm at it?
I just stopped selling myself for a roll.
I've heard that before.
I'm expensive now.
Everyone loves me.
Oh, Edi...
Edi is the dumbest bitch in the history of the world.

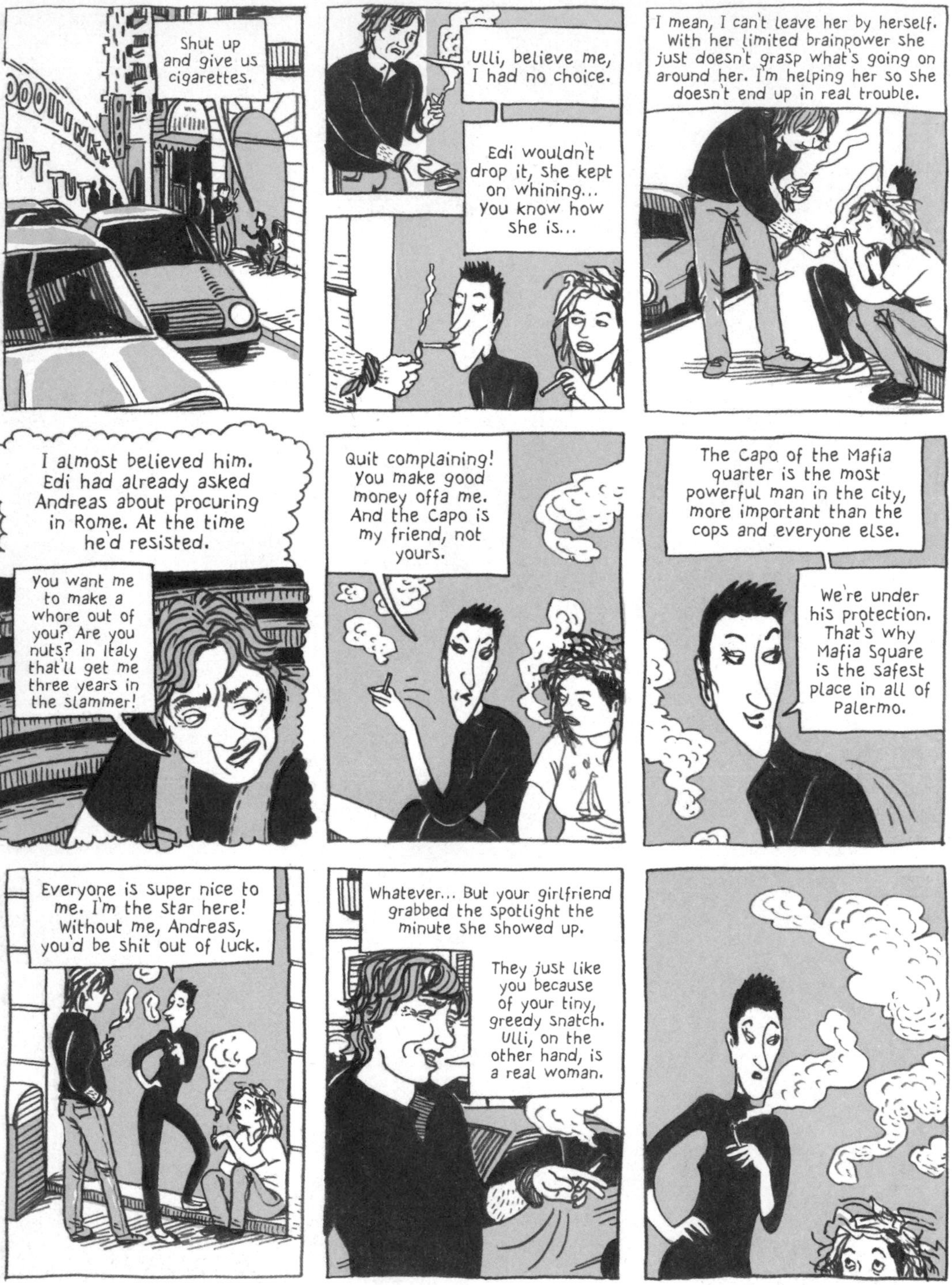
Shut up and give us cigarettes.
OOOIIINKK
TUT TUT
Ulli, believe me, I had no choice.
Edi wouldn't drop it, she kept on whining... You know how she is...
I mean, I can't leave her by herself. With her limited brainpower she just doesn't grasp what's going on around her. I'm helping her so she doesn't end up in real trouble.
I almost believed him. Edi had already asked Andreas about procuring in Rome. At the time he'd resisted.
You want me to make a whore out of you? Are you nuts? In Italy that'll get me three years in the slammer!
Quit complaining! You make good money offa me. And the Capo is my friend, not yours.
The Capo of the Mafia quarter is the most powerful man in the city, more important than the cops and everyone else.
We're under his protection. That's why Mafia Square is the safest place in all of Palermo.
Everyone is super nice to me. I'm the star here! Without me, Andreas, you'd be shit out of luck.
Whatever... But your girlfriend grabbed the spotlight the minute she showed up.
They just like you because of your tiny, greedy snatch. Ulli, on the other hand, is a real woman.

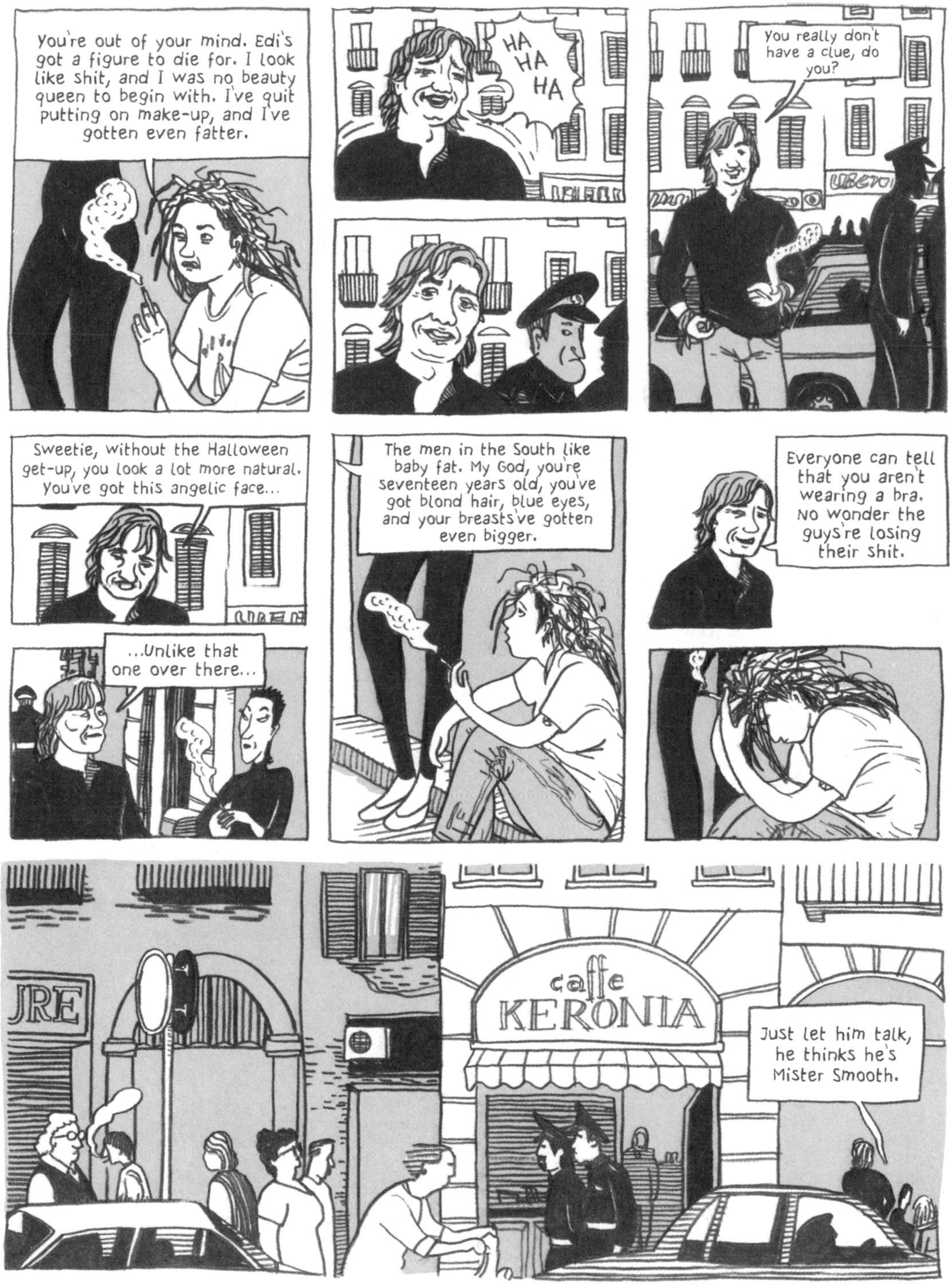
You're out of your mind. Edi's got a figure to die for. I look like shit, and I was no beauty queen to begin with. I've quit putting on make-up, and I've gotten even fatter.
HA HA HA
You really don't have a clue, do you?
Sweetie, without the Halloween get-up, you look a lot more natural. You've got this angelic face...
The men in the South like baby fat. My God, you're seventeen years old, you've got blond hair, blue eyes, and your breasts've gotten even bigger.
Everyone can tell that you aren't wearing a bra. No wonder the guys're losing their shit.
...Unlike that one over there...
caffe KERONIA
Just let him talk, he thinks he's Mister Smooth.

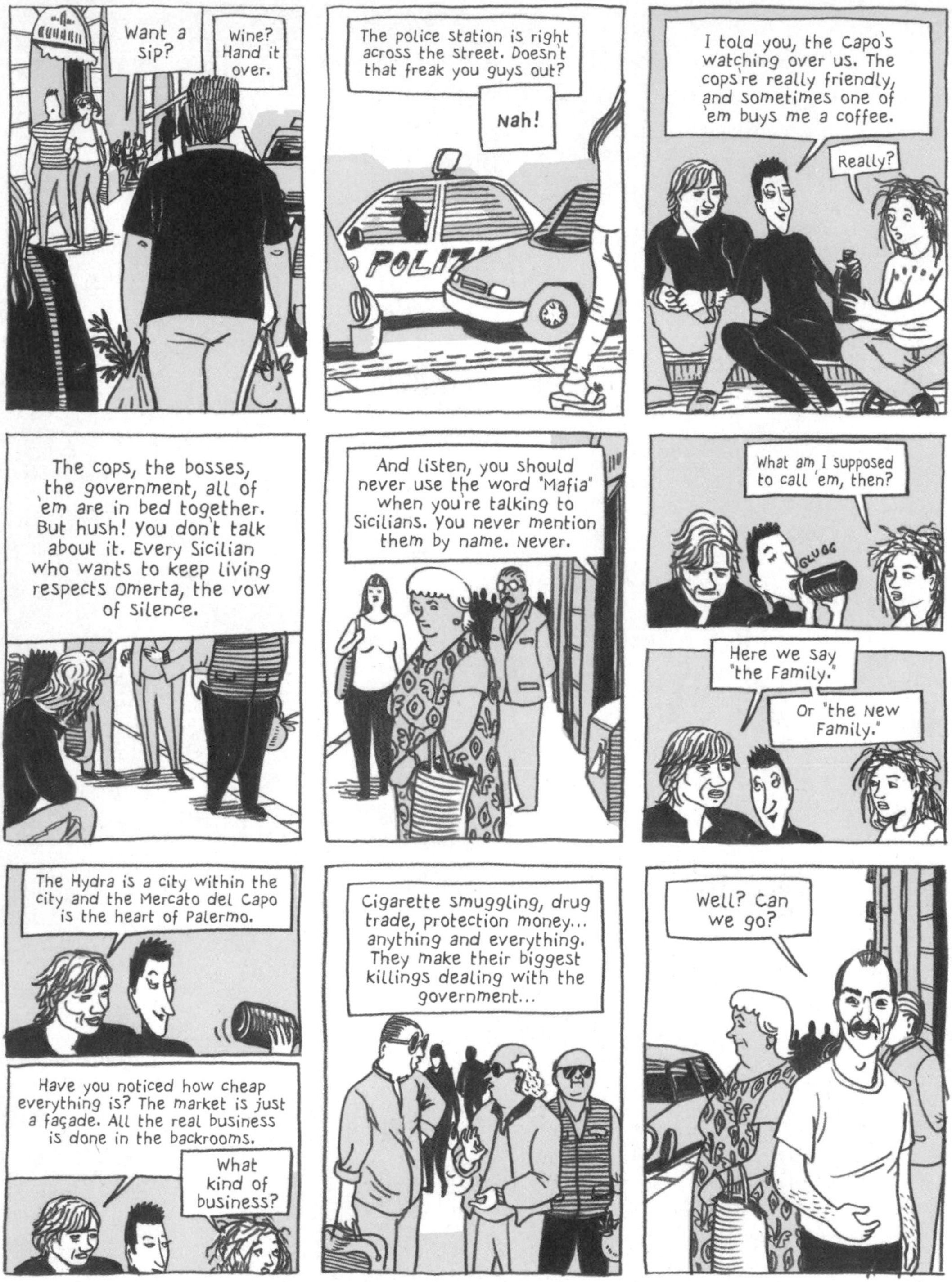
Want a sip?
Wine? Hand it over.
The police station is right across the street. Doesn't that freak you guys out?
Nah!
POLIZ
I told you, the Capo's watching over us. The cops're really friendly, and sometimes one of 'em buys me a coffee.
Really?
The cops, the bosses, the government, all of 'em are in bed together. But hush! You don't talk about it. Every Sicilian who wants to keep living respects Omerta, the vow of silence.
And listen, you should never use the word "Mafia" when you're talking to Sicilians. You never mention them by name. Never.
What am I supposed to call 'em, then?
GLUGG
Here we say "the Family."
Or "the New Family."
The Hydra is a city within the city and the Mercato del Capo is the heart of Palermo.
Have you noticed how cheap everything is? The market is just a façade. All the real business is done in the backrooms.
What kind of business?
Cigarette smuggling, drug trade, protection money... anything and everything. They make their biggest killings dealing with the government...
Well? Can we go?

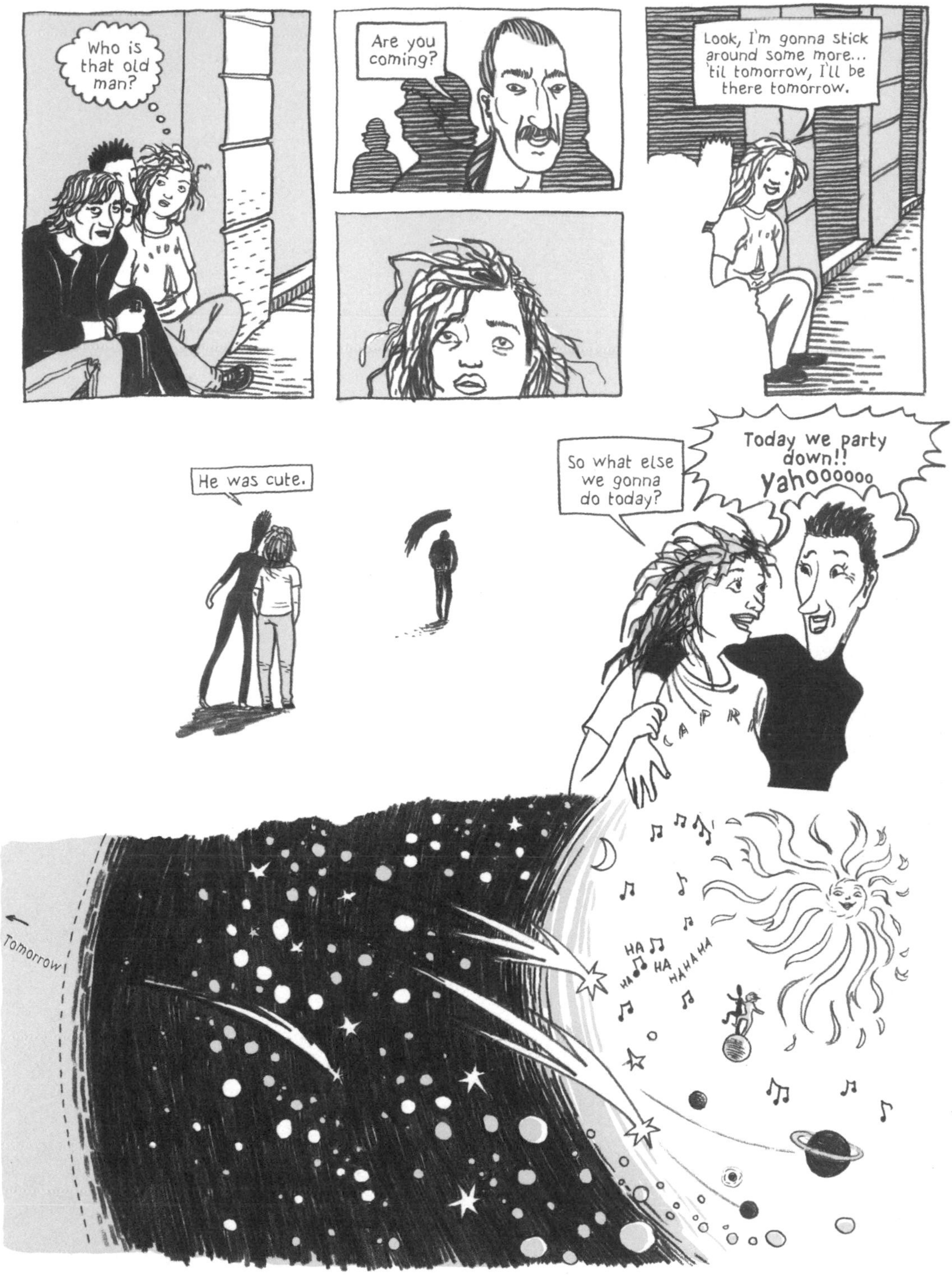
Who is that old man?
Are you coming?
Look, I'm gonna stick around some more... 'til tomorrow, I'll be there tomorrow.
He was cute.
So what else we gonna do today?
Today we party down!! yahoooooo
Tomorrow
HA HA HA HAHAHA

XV. the NEW FAMILY

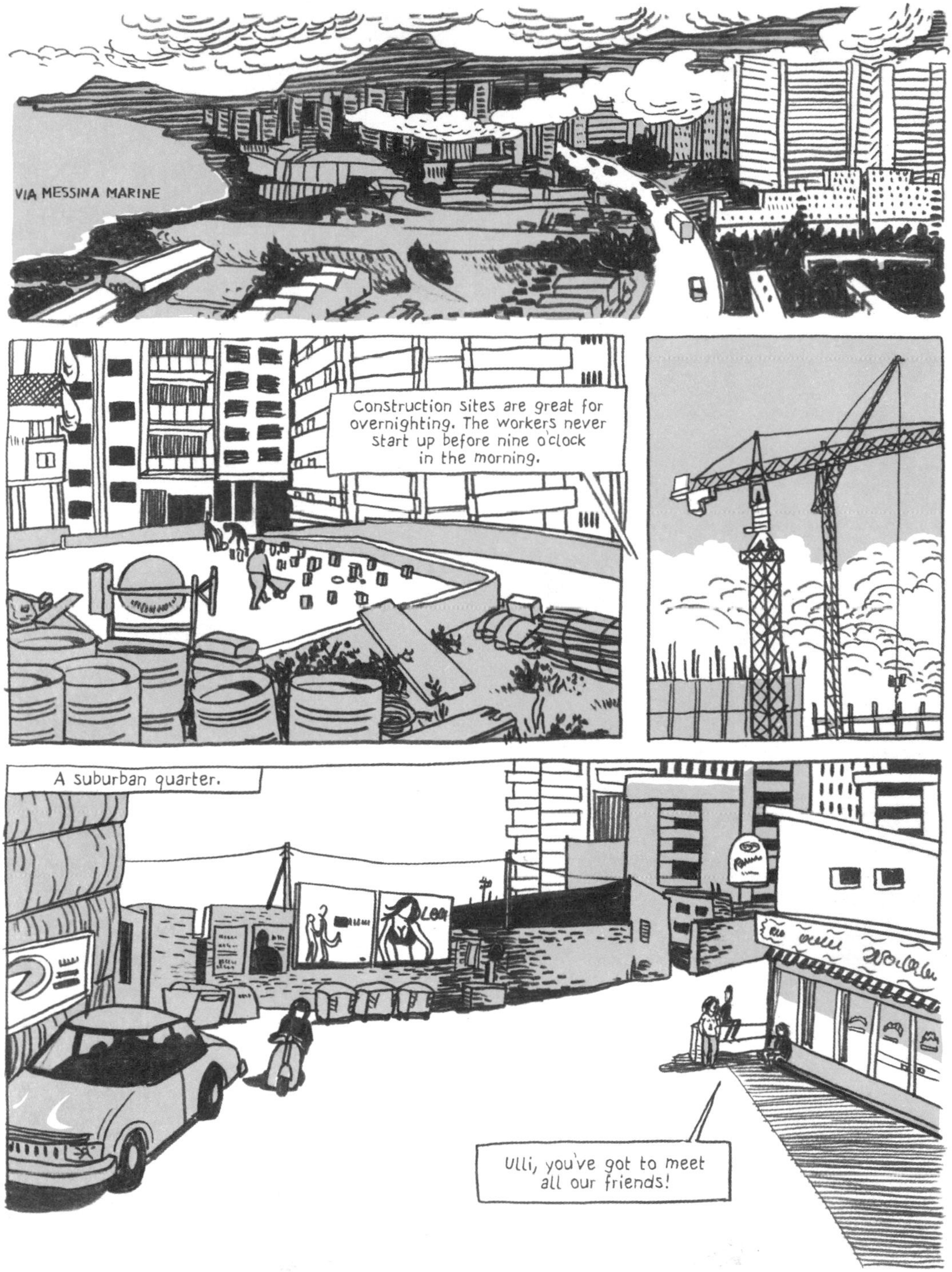
VIA MESSINA MARINE
Construction sites are great for overnighting. The workers never start up before nine o'clock in the morning.
A suburban quarter.
Ulli, you've got to meet all our friends!

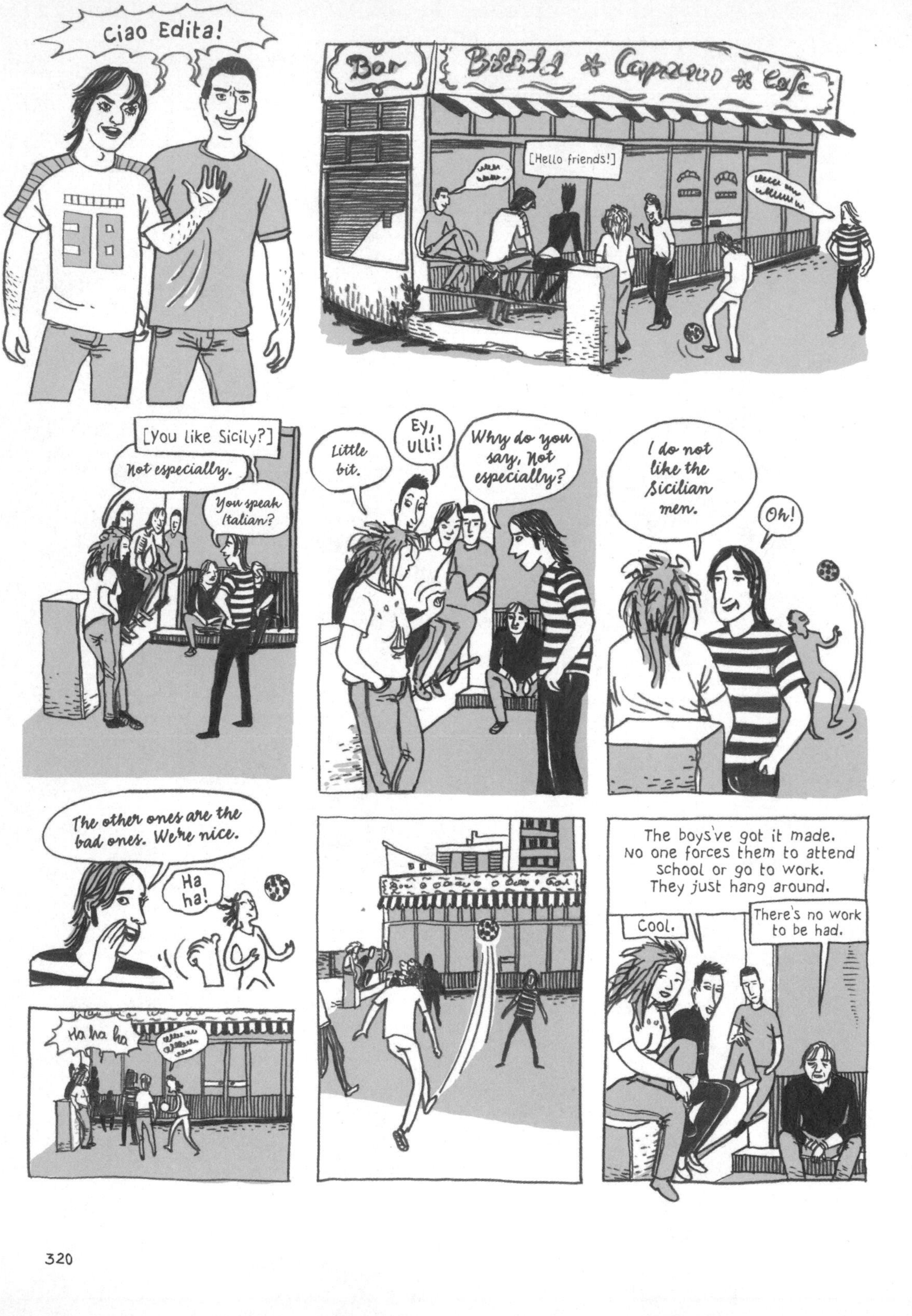
Ciao Edita!
[Hello friends!]
[You like Sicily?]
Not especially.
You speak Italian?
Little bit.
Ey, Ulli!
Why do you say, Not especially?
I do not like the Sicilian men.
Oh!
The other ones are the bad ones. We're nice.
Ha ha!
Ha ha ha
The boys've got it made. No one forces them to attend school or go to work. They just hang around.
Cool.
There's no work to be had.

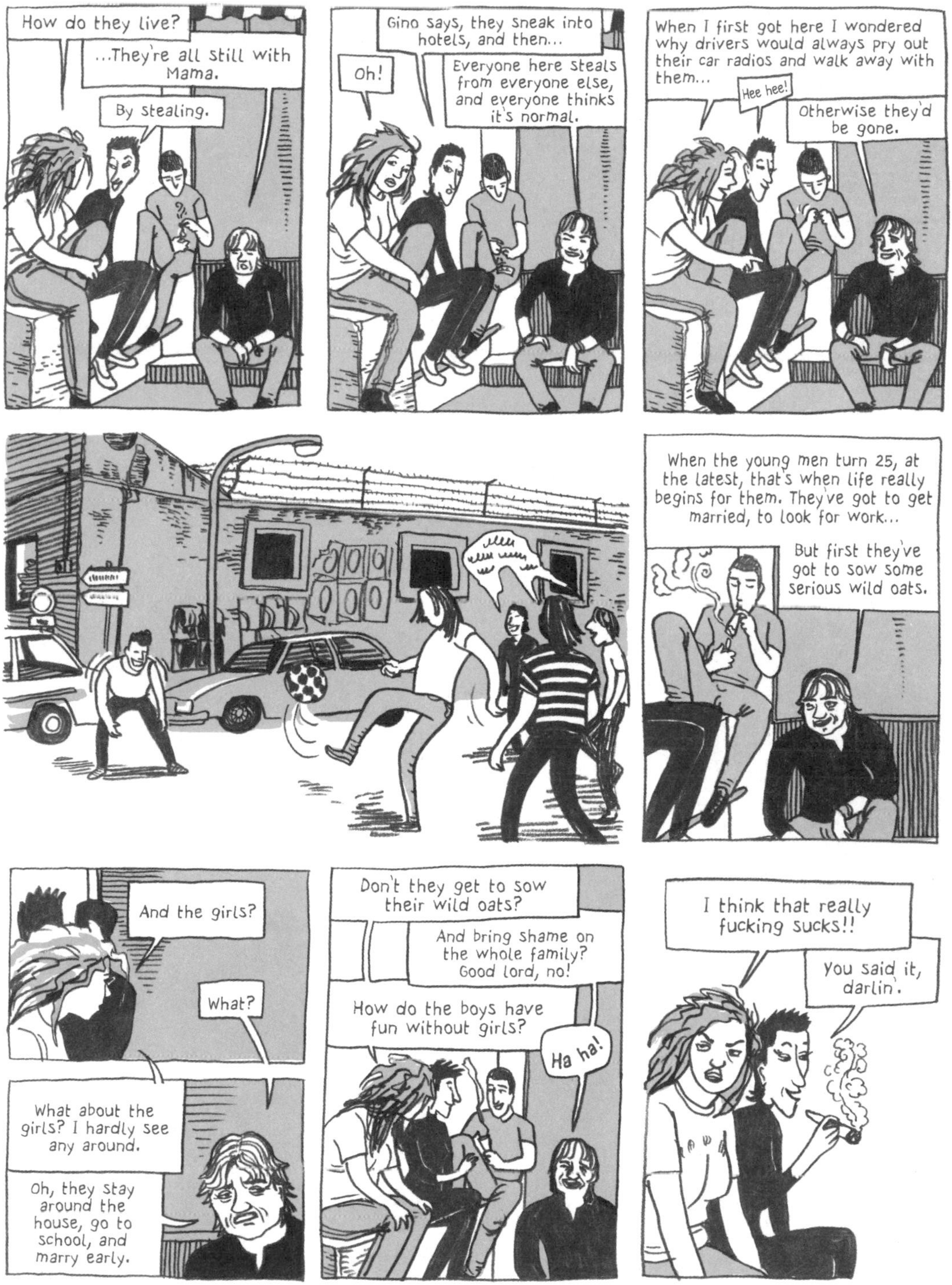
How do they live?
...They're all still with Mama.
By stealing.
Gino says, they sneak into hotels, and then...
Oh!
Everyone here steals from everyone else, and everyone thinks it's normal.
When I first got here I wondered why drivers would always pry out their car radios and walk away with them...
Hee hee!
Otherwise they'd be gone.
When the young men turn 25, at the latest, that's when life really begins for them. They've got to get married, to look for work...
But first they've got to sow some serious wild oats.
And the girls?
What?
What about the girls? I hardly see any around.
Oh, they stay around the house, go to school, and marry early.
Don't they get to sow their wild oats?
And bring shame on the whole family? Good lord, no!
How do the boys have fun without girls?
Ha ha!
I think that really fucking sucks!!
You said it, darlin'.

The girls actually have a better shot at a career, because they go to school and learn things. Which is a waste of time — they're supposed to have children and make good housewives.

Besides, what good is the best education if there isn't any work? These kids get street learning, and hope for a career with the big outfit.

Which outfit?

The Hydra, the Family, the Honored Society.

Its members are men of honor, and highly regarded. Even if they have to go to prison, the company takes care of its members.

But it'd be a disgrace to get caught... wouldn't it?

Nah, not really! Aunts, uncles and children go see the prisoner on visiting day, bring them food and commiserate with their martyrdom.

The biggest disgrace would be to have a traitor in the family.

VROOOM

Traitors are quick to die in Sicily. And because of the concept of liability, they endanger their entire family. They're held in contempt and rejected by their mothers.

I honestly don't understand why anyone would want to join the Mafia.

All they have here are oranges, tourists in the summertime, and subventions from the north. Anyone who wants to do business on the island has to cooperate with the Mafia. Not a penny is spent without the Hydra getting its cut. Nothing can thrive here.

322

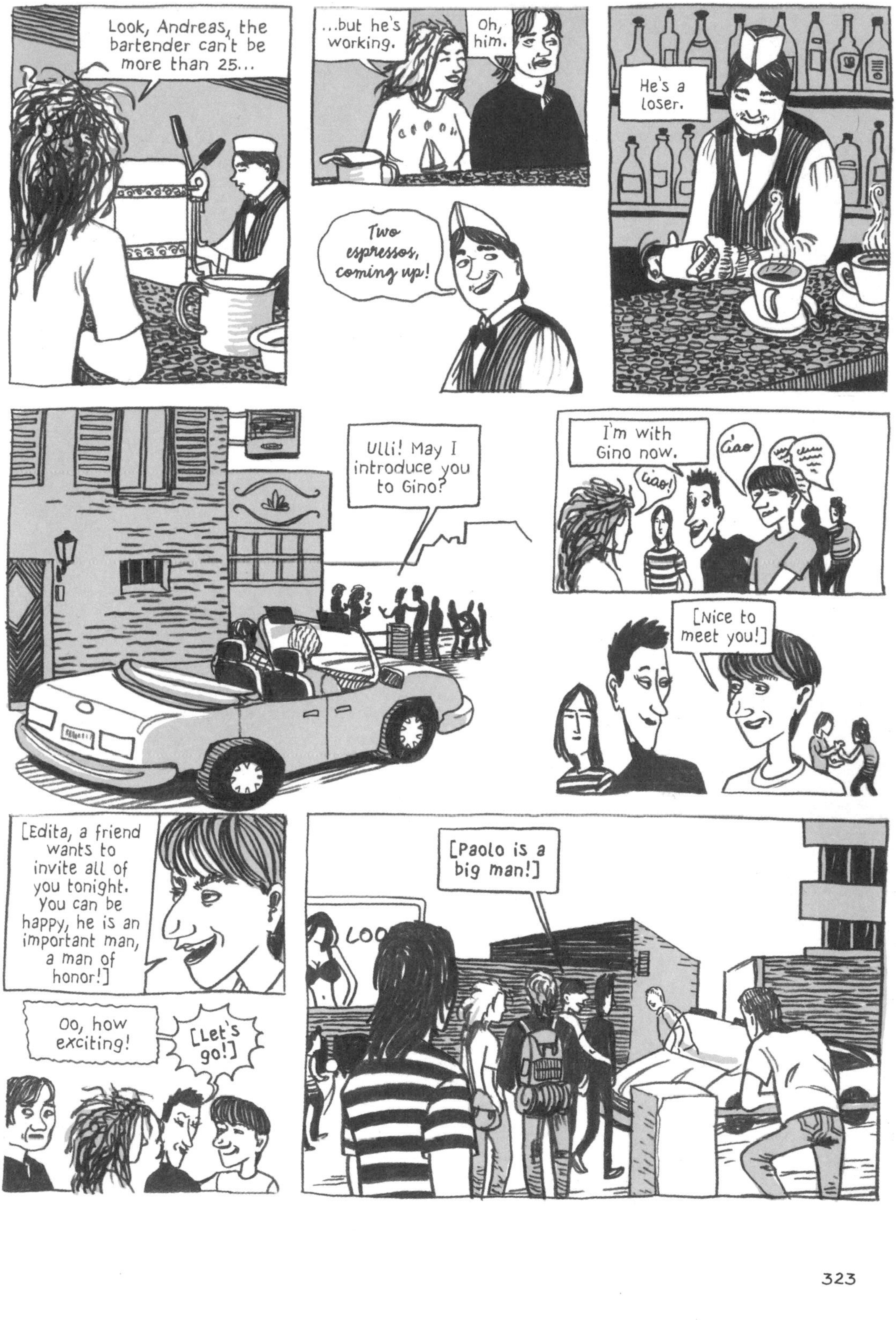
Look, Andreas, the bartender can't be more than 25...
...but he's working.
Oh, him.
Two espressos, coming up!
He's a loser.
Ulli! May I introduce you to Gino?
I'm with Gino now.
Ciao!
Ciao
[Nice to meet you!]
[Edita, a friend wants to invite all of you tonight. You can be happy, he is an important man, a man of honor!]
Oo, how exciting!
[Let's go!]
[Paolo is a big man!]
LOO

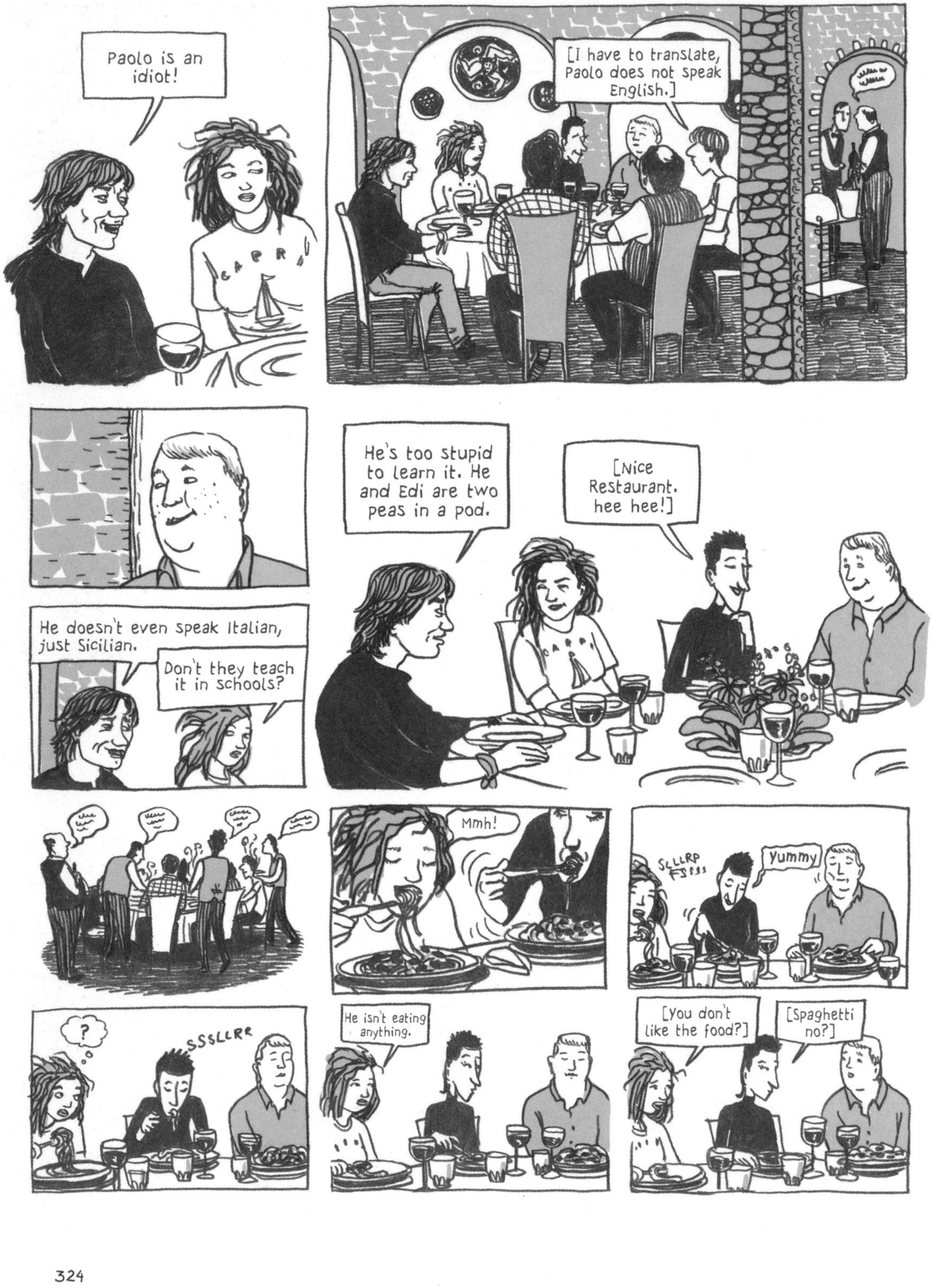
Paolo is an idiot!
[I have to translate, Paolo does not speak English.]
He's too stupid to learn it. He and Edi are two peas in a pod.
[Nice Restaurant. hee hee!]
He doesn't even speak Italian, just Sicilian.
Don't they teach it in schools?
Mmh!
SLLLRP
yummy
?
SSSLLRR
He isn't eating anything.
[You don't like the food?]
[Spaghetti no?]

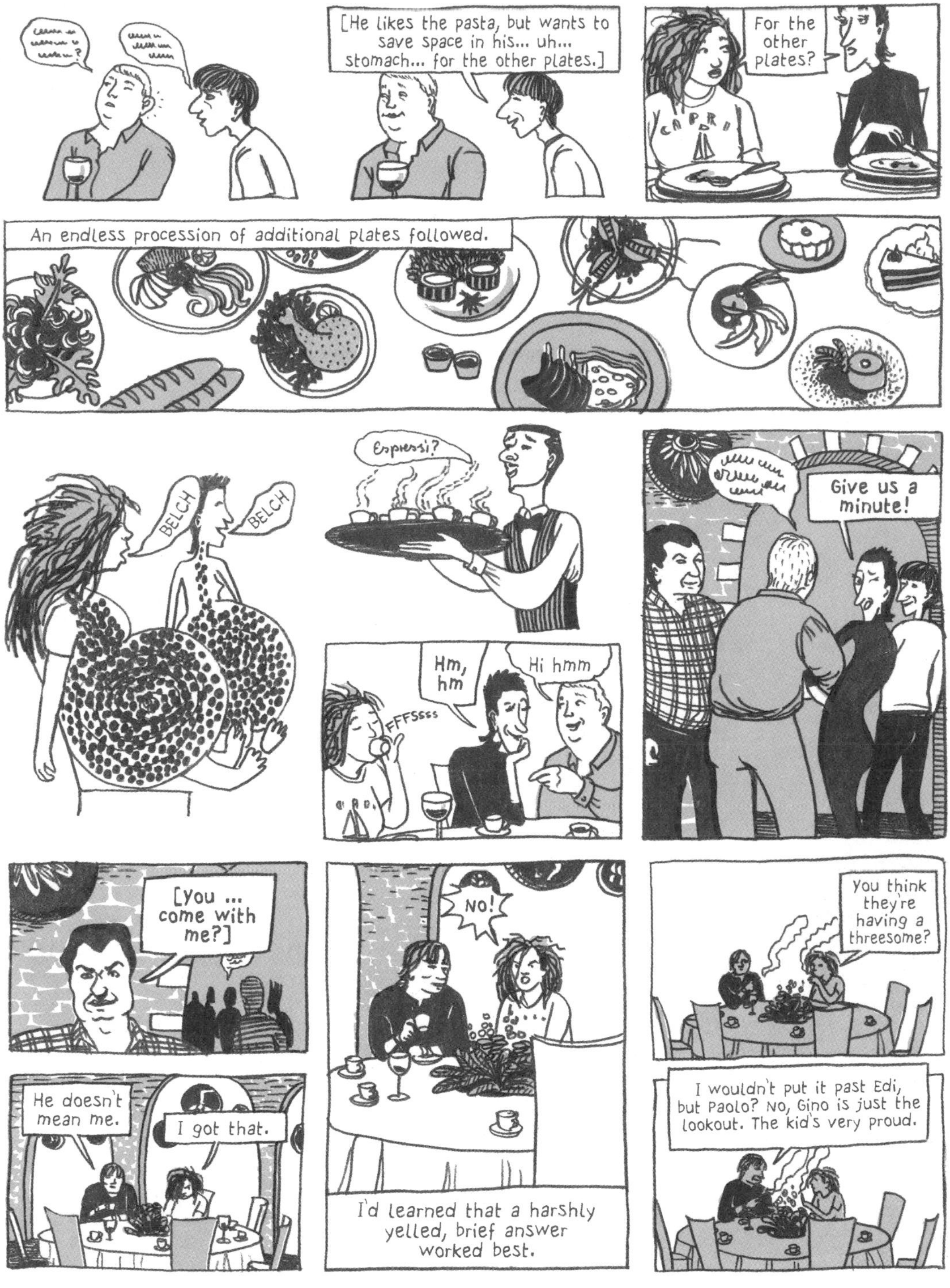
[He likes the pasta, but wants to save space in his... uh... stomach... for the other plates.]
For the other plates?
An endless procession of additional plates followed.
BELCH
BELCH
Espressi?
Hm, hm
Hi hmm
FFFSsss
Give us a minute!
[You ... come with me?]
NO!
You think they're having a threesome?
He doesn't mean me.
I got that.
I'd learned that a harshly yelled, brief answer worked best.
I wouldn't put it past Edi, but Paolo? No, Gino is just the lookout. The kid's very proud.

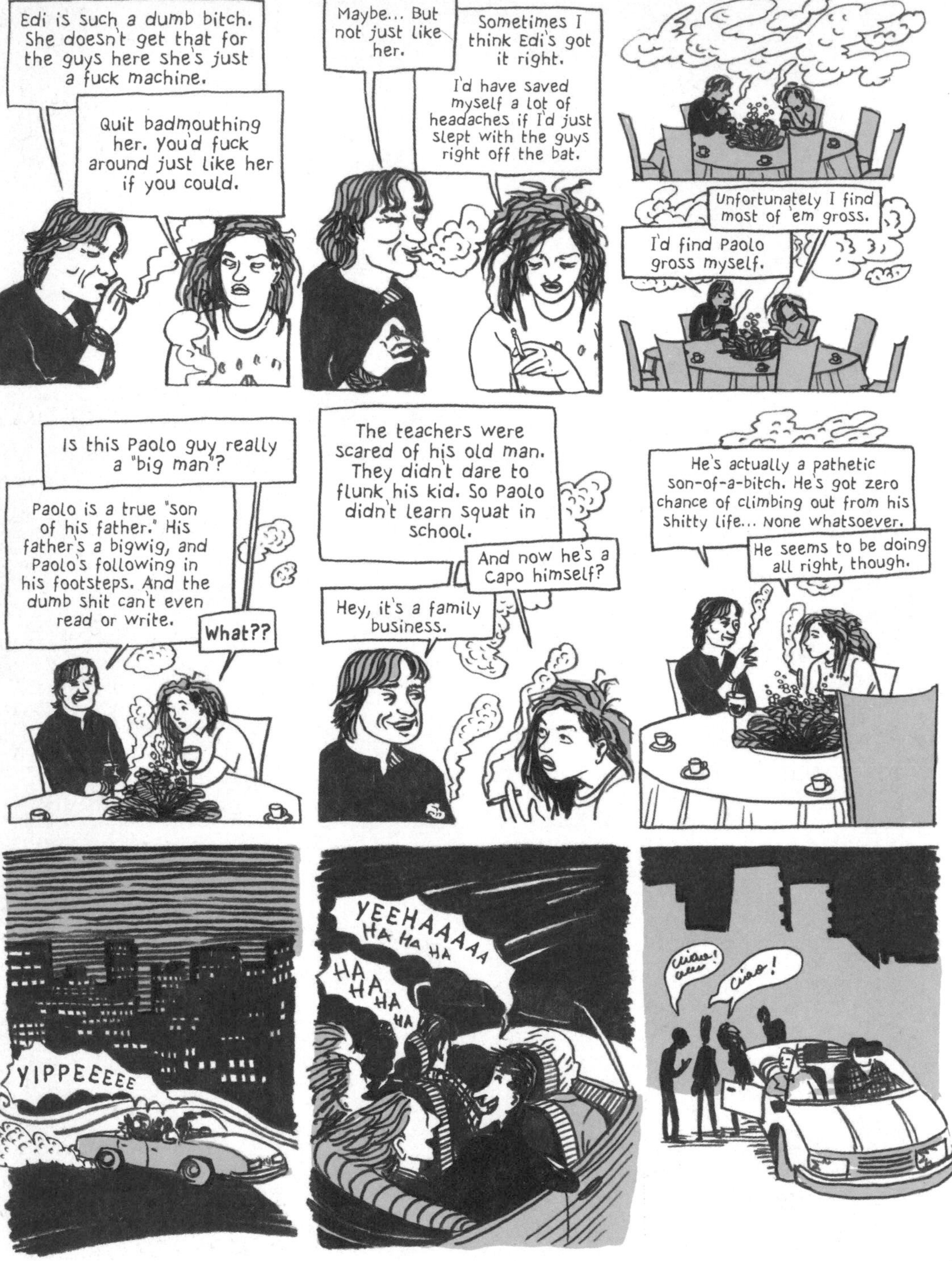
Edi is such a dumb bitch. She doesn't get that for the guys here she's just a fuck machine.
Quit badmouthing her. You'd fuck around just like her if you could.
Maybe... But not just like her.
Sometimes I think Edi's got it right.
I'd have saved myself a lot of headaches if I'd just slept with the guys right off the bat.
Unfortunately I find most of 'em gross.
I'd find Paolo gross myself.
Is this Paolo guy really a "big man"?
Paolo is a true "son of his father." His father's a bigwig, and Paolo's following in his footsteps. And the dumb shit can't even read or write.
What??
The teachers were scared of his old man. They didn't dare to flunk his kid. So Paolo didn't learn squat in school.
And now he's a Capo himself?
Hey, it's a family business.
He's actually a pathetic son-of-a-bitch. He's got zero chance of climbing out from his shitty life... None whatsoever.
He seems to be doing all right, though.
YIPPEEEEE
YEEHAAAAA HA HA HA
HA HA HA HA
Ciao!

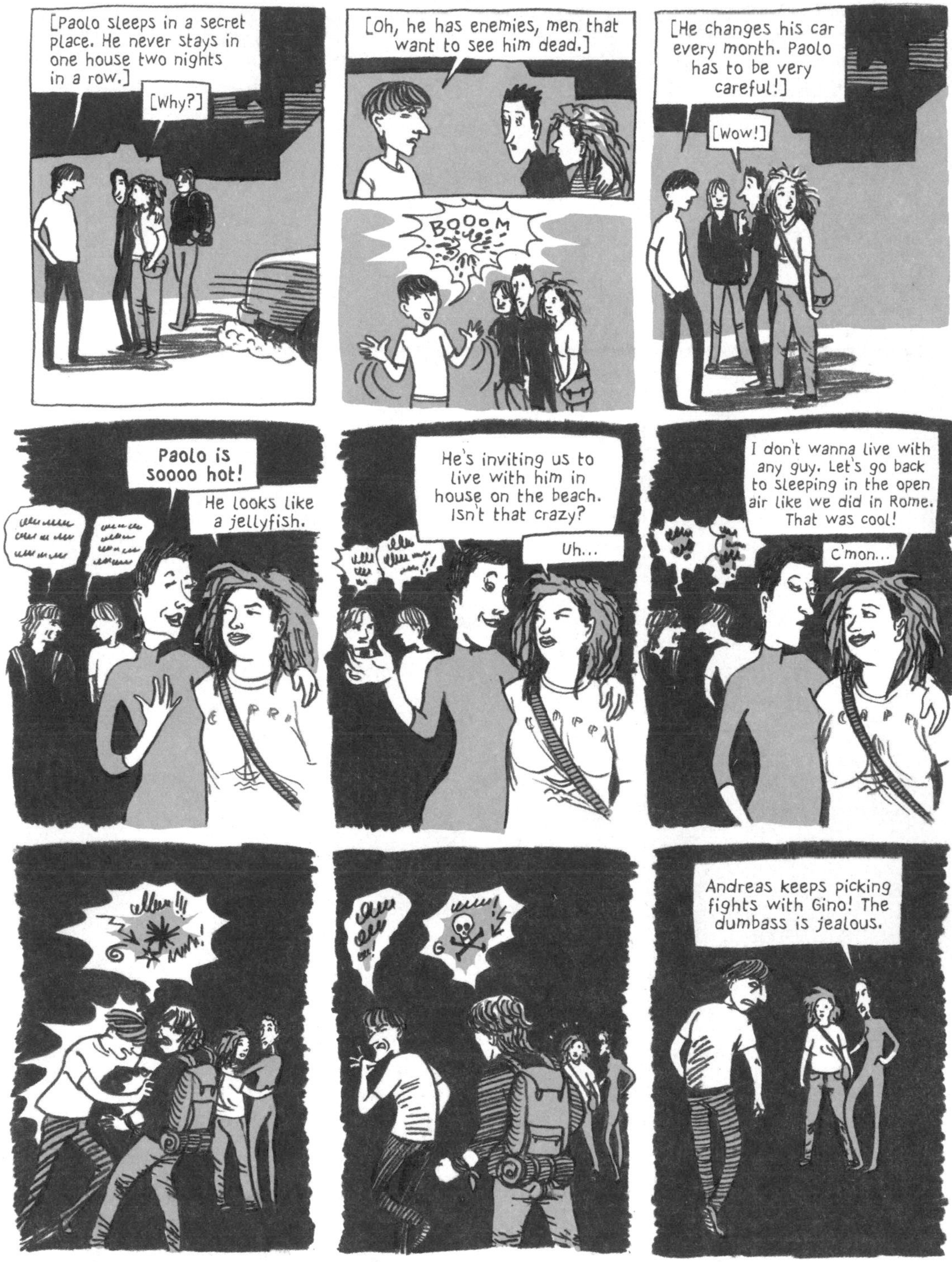
[Paolo sleeps in a secret place. He never stays in one house two nights in a row.]
[Why?]
[Oh, he has enemies, men that want to see him dead.]
BOOOM
[He changes his car every month. Paolo has to be very careful!]
[Wow!]
Paolo is soooo hot!
He looks like a jellyfish.
He's inviting us to live with him in house on the beach. Isn't that crazy?
Uh...
I don't wanna live with any guy. Let's go back to sleeping in the open air like we did in Rome. That was cool!
C'mon...
Andreas keeps picking fights with Gino! The dumbass is jealous.

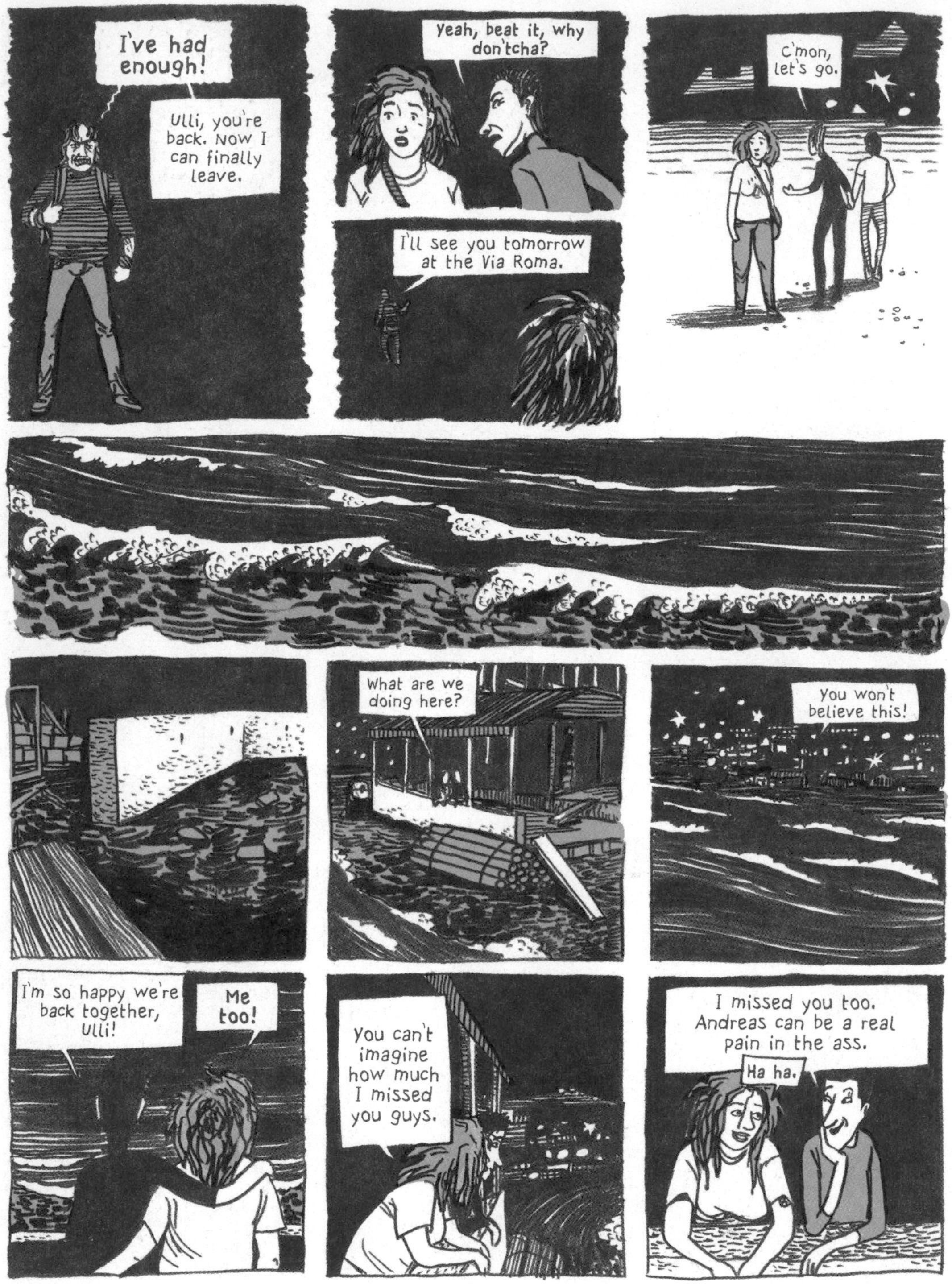
I've had enough!
Ulli, you're back. Now I can finally leave.
Yeah, beat it, why don'tcha?
I'll see you tomorrow at the Via Roma.
C'mon, let's go.
What are we doing here?
You won't believe this!
I'm so happy we're back together, Ulli!
Me too!
You can't imagine how much I missed you guys.
I missed you too. Andreas can be a real pain in the ass.
Ha ha.

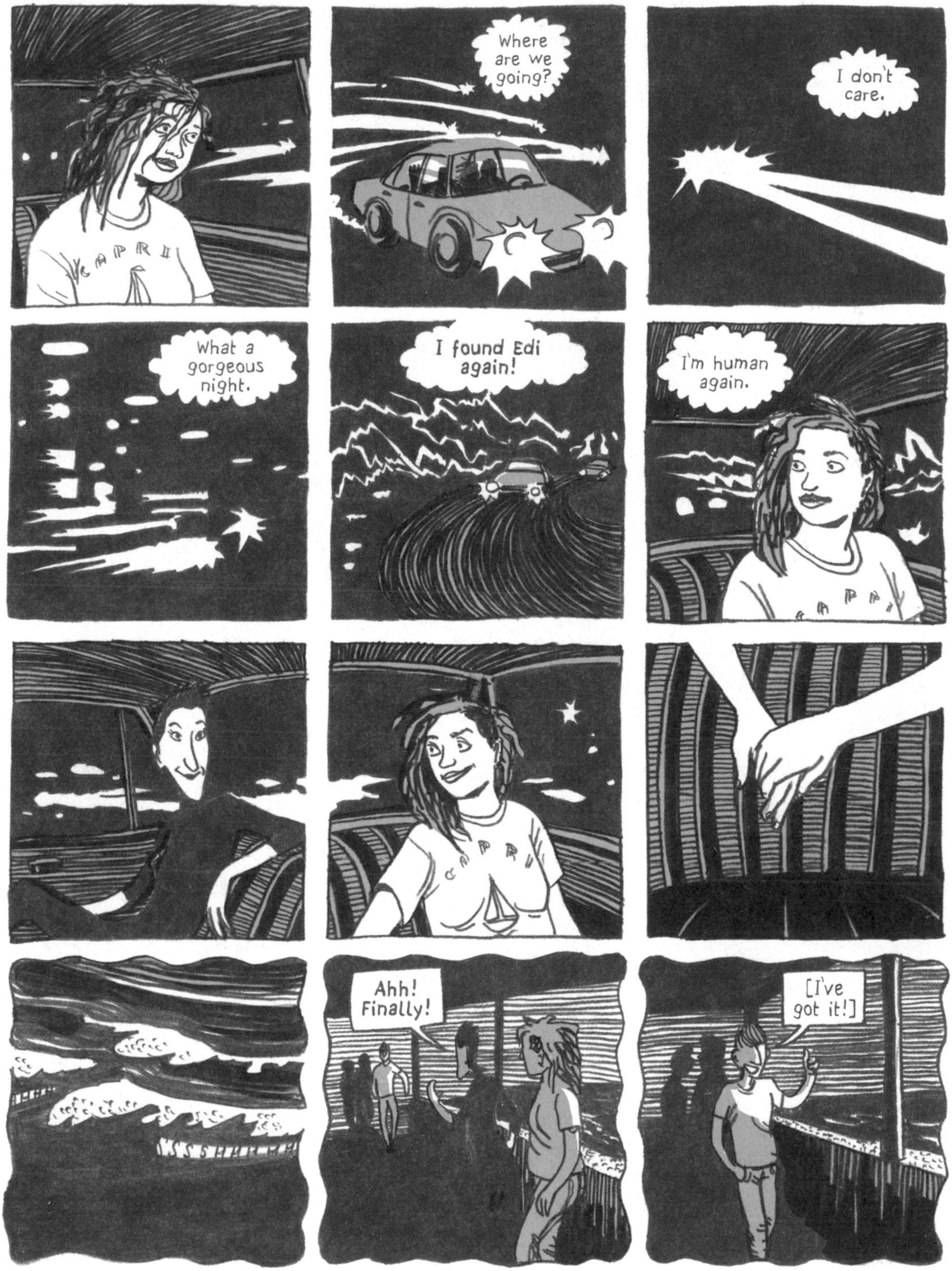
CAPRI
Where are we going?
I don't care.
What a gorgeous night.
I found Edi again!
I'm human again.
CAPRI
CAPRI
Ahh! Finally!
[I've got it!]

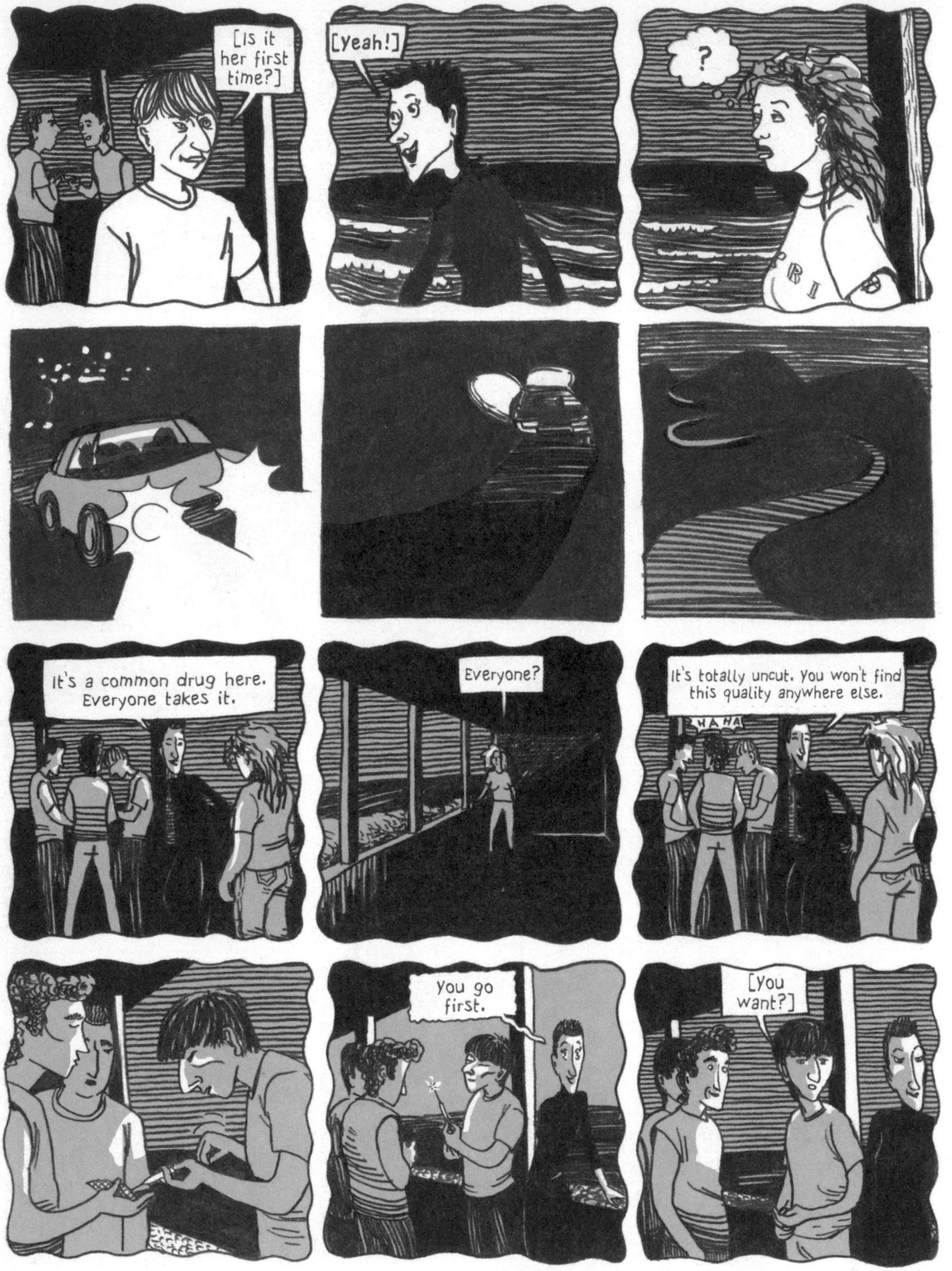
[Is it her first time?]
[Yeah!]
?
It's a common drug here. Everyone takes it.
Everyone?
It's totally uncut. You won't find this quality anywhere else.
HA HA
You go first.
[You want?]

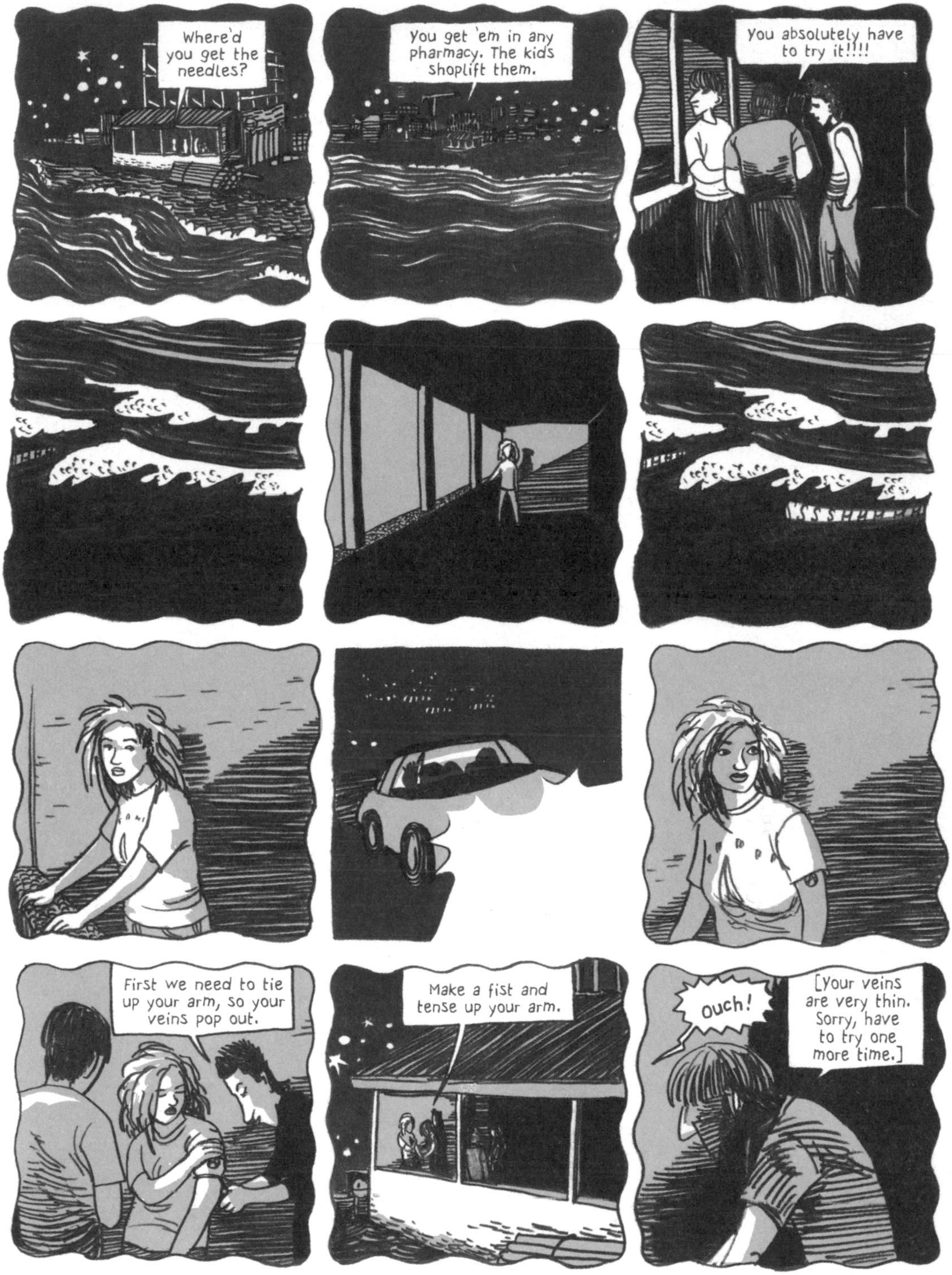
Where'd you get the needles?
You get 'em in any pharmacy. The kids shoplift them.
You absolutely have to try it!!!!
First we need to tie up your arm, so your veins pop out.
Make a fist and tense up your arm.
ouch!
[Your veins are very thin. Sorry, have to try one more time.]

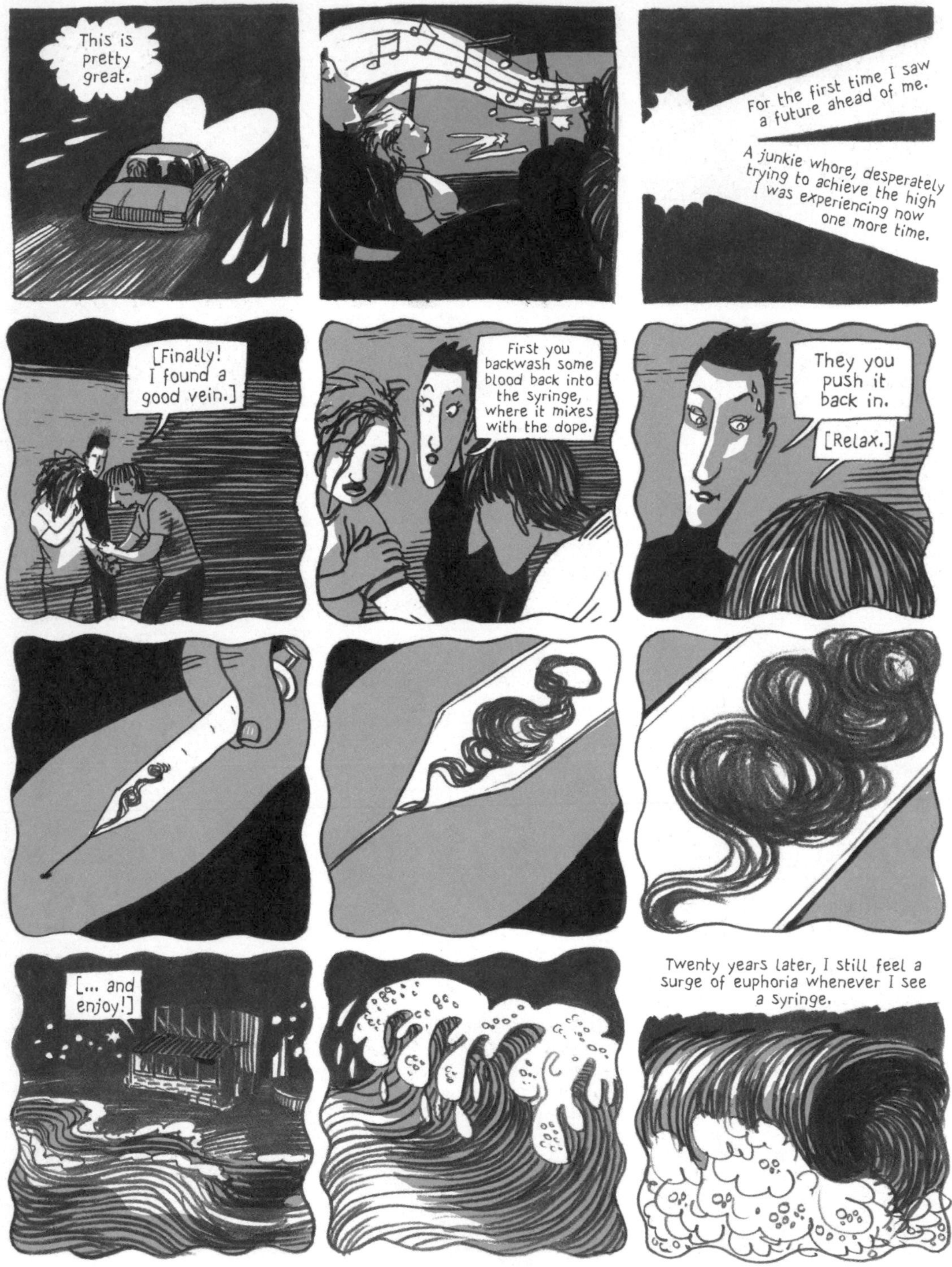
This is pretty great.
For the first time I saw a future ahead of me.
A junkie whore, desperately trying to achieve the high I was experiencing now one more time.
[Finally! I found a good vein.]
First you backwash some blood back into the syringe, where it mixes with the dope.
They you push it back in.
[Relax.]
[... and enjoy!]
Twenty years later, I still feel a surge of euphoria whenever I see a syringe.

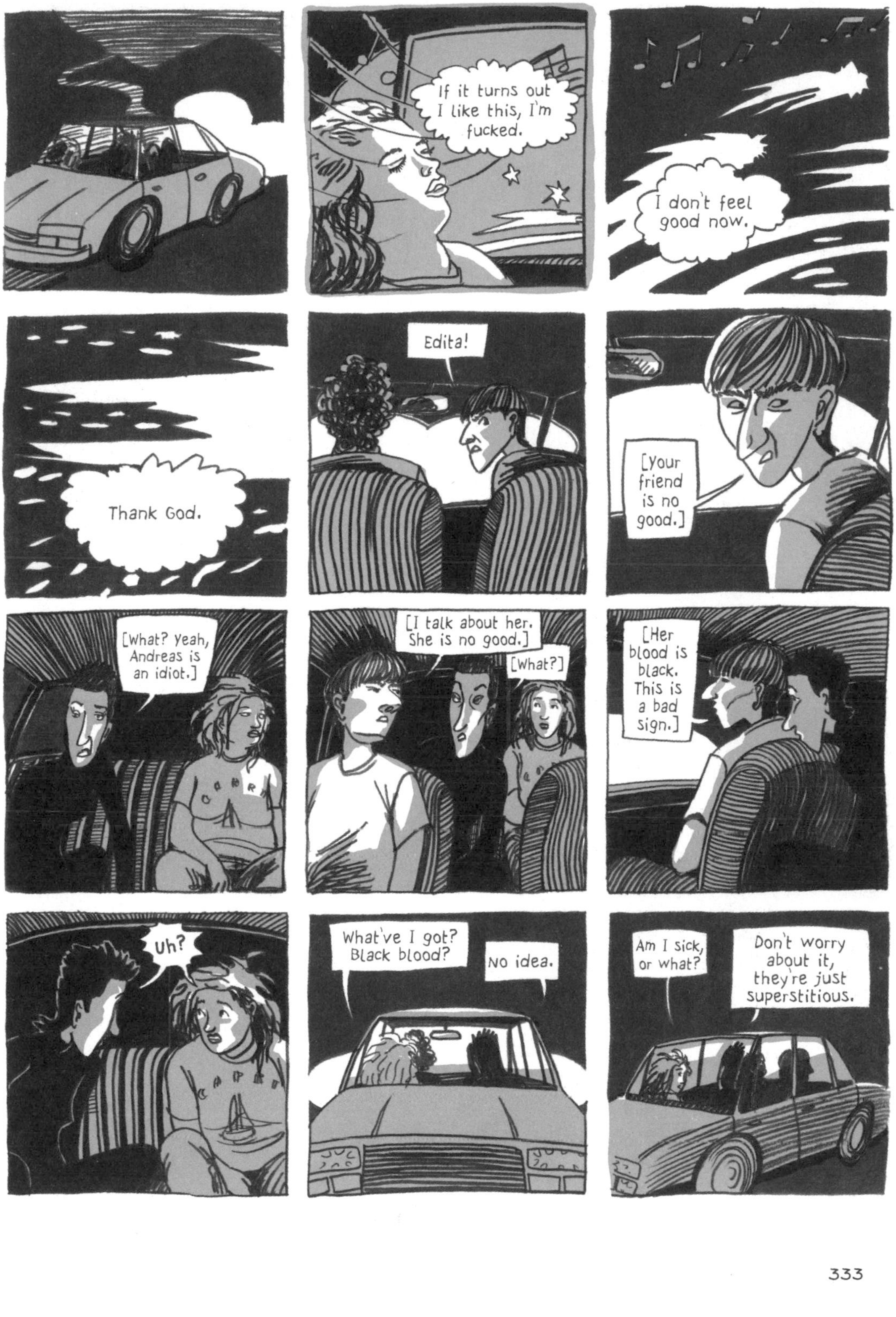
If it turns out I like this, I'm fucked.
I don't feel good now.
Thank God.
Edita!
[Your friend is no good.]
[What? Yeah, Andreas is an idiot.]
[I talk about her. She is no good.]
[What?]
[Her blood is black. This is a bad sign.]
Uh?
What've I got? Black blood?
No idea.
Am I sick, or what?
Don't worry about it, they're just superstitious.

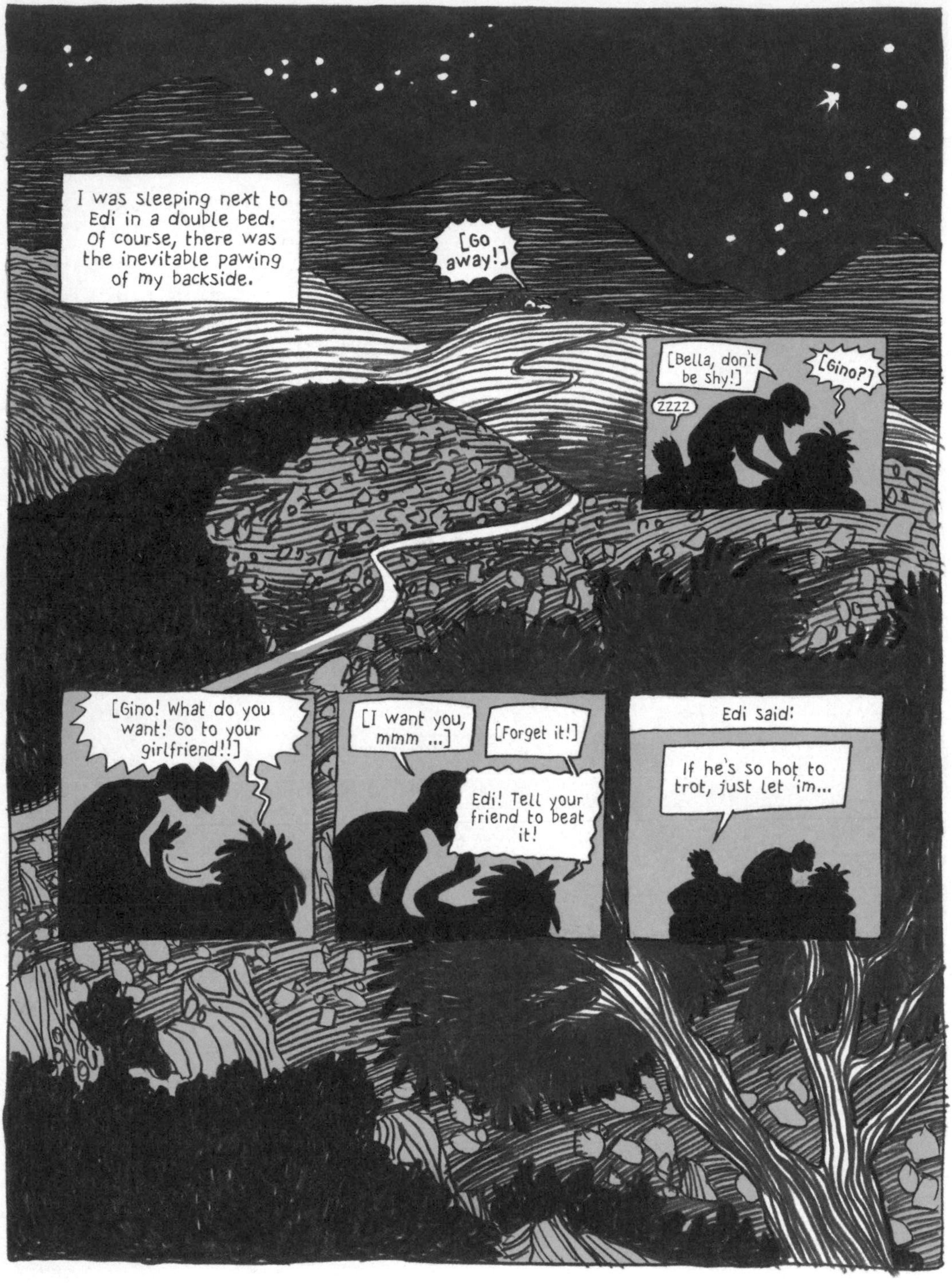
I was sleeping next to Edi in a double bed. Of course, there was the inevitable pawing of my backside.
[Go away!]
[Bella, don't be shy!]
[Gino?]
ZZZZ
[Gino! What do you want! Go to your girlfriend!!]
[I want you, mmm ...]
[Forget it!]
Edi! Tell your friend to beat it!
Edi said:
If he's so hot to trot, just let 'im...

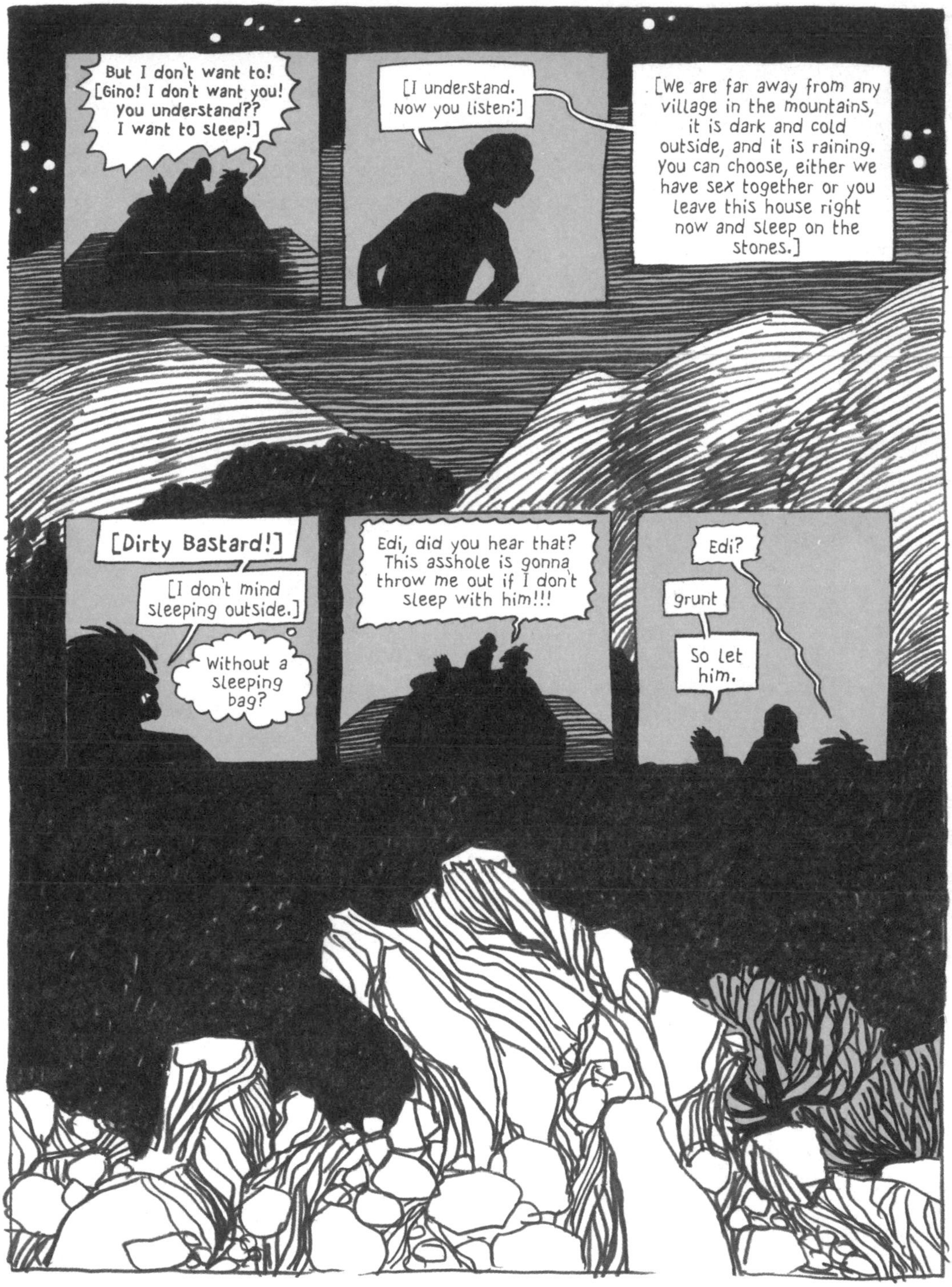
But I don't want to! [Gino! I don't want you! You understand?? I want to sleep!]
[I understand. Now you listen:]
[We are far away from any village in the mountains, it is dark and cold outside, and it is raining. You can choose, either we have sex together or you leave this house right now and sleep on the stones.]
[Dirty Bastard!]
[I don't mind sleeping outside.]
Without a sleeping bag?
Edi, did you hear that? This asshole is gonna throw me out if I don't sleep with him!!!
Edi?
grunt
So let him.

cough
cough

cough
cough
cough

Alone

grunt,
cough

shiver

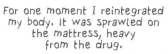

[Hey! Look
at me!]

[Move a
bit! show
some en-
thusiasm.]

[I don't want
to fuck a dead
chicken!]

For one moment I reintegrated
my body. It was sprawled on
the mattress, heavy
from the drug.

[What did you expect?
You can make me fuck
with you, but not to
enjoy it!]

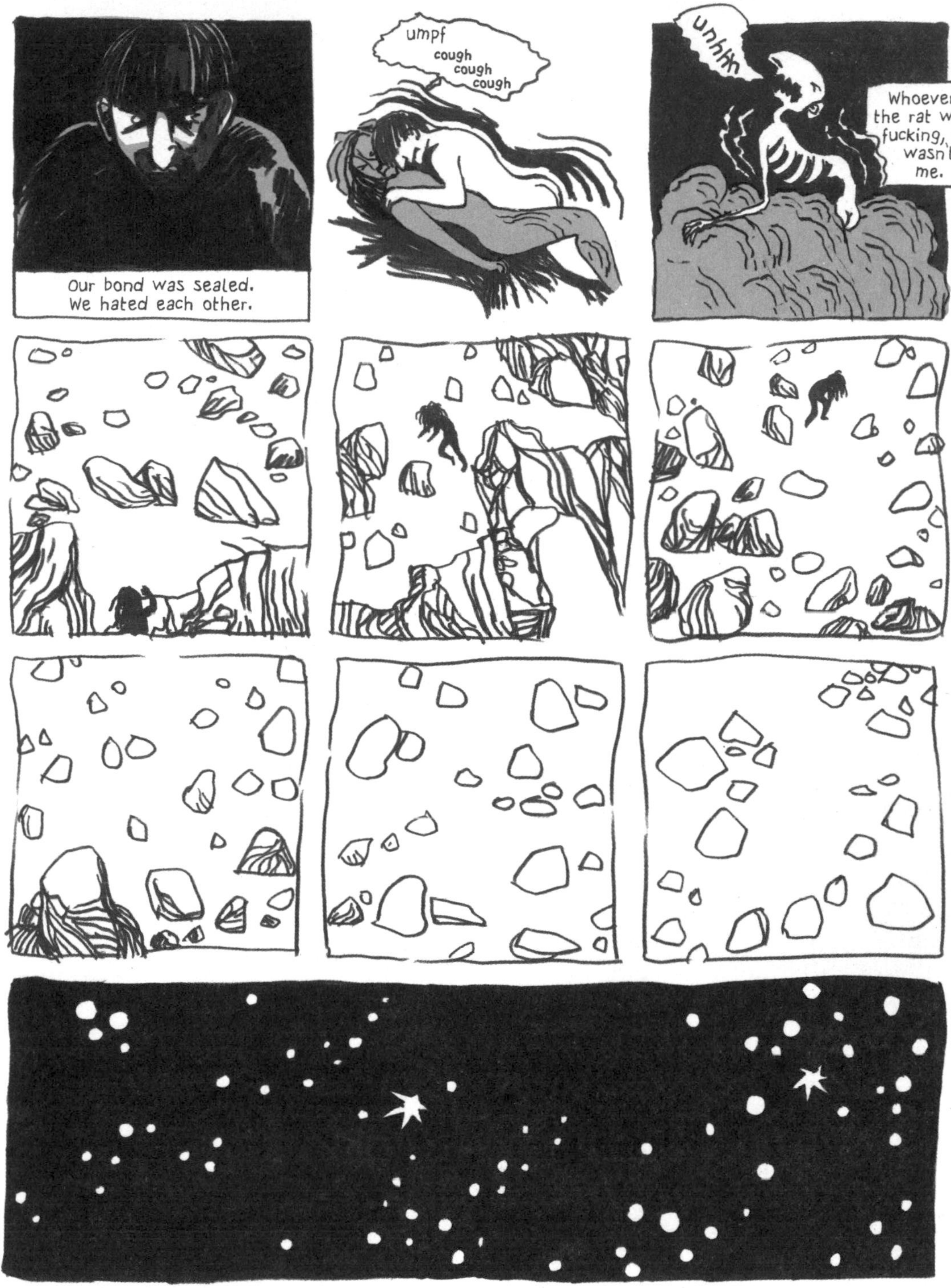
Our bond was sealed.
We hated each other.
umpf
cough
cough
cough
unhh
Whoever the rat was fucking, it wasn't me.

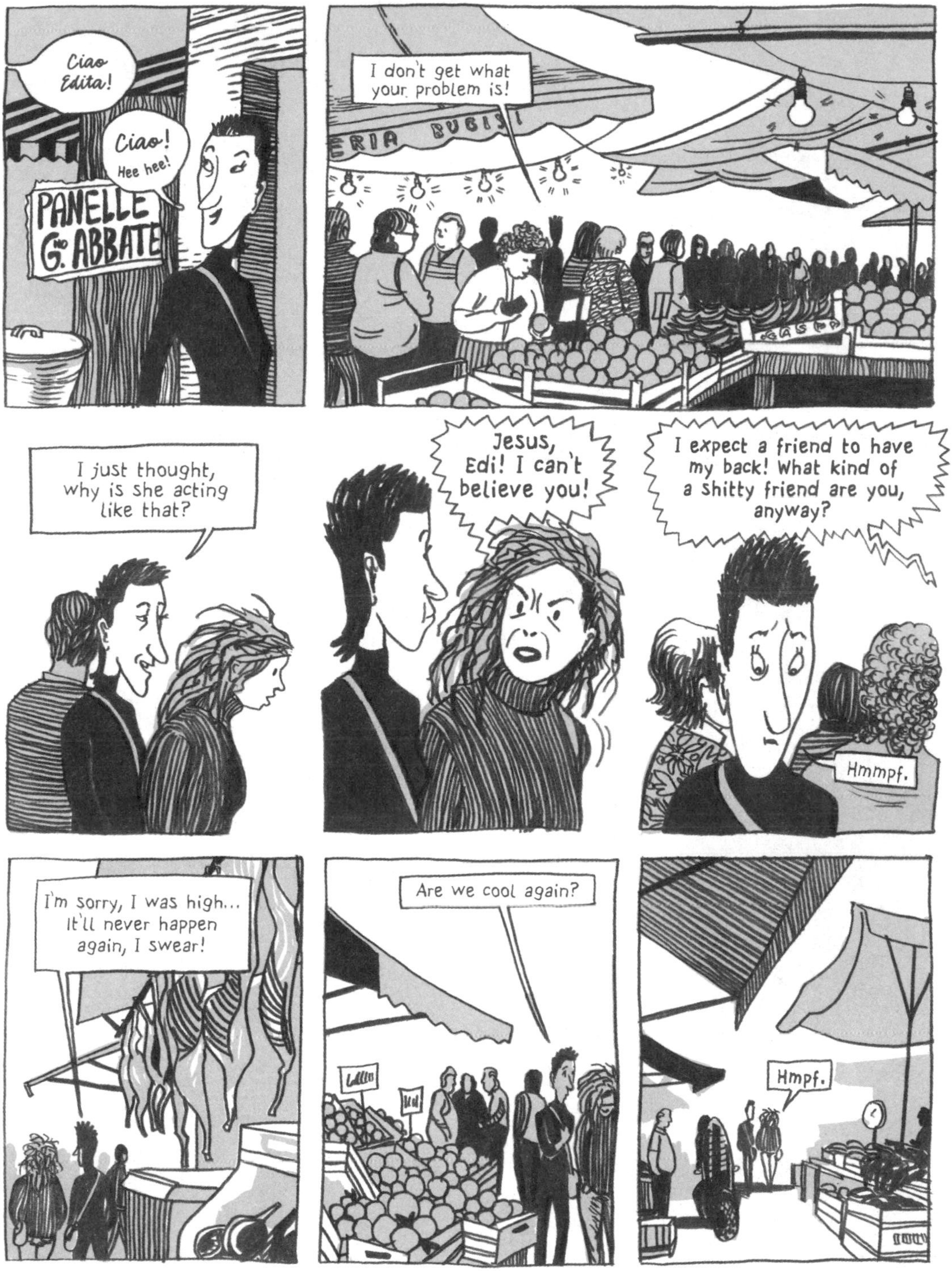
Ciao Edita!
Ciao! Hee hee!
PANELLE G.NO ABBATE
I don't get what your problem is!
I just thought, why is she acting like that?
Jesus, Edi! I can't believe you!
I expect a friend to have my back! What kind of a shitty friend are you, anyway?
Hmmpf.
I'm sorry, I was high... It'll never happen again, I swear!
Are we cool again?
Hmpf.

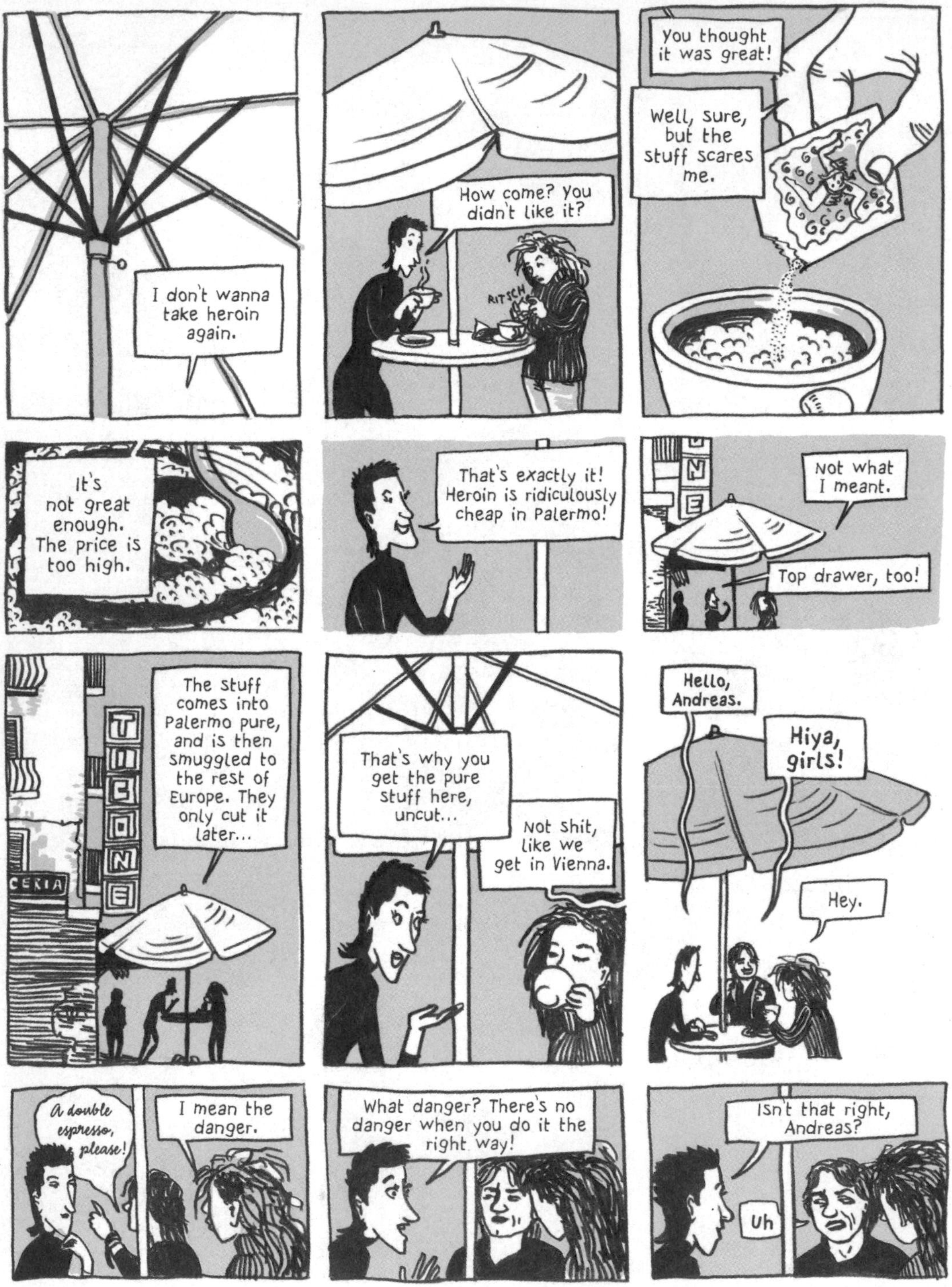
I don't wanna take heroin again.
How come? You didn't like it?
RITSCH
You thought it was great!
Well, sure, but the stuff scares me.
It's not great enough. The price is too high.
That's exactly it! Heroin is ridiculously cheap in Palermo!
Not what I meant.
Top drawer, too!
The stuff comes into Palermo pure, and is then smuggled to the rest of Europe. They only cut it later...
That's why you get the pure stuff here, uncut...
Not shit, like we get in Vienna.
Hello, Andreas.
Hiya, girls!
Hey.
A double espresso, please!
I mean the danger.
What danger? There's no danger when you do it the right way!
Isn't that right, Andreas?
Uh

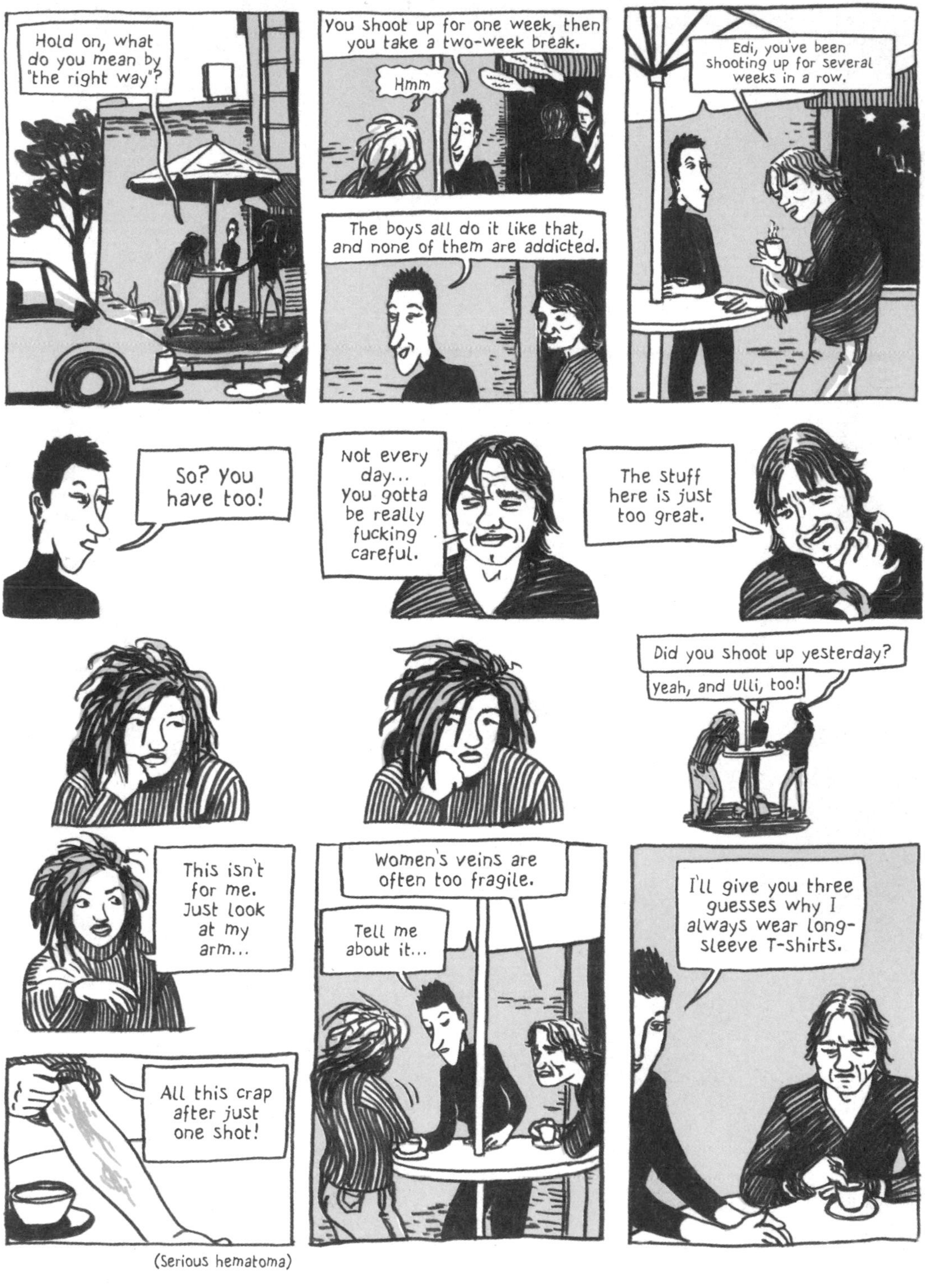
Hold on, what do you mean by "the right way"?
You shoot up for one week, then you take a two-week break.
Hmm
The boys all do it like that, and none of them are addicted.
Edi, you've been shooting up for several weeks in a row.
So? You have too!
Not every day... You gotta be really fucking careful.
The stuff here is just too great.
Did you shoot up yesterday?
Yeah, and Ulli, too!
This isn't for me. Just look at my arm...
All this crap after just one shot!
Women's veins are often too fragile.
Tell me about it...
I'll give you three guesses why I always wear long-sleeve T-shirts.
(Serious hematoma)

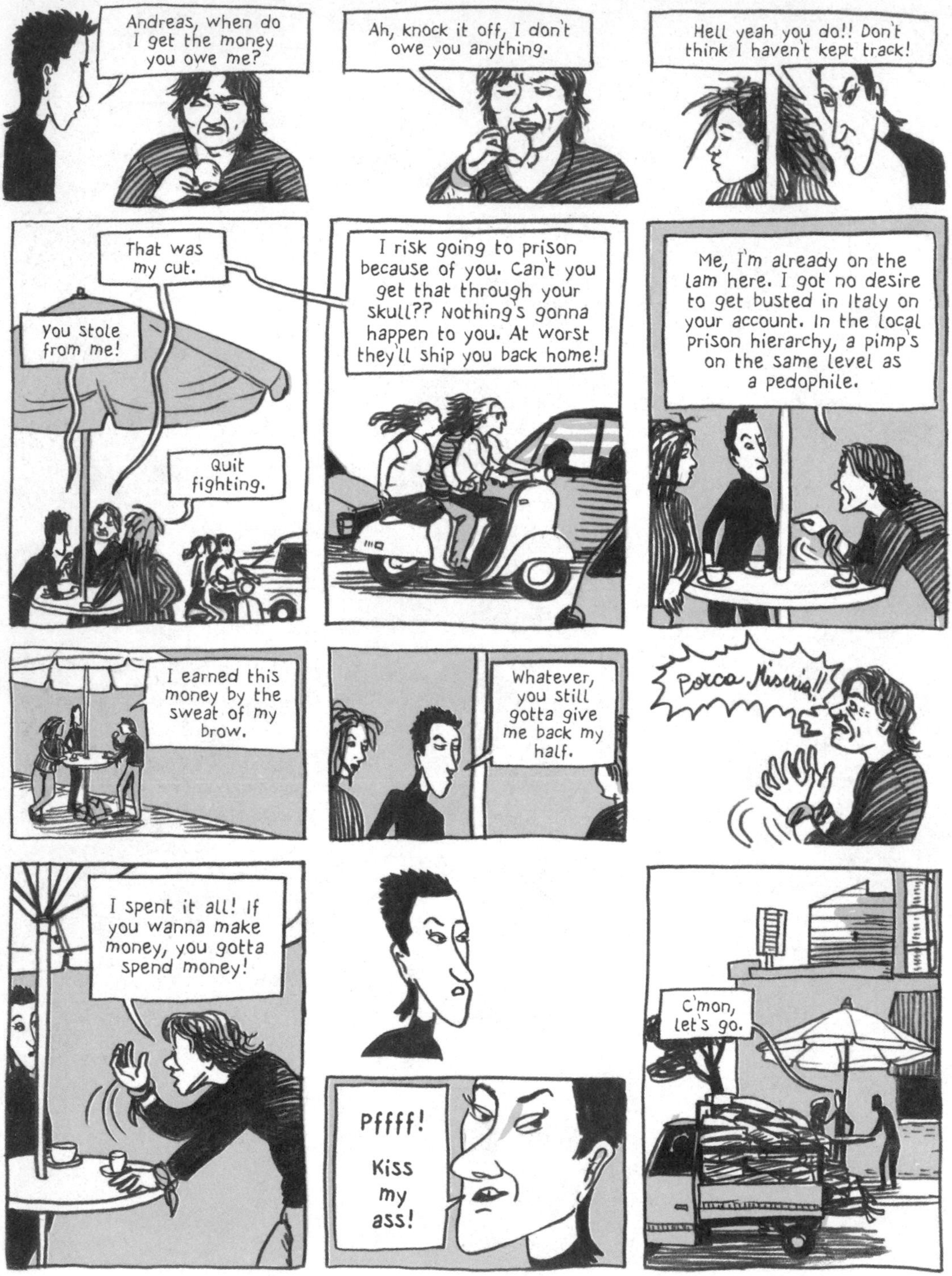
Andreas, when do I get the money you owe me?
Ah, knock it off, I don't owe you anything.
Hell yeah you do!! Don't think I haven't kept track!
That was my cut.
You stole from me!
Quit fighting.
I risk going to prison because of you. Can't you get that through your skull?? Nothing's gonna happen to you. At worst they'll ship you back home!
Me, I'm already on the lam here. I got no desire to get busted in Italy on your account. In the local prison hierarchy, a pimp's on the same level as a pedophile.
I earned this money by the sweat of my brow.
Whatever, you still gotta give me back my half.
Porca Miseria!!
I spent it all! If you wanna make money, you gotta spend money!
Pffff!
Kiss my ass!
C'mon, let's go.

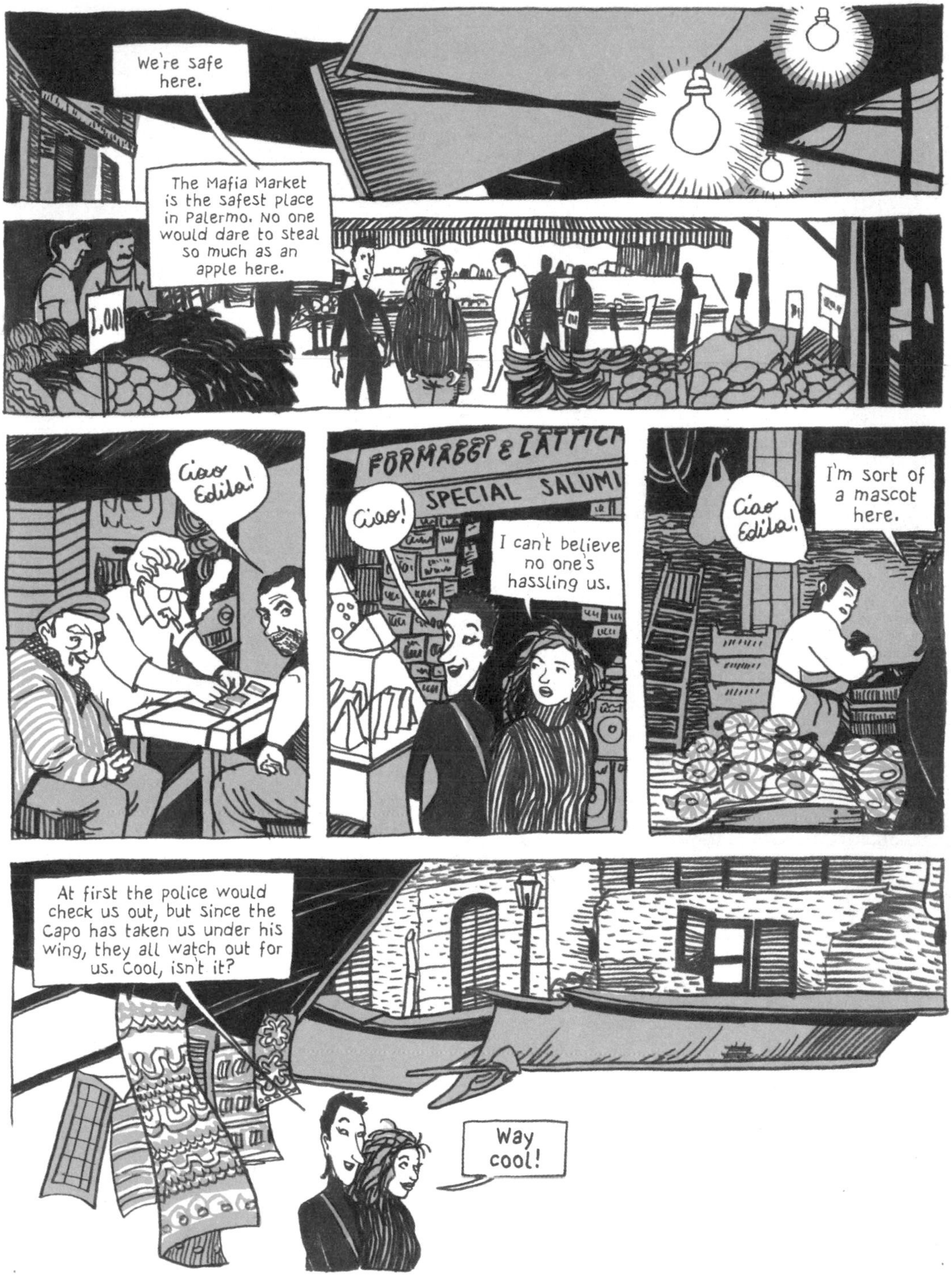
We're safe here.
The Mafia Market is the safest place in Palermo. No one would dare to steal so much as an apple here.
Ciao Edila!
FORMAGGI E LATTICI
SPECIAL SALUMI
Ciao!
I can't believe no one's hassling us.
Ciao Edila!
I'm sort of a mascot here.
At first the police would check us out, but since the Capo has taken us under his wing, they all watch out for us. Cool, isn't it?
Way cool!

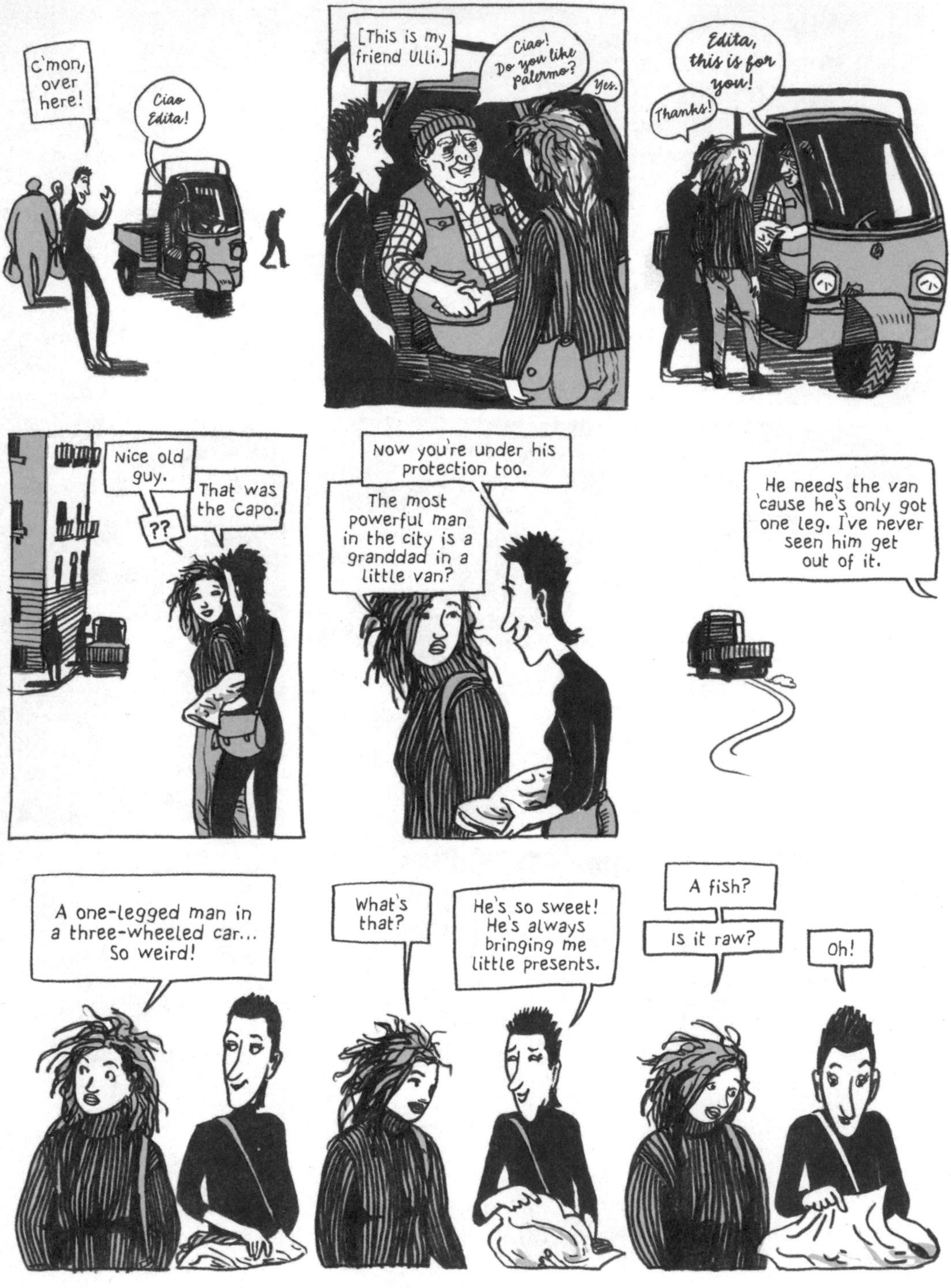

C'mon, over here!
Ciao Edita!
[This is my friend Ulli.]
Ciao! Do you like Palermo?
Yes.
Edita, this is for you!
Thanks!
Nice old guy.
That was the Capo.
??
Now you're under his protection too.
The most powerful man in the city is a granddad in a little van?
He needs the van 'cause he's only got one leg. I've never seen him get out of it.
A one-legged man in a three-wheeled car... So weird!
What's that?
He's so sweet! He's always bringing me little presents.
A fish?
Is it raw?
Oh!

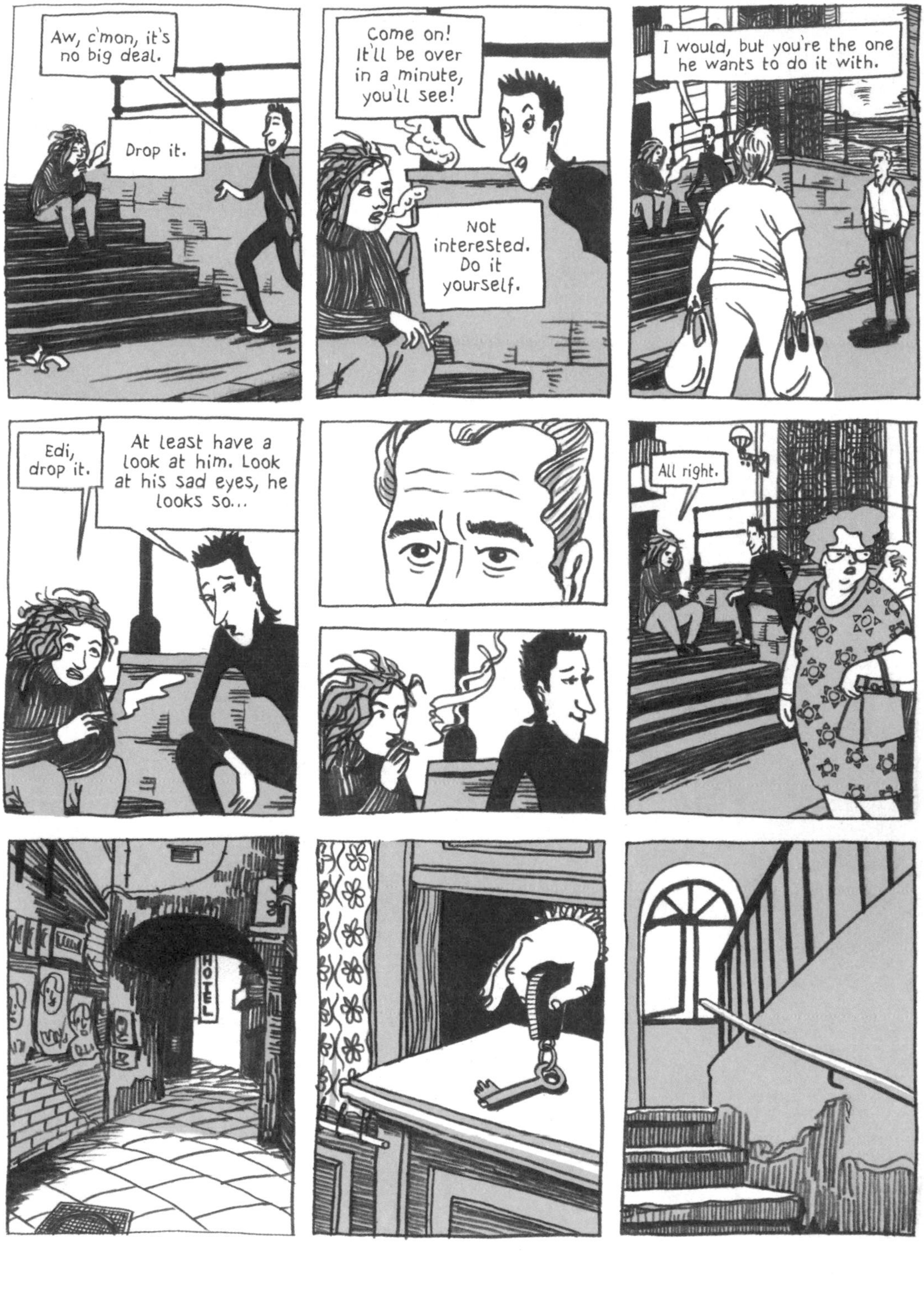
Aw, c'mon, it's no big deal.
Drop it.
Come on! It'll be over in a minute, you'll see!
Not interested. Do it yourself.
I would, but you're the one he wants to do it with.
Edi, drop it.
At least have a look at him. Look at his sad eyes, he looks so...
All right.
HOTEL

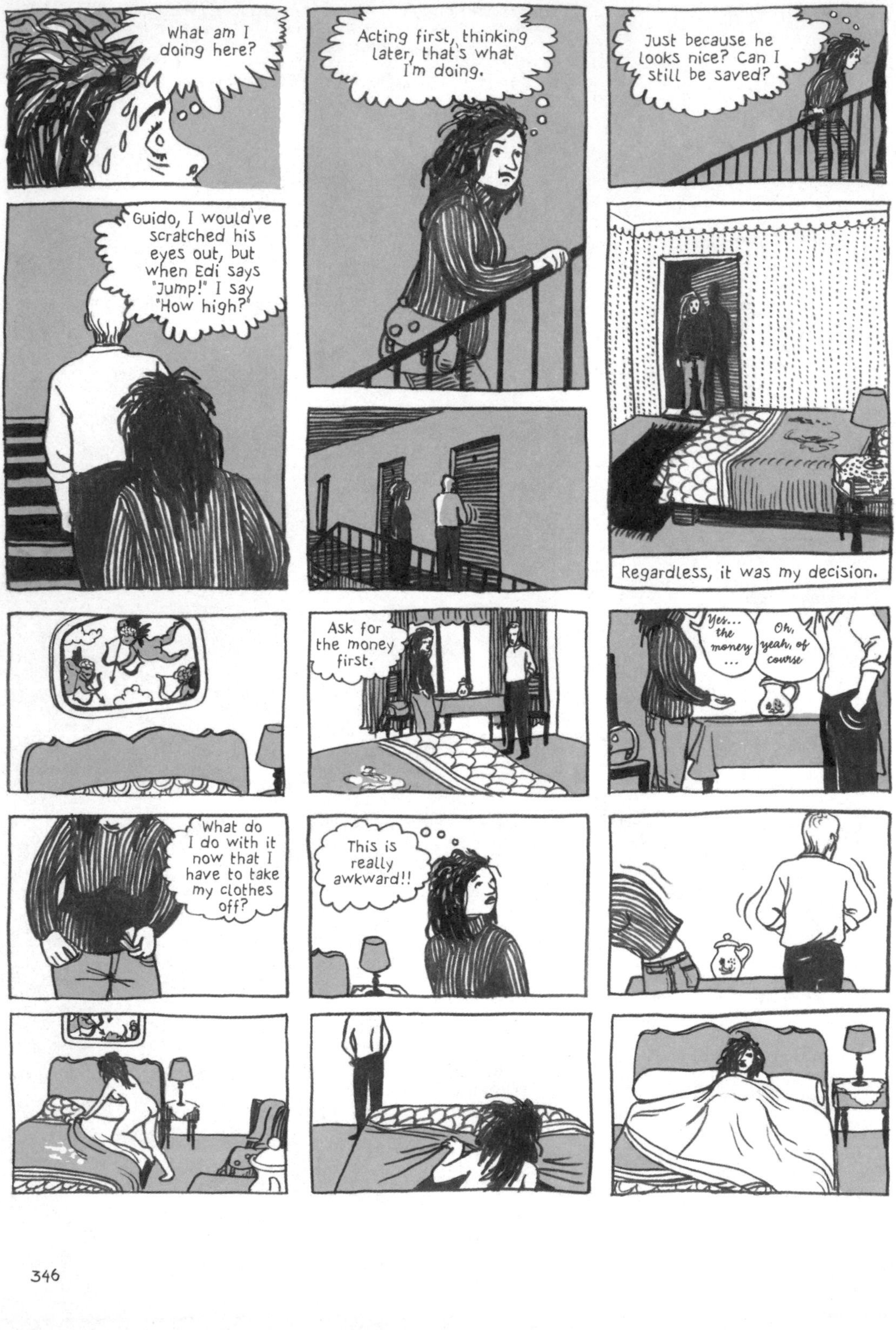
What am I doing here?
Acting first, thinking later, that's what I'm doing.
Just because he looks nice? Can I still be saved?
Guido, I would've scratched his eyes out, but when Edi says "Jump!" I say "How high?"
Regardless, it was my decision.
Ask for the money first.
Yes... the money...
Oh, yeah, of course
What do I do with it now that I have to take my clothes off?
This is really awkward!!

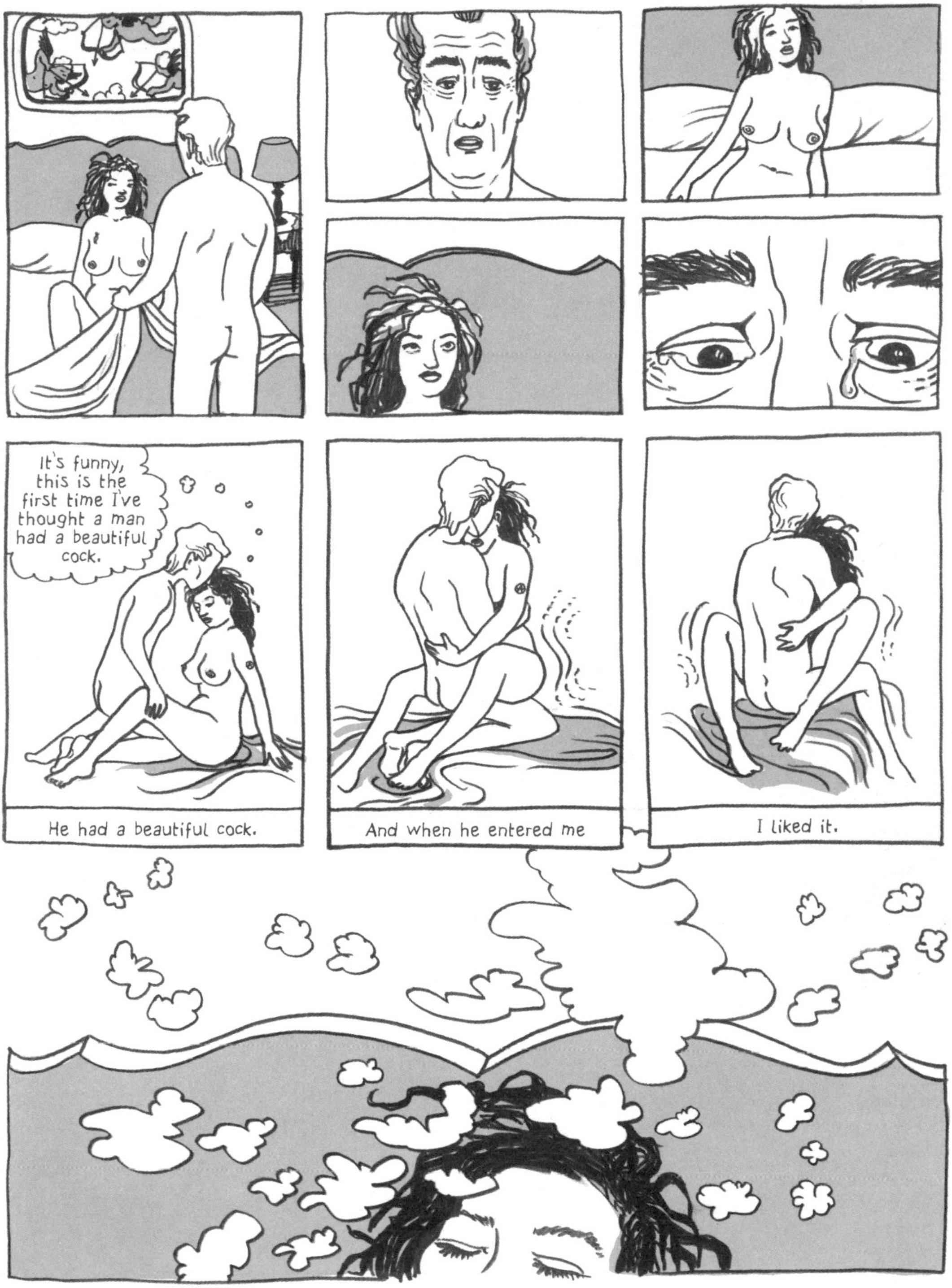
It's funny, this is the first time I've thought a man had a beautiful cock.
He had a beautiful cock.
And when he entered me
I liked it.

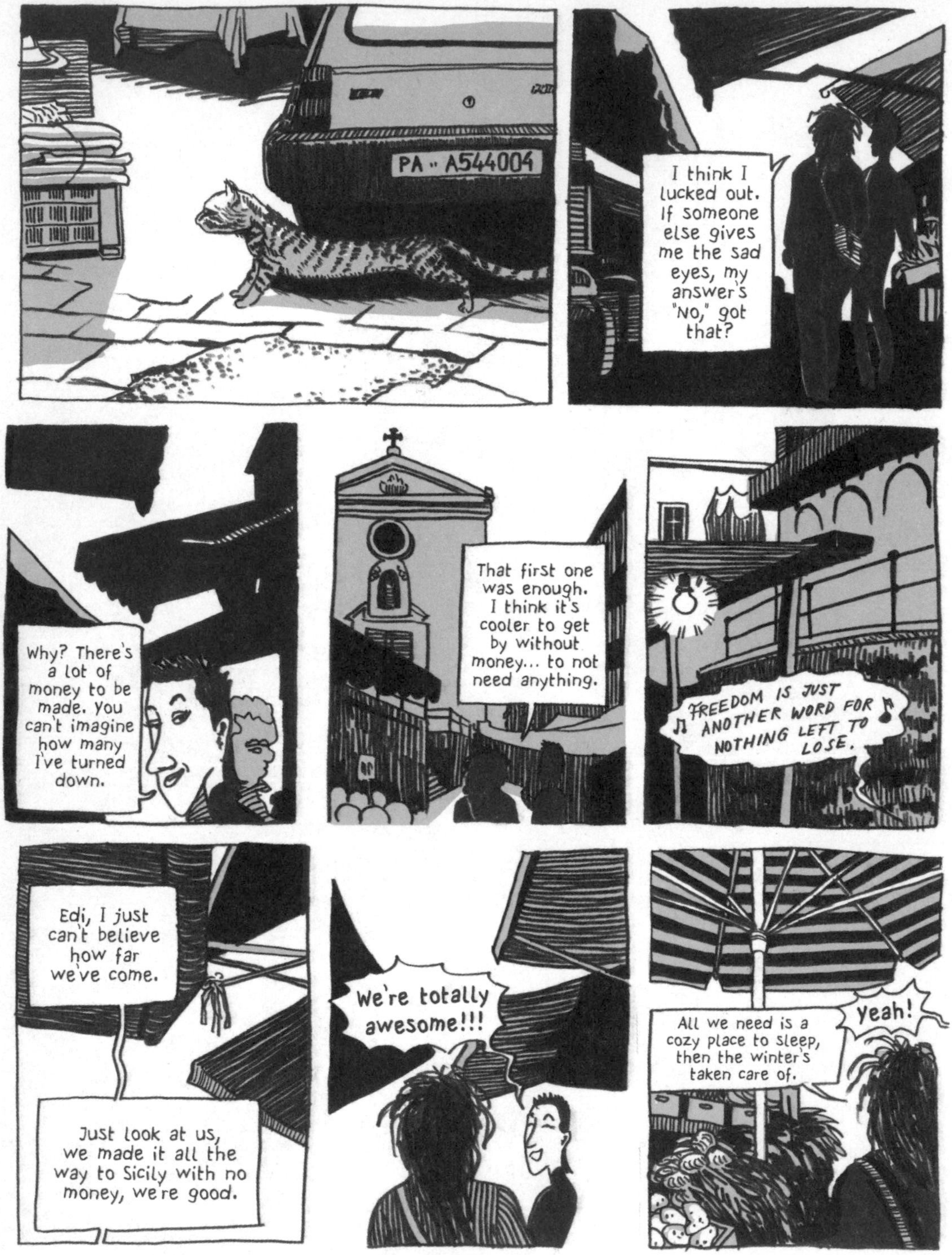
PA A544004
I think I lucked out. If someone else gives me the sad eyes, my answer's "No," got that?
Why? There's a lot of money to be made. You can't imagine how many I've turned down.
That first one was enough. I think it's cooler to get by without money... to not need anything.
♫ FREEDOM IS JUST ANOTHER WORD FOR NOTHING LEFT TO LOSE. ♫
Edi, I just can't believe how far we've come.
Just look at us, we made it all the way to Sicily with no money, we're good.
We're totally awesome!!!
All we need is a cozy place to sleep, then the winter's taken care of.
Yeah!

XVI. the HOUSE

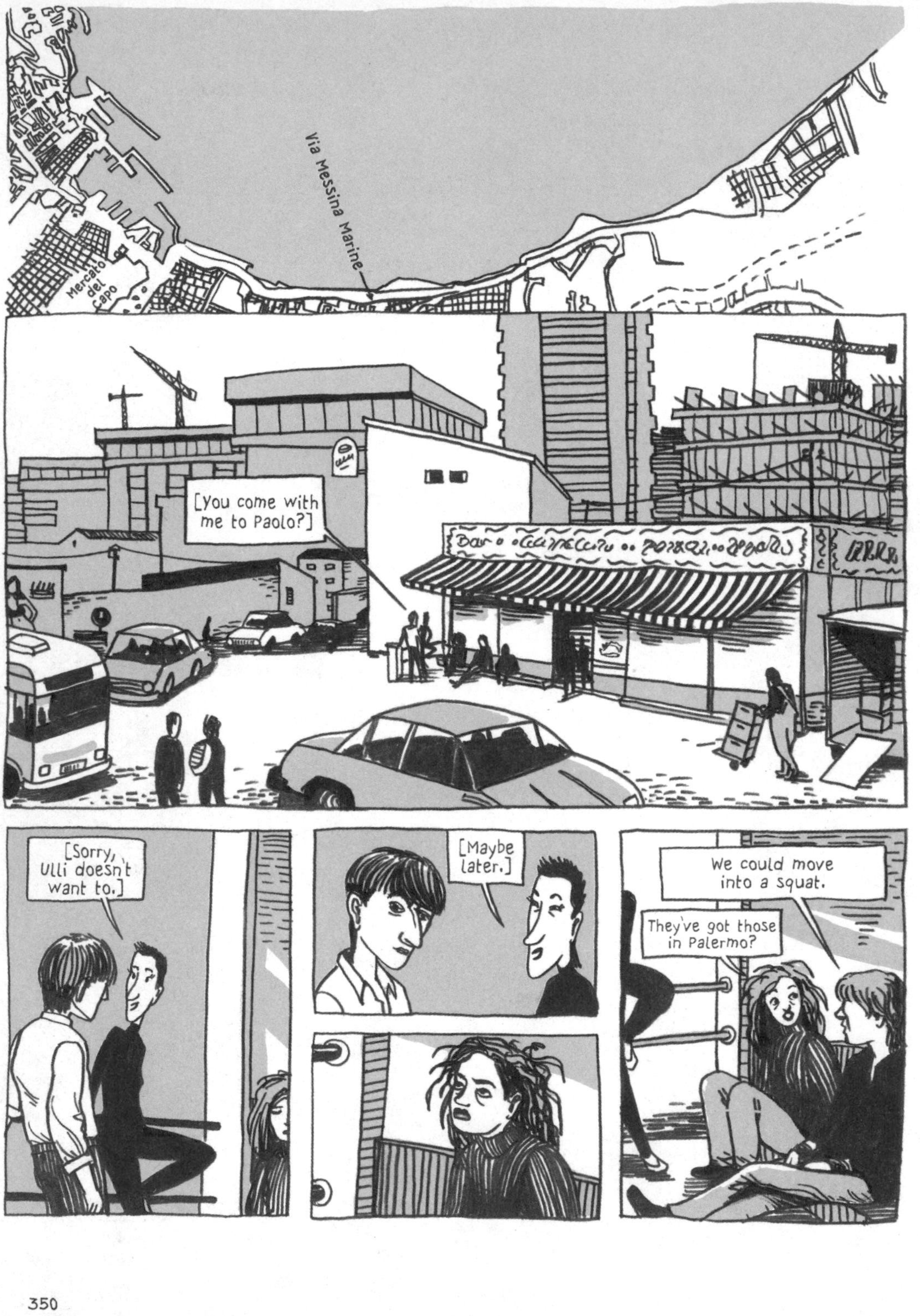
Via Messina Marine
Mercato del Capo
[You come with me to Paolo?]
[Sorry, Ulli doesn't want to.]
[Maybe later.]
We could move into a squat.
They've got those in Palermo?

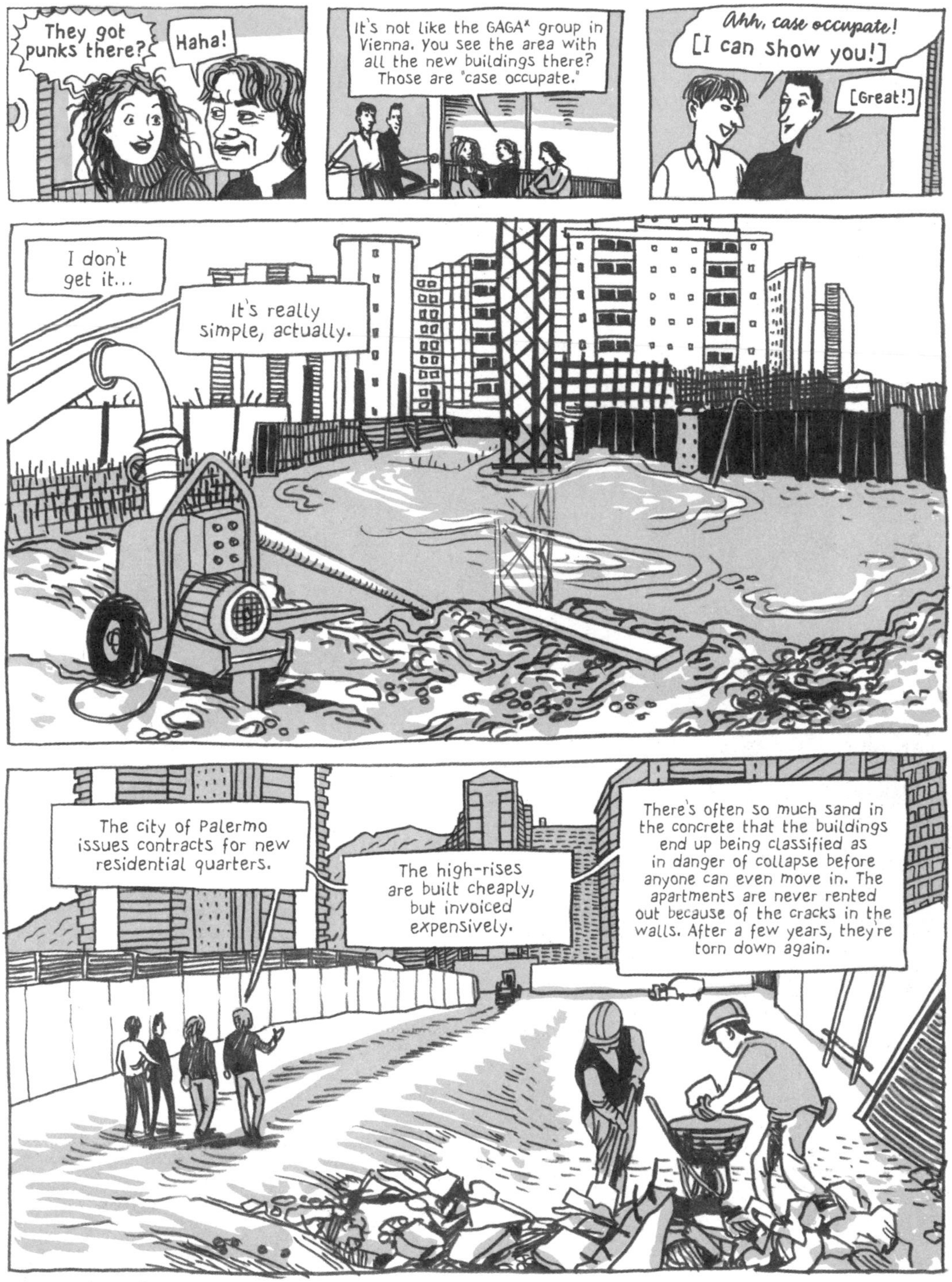
They got punks there?
Haha!
It's not like the GAGA* group in Vienna. You see the area with all the new buildings there? Those are "case occupate."
Ahh, case occupate!
[I can show you!]
[Great!]
I don't get it...
It's really simple, actually.
The city of Palermo issues contracts for new residential quarters.
The high-rises are built cheaply, but invoiced expensively.
There's often so much sand in the concrete that the buildings end up being classified as in danger of collapse before anyone can even move in. The apartments are never rented out because of the cracks in the walls. After a few years, they're torn down again.

* named for the Gassergasse Cultural Center

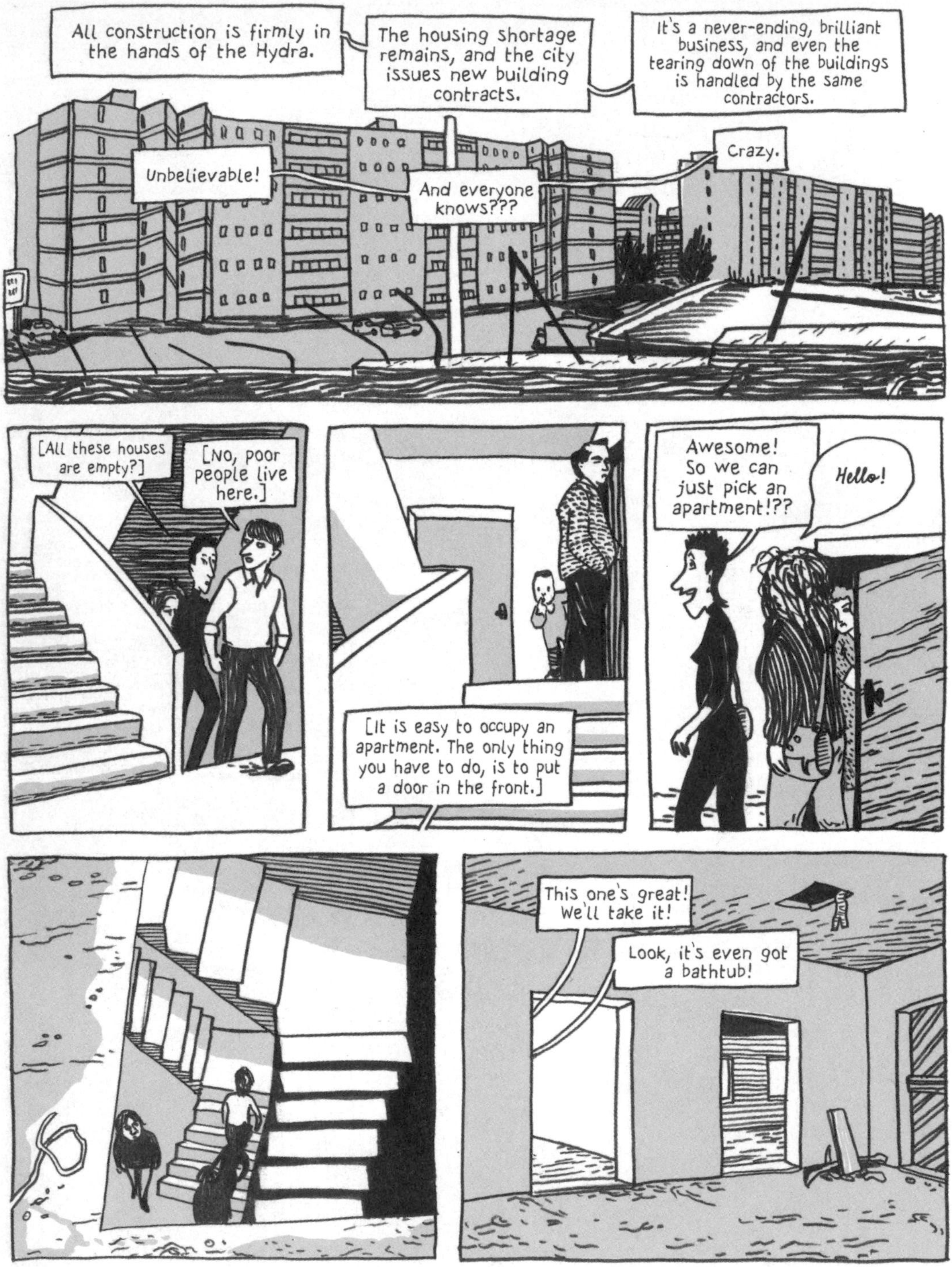
All construction is firmly in the hands of the Hydra.
The housing shortage remains, and the city issues new building contracts.
It's a never-ending, brilliant business, and even the tearing down of the buildings is handled by the same contractors.
Unbelievable!
And everyone knows???
Crazy.
[All these houses are empty?]
[No, poor people live here.]
[It is easy to occupy an apartment. The only thing you have to do, is to put a door in the front.]
Awesome! So we can just pick an apartment!??
Hello!
This one's great! We'll take it!
Look, it's even got a bathtub!

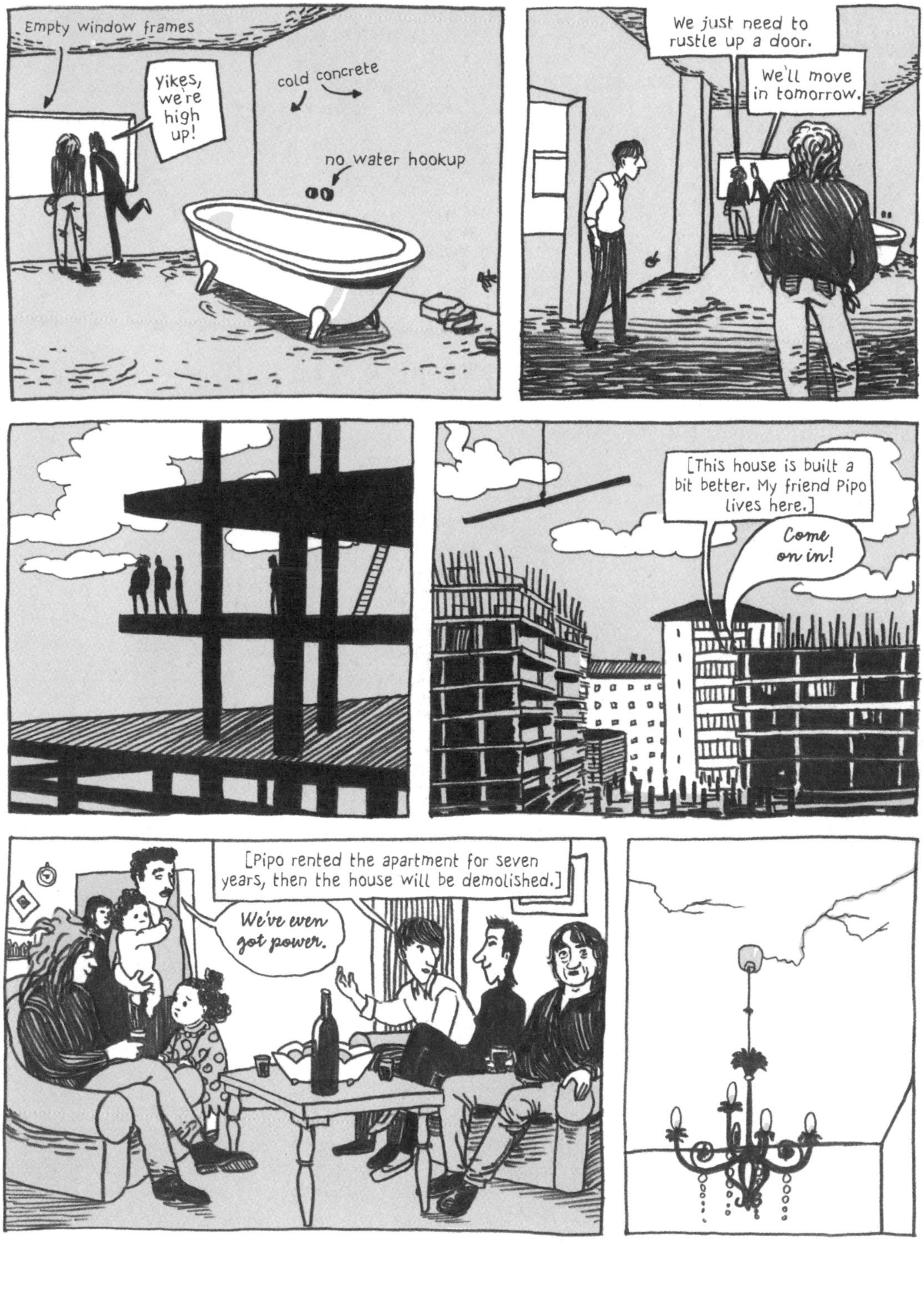
Empty window frames
Yikes, we're high up!
cold concrete
no water hookup
We just need to rustle up a door.
We'll move in tomorrow.
[This house is built a bit better. My friend Pipo lives here.]
Come on in!
[Pipo rented the apartment for seven years, then the house will be demolished.]
We've even got power.

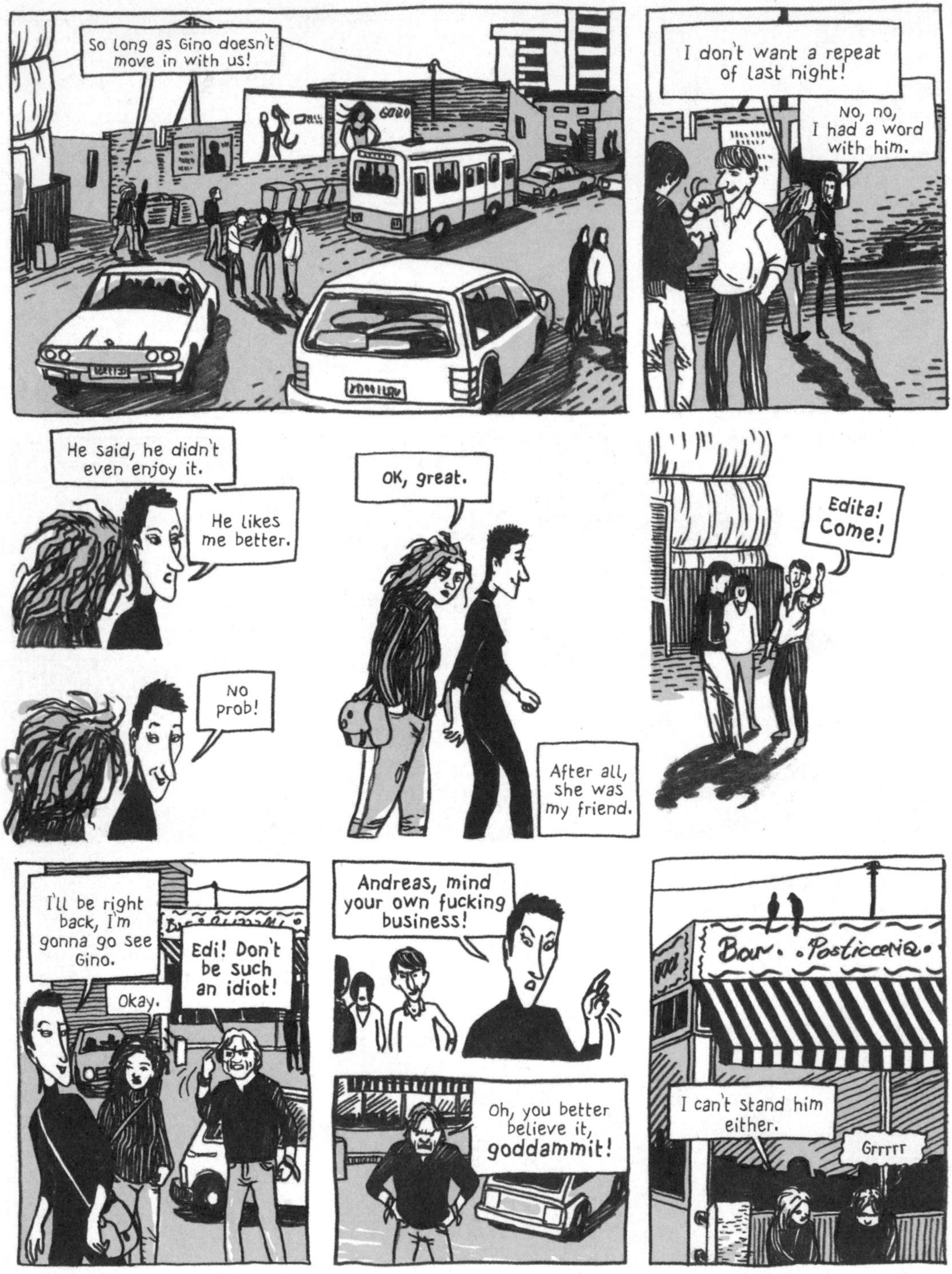
So long as Gino doesn't move in with us!
I don't want a repeat of last night!
No, no, I had a word with him.
He said, he didn't even enjoy it.
He likes me better.
No prob!
OK, great.
After all, she was my friend.
Edita! Come!
I'll be right back, I'm gonna go see Gino.
Okay.
Edi! Don't be such an idiot!
Andreas, mind your own fucking business!
Oh, you better believe it, goddammit!
Bar. .Pasticceria.
I can't stand him either.
Grrrrr

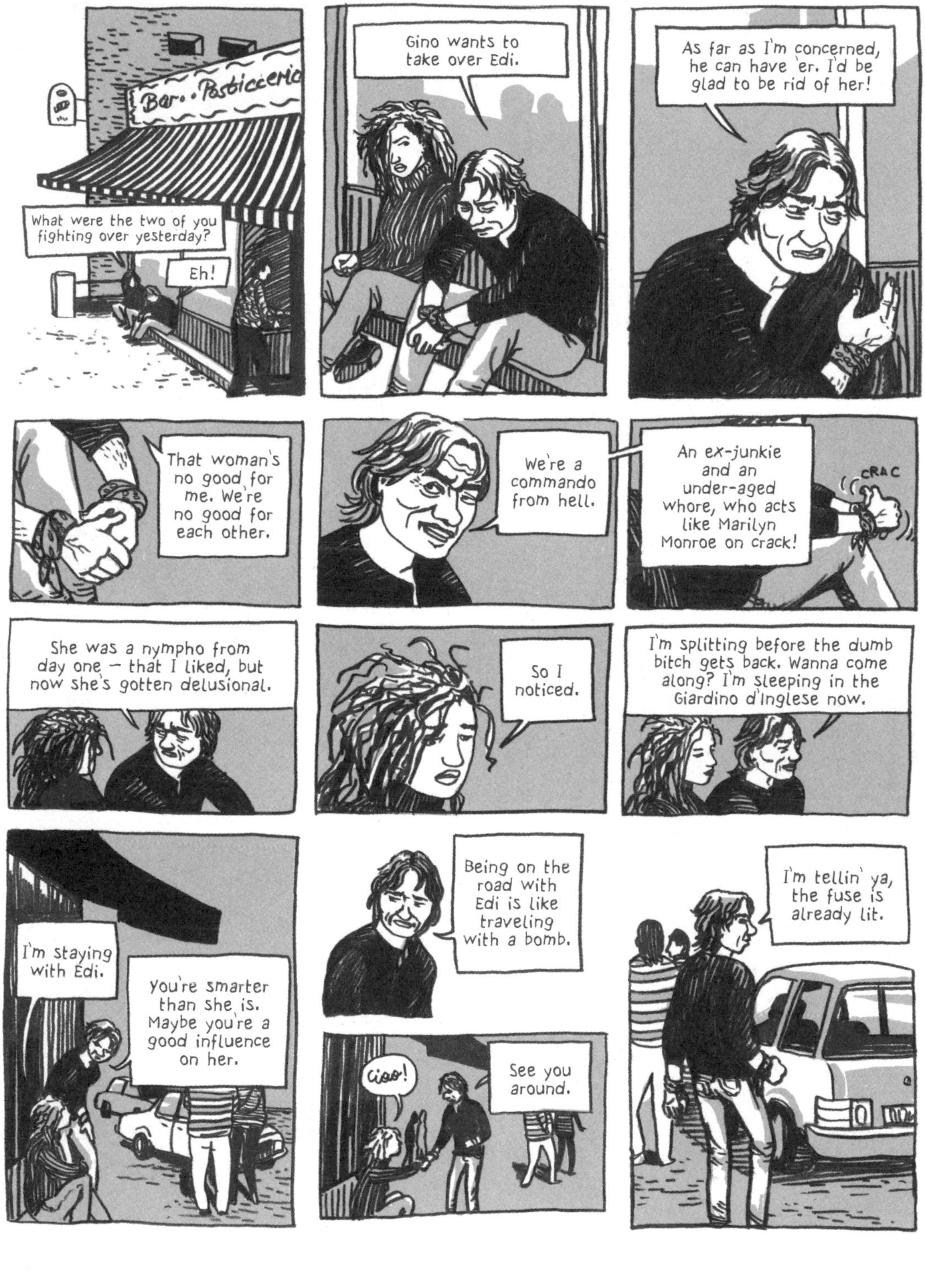
Bar • Pasticceria
What were the two of you fighting over yesterday?
Eh!
Gino wants to take over Edi.
As far as I'm concerned, he can have 'er. I'd be glad to be rid of her!
That woman's no good for me. We're no good for each other.
We're a commando from hell.
An ex-junkie and an under-aged whore, who acts like Marilyn Monroe on crack!
CRAC
She was a nympho from day one — that I liked, but now she's gotten delusional.
So I noticed.
I'm splitting before the dumb bitch gets back. Wanna come along? I'm sleeping in the Giardino d'Inglese now.
I'm staying with Edi.
You're smarter than she is. Maybe you're a good influence on her.
Being on the road with Edi is like traveling with a bomb.
Ciao!
See you around.
I'm tellin' ya, the fuse is already lit.

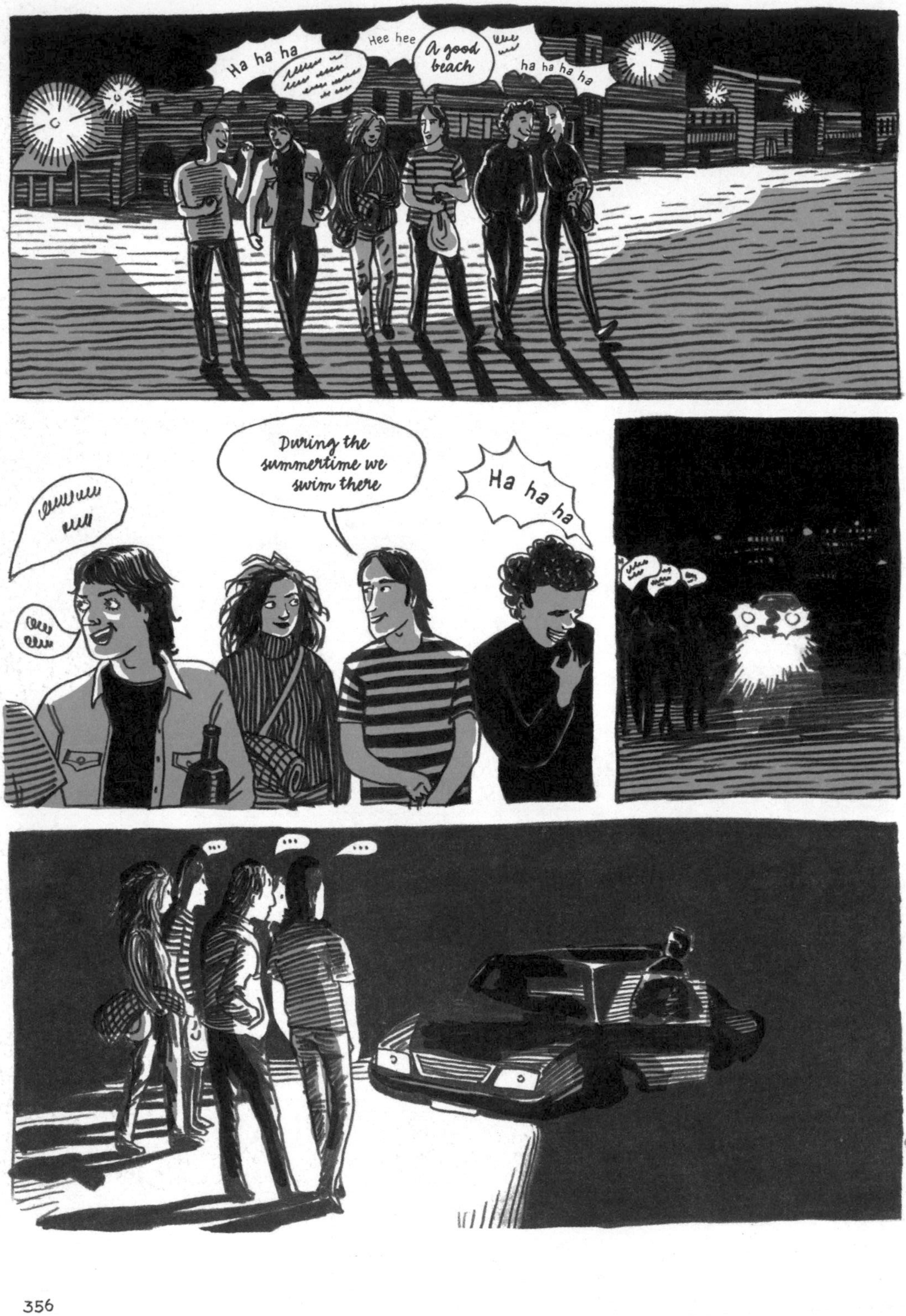
Ha ha ha
Hee hee
A good beach
ha ha ha ha
During the summertime we swim there
Ha ha ha
...
...
...

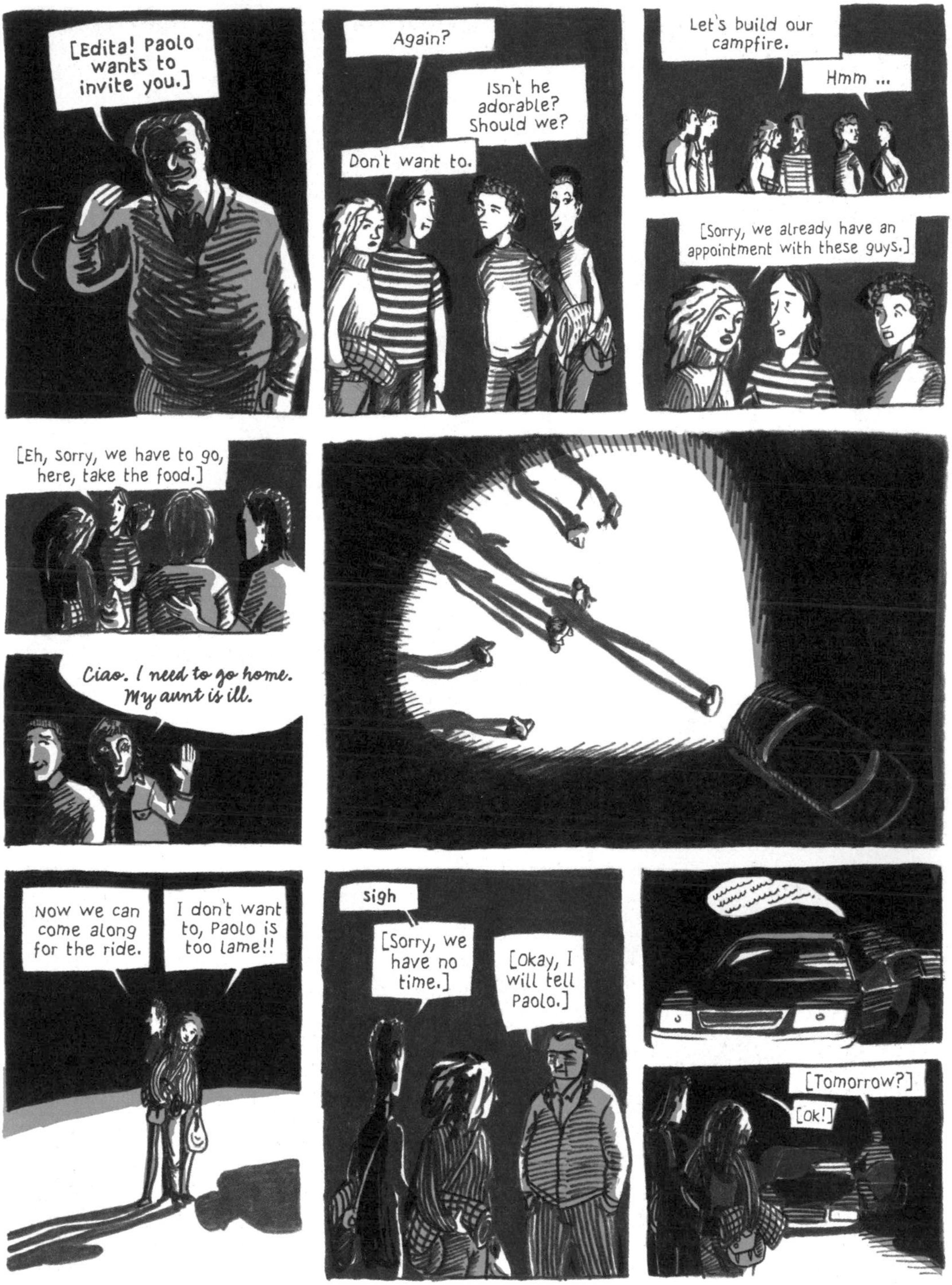
[Edita! Paolo wants to invite you.]
Again?
Isn't he adorable? Should we?
Don't want to.
Let's build our campfire.
Hmm ...
[Sorry, we already have an appointment with these guys.]
[Eh, sorry, we have to go, here, take the food.]
Ciao. I need to go home. My aunt is ill.
Now we can come along for the ride.
I don't want to, Paolo is too lame!!
sigh
[Sorry, we have no time.]
[Okay, I will tell Paolo.]
[Tomorrow?]
[Ok!]

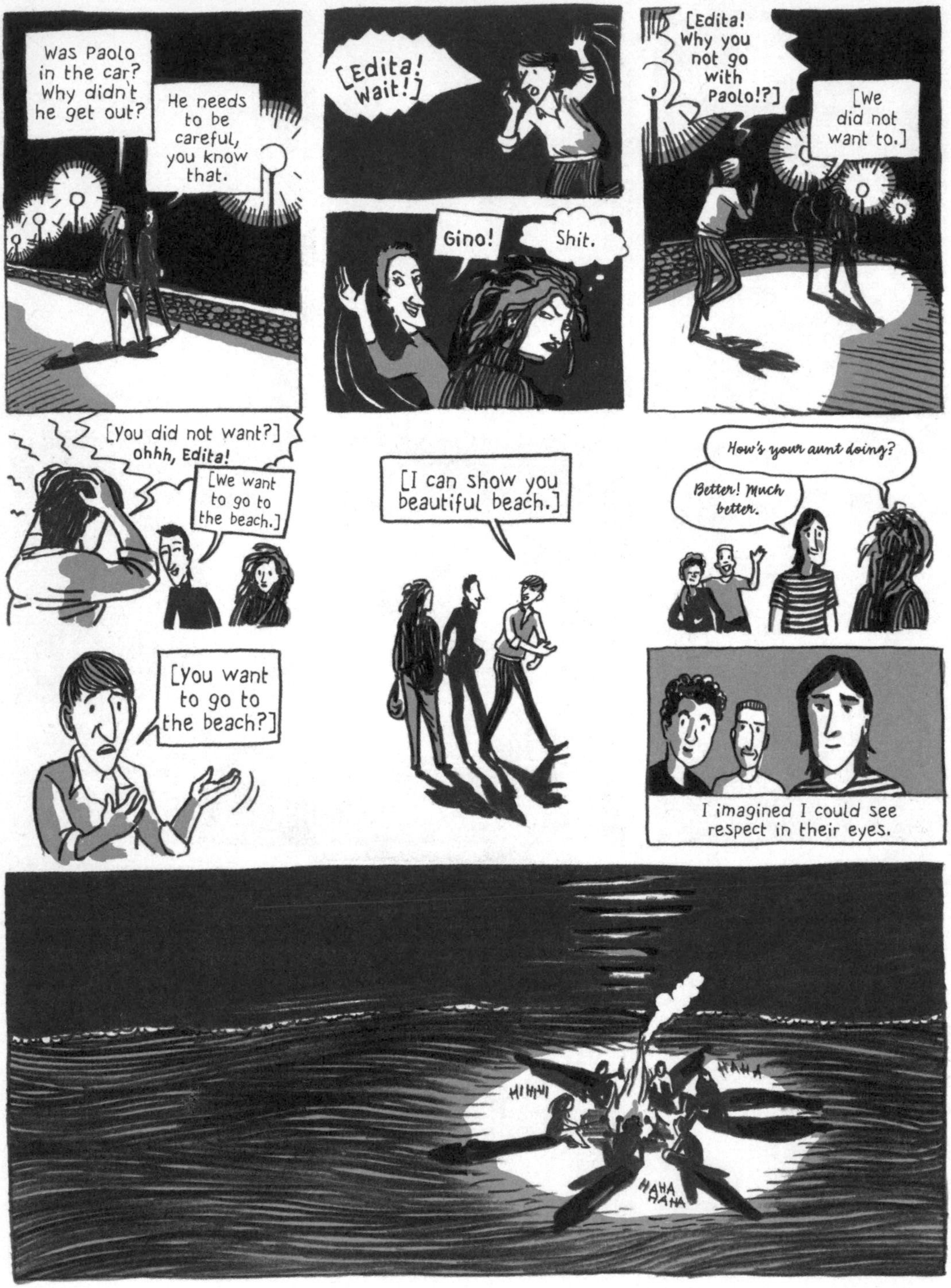
Was Paolo in the car? Why didn't he get out?
He needs to be careful, you know that.
[Edita! Wait!]
Gino!
Shit.
[Edita! Why you not go with Paolo!?]
[We did not want to.]
[You did not want?] Ohhh, Edita!
[We want to go to the beach.]
[You want to go to the beach?]
[I can show you beautiful beach.]
How's your aunt doing?
Better! Much better.
I imagined I could see respect in their eyes.
HIHIHI
HAHA
HAHA HAHA

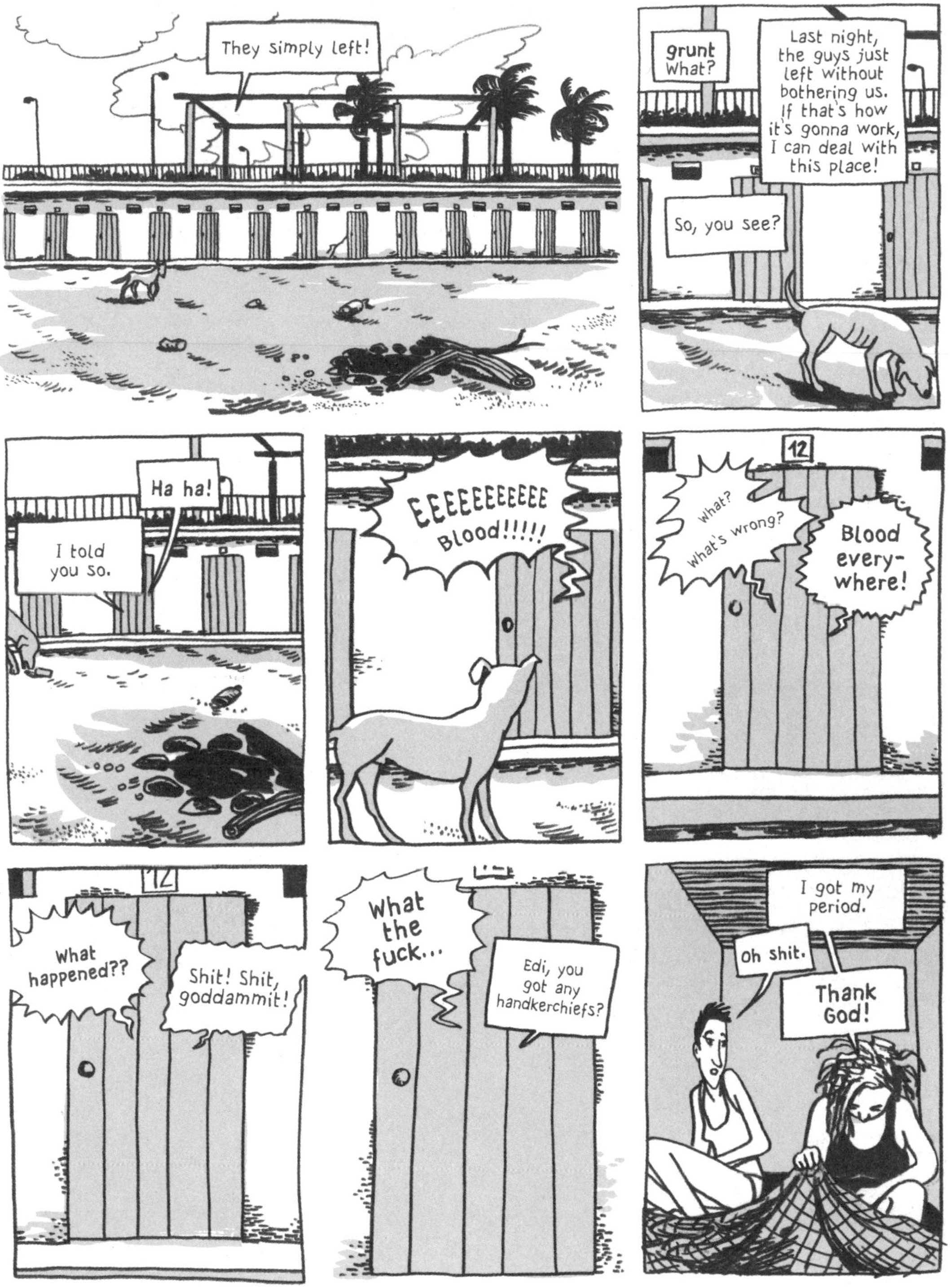
They simply left!
grunt
What?
Last night, the guys just left without bothering us. If that's how it's gonna work, I can deal with this place!
So, you see?
I told you so.
Ha ha!
EEEEEEEEEEE
Blood!!!!!
What? What's wrong?
Blood every-where!
What happened??
Shit! Shit, goddammit!
What the fuck...
Edi, you got any handkerchiefs?
I got my period.
Oh shit.
Thank God!

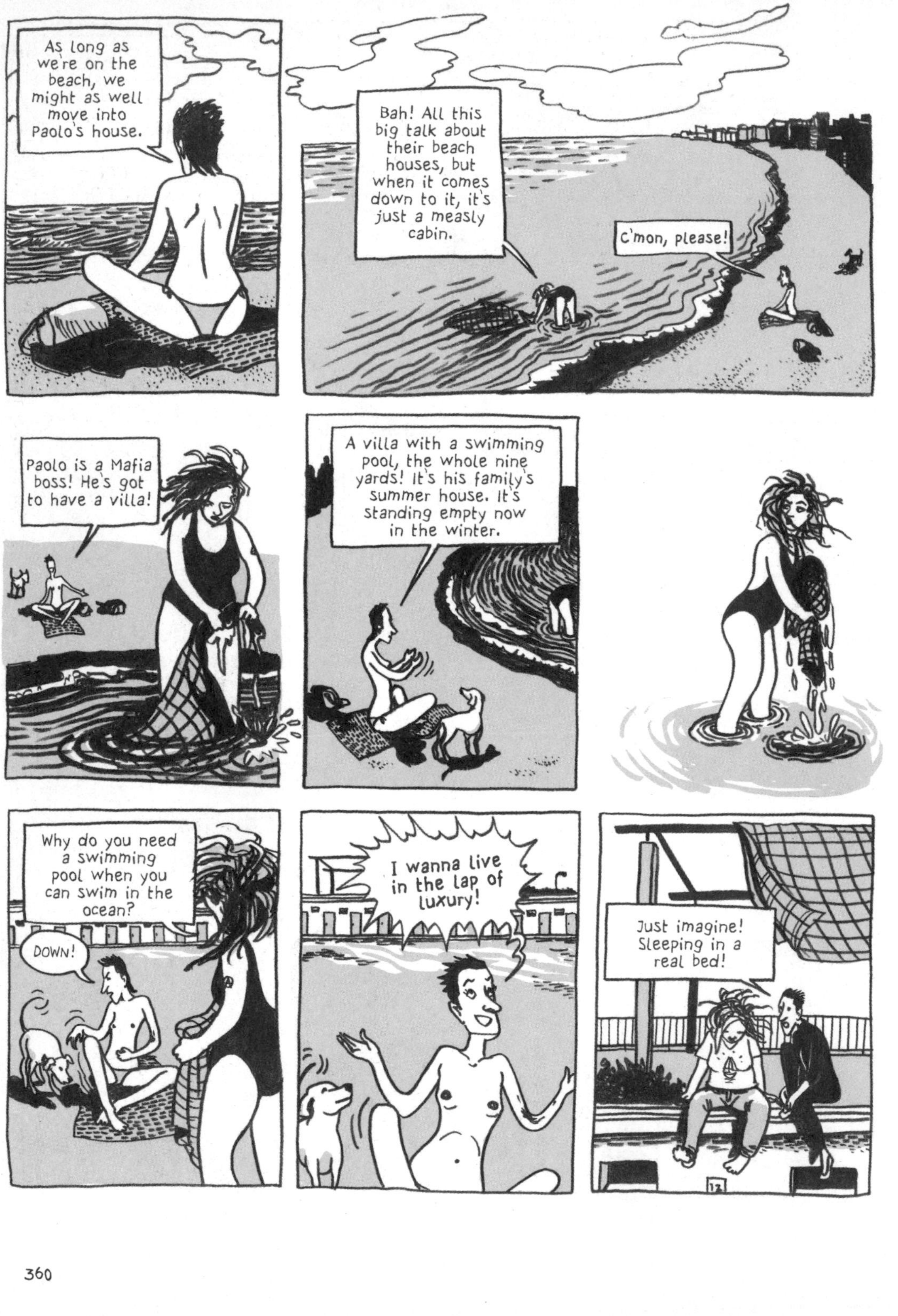
As long as we're on the beach, we might as well move into Paolo's house.
Bah! All this big talk about their beach houses, but when it comes down to it, it's just a measly cabin.
C'mon, please!
Paolo is a Mafia boss! He's got to have a villa!
A villa with a swimming pool, the whole nine yards! It's his family's summer house. It's standing empty now in the winter.
Why do you need a swimming pool when you can swim in the ocean?
DOWN!
I wanna live in the lap of luxury!
Just imagine! Sleeping in a real bed!

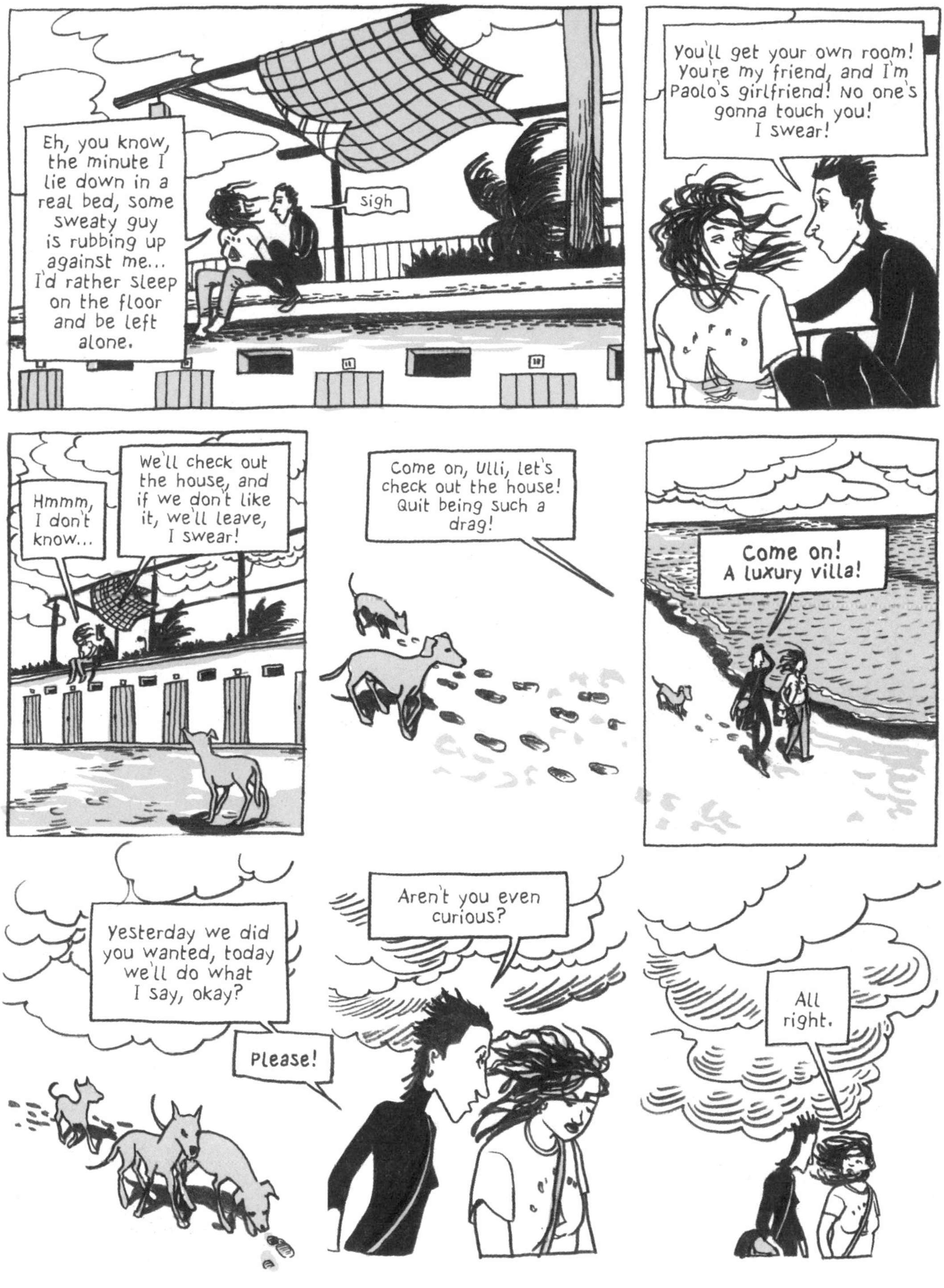

Eh, you know, the minute I lie down in a real bed, some sweaty guy is rubbing up against me... I'd rather sleep on the floor and be left alone.
sigh
You'll get your own room! You're my friend, and I'm Paolo's girlfriend! No one's gonna touch you! I swear!
Hmmm, I don't know...
We'll check out the house, and if we don't like it, we'll leave, I swear!
Come on, Ulli, let's check out the house! Quit being such a drag!
Come on! A luxury villa!
Yesterday we did you wanted, today we'll do what I say, okay?
Please!
Aren't you even curious?
All right.

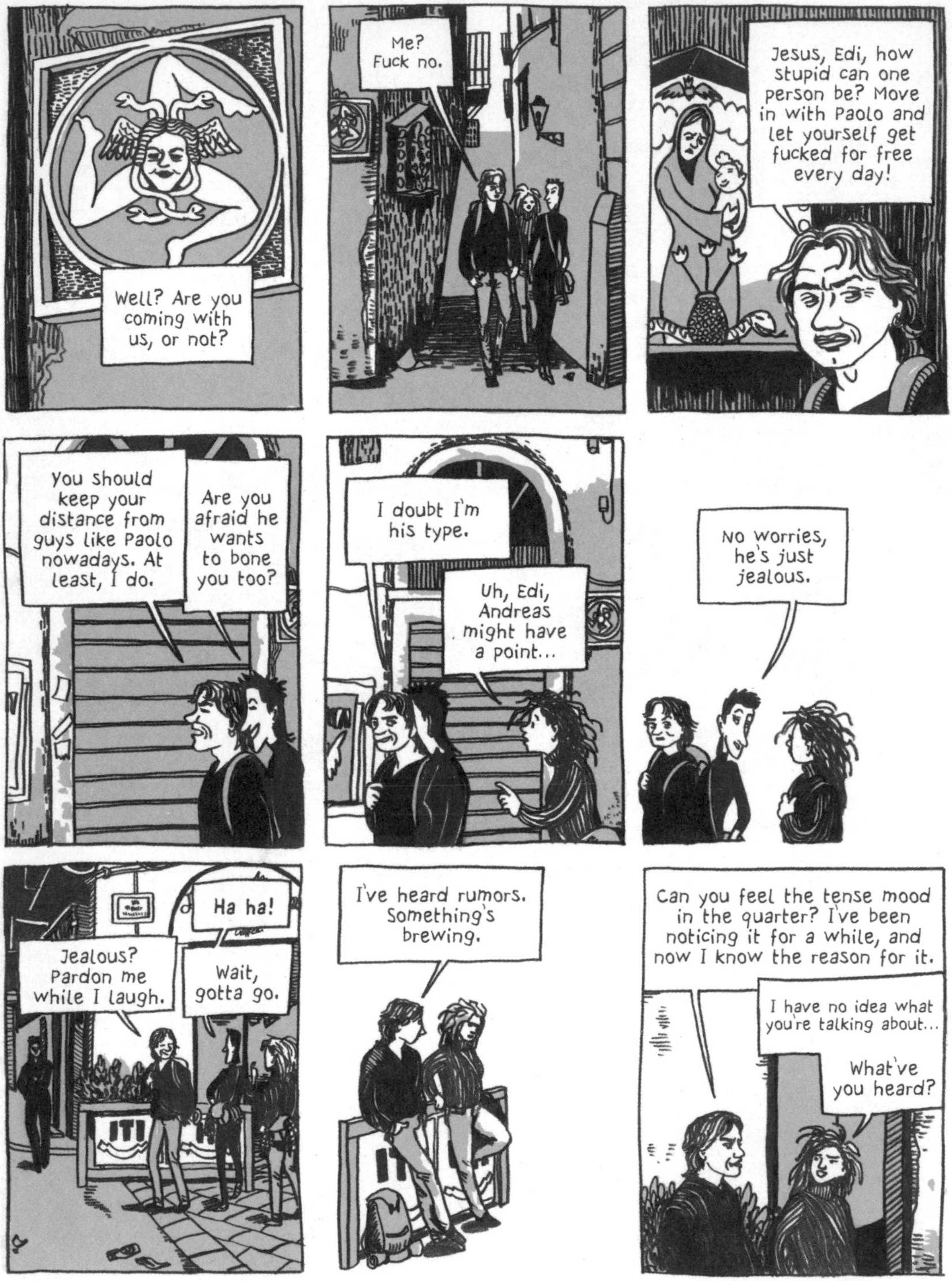
Well? Are you coming with us, or not?
Me? Fuck no.
Jesus, Edi, how stupid can one person be? Move in with Paolo and let yourself get fucked for free every day!
You should keep your distance from guys like Paolo nowadays. At least, I do.
Are you afraid he wants to bone you too?
I doubt I'm his type.
Uh, Edi, Andreas might have a point...
No worries, he's just jealous.
Jealous? Pardon me while I laugh.
Ha ha!
Wait, gotta go.
ITI
I've heard rumors. Something's brewing.
Can you feel the tense mood in the quarter? I've been noticing it for a while, and now I know the reason for it.
I have no idea what you're talking about...
What've you heard?

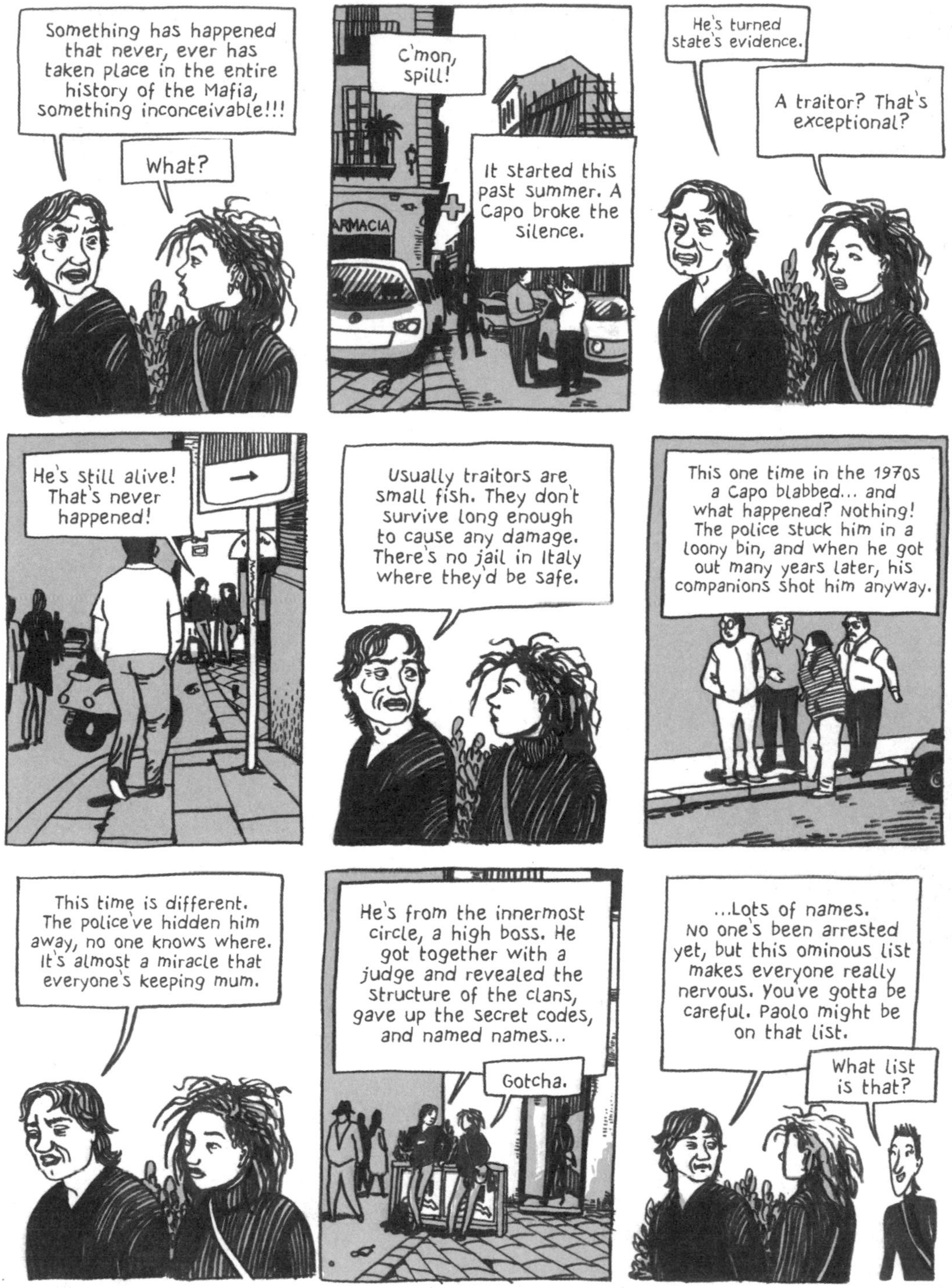
Something has happened that never, ever has taken place in the entire history of the Mafia, something inconceivable!!!
What?
C'mon, spill!
It started this past summer. A Capo broke the silence.
ARMACIA
He's turned state's evidence.
A traitor? That's exceptional?
He's still alive! That's never happened!
Usually traitors are small fish. They don't survive long enough to cause any damage. There's no jail in Italy where they'd be safe.
This one time in the 1970s a Capo blabbed... and what happened? Nothing! The police stuck him in a loony bin, and when he got out many years later, his companions shot him anyway.
This time is different. The police've hidden him away, no one knows where. It's almost a miracle that everyone's keeping mum.
He's from the innermost circle, a high boss. He got together with a judge and revealed the structure of the clans, gave up the secret codes, and named names...
Gotcha.
...Lots of names. No one's been arrested yet, but this ominous list makes everyone really nervous. You've gotta be careful. Paolo might be on that list.
What list is that?

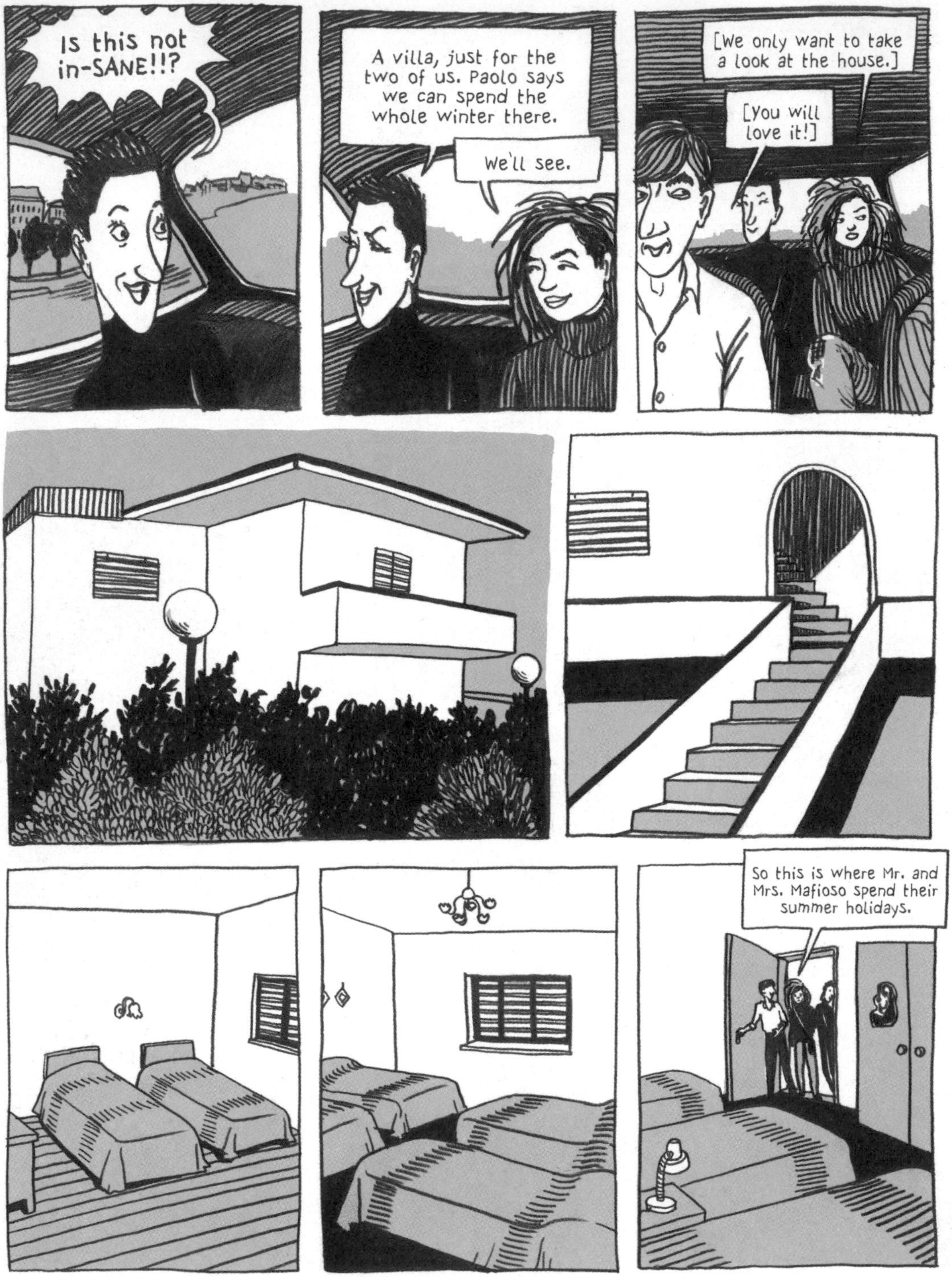
Is this not in-SANE!!?
A villa, just for the two of us. Paolo says we can spend the whole winter there.
We'll see.
[We only want to take a look at the house.]
[You will love it!]
So this is where Mr. and Mrs. Mafioso spend their summer holidays.

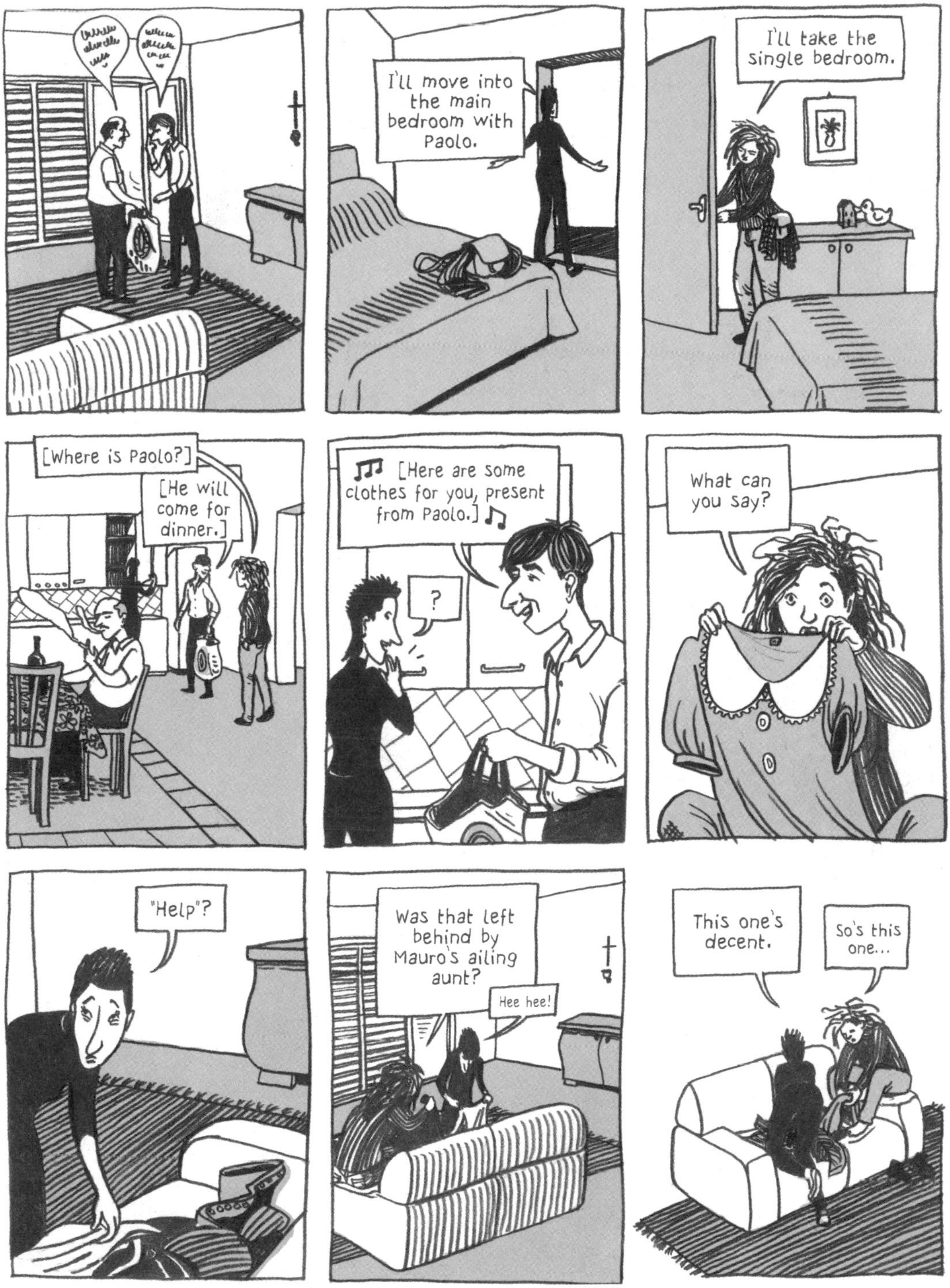

I'll move into the main bedroom with Paolo.
I'll take the single bedroom.
[Where is Paolo?]
[He will come for dinner.]
[Here are some clothes for you, present from Paolo.]
?
What can you say?
"Help"?
Was that left behind by Mauro's ailing aunt?
Hee hee!
This one's decent.
So's this one...

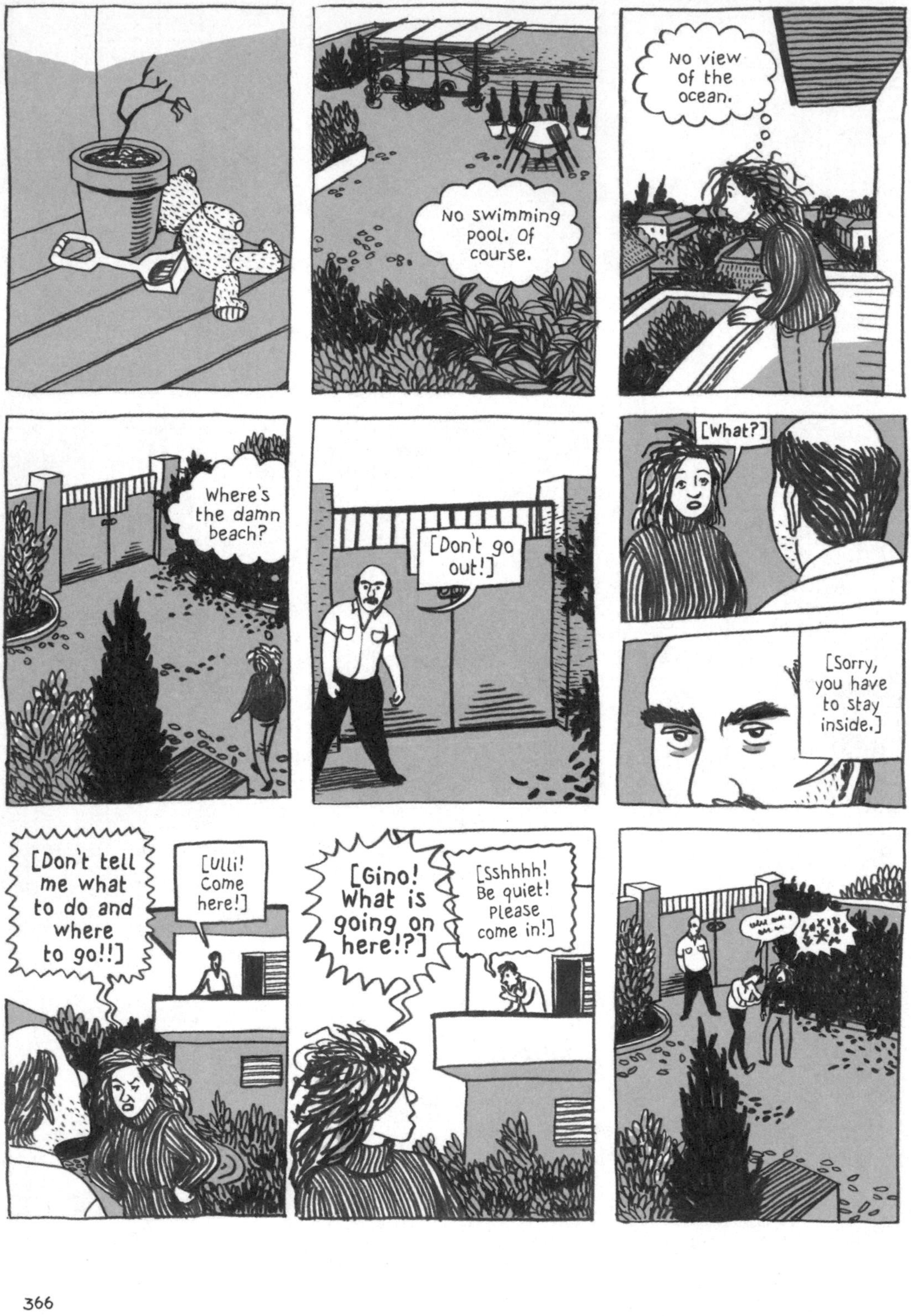
No swimming pool. Of course.
No view of the ocean.
Where's the damn beach?
[Don't go out!]
[What?]
[Sorry, you have to stay inside.]
[Don't tell me what to do and where to go!!]
[Ulli! Come here!]
[Gino! What is going on here!?]
[Sshhhh! Be quiet! Please come in!]

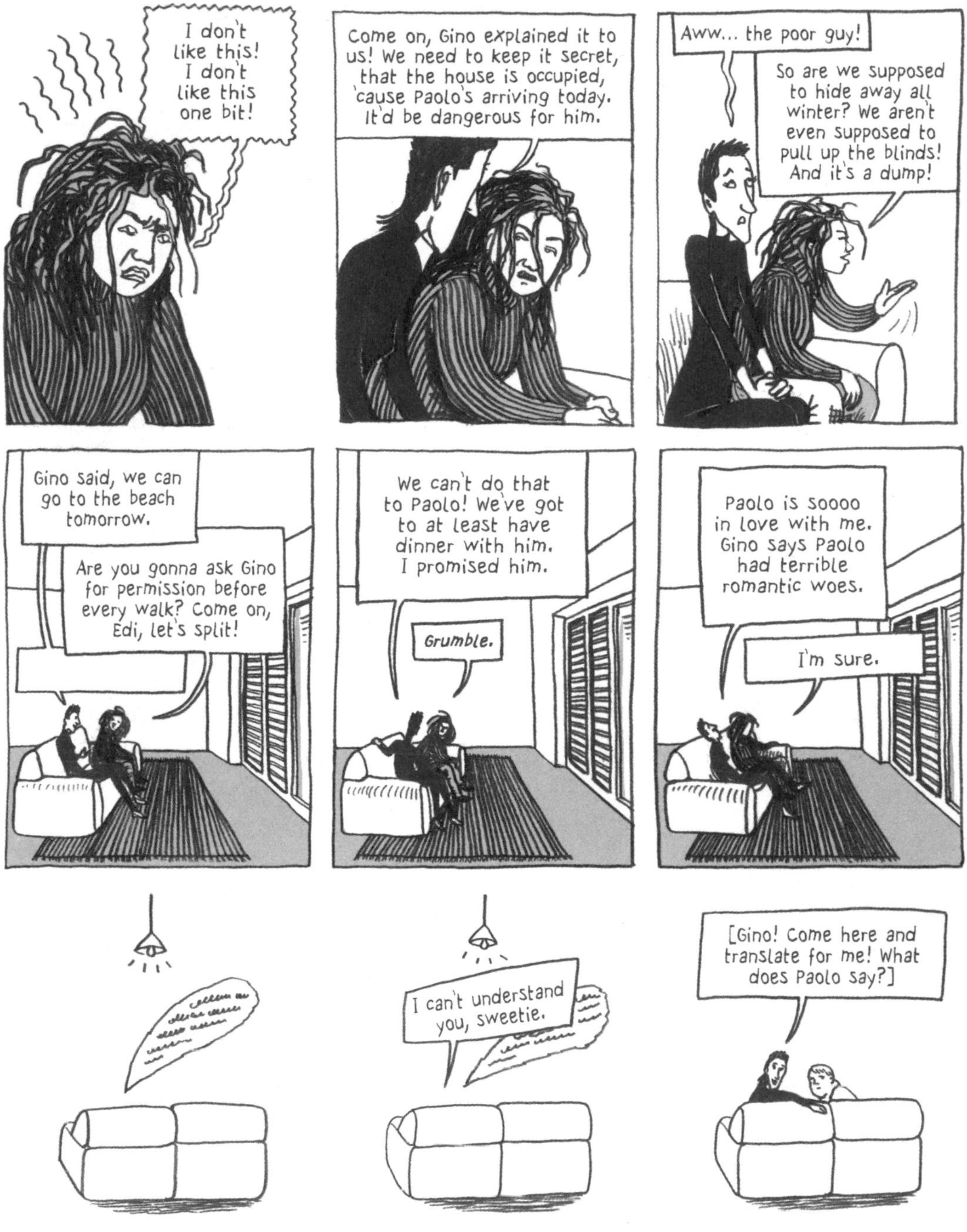
I don't like this! I don't like this one bit!
Come on, Gino explained it to us! We need to keep it secret, that the house is occupied, 'cause Paolo's arriving today. It'd be dangerous for him.
Aww... the poor guy!
So are we supposed to hide away all winter? We aren't even supposed to pull up the blinds! And it's a dump!
Gino said, we can go to the beach tomorrow.
Are you gonna ask Gino for permission before every walk? Come on, Edi, let's split!
We can't do that to Paolo! We've got to at least have dinner with him. I promised him.
Grumble.
Paolo is soooo in love with me. Gino says Paolo had terrible romantic woes.
I'm sure.
I can't understand you, sweetie.
[Gino! Come here and translate for me! What does Paolo say?]

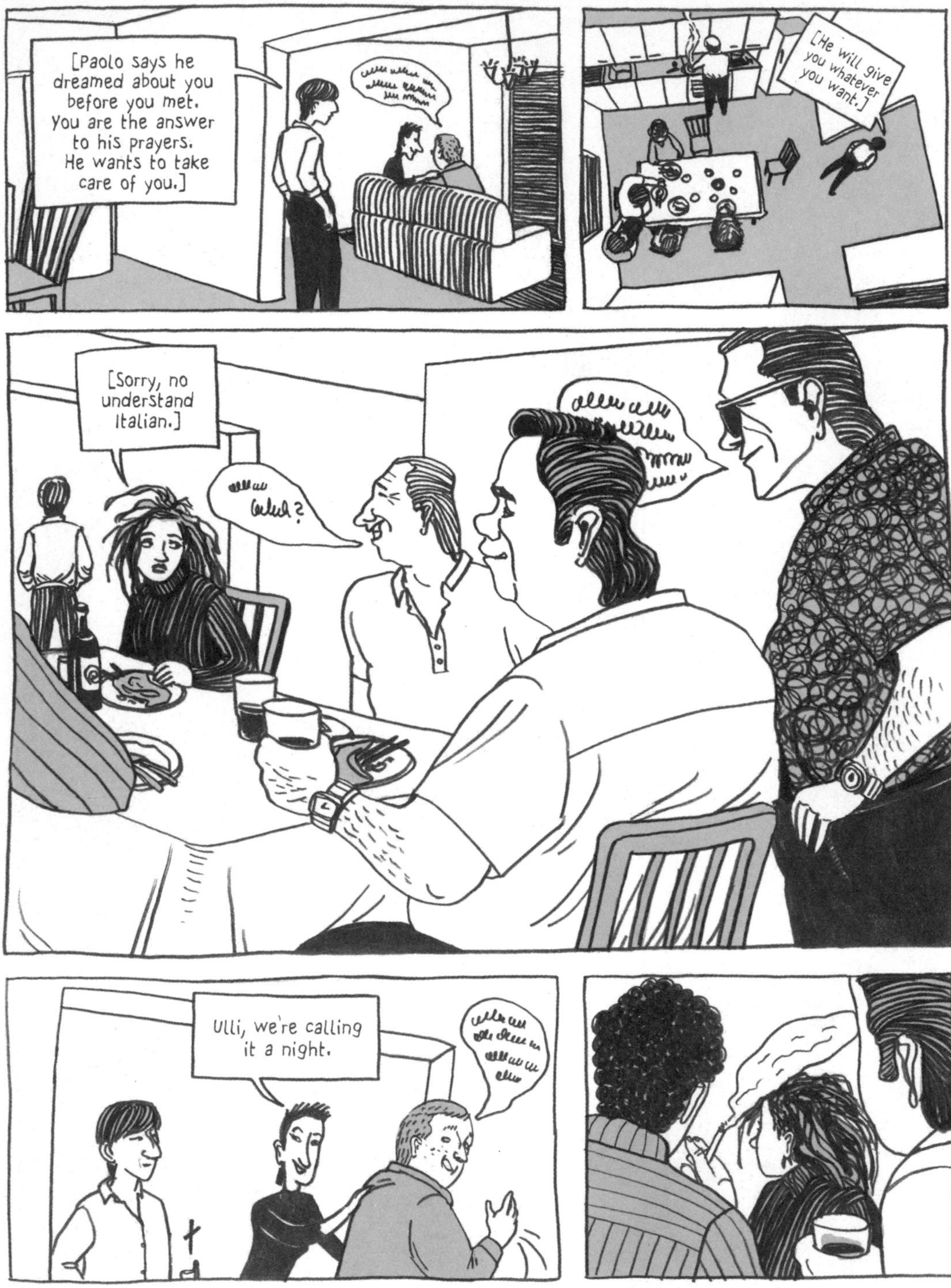
[Paolo says he dreamed about you before you met. You are the answer to his prayers. He wants to take care of you.]
[He will give you whatever you want.]
[Sorry, no understand Italian.]
Ulli, we're calling it a night.

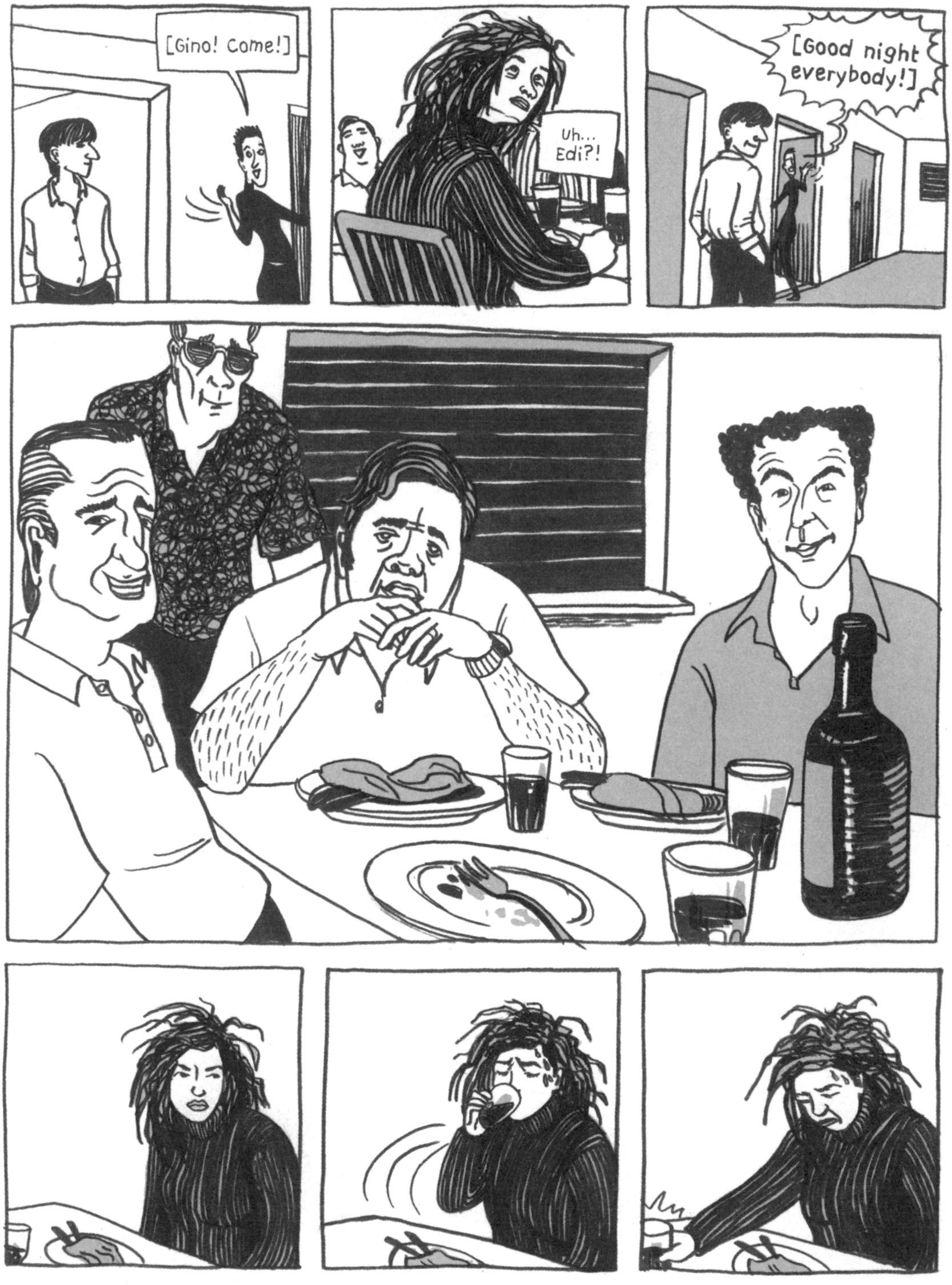
[Gino! Come!]
Uh... Edi?!
[Good night everybody!]

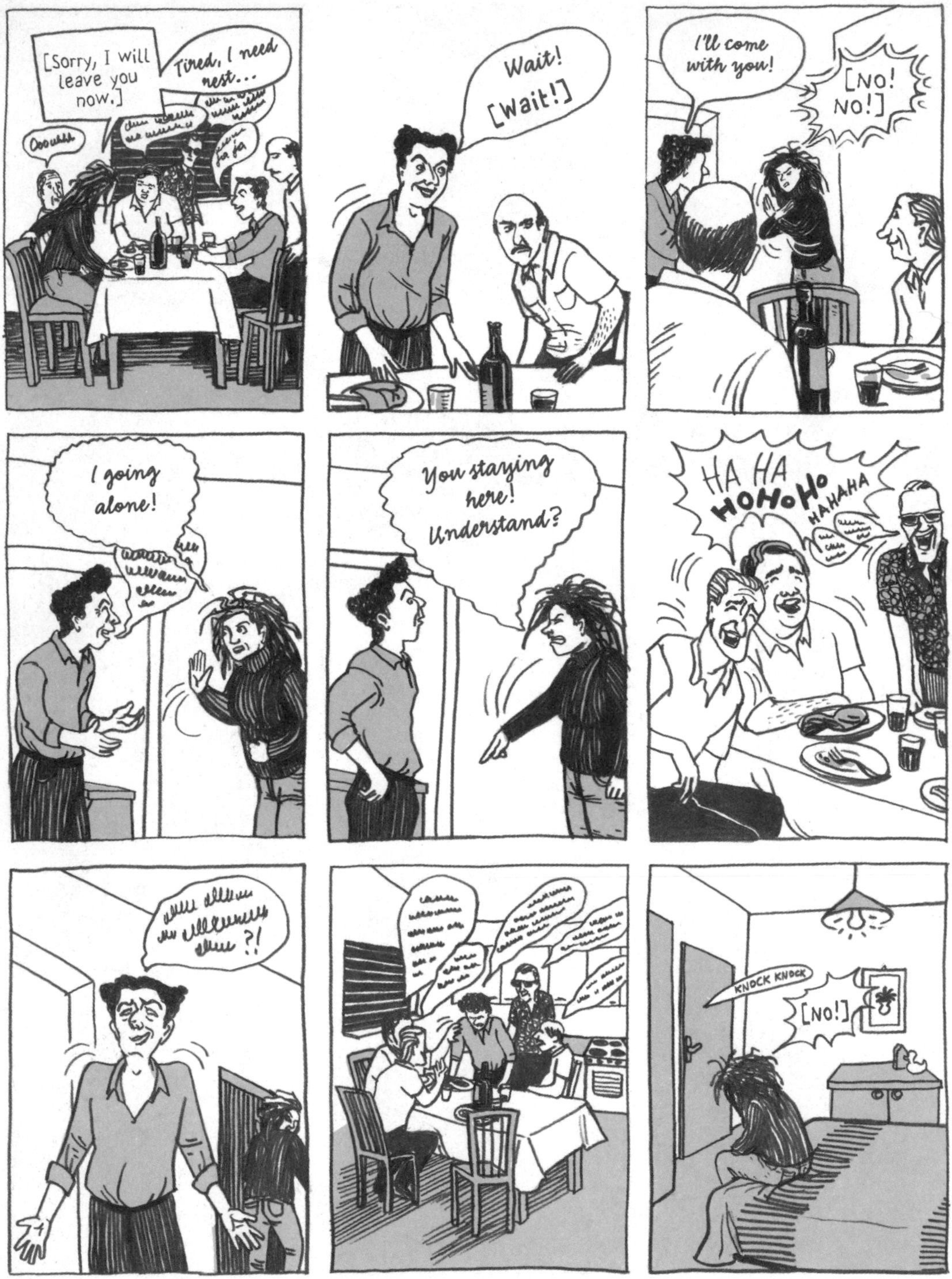
[Sorry, I will leave you now.]
Tired, I need rest...
Oouhh
Wait!
[Wait!]
I'll come with you!
[No! No!]
I going alone!
You staying here! Understand?
HA HA
HOHOHO
HAHAHA
KNOCK KNOCK
[NO!]

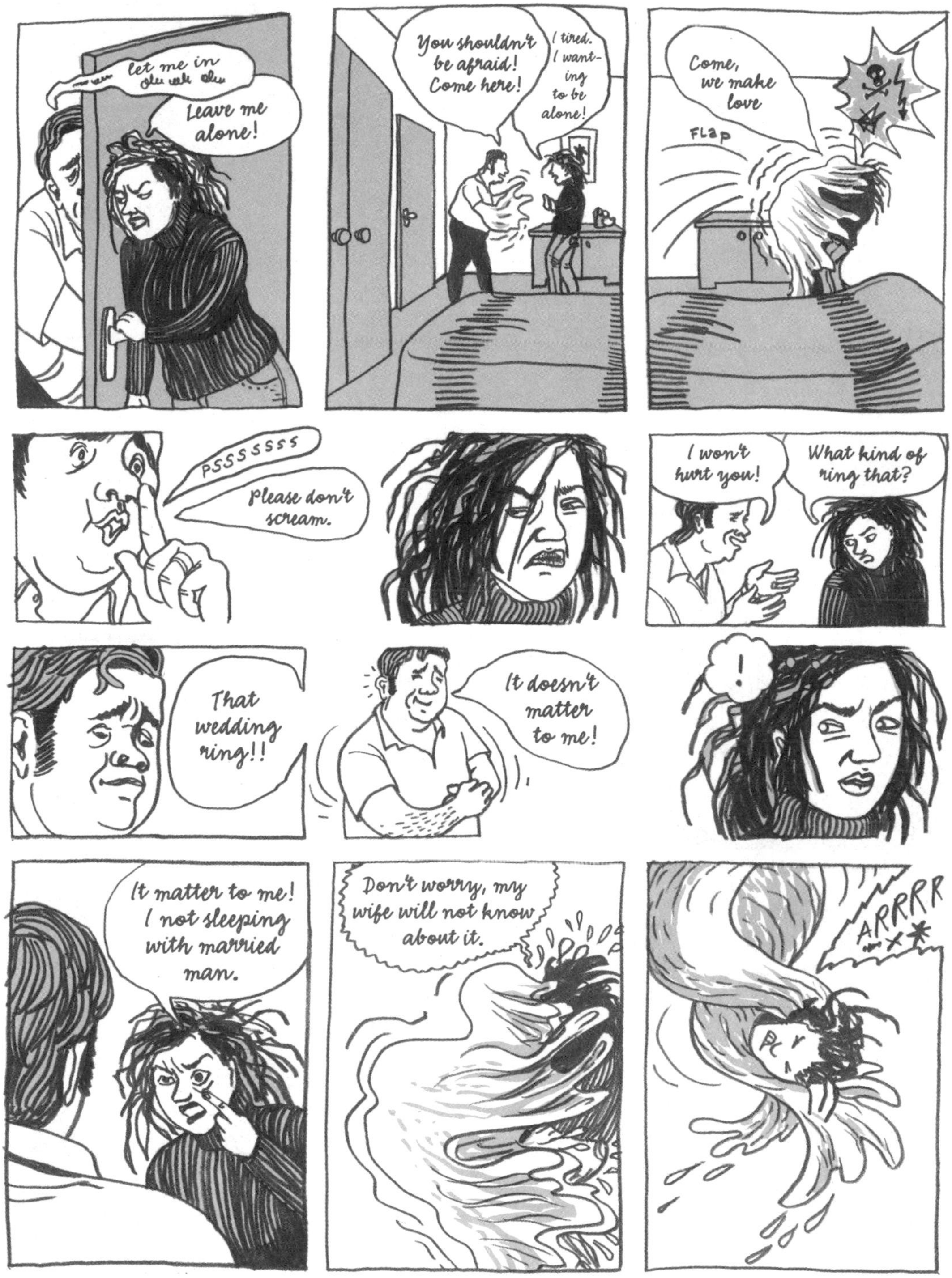
let me in
Leave me alone!
You shouldn't be afraid! Come here!
I tired. I wanting to be alone!
Come, we make love
FLAP
PSSSSSSS
Please don't scream.
I won't hurt you!
What kind of ring that?
That wedding ring!!
It doesn't matter to me!
!
It matter to me! I not sleeping with married man.
Don't worry, my wife will not know about it.
ARRRR

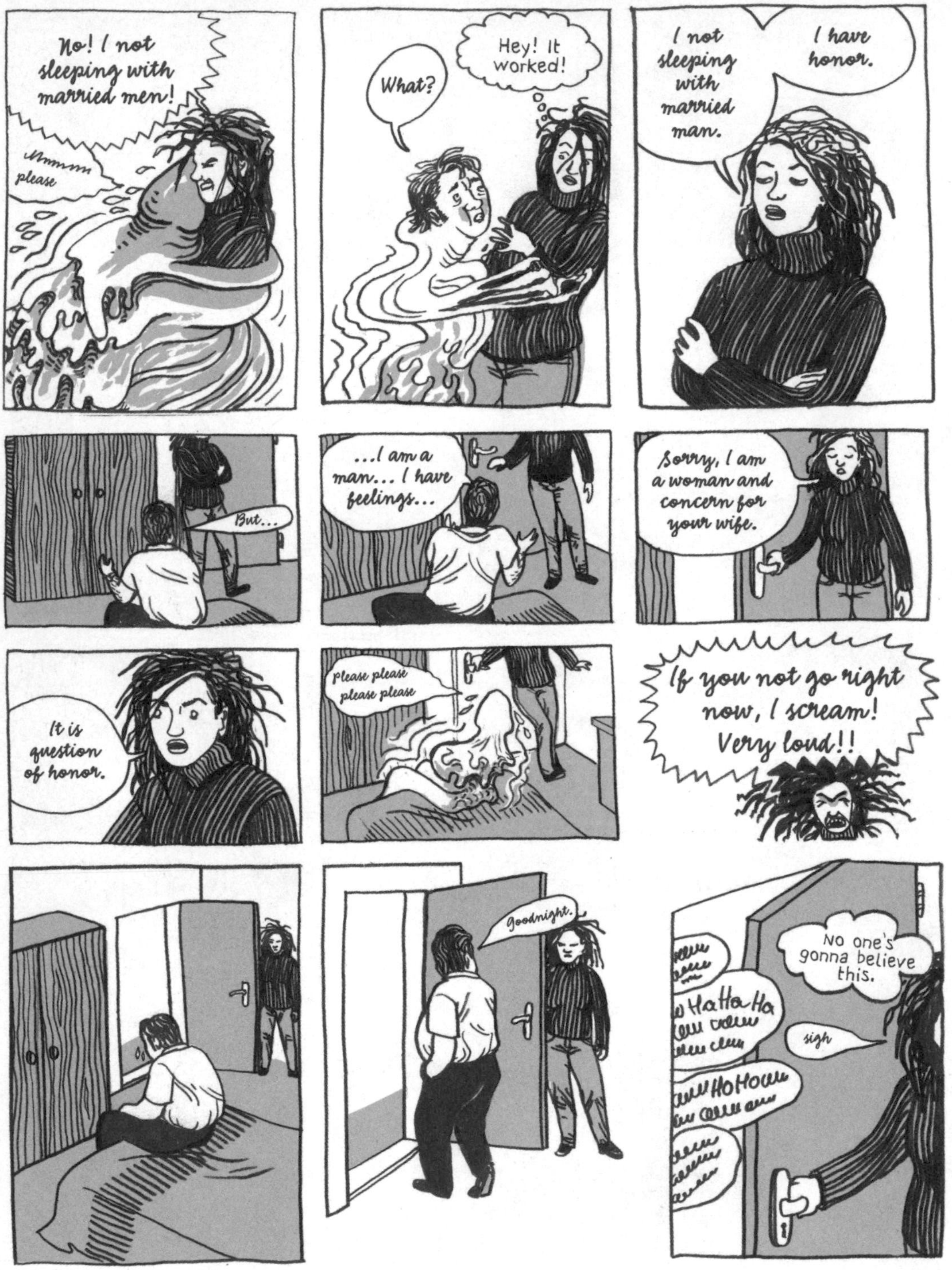
No! I not sleeping with married men!
Mmmmm please
What?
Hey! It worked!
I not sleeping with married man.
I have honor.
But...
...I am a man... I have feelings...
Sorry, I am a woman and concern for your wife.
It is question of honor.
Please please please please
If you not go right now, I scream! Very loud!!
Goodnight.
Ha Ha Ha
Ho Ho
sigh
No one's gonna believe this.

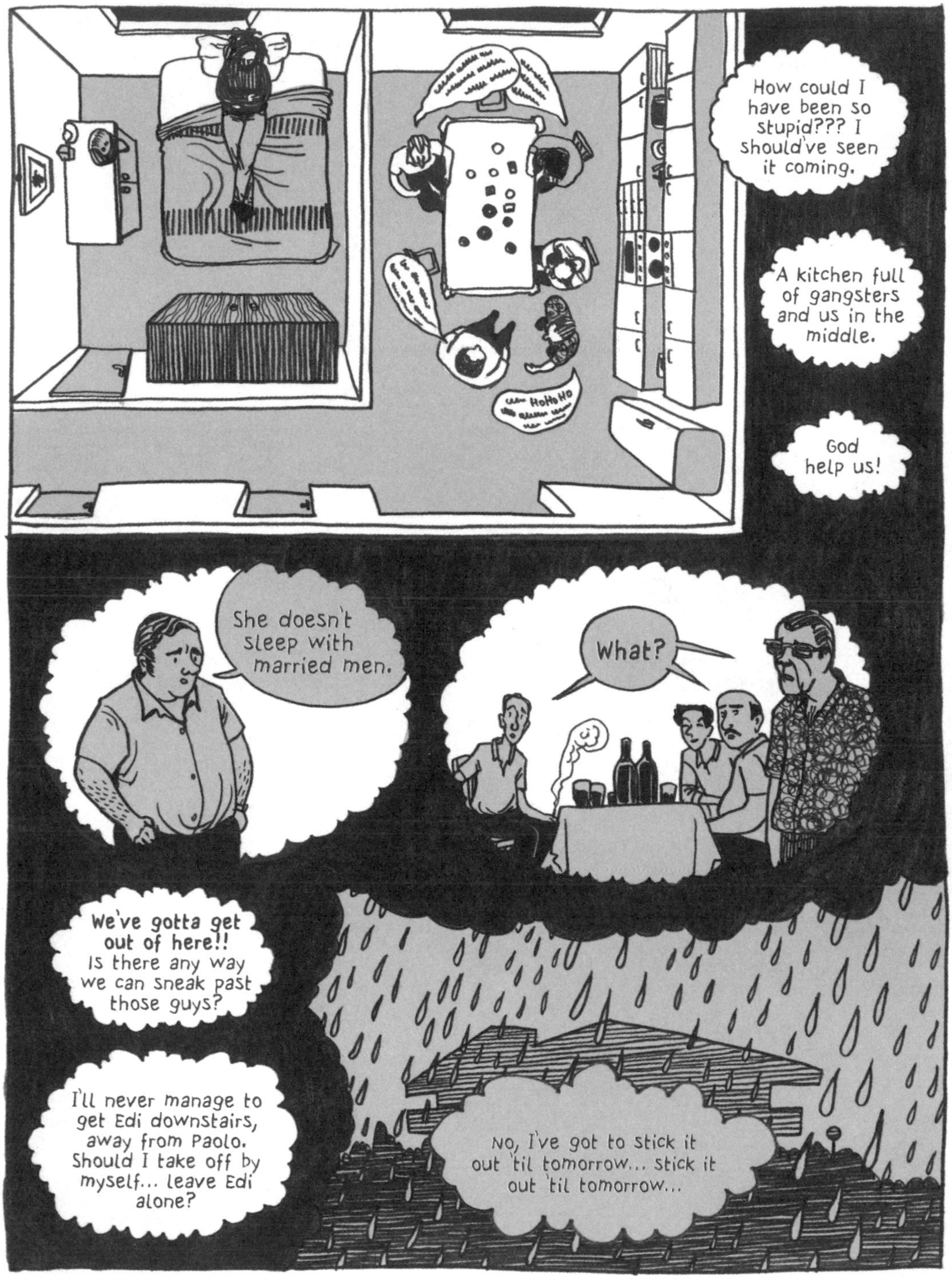
How could I have been so stupid??? I should've seen it coming.
A kitchen full of gangsters and us in the middle.
God help us!
HoHoHo
She doesn't sleep with married men.
What?
We've gotta get out of here!! Is there any way we can sneak past those guys?
I'll never manage to get Edi downstairs, away from Paolo. Should I take off by myself... leave Edi alone?
No, I've got to stick it out 'til tomorrow... stick it out 'til tomorrow...

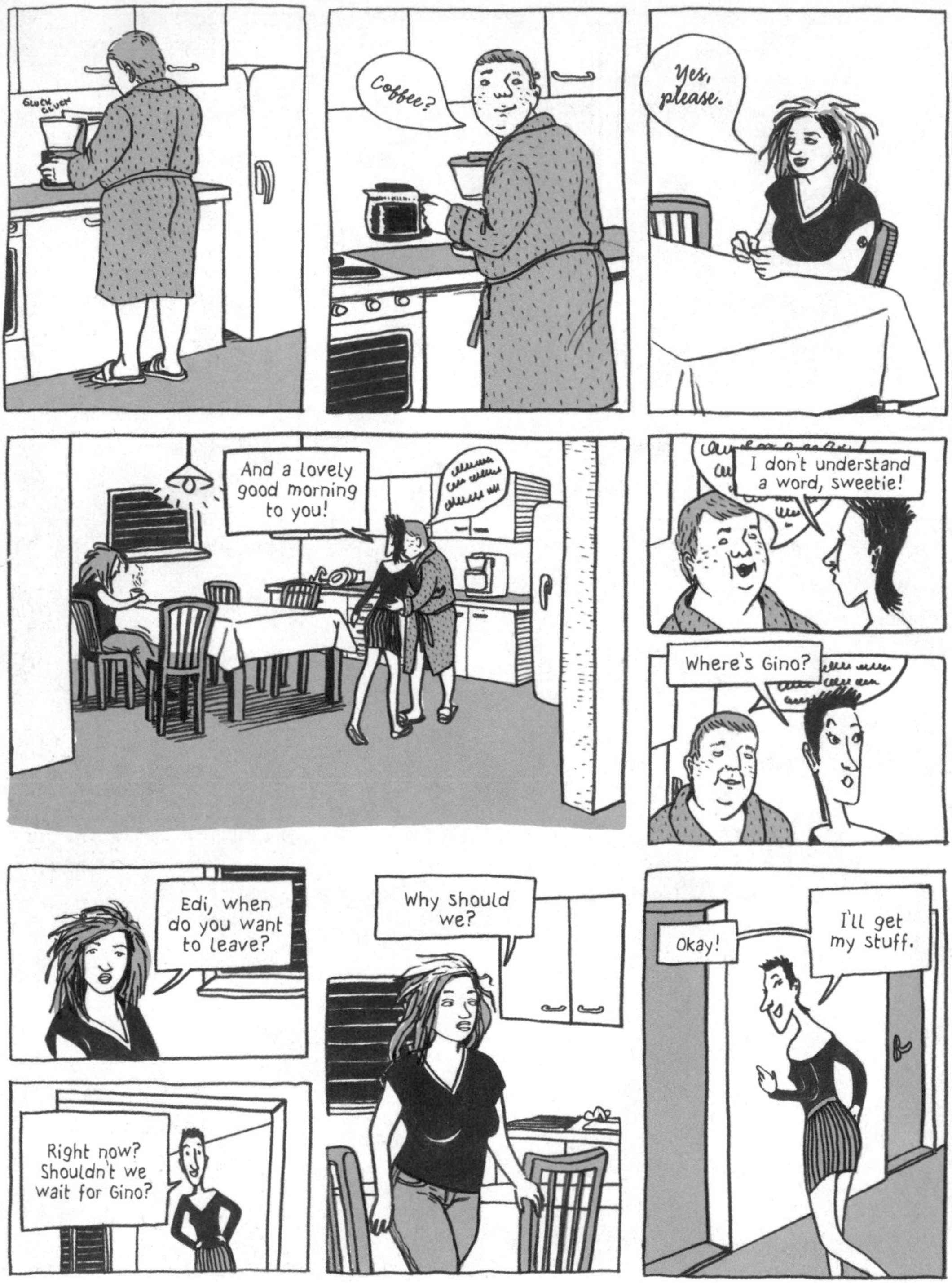
GLUCK GLUCK
Coffee?
Yes, please.
And a lovely good morning to you!
I don't understand a word, sweetie!
Where's Gino?
Edi, when do you want to leave?
Right now? Shouldn't we wait for Gino?
Why should we?
Okay!
I'll get my stuff.

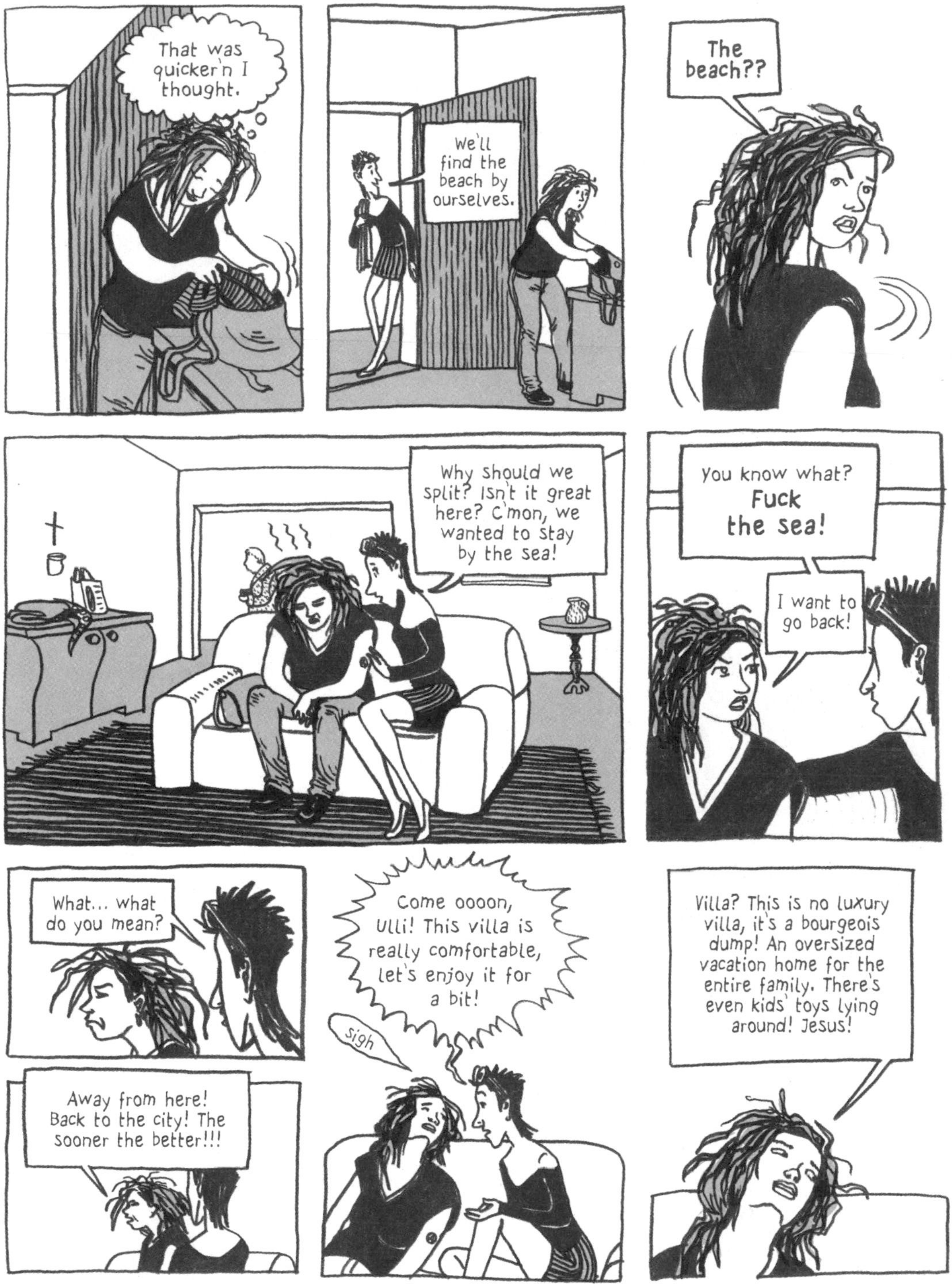
That was quicker'n I thought.
We'll find the beach by ourselves.
The beach??
Why should we split? Isn't it great here? C'mon, we wanted to stay by the sea!
You know what? **Fuck the sea!**
I want to go back!
What... what do you mean?
Away from here! Back to the city! The sooner the better!!!
Come ooooon, Ulli! This villa is really comfortable, let's enjoy it for a bit!
sigh
Villa? This is no luxury villa, it's a bourgeois dump! An oversized vacation home for the entire family. There's even kids' toys lying around! Jesus!

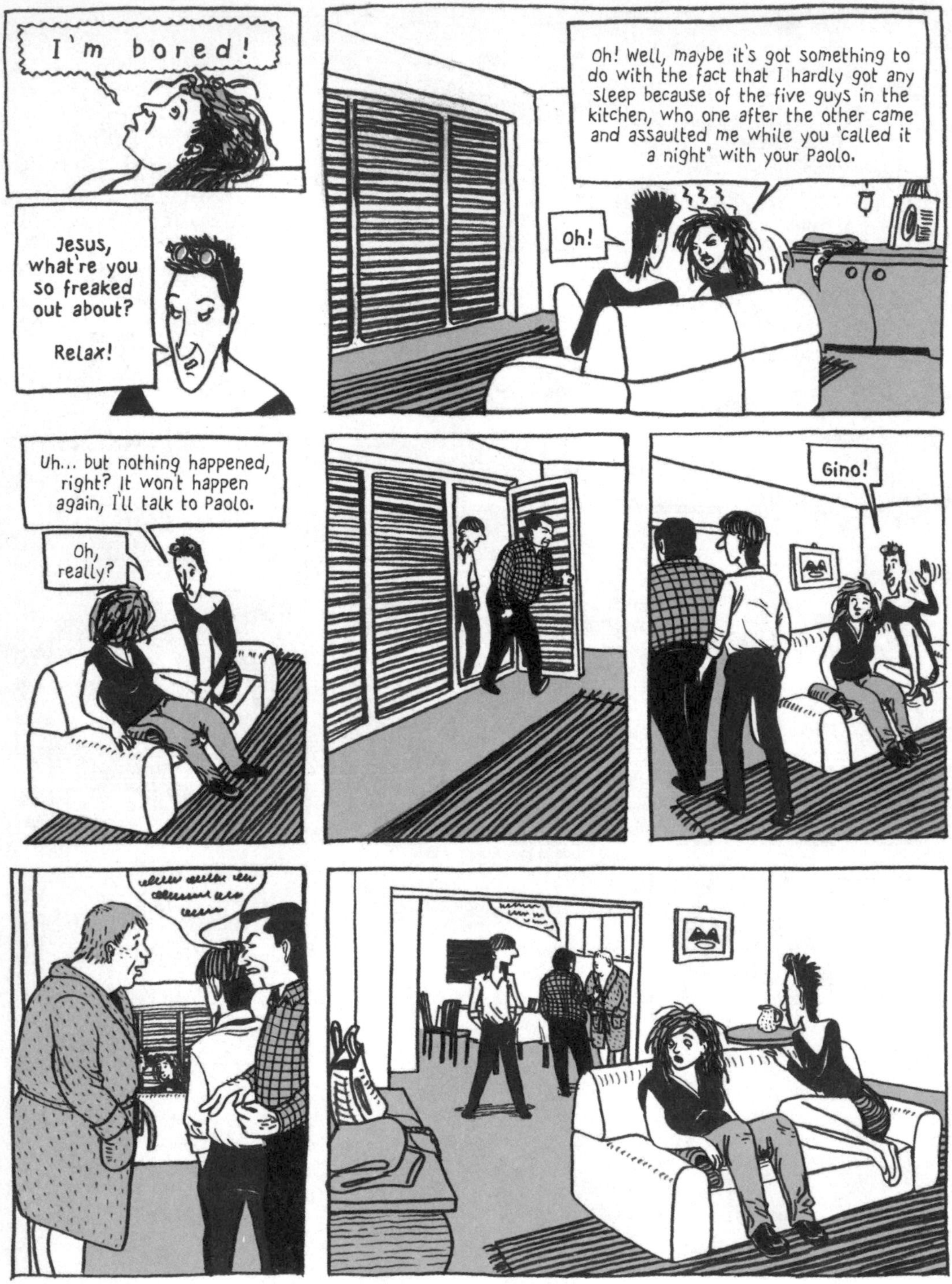
I'm bored!
Jesus, what're you so freaked out about?
Relax!
Oh! Well, maybe it's got something to do with the fact that I hardly got any sleep because of the five guys in the kitchen, who one after the other came and assaulted me while you "called it a night" with your Paolo.
Oh!
Uh... but nothing happened, right? It won't happen again, I'll talk to Paolo.
Oh, really?
Gino!

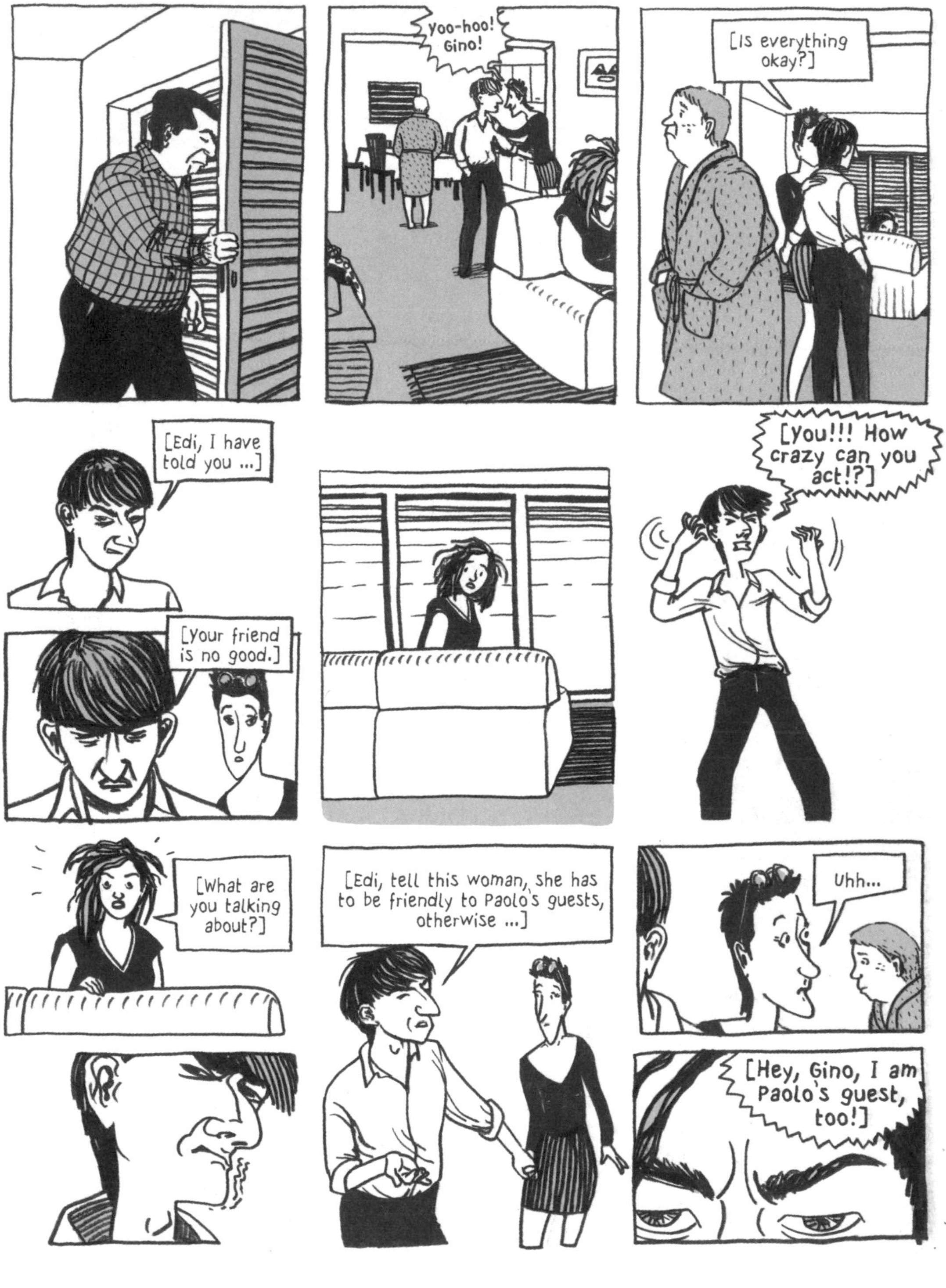
Yoo-hoo! Gino!
[Is everything okay?]
[Edi, I have told you ...]
[Your friend is no good.]
[You!!! How crazy can you act!?]
[What are you talking about?]
[Edi, tell this woman, she has to be friendly to Paolo's guests, otherwise ...]
Uhh...
[Hey, Gino, I am Paolo's guest, too!]

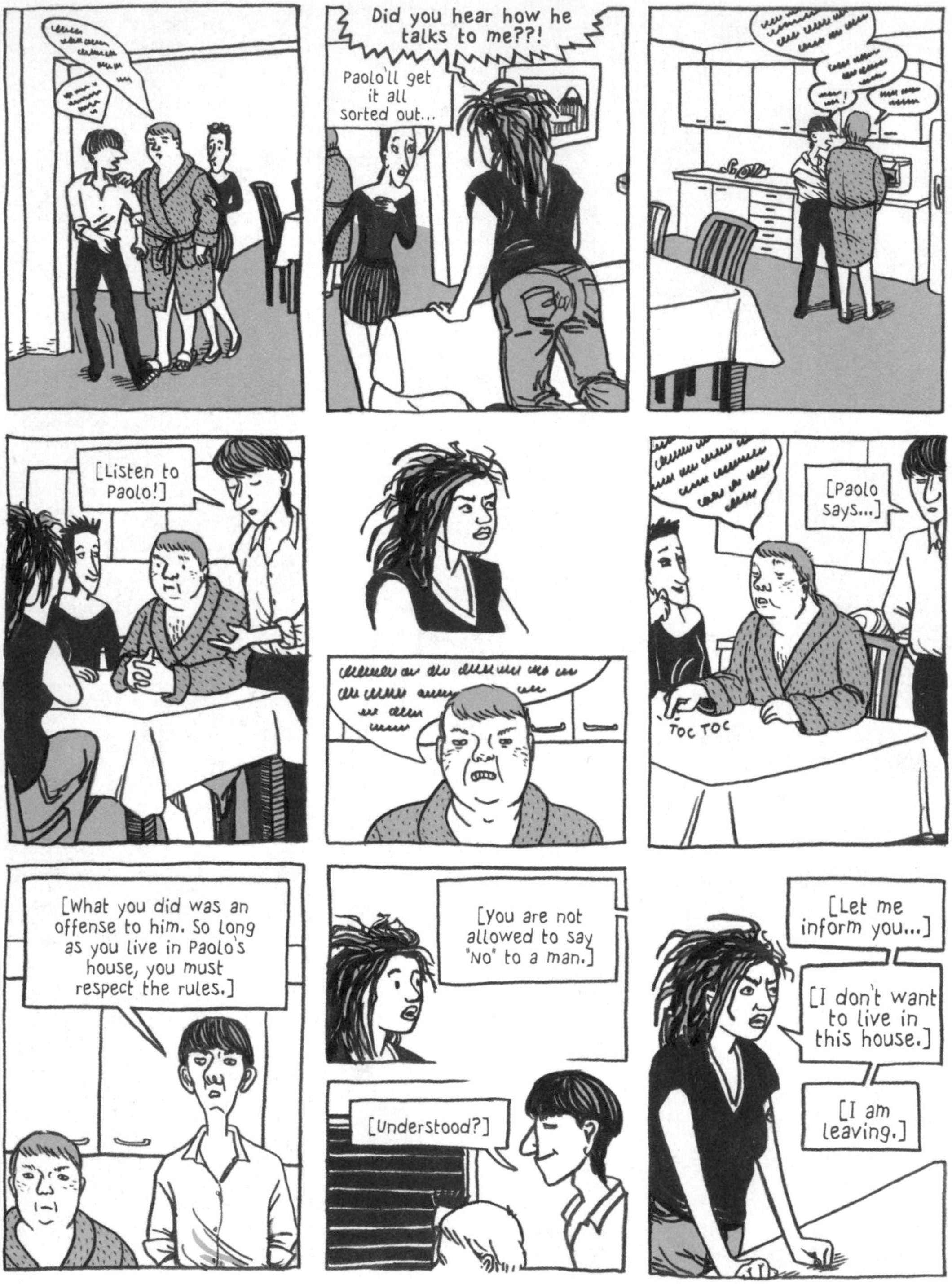
Did you hear how he talks to me??!
Paolo'll get it all sorted out...
[Listen to Paolo!]
[Paolo says...]
TOC TOC
[What you did was an offense to him. So long as you live in Paolo's house, you must respect the rules.]
[You are not allowed to say "No" to a man.]
[Understood?]
[Let me inform you...]
[I don't want to live in this house.]
[I am leaving.]

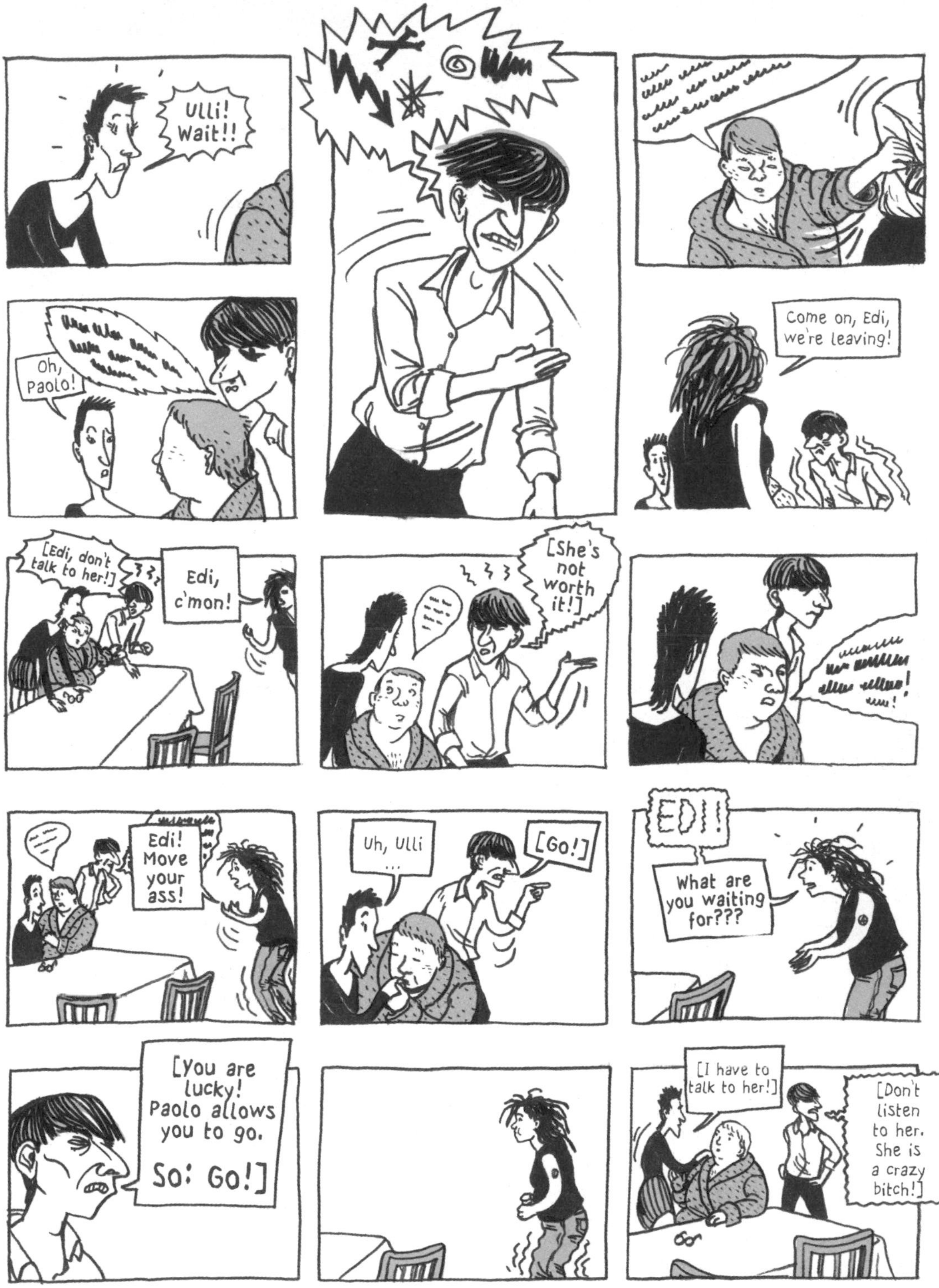
Ulli! Wait!!
Oh, Paolo!
Come on, Edi, we're leaving!
[Edi, don't talk to her!]
Edi, c'mon!
[She's not worth it!]
Edi! Move your ass!
Uh, Ulli ...
[Go!]
EDI!
What are you waiting for???
[You are lucky! Paolo allows you to go.
So: Go!]
[I have to talk to her!]
[Don't listen to her. She is a crazy bitch!]

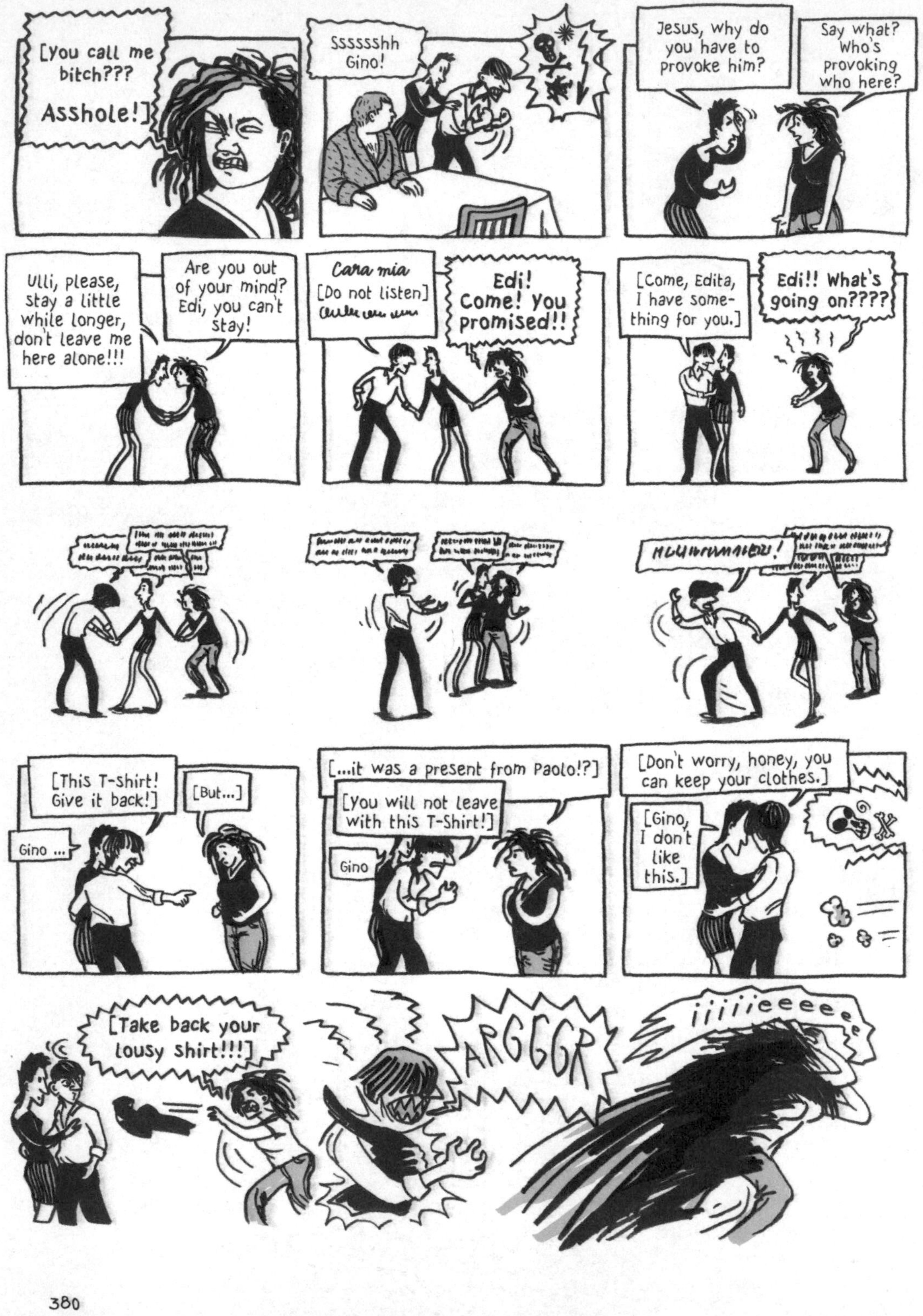
[You call me bitch???
Asshole!]
Sssssshh Gino!
Jesus, why do you have to provoke him?
Say what? Who's provoking who here?
Ulli, please, stay a little while longer, don't leave me here alone!!!
Are you out of your mind? Edi, you can't stay!
Cara mia
[Do not listen]
Edi! Come! You promised!!
[Come, Edita, I have something for you.]
Edi!! What's going on????
[This T-shirt! Give it back!]
[But...]
Gino ...
[...it was a present from Paolo!?]
[You will not leave with this T-Shirt!]
Gino
[Don't worry, honey, you can keep your clothes.]
[Gino, I don't like this.]
[Take back your lousy shirt!!!]
ARGGGR
iiiiieeeee

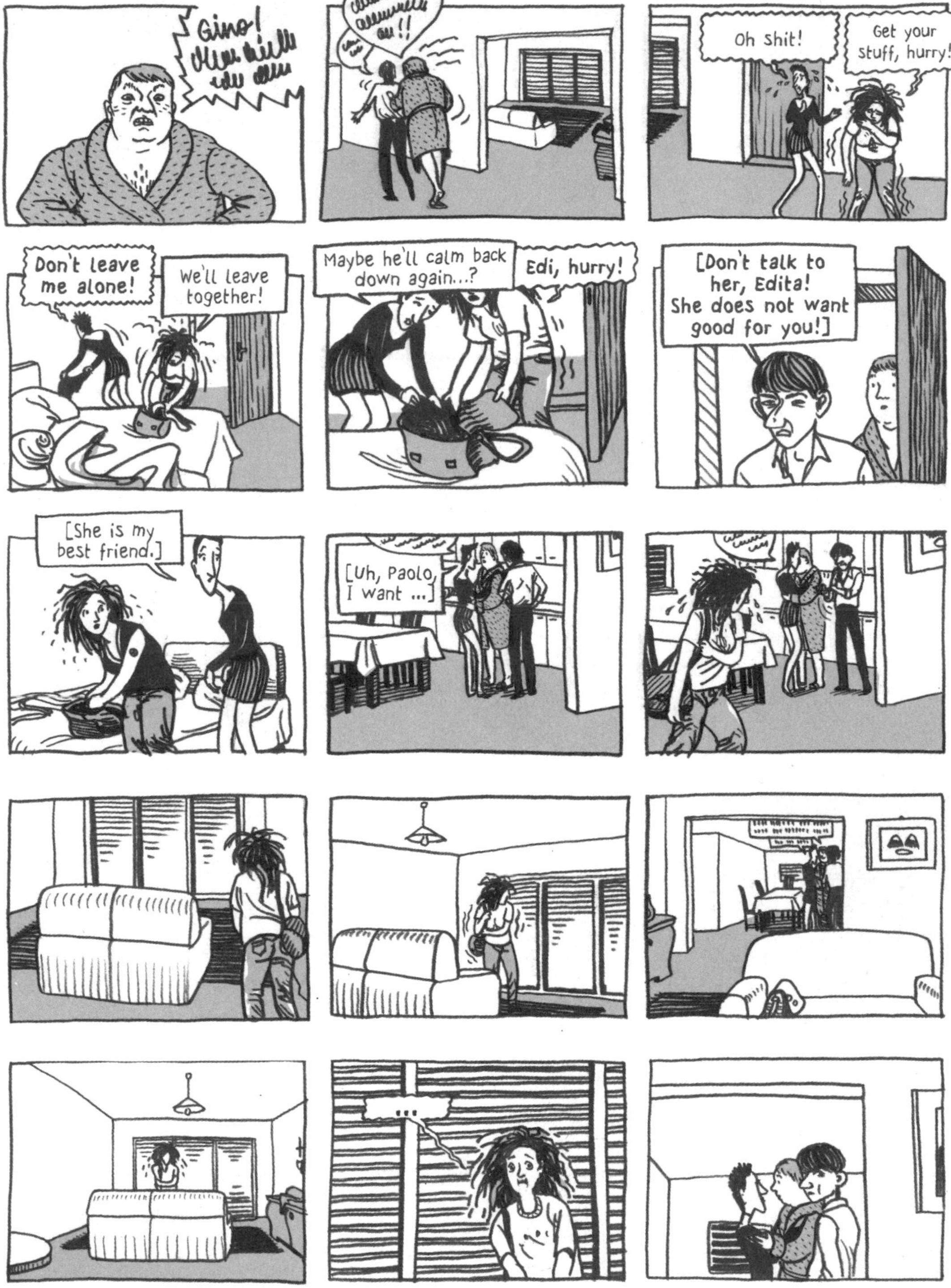
Gino!
Oh shit!
Get your stuff, hurry!
Don't leave me alone!
We'll leave together!
Maybe he'll calm back down again...?
Edi, hurry!
[Don't talk to her, Edita! She does not want good for you!]
[She is my best friend.]
[Uh, Paolo, I want ...]
...

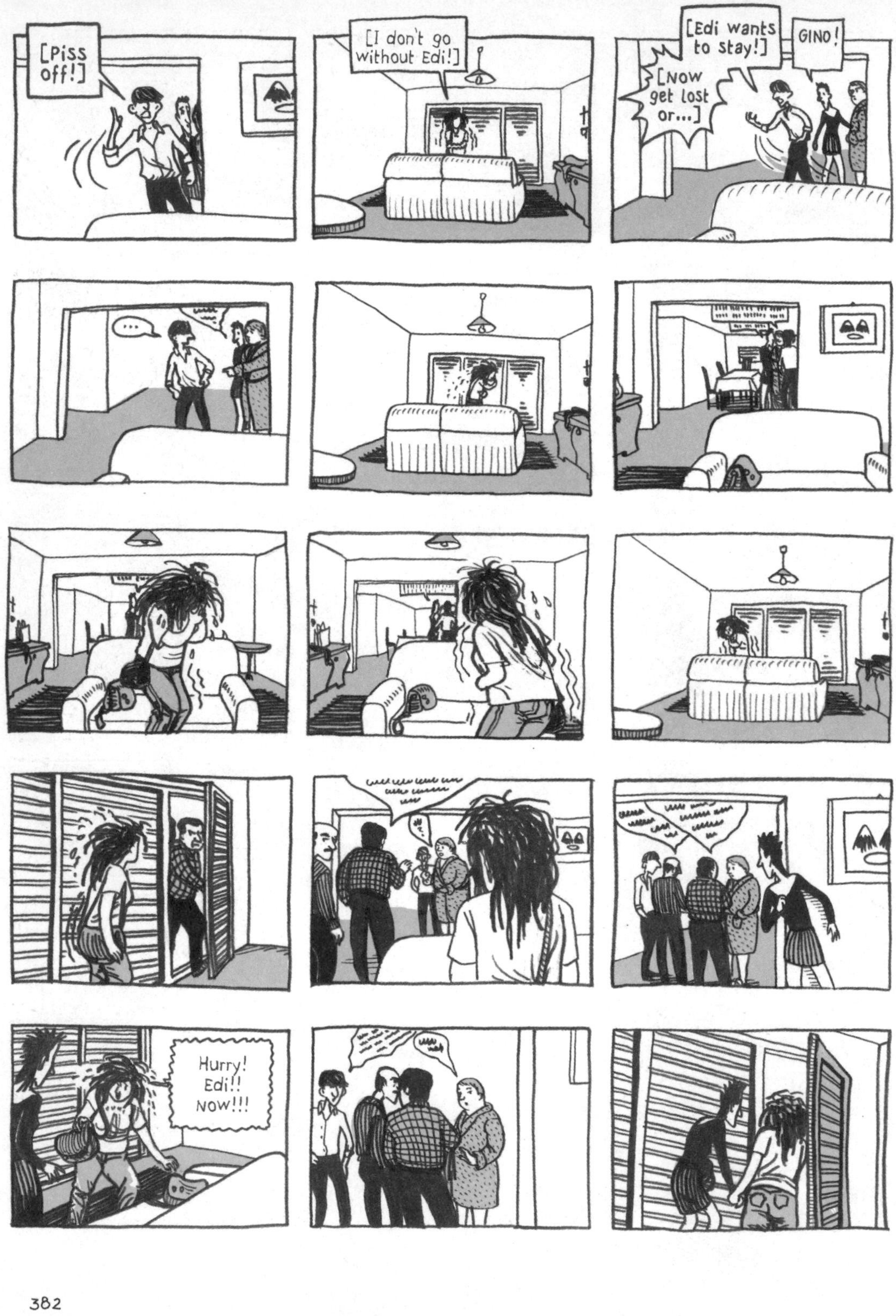
[Piss off!]
[I don't go without Edi!]
[Edi wants to stay!]
GINO!
[Now get lost or...]
...
Hurry! Edi!! Now!!!

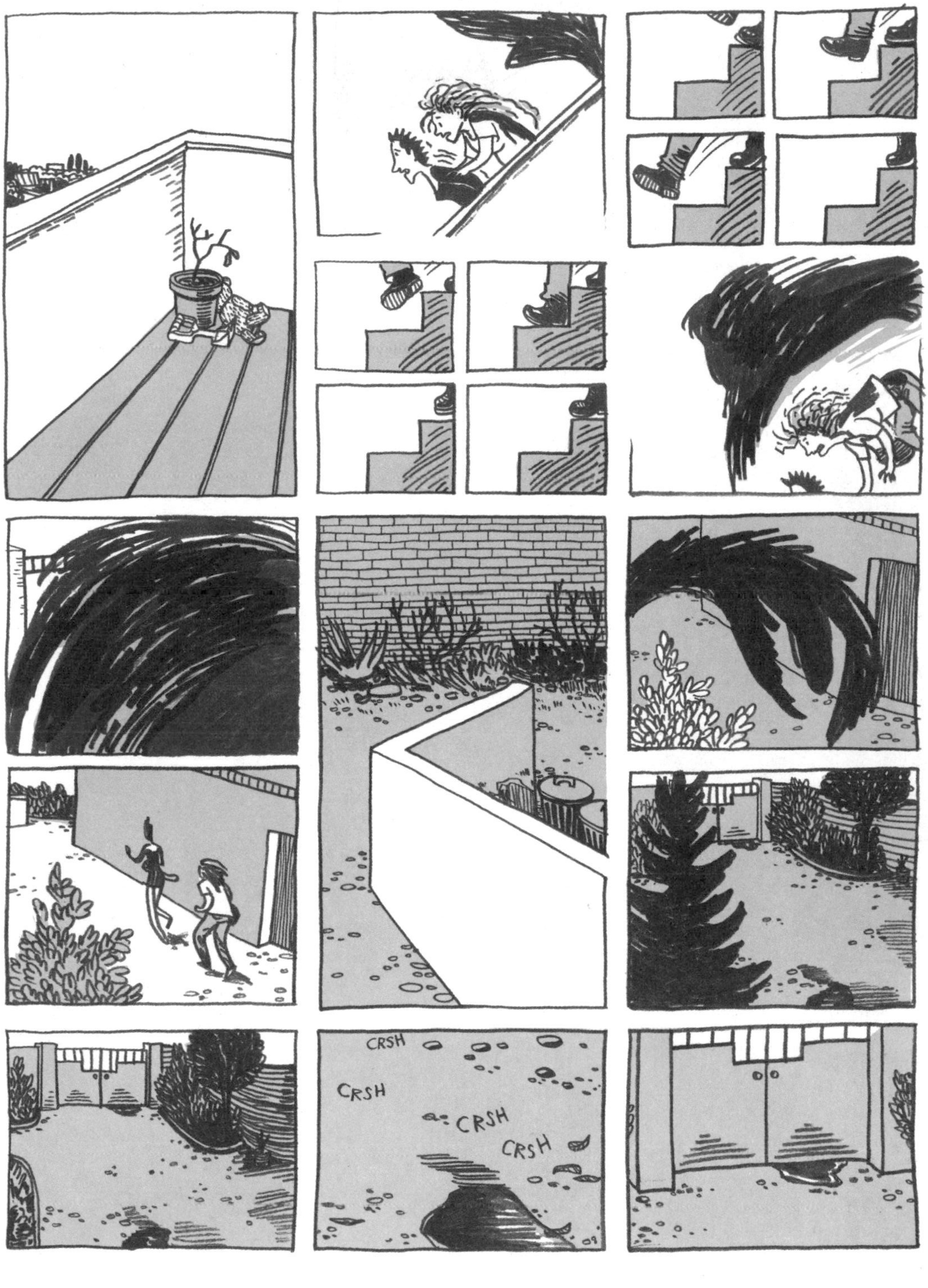
CRSH
CRSH
CRSH
CRSH

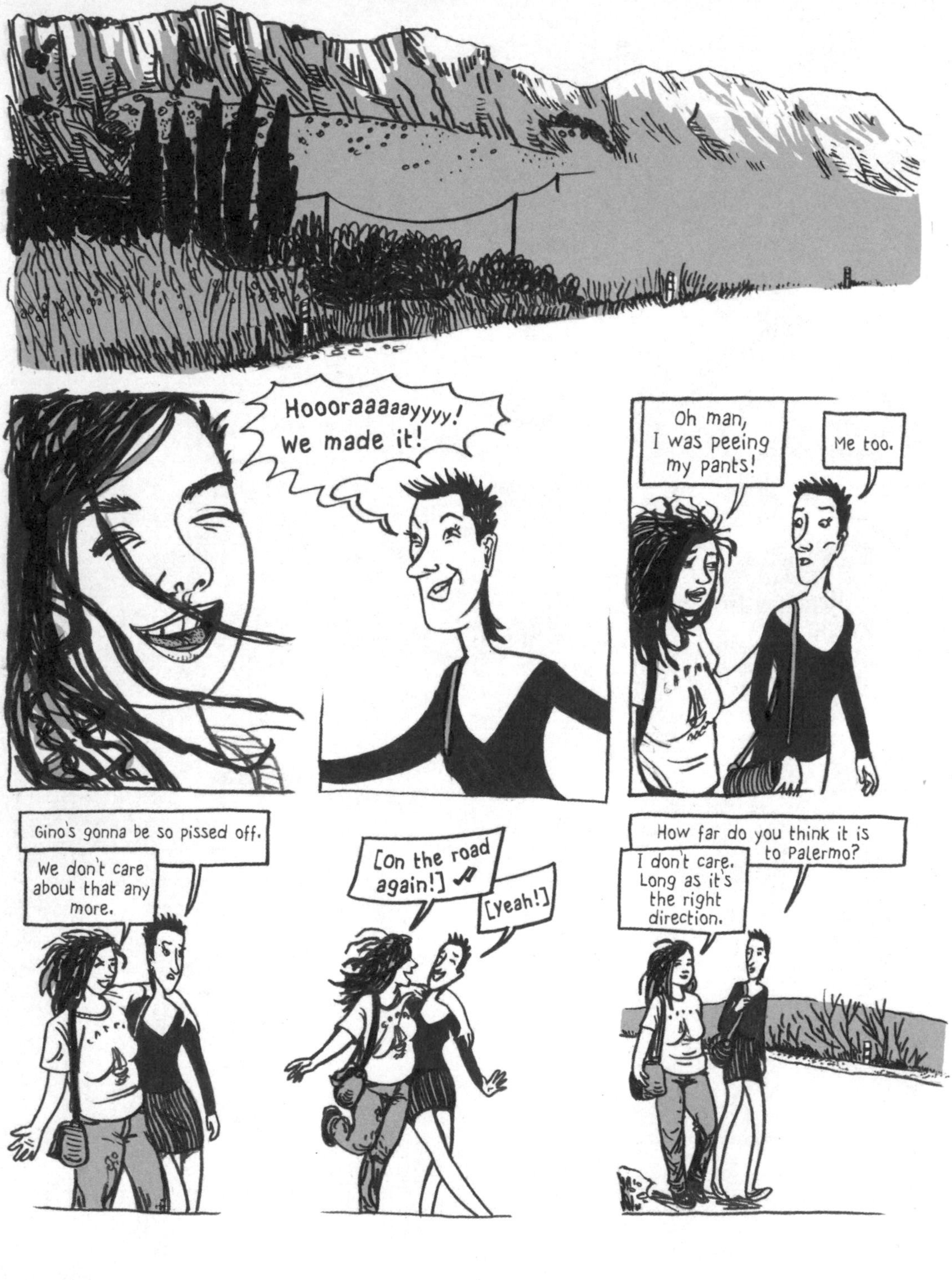
Hoooraaaaayyyy! We made it!
Oh man, I was peeing my pants!
Me too.
Gino's gonna be so pissed off.
We don't care about that any more.
[On the road again!]
[Yeah!]
How far do you think it is to Palermo?
I don't care. Long as it's the right direction.

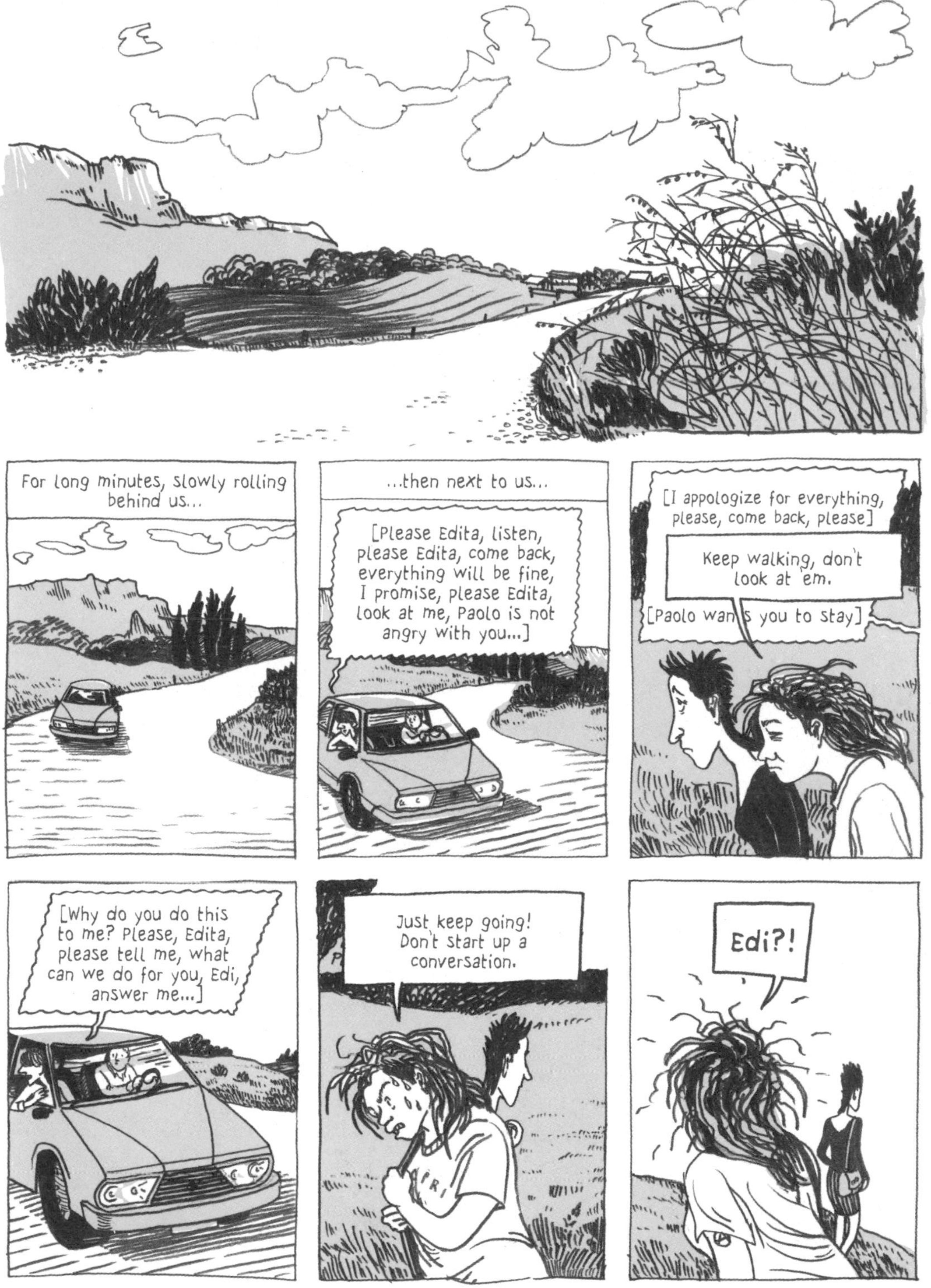
For long minutes, slowly rolling behind us...
...then next to us...
[Please Edita, listen, please Edita, come back, everything will be fine, I promise, please Edita, look at me, Paolo is not angry with you...]
[I appologize for everything, please, come back, please]
Keep walking, don't look at 'em.
[Paolo wants you to stay]
[Why do you do this to me? Please, Edita, please tell me, what can we do for you, Edi, answer me...]
Just keep going! Don't start up a conversation.
Edi?!

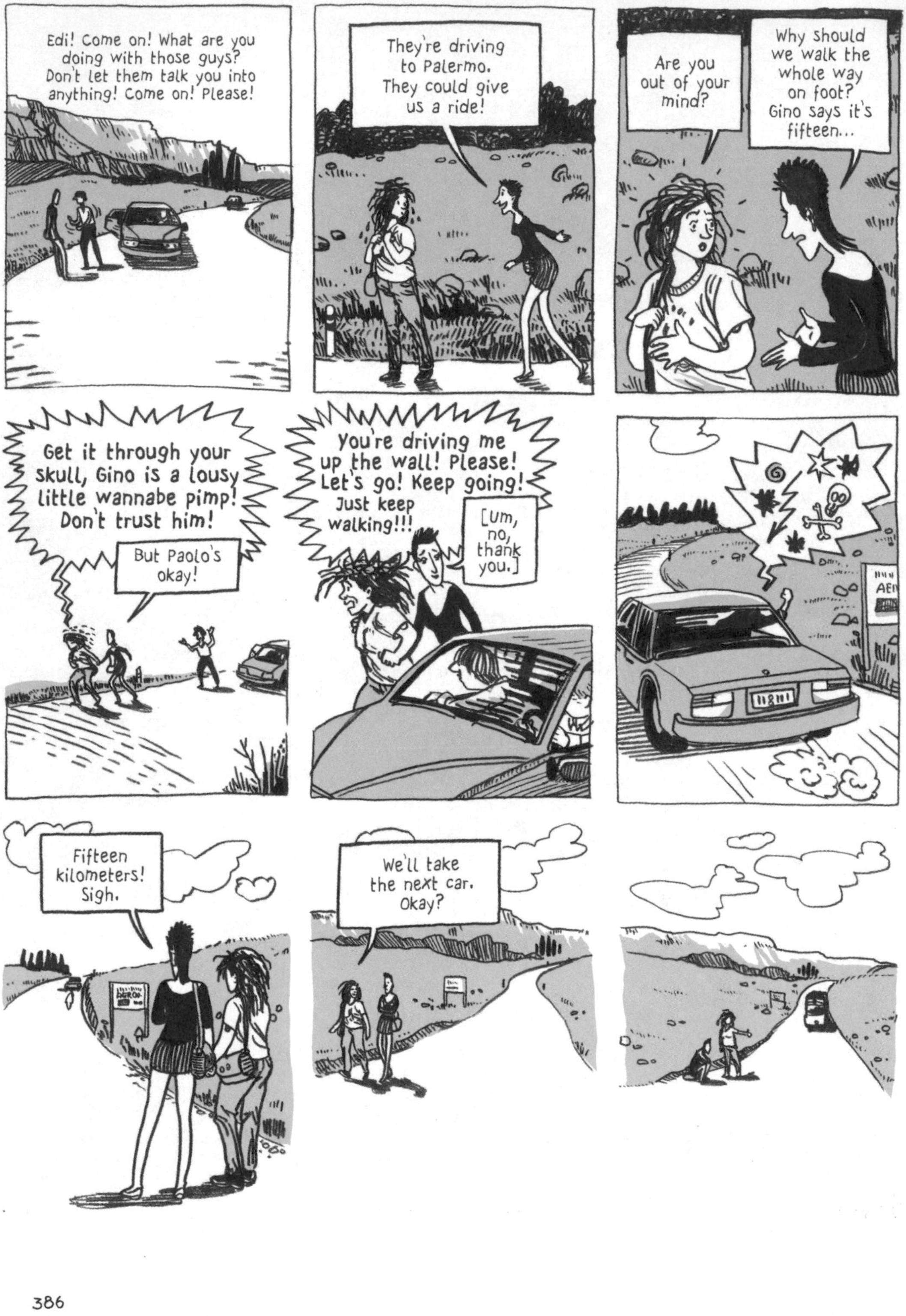
Edi! Come on! What are you doing with those guys? Don't let them talk you into anything! Come on! Please!
They're driving to Palermo. They could give us a ride!
Are you out of your mind?
Why should we walk the whole way on foot? Gino says it's fifteen...
Get it through your skull, Gino is a lousy little wannabe pimp! Don't trust him!
But Paolo's okay!
You're driving me up the wall! Please! Let's go! Keep going! Just keep walking!!!
[Um, no, thank you.]
AEN
Fifteen kilometers! Sigh.
We'll take the next car. Okay?

XVII. the BETRAYAL

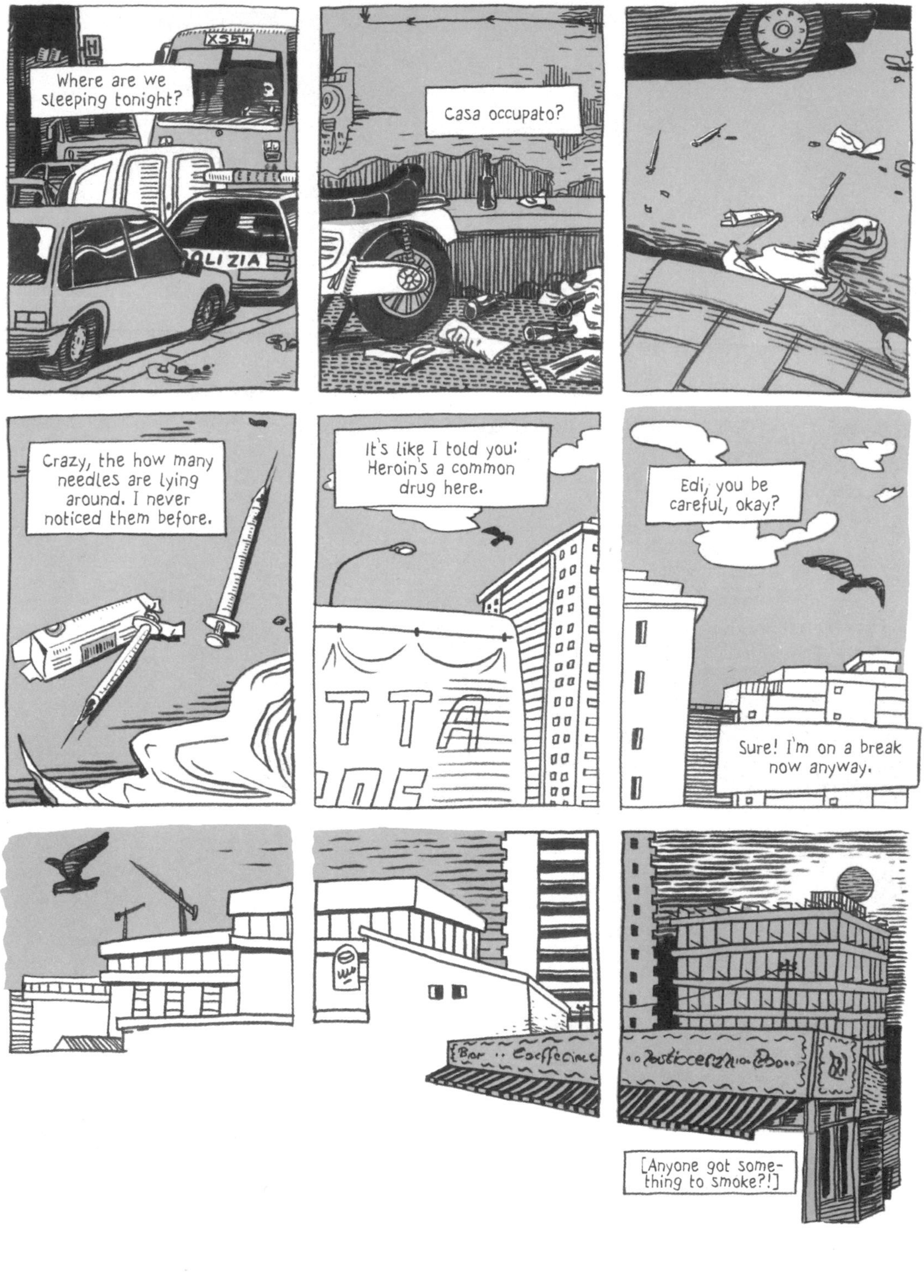

Where are we sleeping tonight?
XS54
OLIZIA
Casa occupato?
Crazy, the how many needles are lying around. I never noticed them before.
It's like I told you: Heroin's a common drug here.
TTA
Edi, you be careful, okay?
Sure! I'm on a break now anyway.
[Anyone got something to smoke?!]

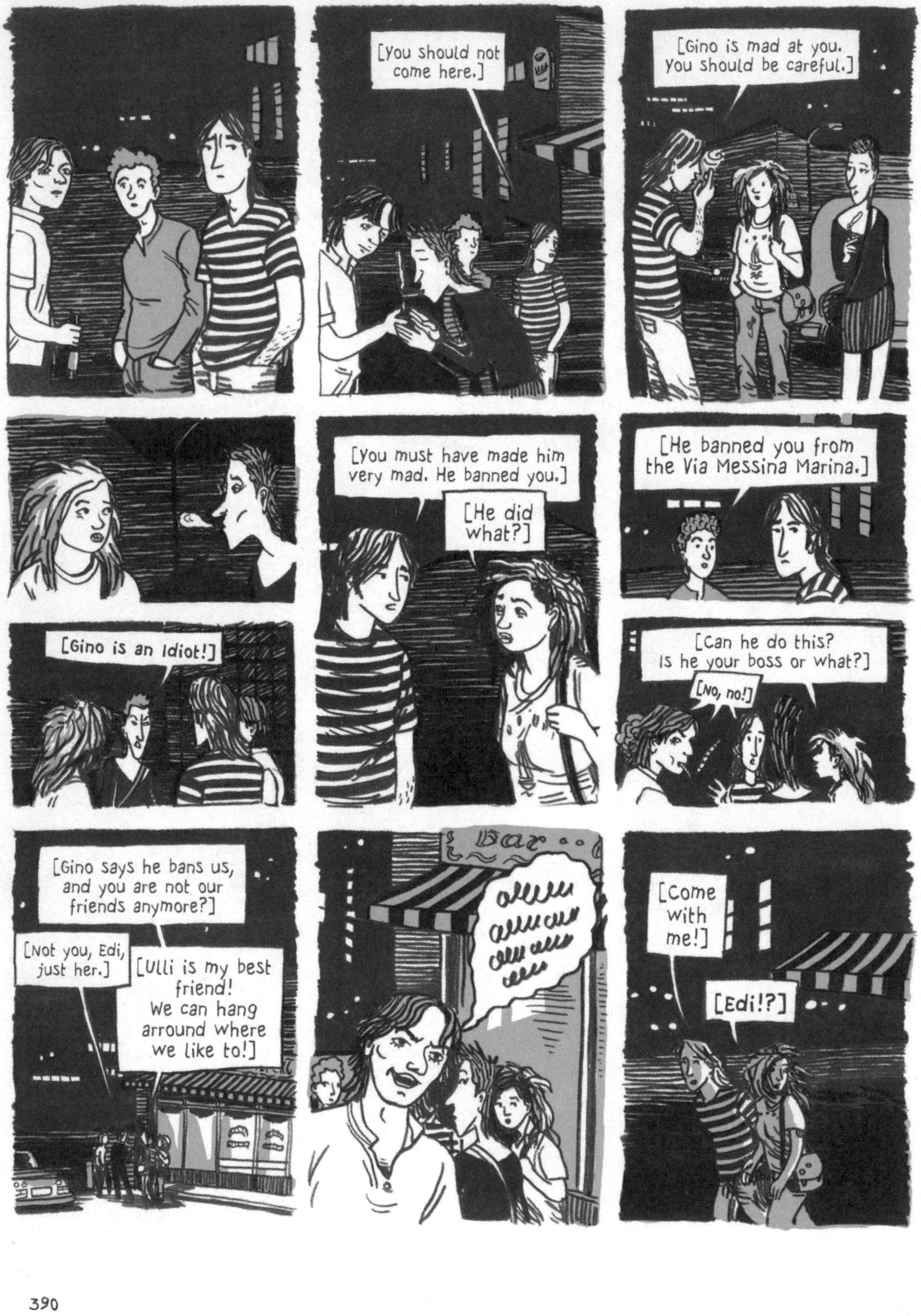

[You should not come here.]
[Gino is mad at you. You should be careful.]
[You must have made him very mad. He banned you.]
[He did what?]
[He banned you from the Via Messina Marina.]
[Gino is an Idiot!]
[Can he do this? Is he your boss or what?]
[No, no!]
[Gino says he bans us, and you are not our friends anymore?]
[Not you, Edi, just her.]
[Ulli is my best friend! We can hang arround where we like to!]
Bar
[Come with me!]
[Edi!?]

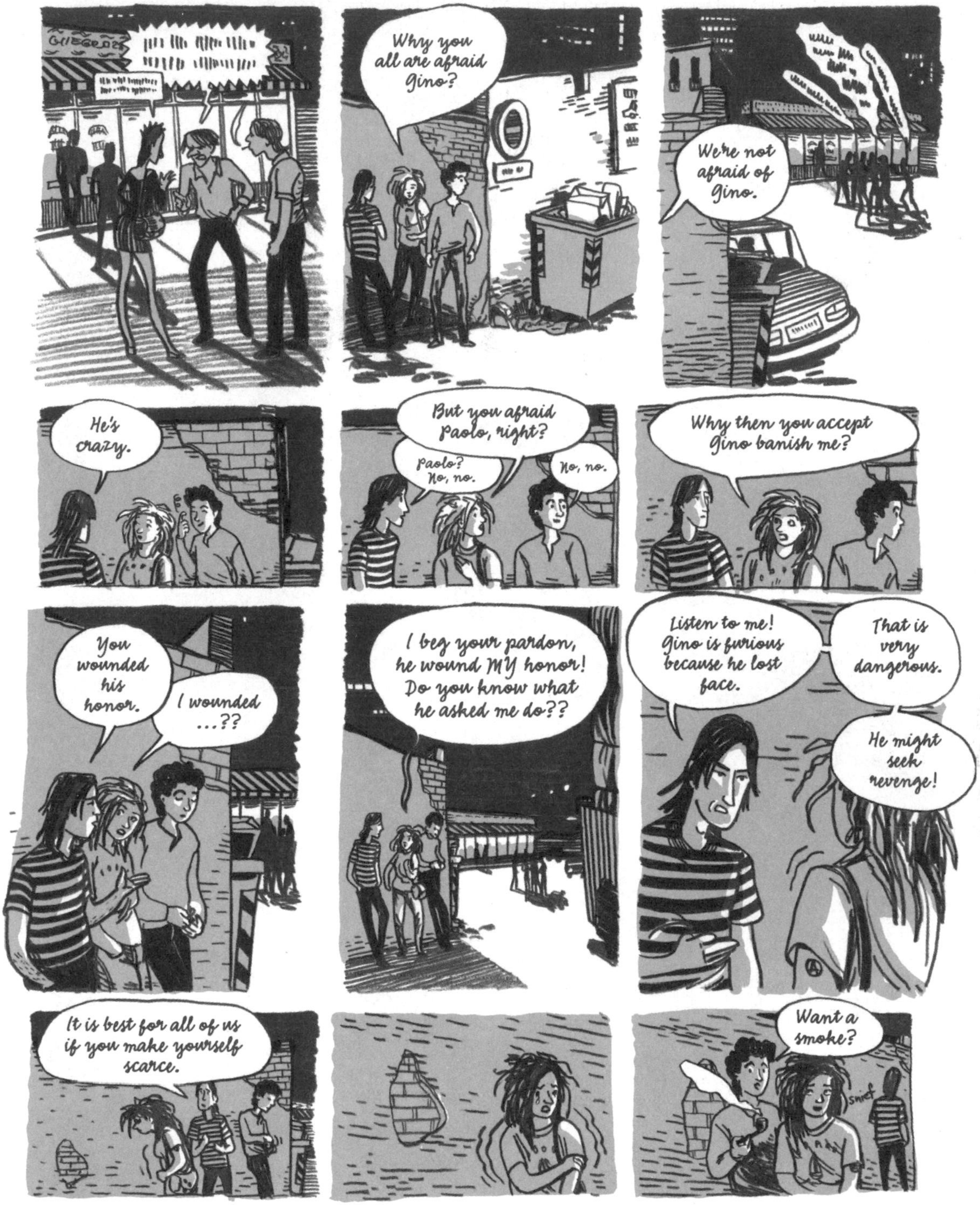
Why you all are afraid Gino?
We're not afraid of Gino.
He's crazy.
But you afraid Paolo, right?
Paolo? No, no.
No, no.
Why then you accept Gino banish me?
You wounded his honor.
I wounded ...??
I beg your pardon, he wound MY honor! Do you know what he asked me do??
Listen to me! Gino is furious because he lost face.
That is very dangerous.
He might seek revenge!
It is best for all of us if you make yourself scarce.
Want a smoke?
sniff

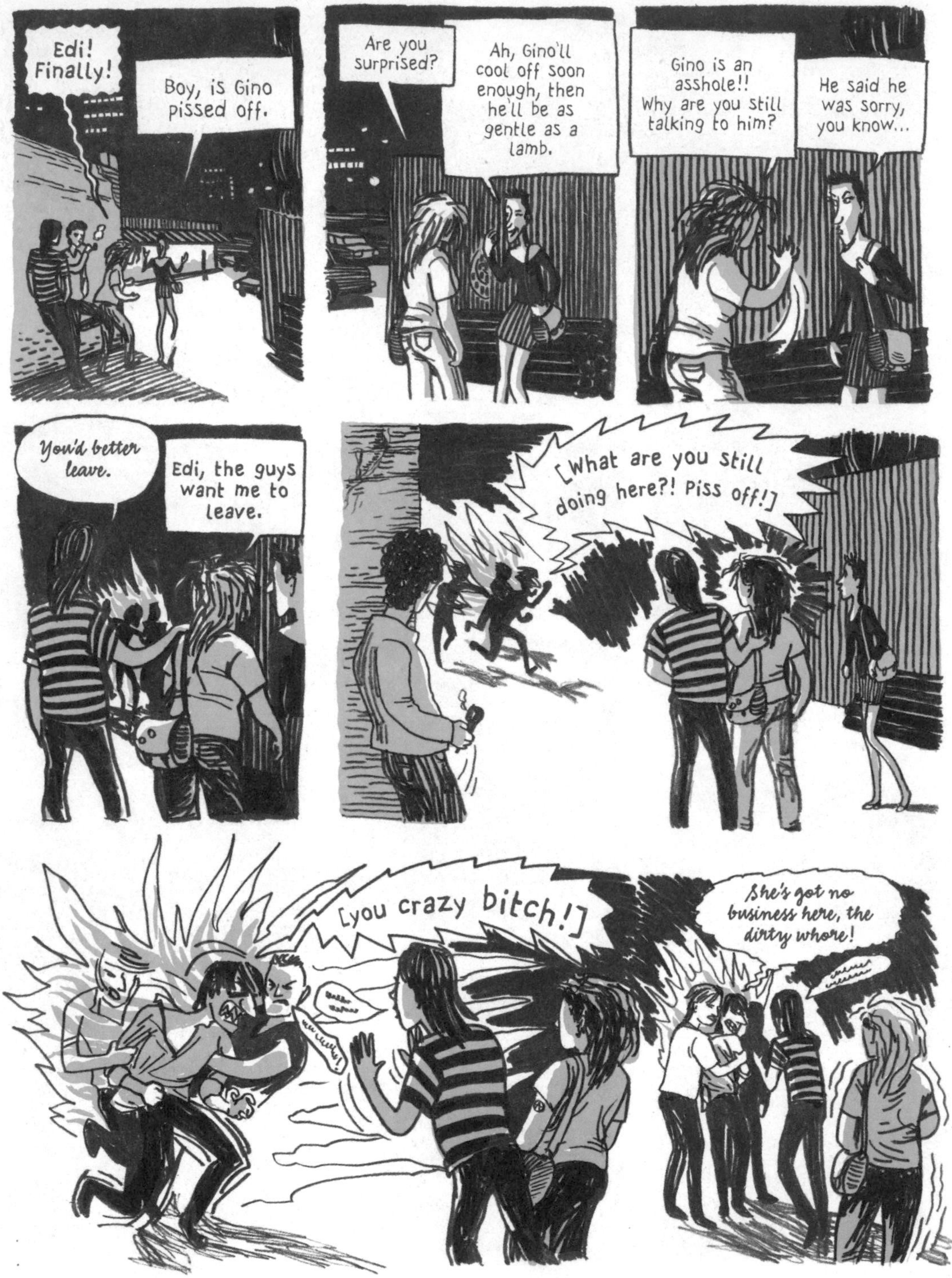

Edi! Finally!
Boy, is Gino pissed off.
Are you surprised?
Ah, Gino'll cool off soon enough, then he'll be as gentle as a lamb.
Gino is an asshole!! Why are you still talking to him?
He said he was sorry, you know...
You'd better leave.
Edi, the guys want me to leave.
[What are you still doing here?! Piss off!]
[you crazy bitch!]
She's got no business here, the dirty whore!

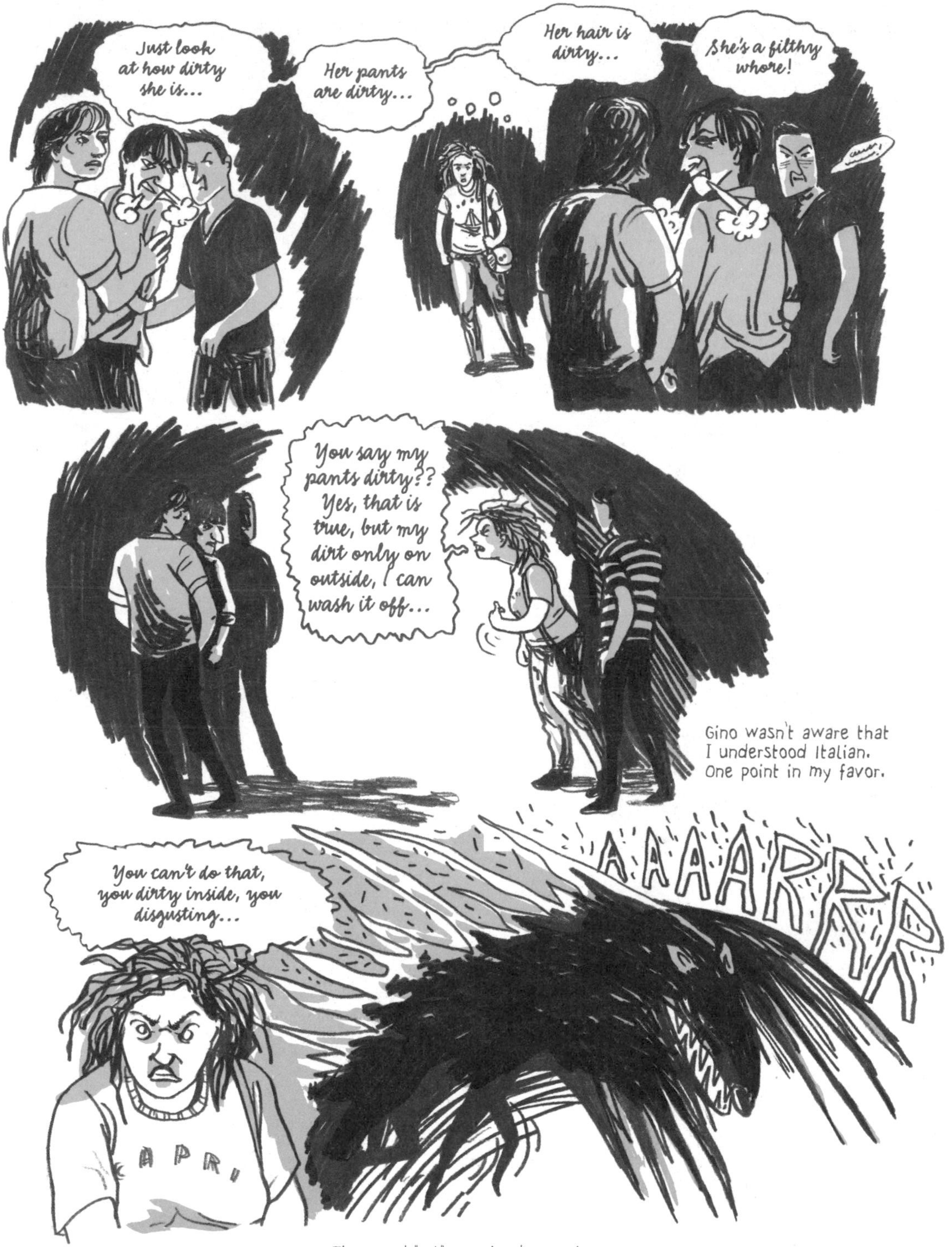
Just look at how dirty she is...
Her pants are dirty...
Her hair is dirty...
She's a filthy whore!
You say my pants dirty?? Yes, that is true, but my dirt only on outside, I can wash it off...
Gino wasn't aware that I understood Italian. One point in my favor.
You can't do that, you dirty inside, you disgusting...
AAAARRR
The word "rat" remained unspoken. It didn't matter what I said anyway.

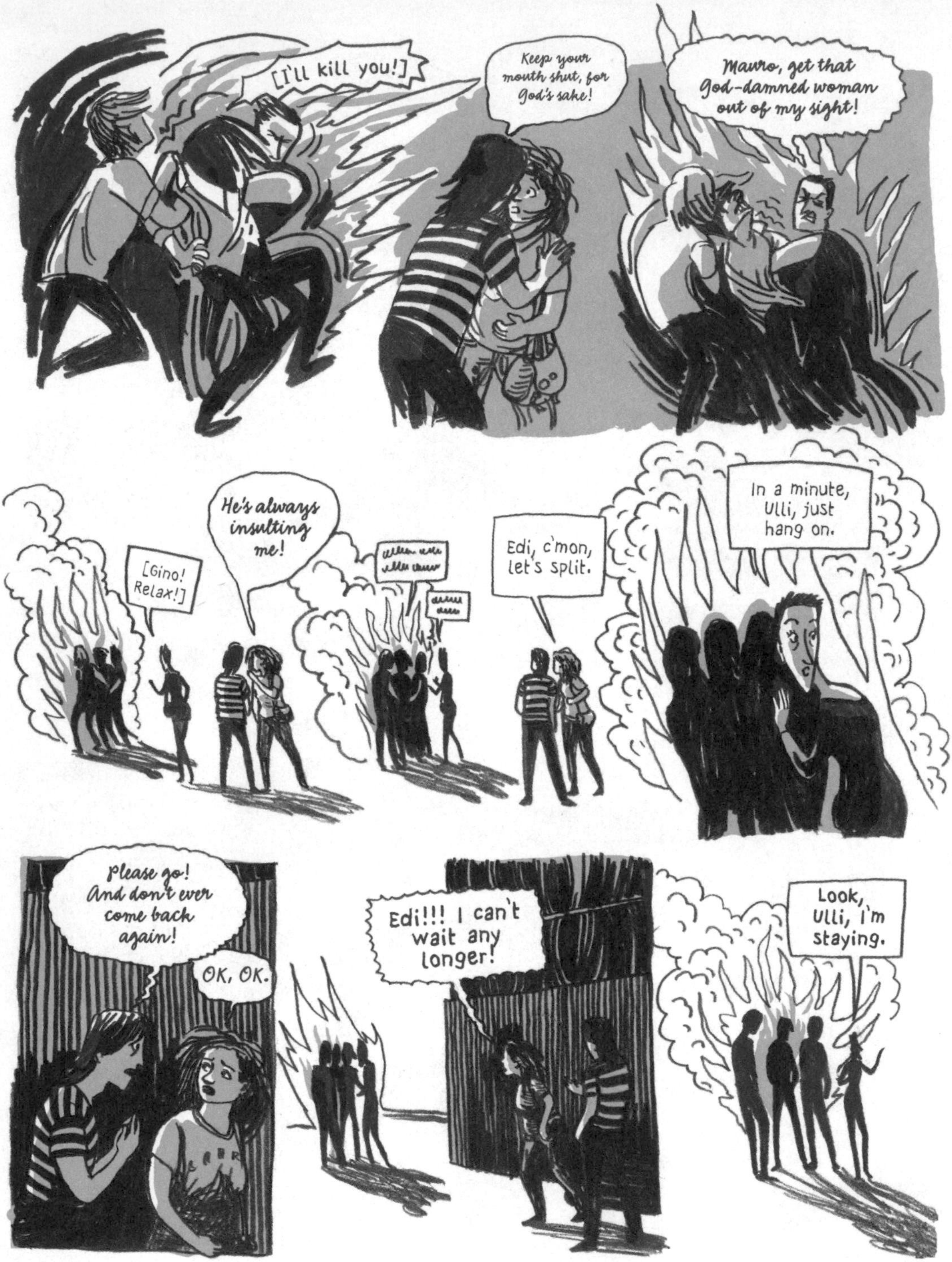
[I'll kill you!]
Keep your mouth shut, for God's sake!
Mauro, get that God-damned woman out of my sight!
[Gino! Relax!]
He's always insulting me!
Edi, c'mon, let's split.
In a minute, Ulli, just hang on.
Please go! And don't ever come back again!
OK, OK.
Edi!!! I can't wait any longer!
Look, Ulli, I'm staying.

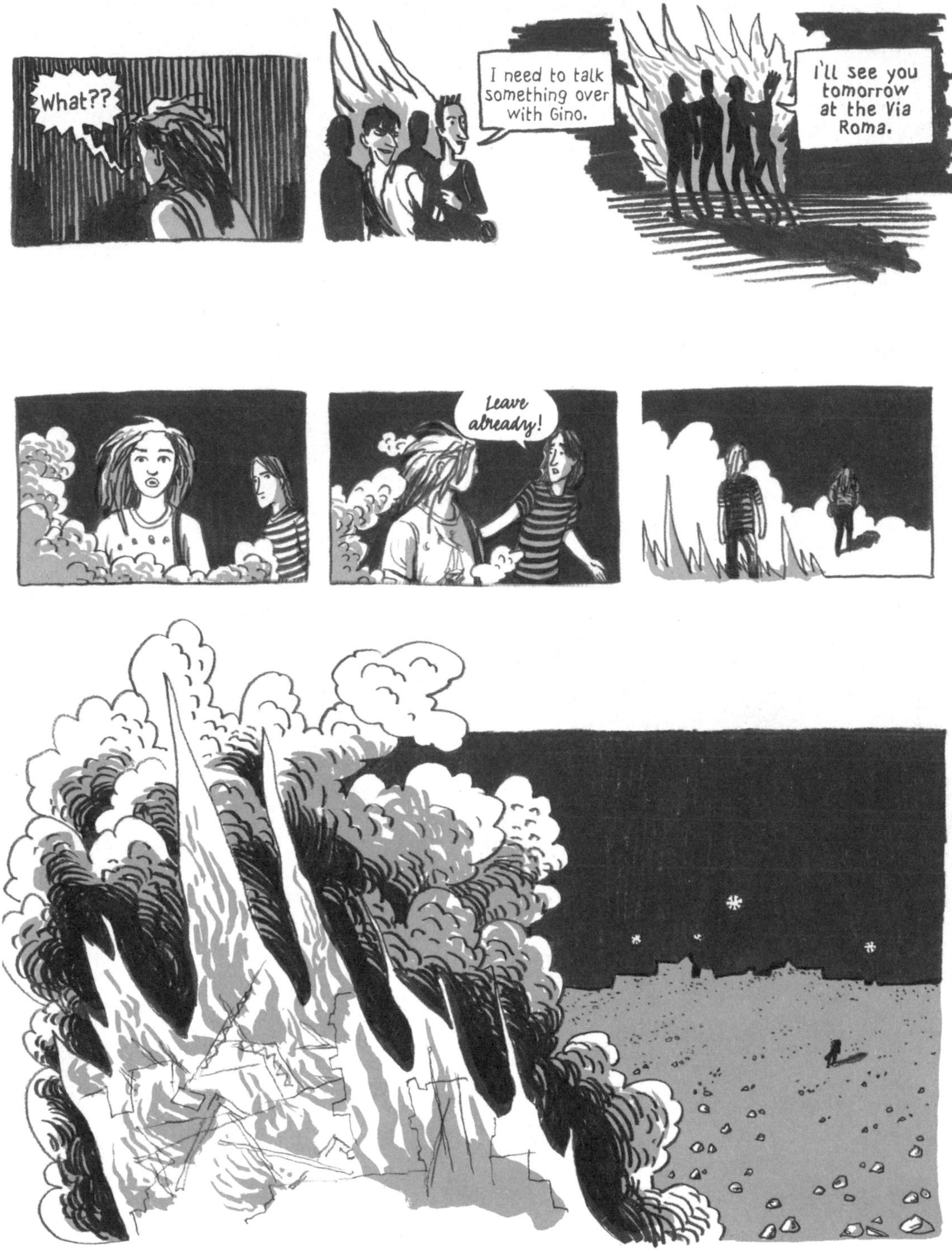
What??
I need to talk something over with Gino.
I'll see you tomorrow at the Via Roma.
Leave already!

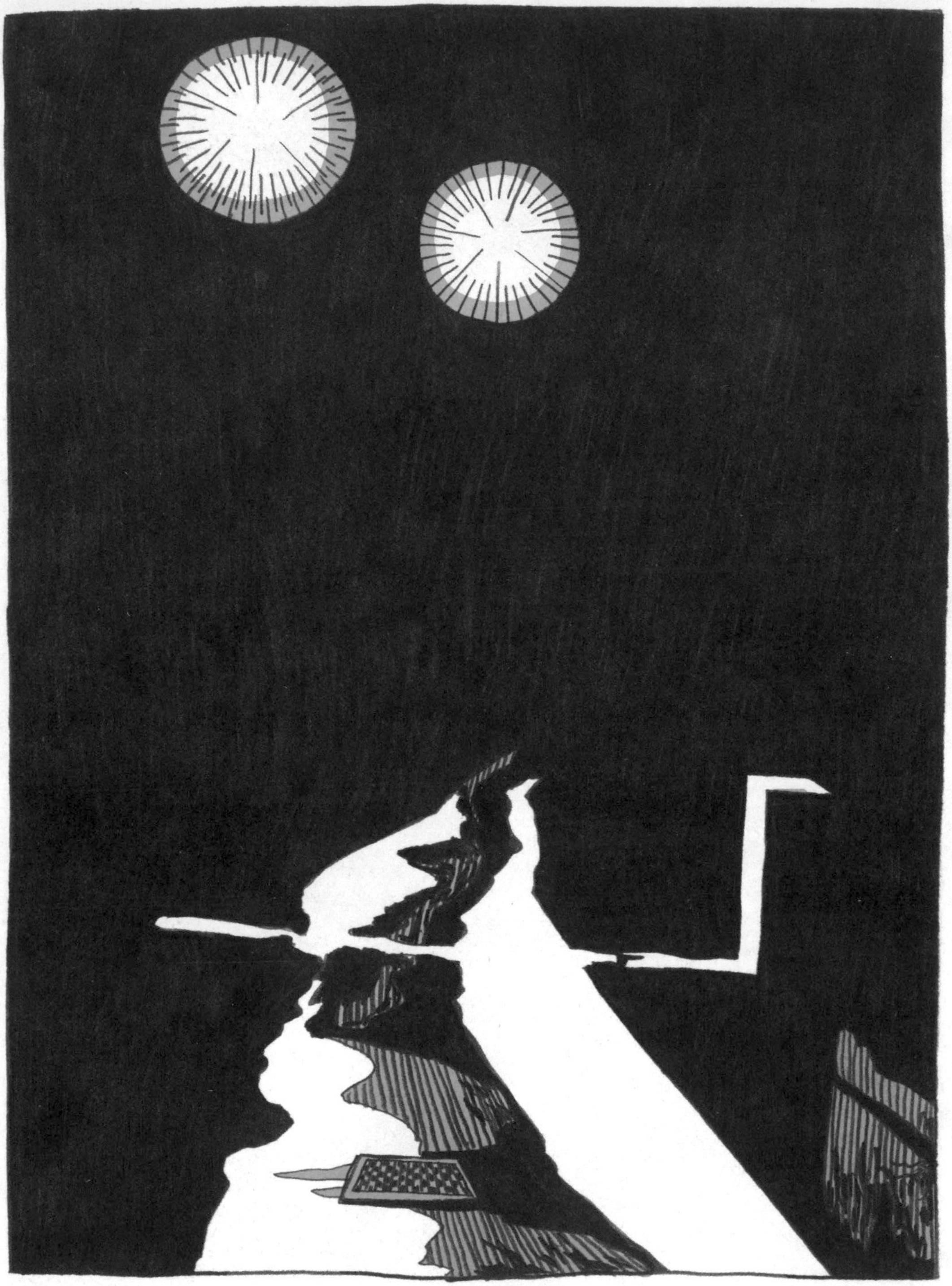

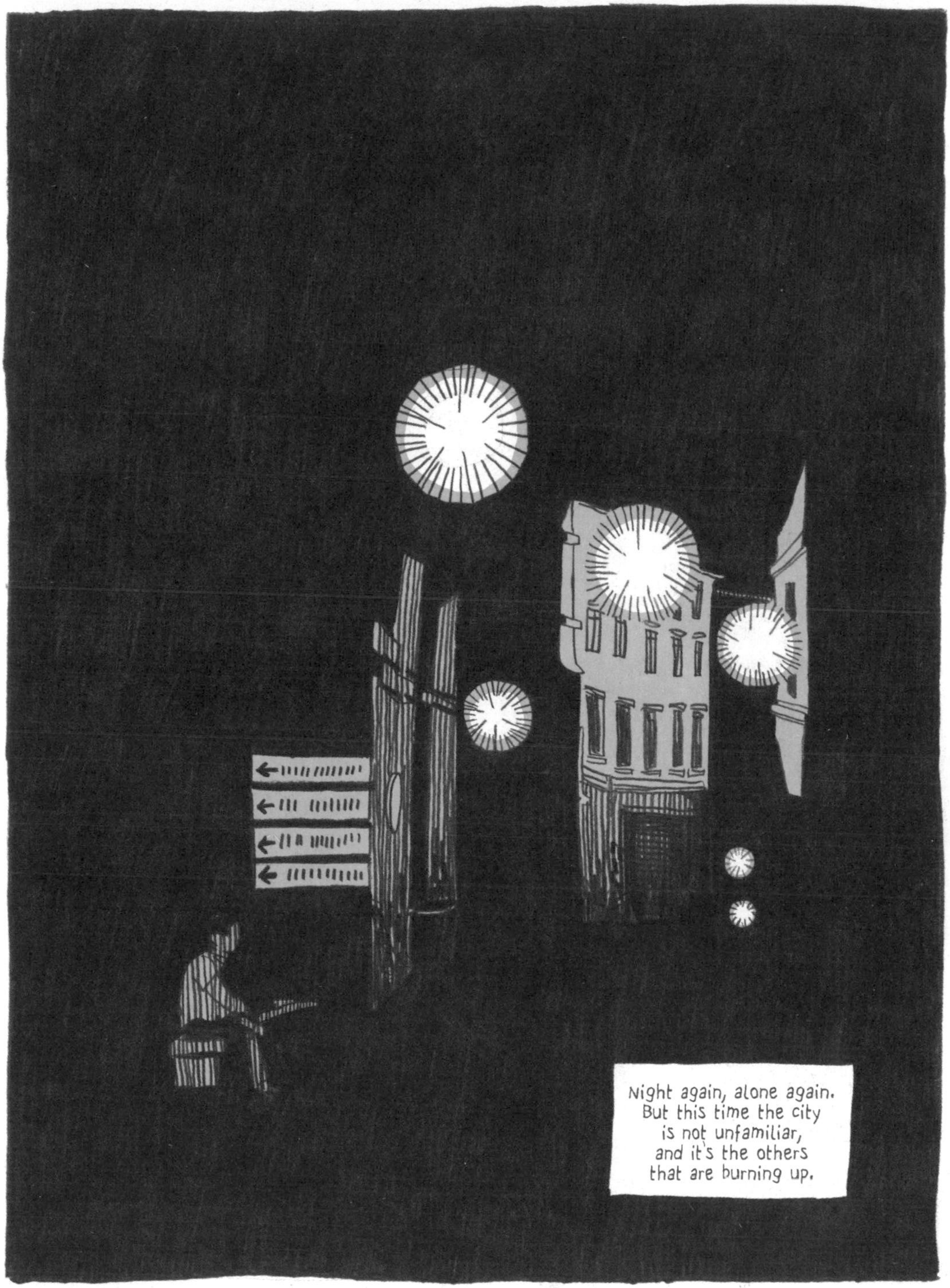
Night again, alone again.
But this time the city
is not unfamiliar,
and it's the others
that are burning up.

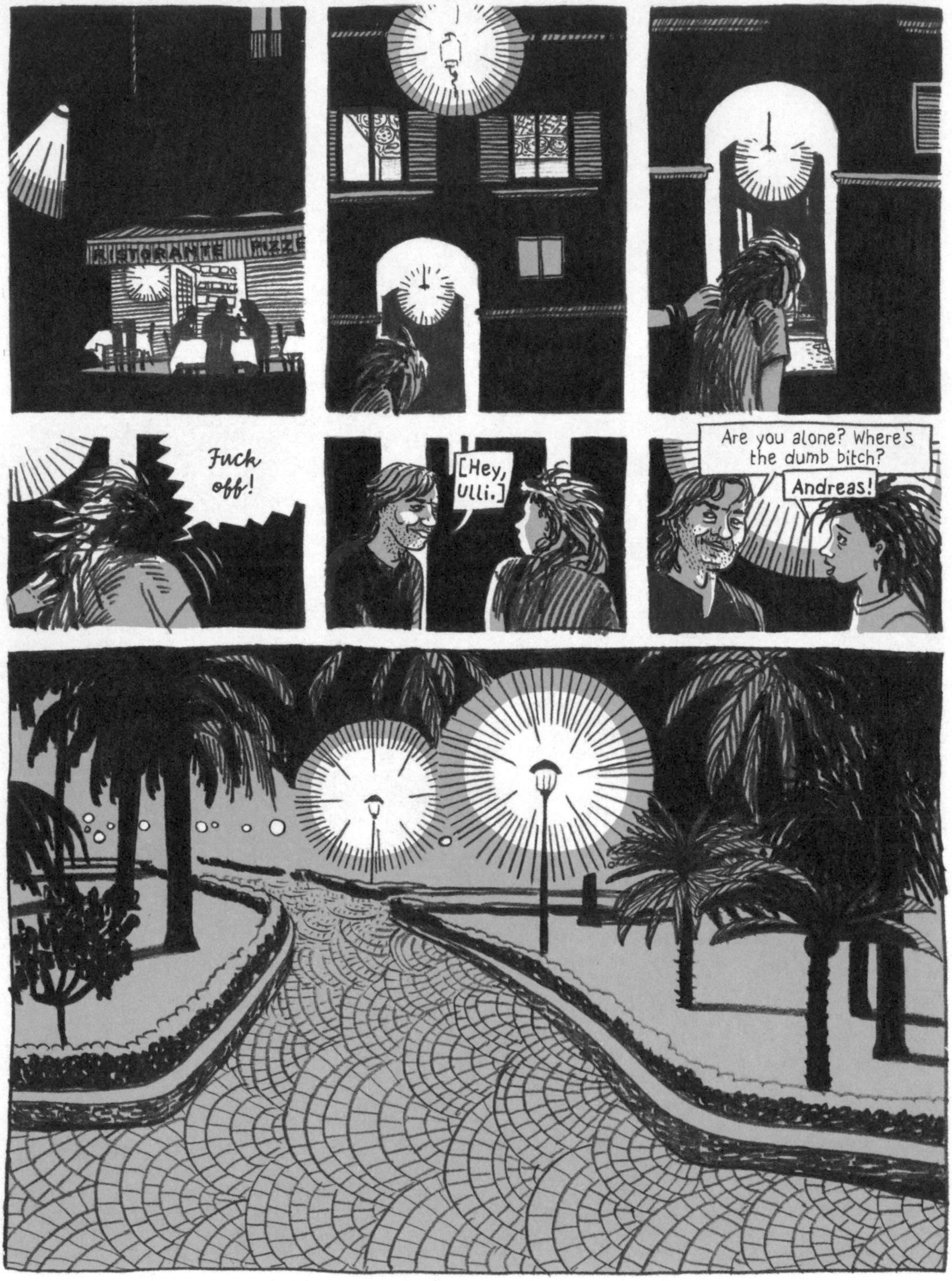
RISTORANTE PIZZE
Fuck off!
[Hey, Ulli.]
Are you alone? Where's the dumb bitch?
Andreas!

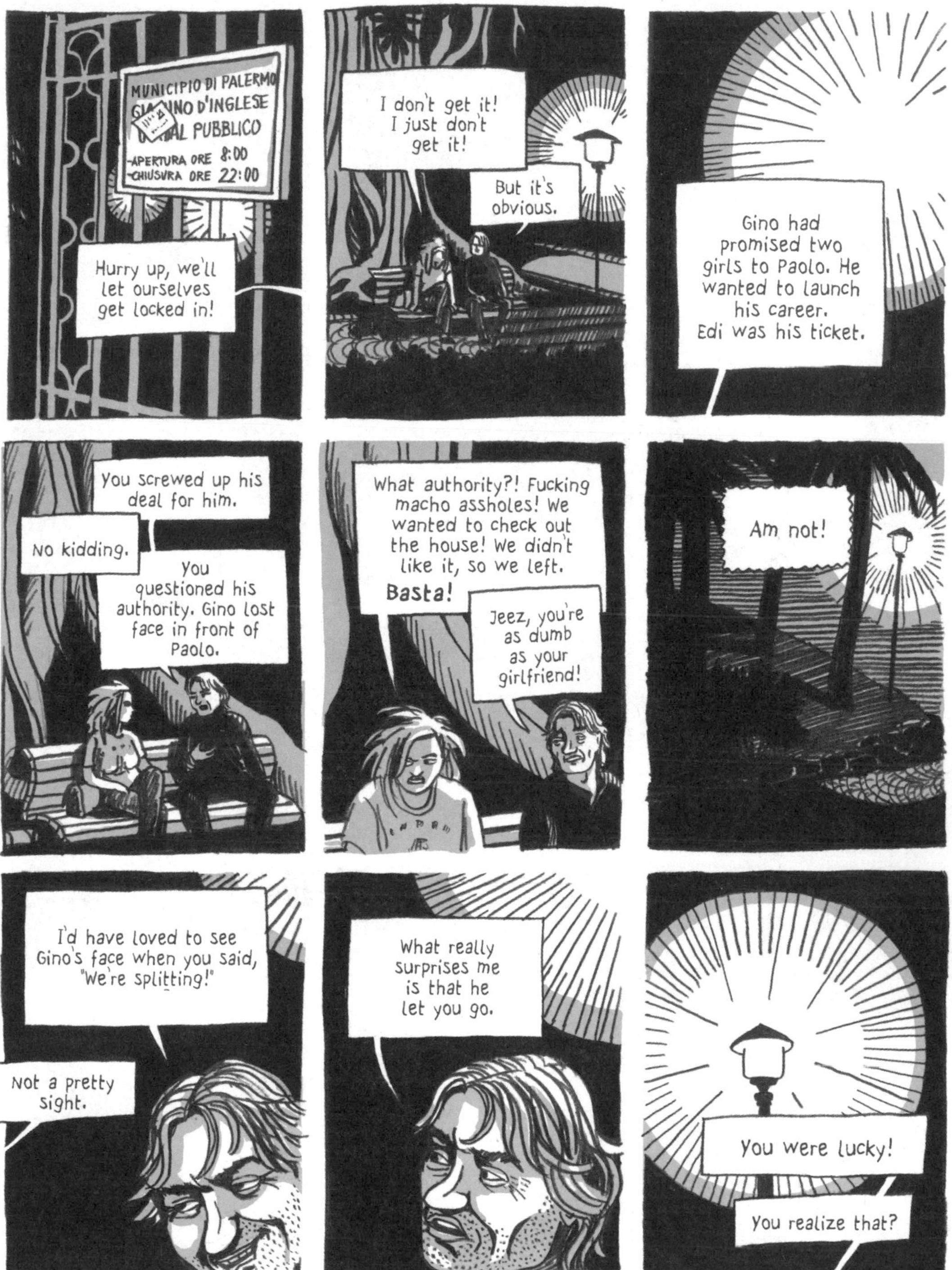
MUNICIPIO DI PALERMO
APERTURA ORE 8:00
CHIUSURA ORE 22:00
Hurry up, we'll let ourselves get locked in!
I don't get it! I just don't get it!
But it's obvious.
Gino had promised two girls to Paolo. He wanted to launch his career. Edi was his ticket.
You screwed up his deal for him.
No kidding.
You questioned his authority. Gino lost face in front of Paolo.
What authority?! Fucking macho assholes! We wanted to check out the house! We didn't like it, so we left. Basta!
Jeez, you're as dumb as your girlfriend!
Am not!
I'd have loved to see Gino's face when you said, "We're splitting!"
Not a pretty sight.
What really surprises me is that he let you go.
You were lucky!
You realize that?

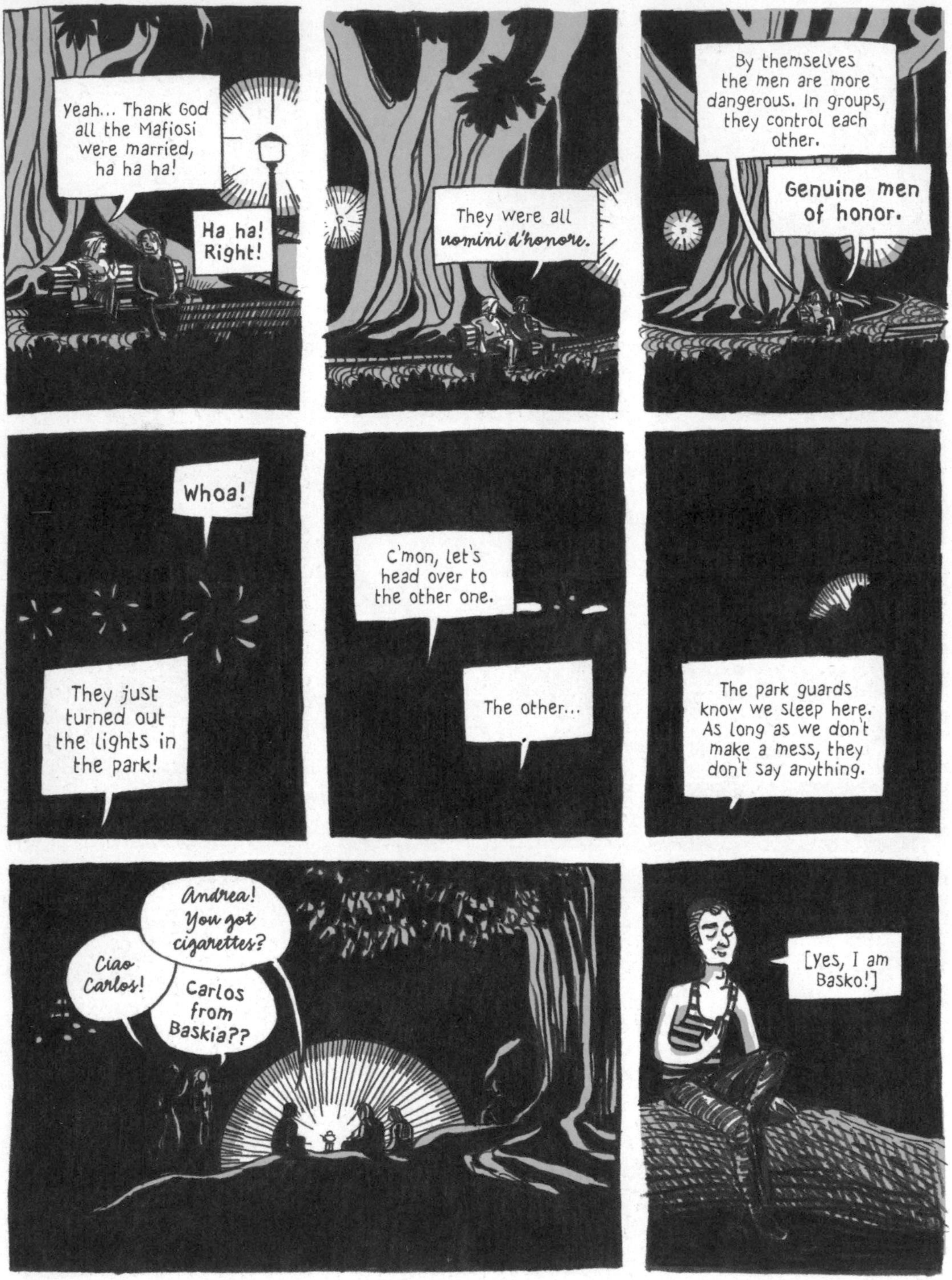
Yeah... Thank God all the Mafiosi were married, ha ha ha!
Ha ha! Right!
They were all uomini d'honore.
By themselves the men are more dangerous. In groups, they control each other.
Genuine men of honor.
Whoa!
They just turned out the lights in the park!
C'mon, let's head over to the other one.
The other...
The park guards know we sleep here. As long as we don't make a mess, they don't say anything.
Andrea! You got cigarettes?
Ciao Carlos!
Carlos from Baskia??
[Yes, I am Basko!]

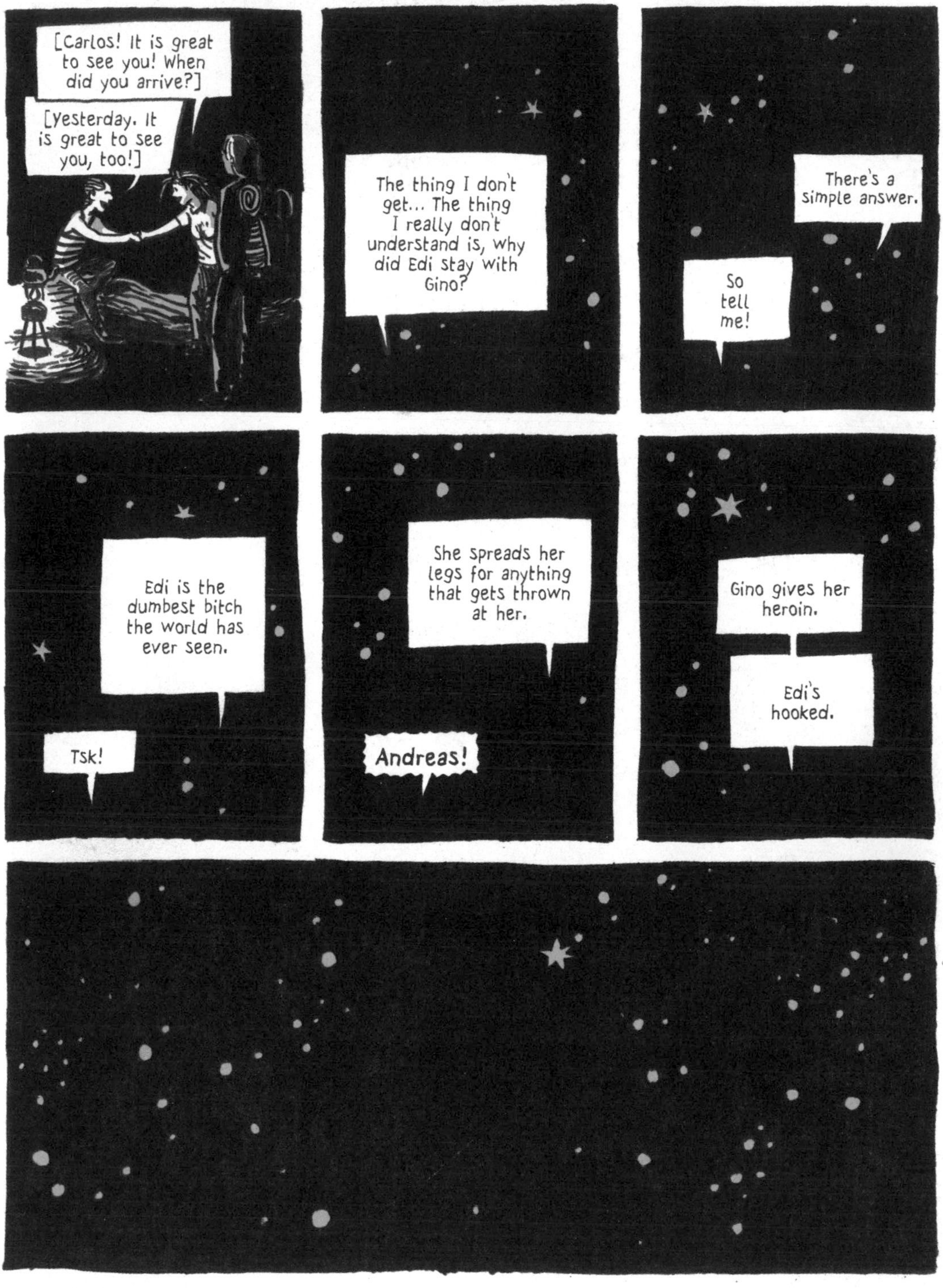
[Carlos! It is great to see you! When did you arrive?]
[Yesterday. It is great to see you, too!]
The thing I don't get... The thing I really don't understand is, why did Edi stay with Gino?
There's a simple answer.
So tell me!
Edi is the dumbest bitch the world has ever seen.
Tsk!
She spreads her legs for anything that gets thrown at her.
Andreas!
Gino gives her heroin.
Edi's hooked.

XVIII. the JOKER

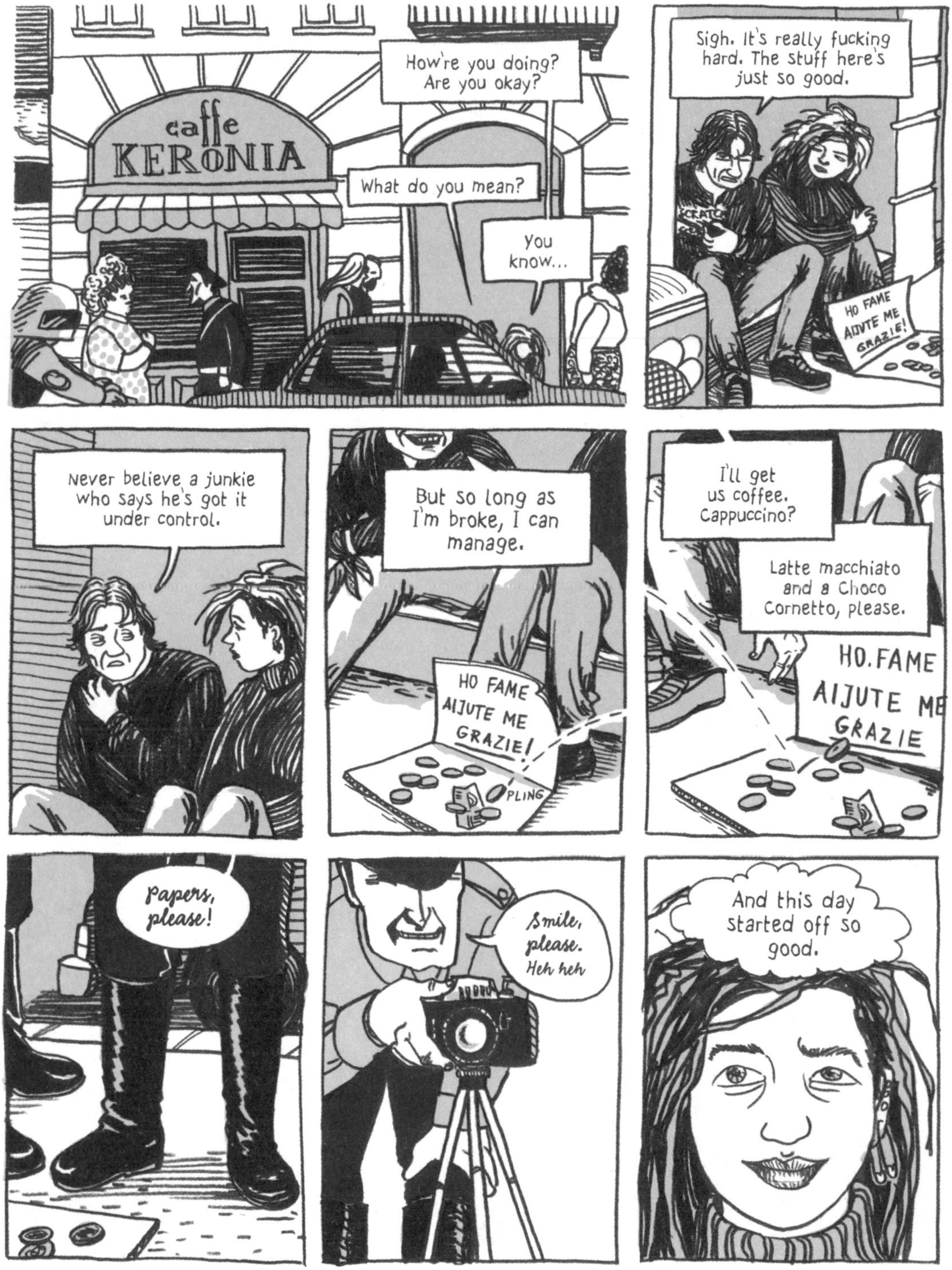
caffe KERONIA
How're you doing? Are you okay?
What do you mean?
You know...
Sigh. It's really fucking hard. The stuff here's just so good.
HO FAME AIJUTE ME GRAZIE!
Never believe a junkie who says he's got it under control.
But so long as I'm broke, I can manage.
HO FAME AIJUTE ME GRAZIE!
PLING
I'll get us coffee. Cappuccino?
Latte macchiato and a Choco Cornetto, please.
HO.FAME AIJUTE ME GRAZIE
Papers, please!
Smile, please. Heh heh
And this day started off so good.

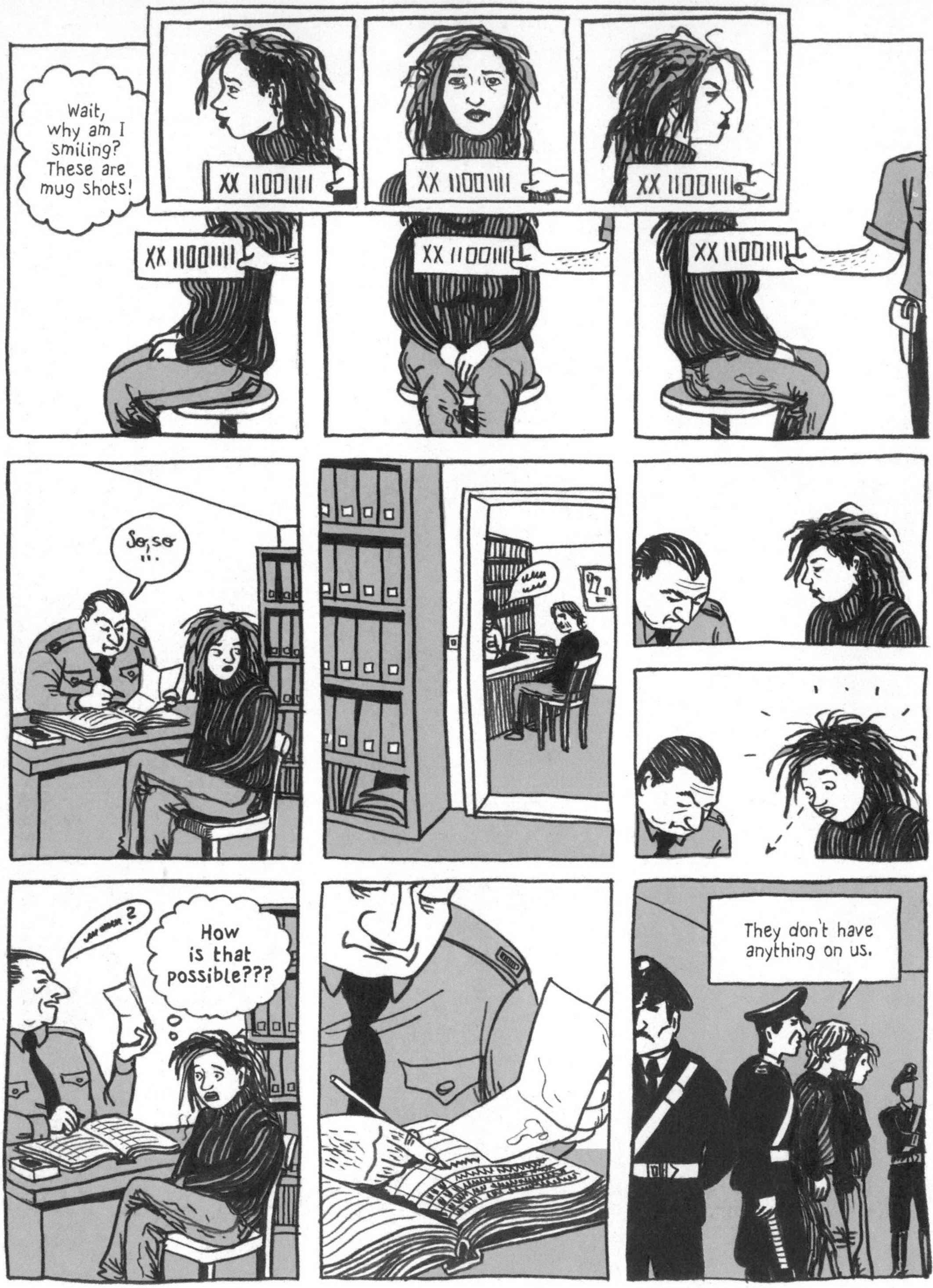

Wait, why am I smiling? These are mug shots!
XX 1100IIII
So, so ...
How is that possible???
They don't have anything on us.

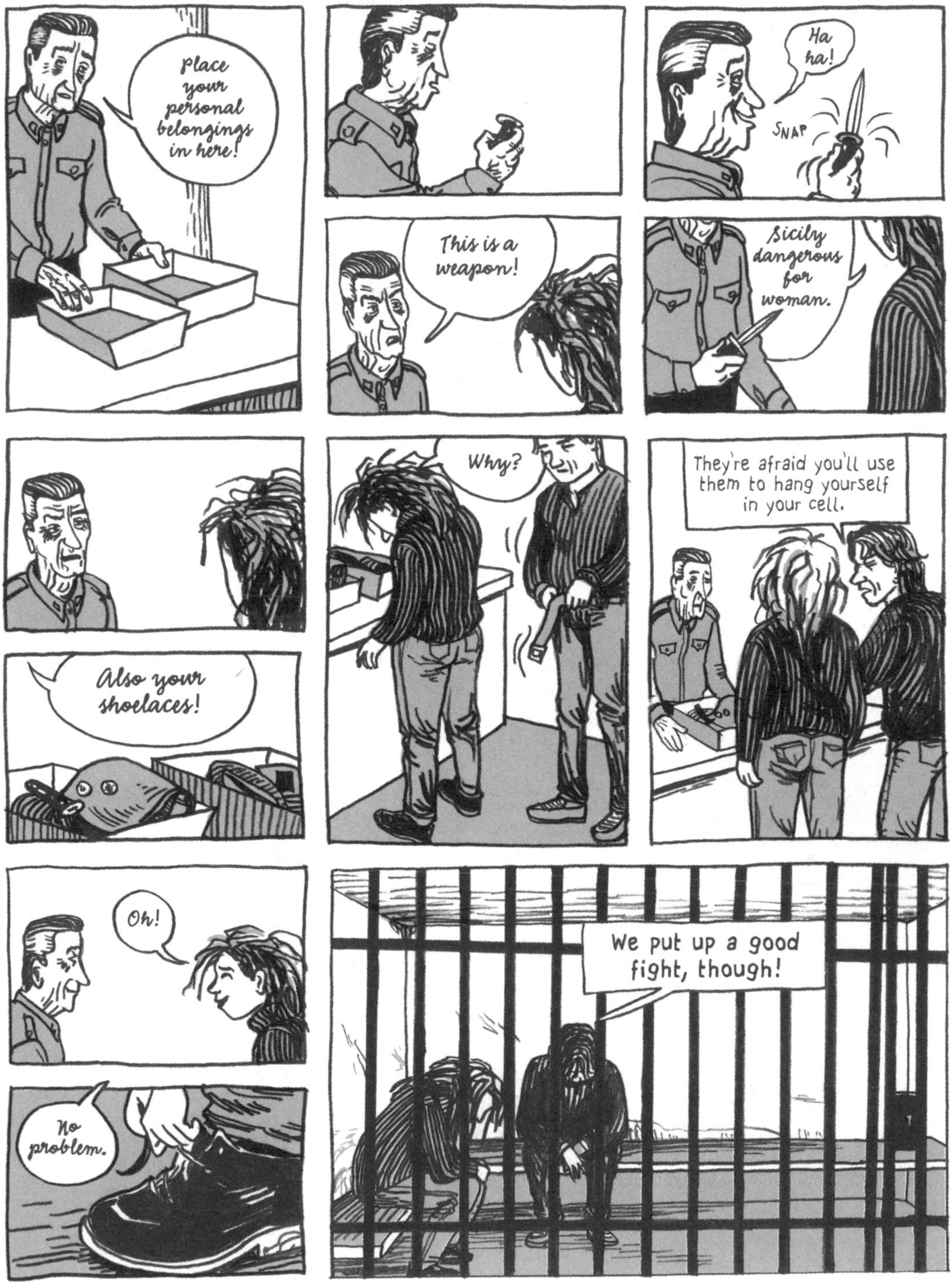
Place your personal belongings in here!
Ha ha!
SNAP
This is a weapon!
Sicily dangerous for woman.
Why?
They're afraid you'll use them to hang yourself in your cell.
Also your shoelaces!
Oh!
No problem.
We put up a good fight, though!

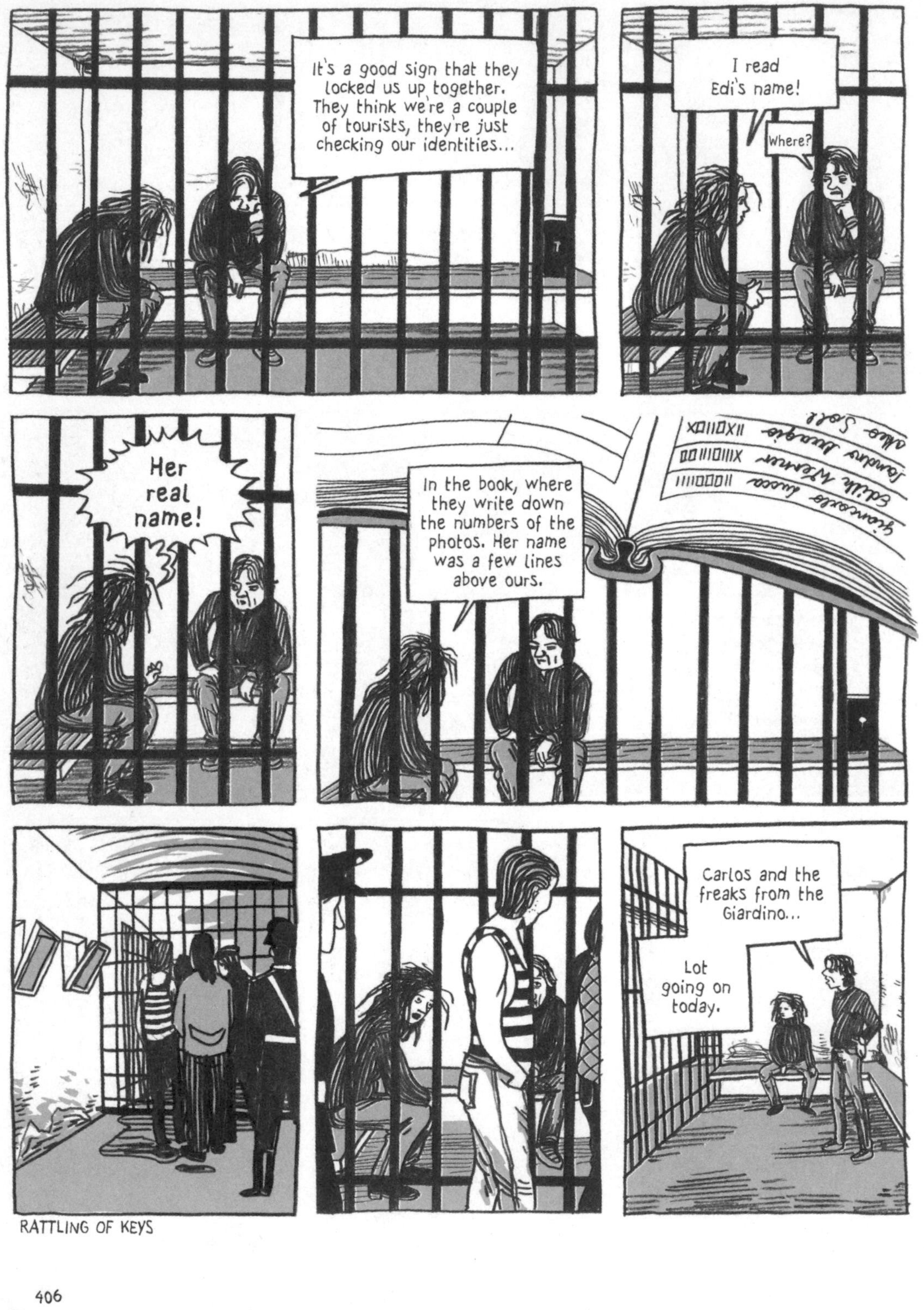
It's a good sign that they locked us up together. They think we're a couple of tourists, they're just checking our identities...
I read Edi's name!
Where?
Her real name!
In the book, where they write down the numbers of the photos. Her name was a few lines above ours.
Carlos and the freaks from the Giardino...
Lot going on today.

RATTLING OF KEYS

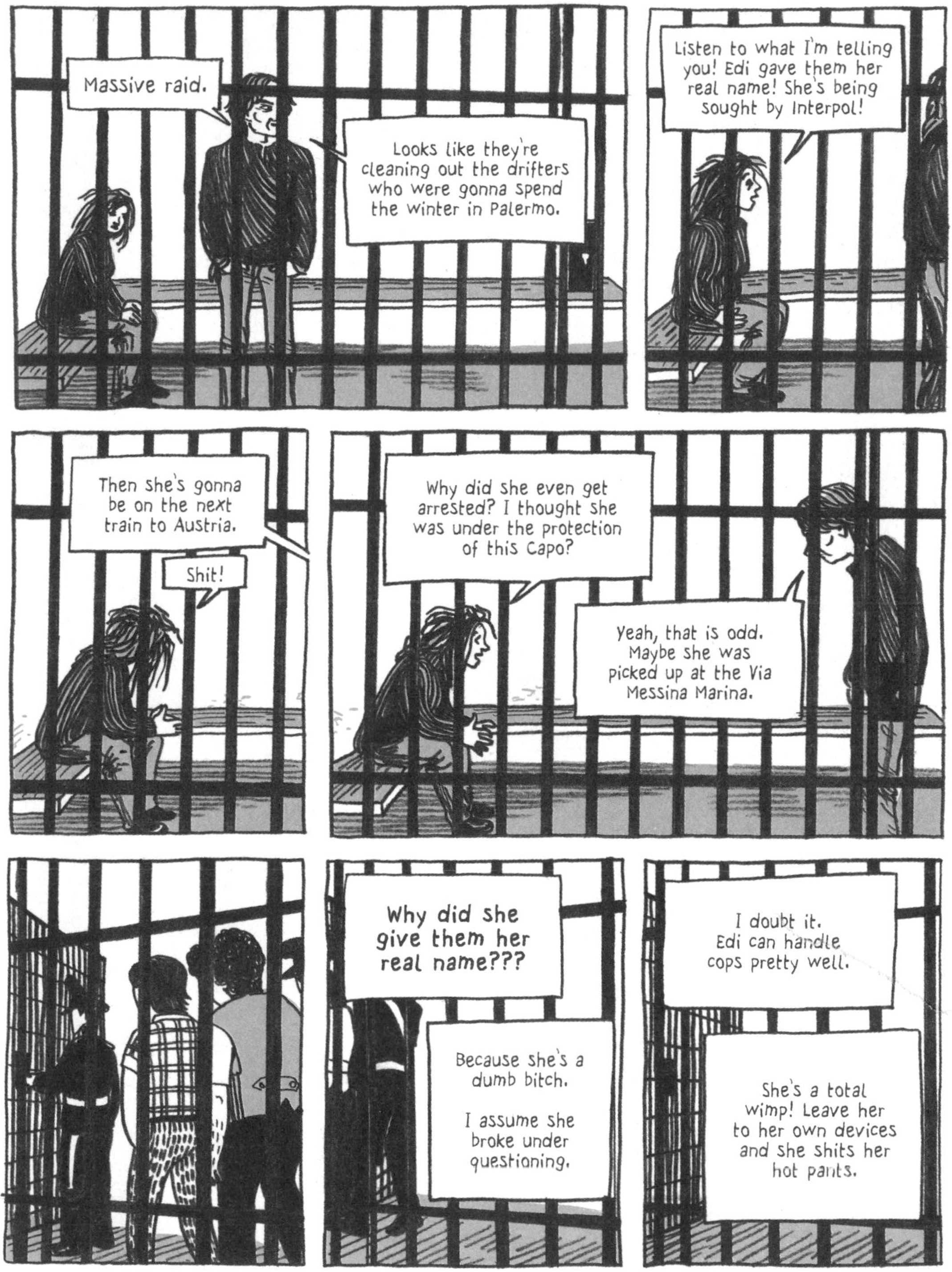
Massive raid.
Looks like they're cleaning out the drifters who were gonna spend the winter in Palermo.
Listen to what I'm telling you! Edi gave them her real name! She's being sought by Interpol!
Then she's gonna be on the next train to Austria.
Shit!
Why did she even get arrested? I thought she was under the protection of this Capo?
Yeah, that is odd. Maybe she was picked up at the Via Messina Marina.
Why did she give them her real name???
Because she's a dumb bitch.
I assume she broke under questioning.
I doubt it. Edi can handle cops pretty well.
She's a total wimp! Leave her to her own devices and she shits her hot pants.

You think our arrest and what happened yesterday are connected?

Then the cops would've mentioned Edi, but they didn't.

Why on earth did she do that?

Maybe she wants to go home?

Edi? No way! If there's one thing I'm sure of, it's that Edi does not want to go home. She thinks everything is awesome here!

You told me that Gino was in a rage yesterday...

What if he took it out on Edi last night?

Oh my God!!

Edi breaks down and crawls back to Mommy and Daddy.

Anyway, she's better off.

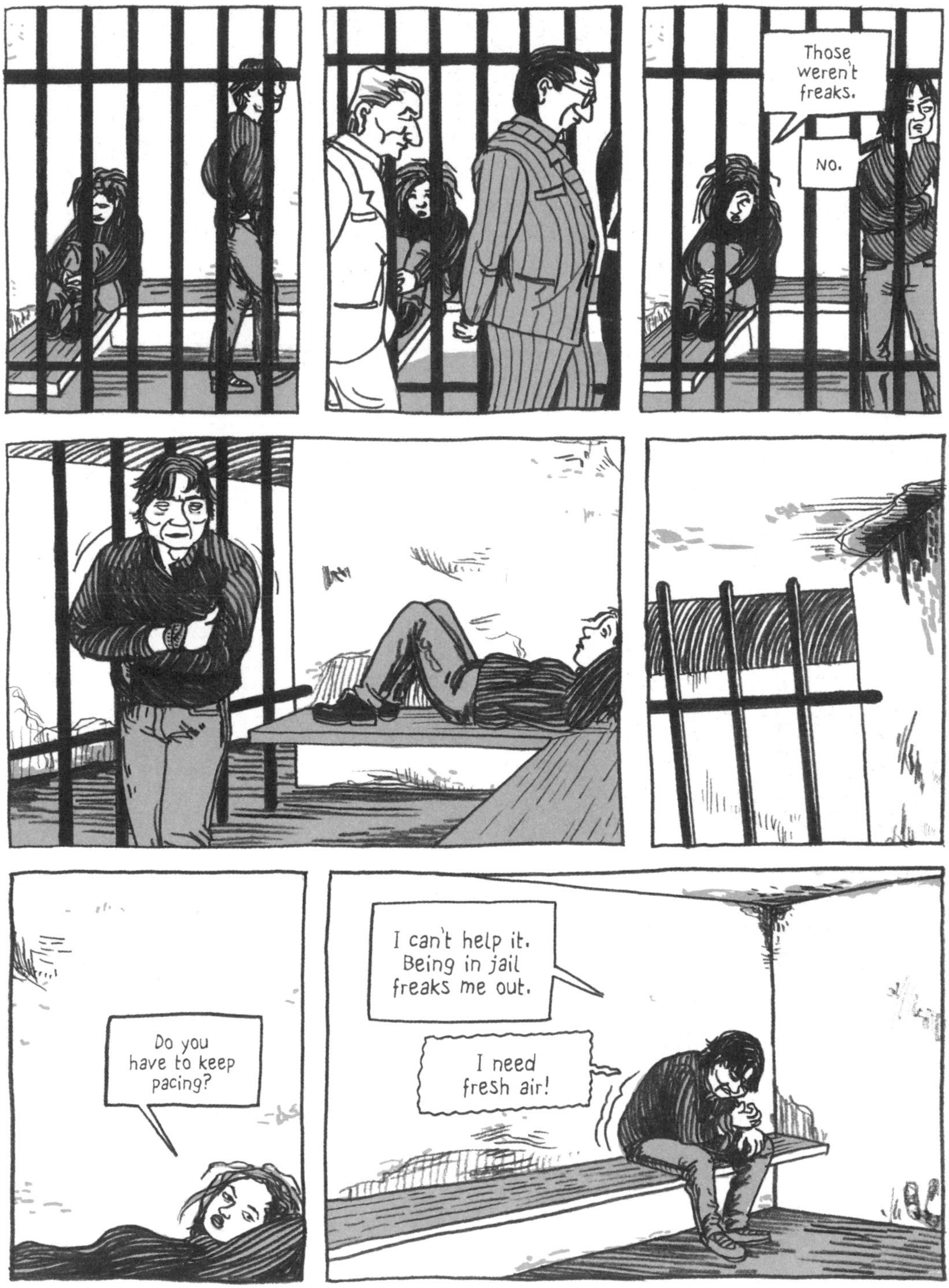
Those weren't freaks.
No.
Do you have to keep pacing?
I can't help it. Being in jail freaks me out.
I need fresh air!

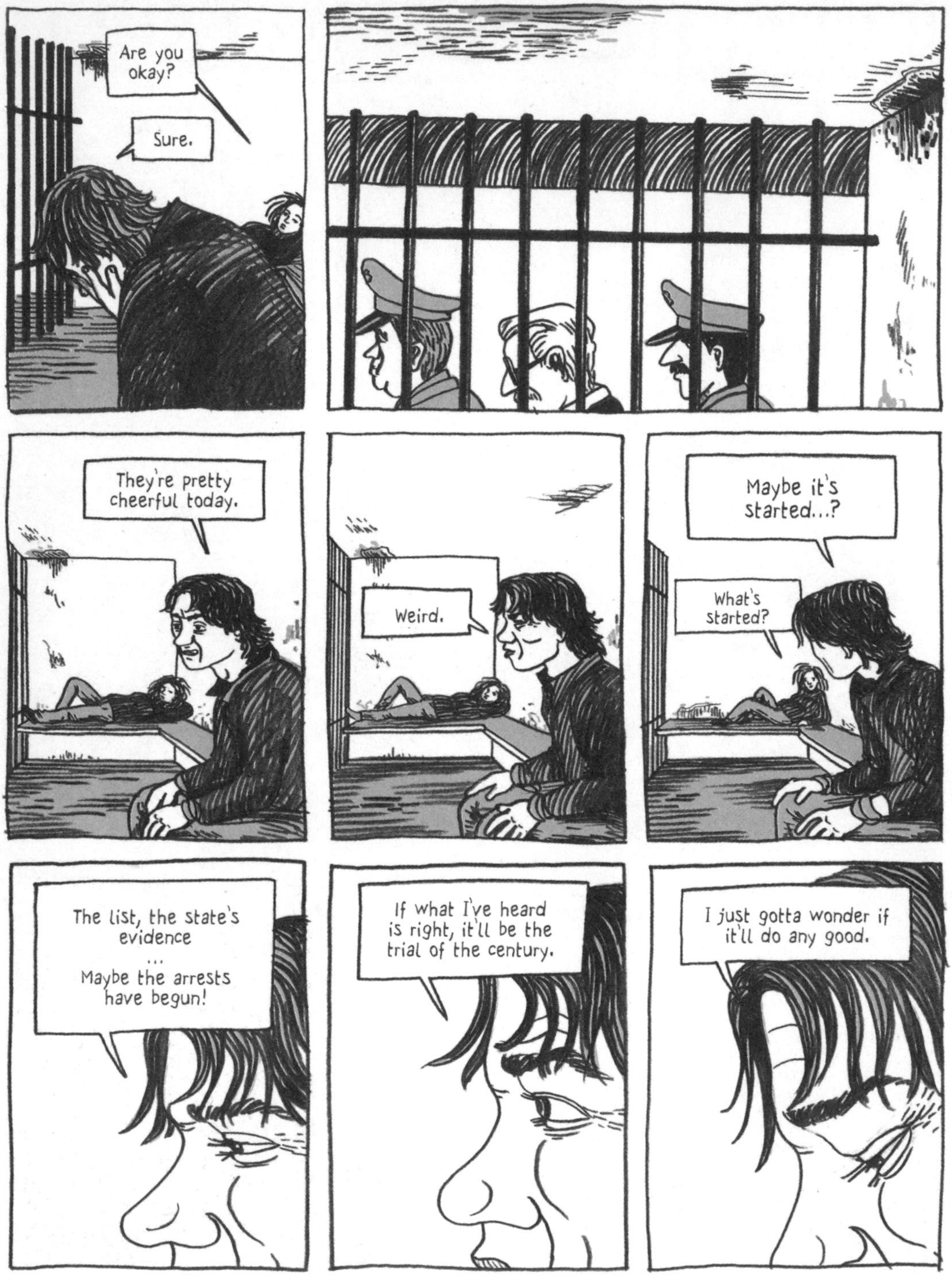
Are you okay?
Sure.
They're pretty cheerful today.
Weird.
Maybe it's started...?
What's started?
The list, the state's evidence ... Maybe the arrests have begun!
If what I've heard is right, it'll be the trial of the century.
I just gotta wonder if it'll do any good.

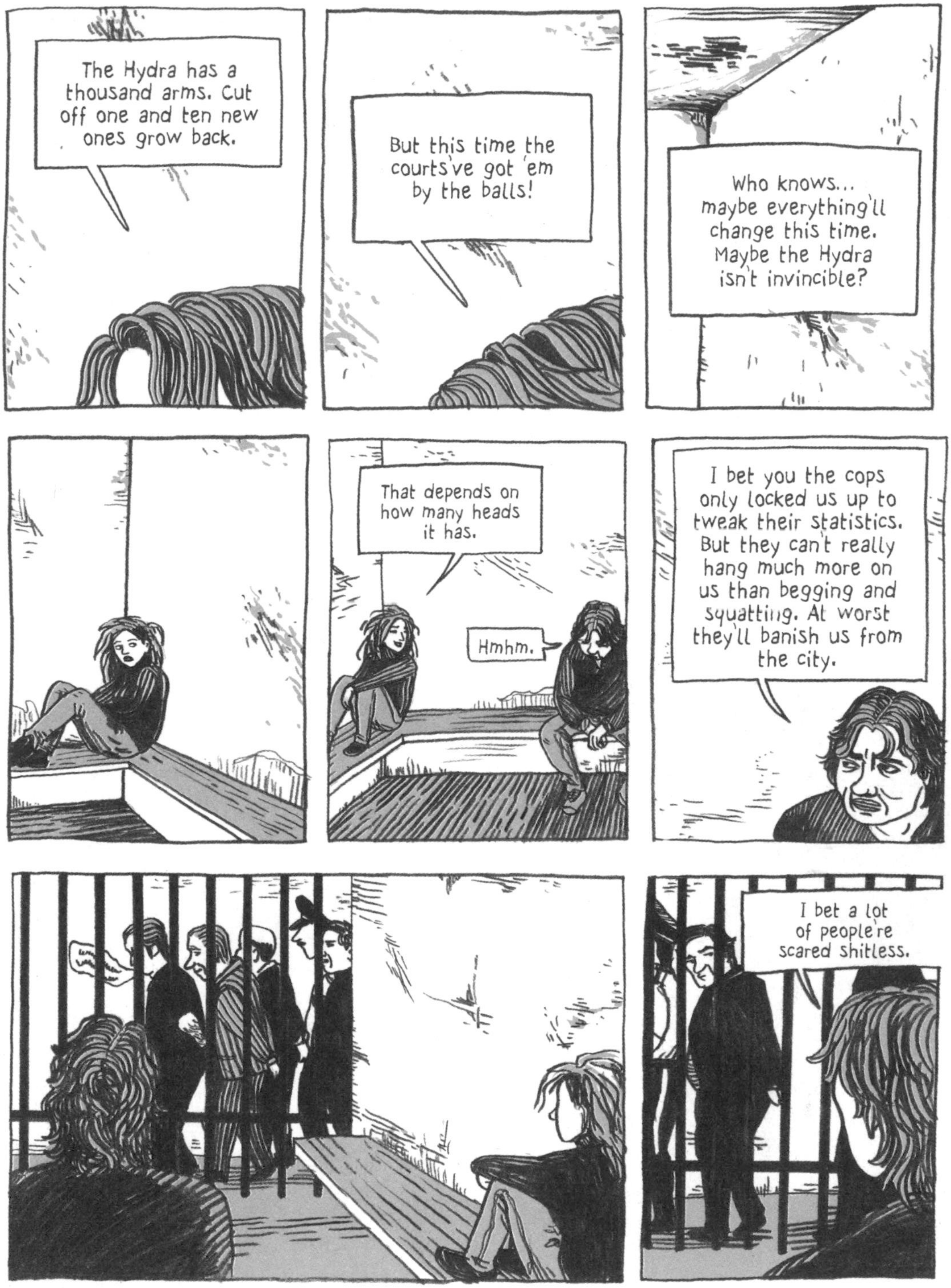
The Hydra has a thousand arms. Cut off one and ten new ones grow back.
But this time the courts've got 'em by the balls!
Who knows... maybe everything'll change this time. Maybe the Hydra isn't invincible?
That depends on how many heads it has.
Hmhm.
I bet you the cops only locked us up to tweak their statistics. But they can't really hang much more on us than begging and squatting. At worst they'll banish us from the city.
I bet a lot of people're scared shitless.

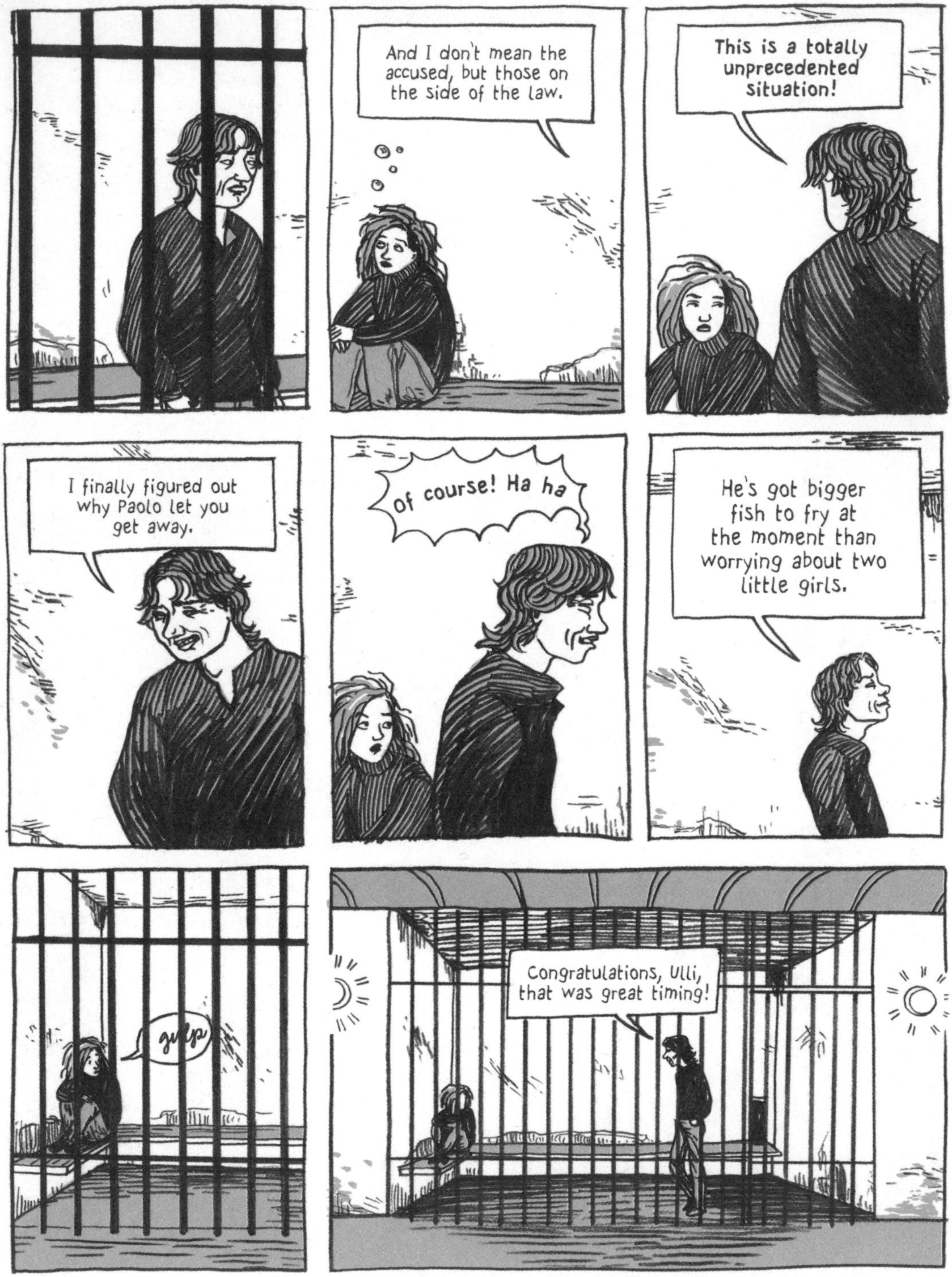
And I don't mean the accused, but those on the side of the law.
This is a totally unprecedented situation!
I finally figured out why Paolo let you get away.
Of course! Ha ha
He's got bigger fish to fry at the moment than worrying about two little girls.
gulp
Congratulations, Ulli, that was great timing!

XIX. the LOST ONES

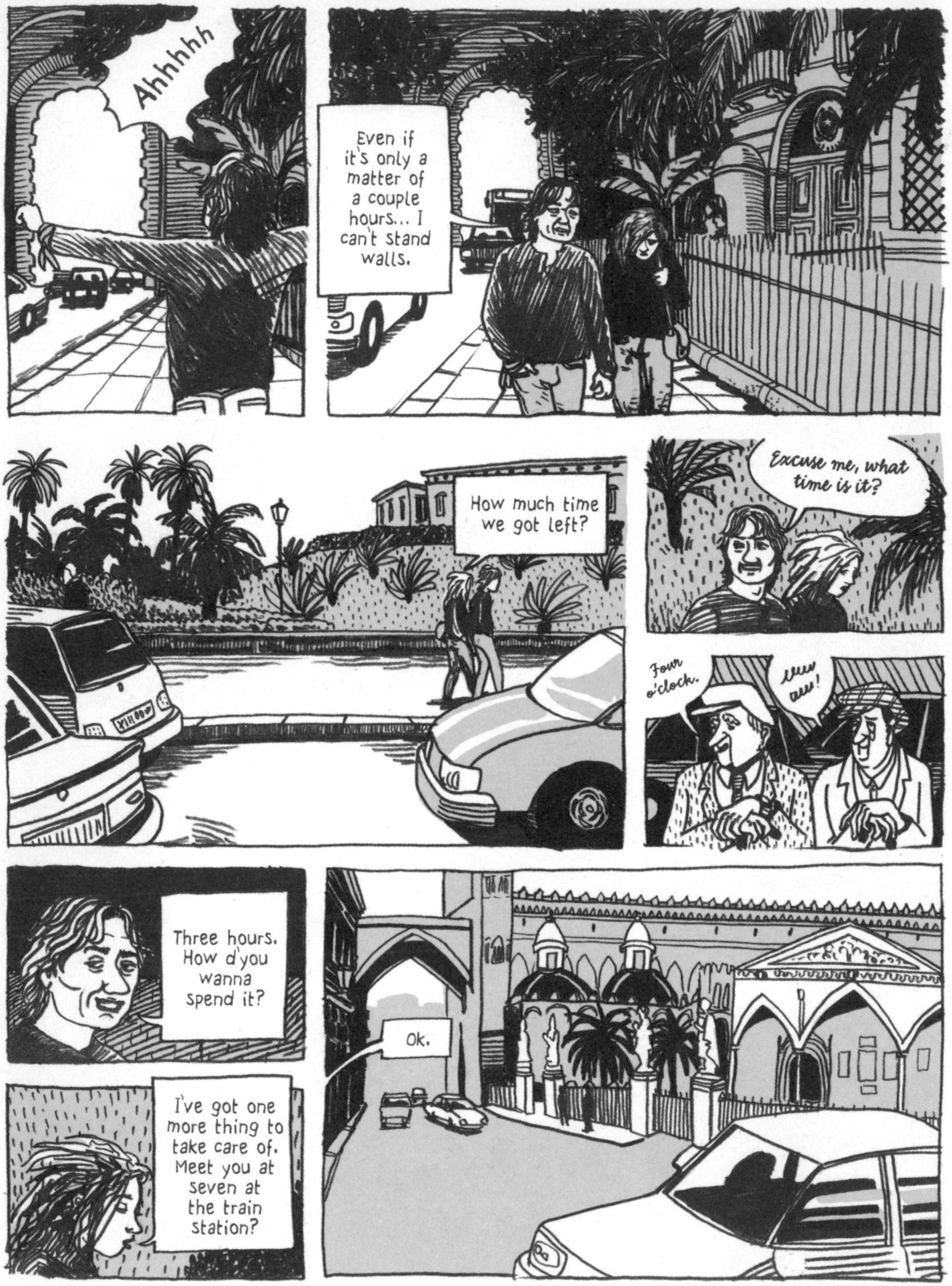
Ahhhhh
Even if it's only a matter of a couple hours... I can't stand walls.
How much time we got left?
Excuse me, what time is it?
Four o'clock.
Three hours. How d'you wanna spend it?
I've got one more thing to take care of. Meet you at seven at the train station?
Ok.

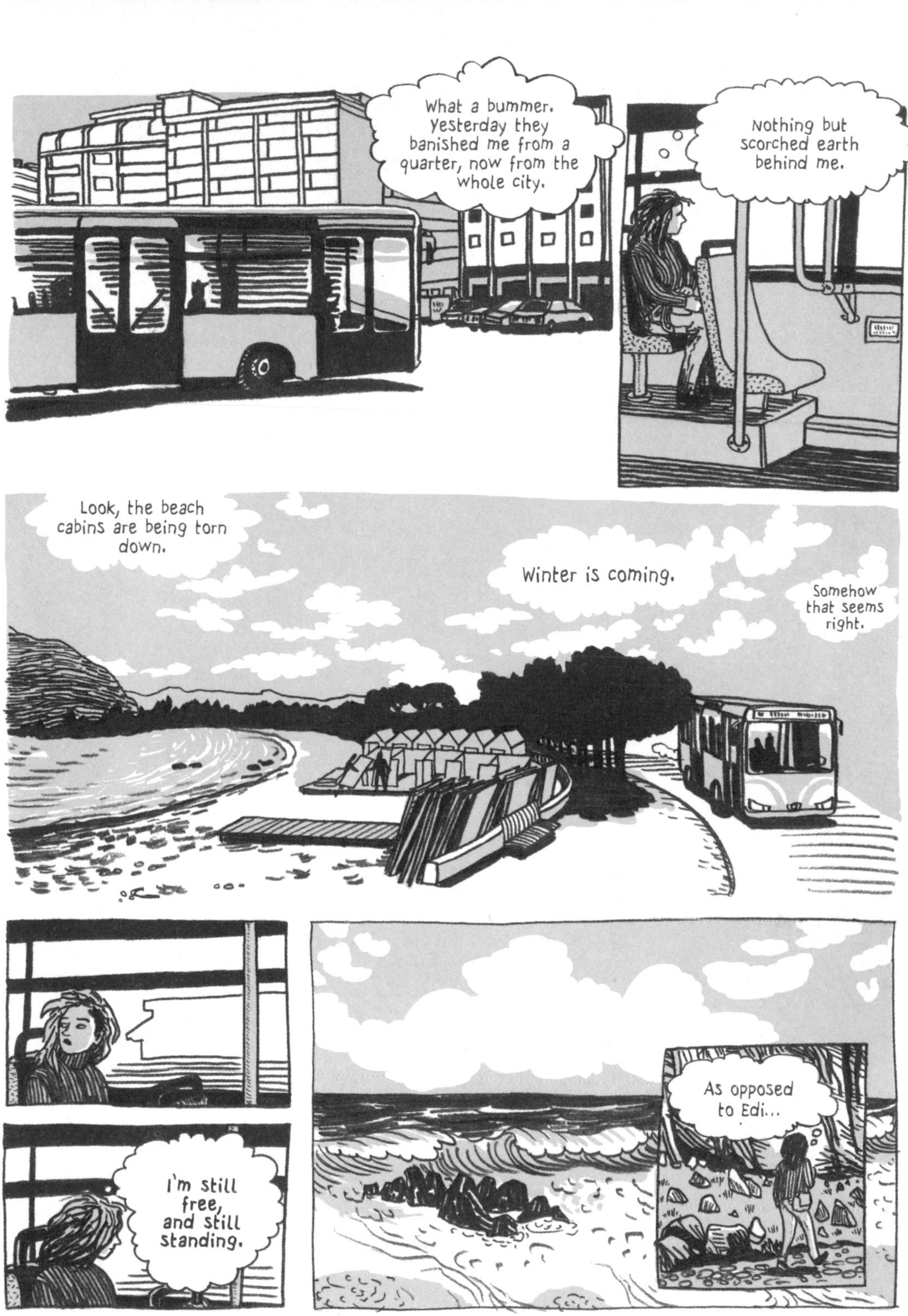
What a bummer. Yesterday they banished me from a quarter, now from the whole city.
Nothing but scorched earth behind me.
Look, the beach cabins are being torn down.
Winter is coming.
Somehow that seems right.
I'm still free, and still standing.
As opposed to Edi...

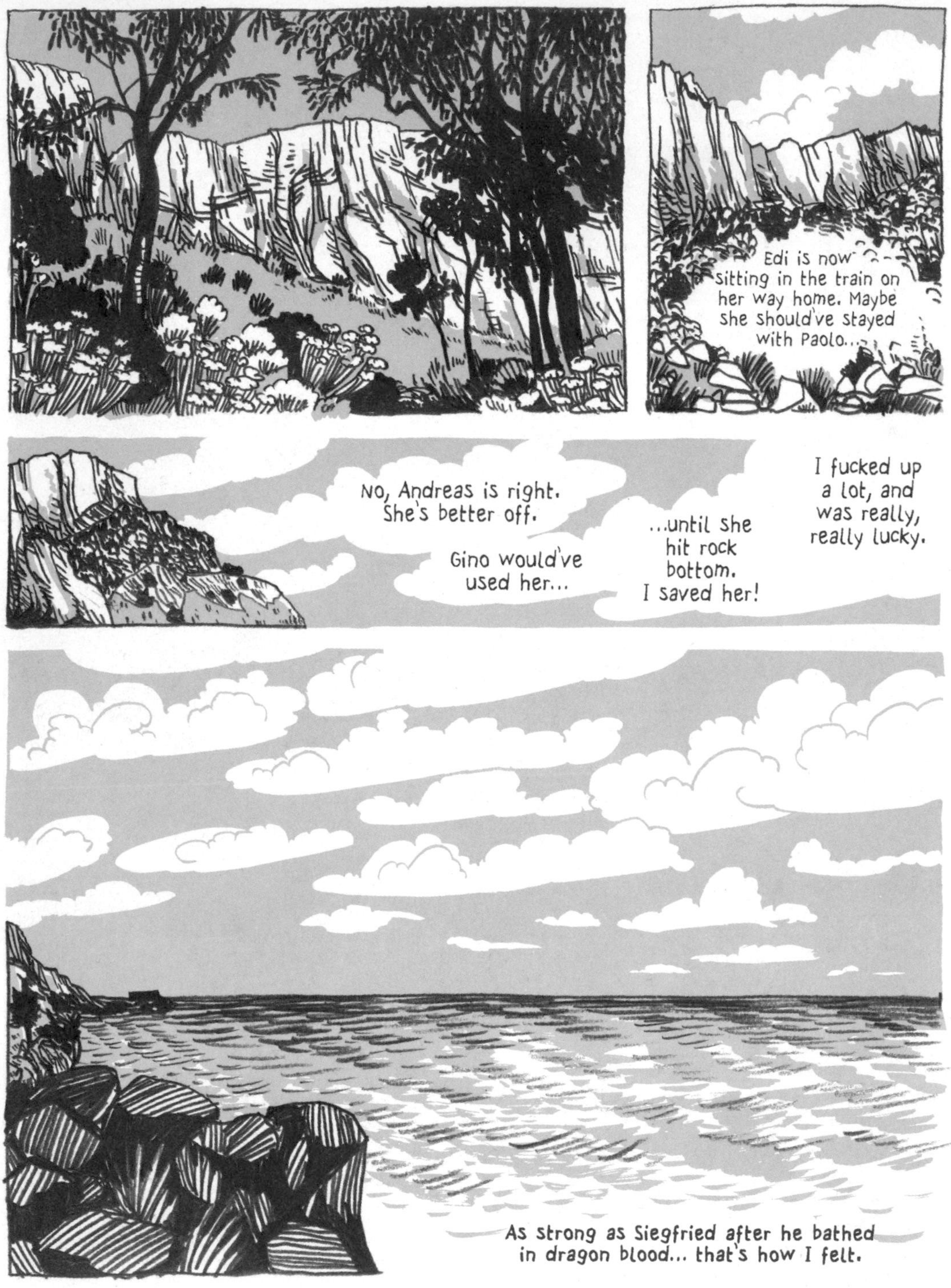
Edi is now sitting in the train on her way home. Maybe she should've stayed with Paolo...
No, Andreas is right. She's better off.
Gino would've used her...
...until she hit rock bottom. I saved her!
I fucked up a lot, and was really, really lucky.
As strong as Siegfried after he bathed in dragon blood... that's how I felt.

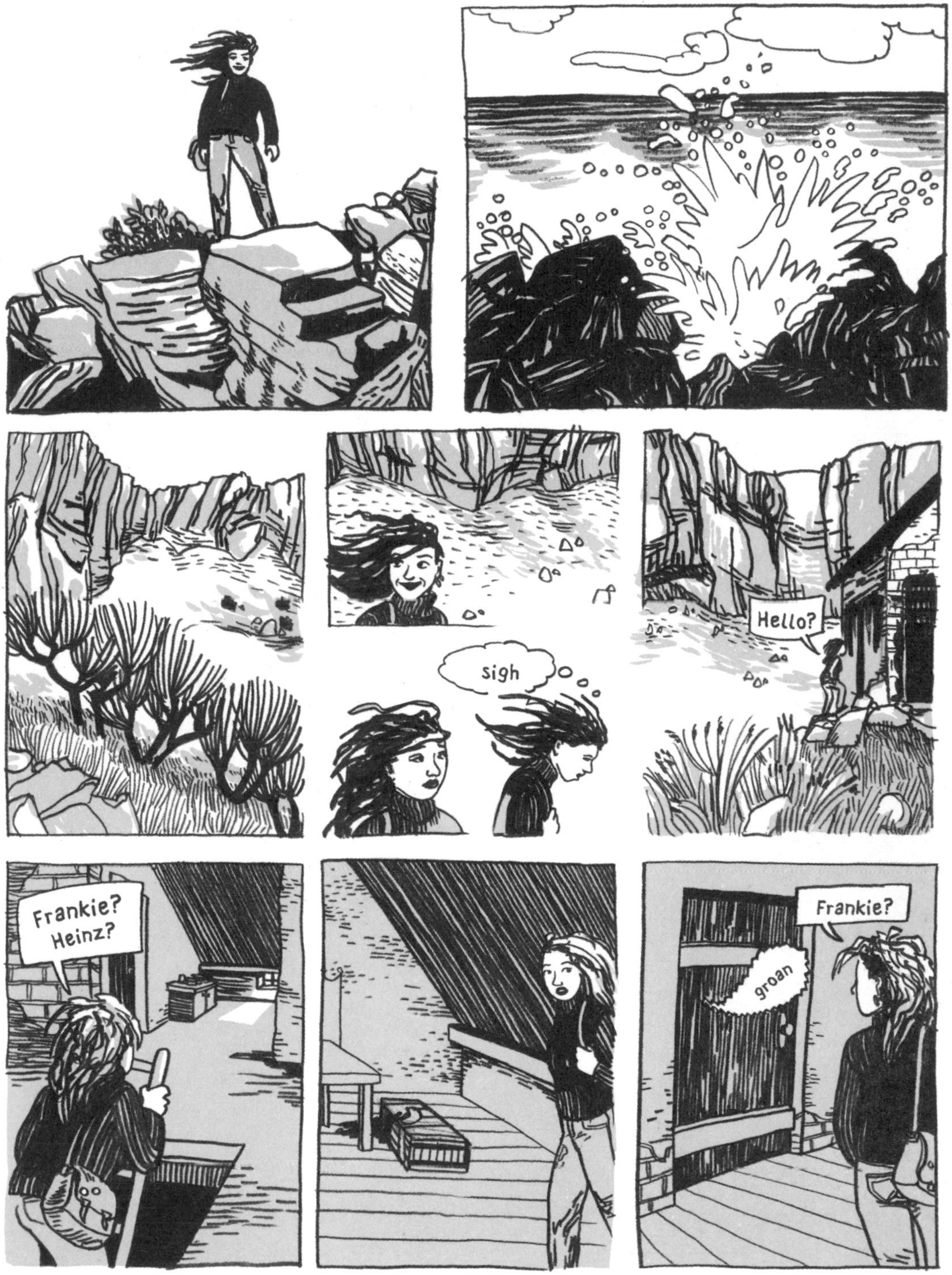
sigh
Hello?
Frankie?
Heinz?
Frankie?
groan

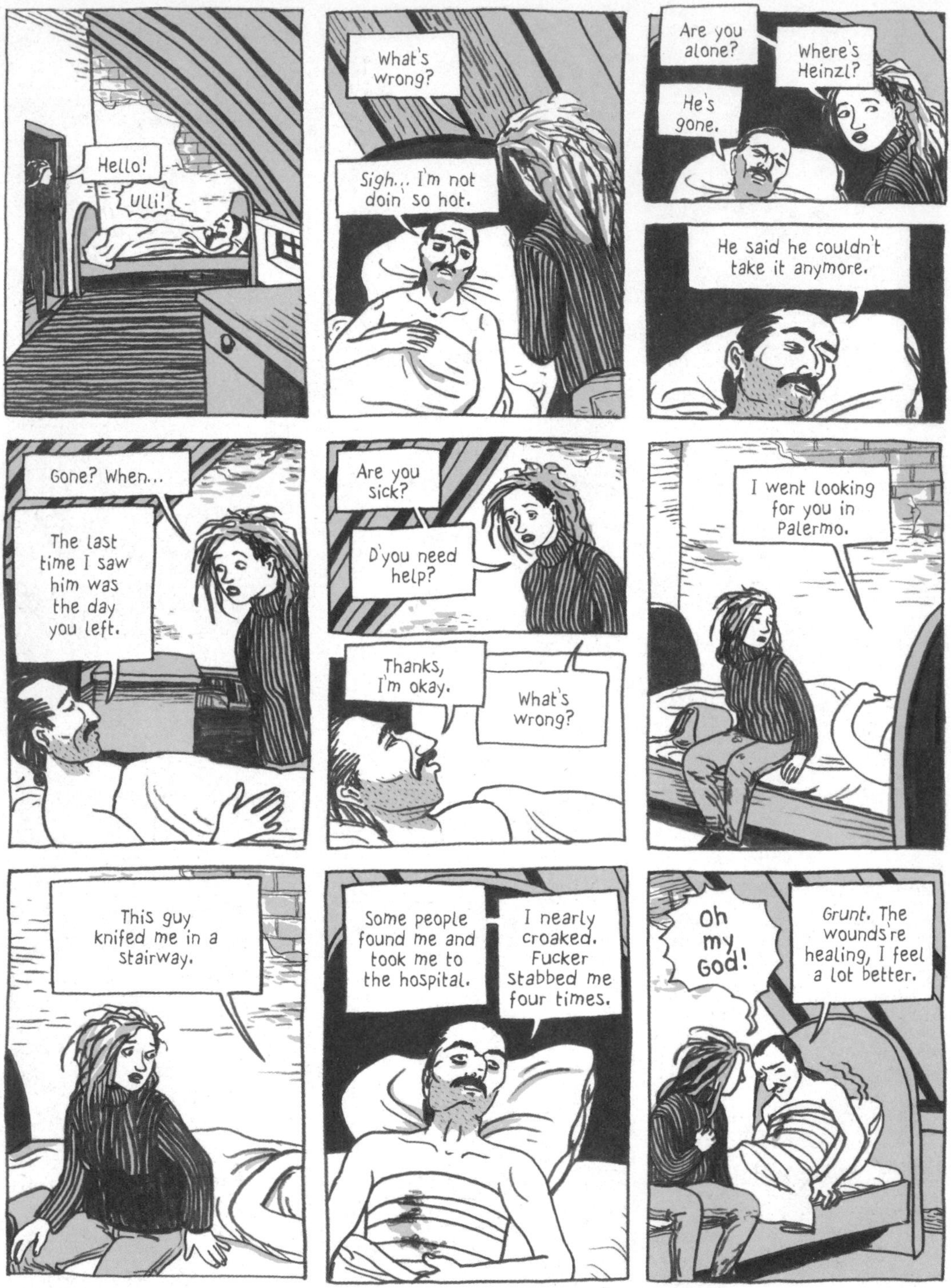

Hello!
Ulli!
What's wrong?
Sigh... I'm not doin' so hot.
Are you alone?
Where's Heinzl?
He's gone.
He said he couldn't take it anymore.
Gone? When...
The last time I saw him was the day you left.
Are you sick?
D'you need help?
Thanks, I'm okay.
What's wrong?
I went looking for you in Palermo.
This guy knifed me in a stairway.
Some people found me and took me to the hospital.
I nearly croaked. Fucker stabbed me four times.
Oh my God!
Grunt. The wounds're healing, I feel a lot better.

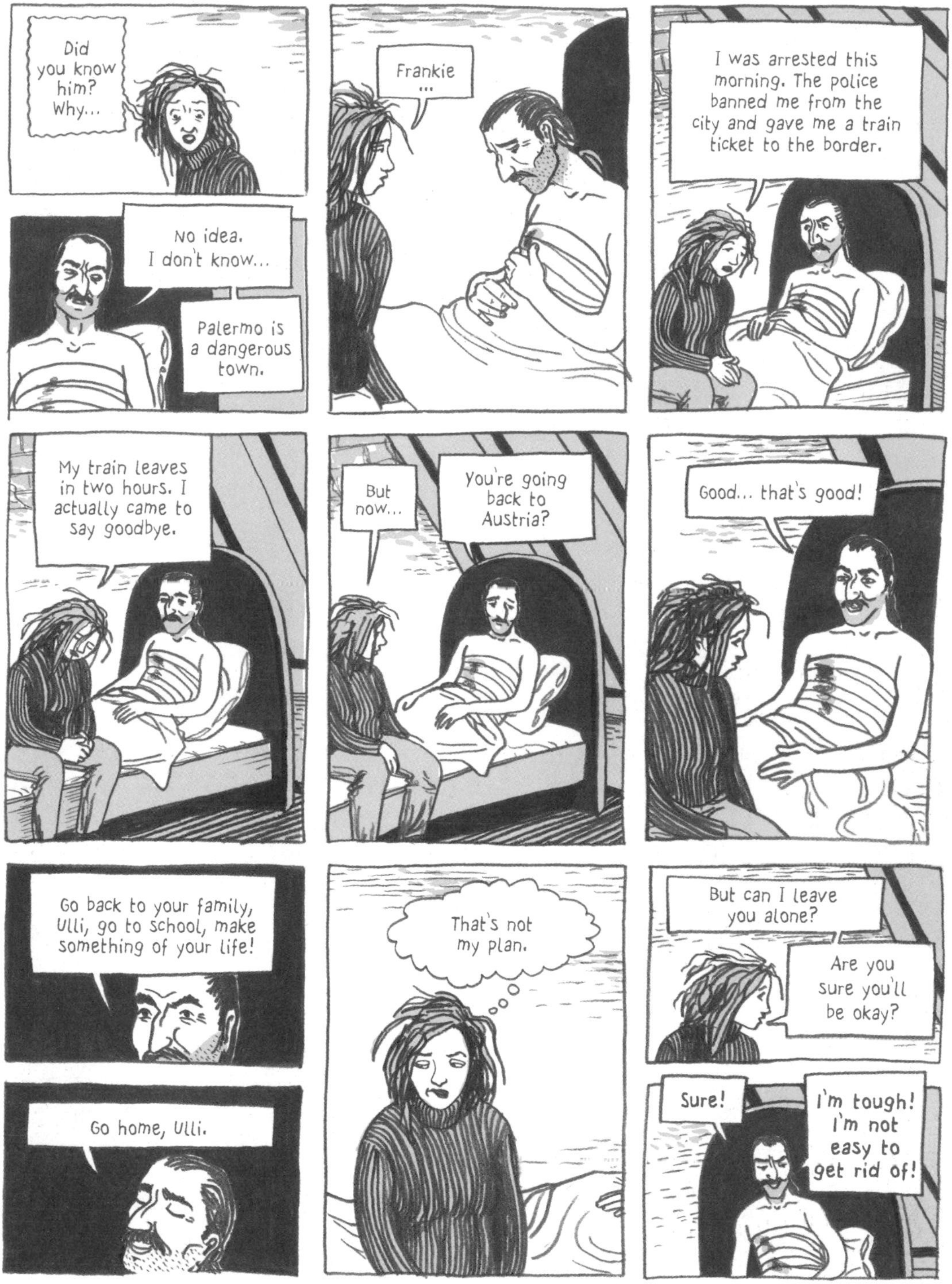
Did you know him? Why...
No idea. I don't know...
Palermo is a dangerous town.
Frankie ...
I was arrested this morning. The police banned me from the city and gave me a train ticket to the border.
My train leaves in two hours. I actually came to say goodbye.
But now...
You're going back to Austria?
Good... that's good!
Go back to your family, Ulli, go to school, make something of your life!
Go home, Ulli.
That's not my plan.
But can I leave you alone?
Are you sure you'll be okay?
Sure!
I'm tough! I'm not easy to get rid of!

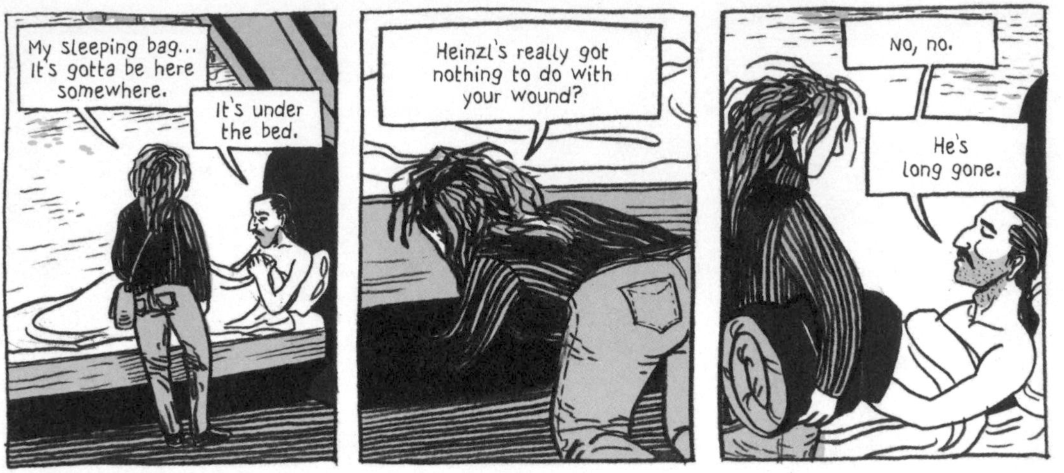
My sleeping bag... It's gotta be here somewhere.
It's under the bed.
Heinzl's really got nothing to do with your wound?
No, no.
He's long gone.

I was ashamed. Ashamed of leaving him alone, and ashamed because I'd dreaded touching the old man.

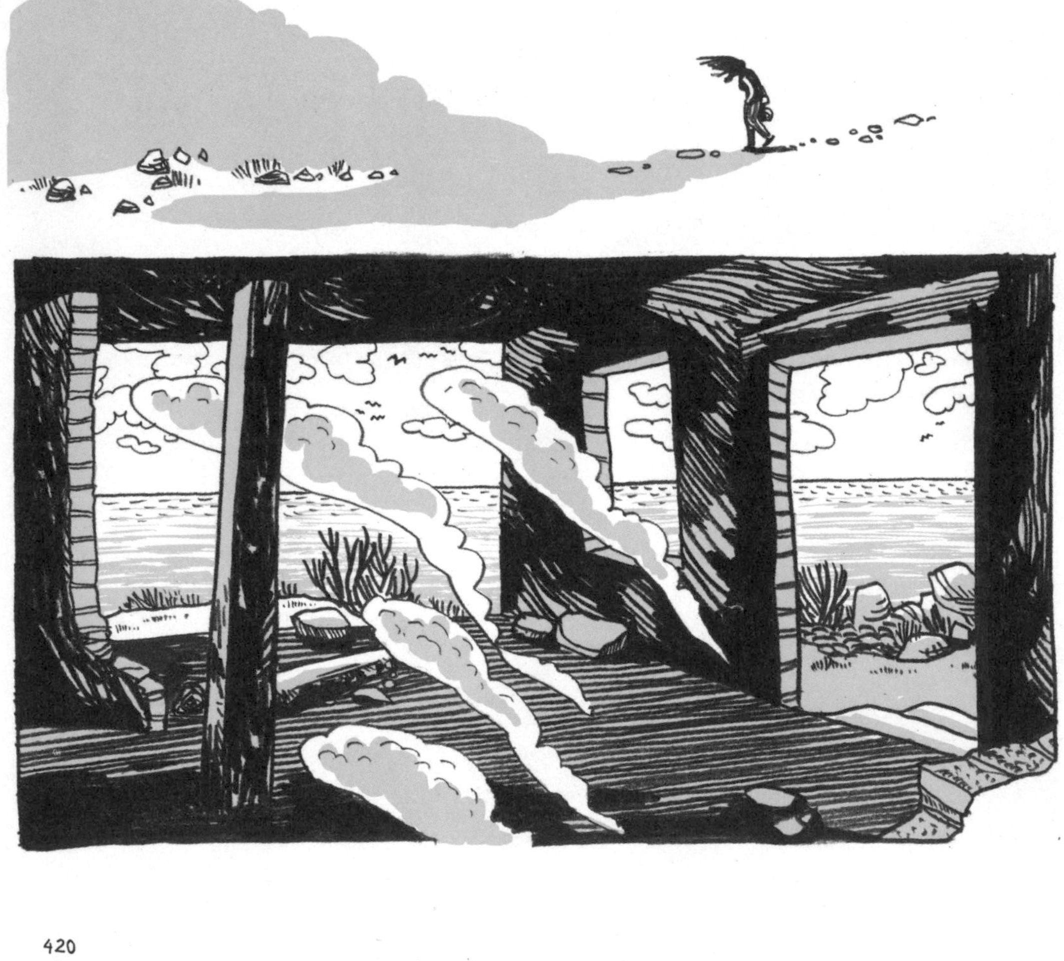

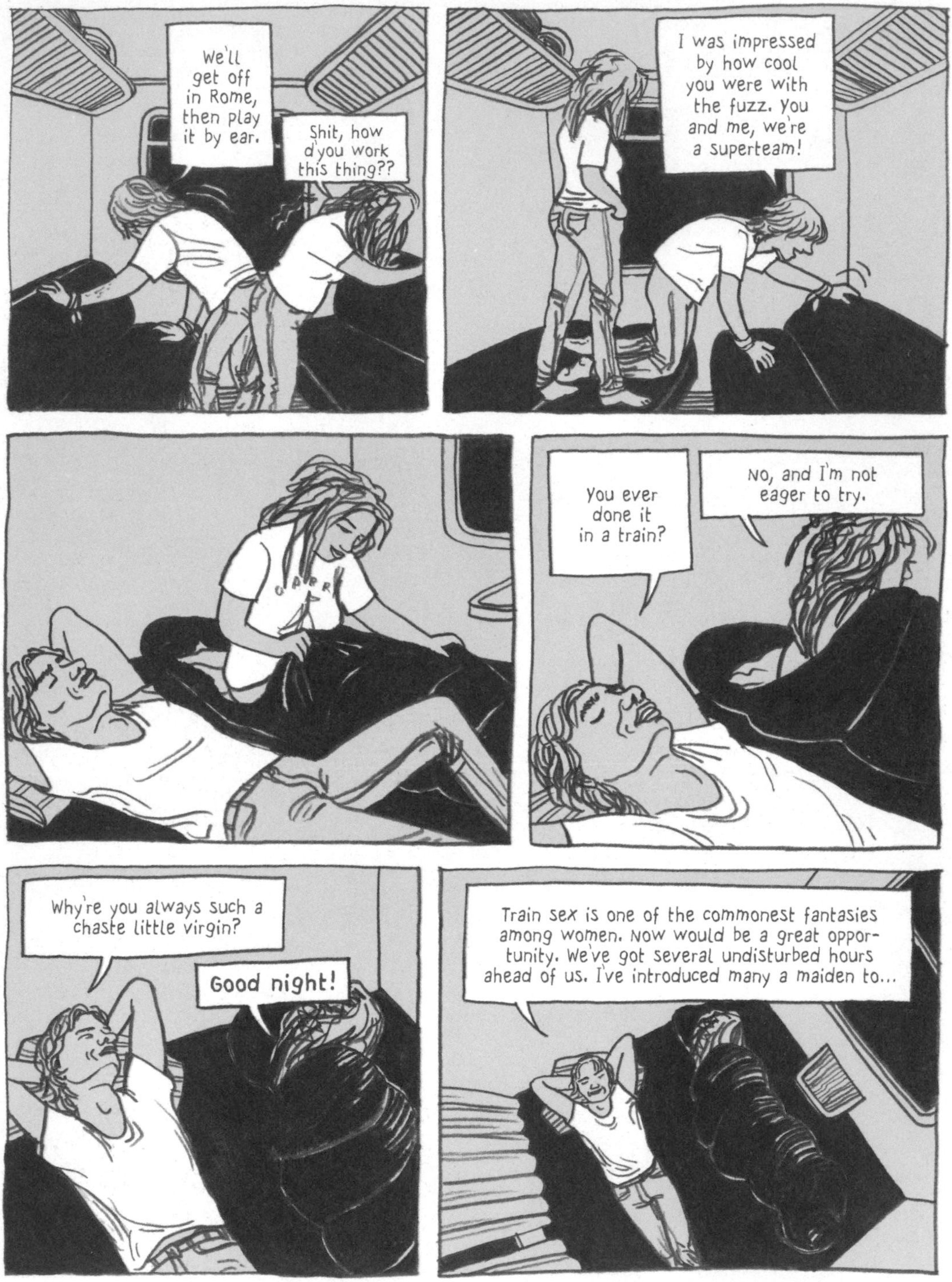
We'll get off in Rome, then play it by ear.
Shit, how d'you work this thing??
I was impressed by how cool you were with the fuzz. You and me, we're a superteam!
You ever done it in a train?
No, and I'm not eager to try.
Why're you always such a chaste little virgin?
Good night!
Train sex is one of the commonest fantasies among women. Now would be a great opportunity. We've got several undisturbed hours ahead of us. I've introduced many a maiden to...

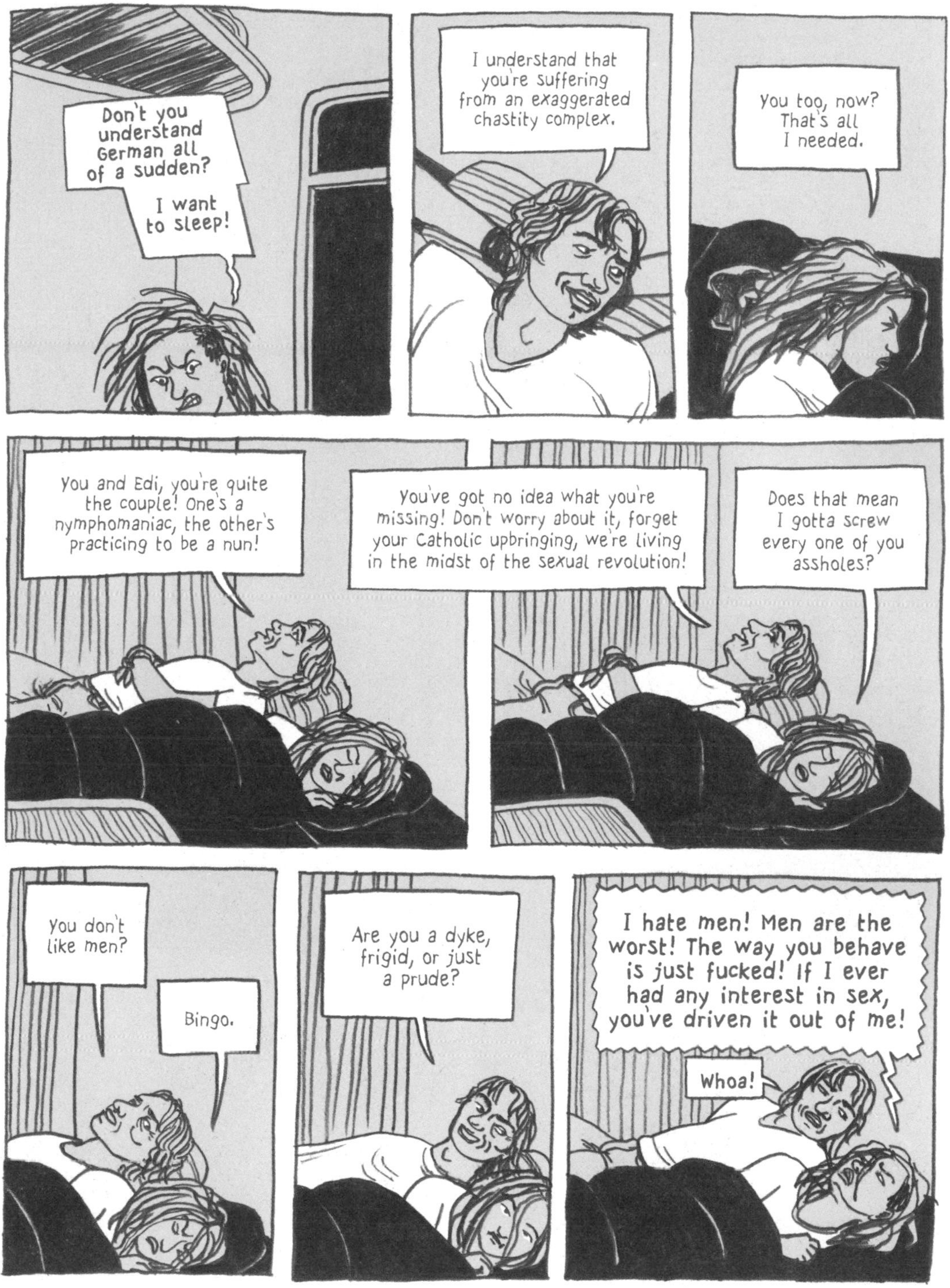
Don't you understand German all of a sudden?
I want to sleep!
I understand that you're suffering from an exaggerated chastity complex.
You too, now? That's all I needed.
You and Edi, you're quite the couple! One's a nymphomaniac, the other's practicing to be a nun!
You've got no idea what you're missing! Don't worry about it, forget your Catholic upbringing, we're living in the midst of the sexual revolution!
Does that mean I gotta screw every one of you assholes?
You don't like men?
Bingo.
Are you a dyke, frigid, or just a prude?
I hate men! Men are the worst! The way you behave is just fucked! If I ever had any interest in sex, you've driven it out of me!
Whoa!

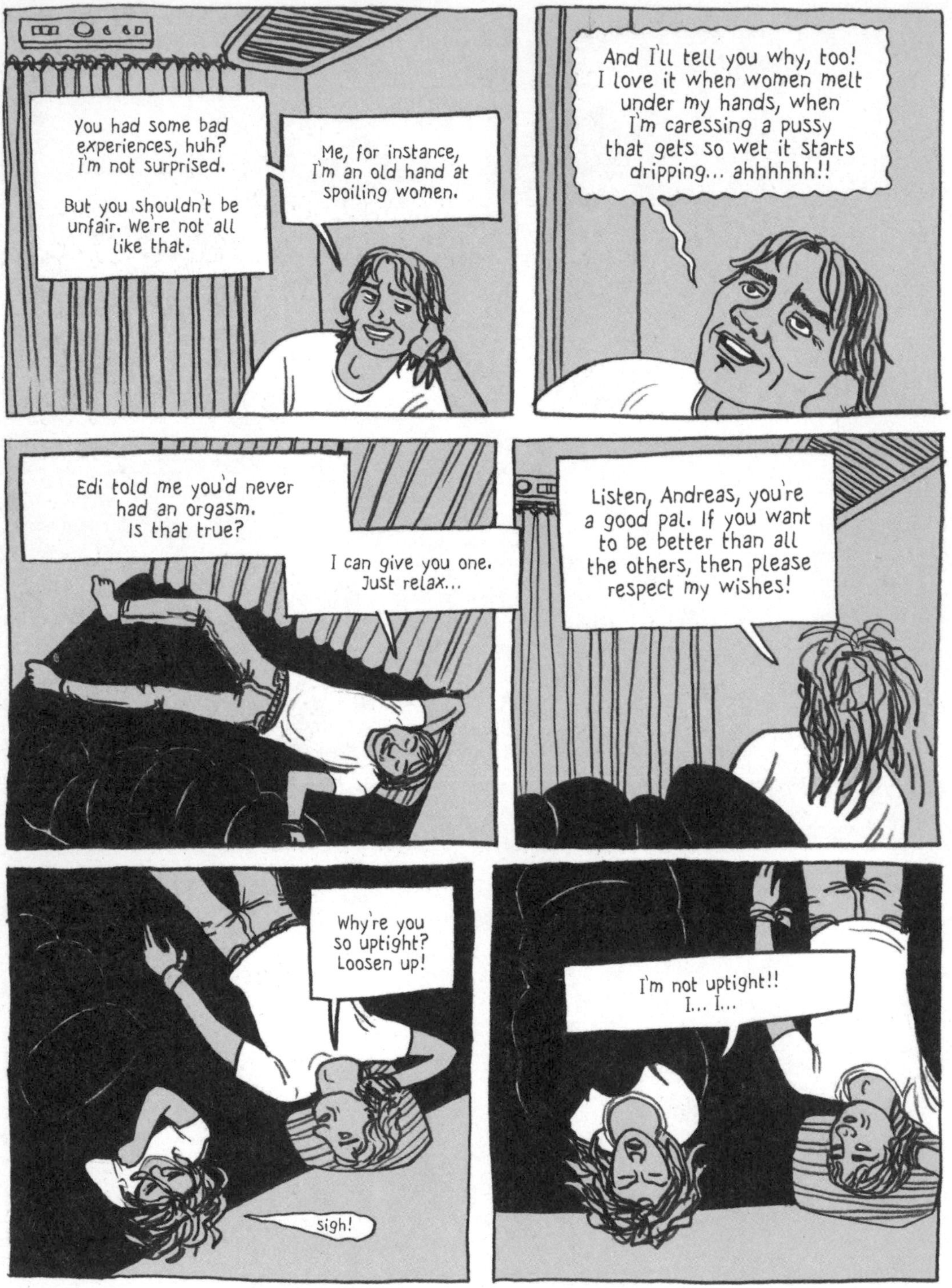

You had some bad experiences, huh? I'm not surprised.
But you shouldn't be unfair. We're not all like that.
Me, for instance, I'm an old hand at spoiling women.
And I'll tell you why, too! I love it when women melt under my hands, when I'm caressing a pussy that gets so wet it starts dripping... ahhhhhh!!
Edi told me you'd never had an orgasm. Is that true?
I can give you one. Just relax...
Listen, Andreas, you're a good pal. If you want to be better than all the others, then please respect my wishes!
Why're you so uptight? Loosen up!
sigh!
I'm not uptight!! I... I...

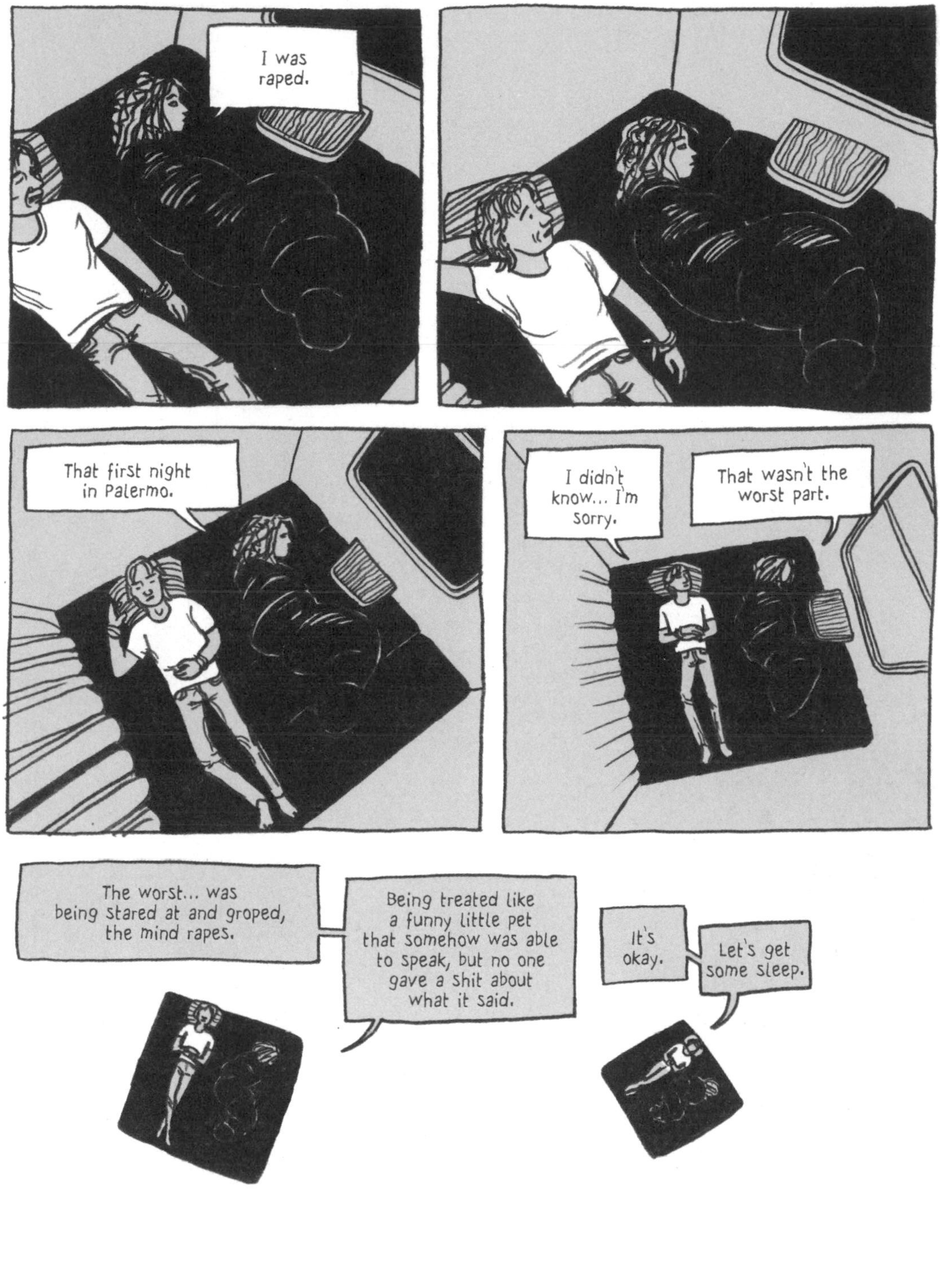
I was raped.
That first night in Palermo.
I didn't know... I'm sorry.
That wasn't the worst part.
The worst... was being stared at and groped, the mind rapes.
Being treated like a funny little pet that somehow was able to speak, but no one gave a shit about what it said.
It's okay.
Let's get some sleep.

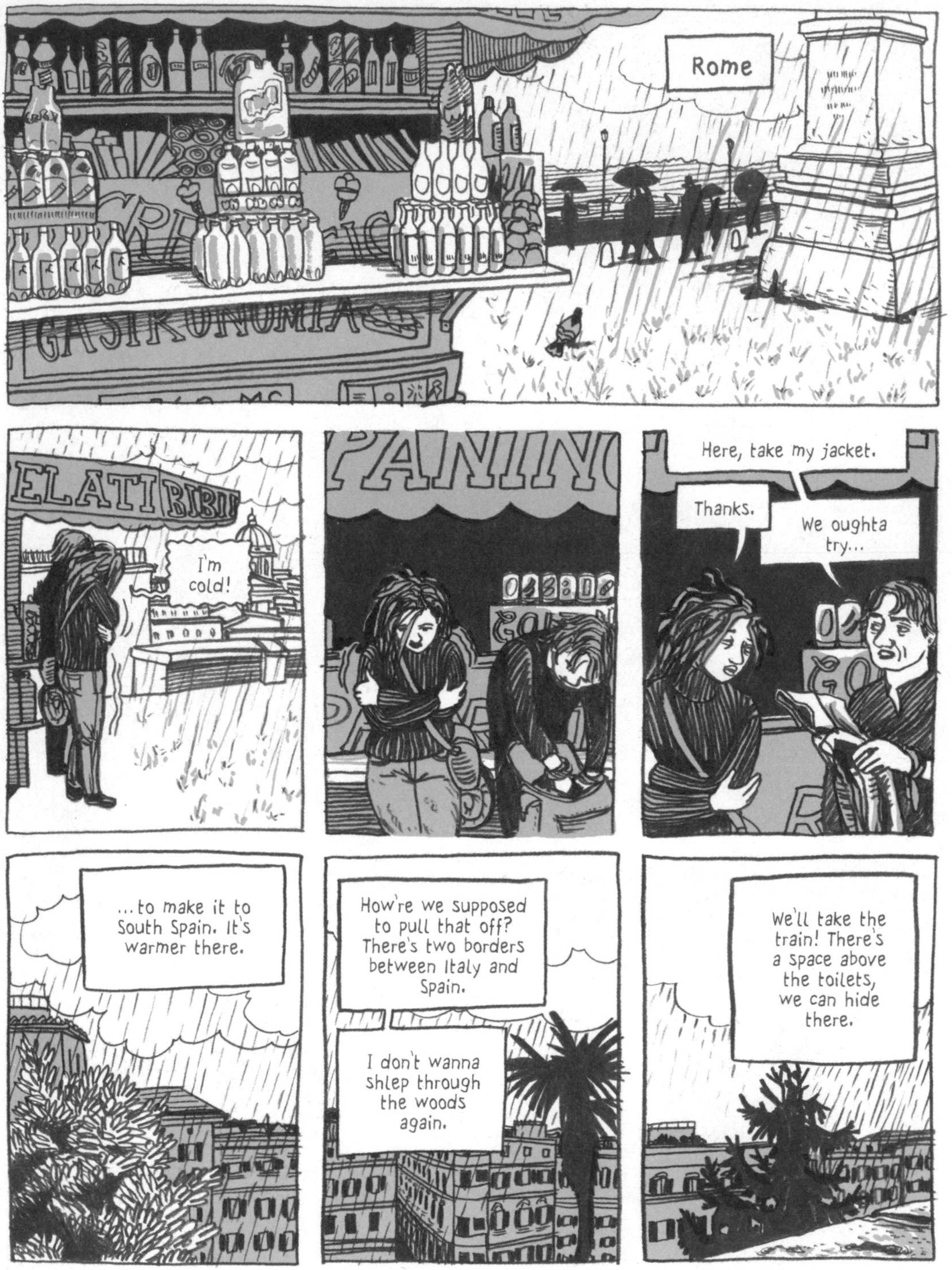
Rome
I'm cold!
Here, take my jacket.
Thanks.
We oughta try...
...to make it to South Spain. It's warmer there.
How're we supposed to pull that off? There's two borders between Italy and Spain.
I don't wanna shlep through the woods again.
We'll take the train! There's a space above the toilets, we can hide there.

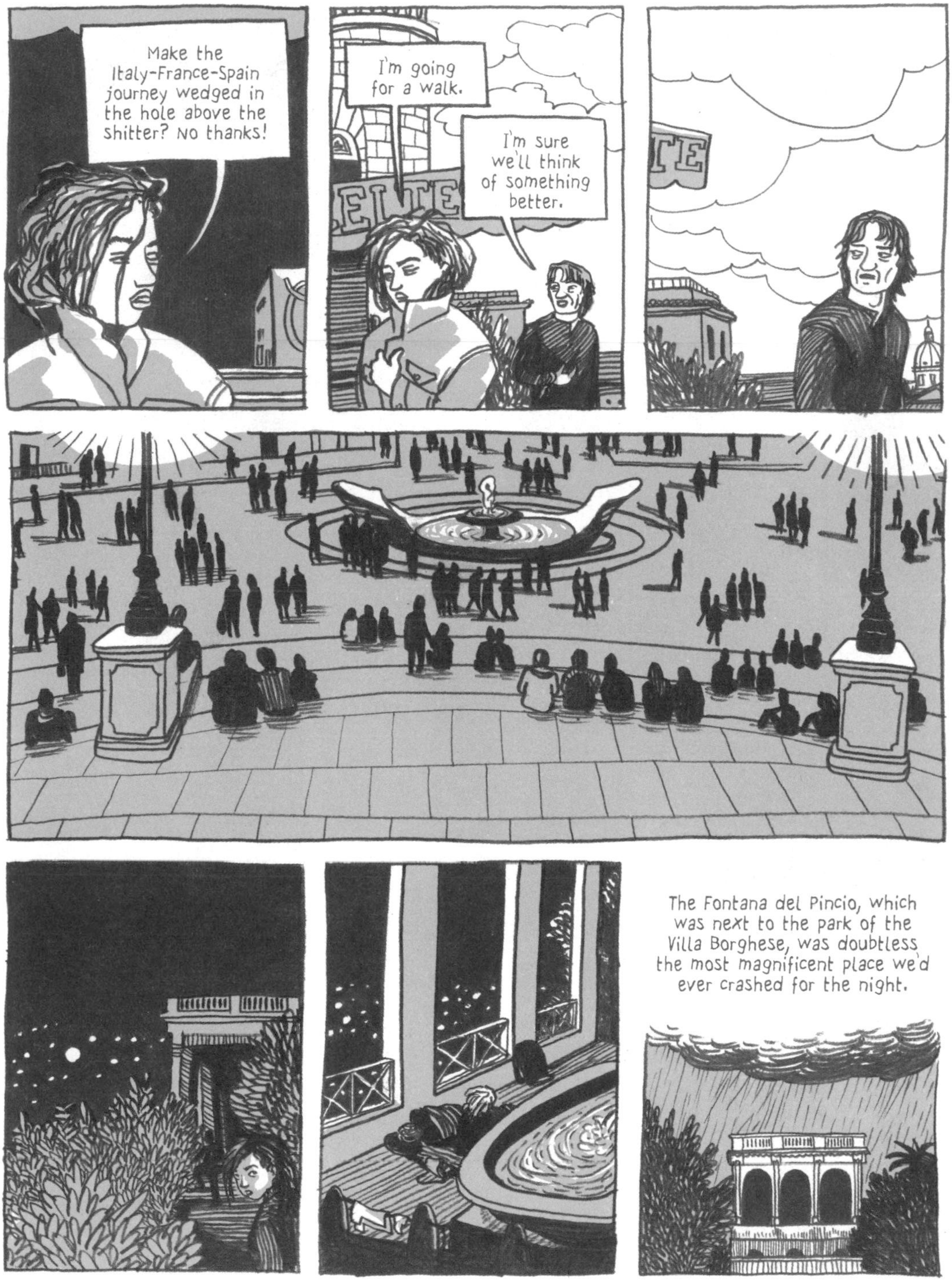
Make the Italy-France-Spain journey wedged in the hole above the shitter? No thanks!
I'm going for a walk.
I'm sure we'll think of something better.
The Fontana del Pincio, which was next to the park of the Villa Borghese, was doubtless the most magnificent place we'd ever crashed for the night.

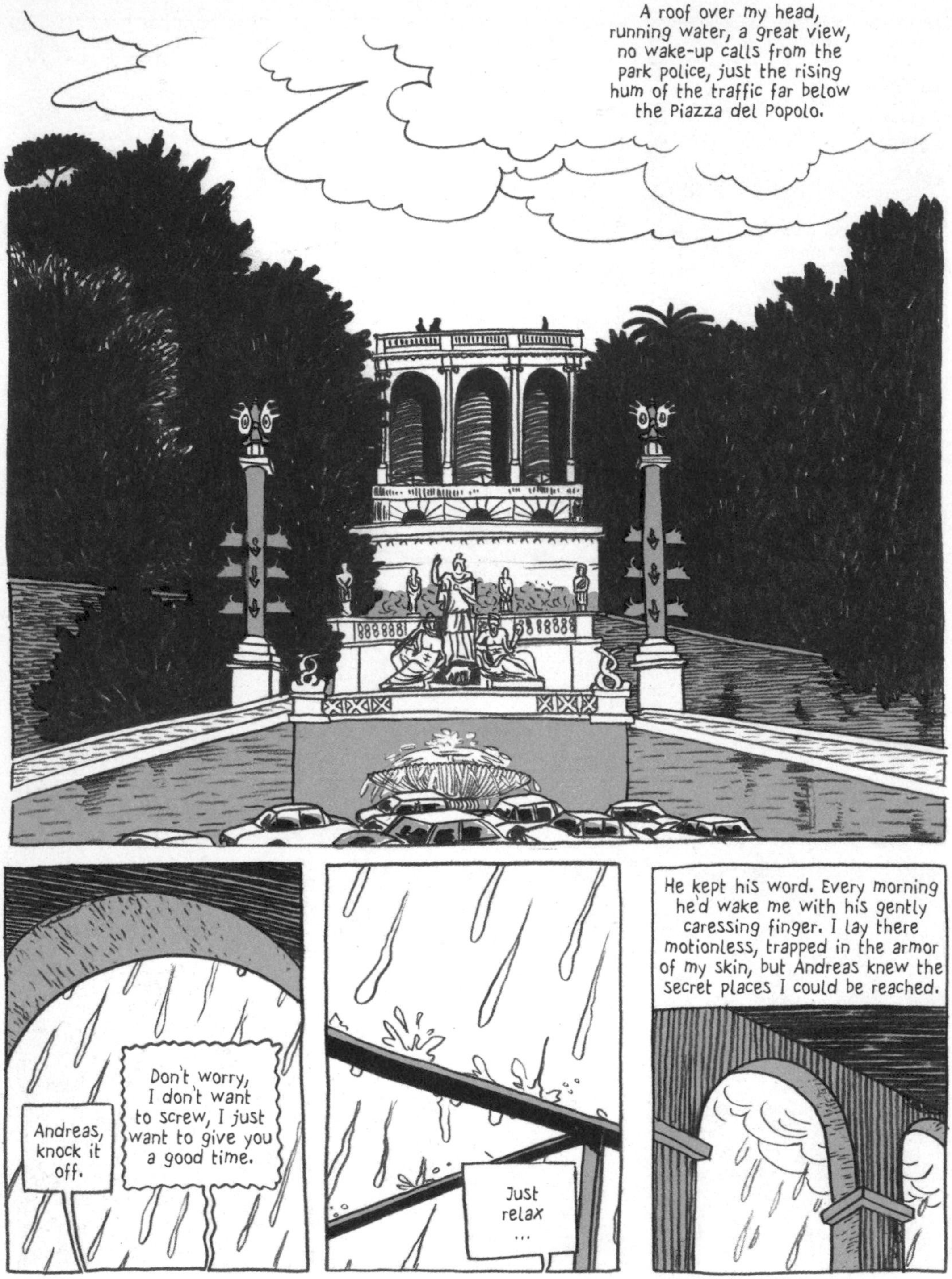
A roof over my head, running water, a great view, no wake-up calls from the park police, just the rising hum of the traffic far below the Piazza del Popolo.
Andreas, knock it off.
Don't worry, I don't want to screw, I just want to give you a good time.
Just relax ...
He kept his word. Every morning he'd wake me with his gently caressing finger. I lay there motionless, trapped in the armor of my skin, but Andreas knew the secret places I could be reached.

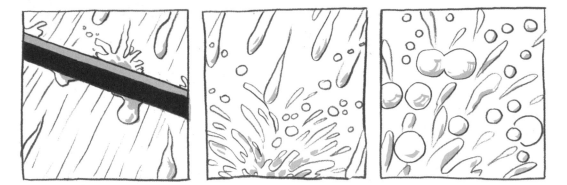

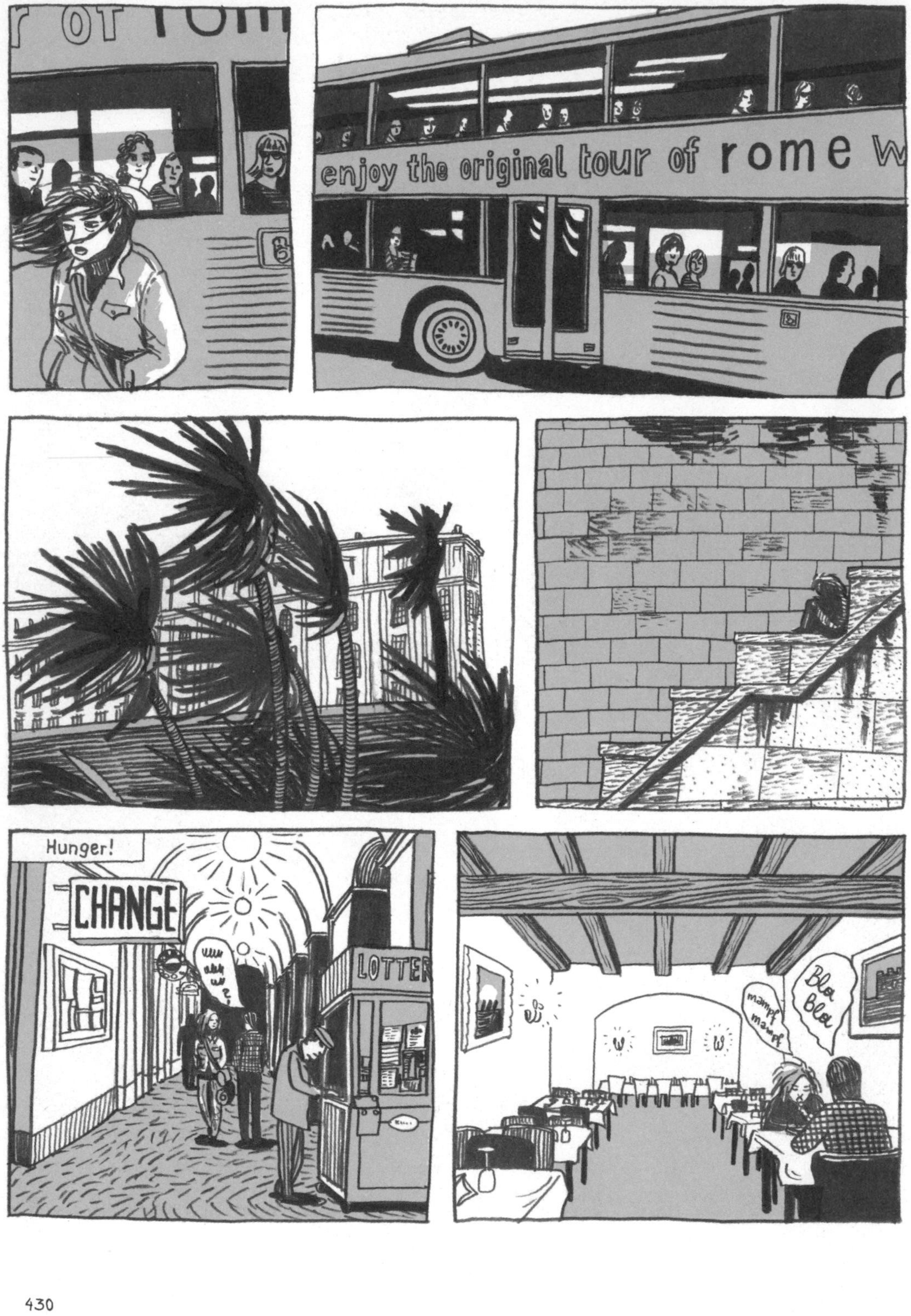
r of rom
enjoy the original tour of rome w
Hunger!
CHANGE
LOTTER
Bla Bla
mampf mampf

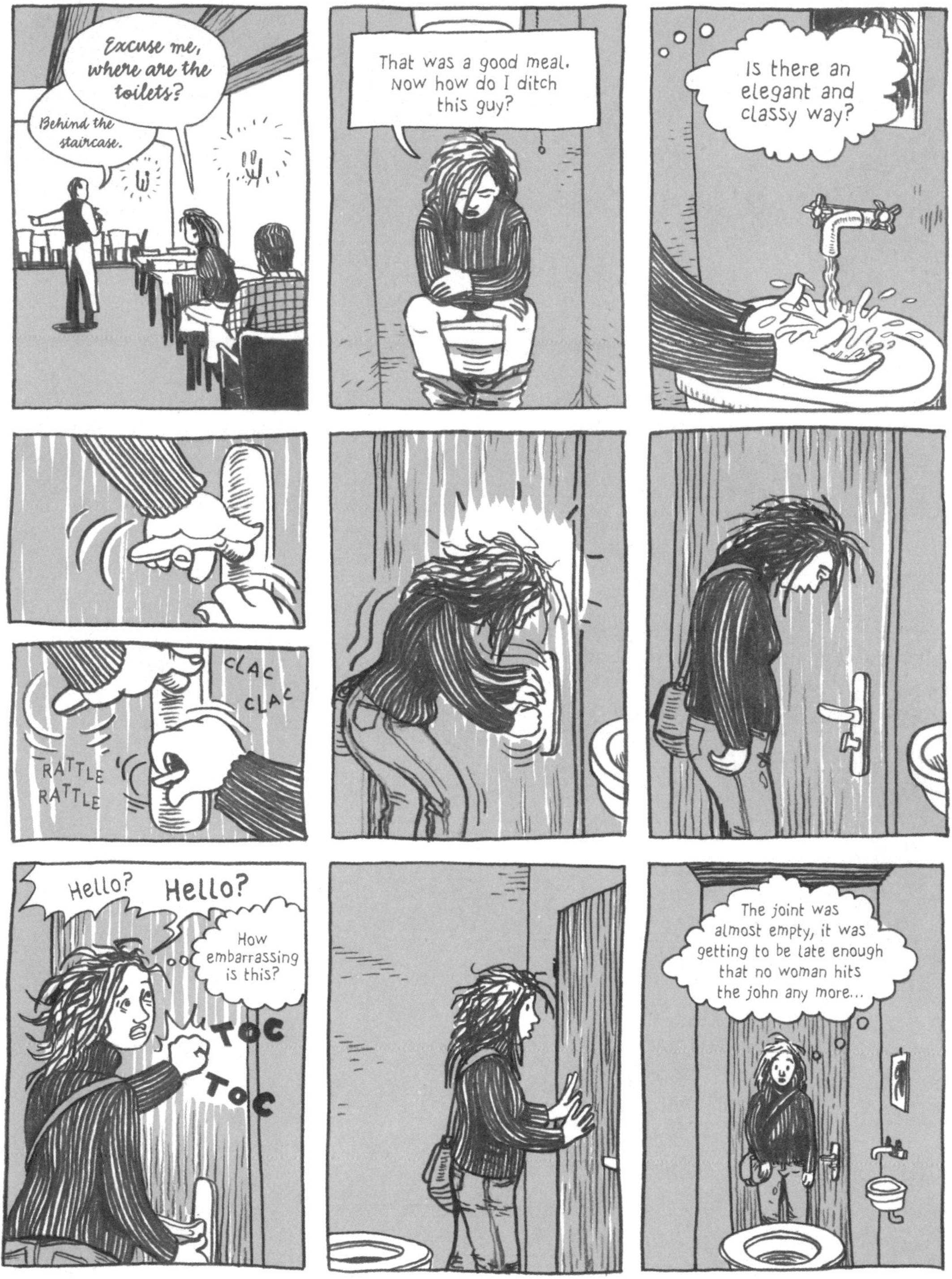

Excuse me, where are the toilets?
Behind the staircase.
That was a good meal. Now how do I ditch this guy?
Is there an elegant and classy way?
CLAC
CLAC
RATTLE
RATTLE
Hello?
Hello?
How embarrassing is this?
TOC
TOC
The joint was almost empty, it was getting to be late enough that no woman hits the john any more...

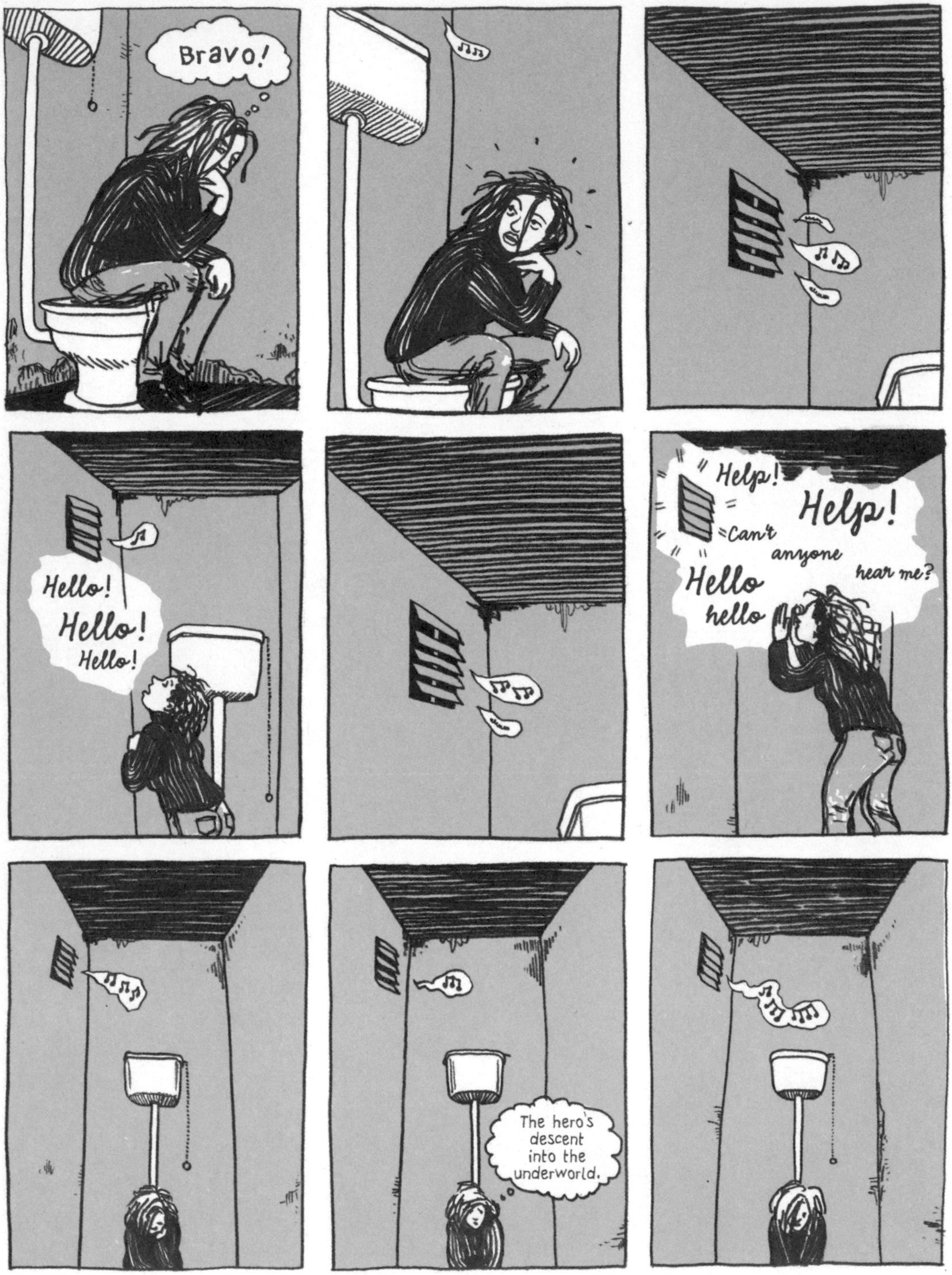

Bravo!
Hello!
Hello!
Hello!
Help!
Help!
Can't anyone hear me?
Hello hello
The hero's descent into the underworld.

XX. the RESURRECTION

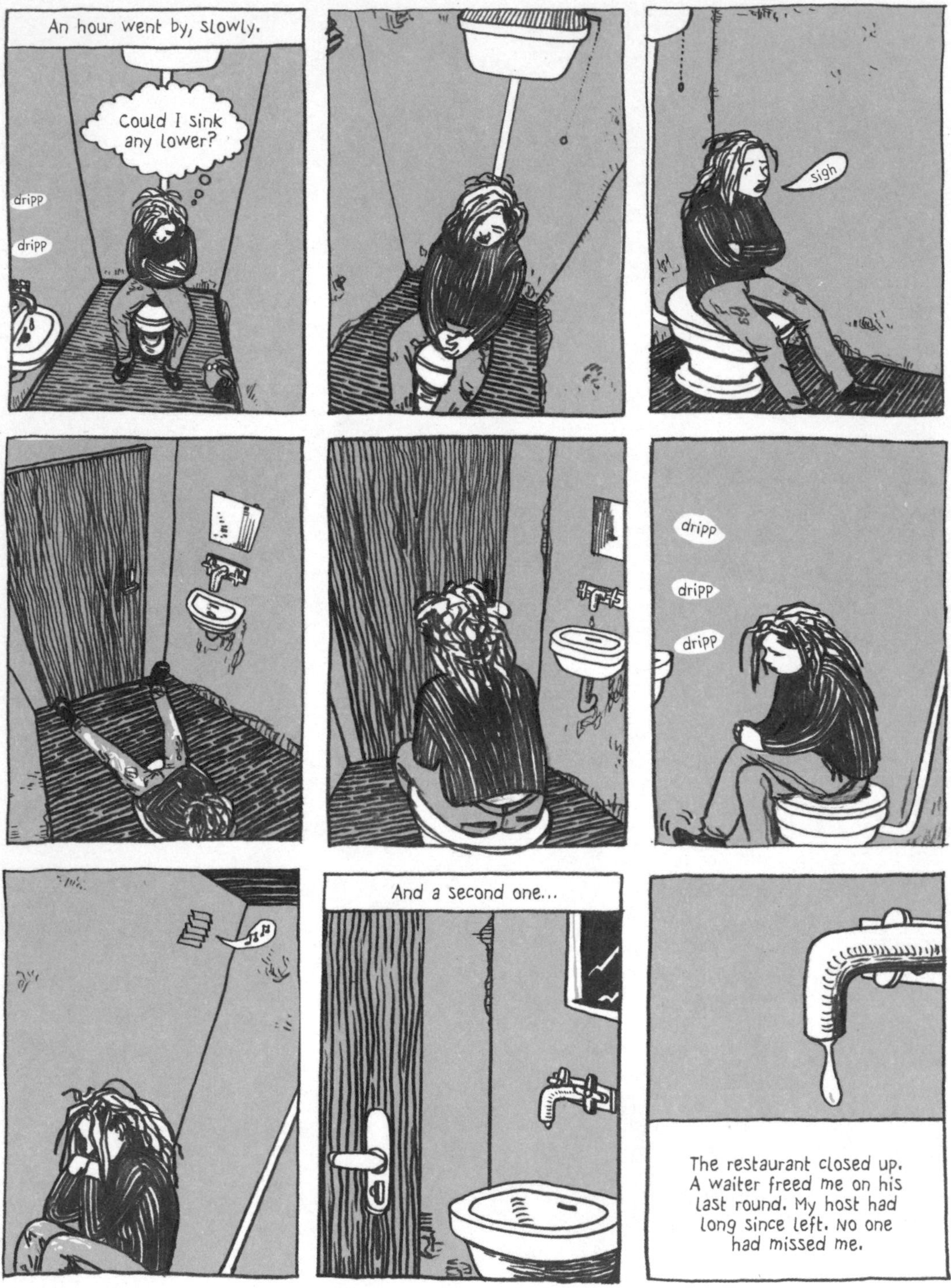
An hour went by, slowly.
Could I sink any lower?
dripp
dripp
sigh
dripp
dripp
dripp
And a second one...
The restaurant closed up. A waiter freed me on his last round. My host had long since left. No one had missed me.

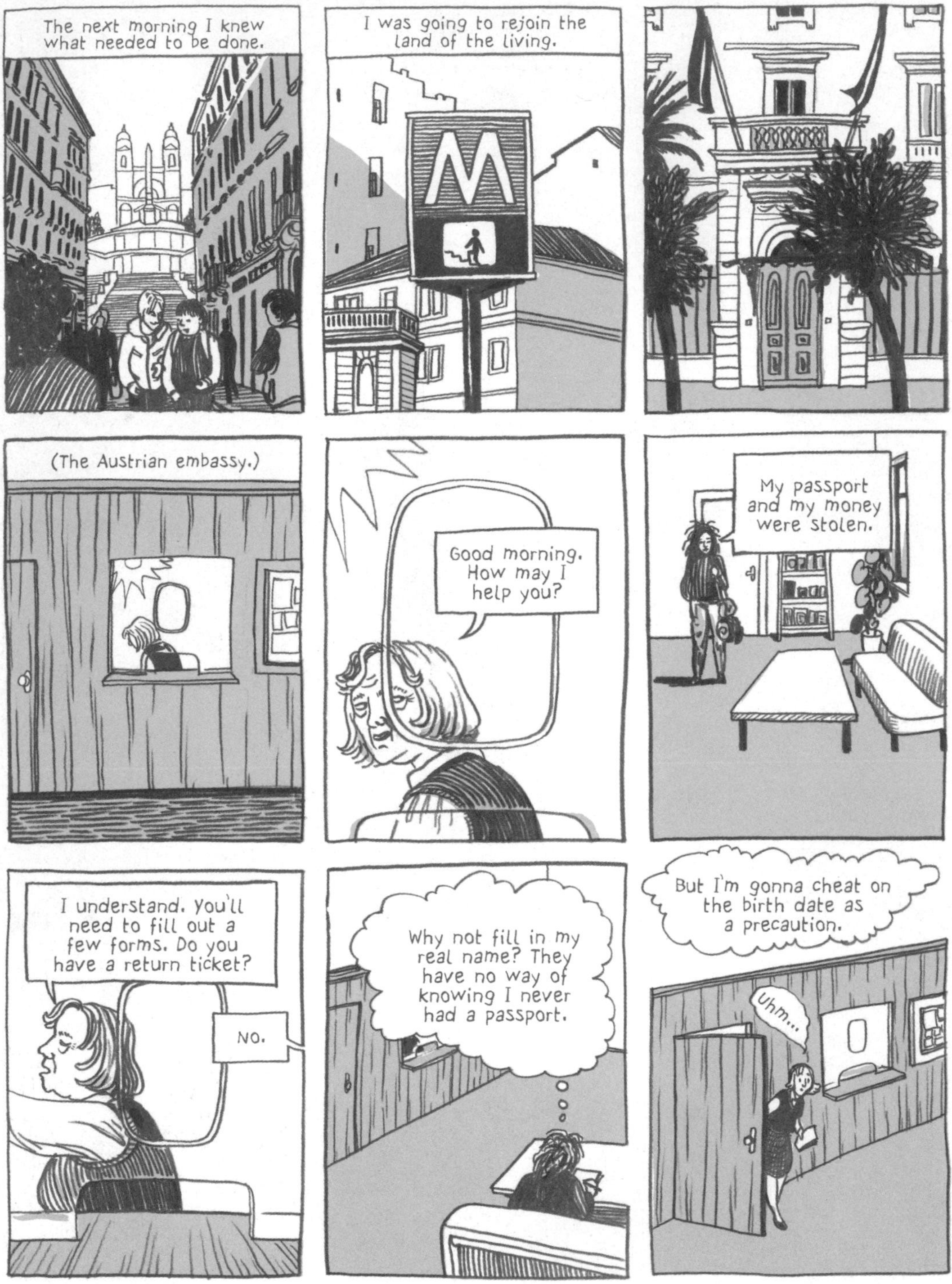
The next morning I knew what needed to be done.
I was going to rejoin the land of the living.
M
(The Austrian embassy.)
Good morning. How may I help you?
My passport and my money were stolen.
I understand. You'll need to fill out a few forms. Do you have a return ticket?
No.
Why not fill in my real name? They have no way of knowing I never had a passport.
But I'm gonna cheat on the birth date as a precaution.
Uhm...

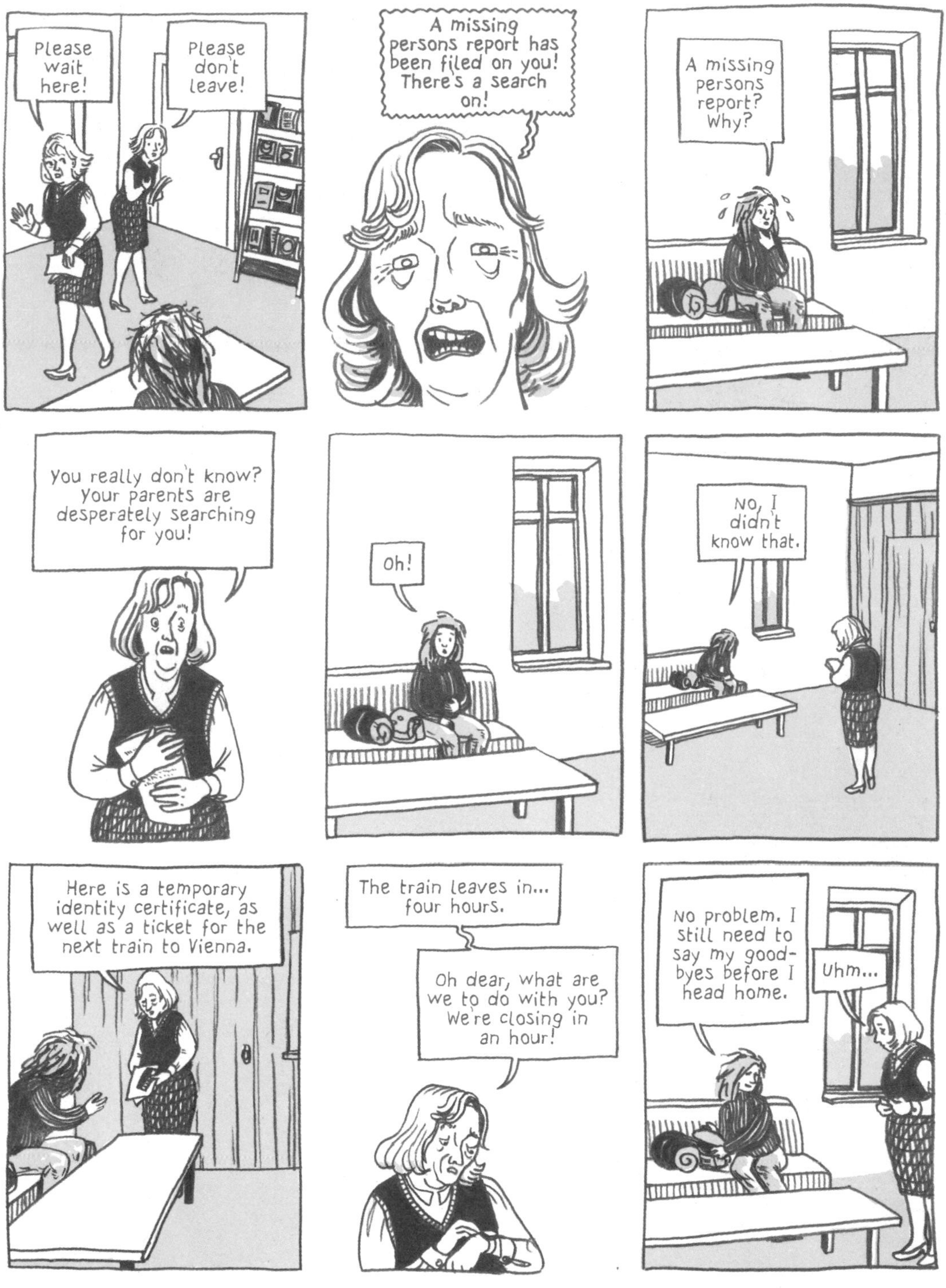

Please wait here!
Please don't leave!
A missing persons report has been filed on you! There's a search on!
A missing persons report? Why?
You really don't know? Your parents are desperately searching for you!
Oh!
No, I didn't know that.
Here is a temporary identity certificate, as well as a ticket for the next train to Vienna.
The train leaves in... four hours.
Oh dear, what are we to do with you? We're closing in an hour!
No problem. I still need to say my good-byes before I head home.
Uhm...

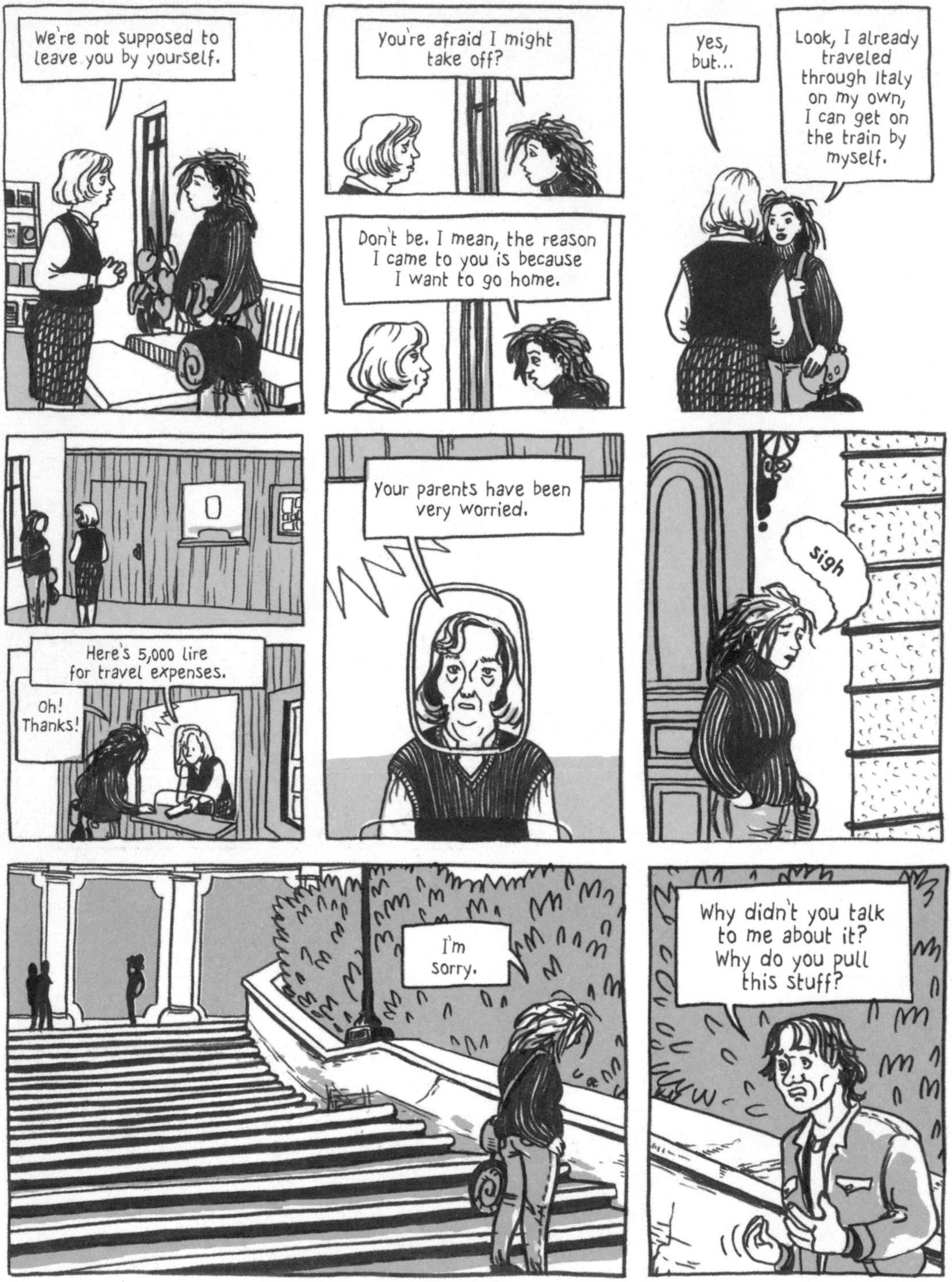
We're not supposed to leave you by yourself.
You're afraid I might take off?
Don't be. I mean, the reason I came to you is because I want to go home.
Yes, but...
Look, I already traveled through Italy on my own, I can get on the train by myself.
Here's 5,000 lire for travel expenses.
Oh! Thanks!
Your parents have been very worried.
sigh
I'm sorry.
Why didn't you talk to me about it? Why do you pull this stuff?

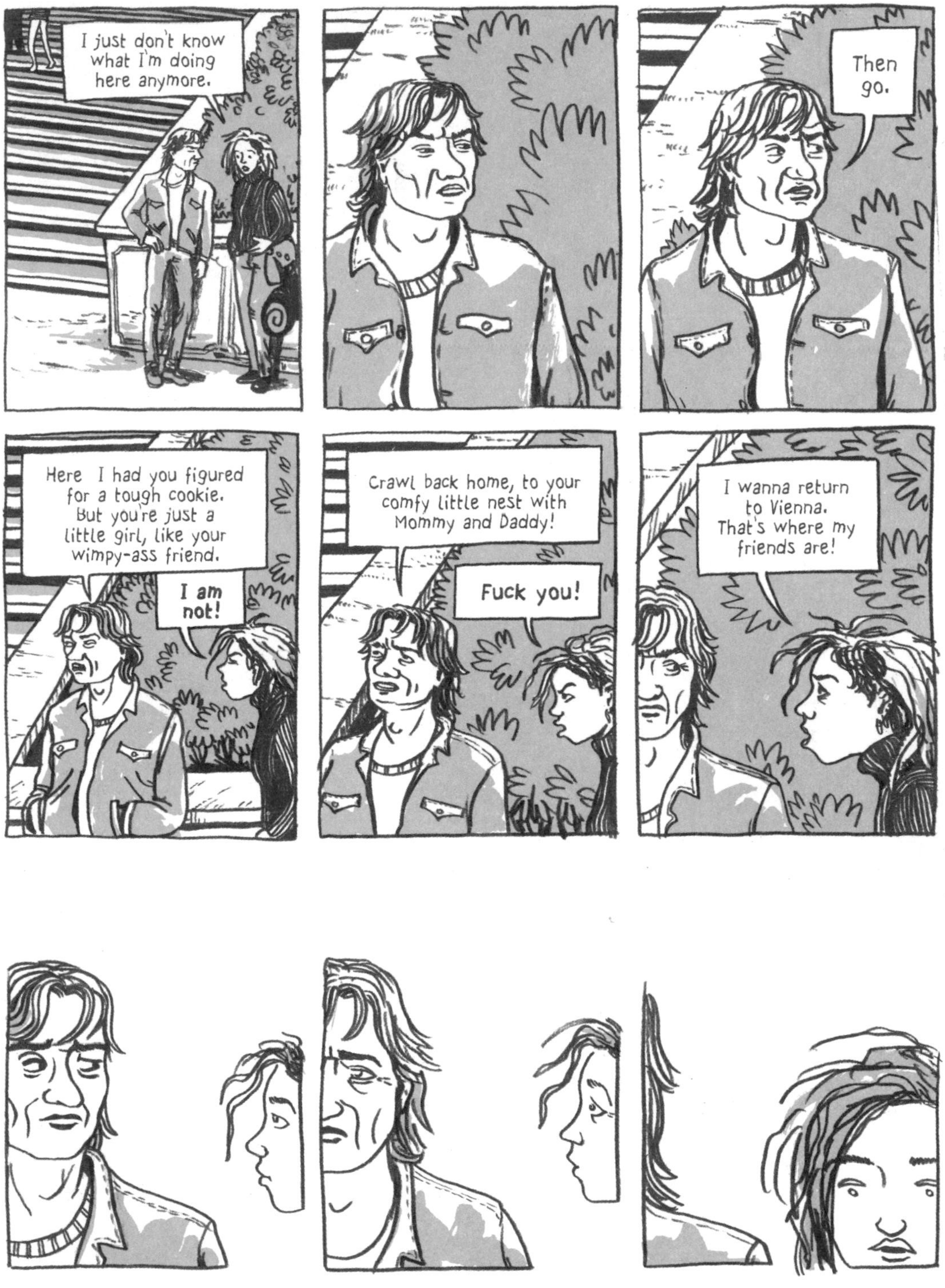

I just don't know what I'm doing here anymore.
Then go.
Here I had you figured for a tough cookie. But you're just a little girl, like your wimpy-ass friend.
I am not!
Crawl back home, to your comfy little nest with Mommy and Daddy!
Fuck you!
I wanna return to Vienna. That's where my friends are!

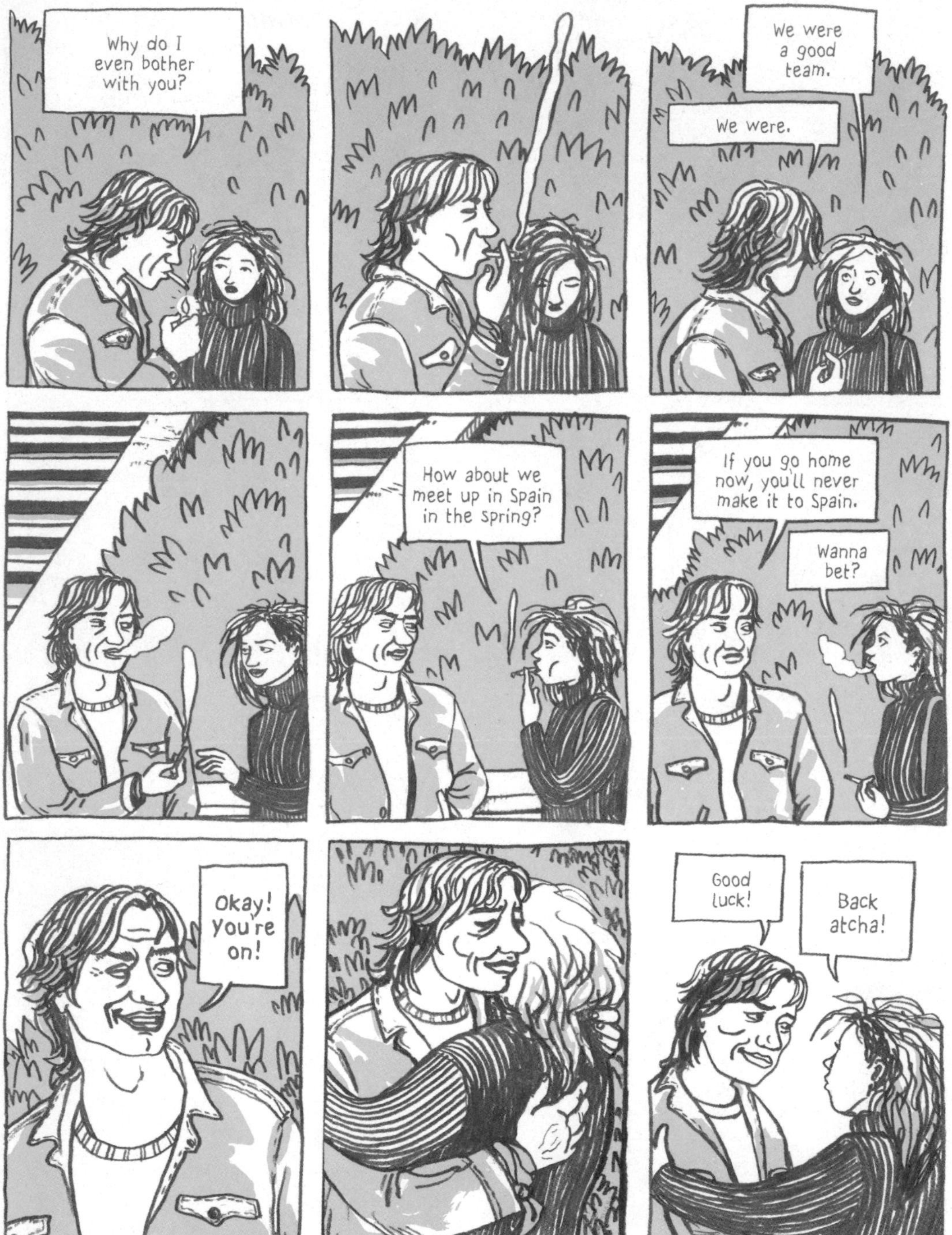
Why do I even bother with you?
We were a good team.
We were.
How about we meet up in Spain in the spring?
If you go home now, you'll never make it to Spain.
Wanna bet?
Okay! You're on!
Good luck!
Back atcha!

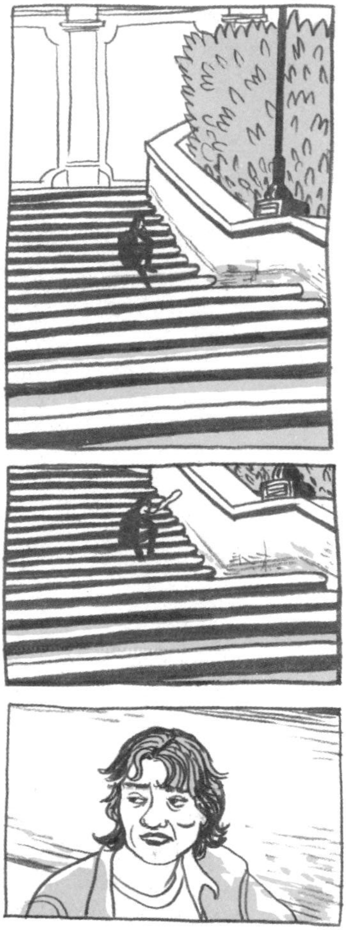

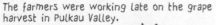

The farmers were working late on the grape harvest in Pulkau Valley.

The police called!

They found Ulli!

Two months earlier, my parents had entered the deserted apartment. They filed a missing-persons report, unfortunately not in Vienna but in the neighboring village.

That girl's a runaway. Between you and me, she's selling herself in Vienna!

There's nothing we can do. Missing kids usually turn back up again on their own.

You should've knocked some sense into her! Why did you even let her go into the city?

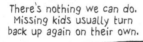

The big carving knife is also missing!

Did you hear about it?

Aunt Maria

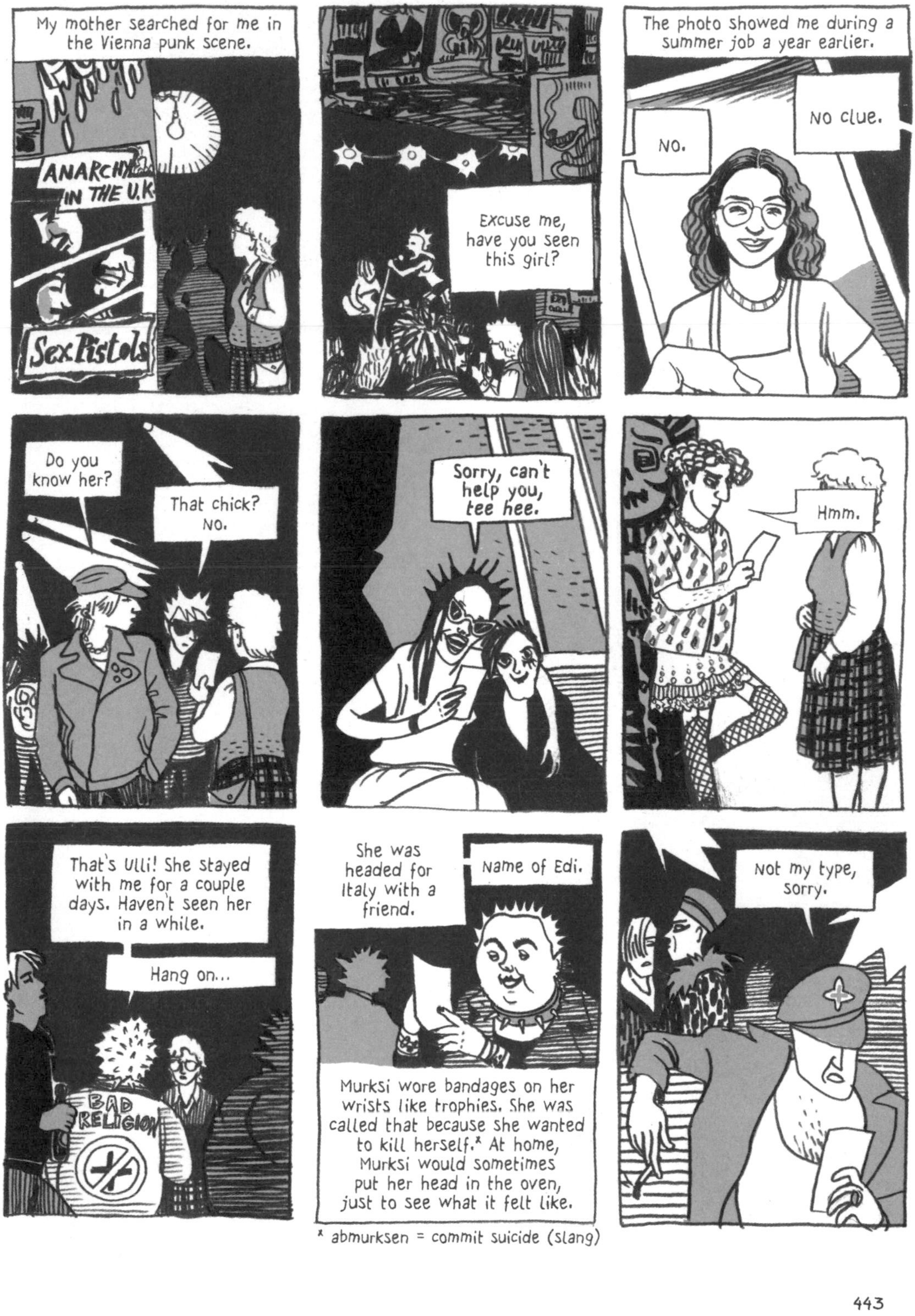
My mother searched for me in the Vienna punk scene.
ANARCHY IN THE U.K.
Sex Pistols
Excuse me, have you seen this girl?
The photo showed me during a summer job a year earlier.
No.
No clue.
Do you know her?
That chick? No.
Sorry, can't help you, tee hee.
Hmm.
That's Ulli! She stayed with me for a couple days. Haven't seen her in a while.
Hang on...
BAD RELIGION
She was headed for Italy with a friend.
Name of Edi.
Murksi wore bandages on her wrists like trophies. She was called that because she wanted to kill herself.* At home, Murksi would sometimes put her head in the oven, just to see what it felt like.
Not my type, sorry.

* abmurksen = commit suicide (slang)

444

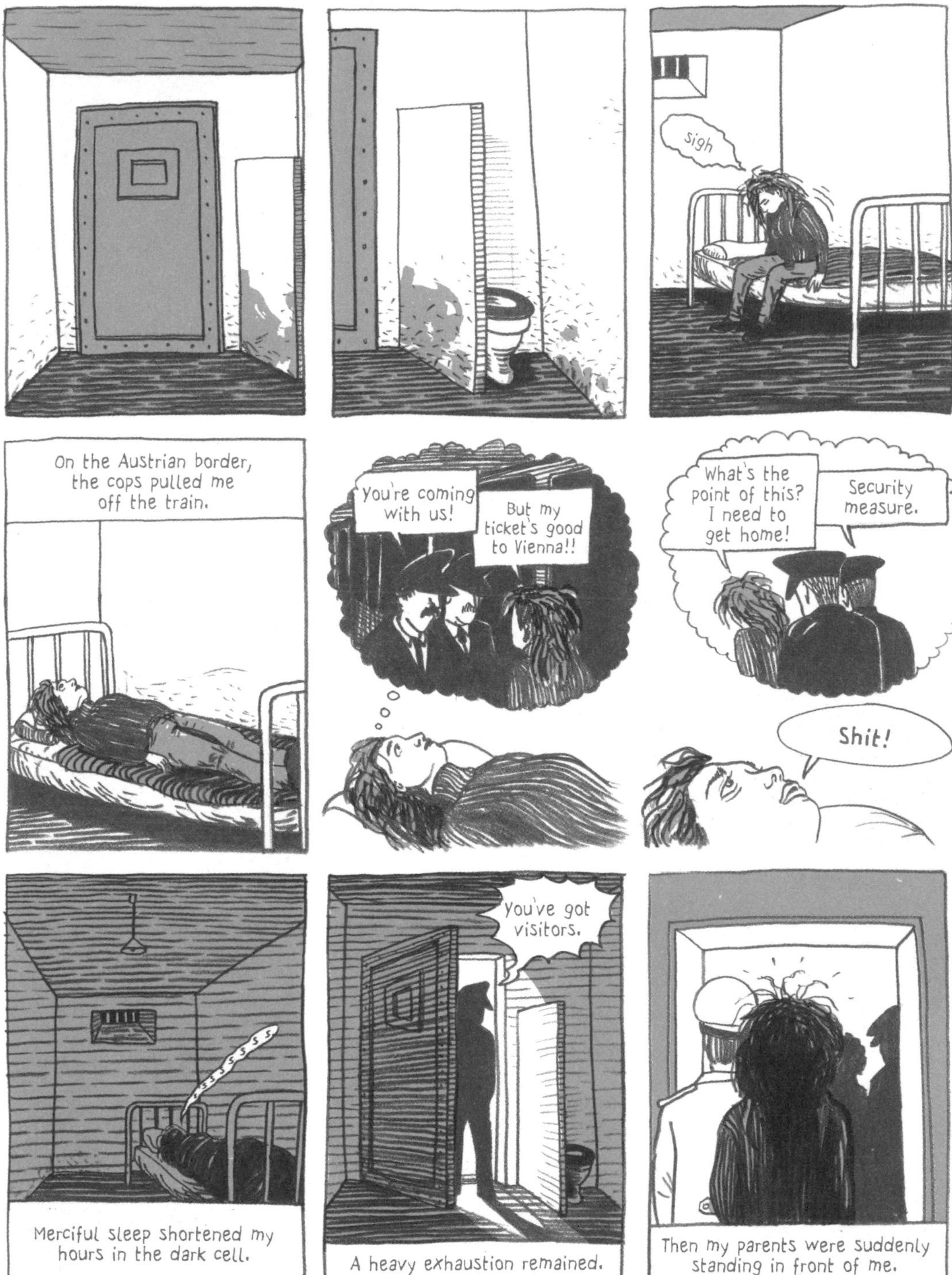
sigh
On the Austrian border, the cops pulled me off the train.
You're coming with us!
But my ticket's good to Vienna!!
What's the point of this? I need to get home!
Security measure.
Shit!
Merciful sleep shortened my hours in the dark cell.
You've got visitors.
A heavy exhaustion remained.
Then my parents were suddenly standing in front of me.

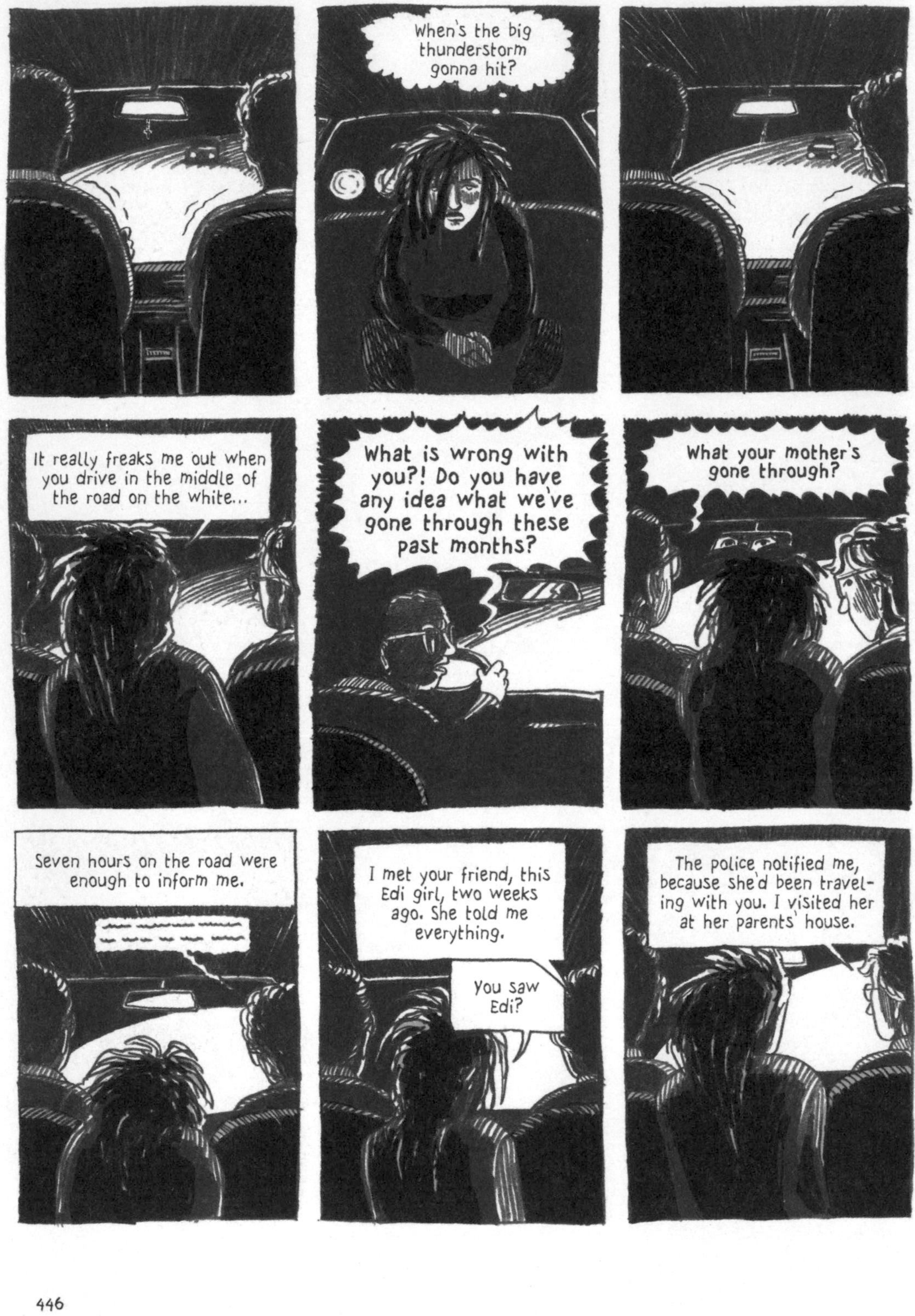
When's the big thunderstorm gonna hit?
It really freaks me out when you drive in the middle of the road on the white...
What is wrong with you?! Do you have any idea what we've gone through these past months?
What your mother's gone through?
Seven hours on the road were enough to inform me.
I met your friend, this Edi girl, two weeks ago. She told me everything.
You saw Edi?
The police notified me, because she'd been travel-ing with you. I visited her at her parents' house.

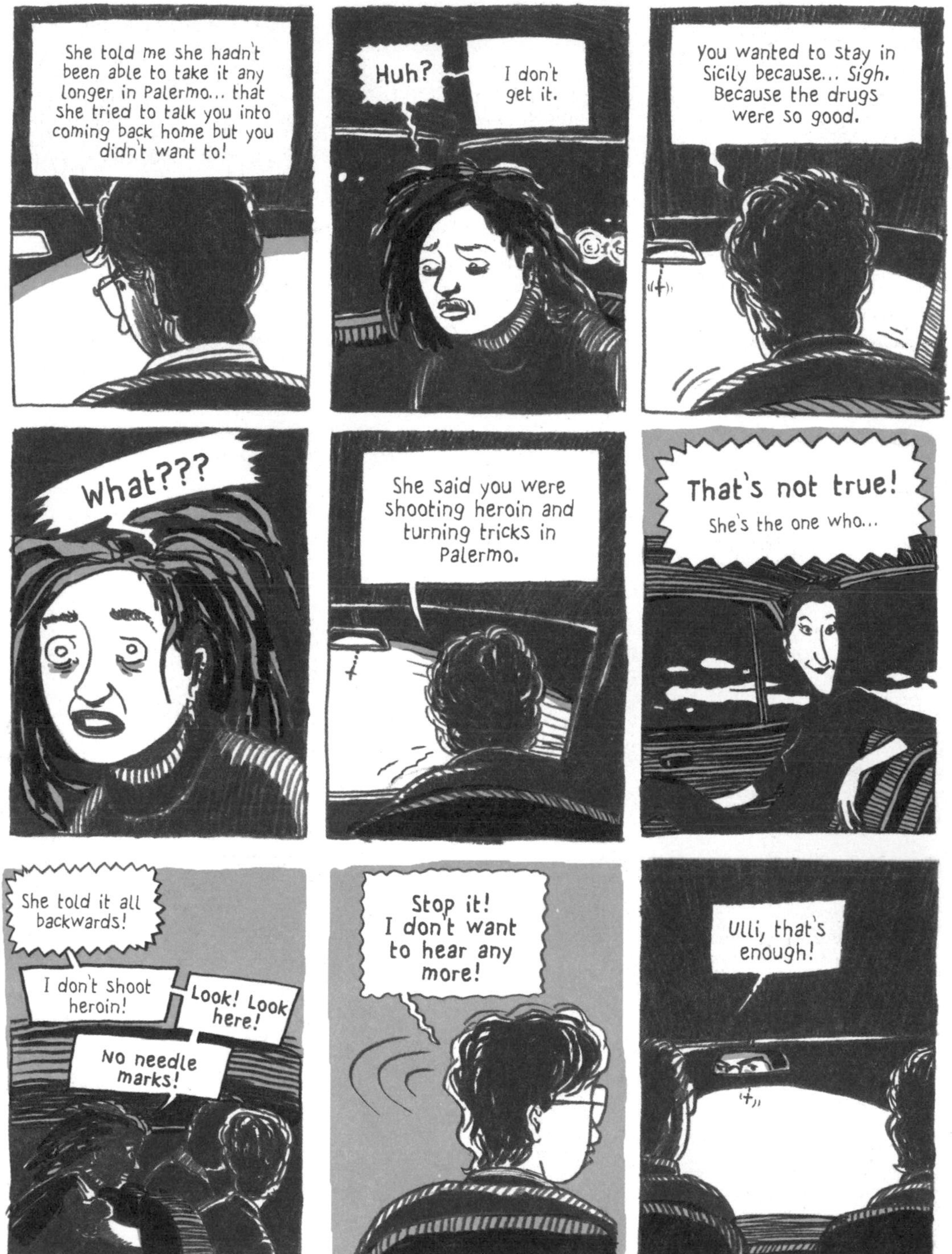
She told me she hadn't been able to take it any longer in Palermo... that she tried to talk you into coming back home but you didn't want to!
Huh?
I don't get it.
You wanted to stay in Sicily because... *Sigh.* Because the drugs were so good.
What???
She said you were shooting heroin and turning tricks in Palermo.
That's not true! She's the one who...
She told it all backwards!
I don't shoot heroin!
Look! Look here!
No needle marks!
Stop it! I don't want to hear any more!
Ulli, that's enough!

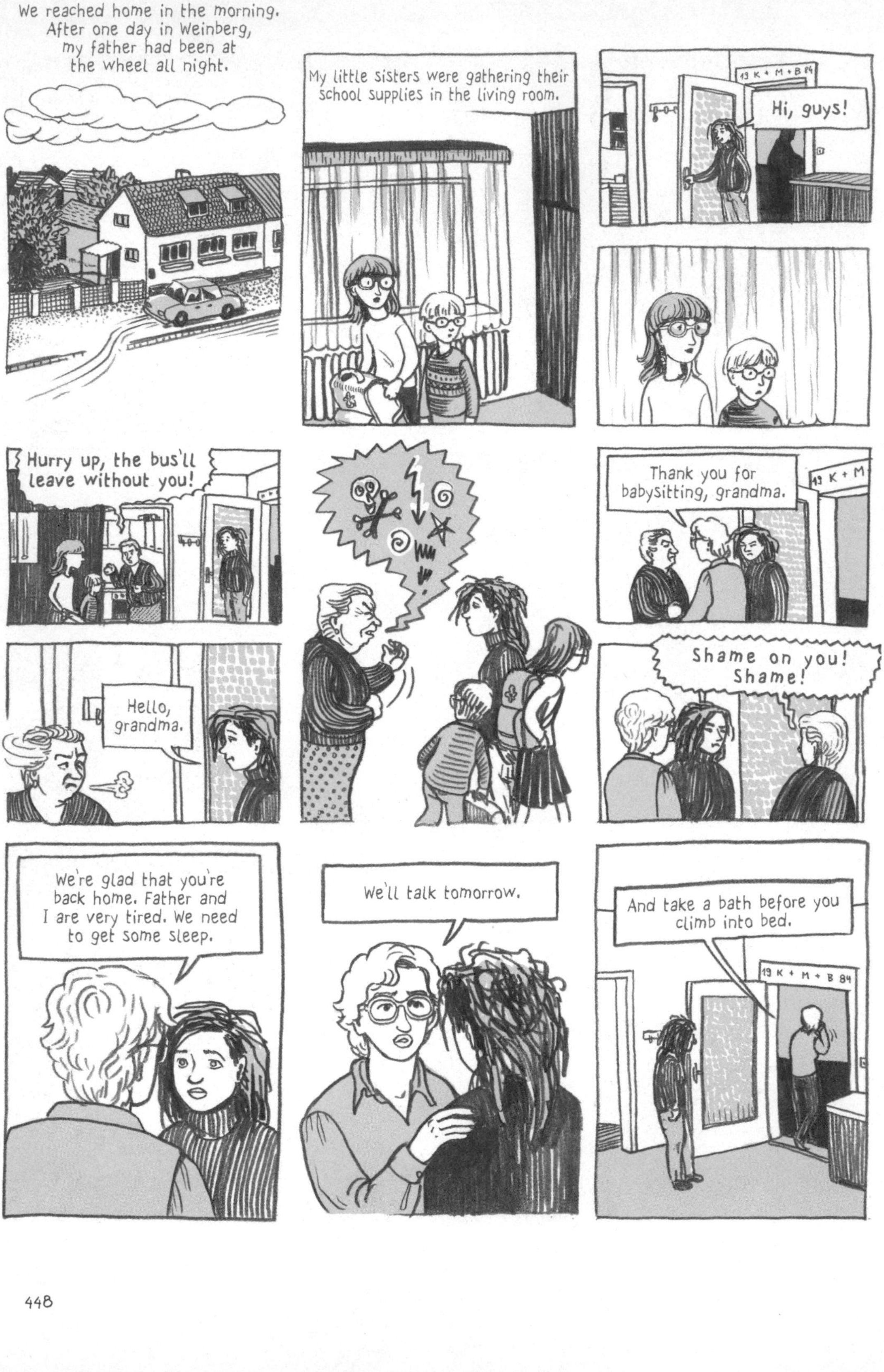
We reached home in the morning. After one day in Weinberg, my father had been at the wheel all night.
My little sisters were gathering their school supplies in the living room.
19 K + M + B 84
Hi, guys!
Hurry up, the bus'll leave without you!
Thank you for babysitting, grandma.
19 K + M
Hello, grandma.
Shame on you! Shame!
We're glad that you're back home. Father and I are very tired. We need to get some sleep.
We'll talk tomorrow.
And take a bath before you climb into bed.
19 K + M + B 84

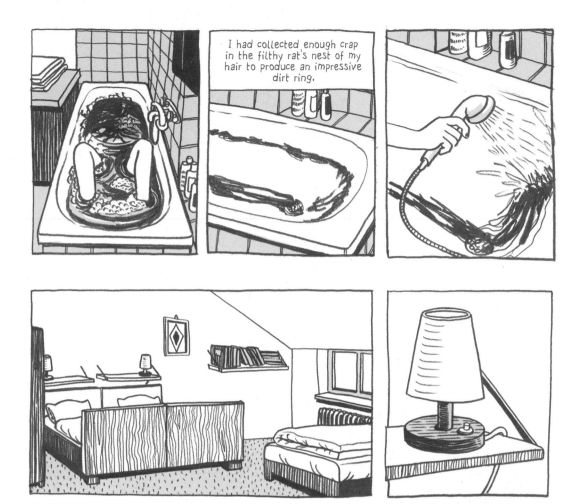

I had collected enough crap in the filthy rat's nest of my hair to produce an impressive dirt ring.

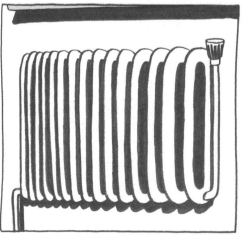

449

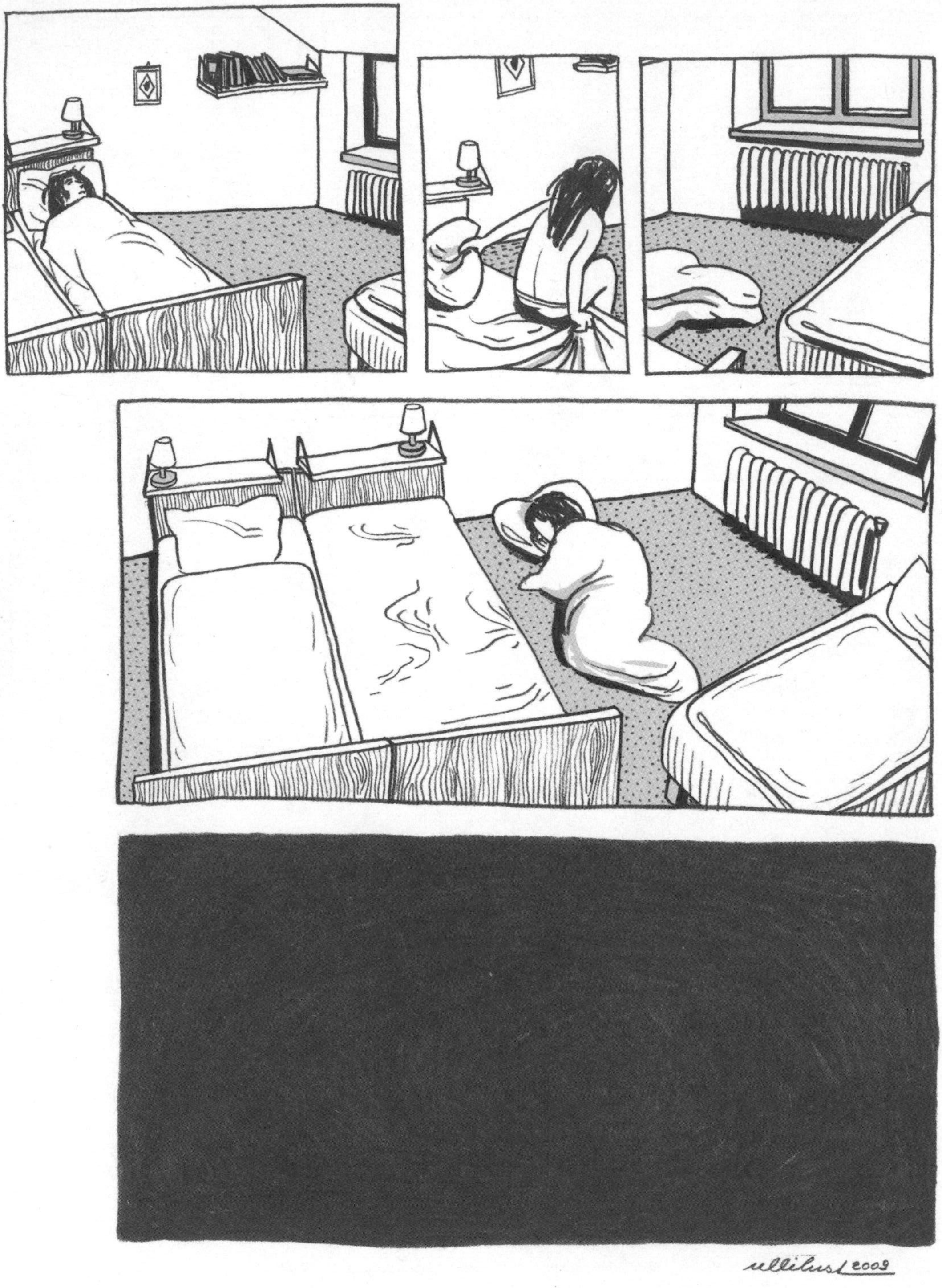
ullilust 2009

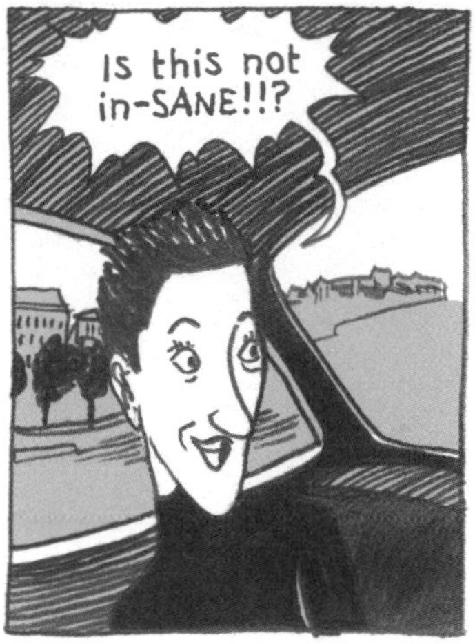
Is this not in-SANE!!?

I ran into Edi again three years later, in Vienna, at a rock concert. She greeted me euphorically: "Wasn't the time we spent together just the coolest?" and "I'm going to a trade school now, it's awesome!"

Had I met an evil spirit, I could not have taken off any faster.

I have changed her name for this book.

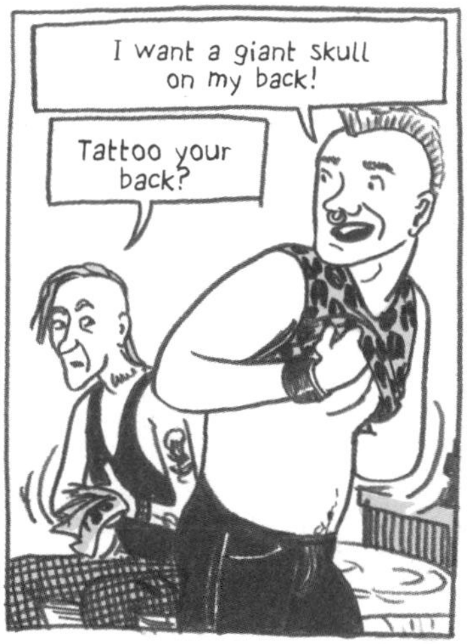
I want a giant skull on my back!
Tattoo your back?

Gerry, on whose back I tattooed the skull, was the only member of the old punk gang to turn up again two years later. His upper arms were now entirely covered in tattoos. "Had it done in prison. I was just in the slammer on account of a fight." He'd ditched the nose ring.

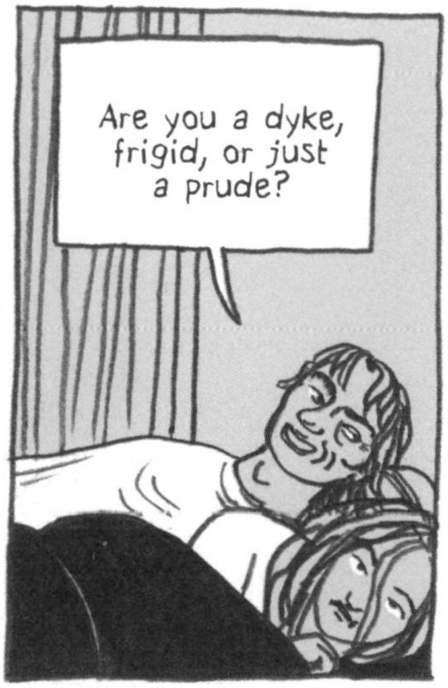
Are you a dyke, frigid, or just a prude?

Andreas never told us his real name. "You might recognize it from the newspapers, that'd cause me problems." We never saw one another again. He'd probably be delighted to hear that he had a hand in the first orgasm of my life. A few months later, when I was alone, I caressed my clitoris as he had done — and exploded (shooting stars, the whole bit).

APPENDIX

Also, verrückt war ich schon immer, aber jetzt bin ich total ausgezuckt!
Angefangen hat alles damit, daß ich Karin kennenlernte.
Ich war seit einem Jahr in wien in einem Klosterheim, und Beginndes
zweiten Schuljahreswurde auch Karin Bewohnerin dieser ehrwürdigen Stätte
Sie war total arg- ich meine verrückt-, aber anfangs merkte ich das
noch nicht,ich hielt sie für ein vollkommen normales Mädchen, etwas
seltsam vielleicht, aber sie interessierte mich nicht besonders.
Dann gingen wir eimal zusammen am Abend aus (zufällig), und ich lernte
sie richtig kennen----ein Wahnsinn!!!!!Sie tanzte total super, und ihr
bisheriges Leben war nur mehr suspekt-Griechenland, England, Italien
München u.s.w. Aufgewachsen ist sie in Innsbruck, was sich ziemlich
auf ihre Aussprache schlug, -ich fands einfach herrlich.Als ich erfuhr,
daß Karin schon seit einiger Zeit bei den Punks war, riß ich nur mehr
die Augen auf!!Punk, das war für mich irgendwie irgendwas undefinier-
bares. Ich hab schon mal zwei gesehen, und sie super gefunden, aber ich
hab sie nicht ganz gepackt.Auf jeden Fallwurden Karin und ich die
besten Freundinnen, und im Heim waren wir bald die" enfants terribles"
,denn wir ließen uns von den beschränkten Weibern dort ziemlich
wenig gefallen.Naja.
Eines Sonntags, als ich gerade von Jetzelsdorf nach Wien kam wurde
erzählte mir Karin nach einer stürmischen BEgrüßung, daß sie die
Punks gefunden habe(!!) - und einenFreund, Roli.Sie ist total abgefahren
auf ihn, denn er redete ziemlich gute Sachen, mystisch, schwarze Magie,
Musik, und philosophierte halt so herum.Karin bewunderte ihn jedenfalls,
er war für sie der Mensch, der die Augen offen hat, der alles so sieht
wie es wirklich ist, so was wie ein Messias eben.Einfach der Größte.
Roli spielte in einer Gruppe,(eigentlich seiner Gruppe, denn er hatte da
das große Wort) den Terror Alarm einer Punkband.Und ihren Proberaum
hatten sie im WUK, wo sich die Punks nach dem Tod der Gaga trafen. Meine
Neugierde war schon einmal geweckt, und ich war total aus dem Häuschen
als Karin mich mal mitnahm. Mein Gott wie ich ausgesehen habe,-
vollkommen normal, sogar Brille und so!!!Naja.
Also das Wuk, also ich kann nur sagen abgefuckt habe ich es mir ja
schon vorgestellt, aber das hatte ich nicht erwartet: Ein riesiges
Gebäude,es wäre eigentlich ziemlich schön, wenn es nicht eine
Ruine wäre. Nun ja, Ruinr ist vielleicht etwas übertrieben, aber im
Hof laüberall der Schutt herum, u,in der mitte des Hofes, war ein
Gebäude, in das ich mich nicht in einer Rüstung hineingewagt hätte, so
zerfallen sah es auch .dann gingen Karin un In der Vorhalle kam man sich
irgendwie vor wie in einer Kirche, so Statuen und so, wenn nicht naja,
alles völlig beschmiertund die Figuren wüst geschminkt gewesen wären.
Es taugte mir irgendwie.Als ich aber die Leute im WUK sah--ich fand
, daß sie wahnsinnig gut aussahen, Nieten , bunte Haare Irokesen,beschmierte
LederjackenKetten und was es sonst noch alles gab. Obwohl ihre Kleidung
eigentlich ziemlich bunt war, wirkten sie total schwarz auf mich-
sie waren mir unheimlich, aber da war etwas in dieser Stimmun g, das mich
magisch anzog.Ich wußte damals selbst noch nicht was es war, aber später
, später merkte ich es......
Mit einem Wrt ich fand sie toll, obwohl ich sie anfangs einfach für urige
Burschen si hielt, mit denen man Gaude haben kann,
Und je lfter ich ins Wuk kam, desto mehr interessierten sie mich.. Natür
Natürlich hatte ich mich nie getraut, alleine hinzugehen, aber da Karin
- man nannte sie dort übrigens Hexe, fest mit Roli verbandelt war....

Journal, 1983 (facing page)

Okay, so I've always been a bit of a nut, but now I've turned into a total lunatic. It all started when I met Karin. I'd spent the previous year in Vienna in a convent, and beginning with my second year Karin joined me as a fellow lodger in this noble institution. She was totally wicked -- I mean nuts -- but at first I didn't notice that, I thought she was a totally normal girl, maybe a little odd, but I wasn't particularly interested in her. Then one evening we hit the town together (by chance) and I got to know her well ---- crazy!!!!! She was an awesome dancer, and her previous life just intrigued me even more -- Greece, England, Italy, Munich, etc. She'd grown up in Innsbruck, which was pretty obvious from her accent. I thought she was a total delight. When I found out Karin had been into punk for a while, that was even more of an eye-opener!!! Punk was somehow something undefinable as far as I was concerned. I'd met two of them, and I thought they were awesome, but I never quite got what they were all about. Anyway, Karen and I got to be best friends, and we soon became the school's "enfants terribles," since we didn't exactly hit it off with the uptight cows who ran the place. Anyway.

One Sunday, I'd just returned to Vienna from Jetzelsdorf, and Karin told me, after a frenzied greeting, that she'd found some punks (!!) -- and a friend, Roli. She was totally into him because he could talk your ear off, about mysticism, black magic, music, plenty of philosophizing. Anyway, Karin was in awe of him, as far as she was concerned he was the one person in the world who had his eyes wide open, who saw everything the way it truly was, even something like a messiah. The greatest, basically. Toli played in a band (actually his band, because he was the loudest), Terror Alarm, a punk band. And they had their rehearsal room in the WUK, where the punks would meet up after the demise of Gaga.* My curiosity had already been aroused, and I was totally out of my mind when Karin brought me along, my God, I must have been a sight -- totally straight, glasses and all. Anyway.

So, about the WUK, all I can say is, I always figured it would be a fucked-up place, but I hadn't expected this: An enormous building, it would actually have been beautiful if it hadn't been in ruins. Okay, maybe "ruins" is a bit of an exaggeration, but the courtyard was piled high with detritus, and in the middle of the courtyard there was a building that I wouldn't have dared to enter even if I was wearing a suit of armor, that's how decrepit it looked. ~~Then Karin and I went~~ The entrance hall somehow reminded me of a church, statues and stuff, well, everything was totally covered in paint and all the statues were decorated. Somehow it all worked for me. But when I saw the people in the WUK -- I thought they looked utterly fantastic, studs, day-glo mohawks, decorated leather jackets, the works. Even though they dressed in bright colors they seemed black to me. They were spooky, but there was something about the mood of the place that appealed to me. At the time I didn't know what it was, but later, later on I'd figure it out...

In one word, I thought they were great, even though at first I just thought they were a bunch of cool guys you could hang out with. And the deeper I got into the WUK, the more it fascinated me... Of course, I never would have dared to go there by myself, but since Karin -- who went under the name Hexe [witch], was going out with Roli...

* WUK: Vienna's biggest cultural center, short for Werkstätten- und Kulturhaus ("artisan and workshop center"). Gaga (named for its location on Gassergasse): an autonomous cultural and communications center that included studios, rehearsal rooms, and an alternative school, which had been closed down by the authorities the previous year.

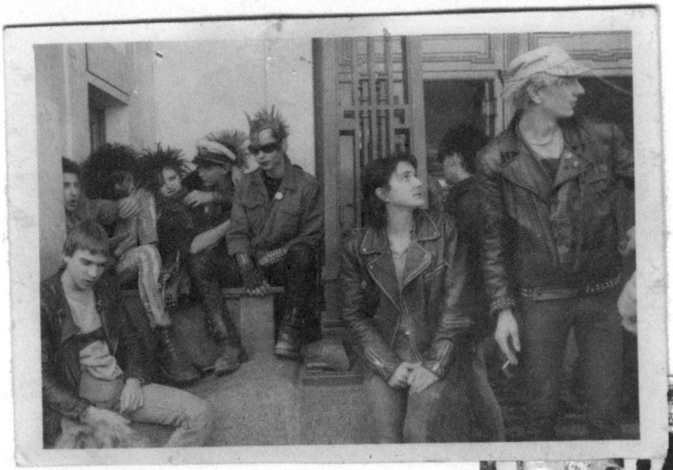

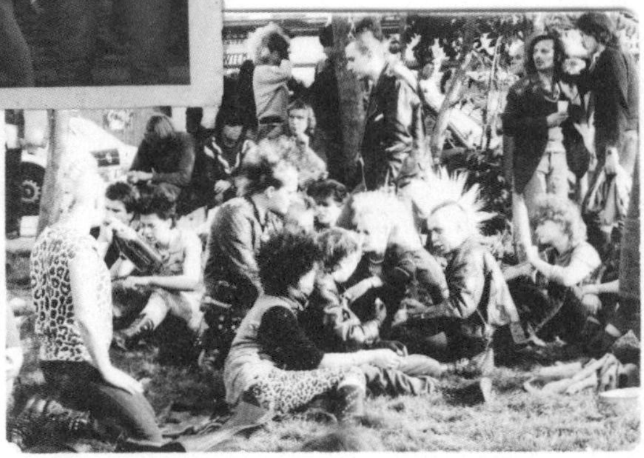

Friends, 1984
2nd photo, far left: Gerry

Page 7

The first written usage of the word "punk" occurs in Shakespeare's *Measure For Measure*. At the time it was a synonym for "prostitute" and had a female connotation. Later on "punk" would frequently be used to define something wretched, worthless, nonsensical; when applied to people: beginner, inexperienced person, hobo, petty criminal, vagabond, or even scum, filth.

Punk as a youth movement took shape in the middle of the 1970s in New York and England, as a reaction against the Hippies. The punks radiated nihilism, subversion, and rage at all forms of institutionalized society and the middle-class life style. They also defined themselves through ugliness: Shredded clothing, safety pins, cheaply produced 'zines, spontaneous dadaistic action art, and above all excessive consumption of alcohol and other drugs. Imperfections were not just accepted but aspired to. Punk musicians were proud of mastering only three chords. Punk stood for a post-materialistic approach to life, for the vulgarity and immediacy of the street. Slogans included "No future," "Destroy yourself," "Trust no one," and above all, "Do it yourself!"

A note to myself

What is the slowest way to
commit suicide?
Being born, and waiting for it
to be all over.

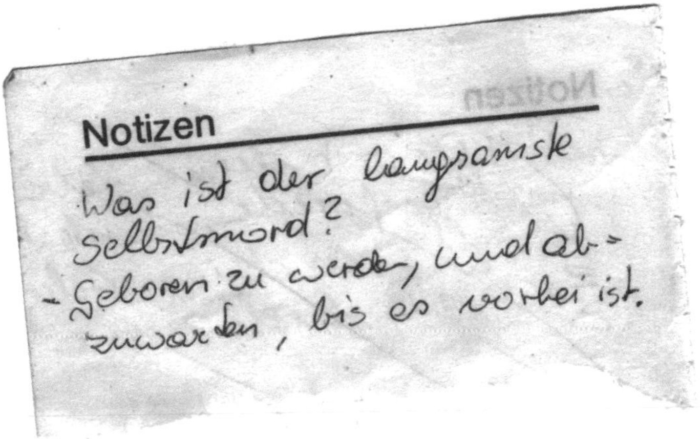

Notizen

[handwritten note, in German:]

Was ist der langsamste
Selbstmord?
– Geboren zu werden, und ab-
zuwarten, bis es vorbei ist.

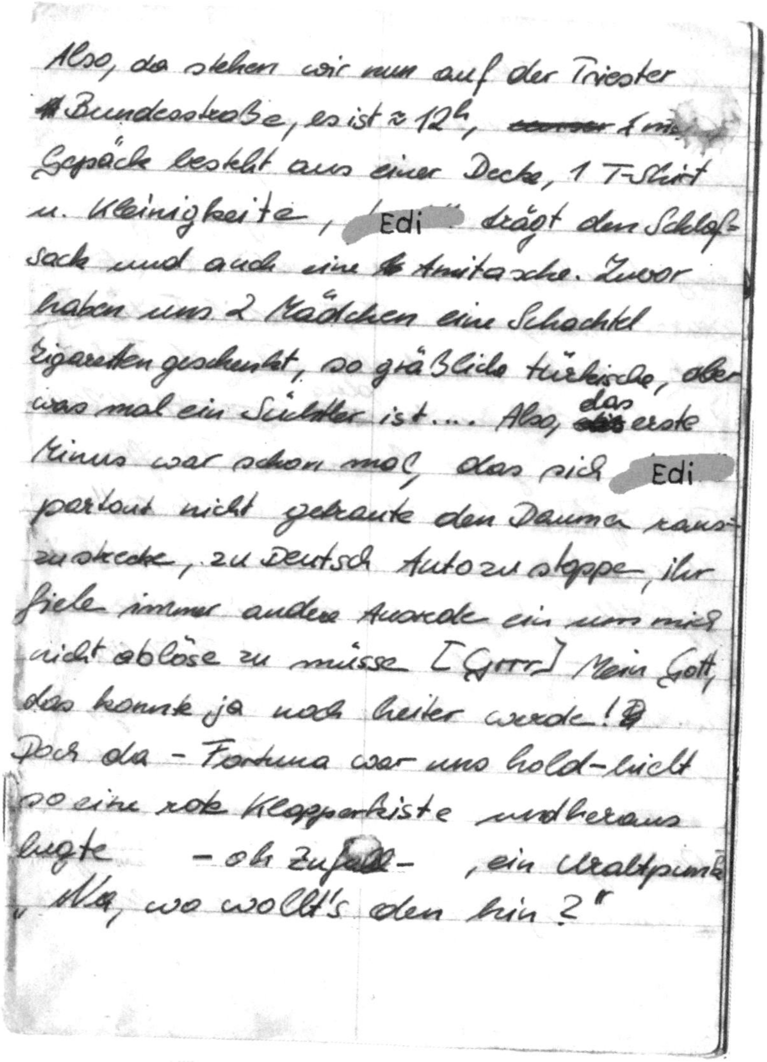

[handwritten travel diary page, in German:]

Also, da stehen wir nun auf der Triester
Bundesstraße, es ist ≈ 12ʰ, ...
Gepäck besteht aus einer Decke, 1 T-Shirt
u. Kleinigkeiten, Edi trägt den Schlaf-
sack und auch eine Annitasche. Zuvor
haben uns 2 Mädchen eine Schachtel
Zigaretten geschenkt, so gräßliche türkische, aber
was mal ein Suchtler ist... Also, das erste
Minus war schon mal, das sich Edi
partout nicht getraute den Daumen raus-
zustrecke, zu Deutsch Auto zu stoppe, ihr
fiele immer andere Ausrede ein um mich
nicht ablöse zu müsse [Grrr] Mein Gott,
das konnte ja noch heiter werde!
Doch da – Fortuna war uns hold – ließ
so eine rote Klapperkiste und heraus
lugte – oh Zufall – ein Uraltpunk
Na, wo wollt's den hin?"

Travel diary, 1984

So we're standing on the Triester
Bundesstrasse, it's around noon,
our luggage consists of a blanket,
1 T-shirt and odds and ends, Edi's
carrying the sleeping bag as well as
a handbag. Earlier today two girls
gave us a pack of cigarettes, it's
those awful Turkish ones, but beggars can't be choosers... Anyway,
the first snag was that Edi could
never work up the courage to stick
our her thumb, to hitch a ride. She
kept coming up with new excuses
not to take over from me (grrr).
Jesus, this could end up being a
real problem! But Lady Luck was
on our side, this red heap stopped,
and an ancient punk -- what a
coincidence -- peered out. "So,
where do ya wanna go?"

459

Page 57

In 1984, the border between Italy and Austria was still controlled. Austria only became a member of the European Union in 1995. From 1997 on there was no longer any control on the borders to other European Union countries (Italy, Germany, France).

Page 179

Edi had seen the movie *Christiane F.*, and I'd read the book, *Christiane F.: Autobiography of a Girl of the Streets and Heroin Addict.* Christiane F.'s autobiographical tale of her life as a junkie, prostitute, and recovering addict was written in such a way as to make heroin addiction appear loathsome. The visuals in the movie gave an entirely different impression, even though it told the same story. In 2007 a journalist in *Vice* magazine wrote, "The best heroin movie, however, the one that is pretty much Carnation Instant Junkie, is *Christiane F.* Every single kid in this movie is a fox, and the more strung out they get, the hotter they get."

Page 266

The hopelessness of my battle for respect was made clear five years later by the discussions that Lara Cardella's 1989 novel *Good Girls Don't Wear Trousers* provoked in Sicily. The 19-year-old author was from Licita, and she took on the macho world of Southern Italy. Her quest for freedom and self-realization peaked with her desire to wear trousers. Because of this book, her father, an insurance agent, lost his clients; her mother, who worked as a nurse, was fired; her sister had to change schools; and Lara Cardella herself was slandered and threatened. As the author wrote, "women can be wives and mothers but they can never be people."

Page 398

Of course, I didn't actually shout "Fuck off." The worst Sicilian curse, the one you use to get rid of bothersome supplicants — or so I was told — was "*Vai a rompere la minchia*" and means something along the lines of "Go break off your dick." Sicilians use the word "dick" in the same promiscuous manner as Germans use "shit" (*scheisse*), or Americans "fuck." They're constantly saying "dick, dick, dick." It can express the entire range from utter loathing to the height of admiration. The fact that the word minchia takes the feminine article "la" did puzzle me, however.

Page 412

Today, the Sicilian word "Mafia" is synonymous with a criminal organization. The origins of the Mafia can be traced back to 17th-century Sicilian brigandage, but it evolved into its current form at the end of the 19th century. The Palermo-born ethnographer Giuseppe Pitrè provided a very precise description of its mindset at the time, even though he dismissed the idea of its being a criminal association: "The Mafia is neither a sect nor a society, it has neither rules nor statutes. The Mafioso is no thief or criminal (...) the Mafia is the consciousness of one's own worth, the exaggerated concept of individual force as the sole arbiter of every conflict, of every clash of ideas or interests. (...) The Mafioso is someone who always expects and is given respect." (*Customs, Beliefs and Superstitions of the Sicilian People, Giuseppe Pitrè.*)

After the end of World War II the word gained traction thanks to the Allies, who had prepared their landing through the Sicilian Mafia. Members were bound by a powerful set of rules: At the top was omertà, the code of silence, then honor, unquestioning obedience, the primacy of the "Family" over the state, the right to personal justice, and, not least, the Catholic patriarchy. A Sicilian Mafioso was allowed to commit murder, but never to cheat on his wife. (*Sicily: Literary Expeditions* by Ralf Nestmeyer.)

With the importation of morphium and its conversion to heroin at the end of the 1970s, "it was the arrival of wealth," a former Mafioso explains. "We'd earned good money with cigarettes, but it wasn't an excessive source of revenue. It was the drugs that changed the life of the Cosa Nostra; they brought in a huge amount of money and allowed us to go crazy."

It was only in 1982 that the first anti-Mafia law was adopted, making membership in the Cosa Nostra a criminal offense and establishing a state witness law.

In July 1984 the drug kingpin Tommaso Buscetta was arrested in Brazil. Buscetta, who also went under the name Don Masino, was the most important state witness in the great "Maxi-Trials" of the 1980s and 1990s. Thanks to his testimony, the prosecutors Giovanni Falcone and Paolo Borsellino gained, for the first time, complete and intimate insight into the organization and day-to-day operation of the Mafia families. The ensuing Maxi-Trials remain to this day the biggest blow the state has landed against the Mafia. The trials took place in a high-security courthouse built especially for this purpose. Buscetta underwent plastic surgery to change his face and spent the rest of his life under assumed names in the USA. On April 4, 2000, he died in New York of cancer. His final book, published the year before his death, was titled *La mafia ha vinto*: "The Mafia won."

Excerpt from a 12/12/1984 newspaper article, *Hamburger Abendblatt* (two months after my return to Austria)

The Mafia suffers its biggest blow to date

Turin, Italy - (...) Over the last weekend of September, a "milestone in the battle against the Mafia" was reached, according to the Italian Minister of the Interior. At that time, 366 warrants were issued, based on testimony by the former Mafia boss Tommaso Buscetta, resulting in 60 arrests. Buscetta's testimony, which filled 3,000 pages of transcripts, would help resolve 121 murders dating back 15 years. Buscetta had revealed his knowledge of the Mafia because the "honorable family" had murdered several members of his family and he believed himself to be at the top of a hit list list drawn up by his former business colleagues. The former Mafia boss had most recently built himself a kingdom in the drug trade in Brazil. Yet competing gangs had gradually taken over the big cities controlled by Buscetta, and seven of his relatives had been murdered by commandos of trained assassins. He was finally arrested by the Brazilian police and extradited to Italy, where he decided to testify. Since then, he has lived under protection in a police barracks in an undisclosed location.

The most prominent "godfather" to be named by Buscetta is the former mayor of Palermo, Vito Ciancimino. His name turned up in the reports of the anti-Mafia commission as early as the early 1970s, but he sued anyone who referred to him as a "Mafioso."

On May 23, 1992, the prosecutor Giovanni Falcone was, along with his wife and his police escort, killed with a half-ton bomb. This resulted in an unprecedented surge of solidarity between the general public and the anti-Mafia crusaders. Paolo Borsellino was chosen as his successor, and charged with carrying on the wide-ranging battle against the Mafia. On July 19, 1992 Paolo Borsellino and five of his bodyguards also fell victim to a bombing in the city of Palermo.

Today the name of the Falcone-Borsellino airport reminds us of these two men. And yet I secretly wonder if this building is designed to commemorate these two men's courage, or to celebrate their murder. Not least because the corrupt Christian Democrats and Socialists who were voted out of office at the peak of the anti-Mafia sentiment during the 1990s have since made political comebacks, mostly as candidates in Silvio Berlusconi's right-wing coalition.

Berlusconi's policies made an ongoing consolidiation of the Mafia possible. The criminologist Letizia Paolio writes about this in her book *Mafia Brotherhoods: Organized Crime, Italian Style:* "It is a subtle process. Take for example the cancellation of the 24-hour personal protection for some of the most important and endangered investigators. Or the barely concealed practice of passing advantageous new laws and repealing those that are inconvenient. Without a doubt, many of these measures have specifically aided the Mafia. And Berlusconi knows that."

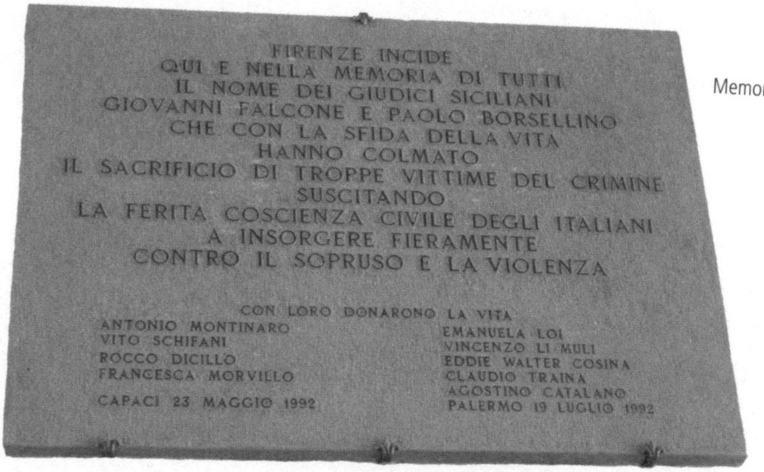
FIRENZE INCIDE
QUI E NELLA MEMORIA DI TUTTI
IL NOME DEI GIUDICI SICILIANI
GIOVANNI FALCONE E PAOLO BORSELLINO
CHE CON LA SFIDA DELLA VITA
HANNO COLMATO
IL SACRIFICIO DI TROPPE VITTIME DEL CRIMINE
SUSCITANDO
LA FERITA COSCIENZA CIVILE DEGLI ITALIANI
A INSORGERE FIERAMENTE
CONTRO IL SOPRUSO E LA VIOLENZA
CON LORO DONARONO LA VITA
ANTONIO MONTINARO
VITO SCHIFANI
ROCCO DICILLO
FRANCESCA MORVILLO
CAPACI 23 MAGGIO 1992
EMANUELA LOI
VINCENZO LI MULI
EDDIE WALTER COSINA
CLAUDIO TRAINA
AGOSTINO CATALANO
PALERMO 19 LUGLIO 1992

Memorial plaque, 1992

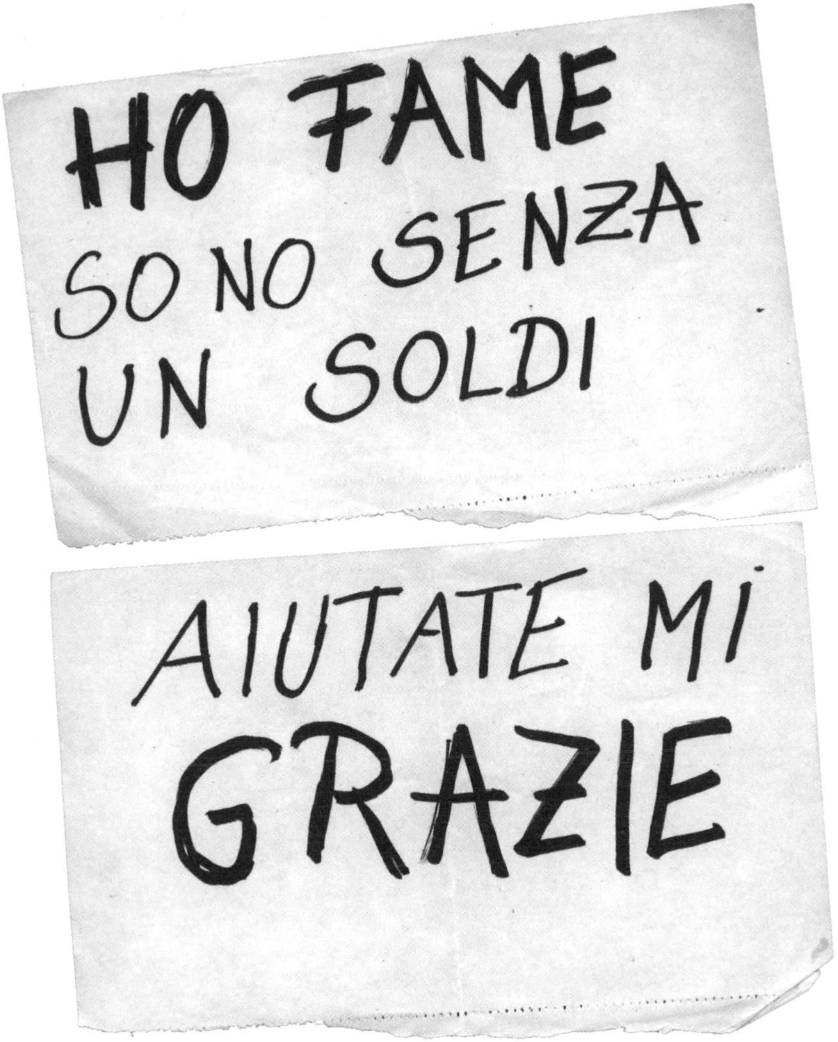
HO FAME
SO NO SENZA
UN SOLDI
AIUTATE MI
GRAZIE

Panhandler's sign, 1984

I apologize to my parents and I cannot thank them enough for their patience and support. I take this opportunity to wish my son Philipp the best, and am delighted that he is such a sensible boy. (Yet again) I thank Kai Pfeiffer for talking me into drawing up this adventure, for his continual encouragement, as well as for his assistance with the writing. Thanks to Ali Decker, Marcie Jost, Peter Zorn for the summer lodgings in the Brickworks and his helpful suggestions; thanks to Dirk Schwieger, Nanne Meyer, Johann Ulrich, Quentin Duclos, Marc de Dieux, Daniele d'Alia, Eric Wunder, Susan Reck, Barbara Hartmann, and all the readers at www.electrocomics.com who have showed their gratitude through donations.

Ulli Lust

Born 1967 in Vienna; moved to Berlin in 1995, where she studied graphic design and now lives as a cartoonist. Her published work includes pieces of comics journalism featuring pointed observations on modern life as well as erotic-mythological poems. She runs the online publishing company www.electrocomics.com, which publishes e-books and online comics by an ever-increasing group of international cartoonists.

Her other work includes:

Fashionvictims — Illustrated Columns and Mini-Reportages From Berlin (avant-verlag, 2008)

Airpussy (l'employé du moi, 2009)

Flughunde (Suhrkamp Verlag, 2013)

Photo: Alexander Paul Englert